20TH-CENTURY ARCHITECTURE

Sweden

Edited by

CLAES CALDENBY, JÖRAN LINDVALL
AND WILFRIED WANG

With contributions by

THORBJÖRN ANDERSSON, CLAES CALDENBY,
EVA ERIKSSON, BJÖRN LINN, EVA RUDBERG,
RASMUS WÆRN AND KERSTIN WICKMAN

Prestel
Munich · New York

First published on the occasion of the exhibition "20th-Century Architecture, Sweden", Deutsches Architektur-Museum, Frankfurt am Main 4 May 1998 - 28 June 1998

Edited by Claes Caldenby, Jöran Lindvall and Wilfried Wang for the Dezernat für Kultur und Freizeit, Amt für Wissenschaft und Kunst der Stadt Frankfurt am Main, Deutsches Architektur-Museum and Arkitekturmuseet, Stockholm

Illustrations editor:
Margit Klint

English translations:
Jeremy Franks, John Krause

Front cover: Aula Magna, Ralph Erskine (Photo: *Åke E:son Lindman*) and the Göteborg Court House extension, Gunnar Asplund (Photo in *Arkitekturmuseet*)

Spine: Stockholm City Hall (Photo: *Max Plunger*)

Back cover: Rosta, Backström and Reinius (Photo: *Claes Caldenby*) and St. Mark's Church, Sigurd Lewerentz (Photo: *Claes Caldenby*)

Frontispiece: Aerial view of central Stockholm (Photo: *Metria*)

Photo credits see page 395

Die Deutsche Bibliothek – CIP-Einheitsaufnahme

20th-Century architecture. – Munich; New York: Prestel
Dt. Ausg. u.d.T.: Architektur im 20. Jahrhundert

Sweden / ed. by Claes Caldenby ... With contributions by Thorbjörn Andersson ... - 1988
ISBN 3-7913-1936-1

Library of Congress Cataloging-in-Publication Data is available.

Prestel-Verlag, Mandlstrasse 26, D-80802 Munich
Tel. (89) 381709-0 Fax (89) 381709-35

Design concept of the series "20th-century architecture":
Gino Lee and Matthew Monk, Cambridge, MA, and Providence, RI.

Designed by:
Anders Ljungman and Johan Melbi, Stockholm

Offset lithography by:
Centraltryckeriet, Borås, Brahe AB, Linköping and Avanti Färgstudio AB, Stockholm

Printed by:
Centraltryckeriet, Borås

ISBN 3-7913-1936-1

Printed in Sweden

Contents

III. Appendix

Introduction

CLAES CALDENBY / JÖRAN LINDVALL / WILFRIED WANG

This book is part of a series of exhibitions and catalogues from the German Museum of Architecture in Frankfurt. It is edited in parallel versions in German, English and Swedish. In earlier exhibitions and publications in the series the 20th-century architecture of Austria, Ireland and Portugal has been presented. The idea of this kind of presentations is to give a picture of architecture in its cultural and social context. Taken together the series will deepen the appreciation of the manifold development of architecture in Europe with its mutual influences and regional characteristics.

The catalogue and the exhibition have been produce in collaboration between the German Museum of Architecture in Frankfurt and the Museum of Architecture in Stockholm. The National Swedish Council of Building Research and the Swedish Institute have given substantial economic support to the project. We hereby thank all those without the support of whom this large project would not have been possible to carry through: patrons, archives and architects.

Up till now there has been no history of Swedish 20th-century architecture written. It has come natural to use this opportunity to remedy that. This means that compared to earlier catalogues of the series this one has been given a longer chronological presentation with the ambition to give a reasonably full description and analysis of the development. To this there has been added two more thematical chapters, one on interior architecture and one on landscape architecture. To the book also belongs a catalogue where some 100 buildings are presented, and also some 100 mini biographies. Even with this rather large volume and high ambitions this can be no more than a sketch of the architecture of a whole country during a whole century. Some periods might be waiting for a different interpretation, other periods have never before been analyzed this broadly. We hope that the book can be a challenge for others to continue working on the subject.

It also comes natural to have the relation between architecture and society as a theme for a work on Swedish 20th-century architecture. This century has to a high degree been about building a country, starting from a poor periphery of Europe going to a welfare state that went its own way and was seen by many as a model, but also, not least in architecture, stricken by some of the backsides of modernization, perhaps before other European countries. Swedish architecture has been described by a foreign commentator as "an elevated plain without peaks". This can be understood not only as a description but also as a goal. In such a culture a presentation of the broad building tasks and of architecture as everyday environment is of course of central importance. Within this framework there are however also individual efforts of high quality, leading to an architecture that is both "basic and intense", what has been called a "passionate" or "sensual" realism in Swedish architecture.

A first golden age of Swedish 20th-century architecture was the development around the last turn of the century. Influenced by international tendencies but with regional roots there developed an architecture with a strong feeling for the program, the place and the materials. It has been called "national romanticism" but could perhaps rather be described as "material realism". Important contributions, that also were formative for further developments, were made by architects like Ragnar Östberg, Carl Westman, Carl Bergsten and Lars Israel Wahlman.

It has been said about Gunnar Asplund that "he stood on the shoulders of Östberg". With the same right it could be said that Lewerentz, Asplund's contemporary and collaborator on the Woodland cemetery, stood on the shoulders of Westman. Apart from these master-pupil relations an important role was also played by the Consumers' Cooperation's architectural office as an academy for the socially engaged architects. The professional culture developed among these architects was in the 1930s placed before a rapid modernization of society, where building both as a metaphor and as an economic activity had a great importance. In Sweden there was developed a form of "lyrical" modernism that during and after the war was developed into a "neorealism" when architects were given a central role in the building of housing organized by society. The social housing, which in Sweden never became a low cost housing for special groups, must be seen as one of the characteristically Swedish contributions to international architectural development. It also had great influence on the rebuilding of war damaged European countries.

The 1950s saw a still faster modernization of society with the scale of building growing immensely. "The strong society" and "the big programmes" also came to mean the marginalization of architects in the building process. "Production adapted design" was a concept of the time and Sweden got an internationally exceptionally large scale structure both of contractors and architectural consultants. Some of these offices, like ELLT and A4, together with the National Board of Building as a strong commissioner, developed a Swedish structuralism realized in a large production of state institutions.

Apart from these broad tasks that demanded new methods of working there were other architects that stood for a continuity. What has been called "the libertarian tradition" meant an architecture that was in many ways associative, popular, wild or even banal, an architecture with connections to the turn of the century and its ideas of a good life in a small scale and based on craftsmanship. Architects like Erik and Tore Ahlsén, Carl Nyrén, Erik Asmussen, Ralph Erskine, Jan Gezelius, Ove Hidemark, Gunnar Mattsson have in different ways been part of this circle. A more severe and basic architecture, often with a reduction of materials and forms, was produced by a number of architects, all with different relations to the aged Lewerentz: Peter Celsing, Klas Anshelm, Bernt Nyberg, Bengt Edman.

During the 1960s Swedish architecture, perhaps more profoundly than other countries was marked by a sort of "dialectics of enlightenment", a separation into a technical-rational way of working in large scale or a more traditional small scale architectural work, foremost in "the haven of beauty" that church building became. This structure and culture of the building trade and the architectural profession is a heritage that Swedish architecture has been fighting to overcome but which it will carry with it into the next century.

But it also carries with it other tenacious structures: The social responsibility and the closeness to popular movements and traditions that have been an important factor behind the after all relatively peaceful modernization of Swedish society and which has left traces in what has been called a "loyal architecture". Further on also the Swedsih closeness to nature, both geographically in sparsely populated country and culturally in an only recently urbanized society. All these characteristics seem to be knit together in what is now being furthered as a new program, to rebuild Sweden for sustainability. The development of a sustainable society is a challenge which stands before all the countries in the world. To solve this task implies a global way of thinking turned into local action. We think that it also presents architecture with tasks that both demand and support a passionate realism in handling the conditions given by nature effectively and justly.

The Swedish example offers a model, based on its own cultural and natural conditions. In meetings across borders it can be compared to other models, thus stimulating mutual development.

Chronology and Themes

Ludvika "first-class station building" (1875) and (left) the railway hotel: buildings of an urban sort in the countryside, part of a network of civilisation cast over the land.

Edebo Church, Uppland, 15th century. Buildings in stone begin to occur in Sweden in the middle ages, when parish boundaries and church building were networks of civilisation.

Nora, Västmanland. Its grid plan (1644) derived from urban planning done centrally in Stockholm but given effect through local resources and building traditions. Such small wooden towns are as characteristic a part of the Swedish architectural heritage as stone-built churches, and are, too, an early part of a planned society.

Building a Country

BJÖRN LINN

Something that can exemplify the factors that gave form to Swedish architecture is a small country railway station built in the 1870s: a small wooden building with an exterior of machine-sawn planks and painted in some light-coloured oil paint. Its symmetrical facades say little of its rooms, but part can be understood to comprise working premises— waiting room, ticket office—and part living quarters for the personnel. The building is not rural in style but the product of a novel, urban or even cosmopolitan culture with machine-technology resources at its disposal, exemplified by permanent way, operating equipment, points, semaphore signals and telegraphs. These premises are a local manifestation of a larger world.

It has created a novel point in the landscape, a knot in a network that attracts other buildings with owners eager to connect themselves to this novel world: artisans and merchants who have moved here, perhaps even a hotel keeper. This bit of the new world, neither large nor urban, in the middle of forests, woods, cultivated fields: those who alight there step down onto not the higher sort of British-Isles platform but a low gravelled or planked arrangement that is less European than colonial, or Russian or American continental, where civilization is still penetrating the woods.

Such a retrospective view of a station is not of an isolated past moment but a scene in constant variation. Building a country, transforming a given piece of its land into a humanised community, is not merely slowly, step by step, to seize the land by erecting one building after another on it. Decisions made elsewhere take form first here, then, at a distance, there. As a process, this could be called a history of merely importing patterns of civilisation were nothing asked as to where such patterns are

applied, and how they are used. Behind the ordered arrangement may be perceived an interplay between different wills and sorts of knowledge on different levels: local and specific or general and generally superordinate.

The result of this interplay becomes visible as architecture, space created around people and their activities, a physical arrangement of buildings that mediate and realise. The exemplary railway station can be interpreted as having three intrinsic factors that derive from problems that its builders had to contend with.

The first is how these surroundings are to be structured, that is, the content of what planners deal with in 'physical planning'. What parts of the landscape shall be coalesced into populated places, and where are the buildings to be put up? This need not entail laying some planned pattern over the landscape, if, in a decisive move, a potentially attractive point be established, such as the exemplary railway station, which presupposes a continuation that cannot be foreseen in detail. This is fundamental to all building, and the history of Swedish building will show it is in large measure the fruit of establishing such cores in different parts of Sweden.

The second factor is that of types and quantities: with what sorts and numbers of buildings will the country be urbanised? The building is rare that is wholly novel: what is usually built is a type. But there is a difference between variations on an established type, which characterised pre-industrial countries, and strict reproduction of a given model that has characterised the industrial stage, despite on-site building work remaining mainly manual for decades. The relevance of a given type to its use in a specific instance is a recurring question. Following a type may save labour, but, if, for an eventual user, its qualities grate

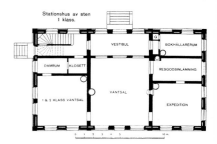

Plan: station building, first class, in stone. A simple, country-house plan applied to a wholly novel function.

against practical demands, justification for this form of rationalisation is nullified.

The third problem is the buildings' qualities, in other words those they should exhibit. As long as it is not ousted by a production of moveable barracks or containers, architecture is an art bound to a given or specified place. Two identical sites cannot be found for even two examples of a single type, while there is the thesis about quality that states the inherent qualities of a place should be a starting point for giving form to a building to be put up there. Architecture as the art of taking good account of and refining the special qualities of a site affords a view quite different from an understanding of what is entailed in producing units to be put on sites prepared for them. The tension between these ways of perception is an abiding source of problems in the history of architecture.

The Core of Swedish Architecture

We distinguish in Swedish history a succession of long waves of phases of expansion and developments of power leading to exhaustion followed by phases of contraction and consolidation. These latter phases, which have been time consuming and have entailed the organisation of land and resources, have given a national administrative structure of fixed but interconnected points.

The initial civilisation network of central planning was ecclesiastical organisation into parishes. Its physical expression was significant, for it coincided with the import in the early 11th century CE of the art of building in stone. As a whole, this building phase was immense. Built to endure, most churches have done so. A modern motoring map of Sweden reveals at once the roles played by churches in the structure of its cultural landscape. Building techniques adapted to the predominantly granite, and such churches became an internationally recognised Swedish type.

The alliance between civil and ecclesiastic powers was a basis for the medieval state that, after the Reformation, subordinated the church. Later, Lutheran pastors and their homes were the intellectual foci of the realm.

Besides churches, towns were civilising elements, of which some (eg Visby on the Baltic island of Gotland, the Old City of Stockholm) were of a German type: high gabled houses in stone inside city walls. Most medieval Swedish towns were small groups of low wooden buildings. From the late 16th century onwards, town streets followed regular geometric grids,

at first within town ramparts, later in open arrangements of buildings encroaching on farms on 'town lands'. These small wooden-built towns are as characteristic of Swedish architecture as their stone-built churches.

During the 17th century, the authorities began seriously to consider the network holding these dispersed but fixed points together. Created to map Sweden, the National Land Survey (Lantmäteriet) had an 18th-century job of rationalising the structure of farming-land ownership. Farms in nuclear villages were shifted to sites in the middle of their lands, which turned members of a community into individual farmers. The Land Survey had then to measure and mark roads, primarily to facilitate travel by servants of the state, as well as organising the system of pre-arranged carriage (skjutsväsen) and inn or bed-and-board services for travellers (gästgiverier) located at intervals of about two Swedish miles (roughly 21.4 km); travellers in pre-railway Sweden looked out for inns, not churches.

In the late 17th century, feudal tendencies among landed grandees were cut down ruthlessly by an efficient royal ruler, Carl XI, who turned them into an upper class of administrators. In the 18th century, they and the farmers were complemented by an enterprising middle class; 18th-century patriarchal owners of generally water-powered 'works' were the models for 19th-century industrialists.

Seventeenth-century Sweden grew wealthy on demand during the Thirty Years' War for forestry and mining (copper and iron) products. The key figure was the Dutch financier, Louis de Geer. Besides financing the Swedish crown's martial contributions, de Geer brought Walloon metal-smiths to Sweden to ensure production by the new industry. The 18th-century industry was based on it, when water-powered industries, generally far from existing towns, led to what the 1940s would call 'planned social development' of brukssamhälle or works' communities. Almost anticipating some 20th-century features, this was the context for the first Swedish building-research project. In 1767, the government commissioned an architect, Carl Johan Cronstedt (1709–77), to devise a means of domestic heating using so little wood that ironworks would not go short of the charcoal they needed for smelting; the result was the Swedish tiled stove (kakelugn), long regarded as the best domestic means of heating in Europe.

The similarities in principle are striking between the works' terraces of metal-smiths' dwellings (following the ordinance of 1766) and the 1930s apartment blocks for urban workers and their families. The works engaged architects to design dwellings in the slightly more-than-average cost class. In the mid 17th century, when architects belonged to a category of artistically-inclined intellectuals a cut above mere builders, being both knowing about the practicalities of building and at home in the literature, Sweden called for experts in their profession: two who responded were Simon de La Vallée and the elder Nicodemus Tessin.

Swedish architects educated themselves, later, through foreign travel. A systematic formal education was introduced in the 18th century, first at the office of the city architect (stadsarkitektskontoret) of Stockholm and, after 1780, at the Royal Academy of Fine Arts, which had been founded in conjunction with the rebuilding of the Royal Palace (Stockholms slott) after the fire in 1697. This work, led initially by the younger Tessin, continued for fifty years or so. Following French style, he was entitled överintendent, around which official position accumulated, in a manner typical for the-then Swedish bureaucracy, an all-embracing organisation of all public-building work. Its disassembly having begun in 1967, it has now been wholly demolished, but, while it existed, it had great importance for keeping up a tradition of knowledge and a culture to do with building.

Even if, institutionally, the 17th century is an important part of the foundations of modern Sweden, present-day Swedes could feel at home first only in some 18th-century conditions, principally those obtaining in the period conventionally called 'the time of freedom': between the soldier's death of Karl XII in 1718, and the absolutism that the young Francophile Gustav III, a nephew to Frederick the Great, introduced soon after his accession in 1772. Its clearly early-modern characteristics include a form of party-political activity, a national policy for industrial and commercial activity, and, in architecture, a creation of building types on a scale approaching that of modern policy. Suitably modernised, 18th-century officer's quarters or small country houses are nowadays attractive, adequately-sized residences. The first golden age of Swedish architecture was gilded by Carl Hårleman, Jean Eric Rehn, Carl Fredrik Adelcrantz and père et fils Carlberg in Göteborg. Erik Lundberg, a historian of architecture, considers that Swedish work then, and during the early 20th century, influenced Denmark; the reverse has otherwise been the case.

This 18th-century foundation has time and again been referred to and taken as a bench

Street (1780–90) at Forsmark ironworks, Uppland, with the church (1794–1800) at one end and the ironmaster's residence at the other: a society planned in function and form. The small houses (for metalworkers) were of a type prescribed by legislation (1766); this housing policy was to further economic development.

mark. When, in the 1930s, Gustaf Näsström, an art historian and critic, presented the new architectural thinking in *Svensk funktionalism*, he devoted his entire long introductory chapter to the link with the 'Swedish building tradition', in which iron-masters' 'works' were prominent. Nowadays, the interiors these architects created have been given emphasis as the general epithet of 'Swedish space'. What is particularly attractive is, perhaps, the charm often found in a movement's early stages, in this case the rationalisation of building work still done manually on a human scale, before the temptation to wring the last drops out of its original ideas becomes overpowering.

This Swedish style ebbed out during the 19th century, as it did elsewhere in Europe with the dissolution of the relatively uniform styles that had united architects and their clients. Until about 1880, European bourgeois society created new institutions needing buildings to house them, while historical and ethnographical studies were giving access to alternative forms. Academic education on French lines made architectural knowledge systematic. Swedish architecture was part of these general conditions.

The Art of Social Engineering, an Architectural Crisis

In about the mid 19th century, an immense wave of energy was released in Sweden, creating not so much large private companies as novel public institutions. In 1848, trade and commerce was liberated from an age-old guild system; in 1864, the last of the other restrictions were abolished. Legislation in 1862 provided a new basis for municipal activity. In 1866, the ancient riksdag of the Four Estates (nobility, clergy, burgers, farmers) voted itself out of existence and became a bicameral assembly.

In the form of railways, a novel network of civilisation spread out over Sweden. A state railway system (Statens järnvägar) built and ran the main lines, with interconnecting lines built and run by private companies. What began as mere railway junctions grew rapidly into urban centres rivalling old formally-established towns. In 1874, a set of building regulations, and one for public health, applied to the country as a whole.

In 1877, with the Royal College of Technology (Kungl. Tekniska Högskolan), in Stockholm, as the principal national institution, technical education was expanded; its basis was elementary schools of technology. With the German polytechnics as a model, further education included a basic education for architects that, in abridged form, was also provided by an embryonic Chalmers University of Technology. The Royal Academy of Fine Arts (Konstakadamien) provided a further stage of artistic education.

What this unique historical epoch contains is better than anything else called the art of social engineering. Having created 'social machines' with decided functions, politicians and administrators delegated their running in accordance with instructions to civil-service 'engineers'. This array of institutions was to carry the burden of modernising Sweden, and—an unrivalled achievement—functioned for about a century.

Its physical expressions included large building programmes to meet the needs of various institutions. Perhaps the best known is

the state railways; in forty years before 1895, it caused about 5,700 buildings, from large stations to huts along the tracks, to be erected; the architect responsible was A.W. Edelsvärd. This sort of programme naturally entails extensive standardisation of types. The job was to master these buildings' new functions that were often much larger than anything previously known; other novelties included materials, techniques following on industrial processes, and social and economic conditions. Architects' only way forward was to try to limit numbers of unknown factors, which can explain the tendency of the time to begin by 'freezing' form to a known size and by referring to a catalogue of accepted styles, which manifested the greatly enlarged historical and ethnographical knowledge at the disposition of middle-class Sweden. The big developments were technical. Drawings were the key: the proper use of modern technology was to reproduce drawn forms with machine-like precision. Both materials and manual skills were subordinated to this form.

Architecture seemed to have a grip on the situation, much as the natural sciences did. But what escaped its grip was the power of industry to produce unexampled quantities of novelties that might impress people but left their feelings untouched. An analogy was novel urban surroundings produced by administrators and planners working as it were over other people's heads. The response was a shift in perspective: turning away from the typical, people now favoured individual products and their qualities as expressions of involvement and work that above all established a real relationship between people, things and their surroundings. Impulses came from British debates, and Pugin's, Ruskin's and Morris' ideas. As the Nordic countries, with the evidence of pre-industrial surroundings before their eyes, had not gone very far down the road towards modernisation, having these ideas contributed to healthy growth in artistic matters.

This shift is one of the most crucial points in the histories of Swedish art and architecture, and, in the latter, displaced drawings from their central position in favour of buildings. Freed from having precisely to copy what a drawing depicted, artisans could leave visible traces of their work and tools. As a slogan put it, architectural form would derive from "real material" and manual work. A teacher whose work seems to have been undervalued for too long, Albert Theodor Gellerstedt, the first professor of architecture at the Royal College of Technology and a

The Wijk Residence, Göteborg, by Adrian Crispin Peterson, about 1880, in an architecture requiring drawings to be reproduced, with machine-like precision, in materials and work by artisans.

builder of lighthouses, had discovered the Swedish building tradition in the course of his work; he caused his students to study simple buildings with just this sort of expression. His teaching did put down roots and begin to grow, but began to sprout only during the second golden age of Swedish architecture: in about 1905 when the world at large began to notice work by Carl Westman, Ragnar Östberg, Lars Israel Wahlman and others.

Twentieth-century art-history research has labelled these currents of thought 'national romanticism', on the grounds of using the same labels for architecture as for painting, literature and music. Consequently, observers may be misled into seeing retrospection of a sort than is seemingly implied: as to quality, this was genuinely one of the most creative and re-enlivening periods in the history of Swedish architecture. Brick is not prominent in the Swedish building tradition, but architects used it plentifully to express their wish for a sense of tangible reality. Were we to choose a better name for the characteristic architectural qualities of this period, it would be 'material realism'.

But expressions from materials and manual work were subdued, while the effects of space became increasingly subtly treated, in the classicism (or as often something of the baroque) of the 1920s that had manifested itself first in about 1910 and was used as both specifically architecturally and for references of a general cultural nature. Whoever consciously moves within space created in this epoch can often perceive how the architect has managed to confer shifting qualities on space itself by causing it to coalesce along frequently intersecting axes, to penetrate a surrounding wall in a dramatic manner, or to create tension in a room through contradictions between exterior and interior elements of form. The Blue Hall of Stockholm Town Hall exemplifies this: the whole building became something of a laboratory for novel concepts. Robert Venturi's 1966 book title, *Complexity and Contradiction*, is apposite here as an indication of what the architects in Stockholm were working with. The emergence of Swedish architecture into general international consciousness was confirmed by the fine book, *Swedish Architecture of the Twentieth Century*, published in London in 1925 on the initiative of Frank Yerbury.

The Swedish architectural profession was then growing strongly. In 1880, when the population was about 4.5 million, there were about one hundred Swedish architects; by the second decade of the new century there were over 400. The work of intellectuals, including

Corner-jointing at Tallom, Lars Israël Wahlman's house, Stocksund (1904–06). He interpreted Ruskin's and Morris' feelings for peoples' relationships to material, and, until 1935, taught the art of building in wood to the functionalist generation.

Ellen Key, a writer, and Carl Larsson, a painter, had caused a general acceptance of the significance of aesthetically ordered surroundings. In a country undergoing modernisation, many industrial but also housing commissions reached young architects, probably from former student friends. Housing began to be understood as the country's major problem. A liberal government appointed a housing commission that made investigations during the second decade of the century; one of its consequences was the appointment in 1919 of the first national commission for planning housing, with respect to small apartments; its report in 1921 was called *Practical and hygienic dwellings* (Praktiska och hygieniska bostäder).

This is symptomatic. Architects' working concerns were widening to encompass matters that would be of central national importance in coming decades. This called for novel knowledge to be developed, around which architects gathered with great interest. Efforts to make this knowledge systematic found form in functionalism: in this mode, the international reputation of Swedish architecture would endure until the 1950s. During the 1920s, the first female architects made their debut, which was also a cultural and social change of great importance.

Functionalism and the People's Home (Folkhemmet)

Thus, as a creation, functionalism was not entirely novel but had been preparing for a long time. The reference to the classical geometric discipline was preserved in its new for-

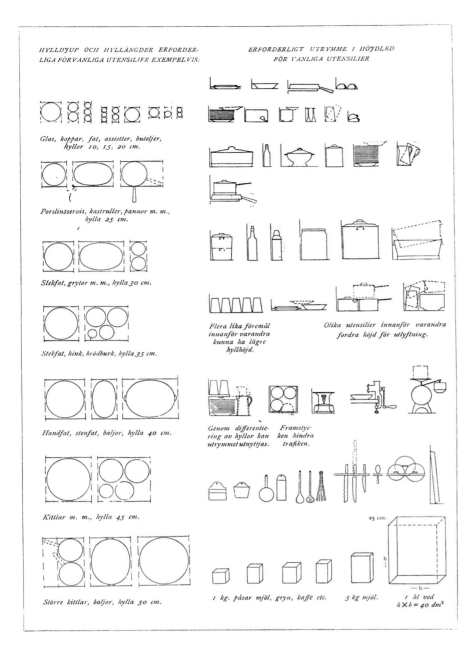

HYLLDJUP OCH HYLLÄNGDER ERFODER-
LIGA FÖR VANLIGA UTENSILIER EXEMPELVIS:

ERFORDERLIGT UTRYMME I HÖJDLED
FÖR VANLIGA UTENSILIER

Glas, koppar, fat, assietter, buteljer,
hyllor 10, 15, 20 cm.

Porslinsservis, kastruller, pannor m. m.,
hylla 25 cm.

Stekfat, grytor m. m., hylla 30 cm.

Stekfat, hink, brödburk, hylla 35 cm.

Handfat, stenfat, baljor, hylla 40 cm.

Kittlar m. m., hylla 45 cm.

Större kittlar, baljor, hylla 50 cm.

Flera lika föremål
innanför varandra
kunna ha lägre
hyllhöjd.

Olika utensilier innanför varandra
fordra höjd för utlyftning.

Genom differentie-
ring av hyllor kan
utrymmet utnyttjas.

Framstyc-
ken hindra
trafiken.

1 kg. påsar mjöl, gryn, kaffe etc.

5 kg mjöl.

25 cm.

1 hl ved
h × b = 40 dm²

Kitchen standards, by Osvald Almqvist (1927). Standardisation of building material and parts was a part of industrial, time-and-motion rationalisation. For a long time, dwellings were at the centre of the development of knowledge by functionalism.

degree. It signifies a national society that did more than erect buildings: it was a metaphor and a symbol.

What would later be called 'the Swedish model' grew out of a widely shared political intention to realise the idea that a general lifting of standards, a welfare society, could be created by favouring industrialisation. Such a society of converging opinions must also be understood as capable of being planned rationally. This sort of thinking had been largely formulated in the Weimar Republic in the 1920s; interrupted there, it lived on as an indisputable basis for Swedish architecture and planning of national society until the 1960s. Since then much of its assumptions have remained as an unconscious basis for ideas.

The functionalism of the 1930 Stockholm exhibition was in a phase of manifestation, in which attention was given to novel elements. As the People's Home emerged, work began to come from everyday life and functionalism kept its striking formal characteristics. The dominating job was to build ready-to-live-in dwellings. Many earlier projects were individual buildings on inner-urban sites; during the 1930s, new districts began to grow outside traditional town centres, in locations with space for novel urban-planning ideas with open, extensive patterns of buildings, initially as long parallel blocks. In the late 1930s, the first apartment point blocks were built, on Gärdet, the park-like open space east of central Stockholm. Signs of this new building culture appeared here and there in Sweden, white cubes like splotches of paint flung out at random: privately-owned houses, often factory-made in wood and ready-to-put-up. Building programmes for the People's Home soon had other aims, among them leisure, tourism and motor cars. After 1938, employees' rights included at least two weeks' paid holiday.

A second phase began in the 1940s. Stylistically, appearances were softer: what had become self evident had no longer to be demonstrated. Romantic elements interrupted rationalism. There were compelling reasons for this: with war in the rest of Europe, cement and reinforcing rods were scarce in Sweden, which favoured a return to manual building methods. Despite houses' changed looks, the working principles of functionalism remained the unquestioned bases for planning.

After 1945, architects' main work was to realise the housing policy decided by the riksdag in 1946–48, on the basis of the Housing-Social Commission's (Bostadssociala utredningen) work since its appointment in 1933.

mal language. But decoration on the body of a building was definitively loosened, to become independent art, and, as a mediating element, skilled crafts' work was finally abandoned. Artefacts had become so habitual that they could be treated as self evident. The task was now to form an architecture that could, but did not have to, be realised through industrial production.

This task was posed in the emblem of the political vision of a People's Home that, as a phrase, had had various uses and senses in Swedish politics before the Social-Democrat party chairman, Per Albin Hansson, used it in a riksdag debate to signify a national society in which all social and economic barriers would be broken down; in other words, a modern welfare society. In 1932, when his party formed the government, its policy was to realise this society. In Swedish history, the People's Home is the political leitmotif for an epoch that has expressed itself visibly to a rare

Selective measures having previously been used, general quality demands were formulated and applied. Subsidies would favour production and keep immediate net rental costs down. In principle, the goal was to offer all the possibility of housing of the same sort. Other countries had a principle of building low-cost housing for low-income families: Sweden offered them rent subsidies. To a remarkable degree, building was of apartment blocks. A detailed array of what were called 'building norms' were established to regulate quality, on a basis of the foundation from the 1940s onwards of building- and housing-research institutions.

Changes After 1945

From about 1950, the Swedish-model housing policy began to look for the befits of large-scale production for municipal-housing and contracting companies. In about 1960, the idea was put forward of production-adapted planning (produktionsanpassad projektering). Architectural expression began to be sought in suppositions about industrial serial production of similar elements: news from yesterday, or Henry Ford's doings on production lines in about 1910. Functionalism was becoming rather remote. Interest was shifting again towards types and quantities, but in more extreme forms than ever before and, thanks to technical resources, on unprecedentedly large scales. This weakened architects' roles: when the scale was of manual work on a comparatively miniature sort, they had been responsible for an important part of the continuity of the knowledge informing the whole. But architectural education continued to expand: being now offered at universities in Göteborg, Lund (from 1964) and Stockholm.

Swedish architecture has always been distinguished as set in Swedish landscapes. There being no really large urban regions in Sweden, most building work has been to extend or rebuilding existing societies. The regional policy of the 1960s entailed moving national-administrative units from Stockholm, not to literal 'new towns' but to small existing ones, which incurred significant social costs. The few examples of building what were really new built-up areas, for example the small coastal resort of Stenungsund, the new national petrochemical centre, were not particularly important from a planning point of view.

The Swedish model did well as long as its relative isolation was kept up. Neutrality in 1939–45 and the relative success of regula-

Dwellings, Nya Bruket, Sandviken, (1973–78), by Ralph Erskine, who followed the 1940s 'people's-home' tradition of preferring a social environment to any one of its buildings.

tions during this long crisis stimulated post-1945 collective thinking about national planning and regulation. The model could no longer be managed once it was exposed to developments and conflicts in the world at large. It had favoured architects by putting them into a central position, close to the big decisions about planning national and municipal societies and the attendant housing policies. When, after 1970, building volumes first wobbled and then shrank abruptly, building regulations were greatly changed, and building norms were discontinued, and the wholly novel conditions that obtained took the architectural profession aback. While the community has at least as great a need as ever of its services, a way must now be found to cope with the problems this poses and to create the novel roles in which architects can best deploy their knowledge.

The main entrance, to the Industry Hall, of the 1897 Stockholm exhibition. Its architecture, festively rich in details, spoke of turn-of-the-century optimism.

International Impulses and National Tradition 1900–15

EVA ERIKSSON

One can see the great 1897 *Stockholm Art and Industry Exhibition* (Konst- och industri-utställningen) as the finale of a century's transforming development. Officially, what was celebrated was the 25th anniversary of the accession of Oscar II to the throne of Sweden and Norway. But the most important role of the exhibition was as a manifestation of industrial advances for a country on the European periphery. In the machine hall, rows of gleaming machines at work thumped and rattled rhythmically. The industry of inventions, with quickly developing production of novel inventions, contributed to the country's rapid inclusion among the advanced industrial nations of Europe.

During the 1890s a period of intense economic growth had begun. Swedish industrialism reached its second phase after that of the steam engine and the breakthrough of the early industrial sectors in the mid 19th century. Now followed the epoch of electricity, large-scale industry and advanced technical development. Being a phase of development with investments demanding much capital, it was a golden age for banks.

The exhibition became something of a fun fair for industrialism, offering the public the industrial advances and scientific achievements of the time along with temptations including balloon ascents, illuminated cascades of water and electric light from thousands of coloured bulbs.[1] But in addition art was prominent: among middle-class Swedes, culture was accorded a high value in questions of national prestige. The late 19th century had comprised a cultural breakthrough for the Nordic countries. The cultural radicalism of the 1880s had called attention to problems of society and opened the way for social engagement. Now a new generation of writers and artists called attention to other questions. Many of these

artists and others had lived for years on the continent of Europe where they had encountered the criticism of civilisation of the time and a fin-de-siècle atmosphere. They returned homewards with their senses wide open for what was particular in the culture and nature of their homeland. Despite its rapid industrial advances, Sweden was still basically an agricultural country. The daily life of most people was closely allied to the conditions of nature and the changes of the seasons. A feeling for nature is also deeply rooted in Nordic tradition and has characterised myths and popular stories since time out mind.

At the 1897 exhibition, the new Swedish art of the landscape that had developed foremost within the Artists' Association (Konstnärsförbundet), a breakaway group formed in 1886 in protest against the conservatism of the Royal

Richard Bergh: "Northern summer evening" ("Nordisk sommarkväll"), 1899–1900. Natural scenes in northern light were depicted suggestively in turn-of-the-century art.

The Nordic Museum, Stockholm (1889–1907), by Isak Gustaf Clason, who intermingled motifs from secular history into a monument having an internal atmosphere that was almost sacred.

Academy of Fine Arts (Konstakadamien). In paintings in the Art Hall there glimmered the light of summer nights over still forest pools and large-scale views. These artists had capture Swedish nature and the light of the north in lyrical, strongly suggestive images, but they also depicted the people of various parts of Sweden and various types of landscape with a realism that was close to everyday experience. Many painters had found their way to Dalarna, where older buildings had been preserved and traditions were still more alive than they were in other parts of Sweden. At the exhibition Carl Larsson's watercolours from his home at Sundborn in Dalarna, for example, were shown for the first time.

The exhibition area included the open-air museum, *Skansen*, a result of efforts by Arthur Hazelius to preserve and make living an old culture that was dissolving. Buildings from different parts of the country were brought there, that, together, formed a map of types of Swedish building traditions. At the time the *Nordic Museum* (Nordiska Museet) was half-way built (1889–1907); for the exhibition, it had been provided with a provisional timber

building. A further ten years would elapse before this immense cathedral of Swedish cultural tradition would be complete enough to be inaugurated. While Hazelius had taken the initiative, Isak Gustaf Clason, an architect, had worked for a long time on the museum project that, earlier, had been formed as a four-square Swedish 16th-century fortress. Now, instead, it became a single volume, with rooms grouped around an immense hall occupying the full height of the building. Its exterior induces thoughts of the Danish renaissance, but, as a whole, the building is a synthesis of architectural forms from different historical times and countries.

Ferdinand Boberg was responsible for the exhibition's most remarkable architectural element. Its immense *Industry Hall* became the emblem of the exhibition; it had an immense central cupola surrounded by four minaret-like towers. Its festively detailed formal language was characteristic for Boberg, who had however received help from his colleague, Fredrik Lilljekvist, primarily with plans.[2] Boberg's *Art Hall* had a wholly different, Spartan character. It was a low, white building originally proposed as wholly smooth except for a wide ornamental frieze. Its final form extended this with a loggia and linked to the *Machinery Hall*, which had a different character that originated in simple constructive forms. It was also designed by Boberg.

The contents of these last two buildings also contrasted. Paintings in the Art Hall could give the impression that Sweden was still a sleeping idyll, while Machine Hall thundered with an atmosphere of bubbling power and energy. It was an eloquent expression of the divided sense of the time. On one side appeared optimism about the future within technology and science, where change implied development and advance. But equally strongly, it expressed an interest in nature, backward looks, and care about tradition, where change could imply a threat to essential values.

Swedish society had began to split under the strain of novel contradictions that industrialism caused. But at the great exhibition the tension could be discharged in a shared feeling of national pride.

A Time of Change

Socially, economically and politically, the first decennium of the 20th century was a time of change. A new parliament building was under construction in Stockholm, which could be seen as a manifestation of parliamentarianism and democracy. But this, the Riksdag, was no really democratic parliament yet. The suffrage was restricted to those who had sufficient income or property and, in addition, the right sex. Ordinary, poor workers were not permitted to vote, nor were women. Political strife over the suffrage began to increase. In 1889, the Social Democrat Party had been formed and the Labour Movement was marching forward. In addition to this, large numbers of people had been organised in other popular movements: the teetotaller movement, the free-church movement. These movements were to acquire an important role in Swedish society. A relatively large part of the population was engaged through them in a disciplined struggle for collective goals and a gathering of forces around shared ideals.

Swedish society was divided into strictly differentiated social levels, conditions of life were very different. The housing question came to be a thermometer for social conditions, as well as a central point in the activity for reform that would gradually begin to grow.

About the turn of the century, architecture was characterised by multiplicity. Architects faced entirely novel tasks in building, a new scale and a new tempo in urban growth, at the same time as new materials and principles of construction began to come into use.

The time was, too, one of searching and change in a purely aesthetic sense. A number of different attitudes towards form existed side by side. As a last element of the otherwise severely criticised architecture of style came different elements from the formal world of the baroque: new baroque, Jugendstil baroque, the baroque of Tessin and of the Swedish late 17th-century great-power period. More or less clear attempts to find an aesthetic expression for modern materials and designs existed alongside or mixed with other formal tendencies. Pronounced Art Nouveau in a French-Belgian mixture was seldom seen. On the other hand it did appear to some extent in a more disciplined Viennese Jugendstil. With Richardson's American architecture and the English Arts & Crafts Movement, medieval and Romanesque forms became relevant together with an increasing interest in materials. Together with inspiration from Swedish 16th-century castles, this became a point of departure in the attempt to develop a new architecture: the national-romantic-style. Finally, middle-to-late 18th-century Gustavian architecture and interior design began to be rediscovered.

Georg Pauli painting a fresco in the main hall of the new Bank of Sweden building (1906).

During the first decade of the 20th century, architecture was to be characterised by this pluralism, but also by architects' attempts to come to terms with the fissile tendencies of the time and find a practical way forward to deal with the problems of modern cities.

Sculptural Freedom and an Interest in Material

The 1897 exhibition became the great breakthrough for Ferdinand Boberg. In the years that followed he was to design many of the important buildings that are characteristic for Stockholm. But, in an architectural history sense, his really path-breaking efforts were over, having been made at the beginning of the 1890s.

Criticism against architecture of style had then found clear expression in Sweden. Younger architects experienced it as a masquerade, in which forms were repeated more and more mechanically. An architect did not proceed from what a building contained, seeking "to give it a characteristic form but took a form onto which he would impress a content", as the young Carl Westman wrote in an article published in 1893.[3]

The attempt to allow the content to find expression in the exterior worked together with the taste of time for an organic formal language, which gave greater freedom in both forms of detail and in the grouping of the masses of buildings. A pioneer in Sweden of this development was Isak Gustaf Clason who, in his *Bünsowska House* (1888–89) on Strand-

(Right) Bünsow House, Strandvägen, Stockholm (1886–88), where Isak Gustaf Clason preferred a freer formal language in brick and stone to the otherwise dominant neo-renaissance plaster.

(Far right) Doorway, Electricity Works, Regeringsgatan, Stockholm, by Boberg (1889–92), embellished with a functionally associating frieze of sculpted light bulbs. The building has been razed, but its doorway was saved and has been re-erected elsewhere.

vägen, Stockholm, had broken definitely with the neo-renaissance schema that still dominated Swedish architecture. The older stylistic pattern emphasised horizontality and a regular modular fenestration that had began to be felt as constricting. Rendered, ornamented facades that gave an impression of being carved in stone were experienced as false. Clason took as his point of departure early French renaissance architecture with its romantically picturesque irregularities of towers and lofty gables. This allowed him more room for variation.

In Gävle Fire Station (1889–91) Boberg used a free, sculptural style associating to work by H.H. Richardson in the US; this photograph predates regrettable change.

Freer fenestration let him create a better agreement between content and form, between floor plans and facades. Finally he made genuine material part of a programmatic demand. The building became a breakthrough in Swedish architecture for brick and natural stone as facade material.

With his *Fire station* in Gävle (1889–91), Boberg introduced a formal language that was to be still more liberating during the 1890s. His inspiration came from H.H. Richardson, the American. Heavy and fort-like, the fire station expresses his ideas. Its doors take the form of deep recesses in the wall that emphasise the mass and weight of the stone, while also providing a means for a rich interplay of light and shadow.

Soon, one of Boberg's characteristics became a thin but rich flood of surface ornamentation with an iconography that could associate to the building's various functions: as was clearly expressed in *Stockholms elverk* (1889–92). Around its deeply recessed door the stone is carved into a frieze of sculptured electric lights in a stylised pattern. This was an attempt to find a modern language, which must clearly have been felt as particularly penetrating for an unprecedented type of building: no electricity building had ever previously been designed in Sweden.

With Richardson and medieval building art as a source of inspiration, the conventional styles of the time could be broken up so as to reach a greater freedom of expression and a more organic context between the inner and the outer, between plan, design and practical usability on the one side and architectural form on the other. At the same time, material moved into the foreground. An architect who, in an unusually powerful manner worked with the effects of material in combination with a sculptural treatment of the volumes of a building, was Hans Hedlund, active in Göteborg. His *Dickson Public Library* from 1895 is an asymmetrical, fort-like building in brick that also has a precise treatment of detail in natural stone.

A Swedish predecessor in trying to use natural stone in facades was the English-influenced Adolf Kjellström. He was not a formally educated architect but through his devoted interest in natural stone he had much influence in his home town of Örebro, where an architecture in natural stone had began to take form as early as the 1860s and 1870s, particularly concerning limestone, a local material that had been quarried in Yxhult since the early 19th century. The breakthrough of natural stone as a facade material about the turn of the 20th century led to an increased demand for it as for the Swedish stone industry as a whole. This was made more easy, naturally, by improved means of quarrying and transporting stone, through explosive and railway developments.[4]

The new feeling for material influenced considerations of the role and character of ornamentation. It was no longer a matter of forming images in stone but of letting the special qualities of different sorts of stone express themselves. Just as in visual art colour acquired a value of its own, in architecture material became an intrinsic reality. This was moving in the same direction as changes in formal language as a whole. The job was not to cover a particular form in a stylistic costume but to give the building a form derived from its own parts—material and design— and to make use of the expressive values that lay in these. Boberg took the first steps in this process, but did not abandon his pictorial view of ornamentation.

In the bank and office building, *Rosenbad* (1899–1904), Stockholm, Boberg contrasted smoothly rendered wall surfaces against sections of ornamented natural stone. His ornamentation is thin and fine-limbed. Only at very close quarters can one see it is clearly his characteristic imagery about the building's intended functions: long rivers of coins form ornamental bands on the stone. For him ornament had an architectural role that empha-

(Left) Skånes Enskilda Bank, Stockholm, by Gustaf Wickman (1897–1900). (Above) Its corner entry leads through to a top-glazed banking hall occupying a former back yard.

sised essential parts in the building's composition rather than its design. Doors, corners, central parts and the extension of the roof is articulated through ornamentation. Close to, there opens up a world of images like that of a rebus.

Modernity and Eclecticism

Similarly to Boberg, Gustaf Wickman worked with a plastic sculptural formal language that

Skåne Bank, Banking Hall, with curved mahogany counter and marble-and-stucco wall decorations. The ceiling arches are in rendered, reinforced concrete.

has a touch of jugendstil about it. But for him the baroque was closer to hand. One can see this on Drottninggatan in central Stockholm, where his building for *Skånes Enskilda bank* (1897–1900) lies next to Boberg's Rosenbad. Here Wickman created large openings for light with the help of internal bearing iron pillars and steel girders. The first two floors form a socle dominated by powerful arcade arches that suggest American architecture. But the building also possesses an expressed neo-baroque character with a great plasticity that culminates in Christian Eriksson's sculptural embellishment of its door. From the entry one goes through the body of the building directly into the top-lit banking hall in the central yard. This resolution became an important pattern for the many bank buildings of the time.[5]

Gustaf Wickman became the leading Swedish architect of banks at the turn of the century. Financial capital had a key role in the economic advances of the time, its architecture gave an expression for self consciousness, solid financial standing and solvency. Practically every Swedish town got at least one new bank building, often with a facade in natural stone and with expensive furnishings. The concept of a 'bank palace' took form.

Wickman was a commercially successful architect with a rich clientele, to whose wishes he was of course sensitive.[6] He represented a neo-baroque that was an element in Swedish turn-of-the-century architecture, but, characteristically eclectic and pragmatic, he combined a baroque interest in details with modern designs and rational ground plans. In some instances he worked in a more severe baroque with more block-like compositions of volumes. But, as he did in the mining town of Kiruna, he could also create an architecture in wood that had a regional association. Even a single architect's work could seem heterogeneous, with partly contrasting elements of modernity and history.

In the many residential buildings along the streets of Stockholm and elsewhere in Sweden neo-baroque united with Art Nouveau into a fertile plastic form. The attempt to get round town-planning decisions so as to obtain as much rentable apartment space as possible contributed to the plumply swollen character of many buildings.

Around the turn of the century, in the sensitive area immediately in front of the royal palace, there were erected two monumental buildings: the *Riksdagshuset* by Aron Johansson and the *Royal Opera* by Axel Anderberg. Both, but especially the first, became the subject of violent criticism. The fundamental argument was that the beautifully balanced place that acquired its character during the 18th century had been destroyed and that the previously self-evident dominance of the palace had been broken. Both new buildings associated to the German-Austrian classicising baroque in Semper's spirit. But the architects of both had sought to associate to the palace and its restrained baroque of the Swedish great-power period in the work of Nicodemus Tessin the younger.

Isak Gustaf Clason made a more precise interpretation of Tessin's baroque in his *brandstodsbolagets hus* on a site on Skeppsbron, Stockholm (1899–1901), which was cleared by demolishing a house owned by the elder Tessin. This had caused strong reactions. The choice of style for the new building was therefore already provided. Clason also followed the historical pattern with academic faithful-

Riksdagshuset, Stockholm, by Aron Johansson (1894–1905). Located near the Royal Palace, the building met severe contemporary criticism.

Royal Opera, by Axel Anderberg (1891–98), also sensitively near the Palace and not unanimously praised.

Hamngatspalatset, Stockholm, by Johan Laurentz (1899).
A department store (demolished), on the model of similar
buildings in Berlin.

This building by Ernst Stenhammar (1908–10) was the
first in Stockholm to use reinforced concrete on a
straightforward skeletal design.

ness to detail but on a scale quite unlike that
of the 17th century. Later, too, he would
remain faithful to the architecture of the
great-power period as an important model.
His strong position as the leading authority in
Swedish architecture at the turn of the century
gave this line of approach a particular legitimacy.

In building for commercial purposes, practical demands led to new tendencies. When,
during the 19th century, cast iron made it possible to relieve walls of bearing functions, larger glazed facade surfaces could be devoted to
display windows and internal arrangements
could be freer. The same effects were sought
in industrial buildings. The reasons for this lay
foremost in that industrial work could be
organised more effectively in larger units,
which demanded large rooms and much daylight.

To begin with, iron and glass were hidden
behind historical facades but began to emerge
as formal elements in buildings for commercial use about the turn of the century. American impulses were mediated here in Sweden
through among other things German depart-
ment-store architecture. The first modern
premises in Stockholm for commercial rental,
the *Hamngatspalatset* (1899) by Johan Laurentz, followed the pattern from Wertheim,
Berlin, with large glazed parts between verti-

cal supports. Earlier a steel frame had been
used in the *Centralpalatset* by Ernst Stenhammar (completed 1898) in a factual form without historical details. The first building in
reinforced concrete in Stockholm that had a
straightforward skeletal design was *Myrstedt
& Stern's* commercial premises on Kungsgatan
(1908–10) by the same architect.

Its large top-lit room became as mentioned
a rational model, much liked in the banking
world. It was excellently suited also for the
interior of department stores, where a well-lit
central space offered extensive vistas and a
place to meet in an international manner. In
this context a light well was introduced to
Sweden in *K.M. Lundberg's* department store
on Stureplan in central Stockholm, 1898, but
it was short-lived. As soon as 1912–1915, its
owners built a new, more modern department
store with a large light well: NK designed by
Boberg.

Covered markets, or saluhallar, were
another sort of commercial building of which
many were built around the turn of the century, where large top-lit spaces met practical
demands. *Östermalms Saluhall*, Stockholm
(1888) by Clason is an example. He combined
'modern' space with historical formal language, while, in *Saluhallen*, Göteborg
(1887–88), Hans Hedlund created a factually
constructive building in steel and glass.

Industrial Hall, 1906 Art and Industry Exhibition, Norrköping, by Carl Bergsten; this style was then very radical for Sweden.

Aesthetically, the most radical architecture in the first decennium of the 20th century were Carl Bergsten's buildings for the 1906 *Norrköping Art and Industry Exhibition* (Konstoch industriutställningen i Norrköping 1906). He received the commission after a competition to which he was invited to contribute in autumn 1904. Then 25 years old, he had just got home from his first lengthier study trip. His formal language is a testimony to its goals. He was one of the few Swedish architects who were then deeply impressed by Vienna and the Wagner school.[7] His student friend Gunnar Morssing, who followed the same line, helped him to work through the competition drawings in the final project work.

Bergsten's commission concerned the most important buildings and the planning in general. The dominant feature was the Industrial Hall with a peculiar tower crowned by a parabolic cupola on a large protruding horizontal part. Most pared down and simple was the Art Hall with clean white surfaces. It followed the praxis begun in the remarkably simple one at the 1897 Stockholm Exhibition by Boberg, but, in comparison, Bergsten's work seems revolutionarily modern. In this context, ornamentation à-la-Boberg would have been unthinkable, seeing that the walls were so abstract and devoid of material. The entry was formed as a large semi-circular niche, decorated with a blue pattern; this recalls Olbrich's studio at Matildenhöhe in Darmstadt that Bergsten had visited on his way home from Vienna.

The Norrköping exhibition was much too radical to win general acceptance in Sweden. A comment by Ragnar Östberg says much about the views of the time besides showing his personal ability to appreciate Bergsten's talent and artistic seriousness. "In this build-ing, the Industry Hall," he wrote "there lies something of flinty consistency, intensive ruthlessness, and radical energy that are extremely rarely found in a Swedish artist and in general in the Swedish temperament. That the architect of this work possesses both a powerful and rare talent is evident. We greet him with pleasure. He is needed. His temperament takes pleasure in a saltiness that becomes a power of good at once in the saucepan of Swedish architecture. For all together too often our work suffers from a spineless talent for agreement, where masonry may degenerate into pastry cooking and the tones of history replace an artistic touch."[8]

Born in Norrköping, Bergsten soon received two more commissions in the town. For the exhibition year he designed a restaurant, *Strömsholmen*, with interior design in a Viennese Werkstätte-style. And he reworked his earlier drawings for a school, *St. Olof School*, giving it a more geometrical character and further simplifying it. In addition, he designed a bank in the same town, *Skandinaviska banken*, where he reinterpreted the architecture in brick of the time in a personal way. The effects of the material are held back so as instead to give an impression of flat surfaces, where areas of rendering in contrasting colours contribute an abstract character.

Bergsten shared an interest in severity and a geometrical tendency in Viennese Jugendstil

In its form, Georg A. Nilsson's own house, at Regeringsgatan 88, Stockholm, 1906–07, almost anticipated functionalism.

with Georg A. Nilsson, an architect who came to devote the greater part of his professional activity to school buildings, on which he came to be an authority. He was also known as an unprejudiced and advanced designer of a couple of modern commercial and residential premises in central Stockholm. He achieved his breakthrough with Matteus skola in Stockholm (1901–02) that, without seeming radical, was unusual at the time for a stringency and clarity in volumes and details. Cubical blocks and a certain geometrical tendency in bands of white rendering on its brick walls were balanced by softly rounded forms in doors, windows and parts of roofs. It became exemplary through its simple natural designs and absence of decoration. In the building of Swedish schools it was epoch-making in its resolution of plans and manner of building.[9]

In designing an industrial complex for Luth & Rosén's engineering works, Stockholm, that was an early Swedish example of large-scale fenestration in industrial architecture, Nilsson cooperated with the designer, Ivar Nyqvist.[10] Nilsson was more radically modern in his own house on Regeringsgatan 88 (now spoiled) from 1906–07. This commercial and residential building had an extremely simplified facade that revealed its early origin in few details. Its top floor balcony rail belongs more to the formal world of functionalism.

Nilsson took this modernistic line further with a *commercial and office building for Felix Sachs* at Regeringsgatan 9, Stockholm, which he did with Nyqvist, now his partner. Nilsson had begun work on these drawings in 1908 and twice reworked and simplified them later, until all was complete by 1912. This cleaned out Art Nouveau details, so that the modern design (steel skeleton with a concrete beam construction), became more and more simplified, but was also artistically well balanced. Above a ground floor with large shop windows the facade was formed as three large bay windows covering four stories, over which lay two floors recessed behind a terrace. The premises extended over two sites, which included two inner courts and a further street facade, which was also radically simplified. Equivalent tendencies to simplified constructive design forms were exhibited by a couple of other commercial premises in Stockholm, but without the consistent and aesthetic control exhibited by Nilsson's building. Even in an international prospective it was in advance of its time.[11]

In 1908, two years after the Norrköping exhibition and in the same year as Bergsten's Norrköping bank and school, and after a lengthy building period, a more noted inaugu-

Royal Dramatic Theatre, Stockholm, by Fredrik Lilljekvist, 1901–08, encountered a certain degree of criticism for its festively embellished Art Nouveau architecture.

ration took place in Stockholm: the new *Royal Dramatic Theatre* designed by Fredrik Lilljekvist that also contained certain elements of Viennese Jugendstil but without the severity and consistency that distinguished Bergsten's and Nilsson's building. It expresses a festive atmosphere not least in its ornamentation and richly artistic embellishments. In contemporary eyes this theatre building seemed new and modern. The question was whether it would set a new tone in Swedish architecture.

Westman's critical commentary in *Arkitektur* was caused by precisely the worry that it might become the norm.[12] His objections were therefore those of principle. To begin with he criticised the gap between its design and expression, a theme repeatedly addressed in the debate. Its dominant central tower was motivated aesthetically, but, in his opinion, was merely an empty form lacking any equivalent practical function, while the fly tower over the stage, for which there was a practical reason, was not indicated architecturally, but rather pressed down in form. Further, in Westman's opinion, the theatre's embellishment was divided and lacked a consistent scale. He and other critics sought a clearer entity, in which essentials were emphasised and inessentials restrained. They objected a muddle of decoration and architectural forms.[13] In Westman's eyes, a certain severity had always characterised the Swedish art of building.

For himself, Westman had already made himself clear in a building of his own, *Medical Association building* (1904–06), Stockholm,

Medical Society's House, (1904–06), Stockholm, by Carl Westman, epoch-making for national romanticism.

that, in contrast to Dramaten, did become a Swedish architectural norm. In the whirligig of tendencies and expressions of form that characterised turn-of-the-century work, a group of architects now sought answers to the problems of principle they faced in contemporary architecture.

Not the Drawing Board but the Building Site

Stockholm was a city of plaster. Bare brick, by contrast, was most used in Skåne, in the south of the country, adjoining the Danish and northern German brick area. Further north, timber was usual in simpler houses; more distinguished ones were rendered, except on the

west coast, where winds off the sea affected plasterwork. But one cannot claim brick was a national material, so it is paradoxical that brick walls should become the most characteristic early 20th-century expression of national architectural style.

Medical Association building became the breakthrough work. To a high degree, Westman brought international currents of thought down onto Swedish ground. Traces are evident in his work of Ruskin, Morris and the Arts & Crafts Movement. But when this building was complete, its feeling, if not directly its material and forms of detail, was very Swedish: its seriousness, factual appearance and unadorned simplicity were deemed to be national characteristics.[14]

The beautiful hand-made brick Westman chose gave the wall a shifting surface with a painterly effect of a richly chromatic effect. The strong reddish roof and walls were deepened in colour through contrasts with white woodwork of windows and grey natural stone. The windows were halfway up the facade in a manner traditional in the latitude of Stockholm: brought to the surface of the wall, the glass effectively catches and reflects the low sloping winter sunlight down into the street. The white painted woodwork on the surface also gives the wall a textile character, on which the bays of the windows hang like simple jewellery, while the door has the impression of breaking through the wall. The building contains club premises for doctors, various public rooms, an auditorium and a dining room. The suites of rooms were worked by Westman in a restrained Art Nouveau.

Westman had limited his means of expression to the fundamental elements of the building: walls, doors, windows, roof. He sought a new simplicity, a restrained factuality. At the

Hall and staircase. Medical Society's House: a light interior with yellow-glazed bricks and a touch of Viennese Art Nouveau.

Assembly room, Medical Society's House: Art Nouveau furniture and fittings by Carl Westman.

same time he wanted to achieve a sensual richness through colour, the texture of materials, and the play of light and shadow. Brick expressed this textile quality and workmanlike character better than plaster.

Influences from England were part of the basis of his ideas but they had been strengthened by influences lying closer to Sweden. Martin Nyrop's city hall in Copenhagen (1892–1905, following a competition in 1888) had aroused great interest throughout the North. There was here a Northern example of the same tendencies of development as Berlage had shown in his stock-exchange building in Amsterdam, while large German town halls were still being built in neo-Gothic. This stimulated Swedish architects' interest in the Danish tradition. Brick buildings in Stockholm at the time included *Tjänstemannabanken* (1906–08) by Ernst Stenhammar, *Östra Real school* (1906–10) by Ragnar Östberg and, for the 1912 Olympics, the *Stadium* by Torben Grut.

More clearly than any of his generation, Westman had during the 1890s formulated the surfeit of the time with old forms of style. In his opinion, it was necessary to begin again from the beginning, to get away from the sort of imagery cultivated on drawing boards and, instead, begin with the realities of building: materials, designs, plans. This attitude can be said to be more realistically practical than romantic. Some historians of Swedish architecture have claimed that, as a name, 'national-romantic' is misleading; 'national-realism' or, later, 'material-realism', have been suggested as better. But the first, being now established, cannot easily be replaced only in Swedish architecture, for it has been used in other arts and in other countries. This makes it more important to point out its internal contradictions.

Historicism, but not an interest in inheritances from history, was thus to be rejected. On the contrary, people perceived a knowledge of history as an important way toward renewal. But, instead of copying detailed forms of historical style, people began to search for the essence in the more anonymous tradition formed during centuries of practical needs and usage of local materials. Despite inspiration coming to a great extent from outside the country, this implied a new interest for Swedish building culture and its historical roots. In Westman's version national romanticism was a programme for a functional, practical and economic way of building to satisfy people's needs for agreeable surroundings. And it contained a certain social engagement.

Östermalm Teachers' College, (1906–10), by Ragnar Östberg, a monument in the brick-building period c. 1910.

But national romanticism was coherent. It had an undeniable weakness for romantic atmospheric art that could sometimes lead to self indulgence, as, for instance, in Östberg's comment above on the Norrköping Exhibition. Fascination with the play of light and shadow over the rough surfaces of stone and in mysterious apertures in the bodies of buildings recall 19th-century romanticism over ruins. Beautiful superficial effects and picturesque variations were then modish, a freak of taste, in contrast to long-term, more significant efforts to simplify that were particularly clear in Westman's work.

Church Space and the Values of Atmosphere

The cultural currents of the 1890s had brought a strong individualism with them. And, naturally, there were wholly different personal expressions within the framework of a common style. To capture its width we can go from Westman's factual, robust houses to an architect of another character and to a sort of commission in which atmosphere has a wholly different role and legitimacy: churches.

The years after the turn of the century were an apogee in church building. Through the growth of the large towns, and the spread of built-up areas, new parishes were formed and old ones divided. At the same time, the (established) Church of Sweden was renewing itself and becoming more vital. Opinion in favour of a popular church, or one open and welcoming to all protestants, had begun win ground. This led to different attempts to alter the space within churches so that the pulpit would become more central in relation to the congregation. As an idea, a centralised church

Engelbrekt Church, Stockholm (1909–14), Lars Israel Wahlman, dominates its vicinity.

Interior, Engelbrekt Church: an atmosphere of height, light and shadow.

began to spread, but forming it in an artistically convincing way, and mastering its acoustics, proved difficult.[15]

The most creative of the churches built at the time was the *Engelbrekt Church*, Stockholm, by Lars Israel Wahlman for a competition in 1906; he reworked it the following year and it was built in 1910–14. Sited high on a rocky outcrop in the centre of an area that was about to be built over, it was also to be visible along the sight lines of a number of streets.

Wahlman used the rubble from blasting foundations to terrace the outcrop, to create surroundings as a entity, where he could deploy the full register of contemporary aesthetics. On foot, one ascends a rich sequence of steps and terraces, enveloped by walls and greenery.

Externally, the church seems to be composed of elements independent of one another. If its distant silhouette is effective, closer views get swamped in picturesque details and other singularities. Inside, however, one encounters a light, unifying form. Exterior weight becomes lightness. One has a sense, in part from Wahlman's contrasting effects, of immense height, of space that seems to expand. The lofty vaulted arches have counterparts in low, shadowed, intimate niches. Contributions to this include the arches' parabolic form that reinforces the sense of energy, tension and movement. Wahlman sug-

gested a space without definite boundaries, extending into infinity.[16]

With the Nordic Museum, Isak Gustaf Clason attempted a large-scale synthesis, and, as one might say, illustrated the possibilities of the final phase of 19th-century eclecticism. His encyclopedic knowledge enabled him to assemble forms from different times and cultural areas into something novel.[17] But he was still closely constricted by looking at form in terms of historical style. In this connection, Wahlman illustrated a way of looking of a new period. His goal was a personal synthesis of all such material, so well digested that, subordinated to the idea inspiring them, all its forms dissolved and became a novel entity. He who achieved most in this spirit, better than all others of his generation, was Ragnar Östberg, in his Stockholm Town Hall.

The Engelbrekt Church was an individual work on a separate line that Westman represented. In the eyes of a critic, August Brunius, writing in a leading Stockholm daily paper, this church would always be a crux for the proponents of the simplicity and Northern severity of the Swedish art of building.[18] Like him, the editor of *Arkitektur*, Carl Bergsten, found its exterior less coherent than its interior, while he called its tower a "masterpiece in the art of achieving proportions and a play of lines."[19]

Nine years younger than Wahlman, Bergsten had, as mentioned, a different interna-

Hjorthagen Church (1904–09), by Carl Bergsten, unusual in its stereometric forms.

Interior of Hjorthagen Church: a factual form full of light.

tional orientation. He had himself designed a smaller church for an outer, working-class industrial area of Stockholm, *Hjorthagen*. He had got the commission after a competition in 1904, in which his radical architecture had no worthy competitor; but the parish authorities had difficulty in accepting it. So the whole project developed into a parodic dispute between a conservatively-minded building committee that wanted only a conventional church and a determined young architect wholly inspired by novel, radical ideas.[20] Conducted mainly through the parties' agents, their discussions led to certain reworking and lesser modifications in the completed church that got built by 1909.

This church, too, lies on high ground, is visible over a wide area and seems to be composed of parts independent of one another; but its exterior is more melded together and rounded off, its forms are cleaner and more severe, having a clearly stereometric character. Built earlier than the Engelbrekt Church, it now seems more 'modern'. The effects of its materials are strong but not dominant. Its lines appear more distinctly.

Its interior is clear and illuminated throughout. Bergsten worked with a rhythmic succession of parabolic vaults that, even so, wholly lack the dynamism and striving towards height of the Engelbrekt Church. The space in his church is more static, more factual and almost profane. It associates more to the rational

design of railways stations built in iron than to the interior of a church. While, with its bearing elements concealed in its walls as bones are within the body, the Engelbrekt Church seems organic, the comparable elements at Hjorthagen are free standing and emphasised.[21] The reduced simplicity and geometric clarity of the Hjorthagen Church were distinctive in the Sweden of the time.

A wholly different atmosphere exists in *Masthugg Church*, in Göteborg, by Sigfrid Ericson. Externally it has many similarities with the other two: a conspicuous landmark on its eponymous scar of rock, it rises, in the eyes of seamen and landsmen, like a lighthouse over its harbour town. Its silhouette is also effectively distinct thanks to its powerful tower, its height and dominance being strengthened by the low posture of the rest of the church. And, even more expressively than Wahlman, Ericson worked with the emphatic power of his material's texture and colour: deep-red brick, walls of rounded stones in shifting colour, weathered copper gutters and down pipes, cave-like entries to doors and arches that emphasise the walls' thickness. Its interior, by contrast, is quite different. Its relatively low vaults are formed from heavy timber balks, which makes the space heavy. Its atmosphere is old fashioned, lacking anything of the undogmatic, novel interpretation of space and spiritualised atmosphere expressed by the Engelbrekt Church.

Detail of Masthugg Church, Göteborg, Sigfrid Ericson, 1910–14. Powerful effects of material: brick and granite on a large scale.

Kiruna Church (1909–12) by Gustaf Wickman, The large gable-window illuminates a lofty interior associating to old northern practices of building in wood.

An illustration from the second-prize proposal (Nils Gellerstedt and Torben Grut) for the 1901 urban plan for Göteborg: an image of a town full of atmosphere.

The Gellerstedt and Grut plan for Göteborg (1901) used local topography to get picturesque variety and great monumentality.

striving for entire, pure forms, for natural simplicity, is evident here, with associations to old parish churches in the country. Tengbom was later to describe the strong impression such a Danish church once made on him: it was "free from the false employment of form that follows in the track of the art of drawing."[24]

Camillo Sitte's Ideas Replanted on Swedish Soil

More than anywhere else, re-orientation had arrived more quickly and brought about a superficially more dramatic change in urban planning. Camillo Sitte had supplied the argument. And, because, at the time, Swedes learned German as their first foreign language the original edition of Sitte's *Der Städtebau nach seinen künstlerischen Grundsätzen* was quickly influential in the Nordic countries. According to the Collins, it was hardly known outside Germany until 1902, when it appeared in a partly distorted translation into French. But, as Sitte himself noted, his point of view was "in the air" at the time.

During the 1890s in Sweden, the pioneers, Per Olof Hallman and Fredrik Sundbärg, set off a debate that quickly gave practical results. In 1897, writing in *Ord och Bild*, Sundbärg took a hard line against the engineers' art of the ruler: Swedish country towns were, he wrote, so confusingly alike that they might all be from the same factory, for "wherever you turn, in small towns and large ones, on flat or undulating land, you see almost only the same chessboard system."

He asserted that contemporary urban planning had been "thoroughly and with genius" investigated by Professor Camillo Sitte in Vienna, before going on to outline the professor's principles and argument, backing this up with eloquent Swedish examples. He pointed out the hermetic character of older towns' squares, on which public buildings were sited in picturesque groups, while the contemporary rule was that streets should intersect at the corners of what was misconceived as no more than an unoccupied square on the urban chessboard. The streets of old towns permitted variations of open and closed views; the backdrop seen along any typically curving street would change constantly.

An architect, Fredrik Sundbärg aimed his criticism at supposedly stale doctrines in urban planning, as well as at an entire professional group: engineers. In his view, their rapid advance had been devastating for towns. Urban planning had now become a central question for architects. It was a natural conse-

Masthugg Church was reviewed in Arkitektur by Gunnar Asplund who noted its feeling for material with respect, but was reserved in his assessment of its heavy roof: "Any light, liberating feeling of hope is not much at home inside this church."[22]

A powerful effect of interior space, combined with the Northern tradition of building in wood, came into being the remote iron-ore mining settlement of Kiruna, north of the Arctic Circle, that came into existence in a short time under the most adventurous conditions. Thanks to the company's director, Hjalmar Lundbohm, artistic ambitions were as superlative. He commissioned Gustaf Wickman to design a church and living quarters for the miners, indeed most of what got built during the first years. In his *Kiruna Church* (1909–12), Wickman combined extensive fenestration with a deeply drawn-down, tent-like roof that recalled contemporary American styles for private houses. The church is a central one, on a quadratic ground plan, its walls having the forms of immense triangles with glazed upper parts. Externally, he gave the church a look of a Lapp kåta, a portable building of poles covered with skins and the like, but its interior recalls the building style of the Northern stave churches.[23]

The more prominent church buildings of the time included *Church of the Revelation*, Saltsjöbaden, by Ferdinand Boberg, and *Arvika Church*, by two young architects, Ivar Tengbom and Ernst Torulf. The latter includes a high central nave flanked by low aisles and crowned by a wooden roof. The vaulted opening to the choir is parabolic. A

quence of contemporary striving for unified views. All should work together towards a deliberately created artistic harmony: an individual house with its furniture, fittings and interior decoration to the town as a whole.

Sundbärg's career was cut short by early death, in 1912, before he could give much practical expression to his ideas. Per Olof Hallman, on the other hand, became the early 20th-century Swedish authority in the practical work of urban planning. Employed in 1897 by the city of Stockholm, he worked there but also drew up to a greater or lesser degree the town plans of some seventy other places in Sweden, even if by no means all were put into practise. Not the least of his achievements was as a teacher in urban planning at the Royal College of Technology, an important centre of influence on Sweden.

In 1901, Hallman's and Sundbärg's first prize in the international competition for an urban plan for Göteborg was the official break-through in Sweden for the new principles. The second prize was awarded to Nils Gellerstedt and Torben Grut, who applied the same ideas as the winners. Gellerstedt was to become a leader in urban planning, while Grut belonged to the kernel of the national-romantic architectural troupe. All the prize-winning proposals contained picturesque and varying urban images of a curvy network of streets and effective views. The ideal of the time was well exemplified by Grut's perspective drawings of monumental buildings rising up in eloquent lighting to crown the image of the town.

An undoubtedly romantic atmosphere envelops these images, but, while contemporary plans did deliberately try for effects, they were basically adapted to a reality. The plans employing regular networks of streets had been poorly adapted to reality because, as Sundbärg had pointed out, they took no account of how things really were on the ground. Now the question was how best to use the lie of the land, and to accept existing roads, buildings and site boundaries. In Hallman's opinion, one should first map the contours, then (as he did systematically) make a model.

Making use of height differences was particularly interesting, because many of the areas that were to be built over included scars, or (typically Swedish) abrupt, irregularly shaped outcrops of bedrock. Many towns included unbuilt areas in which the planned regular network or geometry could not easily be realised. The new urban-planning ideal was as if heaven-sent to resolve such matters. An

expression of this novel view was embodied in the 1907 urban-planning law that came into force in 1908. Giving municipalities a new role in urban planning, it permitted them greater possibilities of regulating building in a more differentiated way so as to accord with conditions obtaining in a given area. In contemporary European terms, it went as far as did only Dutch legislation.[25]

Urban planning in Göteborg was led by Albert Lilienberg, who was soon to be the equal in Swedish urban planning of Hallman. Besides his work in Göteborg, he drew up town plans for a large number of places elsewhere in Sweden during the following twenty years. One of his earlier plans, done in 1908 for the working-class area in Göteborg called Christinedal-Bagargården, aroused international interest. It was presented in *Der Städtebau* and, in 1910, at the urban-planning congress in London, where Lilienberg gave a much remarked lecture. His plan was centred on a plateau, on which he sited a church and other public buildings along a main axis that

Novel urban-planning ideas from an urban-planning competition (1901) for an extension of Göteborg: a proposal by Torben Grut and Nils Gellerstedt won the second prize.

was surrounded by long residential blocks that delimited the plateau. The buildings were also differentiated between closed quarters of a more urban character and open areas of small houses. Linn has stated that this is one of the first plans to combine sequences of spaces inspired by Sitte with closed quarters of the type he designated as literally a "large-court-yard quarter" perimeter block.[27]

Internationally, the time was one of lively activity and newly-aroused enthusiasm in urban-planning circles. Probably because Sitte's ideas had been absorbed and put into practise so quickly in Sweden, and that possibly most and the most undiluted examples of his basic ideas were to be found in the Nordic countries and especially in Sweden, the country soon had a relatively prominent role at urban-planning congresses and exhibitions.[28] The Swedish architects who kept up with urban-planning matters read *Der Städtebau* regularly (Hallman was for a time on its editorial committee) and were fully aware of the German debate. Even if, for linguistic reasons, German was the channel through which thinking of the time reached Sweden, influence from the British Isles was also substantial: Ebenezer Howard's ideas were well known, Raymond Unwin's books were reviewed thoroughly, and practical examples from, for instance, the English garden-city movement were a rich source of inspiration.

In 1910, a change occurred in points of view and methods. A large international competition for Berlin was held that year, as well as a number of large exhibitions and congresses in various parts of Europe; they gave new impulses. Although Lilienberg had thought the Sitte tradition had played an important role in the development of modern urban planning, he began to take exception to it. He was younger than Hallman and was better than him at adapting urban planning to new conditions. The development of trams in Sweden caused towns quickly to expand into the land around them, which called for new perspectives and analyses that were wider in scope. Views of built-up urban quarters were more subtle: the spaces between buildings, their 'yards', began to be remarked as an important element.

In 1910, a group of younger architects felt they had had enough of the teaching of the Royal Academy of Fine Arts: for them, it had congealed into exercises in form and lacked contact with the problems of contemporary reality. They approached Bergsten, Tengbom, Westman, Östberg and Grut to ask whether they would function as teachers in an alternative, private school; only Grut declined. The result got the name of the Klara School. Although it existed for only one academic year, it won great significance for the unique assembly of talent among its six students: three were Gunnar Asplund, Sigurd Lewerentz and Osvald Almqvist.

Teaching was to be anchored in realistic projects. Bergsten and Tengbom, having been commissioned by the Swedish Association of Engineers and Architects (Teknologföreningen) to study the housing question, chose an aspect of it "that has hitherto not been given enough attention", namely, particularly to investigate the possibilities of the 'yard'.[29] To make their exercise as realistic as possible, they located it in what was popularly called the 'Gossip Square' (Samtalstorget) in Bergsten's birthplace of Norrköping, a town south of Stockholm well furnished with trams.

Two quarters were planned in detail. Each would have the form of a perimeter block that held a continuous long housing block designed to meet the criteria that would have applied had they given onto the street. Thus each would contain large, light apartments stretching from side to side, with windows on both, while, around them, there would be not the usual cramped muddy backyards but a semi-private zone, where the apartment blocks would be—a novelty in urban building—like private houses in a park of greenery. As if they

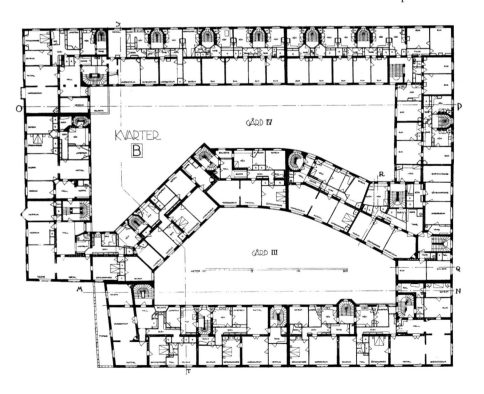

Klara school students' (1910–11) plan an apartment block, Skvallertorget, Norrköping: the upper length (kitchens towards the street) by the young Lewerentz, the bent central one by Asplund.

really were, they were aligned by reference to the points of the compass rather than in the kitchen-facing-the yard and the front-room-giving-onto-the-street convention. By locating large apartments in the yard and small ones in the buildings on the street, accustomed social practise was turned metaphorically and literally inside out.[30]

Although this project was never realised, its models, plans and perspective drawings were exhibited in Stockholm in summer 1912, together with other work by the group on similarly realistic jobs.

The Tradition is Researched and Reinterpreted

The intensive building activity around the turn of the century began to break the prevailing uniformity of the Swedish urban scene. Among the homogenous two-story buildings in wood, new ones, double their height or more, and built in stone, stuck up. Their individual forms that were nourished by different contemporary stylistic tendencies contributed to the impression of division and disharmony. A planned penetration for traffic of the small town of Ystad (it had been Danish until the mid 17th century) that was still medieval in character caused something of an uproar.[31] The situation was a forcing ground for some new criticism that, once again, was most clearly articulated by Carl Westman. Lecturing in 1908 to his professional architectural colleagues, he depicted in glaring colours the devastation of the country towns of Sweden. In opposition to this new, vulgar diversity, he proposed the uniformity and harmonic tonality of the older buildings.

In 1908–09, deriving from these domestic reactions as well as from exotic impulses, a new orientation affected Swedish architecture: uniformity became a key concept, implying careful respect for the whole, while respect for the anonymous tradition of building was given more and more emphasis.

The Arts & Crafts Movement had directed attention to traditional English houses built in local materials to meet practical demands and characterised by an artless simplicity. Another component in the new Swedish orientation was Sitte's strong influence. Both he and the Arts & Crafts Movement had sought to filter timeless principles out of the anonymous tradition in architecture and urban building. A reaction against the architecture of styles, this was a general tendency of the time.

George and Christiane Collins have pointed out the correspondence between Sitte and Loos in this respect. In their view, Loos argues (and uses formulations that are strikingly recall of some of Sitte's) for a return to basic building traditions free of the trappings of style and free of its most obvious manifestation: ornament. According to Loos, it was possible to find a true expression for one's own time only by returning to the fundamentals.[32] They also state that Josef Frank, an Austrian architect who later made his home in Sweden, transformed Site's principles for the architecture of the private house in his essay *Das Haus als Weg und Platz*.[33] In Sweden, architects including Asplund, Lewerentz and their contemporaries would develop this theme: architecture experienced as spaces consequent on a movement through a building. Sitte's contribution had been to articulate a novel awareness of space.

While historical accounts have proposed Loos as a pioneer of modernism, they have written down Sitte as a nostalgic romantic. In reality, and in a manner that was typical for the time, both sought for a starting point in tradition whence they could formulate a critique of their own time and find a means of addressing its problems. In contrast to Morris, both also took a positive view of towns as products of culture.

Swedish architects could attach to the international impulses their interest for their own country's specific building cultures and anonymous traditions, which was itself both typical of the 1890s and a natural development of contemporary artistic impulses.

The annual meeting of Swedish architects in 1908 decided to publish a series of papers to demonstrate the value of older urban environments that, as *Gamla svenska städer*, began to come out the year after. Its purpose may have

Cover, "Old Swedish towns" "Gamla svenska städer"; it presented many older towns that had kept their uniform architectural character.

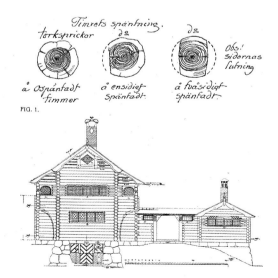

Lars Israel Wahlman presented his own house, Tallom, in *Arkitektur* (1908), with useful hints on timber work.

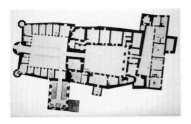

Plan, Läckö Fortress. Its irregularities that had accumulated since the 13th century inspired Östberg.

been to spread knowledge to a wider public outside the profession, but it became an important source of architectural inspiration. With Paul Schultze-Naumburg's *Kulturarbeiten* and Paul Mebes' *Um 1800* as the most significant, impulses from Germany were influential. In 1908, the architectural students at the Royal Academy of Art formed the *Architectural Memorial Association* (Arkitektur-minnesföreningen) with the aim of arranging journeys to undertake measurements and to publish papers. A important source of inspiration was the Danish association, *Foreningen af 3. December*, that had been formed 15 years earlier. The importance of tradition for creativity was illustrated in *Svenska Allmogehem*, published in 1909, in which different architects contributed with proposals for types of building suited to different parts of the country. Published in 1912, *Gamla svenska allmogehem*, an illustrated documentation of older rural Swedish building culture, was edited by John Åkerlund and Ivar Tengbom.

Many architects made their own excursions into the countryside, took measurements and sketched various sorts of old buildings. It was typical that they should try to look into older building principles. Wahlman was to acquire a dedicated knowledge of the art of building in wood, and, as a teacher, was to persistent in passing on this knowledge to student architects into the 1930s. In *Arkitektur* for 1908 he presented his own house, *Tallom*, that he had built in accordance with old techniques of building in timber; at the same time, he made himself a proponent for this traditional technique that, in his opinion, represented a suitable, well-tested means of building in the Swedish climate. Its quality was demonstrated through wooden buildings that were several centuries old.

But, while there might have been this powerful interest in Swedish building traditions, it was not nearly as clear how it should actually be characterised. As a whole, the tradition contained elements that differed, besides coming from different times, but, bit by bit, architects began to pin them down and interpret the tradition. In actual fact, this interpretation was steered by the taste of the time as well as by the building jobs that began to emerge as most central in status and most comprehensive. During the first decade of the new century, important sources of inspiration were the 16th-century castles and fortified residences, late 17th-century Baroque buildings of the Caroline period (1660–1718, or the successive reigns of Karl X, XI and XII), late 18th-century Gustavian (= King Gustaf III, 1772–93)

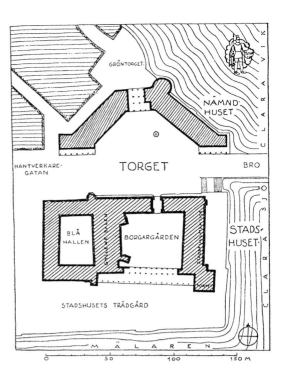

Östberg's plan for the Stockholm Town Hall, at the stage work had reached in 1913.

buildings, early 19th-century classicism, and, not least, study trips by the young architects to Italy.

Monumentality on a National Foundation

Against a background formed of influence from Richardson and contemporary interest for material, it was not strange that Swedish architects should have been attracted by the immense walls and coarsely-dressed stone surfaces of 16th- and 17th-century Swedish Vasa-dynasty castles. Their heavy volumes contained a power and severity that architects deemed to be national characteristics that also accorded with contemporary international tendencies. What was more specifically Swedish about them was their cubistic simplicity: it was perceived that monumentality could be achieved much more convincingly through a sense of enclosing weight than by means of even the most liberal application of decorative embellishment.

Swedish towns, growing about the turn of the century, engendered a need for new public buildings for use on formal occasions: town halls, courts, schools and so on. The greatest interest settled on a town hall and a law court for Stockholm, the projects for which originated in a competition held in 1903 to make use of the site where the Town Hall now stands.

In the first of the two stages of the competition, six proposals would be selected: they included work by Östberg, Westman, 25-year-

Court House (1909–15), Stockholm, by Carl Westman. Its closed volume and central tower suggest influence from 16th-century Vasa-dynasty buildings.

Vadstena: a palatial Renaissance-style building (1550s–1620s) that was a model for the Stockholm Court House.

old Tengbom jointly with Ernst Torulf, and the 24-year-old Bergsten. The jury included Martin Nyrop, whose Town Hall for Copenhagen was building at the time. Östberg won the second stage, after a further competition with Westman.

His winning proposal was for a complex of buildings, including a powerful tower, around a core. Östberg was later to adopt some of Westman's ideas, including a placing nearer the water and the tower on the corner of the site, also by the water. In 1908 the town council decided to divide the project: a town hall for administrative and formal purposes on this site, and a law court on another, which Westman was commissioned to design, while Östberg re-worked his proposal to accommodate only the town hall.

For a decade, while it was being built, the town-hall project underwent constant, creative development. In re-working the project, Östberg was influenced by Vasa-dynasty architecture, among other things, being captured in spirit by the informal charms of the skewed lines and irregularities of the castles that had come with the years. In summer 1909, he was at Läckö, basically a late 17th-century building on one of the great Swedish lakes, where, with the help of his Norwegian colleague, Eliassen, he reworked his town-hall project, and, as Elias Cornell has shown, began to cultivate a particular interest in irregularities, which interrupted the symmetry that had hitherto characterised his proposal. And he developed the covered yard (now the Blue Hall) that, through its unsquared corners, caused the entire project to become asymmetrical.[34]

His study of the Vasa-dynasty castles also contributed to his interest in the enclosed yard (now the Great Courtyard). In 1909, when Östberg was working on the Blue Hall, the big

glazed Winter Garden of the *Grand Hôtel Royal* by Ernst Stenhammar was completed. Östberg reviewed it favourably in *Arkitektur*, especially the large concept to which fundamental idea all details were subordinated.[35] The Winter Garden comprised an assembling space, in and around which dining rooms and the cafe were grouped.

The most direct expression of interest in the Vasa-dynasty castles was in Westman's *Stockholm Court House* (1909–15). Its norms, and its simple, powerful walls and heavy tower in the centre of the facade derive from Vadstena Castle. Inside, traditional brick vaulting has a bare, clean form: its making had entailed reviving defunct knowledge. Westman's wish to get away from the drawing board into practicalities was illustrated by his manner of organising the building work in an old-fashioned way, with everything done by hand, on site. That this was not something exclusive for the time is shown by the fact that Westman incurred lower costs than had been estimated. The old-fashioned character of the building can be seen as an expression of rationality and economy of means derived from well-tried knowledge, rather than nostalgia and historical romanticism, but it did represent a technique of building in brick that was soon to give way to more modern methods using concrete.

As we have seen, the Vasa-dynasty castles inspired developments towards unadorned simplicity and the effects of three-dimensional volume, but, especially for Östberg, they led the way to more subtle architectural effects through hardly noticeable line shifts, and departures from symmetry and right angles. Attention towards the interplay between the simple whole and its articulating details became keener. The covered yard began delib-

Stockholm Court House: this vaulted passage has an old-fashioned look, despite paintings by Filip Månsson. Staircases and corridors are in traditional styles of building in brick.

Pressens House (1901–02, not preserved), Saltsjöbaden. An early house by Carl Westman with English elements.

erately to be given form as a space with historical references, where experience swung between "outside" and "inside". All this was the theme that would continue to live in Swedish architecture.

Private Houses — a Subject for Experiment

In the years after the turn of the century, built-up areas of private houses began to surround many towns, partly on account of tramlines stretching outwards, partly because a

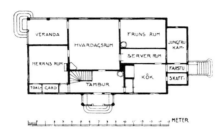

Ground floor, Ebbagården, Stockholm, 1901–03. Östberg began with the traditional plan of a double "stuga" but made it slightly irregular.

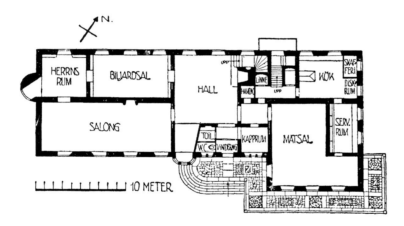

Östberg's Pauli House, Djursholm, Stockholm, 1904–05. Ground floor with free grouping of its rooms.

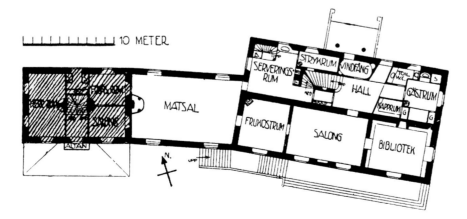

Östberg's Nedre Manilla, Stockholm, 1909, for K.O. Bonnier, a publisher. Ground floor: shading indicates the house Östberg extended.

middle-class ideal was to live in such houses. This led to interesting architectural jobs, for the small scale of a single house allowed different architectural ideas to be tried out.

Inspiration came mainly from England, as shown for example by the *Pressen House* (1901–02) at Saltsjöbaden, a southern suburb of Stockholm, by Westman. Its rooms were conjoined informally, and its exterior walls formed an irregular ground plan. Later, however, Westman's plans for houses became (more) taut and cohesive. Swedish buildings have developed from what is called a parstuga: the two rooms on either side of the central entry of this small wooden dwelling. This customary fixed plan had shown itself to be most suited to the Swedish climate, in which heat had to be kept in and fuel (split logs) eked out. The country houses of those with positions in the world were also symmetrical, with public rooms aligned with their main facades. After 1905, like other architects, Westman increasingly used traditional Swedish types of plan. A closed cube, often on heavy stone foundations, became characteristic for Swedish private houses, but the cube had to contain modern amenities for comfortable middle-class life: bathrooms, wardrobes, lesser or back stairs and so on, features that conferred a certain informality on the enclosed plan. In addition, there was a certain contradiction between the closed nature of the house in winter and the wish, in summer, that it should be open to the light and outdoor greenery. To complement their town apartments, late 19th-century middle-class Swedes had begun to acquire summer places that, if they were built to order, had an informal, open architecture: large glazed south-facing verandas affording views including (where possible) nearby water. They affected the architecture of all-the-year-round residences, manifesting themselves in the form, for instance, of verandas and bay windows. Tensions arose between strictly circumscribed and unrestricted plans: Östberg showed that such tensions could be exploited artistically.

Östberg had begun his career as an architect of domestic houses: he built the *Ebbagården House* (1901–03) at Edsviken, Stockholm; it was reddish with white corners and window frames, and had a mansard roof and a small veranda in front of the entrance. Its exterior gave a traditional Swedish impression — 'the little red stuga' — while its interior followed the layout of the two-roomed parstuga, but with a slight shift in its lines. As Cornell has pointed out, Östberg's resolution exemplified the artistic use of the circumscribed v. unrestricted tension in layouts.[36] Östberg's *Pauli House* (1904–05), in the new but exclusive Stockholm suburb of Djursholm, exhibits more of the informal English grouping of reception rooms around a large central hall carried up to the second floor. By placing a wall obliquely, Östberg created a funnel-like entry into the hall that also gave an outlook through the opposed window. He expressed his interest for effective irregularities in the large house he designed for a publisher, Karl Otto Bonnier, *Nedre Manilla*, on Djurgården, in central Stockholm. This was in 1909, the year he was working at and influenced by Läckö in his work on Stockholm Town Hall. As Cornell has noted, the hall at Nedre Manilla contains "effective shifts of line in its spaces and walls aligned crookedly that added to comfort at the same time as they were picturesque and gave an impression of freedom and chance to the whole arrangement."[37] Östberg went furthest in these experiments with ground plans at the *Geber House* (1911–13), Stockholm, when he was working intensively on the Town Hall.

During this earlier phase of designing private houses, an important contribution was made by Elis Benckert at the start of what looked like a promising career. His *Lagercrantz House* at Djursholm (1909–10) refined contemporary demands for simplicity in an almost archaic way, to create an interplay with its nearly rural surroundings: in presenting his work, Benckert significantly began by describing the trees on the site and their connection with the house: on opening the front door to enter the house, one can see, looking straight through the house and a glazed door, a beautiful birch tree.[38] By angling a wall, the entry is tapered and thus concentrates the line of sight on just this view. In this, the house resembles Östberg's Pauli House. Benckert's main staircase is unnoticeably narrowed. But he emphasised even more clearly the intimate relationship between his architecture and the surroundings of the house: lofty windows carried lower down than usual and window openings angled through the thick walls to concentrate on views also admit light into the room in a beautiful way.

Benckert's presentation gives particular attention to material and its treatment. The simplest forms and material are never cheap when they are treated with respect and are used in the right place, but all real expressiveness requires restriction of means. He proposes three mottos for "our Vignola": "Never use forms more demanding than their purpose requires; never use material more costly than

Lagercrantz House (1910), Djursholm, Stockholm, by Benckert. Contemporaries admired its reduction of forms and materials.

what is needed to meet practical and artistic demands; do not overwork material or the character of its eventual form more than is required."

Two years later, he took his own life, on New Year's Eve 1912. He had been the first in Sweden to introduce classicism, in a couple of works from 1911–12: an exhibition in *Arvika* in 1911, and *Borgen i Skuru*, an 18th-century house in Stockholm, where he introduced a novel symmetry and a coloration that gave it a clearly Empire character. This classical touch appeared, but only after his death, also in his *Norrgården* on Ägnö, a house on an island in the skerries off Stockholm, and in the *de Jounge House* in Gävle, a coastal town north of Uppsala. His work thus introduced a theme that was to be outstanding in Swedish architecture for the next ten years or more.

The Gustavian Inheritance

The Gustavian period is named for King Gustav III (b. 1746, reigned 1771–92), the first Swedish-born prince of his century, who was, like his uncle Fredrick the Great, a Francophile and fascinated by the arts. During Gustav's reign, art, architecture and design (and much else in Sweden) reached an apogee of distinction that was not at all diminished in the eyes of ensuing generations by his assassination. At the end of the 19th century, the drawing room at Sundborn, the house created by Carl Larsson, a painter, and his wife Karin, herself a painter, with its pretty furniture, blue-and-white textiles, white joinery and rose-coloured walls can be seen as a tribute to

18th-century Swedish country house interiors in Gustav's day. The turn-of-the-century ideal of light, well-lit interior design associates partly to this blonde ancestor.

The Swedish 18th century received attention in another context, for, during the latter part of the 19th century, the old mining and ore-refining industry went through a period of structural rationalisation, and many of its originally (water-powered) works were discontinued. At the turn of the century, when the question arose of how these works might be preserved, architects' trips for study purposes took them into the deep countryside to the north, west and north west of Stockholm (respectively to Uppland, Västmanland and Dalarna), as well as elsewhere. They began to become fully aware of the size and richness of the cultural treasures comprised by these uniformly built early industrial centres that featured simple but well proportioned houses for their workers. The designs of not only costly upper-class residences but also and to a higher degree of mass housing of a simpler sort could be used as models. And, as urban housing problems became more and more acute, they were so used.

The same applied to the exemplary character of the uniformity of the Swedish towns that had been built in wood, and their well-considered panelled architecture, often in restrained classicistic forms. These models simply gained in relevance as architects increasingly sought to achieve uniformity and balance in entire urban scenes.

From the Tessins' Baroque to Budding Classicism

Early 20th-century Swedish architecture exhibited an increasingly prominent element of influence from the 17th-century Great-Power period, and, as national rhetoric swelled, it often sounded the national overtones in this style. The appreciation of cubic space corresponded to a tendency that began to be noticeable about 1910, and, during the following decade, models were often enclosed, 17th-century volumes with lofty hipped roofs. Private residences, often with quoins, often took this form. Westman favoured this pattern in his houses, but used it also on a monumental scale in his *Court House* in Nyköping (1907–10).

Thus, this Caroline baroque dominated tendencies in form during the second decade of the century, side by side with a diminishing national romanticism and a budding classi-

Stockholms Enskilda Bank (1912–15), by Tengbom. Rationally planned bank premises exemplify an early stage of a returning classicism.

cism. This later originated in influences from Denmark and other sources outside Sweden, and, from domestic sources, from Gustavian architecture and interior decoration, as well as the classicism at the end of that century. But it can also be said to be a natural development of the Tessins' baroque.

This continuity can be exemplified by a building, *Enskilda Banken*, Stockholm, that revealed Ivar Tengbom's great talent. He won it with a proposal, made by invitation, under the motto of "Classic ground", to a competition in 1912 for a prominent site overlooking Kungsträdgården owned by the Wallenberg banking family, where a dynastic change ushered in a changed attitude towards building questions. Gustav Wickman's proposal of a heavy baroque facade in natural stone that followed German patterns having been rejected, the competition was arranged. Tengbom's winning proposal was discreetly distinguished: its volume, high roof, flat walls and a heavily rusticated basement are together reminiscent of the Caroline baroque as well as the closed character of Renaissance classicism.[39] The stark contrast between the rusticated and flat walls and the excessive size of the sculptures around the doors, gives the facade a certain mannerist tone. Tengbom avoided the brickwork that was in general use by his contemporaries, preferring the more traditional Stockholm plaster. Among those who had spoken out for greater urban uniformity, he had been to the fore.

Behind the closed exterior, a strikingly light and airy interior conceals itself, with a central banking hall that associates to the courtyards of Renaissance palaces. This comprises the centre around which the building's other parts are grouped. While its facade is walled in a traditional way, the interior of the building is constructed in concrete, but the pillar-and-beam system has been done as arcaded galleries with a classicising form. A rational construction and a functional ground plan have been brought together with a historically associative expression.

We can thus state that both Westman and Tengbom expressed a connection between construction and form, as had been sought even since the end of the 19th century. But Tengbom worked with a more modern type of building and with another technique of building than did Westman. His Rådhus building was thoroughly unified, being consistently formed through a walling technique following older patterns. Tengbom chose a more sophisticated, eclectic attitude.

As we have seen, Carl Bergsten appeared as an avant-garde inclined architect, strongly influenced by the Viennese Wagner School, which became more or less a burden on his career in Sweden. Around 1909, he had abandoned his experimental style, partly on account of the journey to Denmark, but also because of international tendencies. His factual, constructive inclination and his interest for simple reduced forms found a release in classicism that became a means for him to express the fundamental play of forces in a design between bearing and borne elements. He made this clear in *Liljevalch Art Hall*, Stockholm, designed for a competition in 1913 but built and completed only by 1916.

Relatively controversial when new, it became a epoch-making building in Swedish architectural history. The leading critic, August Brunius, hardly understood it, despite appreciating some individual parts.[40] He thought the extensive simplification of the building indicated a lack of dignity and monumentality, while it got popularly nicknamed the 'herring box', which showed at least the general public had appreciated its leading characteristic was a cubistic simplicity. Among young architects it was taken as the first sign of an architecture of the novel technique of building in reinforced concrete.[41]

One passes from the vestibule to a lofty sculpture hall, top-lit by a row of windows high up in the entry facade. Two lofty rooms for paintings lead off the hall, each surrounded by a suite of lesser rooms. At the far end of the

building, a yard, like an oasis ringed by buildings, is the focus for the narrow lengths of the cafe. A stylised portico of classical columns marks the transition from the art hall to the yard, well exemplifying the ability of classicism to express the play of forces in constructions in concrete.[42]

Bergsten proceeded from the fundamental demand of function. He created a beautifully lit space with a multiplicity of uses, and a natural succession of rooms, combined with a yard and a cafe that offer intimate pleasure. The great stairway of the sculpture hall implies the source of inspiration of this factually restrained classicism: Heinrich Tessenow's Dalcroze Institute in Hellerau (1910–12). The character of an exterior yard may be recognised as a theme in Swedish architecture of the time.

A long tradition among Swedish architects has been to undertake long educative travels in Europe south of the Baltic and, particularly, south of the Alps to Italy; and to return home with full sketchbooks. In the 19th century, these records of detailed forms would later serve as a store to be drawn on during the architect's career. In 1912–14, many young architects went to Italy with a renewed interest in classicism but not the detail of its forms nor its great monuments but more the anonymous houses, streets and atmosphere in towns such as Siena. It was *architettura minore*, minor Italian architecture that captured their interest. Together with his friend Folke Bensow, Gunnar Asplund made such a trip in 1913–14, and returned with a diary full of sketches and

Snapshot by Asplund (1913–14) of an Italian street, one of many he made of everyday scenes.

Liljevalch's Art Hall (1913–16), by Carl Bergsten. Its factually classical form, stringent planning and beautiful lighting introduced an epoch in Swedish architecture.

observations that were written with an intensity close to euphoria. He returned home, the European war broke out, frontiers were closed for years and Scandinavia entered many years of isolation lessened only by increased contacts between architects from its individual countries.

The Housing Question and the Owner-Occupier Movement

The housing enquiries that were made in certain towns were clear in their conclusions: class differences were profound, living conditions for the urban working class were cramped in the lived in extreme. In local-government elections after the turn of the century a certain political radicalisation occurred in many places, when the liberals who were sympathetic to reform and Social Democrats strengthened their positions. "The social question" had got onto the political agenda.

The most influential representatives for the liberals had political roots in the cultural radicalism of the 1880s, and it was their point of view and social engagement that were carried on into a phase of definite initiatives and proposals. Locally, working-class families' concerns about housing were an urgent matter in the larger towns. "Workers' barracks" were mentioned with indignation, along with everything associated with them in the form of crowded living and social degradation. Middle-class sympathizers with reform considered their own houses as an ideal for the working class, too, and the housing question became more and more synonymous with the owner-occupied question. A better, longer-term control was demanded over the growth and expansion of the towns. Land policy became a central concern.

Emigration to the United States was an inflamed question, flaring up regularly towards the end of the century. By then emigration had culminated numerically, but its emotional charge was greater than ever, for it got attached to the national feelings of the time. Conservative-minded people felt that, as young families moved overseas, the nation was being drained of healthy blood; they became engaged in proposing countermeasures. When, in 1904, the national government, for the first time, formulated a means of direct support for housing, it was reached through a compromise that says much about the economic and political structures of the time: the riksdag decided to introduce national loans in support of owner-occupier homes, intended

primarily for smaller family farms in the country, but also available to associations of owner occupiers around towns and industries.

For the riksdag, the problem was primarily not to offer the means whereby the urban proletariat could acquire good homes but rather to check urbanisation and find a solution to "the social question". The family was seen as the self-evident basis of society, and this housing policy would provide a solution that would in part stabilise society at a time of upheaval and change, in part help individuals to better lives. To a high degree, the impact of the vision was due to the symbolic role performed at the time by "the home".[43]

Thus this national policy for owner occupiers was the fruit of a political consensus, in which the powers driving it were variously motivated. The conservatives saw as central its aspects that would preserve society, the social-liberals those that were emancipatory. For those without property, it was a means of coming up in the world. But the policy was also part of an effort to integrate the working class into middle-class life, to gloss over class differences and bring together the polarised layers of society into a single big family. In this lay one of the foundations of what would later be called det svenska folkhemmet, or the 'people's home'.

An oddity about Swedish industrialisation was that industries, having grown up around ironworks and sawmills using local (water) power to refine local material, were often deep in the countryside; this dispersed pattern endured far into the 20th century. The old 'works' tradition survived in many industrial centres: as the owners had been, the new managers were responsible for seeing the workers had somewhere to live. Having thus in many earlier instances built workers' barracks, representatives of industry were now more closely engaged in owner-occupier matters.

The Little Red Stuga

The powerful symbolic value of a home of one's own, and especially of its emblematic little stuga (a small, typically rural wooden house, painted red but with white corners) flanked by its flagpole supporting a blue-and-gold Swedish flag, was thus nourished from various sources. Its emblem expressed more clearly than anything else the national identity that people now tried to capture and depict in the arts. A writer Ellen Key, who was one of the most active of the intellectuals engaged in

"Beauty for all", a turn-of-the-century publication in which Ellen Key, a writer, argued in favour of beauty in everyday things for all classes of society; public debate focussed on it.

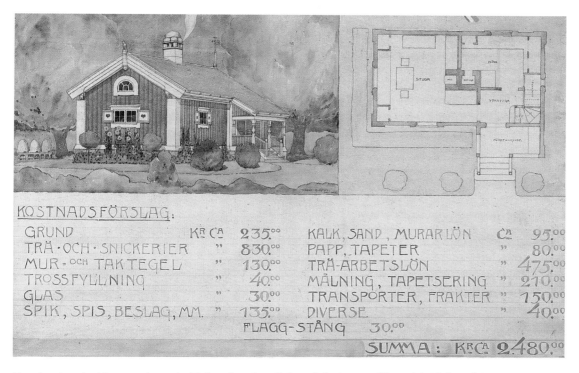

Drawing (1905) with cost estimates by Torben Grut for a little, red, do-it-yourself 'stuga' (with flagpole).

public debate, located the home and the family at the focus of her view of society. The influential periodical, *Skönhet för alla* ('Beauty for all'), presented an amalgamation of social policy and aesthetics. Society was good to the extent that it was characterised by cleanliness, worthiness and beauty, and when, in 1889, Carl Larsson published in book form his watercolours of his home at Sundborn, Dalarna, it provided a powerful argument for this view of society.

In addition, after the turn of the century, young architects who were establishing leading positions in their profession were engaged in this novel striving. Westman designed simple, working-class furniture that he exhibited according to a programme that Ellen Key had begun in 1899. With Östberg, he opened an advisory office in Stockholm for working-class families who wanted to discuss practical forms for and furnishing of their dwellings. A result of this was Östberg's small publication *Ett hem* that showed how a poorly-off family's stuga might look. Torben Grut's drawing (1905) of a type of an owner-occupied house, with ground plan, budget and all, is illustrative.

Stockholm was surrounded by an extensive network of jerry-built and middle-class housing built on private initiatives. If the town was to have any possibility of steering the continued development of its built-up areas, it had to hurry. Among those who were elected to the town council for the first time in 1903 was the man who also became mayor that year, Carl Lindhagen: he was to be a driving force for a land-and-housing policy for the town. In 1904, much land began to be acquired by the

town. In 1907 a board was appointed to lead the use made of this land. The first area to be built up by the town was *Enskede*, where plots for building were leased and built according to a plan by Per Olof Hallman from 1908.

Enskede is usually regarded as the first garden city in Sweden, inspired primarily by English examples, but no independent garden city, as conceived by Ebenezer Howard, was in fact built here, only in practice traditional estates of larger and smaller private houses on urban peripheries that grew rapidly as horse-

Plan (1908) for Enskede. Per Olof Hallman conceived the area as an enclosure of many terrace houses and some detached ones surrounded by three-story apartment buildings; in fact, it was built over mainly with detached houses.

Björkvägen, Enskede (1910), where the town built semi-detached houses modelled on traditional Swedish "works" communities.

drawn tramways, having been electrified, spread out even more quickly. But leases of sites for building, which can be seen as a rudiment of Howard's social-reformist ideas, were granted on a large scale in Stockholm and a number of other towns. Both domestically and internationally, this was a relatively radical way to conduct land policy, giving municipalities unique possibilities of steering developments in built-up areas, especially when used in combination with the 1907 legislation that gave municipalities a driving role in planning.

The Baltic Exhibition

The National Association To Counter Emigration (Nationalföreningen mot emigrationen), having been a constant motive force in the owner-occupier movement, opened a permanent exhibition in Stockholm in 1912, demonstrating exemplary arrangements from all parts of Sweden. The association published a handbook in 1915 that listed all the owner-occupier estates in Sweden, which included a number by leading architects. The most interesting included some projects by two young architects, Torsten Stubelius and Sigurd Lewerentz who, having worked and studied in Germany, had made close contact with the circle around Deutscher Werkbund. Stubelius had made use of a travelling scholarship that extended over a number of years.

Lewerentz worked for Bruno Möring in Berlin, and, later, in Munich, for Theodor Fischer and Richard Riemerschmid.[44] With the latter he worked on dwellings in Hellerau, in connection with which job he probable came into contact with Heinrich Tessenow. Staying in Germany until May 1910, on his return home he joined the group around Klara School. In 1910–11, he worked for Carl Westman, whose thorough knowledge of building in brick, and factual approach and demand for

manual quality were important for the direction of Lewerentz' later work. His next move was to start an office with Stubelius.

In a Deutscher-Werkbund spirit, they devoted time to designing simple objects for use but also, for a couple of companies, as well as for the town of Helsingborg, to design workers' premises—small apartments—that followed roughly the pattern of those at Hellerau: a kitchen and dining-living room on the ground floor and smaller bedrooms upstairs. The separate dwellings were either linked together, or detached, and arranged village-fashion along streets and round small squares. Their exteriors were very simple but reflected local styles: the Danish-Swedish liking for brick in Skåne (ie at Helsingborg), panelled in northern-Swedish style in the far north.

In the summer of 1914, they exhibited these projects at the *Baltic Exhibition* (Baltiska utställningen) in Malmö, which was held at the same time as the Werkbund exhibition in Cologne, but, while the second became well known later for its radical elements, the first was criticised most for its lack of renewal. It has been seen as the swan song of art nouveau, which had made a big impression in Sweden at the 1897 Stockholm exhibition. Malmö proved to be the perigee of Boberg's comet-like career as an exhibition architect: he withdrew from the scene, probably because, politely but firmly, his colleagues and many critics cried down his work, which was a reflection of an altered view of architecture. His formal language that had been considered as full of imagination was now decried as slack. The Malmö exhibition was still open when the European war broke out, extinguishing the glow of the triumphant optimism of the Stockholm exhibition about the future.

The Malmö exhibition had an ambitious architectural department, with large models on view, including work by the-then well established architects who followed national-romantic directions but also by young, relatively unknown men including Asplund, Lewerentz and Stubelius. The latter two exhibited a project that attracted particular attention: a small funeral chapel for Helsingborg that was significant in view of what happened later. In commenting on the exhibition, Bergsten stated that neo-classicism had returned: "Then let us not stop with classicism, as we did previously, but aim at its continuation, and may we hope that the new period of neo-antiquity that seems from all that we can be see to be about to open will be the springboard to novel forms for architecture."[45]

Baltic Exhibition, Malmö, 1914, designed by Ferdinand Boberg.

[1] Well described in Anders Ekström's dissertation *Den utställda världen* (1994).

[2] They had worked their separate competition proposals into the final project. See Ulf Sörenson, *Ferdinand Boberg. Arkitekten som konstnär* (Höganäs, 1992), 94, 102 ff.

[3] Carl Westman, "Är vår moderna arkitektur modern?", *Dagens Nyheter* 19 April 1893.

[4] Fredric Bedoire, *En arkitekt och hans verksamhetsfält kring sekelskiftet. Gustaf Wickmans arbeten 1884–1916* (1974), 42 ff.

[5] Fredric Bedoire (1974) has exhaustively described Wickman's career as an architect, his clientele and his incomes.

[6] Bengt O.H. Johansson's dissertation describes Bergsten's development and work up until 1910. *Carl Bergsten och svensk arkitekturpolitik under 1900-talets första hälft* (Uppsala, 1965).

[7] Ragnar Östberg, "Utställnings-arkitekturen Norrköping", *Arkitektur* 9/1906, 109 ff.

[8] Björn Linn, "Den stillsamme revolutionären", *Arkitektur* 7/1964, 157 ff, is an excellent presentation of Nilsson's architectural work.

[9] Lisa Brunnström, *Den rationella fabriken* (Umeå, 1990), 37.

[10] Martin Rörby et al., *Georg A. Nilsson arkitekt* (1989).

[11] Carl Westman, "K. Dramatiska Teaterns nya byggnad", *Arkitektur* 4/1908, 45 ff.

[12] See Axel Lindegren, *Ord och Bild* (1908), 129 ff; & August Brunius, *Svenska Dagbladet* 15 February 1908.

[13] See Torben Grut, "Svenska läkaresällskapets nybyggnad", *Arkitektur* 1/1907, 1 ff.

[14] Summarised in Hakon Ahlberg, "Carl Westman och nationalromantiken", *Byggmästaren* 11/1954, 254 ff.

[15] This change has been addressed by a number of writers, of whom some have considered Engelbrektskyrkan, among them Göran Lindahl, *Högkyrkligt, lågkyrkligt, frikyrkligt i svensk arkitektur 1800–1950* (1955); Rudolf Zeitler, *Skandinavische Kunst um 1900* (Leipzig, 1990); & Krister Malmström, *Centralkyrkor inom svenska kyrkan 1820–1920* (1990).

[16] Zeitler (1990) 212, Lindahl (1950) 112.

[17] With Nordiska museet as its point of departure, Johan Mårtelius' dissertation, *Göra arkitekturen historisk* (1987), has deeply analyzed Clason's stylistic models and striving towards synthesis.

[18] *Svenska Dagbladet* 18 & 22 January 1914; see also August Brunius' *Det nya Stockholm* (1926) that gives the year of original publication, erroneously, as 1913.

[19] Carl Bergsten, "Engelbrektskyrkan", *Arkitektur* 2/1914, 17ff.

[20] Johansson (1965), 172–180.

[21] This organic character is strongly emphasised by Erik Lundberg in his *Arkitekturens formspråk*, X, 525 ff (1961).

[22] Gunnar Asplund, "Masthuggskyrkan i Göteborg", *Arkitektur* (7/1915), 70.

[23] Fredric Bedoire, *Kiruna kyrka*. Sveriges kyrkor Vol. 153. (Uppsala 1973).

[24] Ivar Tengbom, "Ett ungdomsprogram.", *Trettiotalets byggnadskonst i Sverige*. (1943).

[25] Collins, George R. & Collins, Christiane Crasemann, *Camillo Sitte: The Birth of Modern City Planning* (New York, 1986), 51.

[26] Hans Bjur, *Stadsplanering kring 1900* (Göteborg, 1984), 52.

[27] Björn Linn, *The Importance of Sitte in a Swedish Perspective*. Manuscript of a talk given in Venice in 1990 and published as "Sitte secondo una prospettiva svedese", in Guido Zucconi (ed.), *Camillo Sitte e i suoi interpreti* (Milan, 1992).

[28] Bjur (1984), 103.

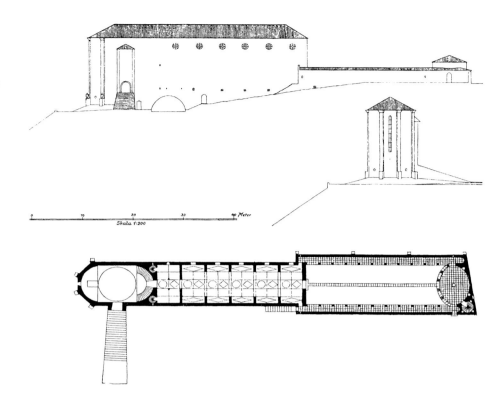

Sigurd Lewerentz' and Torsten Stubelius' proposed crematorium (1914), Helsingborg, influenced ecclesiastical architecture until 1939, both architecturally and in its ideas.

[29] Carl Bergsten & Ivar Tengbom, "Ett bidrag till belysning av bostadsfrågan i stad" *Arkitektur* 9/1912, 105–108.

[30] *Arkitektur* 11/1908, 130; *Svenska Dagbladet* 28 October 1908, 24 January 1909.

[31] Collins & Collins (1986), 14.

[32] Josef Frank, "Das Haus als Weg und Platz" (*Baumeister*, 1931).

[33] Björn Linn, "Ivar Tengbom och arkitektyrket", in *Stenstadens arkitekter* (ed.) Thomas Hall, (1981), 162.

[34] Elias Cornell, *Ragnar Östberg. Svensk arkitekt* (1965), 114, 109, 136 ff.

[35] Ragnar Östberg, "Grand Hôtel Royal i Stockholm", *Arkitektur* (3/1909), 33 ff.

[36] Cornell (1965), 44.

[37] Cornell (1965), 167.

[38] Elis Benckert, "Ett hem på Djursholm", *Ord och Bild* (1912), 14 ff.

[39] Henrik O. Andersson & Fredric Bedoire, *Bankbyggande i Sverige* (1980), 188 ff, 422 ff. Bedoire (1974), 119 ff.

[40] *Svenska Dagbladet* 14 October 1910, 10 August 1913, 29 February 1916, 2 March 1916. Brunius, who was inclined to the English-speaking world had criticised Bergsten's work, including his bank and school at Norrköping, in 1910.

[41] Johansson (1965), 210.

[42] In his "Scandinavian Doricism" (*Architectural Design* 5-6/1982), Demetri Porphyrios considers Bergsten managed to cause the design here to appear in its mythological dimension.

[43] For a penetrating study of the Swedish owner-occupier movement about the turn of the 20th century, see Nils Edling, *Det fosterländska hemmet* (1996).

[44] Janne Ahlin, *Sigurd Lewerentz, arkitekt* (1985), 244 ff.

[45] Carl Bergsten, "Omkring arkitekturutställningen", *Arkitektur* 1914, 95 ff.

Rationalism and Classicism 1915–30

EVA ERIKSSON

In an article published in 1916, Gunnar Asplund asked his readers to call to mind pictures of Old Stockholm. "We must envy the uniformity and the calm modest middle-class characters of the private houses, admire the generally good taste of their builders or those who commissioned them, their instinctive tendency to go on building with the traditional motifs that had been used before in the town or by their neighbours, their sense for the self evident and correct, that these private residences ought to subordinate themselves to the public scene and keep themselves within the order of their surroundings."[1]

He had no small-town circumstances in mind. The four-and five-story 18th-century houses in the centre of the town, where the ground had been used with the greatest economy, were, he emphasised, fully comparable with contemporary apartment buildings. But it was extremely rare that houses which had just been built seemed to have grown up naturally in their surroundings. He wrote that "one forgets that it is more important to follow the style of the place than that of the time."

To restore the interplay between houses having different urban roles, residential buildings must be toned down and bound together into a tranquil unity. In this, thought Asplund, the straight horizontal roof line would be an important means.

Interest in old towns and older building traditions had widened into a more comprehensive view of urban organisation and architecture. During the latter part of the 19th century, the older bourgeois urban image, with its clear separation of roles between anonymous residential buildings and prominent public buildings, had been lost. In both size and embellishment, residential buildings and banks were appearing to claim as much attention as town halls; what was now sought was a greater urban clarity and a comprehensive urban view.

In the autumn of 1915, Sven Wallander presented a proposal accompanied by drawings for how the new central-Stockholm street, *Kungsgatan*, should be formed.[2] He thought of it as a busy commercial street in a uniformly classical style, but, as a dramatic element, with two high buildings of the sort that were becoming known as skyscrapers. With their help, he could resolve an architectural problem: how, elegantly, to connect the two levels that had been formed when blasting had excavated a way through the glacial ridge called Brunkebergsåsen. Wallander's proposal expressed a bold modernity and was met with great interest. Carl Bergsten admired its architectural value; the uniformity he spoke so warmly of evidently did not exclude such bold novelties as skyscrapers.[3] In this, his opinion was shared by other architects. They strove to give every function in a town an adequate expression with a comprehensive framework and here Wallander had found a form suitable for modern commercial life. To treat an entire street as an entity was seen as a great gain. The thought was to use building regulations to induce individual property owners to subordinate their new buildings to general principles for giving form.

The same striving towards larger comprehensive units was relevant to residential quarters. In Gregor Paulsson's opinion, expressed in *Den nya arkitekturen* (1916), lumping together "the many disparate individuals" in a quarter into a block with a shared courtyard would achieve a novel architectural urban unit.[4] Thanks to the central courtyard, residents would get more light, air and greenery.

Paulsson was an art historian and strongly engaged in contemporary social and aesthetic questions. He had been much influenced by

Norra Kungstornet (1920–23), Stockholm, by Sven Wallander; one of the first two European skyscrapers, a part of his vision of this central street.

the German reform movement in the circle around Deutscher Werkbund; he propagated actively in Sweden for their ideas. He was a motive force in the Swedish Handicraft Association and was to play a central role in the architectural debate in Sweden in the 1920s and 1930s.

The 1914–18 war had large effects on the Swedish economy and social conditions. The spirit of the times was different. There was a reaction against individualistic self assertion in many respects. Paulsson argued strongly in favour of collectivism and described it as almost a phenomenon of the time. Art should not be an occurrence in a superior class, produced by private individuals for an elite. It must undertake new tasks, not only monumental buildings. He wrote that "a movement is proceeding through time that definitely requires that there be 'beauty' in all the details of our everyday surroundings;" his formulation reveals influences from Ellen Key and, ultimately, from the Arts & Crafts' Movement.

The Crisis of the First World War

The intrusive social questions of the time opened entirely novel perspectives for architects, too. The large building jobs that, in a democratic spirit, could be seen in the future, seemed mostly of all to be collective. More than anything else this was a question of the long-neglected need of dwelling for the broad majority. The conflicts were sharpened by the supply crisis that the war brought with it. In 1916–17, foodstuffs and housing for the most people in Sweden became increasingly scarce, while a few made a great deal of money out of meeting demands in Europe. This challenging contrast contributed to raising the political temperature in Sweden. During a number of weeks in spring 1917 it reached boiling point. Demonstrations and food riots were reported from town after town.[5] The Swedish establishment was shaken. The following year the suffrage was extended to all men and women of 21 and older.

The housing question was at the centre of the debate about the national society. Within only a few years, building costs had tripled. Private-sector building companies had become almost completely inactive. The result was severe housing shortages and rising rents, which was most hard on the working population that was already living in cramped conditions.[6] Cramped living conditions were worsened by heating costs, which became high in Sweden, being in direct proportion to the floor area of apartments. Working-class families in hardly any other European country lived in such cramped conditions as those in Sweden.

Not until 1923 did inflation slacken its crippling grip on private-sector building activities. But in 1917 the crisis was so acute that circumstances forced municipalities to built emergency dwellings. The whole initiative went automatically over to the public sector, which, comprising the municipalities, the state and housing-cooperative organisations, had accounted for 10 per cent at most of what had been built before 1914; now it was to account for 60 to 70 per cent, but of a very small sum of building.[7] With this form of building it became possible to organise larger projects that had whole urban quarters as units. The crisis years became a period of experiment and novel thinking, when a new foundation was laid for building Swedish housing.

In 1913, the Västerås municipal housing

Working-class housing quarter, Västerås, 1915–17. (Left) The Josef quarter, by John Åkerlund. (Right) Erik Hahr's Ivar quarter, and (background) the blocks in his Julius and Jörgen quarters.

Crisis housing (Stativet & Tumstocken quarter) by Asplund for the city of Stockholm to a simple standard but with an idyllic small-town atmosphere. Now demolished.

committee had commissioned an architect, John Åkerlund, to design the *Josef* urban quarter as a storgårdskvarter, a perimeter block, or a building around an internal courtyard. It was built in 1915 but the commission had been taken over by the ASEA company. Later, a further two such quarters were built; the one called *Kåre* was designed by the municipal architect, Erik Hahr.[8] During the crisis years, he also designed some areas for a semi-municipal housing company, AB Arbetarbostäder i Västerås. They included the *Julius* and *Jörgen* quarters (1917), which comprised eight long blocks; their short ends, which gave onto a road, were joined a low wall running parallel to it, which was an unusual form for the time. Hahr can have sought models in older Nordic examples. Gunnar Asplund used the same pattern in the *Stativet* and *Tumstocken* quarters, which he designed in 1917 for the town of Stockholm: he placed a row of small freestanding blocks at an angle to a slightly curving longer block. The buildings were beautifully proportioned, and had an idyllic small-town atmosphere; but they were extremely simple in construction and standards. They were among a number of straightforwardly emergency dwellings that had a simplified but eventually problematic wall design; they were torn down later.[9]

A house designed by Cyrillus Johansson and built in 1915 at Enskede for the *Framtiden* housing association became a model for Stockholm. It contained apartments that contained, besides a kitchen either one or two rooms. The facades of the first block were brush-finished in different shades of yellow, to look as if it were a number of buildings brought together in a single length.

The years of crisis became a starting point for Swedish housing cooperative movement. Formed in 1916, Stockholm Cooperative Housing Association (*Stockholms Kooperativa Bostadsförening*, or SKB) built among other things the *Motorn* and *Vingen* quarters (1916–19); they comprise three-story buildings grouped around large planted courtyards. Their simple brush-finished facades are the same back and front, with entries from the courtyard. In all their simplicity, these quarters, which were designed by Gustaf Larson, became an important model for housing architecture during the novel conditions that then obtained.

Many other urban municipalities now set about building small, carefully laid out apartments to simple standards, well exemplified by the buildings on *Konsistoriegatan*, Linköping; designed by Gustaf Linden for the municipal

housing company AB Smålägenheter i Linköping and built in 1918, they contained one- and two-room apartments, each with a large, rather countrified style of kitchen, a bostadskök. Osvald Almqvist designed a housing area at Borlänge for the *Domnarvet Ironworks*; called *Bergslagsbyn*, it was built in 1915–20 and contained dwellings for blue-collar and white-collar employees. Almqvist combined contemporary ideas in a mature, well-thought-out way (see also catalogue). He combined influence from English garden-city planning with elements from Swedish works' and vernacular traditions. The buildings are ranged along the streets, giving a closed impression when so viewed, while the open spaces behind them were left open to provide for shared green areas. Looking like so many classical little red Swedish stugor, the surroundings have a Swedish village-like atmosphere, even though these buildings were in fact manufactured in a rational way with a high degree of standardisation.[10]

As mentioned above, the firm of Lewerentz & Stubelius had designed workers' dwelling before 1914: some for various companies, some for the town of Helsingborg, where they had done drawings for the buildings and their general plan in two owner-occupier areas called *Pålsjö* and *Eneborg*. In 1917–18, 12 houses were built at Eneborg, in size varying from one for a single family to one for twelve. They

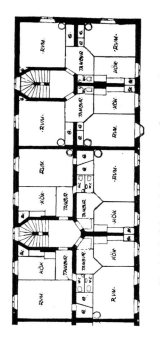

Apartments for a Stockholm-co-operative association at Enskede (1915), by Cyrillus Johansson: a high standard at the time.

Landala owner-builder area, Göteborg; Sitte-style plan (1908) by Albert Lilienberg. These one- or two-family houses (1914) were types designed by Carl Westman; all were painted brown, which made for overall uniformity but variations in its details.

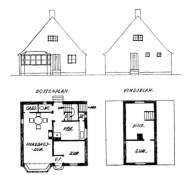

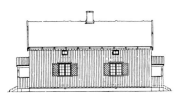

Two designs by the Lewerentz & Stubelius firm: (above) plan for an owner-builder family house in brick, Helsingborg.

(Below) a wooden house for two working-class families (1912), to be made by Luleå Träsliperi, Karlshäll, and to be painted in the traditional red; such houses were intended for an owner-occupier area designed by the architects.

reveal, however, Lewerentz' severely factual approach, in which materials and proportions are decisive for their overall impression. The dark-red Helsingborg brick gave the area a character traditional in this part of Sweden, called Skåne.[11]

In 1917, Swedish Handicraft Association arranged the Home Exhibition (Hemutställningen) in the newly-built Liljevalch Art Gallery in Stockholm; it was wholly dominated by the Swedish problems of the time. On display in the smaller rooms were various proposals for how an unexceptional apartment for a worker could be furnished so that, despite modest means, a pleasant domestic atmosphere could be created. Furnishing had been done by various architects. The interior by Asplund was the most admired; and has come to a high degree to characterise the exhibition (see p. 206). One of the large rooms presented new municipal building projects from all parts of Sweden: many had lightly classical touches, with pitched roofs, rhythmically repeated and well proportioned fenestration, and, in some, pilasters that added more rhythm. This retrained classicism, based on rhythm, proportions and repetition, was well suited to a rationalised manner of building.

But architects still emphasised local associations, the 'architecture of the site'. So did Gregor Paulsson, despite taking definitive exception now to the spate of "hembygds-svärmeri", meaning roughly parish-pump enthusiasm, that had flowed through early manifestations of national romanticism; he called all interest in old vernacular objects a "neurasthenic upper-class mania," and though it ridiculous to attempt to arrest the passage of time.[12]

In Paulsson's view, a new time required new forms. "The first railway carriage was a stage-coach on rails, the flywheels of steam engines were decorated with chariot spokes, gaslights were fitted to Empire candelabra." His formulations would be repeated in the Swedish functionalist programme pamphlet acceptera, published in 1931. As early as 1916, Paulsson was convinced in his belief in the movement of development.[13] In his opinion, the style of a new time would automatically grow out of new methods of construction, just as had happened earlier in history.[14]

Industrial Buildings

Industrial buildings formed an area of activity in which functional and economical demands were more penetrating than elsewhere; it was one in which architects were concerned to only a limited degree. In so far as they existed, architectural ambitions reached as far as to facades, while plans and designs were decided by engineers. Architects had good reason to wonder what they could do in the present and likely future circumstances. In 1918, Carl Bergsten opposed a document from the Industrial Federation (*Industriförbundet*) that claimed pre-eminence in responsibility for industrial building for engineers, with a "lateral access to architectural knowledge." The document declared that, in this context, what was architectural would be subordinated, because "all questions concerning the position and design of buildings, and their suitability for use, lie within the scientific competence of engineering, economics and technology."[15] In Bergsten's view, this was an outmoded way of looking at the work of architects, which interpreted it as merely historical decoration. He claimed that now, instead, the effect of the whole was to be emphasised, and thus architects dealt with precisely position, design and function.

This number of the periodical also presented some industrial buildings of which architects had designed at least their exteriors.[16] An early example of an industrial building of a modern sort was Erik Hahr's ASEA *Mimer-verkstaden* in Västerås. At the time, ASEA was as advanced and as rapidly expanding an elec-

Textile factory on Laxholmen Island, Norrköping, by Folke Bensow (1916–17). Ove Hidemark (1991) restored it; it now houses the Museum of Work.

tro-technical company, and as technically distinguished, as AEG in Germany. ASEA's managing director was internationally oriented and a keen proponent of Taylorism in Sweden. He wanted a new building to make it possible to rationalise production of electric motors as far as possible. At AEG, he had found a model both to organise production and form the factory, and, as AEG had done, he engaged an architect as the designer of the new factory's exterior.[17] Its first stage was built 1911–12, the second in 1914–15; it was thus almost contemporary with Peter Behren's celebrated turbine hall in Berlin. With the second stage complete, the workshop was 200 metres long, and built in a design in iron, with bricked facades. Large-scale fenestration dominated its long facade, which was given a rhythm through supports in the form of brick pillars that seemed to support the protruding upper floor with its fenestration as an accentuating horizontal line.[18]

The building had been shown at the Baltic exhibition in 1914. So had another, which the Lewerentz & Stubelius firm had designed for *AB Baltic* in Södertälje that year; it was a design in concrete clad with brickwork. In its general appearance it resembled the Mimerverkstaden but was much more severe in form. Its ground plan was based on a scheme for production drawn up by an engineer, T.A. Bergen; he worked for a consultancy, *Industribyrån* that, specialising in planning according to Taylorism's ideas, gained great importance for Swedish industrial buildings.[19]

The industrial and utilitarian buildings shown in the same number of the periodical included a prototype silo for the National Grain-Storage Agency (*Statens spannmålslager*) (1917–18), of which nine variants were erected in different places. These were designed by Asplund who, in presenting them, pointed out that his commission had been limited to a general tidying up of their external forms: lofty volumes to which, despite their large scale, he succeeded in giving a certain delicate elegance. A textile factory on *Laxholmen* (1916–17) that Holmens bruk, Norrköping, commissioned Folke Bensow to design was beautifully free and self evident in its form. In his opinion, he used every bit of the site, a holm in the river running through Norrköping, so that the building seems to rise straight out of its reflection in the water. Lightly rendered in yellow, beautifully proportioned and having only a few decorative details, the building has given great character to the town; it is now used as a museum (page 174).

Mimerverkstad, Västerås, (1911–12, 1914–15) by Erik Hahr who followed contemporary international ideas. The factory produced advanced electrical goods. Section below.

The periodical thus brought industrial building to the fore as an important task for architects and contributed to raising their status. An argument was that factories were becoming physically larger and more dominant over their urban surroundings, which motivated giving attention to their form. But in contrast to urban planning, to which architects had contributed a wholly novel way of seeing, they accepted the necessity of a basically engineering point of view. As a consequence of the systems according to which they were built, industrial buildings got a factual appearance, so that they can be understood as representing a stage preceding functionalism.[20] But it is also important to keep in mind that contemporary architects still clearly distinguished between different types of commissions and the formal language suitable to them.

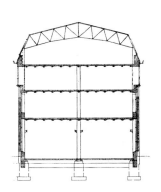

Contacts Between the Northern Countries Become More Intensive

During the years after the turn of the century, those participating in the Swedish debate about architecture referred increasingly often to Denmark. Nyrop's town hall in Copenhag-

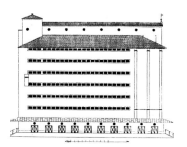

Official grain silo, a variant of Gunnar Asplund's (1917–18) prototype.

Liselund, Danish country house (c. 1790), island of Møn; it inspired a renewal of classicism in the northern countries shortly before 1920.

en had contributed to a renaissance for brick architecture. The study of older buildings that had been undertaken as a consequence of the founding in 1892 of an association of architects was even more important; it became a model for equivalent studies in Sweden.

Compared with the other, lightly populated countries of the north, Denmark had urban populations, cultures and architectural styles that had long been more bourgeois in character, while Danish building traditions were expressed in refined craftsmanship, sound materials, a firm sense of proportion and a sparse simplicity. During the golden age of Danish art, ie around 1800, the simple classicism of the Danish bourgeoisie became closely united with the country's tradition and identity. The path of the return of classicism to Danish architecture was opened by an intellectual feud in 1911 over a proposal to build a new spire on a church, *Vor Frue Kirke*, that was one of the main early examples of 19th-century classicism. The church was by C.F. Hansen, but the proposed spire was a reconstruction of a 17th-century Baroque design. This led to Hansen's work being wholly re-evaluated and to the younger generation taking it as an essential model.

The breakthrough work for classicism in the north was Carl Petersen's *Museum in Faaborg*, Denmark (1912–15). Seemingly modest and squeezed into a very narrow site, it comprises a series of exhibition rooms along an axis. Impulses from Hansen may be seen foremost in its small facade, the small dimensions of which are enlarged through whole surfaces. Its powerful pure interior colours and its mosaic floor's effective patterns associate to the *Thorvaldsen Museum*, Copenhagen, an important early 19th-century Danish monument. But Petersen reinforced the rhythm of the succession of rooms with effective interruptions. Similarities and dissimilarities in size, height, form, coloration and lighting of the rooms emphasise this. In a celebrated arti-

cle that was given the headline of Modsætninger ('Contrasts') Petersen wrote that "there ought not to occur something at every point in a building."[21] The "surfaces and rhythmic divisions of a structure ought to calmly build up to the contrast with the focal points where efforts have been concentrated." He wanted to achieve an interplay, at vital points, between whole uninterrupted surfaces and contrasting effects. This way of seeing things became characteristic for classicism in Sweden in the 1920s.

Contacts between the Nordic countries were strengthened during the 1914–18 war, which cut all of them off from the rest of Europe. To a high degree, Denmark made contributions, but mutual contacts between Denmark and Sweden were particularly fruitful. Leading Danish architects, including Kay Fisker and Aage Rafn, received decisive impulses from Asplund and Lewerentz. In 1917, these two Danes and others took measurements from a small country house, *Liselund*, on the island of Mön: this whitewashed house from the 1790s with a high thatched roof unites a delicate classicism with a rural tradition. They published their work in a book in 1918; but their drawings and measurements, and the museum at Faaborg, were included in an exhibition of Danish architecture and arts and crafts that had opened at Liljevalch's gallery in Stockholm in February that year.[22]

Cemeteries

In quickly growing towns space was needed not just for the living but also for an increasing number of graves. Cemetery facilities became a new task for architects: old conventions had to be tried and new attitudes created. The subject of this work was components of the natural world as much as buildings, but most of all the question was to create dignity and a cultural anchorage for a function that, in a modern community, had to be coped with in a commonsensical and hygienically acceptable way, at the same time as it contained large questions concerning human life and existential dimensions.

In Sweden, using arguments motivated strongly by sanitary reasons, the Cremation Society (*Eldbegängelseföreningen*) proposed coffin burials should be replaced but, at the same time, proposed that a merely rational view of death should be opposed.[23] Cremation must therefore be accorded the same dignity as a traditional burial. A few crematoria had been built in Sweden, but the movement had devel-

Air view, Woodland Cemetery (1934), showing the general layout before any chapel or other building had appeared.

oped most in Germany, where there was a number of facilities that inspired the Swedish proponents. The most energetic of them was the chairman of the association mentioned above, Gustaf Schlyter. He had worked out a programme of ideas for the ceremony of cremation as well as the principles for giving form to the relevant buildings; they had been the basis on which Lewerentz & Stubelius prepared the drawings for their proposal for a crematorium for Helsingborg (page 44).[24]

These architects were well acquainted with the German discussions of the question. they had both lived in Munich, where an important pioneering facility lay: Münchener Waldfriedhof. Stubelius took an active part in the Swedish architectural debate, among other things having written an article on the art of laying out cemeteries. While the drawings are clearly from Lewerentz' hand, Stubelius was supplying the ideas of their proposal.[25]

The chapel was conceived as a long, high, slender building through which mourners would proceed in a way that matched the different phases of the ritual of cremation. A long ascending set of stairs led up to the entry and into the 'room of death,' where the main ceremony would be held in the presence of the catafalque. At the conclusion of the ceremony, once the coffin had been lowered into the furnace on the floor below, the mourners would proceed up a small stairway, to the accompaniment of choral music from a gallery, to the 'room of life', which was on the uppermost floor of the crematorium, high up on a ridge, and with extensive views over the landscape. It was also well lit, and, while they waited to receive an urn of ashes from the deceased, the mourners could obtain a sense of reconciliation and of returning to life.

Towards the end of summer in 1914, two former students of the Klara School, Asplund and Lewerentz, fell into conversation by the model of this crematorium at the Baltic exhibition. An architectural competition for the *Woodland Cemetery*, Stockholm (see catalogue) having just then been announced, they agree to prepare a joint entry. Their long cooperation over this job had thus begun.[26]

The burial ground was to lie on land owned by the town at Enskede and be accommodated within a large mostly undisturbed wooded area with pines that included a couple of small gravel pits. In their first proposal, the architects let these features of the site dominate; they presented it lightly retouched. They kept the existing old roads and made skilful use of the absolutely straight boundary lines. Graves would be placed directly in the wooded parts. Located in a ravine on the edge of the largest gravel pit, the main chapel would accommodate the ceremony, which would be formed as a procession from darkness to light. This theme from the Helsingborg crematorium has been shown to have been a leading motif in giving form to the burial ground at Enskede.[27]

Compared with some German and more formalistic entries for the competition, for example, the lyrically natural proposal by Asplund and Lewerentz was of a different species. It reflected a specifically Northern feeling for the untamed natural world, as it had particularly been expressed in art in the 1890s. In announcing it as the winner, the prize board emphasised the great qualities in the two architects' proposals but asked for a certain

The Way of the Cross, drawing by Lewerentz (1915) from his and Asplund's original proposal for the Woodland Cemetery.

A gouache by Asplund (1918) from his work on the Woodland Chapel, with small columns as dark as the pine trunks.

(Right) Asplund's chairs are subordinated to the chapel but, as here, emphasise its focus on the illuminated circle beneath its cupola.

amount of reworking. Influenced by Osvald Almqvist's proposal, their new proposal entailed a greater disturbance to the land: the gravel pits would be widened, deciduous trees would be planted and extensive felling would be undertaken.[28]

The complete cemetery came into being in the course of a very long time. Its realisation proceeded by stages and in an order that was the inverse of what the architects had originally intended. The main chapel that was to be the centre of the whole facility was postponed

time and again. At first economic resources were altogether to limited. In 1918, a year of crisis in Sweden, the overall plans were was decided for the first small chapel, a modest building in wood that was to be located well into the area.

In 1918, Asplund was editor for *Arkitektur*. In the March 1919 number of the periodical, he reviewed the Danes' "delightful book on a small refined country house in a rich natural setting." His further comments have often been repeated: "Altogether too beautiful historical books on architecture can have their dangers for a modern architect, who can too easily be induced to borrow beautiful motifs that do not belong to his time or buildings. But they can also confer artistic impulses, give a jerk to artistic ambition. And such is the book on Liselund: when studying it, one grabs a clean bit of paper and begins freshly reworking one's old drawings."

At the time, Asplund's drawing board had his drawings for the small *Woodland Chapel* (1918–20) on it, and he changed its character radically. Instead of the severe classicistic volume he had been thinking about, an intimate, modest chapel begins to appear among the trees, like a woodland hut. A drawing from December 1918 shows columns of its antechamber as black as the trunks of the surrounding pine trees, the forest seemingly comes in beneath the dark shingled roof as if it, too, were something natural. But with the white columns he intensified the contrast between the rusticity of the Northern tradition and the slender, refined classical culture.

In his presentation of the building, Asplund asserted that the chapel would meet the immediate need of less elaborate burials once the burial ground begun to be taken into use

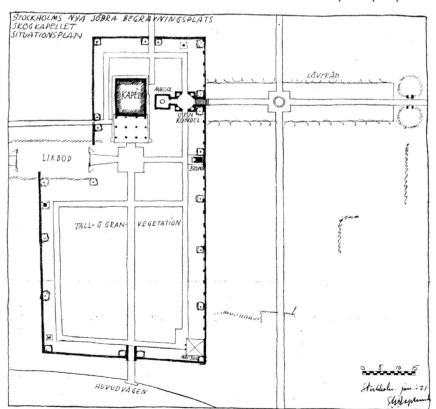

Plan of the walled vicinity of the Woodland Chapel and its conifers and (upper right) the path leading through deciduous trees to the children's place of burial.

in the autumn of 1920.[29] It was to be small, as inexpensive as possible and ready for the inauguration; later its role would entirely subordinate. Because its volume was not large enough to have a monumental appearance in the wood, he chose instead to depress it: he wanted nothing that would be in between.

Asplund worked deliberately with contrasts. The darkness of the woods elevated the experience of the light space of the interior of the chapel. In contrast to the organic character of the exterior, the interior has a bare simplicity of flat surfaces and geometric forms. Sensualism and abstraction balance. The room is quadratic, but Asplund has concentrated it into an illuminated circle around the catafalque that a ring of columns define; they carry a cupola with an aperture for light in its middle, as if it were a small pantheon. The light creates an enchanted circle drawn against the obscurity of the corners of the square. Asplund himself expressed a certain dismay over the room not being exactly as he had intended. The cupola should have raised itself lightly and airily above the depressed antechamber and entry, "but [it] has in reality had a lower and flatter effect than the drawings promised."

The chapel lacks any fixed seating. Its intimate and informal character is strengthened by the chairs that can be moved and placed in a ring; small and neat, they are painted in a light-grey tone and have a bit of an Empire character. The thin and elegant patterns of the open-work doors contrast with the external doors, which are flat, dark and iron bound.

Facing the door to the cemetery, the observer sees to the left a small building half sunk in the ground: the bodies of the dead rest on their way to their final interment in a place already well down in the earth.[30]

As we know, in reviewing the church at Masthugget, Asplund had reacted against its burden of a roof and its lack of "a light and liberating feeling of hope." Here he showed for the first time his striving to give form to light, floating roofs.[31] Wahlman's Engelbrekt church can have inspired him, for its roof seems to be almost incorporeal; its contrast with the heavy exterior astonishes, and, thanks to the long ascent to the church, does so dramatically. Lewerentz' contemporary Helsingborg chapel obtains its form from a succession, a sequence of experiences.

A self-evident sounding board for the Woodland Chapel is the architecture and gardening art of late 18th-century Gustavian Sweden, such as it is expressed, for example, in Hagaparken in Stockholm. It contains a clear

dialectic between nature and culture, between organic form and sharp-edged classicism. A further natural source of inspiration is the Romantic funeral culture. In the 18th century, hygienic considerations had led to demands that churchyards should be removed from urban surroundings;[32] they accorded with the fanciful interest in graves set in a landscape that were required in any contemplation of the currency of life.

Louis Jean Desprez, Gustav III's favourite architect, was also among other things a very skilful designer and decorator of theatrical effects; beside the severe neo-classicism he displayed in some formal building commissions, he could playfully stage the dramatic image in Hagaparken of the multiple Copper Tent. They have often been claimed as a putative inspiration for Asplund's creation in 1922 of a *services' facility* for the Woodland Cemetery: a wilful building that demonstrates how undogmatic, even to the point of being irreverent, Asplund could be in so deeply solemn a context as this one. It looks like a small encampment of tents—small pavilions with high pyramidical copper-covered roofs over linking lengths of buildings in wood. In their centre a conical roof points upwards; its interior is painted blue, a captured bit of heavenly sky. Its form associates to Egyptian burial cultures, French revolutionary architecture.

So far as concerns the Woodland Cemetery as a whole, Lewerentz made the greater contribution, as Asplund emphasised in his presentation of the chapel. As he wrote, the chapel was far from being the most important bit of work that had hitherto been done. "The arrangement in detail of the area, with its entry, boundary walls, roads, burial grounds, all of which have been undertaken by the architect Sigurd Lewerentz, is a long, difficult and, at first sight, not so rewarding or eye-catching a job but is perhaps the most remarkable hitherto and will in the end certainly be what will give the cemetery its character."[33]

Lewerentz had a rare ability to perceive in respect to any given site the specific possibilities it offered. This is exemplified well in his contemporary work on *Malmö Östra cemetery*, a commission he received after a competition in 1916. The site was an open stretch of farm land, with a slight ridge along one edge: he took its slope as the central point of departure for his work on the whole, orienting paths and viewing points by reference to it, as well as the site of the first chapel, and, along its edge, the line of the central road. And he laid out a circular glade of memory beside it. All is minute-

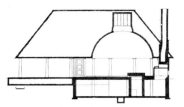

Woodland Chapel, section: the high dark roof conceals the cupola and its fenestration.

Lewerentz continuously re-designed the entry to the Woodland Cemetery by reference to his and Asplund's thoughts about forms for the main chapel and its surroundings that they would place just inside the entry.

The oldest part of Lewerentz' cemetery at Malmö, a design from 1916; he caused the chapel building, which contains three small chapels and four adjoining rooms, to fit well into the open landscape around it.

ly worked through but with the sparsest possible means. Without departing from the natural topography, Lewerentz structured the vegetation architecturally.

As we have mentioned, the Woodland Cemetery in Stockholm grew for many years, the result of a constant dialogue between the two architects. Among the first things to be built was the wall, which was designated as a labour-market project in a period of unemployment during the 1914–18 war. Lewerentz worked in the initial stages with the entry; we

Constantly changing light between tree trunks contributes powerfully to the Woodland Cemetery's special character.

shall recur to his chapel and the later parts of the project (p. 70, 75).

In a thorough study of the Woodland Cemetery, Caroline Constant has tried to define the specifically Swedish situation out of which a work of this sort could emerge. In Sweden, in contrast to what often occurred in continental Europe, the engagement in national society that was associated with modernism lacked a utopian direction; in her view, it was characterised by a more realistic, socially responsible attitude that entailed engagement and care for human life in a practical way that also entailed having to do with death. In her opinion, the conflicts of the time between modernity and tradition could be bridged uniquely in this work of art. Rather than a nostalgic confirmation of traditional values, it expresses both a timelessness and a modern spirit. She further asserts that it is striking how spiritual values have been given form without the use of traditional ecclesiastical symbolism. In her opinion, this formal language is charged with feeling but without confessional linkage; as a symbol, the greatness of the natural world has replaced the superordinate church.[34]

The many anonymous gravestones in the woods give an impression for the endless cycle of life, death and rebirth, but also for the equality of all before death, and community with the natural world. It can perhaps be interpreted as the Swedish ideal of equality, the thought of the folkhem in association with an agricultural community with its being rooted in the natural world.

Both Asplund and Lewerentz received a number of other commissions for cemeteries in different places; each treated his commis-

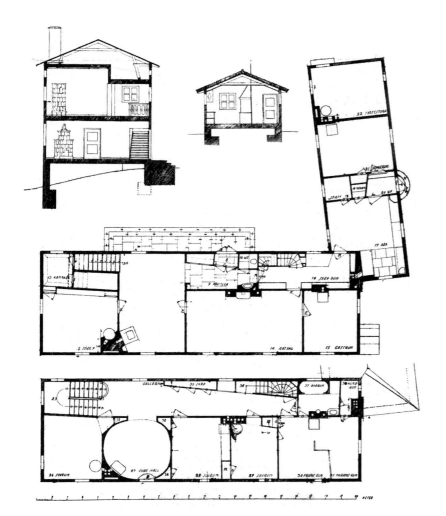

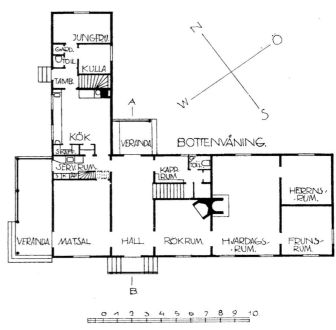

(Above) Ground-floor plan, Ahxner House, by the Lewerentz & Stubelius firm (1914).

(Left) Ground- and upper-floor plans, and sections, of the Snellman House, Djursholm, north-west of Stockholm, by Gunnar Asplund (1917–18).

sions individually in accordance with their separate preconditions. The Woodland Cemetery never became a standard pattern.

Two Private Houses and a Court House

In the last 1919 number of *Arkitektur*, Lewerentz and Asplund each presented a private house in Stockholm. They were similar and different. The *Ahxner House* by Lewerentz & Stubelius (1914) is a low, robust and in its exterior quite modest two-story house with a lower kitchen wing extending at right angles from the back. Its main volume is narrow, its hall and living room extend across it. Along the entry facade, which faces south west, the reception rooms are aligned in the file that was customary in Swedish country houses. Björn Linn has observed that the flood of light through the hall thus encounters the light penetrating the file of rooms, and that this principle was used by Asplund in his *Snellman House*.

The latter is the more sophisticated. Its principal character is different: light rendered walls and white-painted window arches. It is high and slender, reaching the ground without a mediating foundation. Empire-style details including festoons, lunette windows and doors give a delicate, graceful impression. The garden facade seems on first sight to be simply regular, with rhythmically repeated window rows, until it is noticed that the lower windows are not aligned with those above them, which is felt as tension in the facade.

The narrowing form of the porch, staircase and upper gallery is a familiar theme in the house, which accords with the type of oblique ground plan that Östberg has worked with. The upper floor includes a hall, which has a peculiar, organically rounded form; it is panelled in warm, brown wood. The ceiling of the ground-floor hall is also panelled in wood, and, according to Asplund's presentation of the house, was to have been painted with figures of landscapes and human beings.[35] Some of the interior parts of the house have thus a character of cosy, organic rusticity that seems to oppose the facade's materially neutral surface and almost abstract character. Such a contrast could be found at the Woodland Chapel but, here, it was, so to say, turned inside out.

Asplund described the Snellman House as an attempt to resolve the design of a modern dwelling in a building of a width of only one-and-a-half rooms. In his opinion, modern living with its demands for subsidiary space,

Asplund's Snellman House: garden facade, with subtle fenestration irregularities.

heating and communication was no longer possible in an old parstuga and its offshoots of only a single room's width. On the other side, he wanted to admit as much light as possible. Therefore all rooms give onto the south and a view of the garden, while space for practical purposes lies on the north, a principle that Westman and Östberg had applied.

The seemingly identically equal doors in the entry facade are puzzling. The French door has the evident function of admitting light so that the hall should be illuminated from two directions, as in the Ahxner House. But it can also stand as a symbol for a cleft in Swedish mentality between winter introversion and its opposite in summer. As days shorten in the autumn, the occupants of the house try to shut out the winter, for example, closing the shutters on the French door; in summer, when light returns, the doors are opened. The Snellman House is richly filled with puzzles and contradictions, as if Asplund needed to balance a sense of over-cultivation and style against one of naive simplicity and something primitive. As if the precious must be weighed against the playful, and the solemnly elevated must be undermined by a mocking manner, a certain distance.

Asplund designed the *Lister Court House* for the small town of Sölvesborg, which was built in 1919–21 (see also catalogue). It lies on top of a hill on the line of sight of a straight street. Seen along this perspective, its main facade, having the form of a gable although it is actually the longitudinal side of this rather narrow rectangular building, gives it a look of being bigger than it is. On its smooth rendered yellow wall surface, a round flat clock-face, painted black, appears distinctly. Its entry is embodied in a "sunken vault" with Empire-inspired patterning.

Here, as in the Snellman House, Asplund's use of flat surfaces and the abstract character of the Empire style represents a complete abandonment of the previous generation's striving to try to express a powerful effect of material. It associates most immediately to C.F. Hansen's work. As is so in the 19th-century neo-antique, a few expressive, independent details outline themselves against the body of the Sölvesborg building that, as a whole, is constituted by powerful geometric forms and smooth wall surfaces. The court room itself protrudes from the back of the building like a half cylinder, a motif that can be found in many early 19th-century classicistic buildings. But, here, windows extrude from the wall in a peculiar way. The vestibule is incised by the other, round side of the court room, in a way that resembles the altar circle in Vor Frue kirke in Copenhagen. Hansen's balustrades are borne on obviously plumply rounded balusters. Asplund greatly over-emphasises their roundness.[36] In such manneristic indications he demonstrates his distance from academic classicism.

Asplund's Lister Court House (1919–21): this straight street is terminated by what is only apparently a facade.

From Crisis to Boom

The 1920s in Sweden began and ended with crises; in between lay an uninterrupted period of steady economic growth, when wages rose in real terms and working hours were shortened. Agriculture declined while industry developed dynamically. The country became literally electrified, production was mechanised and, in a spirit of Taylorism, made rational. New goods could thus be produced more efficiently; motor vehicles distributed them more quickly, and, in conjunction with railways, contributed to an increasingly finer-meshed transportation network. As real wages rose, so did purchasing power, laying the foundations for a mass market of simpler utilitarian and other goods. Trade and commerce flourished.

The political situation was labile, with a succession of minority governments of various political hues. The centre of political gravity thus lay in the riksdagen and its special committees, where solutions were reached through compromises. Unemployment remained high; the level of recompense to be paid for labour-market measures to relieve it was one of the hottest political questions. Strikes and lock-outs were relatively frequent. Despite all this and structural changes, developments in Sweden were calm compared to those elsewhere in Europe.[37] A reason for this was that Sweden was not affected so badly by international economic swings. Sweden was not (yet) as highly industrialised as other countries. In the years when international economic factors had most impact on Sweden, domestic investments in housing stimulated domestic production.[38] Building thus came unintentionally to function as a regulator of economic activity, a valuable experience for future Swedish policy.

Intensive rationalisation of industry was a basic characteristic of the 1920s. The spirit of the time was characterised by a belief in commonsense derived from calculations of an engineering sort, and a factual concentration on practical problems. Because modernisation had showed it could contribute to rising real wages for a majority of the population, it was appreciated as a force for progress, and assented to by a wide range of the population. In the Labour Movement, economic efficiency and social reform activity began to be associated: possibilities began to appear for a pact based on a balance of power between company owners and workers that would benefit both. This was the basis for what would be called the Swedish model. Within the Social Democratic Party, class warfare was toned down and demands for socialisation were abandoned. Instead, negotiated solutions were spoken of with favour; the Labour Movement would close ranks around making the national economy more efficient, with the central government as the controlling hand. In return, politics could aim at equality, while increasing resources could be devoted to social reforms. Values of national symbolism were integrated with tactical skill into this model, which entailed twisting a demagogic tool out of the hands of the right wing.[39] In a debate in the riksdag in 1928, Per Albin Hansson summarised for the first time this novel orientation of politics by invoking the image of 'the good home', where all would be accorded equality (page 81).

As a metaphor that derived from the debate about culture at the turn of the century, 'the home' showed it had kept its political clout. The 1920s was also to be the first decade when dwellings were built on a broad front with qualitative goals. Building dwellings acquired a stabilising role in the economy and results made positive signals. For many working-class families, a good dwelling seemed no longer out of reach, even though much time would elapse before a national housing policy could be established and a majority of the population got an acceptable standard of housing.

Building matters were good in other sectors. New offices and shops grew in urban centres. Motor vehicles got their first breakthrough, and traffic on urban streets beat with a novel pulse in town life. The cinema became a popular entertainment, and the new cinemas contributed to urban evenings bubbling with life. Many new public buildings, including libraries, concert halls, schools and so on testified to lofty cultural ambitions not only for the elite of the bourgeoisie but also for a democratised cultural life on a broader base.

The Soil of and Developmental
Tendencies in Architecture

Since the turn of the century, Swedish architects had often expressed a wish to achieve a uniform style for the times. This striving seemed now to be bearing fruit. During the whole of the 1920s, classicism was so dominant that its architecture has been called 20-talsklassicism, '1920s' classicism'. But, despite its outward uniformity, it spanned a great width and included a number of different possibilities of expression.

Let us recapitulate some of the strands of the inheritance from the preceding decades. In starting from the basics of architecture—design, function and tradition—Carl Westman had tried to reduce formal language, while also employing material and texture as sensually expressive. To speak pointedly, he strove to unite the archaic with what was sensual, which was further developed by Lewerentz, who could extract from such a unity both a general validity and the utmost refinement. Ragnar Östberg, on the other side, worked with a broad register of architectural references. He made use of inherent contradictions and departures from symmetry to achieve a richer expression, but his striving was also to mould together separate bits and detailed forms around superordinate formal themes and sequences of rooms. Asplund inherited and carried on this theme.

Another tendency was to seek, in the rhythm, proportions and balance of classicism, to hold larger parts of towns together in beautiful unities. Sven Wallander, among many other, anonymous architects, worked in this way to give form to 1920s' housing areas. The basis for this was studies of anonymous architecture, partly of Swedish traditions from wooden-built towns and from works' communities, partly from stimuli of Danish and German classicism around 1800. The latter had been reinforced by the book *Um 1800* by Paul Mebes, which was much read in the Nordic countries. Heinrich Tessenow's much reduced classicism that was balanced by an intimate middle-class cosiness attracted much attention. *Hausbau und dergleichen* (published 1916) was well received especially in Denmark and Sweden.

Tessenow's significance in the Nordic countries can be explained as a factor of his formal language, which resonated with domestic tradition. In old, wooden-built Swedish towns the proportions of houses derived from joiners' customary dimensions for timber. This had resulted in stretches of street that were divided rhythmically but looked very uniform; the houses were embellished simply and finished in light hues of oil-based paint. In Denmark the regularity and standardised dimensions of timber framing had had a similar effect.

The reaction against 19th-century style architecture had created a strong distaste for a formally constrained and stylistically articulated architecture. Classicistic forms could be used only if classicistic conventions were simultaneously undermined or controverted. To create monumentality through a hierarchy of systems of columns with emphasised central parts and strictly determined axles of symmetry was uninviting. Architecture in Sweden in the 1920s differs from the sort of representative neo-classicism that manifested itself in the European 1920s, among other things on account of its modest scale and absence of monumentality. The Swedish attitude to the traditional language of classicism was sophisticated and a little remote. This remoteness could express itself in manneristically drawn-out proportions or an abstraction of formal language and a deliberate demolition of monumentality and hierarchy.[40] A model was offered by the unorthodox point of view of the architecture of the French revolution. One can compare the situation with late 20th-century post-modernism, in which architects have begun to draw on a store of older forms. But because they felt worn out if used seriously, they were taken up as citations or in a fragmented form. Post-modernism has not plumbed traditions as deeply as architects in the 1920s could do at the break between tradition and modernism, but there was a certain similarity in their attitudes.

During the second and third decades of the 20th century, Swedish architects took marked exception to the individualism of the 1890s. While striving towards the anonymous and generally valid, they retained the turn-of-the-century lyricism of nature and the feeling for an interplay between nature and culture. They retained, too, something of the informal character of the Swedish national romanticism and organic formation of plans, as well as its predilection for undecorated wall surfaces and the effects of cubic volumes. Younger architects, however, reacted against the weight and expressive interpretations of the intrinsic qualities of material. A novel lightness characterised the architecture of the 1920s.

Classicistic formal language functioned as a means to strive for a number of important things at the time. Besides making visible the play of forces in designs in concrete and to make rhythmic large coherent parts of towns, it was used to give form to an appreciation of space. We have observed that some architecture proceeded from sequences of rooms. The transition from one to another occupies a zone that Björn Linn has called one of *interpenetration*.[41] Columned porticos, arcades, antechambers: superficially appearing to be stylistic elements alone, they have in fact this role in a successive of rooms. During the period in question, these historical forms are not ends in themselves but means to achieve architectural effects. The similar intermediate zones that can be seen in the classicism of the early 19th century comprise a putative source of inspiration: Schinkel's *Altes museum* in Berlin, for example, or Hansen's *Domhus* in Copenhagen, in which an antechamber mediates a transition between the town and the building.

Towards a More Rational Production of Dwellings

Early 20th-century urban apartments for workers had been severely criticized for being cramped, dark and unhygienic. Their plans were often done unthinkingly, sites were over-exploited, with many apartments on each staircase and privies in the yards below, which was a manner of building the old building regulations favoured. But if this sort of building was done almost entirely by the private sector, and included a large element of speculation, there was no real public-sector housing policy.

The crisis from 1917 to 1923 was a turning point. As already mentioned, municipalities and housing-cooperative associations had already displayed examples of better housing premises. It was important that, in the background (1912–18), a national housing commission had been working to determine housing demands. It was followed in 1919 by an investigation to formulate demands for quality that might have been linked to a form of national official support had this not been stopped in 1923, when the economy began to recover. Thus the report of the 1919 investigation, Practical and Hygienic Dwellings (*Praktiska och hygieniska bostäder*), published in 1921, did not have its intended guiding role. But its firm, down-to-earth discussion of how to plan apartments to be as good as possible despite scarce means became significant as a source of data. It did not consider it realistic to suppose a normal worker's dwelling should contain more than a room and a kitchen, but, for this reason, considered it highly important that this tiny space should be used as best it might. So various actual layouts were analyzed in detail. It was decisive that dwellings' surroundings were good. The investigation prescribed apartments stretching from side to side of three-story 'narrow' buildings with large airy courtyards. Osvald Almqvist played a central role in the investigation. He wrote a supplement on planning housing areas, in which he gave a good summary of the nuances of contemporary knowledge of the art of urban planning.

It was important that demands of quality were formulated, for now questions of costs dominated the debate. The crisis had made it necessary to depress building costs. Floor space in even larger apartments had to be used more efficiently. Sven Wallander wrote in 1920 that "for us architects, demands have become stricter, so that if a house is to be inexpensive, its plan must be as simple and lucid as a chessboard."[42]

The building industry was still working in its old way, and on-site construction of buildings' frameworks and fixed equipment made this work seasonal. Systematic standardisation work was introduced so as to create good patterns for joinery work that could be made industrially. In 1919–20, working in conjunction with the architects' department of the Swedish Association of Engineers and Architects (Teknologföreningen), the Indus-

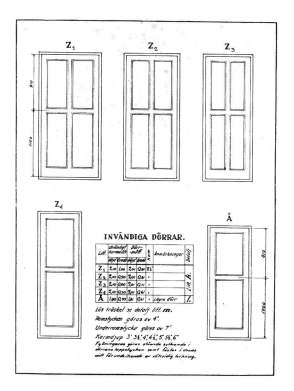

Catalogue page, showing standardised door types (1920) by Sven Markelius.

trial Federation (Industriförbundet) appointed a standardisation committee with its own drawing office; Sven Markelius was appointed to run it.[43] In 1920, he presented its first results, which concerned doors and windows.[44] The work of standardising kitchen joinery was much more comprehensive; led by Osvald Almqvist, it continued for years (1922 to 1934). Cupboards, shelves and working surfaces were seen as building blocks to be used variously in various types of apartment. Almqvist's kitchen studies became a pioneering work, a predecessor of investigations during the 1940s (page 112).

One of the housing cooperatives, *HSB* for short, which had Sven Wallander as its head, was a national organisation and was the most important motive force for good dwellings for working-class families during the 1920s. It began its activities in 1923, when the economic turn-round began, and got off to a flying start. It built only small apartments and could thus rapidly develop resolutions of types of plans and, in conjunction with Osvald Almqvist, kitchen furnishings.[45] Because the housing-cooperative movement grew quickly it enjoyed certain advantages of size, for example in purchasing, when it could put pressure on production costs.[46] Even though its means were limited, it did not compromise over modern conveniences including hot and cold water, showers or baths, central heating and up-to-date laundry rooms, a standard that was by no means self evident for small apartments of the time. Reasons of costs led to the build-

Do-it-yourself houses rationally arranged.

ing of what were called 'thick' apartment
buildings.

Small single-family houses began to be built
more rationally. A private-sector company, *AB
Industribostäder*, made an early start, in 1918,
with prefabricated houses. Its managing director was Hans O. Elliot, a pioneer within the
Swedish movement for standardisation and a
committee member of the Swedish Handicraft
Association. As we have mentioned, the city of
Stockholm owned large land areas, which it
augmented with further purchases. These
small houses spread out over these areas in
what were called literally 'garden towns'. Sites
were made available on a form of lease that
enabled the city to retain control over land
use, especially because subsidised loans were
offered for such small houses. When it was
found that merely inspecting drawings did not
ensure a sufficiently high quality, the building
board worked out sets of standard drawings to
which individual additions and changed could
be made. In 1922, the National Building
Office (*Statens Byggnadsbyrå*) published a set of
such drawings, which contributed to both
conferring a uniform character on these areas

Using factory-made elements, a do-it-yourself owner and
friends build his house.

and enabling building work to be more rational. These possibilities were exploited in an
organised form in what might nowadays be
called do-it-yourself building in Stockholm in
1926; this was led by the Office of Small
Houses of Stockholm (*Stockholms stads små-
stugebyrå*) which employed its own drawings.
Using prefabricated elements, and with the
organisational, instructional and purchasing
help of the city, owners built their own houses.
Loans could finance up to 90 per cent of the
costs.[47] In this way, even people with very little
cash in hand could get a house. Initially 200
small houses were built in this way.

Rationalisation was a strong under-current
throughout building activity during the 1920s.
In Elliot's opinion, besides the housing crisis,
the reason for this was a characteristically contemporary "demand for choice, order and
system" in production that had hitherto been
altogether too splintered and unpredictable.[48]
In 1927, he stated that this had become internationally a sign of the times, exemplified by
Le Corbusier's programme based on types and
standards (Elliot deemed it over-distant from
reality) and the German *Rationeller Wohnungs-
bau, Typ-Norm* programme of reform (than he
deemed strongly dogmatic). It seemed also, he
wrote, as if Sweden were sheltered, despite the
fact that "we could still in essentials count
ourselves among the pioneers", although this
came because "we deliberately chose methods
that were based on 'natural growth'."

In another context, Elliot wrote that "it
seems to me as if we, here in Sweden, already
possess, admittedly to a strictly limited extent,
a culture of dwelling that is sufficiently suited
to its purpose in a modern way and in addition
derived from tradition for us not to need,
unlike Le Corbusier in a France that is
weighed down and bound by style, to revolu-
tionise what exists, to address the problem
anew and fundamentally, and seek our way
forward to what L.C. calls a 'functional' art of
building."[49]

Elliot asked whether in a hectic and fluid
time there were something "that should be
allowed to retain its static character as the
fixed point in existence that it ought to be, so
it is just the dwelling house, the home, and its
'function' is and will continue in large measure
to be the same as it has always been."

Housing Areas and Garden Cities

After the national economy had stabilised in
1923, a period of intensive building activity
followed, when new areas appeared that, in

A 'landshövdingehus', Göteborg, (1920) with a stone bottom floor and two upper floors and an attic in wood.

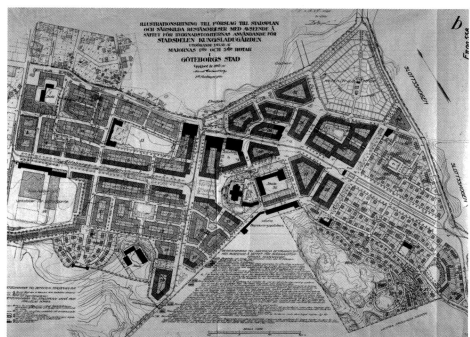

Kungsladugård area, Göteborg (1911–16), by Albert Lilienberg: monumentally wide main streets contrast with progressively narrower roads and more intimate dwelling quarters.

many instances, comprise apogees of Swedish 20th-century housing architecture.

In the west-coast harbour town of Göteborg, the traditional type of working-class dwelling, which had been established since the 1870s, was a *landshövdingehus*, a three-story building, with a brick-built bottom floor on which the upper two floors were built in wood. For reasons of economy and fire prevention, the houses were 'narrow', with only two apartments giving off each landing; kitchens gave onto the yard, the other rooms onto the street.[50] The investigation that produced Practical and Hygienic Dwellings took such narrow buildings as exemplary, but, in Stockholm, they were not so treated. In Göteborg, this type remained in building work through the 1920s and into the 1930s as the unique, dominant type. Streets of these houses acquired much of the appearance of traditionally built wooden towns. During the time that Albert Lilienberg was head of urban building in Göteborg, its urban plans were further developed, as already mentioned, with greenery in courtyards and accommodation to local topography.

The plan for *Kungsladugård* was approved in 1916; during the 1920s, the area was built up in successive stages. A rich example of contemporary, sensitive urban planning, it clearly distinguishes between public buildings, monumentally laid-out main thoroughfares and intimate housing quarters with varied perspectives of courtyards and streets.[51] It also contains terrace houses, a type that had not been very well received in Sweden, but which now did relatively well in Göteborg, primarily as a middle-class form of dwelling. The type had been

launched during the crisis of the early 1920s because it was more economical for municipalities than small private houses, and, in addition, did more for the urban image of Göteborg. The town authorities planned and built some experimental terraces, before the private builders took over.[52] The area called *Änggården* is a good example.

Building in Göteborg of dwellings was thus developed within local traditions and also according to influences of international urban-planning ideas, primarily from England and Germany. Under Lilienberg's supervision, this was given form by architects who were active locally, who have remained relatively little known; but their work maintained a very high quality. Arvid Fuhre should be mentioned, among other things for the beautifully coherent *Standaret* quarter (1921–22); it was built by HSB and has a monumentality that is otherwise seldom seen, in which associations to 18th-century country houses have been translated into simple timbered architecture.

Building in certain towns during the 1920s

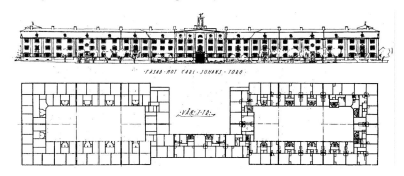

A monumental 'landshövdingehus' with apartments of one to four rooms, plus an inward-facing kitchen. This is the Standaret dwelling quarter, Göteborg (1921), by Arvid Fuhre.

Dwellings at Norrköping for white- and blue-collar employees of the national telephone corporation, (1919, 1922), by Erik Lallerstedt.

Rödaberg area, Stockholm (1920s), with a revised, more urban plan for the area by PO Hallman from 1922. The variated streets in the spirit of Camillo Sitte work well together with the strict facades of the 1920s.

was undertaken by their municipal architects who not only drew up urban plans but also designed a very large part of both housing quarters and individual monumental buildings. By way of example, Gunnar Leche designed housing in *Uppsala* of various sorts and even developed a certain local style with rendered three-to-five-story lengths of buildings that he arranged in quarters. A small pearl of an area in this small format is the one called *Kungsgärdesplan*, from 1925: it contained simplified dwellings intended to relieve the critical situation that still obtained in Uppsala in 1924 for families who had to make do with small apartments.[53]

A similar sort of semi-detached house that could contain four apartments can be found at Norrköping, among other places; these timbered houses at *Fågelsången*, a wooded place at Oxelbergen, are from 1919 and have typically contemporary pitched roofs and small glazed verandas; they were designed by S.E. Lundqvist, who got the commission after a competition. Norrköping also contains the beautiful small terraced-house area by Erik Lallerstedt (built 1919–22) for the employees of the national telephone corporation. The municipal architect of *Kalmar*, J. Fred Olson, followed the guidelines laid down by Practical and Hygienic Dwellings: two-story buildings with two apartments on each landing form a well-balanced small-town area, with closed views along its streets and with open, leafy courtyards behind the houses.

At the time, parts of the centre of Stockholm were being built that had previously

been left alone because their topography did not fit into the squares of the urban-planning map. They were smaller steep bits of ground, appreciated in the more picturesque pattern of Hallman's plan. He had originally planned that single-family houses should occupy the inner part of the *Rödabergsområdet* area, but a revised plan provided for a more urban, differentiated mixture of higher buildings on larger streets around the area, and three-story buildings with a small-town atmosphere on the smaller streets. The buildings enclose larger leafy courtyards that form park-like oases, comprising fine transitions between public and private space in the town. A large part of them was designed by Sven Wallander and the HSB drawing office. *Helgalunden* and *Blecktornsparken*, lying in the Söder area of Stockholm, have similar qualities; Hallman did the general planning; HSB and Stockholm Cooperative Housing Association (SKB) respectively designed them. The *Ryssjan* section of the latter, designed by Edvin Engström and built in 1927–29, is perhaps the best of this very fine bit of building.

The literally named 'garden towns' grew up around the core of Stockholm; the city tightly controlled them and what was planted there. The strong feelings during the 1920s for forming space found a clear expression here, in a striving to place the houses by their plot edges so as to get a closed space in the road and a perspective in depth. A fine example is provided by *Magnebergsvägen*, Enskede.

With the help of new urban plans, attempts were made to differentiate and bring out the nuances between buildings in the parts of the town that were already built. In a couple of places, new roads were led through existing, partly-built quarters, where some lower buildings were added, thus conferring a more small-town, tranquil air to parts of the town: for example, Danderydsgatan and Tysta gatan.

Sven Markelius used a similar means in his plan for an area of larger houses on Lidingö, which he intended to display as a model at the Building and Living Exhibition (Bygge och Bo) in 1925. He caused a street to cut through the large quarter, with houses on either side of it as that they would form a closed, urban space on the street, which leads to a square with a strong sense of space. Beyond it, on a hill, a house forms a backdrop. Markelius used high, traditionally Swedish wooden palings to bind the area together and give a sense of closure and intimacy. He designed a number of the houses himself, while other architects contributed designs for single houses. These middle-class residences have an aesthetically refined character: lofty slender volumes, with pitched but flattish roofs. As part of the elongated plan of the whole, they form roads into spaces, while, at the same time, their closed facades giving onto the roads are contrast sharply with how, at the back, they open onto their gardens. Smooth rendered walls dominate but the very few, restrained instances of ornamentation—for example, window brackets and balusters—can be strongly emphatic.

Elegance and Abstraction

Stockholm Town Hall was inaugurated in summer 1923 (see also catalogue). From his first competition proposal, Östberg had developed the project into an increasingly refined interpretation of the spirit of the site: the town on the water. It had shed weight, its volumes had been slimmed down into a greater elegance.

In some respects, Östberg had made use of elements in some of his colleagues' competition proposals (page 36). In a move of genius and inspired by Westman, he placed the tower close to the water, causing the silhouette of the building to have its maximum effect on the image of the town. Östberg had got the main lines in his ground plan from Tengbom's and Torulf's joint proposal in the first round of the competition. But more than anything else, Östberg took the building through a creative development throughout its long gestation, while he tried out various themes that would live on in Swedish architecture in the rest of

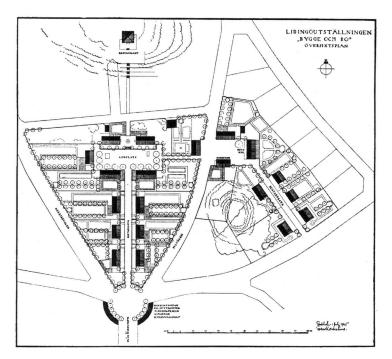

Differentiation between urban streets and private-house privacy in an area designed by Sven Markelius for the 1925 Building and Living Exhibition.

the 1920s. The unique character of the site had supplied the main concept: through the arcades that open from the inner courtyard onto Lake Mälar, building and water are bound together in a way illustrative of the 1920s' characteristic of spaces brought together.

The interior exhibits, and is wound together

Blue Hall, Stockholm Town Hall: while this fascinating contradiction between outdoors and indoors was inaugurated in 1923, Ragnar Östberg had got its character down on paper as early as 1909.

Stockholm Town Hall: view from the south east, whence its symbolism of the town's encounter with the waters of Lake Mälaren is beautifully clear.

by, a series of motifs on which Östberg had worked during these years. He created a magnificent series of rooms that, running through the *Prince's Gallery* and the *Golden Room*, obtains its rhythm from including a couple of smaller rooms. It reaches its crescendo in the ambiguous character of the *Blue Hall*: a room that is also a courtyard. The departure from a right-angled ground plan that his room expresses is another theme. Björn Linn has observed that Östberg's discarding his idea of glazing over the room in favour of top-lighting it from lateral windows played its part in developing a richer effect of space.[54]

The rooms intended for festivities and formalities open onto the lake, while the workaday rooms are in the background, with the town-council session room is an extension of the tower. A number of younger architects, including Asplund, contributed items of furniture, and many artists had a hand in the embellishments. The Town Hall had functioned as a forcing ground for arts and crafts; together with the embellishment of a number of other public buildings at this time, this activity contributed to raising the already high quality of this work.

In 1923, when the Town Hall was completed, so was *Högalid Church*; designed by Ivar Tengbom for a competition in 1911, it had been begun in 1917. Its large, wholly brick-built surfaces and effective silhouette effect gives it a certain relationship to the Town Hall. Compared with the Engelbrekt church, it is benevolently calm, thanks to its clear contours that terminate upwards in the soft play of forms of the cap of its tower.

Swedish architecture now began to be noticed internationally, partly on account of the Town Hall, but thanks also to the 300th Anniversary Exhibition (*Jubileumsutställningen*) in Göteborg in 1923. Incomparably the largest exhibition to have been held in Sweden, and large even by international standards, its antecedents were closely associated with forming *Götaplatsen* (see also catalogue), a monumental open space that terminates a main street, Kungsportsavenyn.[55] Its basic appearance had been determined by Lilienberg's 1910 urban plan, which formed the basis for an architectural competition in 1916–17 for the square's eventual appearance. The competition was controversial: the plan and its locking effect were objected to.[56]

In Östberg's opinion, and his was the most authoritative view, emphasis had been given to the form of the place rather than to the basic urban-planning problem with the area; he preferred Asplund's and Lewerentz' proposals that had each departed from the terms of the competition. The first proposed an elongated, coherent place on rising ground, a beautifully formed Piazza Navona, but the second had more than any other proceeded from what Östberg called the "real conditions": he meant the lie of the land, the points of the compass, their interrelationships and the street running downhill to the north. But the competition was actually to do something else altogether: to create a closed square with an art museum that, in the background, would act as a screen. In addition, the place would be further delineated by a pair of monumental buildings. After competition and repeated competition, the commission for the art museum went to the ARES group of architects: Arvid Bjerke, R.O. Swensson, Ernst Torulf and Sigfrid Ericson. It

An impressive element on the Stockholm skyline: Högalid Church (1917–23), by Ivar Tengbom.

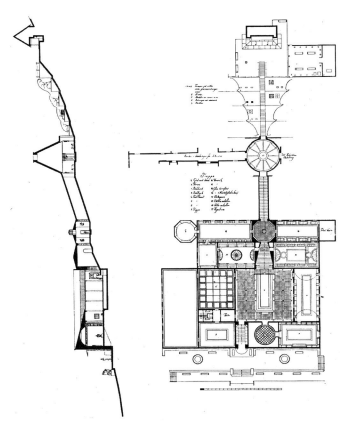

Tercentennial Exhibition, Göteborg (1923), designed mainly by Sigfrid Ericson and Arvid Bjerke. Festively supporting the town's heraldic lion and crown, the two towers have been called 'minarets'.

(Left) Plan and section of the exhibition's arts-and-crafts' building; and (right) steps leading to the plateau and cremation-society display; it and the upper part of the steps, were by Lewerentz.

was ready for the 1923 exhibition, but some time would elapse before the other public buildings on the square were completed.

The content of the exhibition was extensive and included a multiplicity of various subject areas, including a very ambitious urban-planning department. Two of the members of the ARES group, Ericson and Bjerke, were responsible for its architectural form, which was built around a series of stretches and courtyards that extended between the newly laid-out Götaplatsen square and an amusement park called Liseberg. The tone of its architecture was festive and easy-going, with gracefully formed details and patterns that were effective in their contrasts; these were set

Facade, arts-and-crafts' building, by Hakon Ahlberg: it typically combines unrelieved surfaces and delicate detailing.

off by unbroken smooth surfaces. Two high, slender minaret-like towers with a decorative striped pattern were landmarks. An element of exoticism and the mysterious orient was noticeable, an element that was typical of contemporary architecture intended for enjoyment.

Other architects than the two principals did some lesser work at the exhibition. The arts-and-crafts building was by Hakon Ahlberg, a cremation facility by Lewerentz and pavilions for the exhibition of interiors for the Workshop Association (Föreningen Verkstaden) were by Lewerentz with the assistance of Melchior Wernstedt. Grouped around a flight of steps, all these buildings were linked to each other. Asplund commented on them, for, in his opinion, they displayed something "that one would like to believe is today's and tomorrow's will in our young art of building."[57]

At the instigation of the principal architects, Ahlberg had added a certain degree of exterior decoration to his building, which he had conceived as having a wholly smooth, windowless rendered wall surface down to the ground.[58] A high, narrow entry was cut into the centre of the facade and framed by a light rendered part with thin horizontal ashlar markings. A fan-shaped canopy is borne on two decoratively formed pillars that, looking as thin as a spider's web, are more like suspended cords. A more academic classicism would have caused the centre entry to lead a visitor into the space behind along its axis, but this one led into one corner of this space: typical 1920s classicism. From the pavilion a long flight of steps ran upwards with the exhibition rooms grouped along it.

Asplund wrote how "amazing [it is] with this long flight of steps: it does not frighten off, it attracts." In it he perceived the principal idea of the whole arrangement, which he found superb, for, from it comes "the clear rhythmic composition that is the characteristic of good architecture." Divided into sequences, the flight was broken first by an octagonal, then by a circular, space; each was roofed with a cupola. Then it continued to the Cremation Society's department, where it was flanked by terraces of graves, which grew higher as the flight of steps became steeper. Asplund felt that, on approaching their top, a visitor would reach a peak of excited fulfilment.

In his appreciative assessment of the three exhibition arrangements, done mainly by Ahlberg and Lewerentz, Asplund concludes by summarising his views of architecture's development.[59] "In relation to most of yesterday's and today's building art that is characterised by detail of demands to disorder and looseness of control resulting in unclarity, they [the three arrangements] stand on common ground. Today's architectural will, when it is at its best, proceeds towards subordinating detail, an ordering of all heterogenous needs and demands and dimensions to a strong architectural grip, around a central idea; it seeks order and character."[59]

In September 1923, the cinema called *Skandia* in Stockholm was ready. Asplund had created a spiritual, festive four-part sequence of rooms: portico, hall, foyer, cinema. The portico mediated the transition from outside to in, between the older 19th-century facade and, as Asplund put it, the cinema's "colourful and rather overdone modernity."[60] Tickets were sold, and customers waited, in the vestibule. Two public rooms gave off it: one, also for waiting, was in deep-green plaster with a frieze by Hilding Linnqvist, an artist, and metal benches with black leather cushions to sit on; the other was a rotunda, a small pantheon, intended for portraits of film actors.

From the vestibule one passes down to the lower foyer, which has the form of a space in a street or courtyard, in which the cinema itself seems to stand as an independent building: Asplund wrote that its walls are to appear to be as an exterior facade of attractive entertainment premises. The character of this facade is emphasised by thin ashlar markings, a canopy and globular lanterns. The upper foyer contains the entry doors to the balcony: a row of small entries, each different, embellished with battens, capitals and Empire details in red, black and gold. The apogee of this procession through rooms is the entry into the cinema.

Asplund wrote that, to get the greatest possible tranquillity and repose in this large room, he had "the entirely un-architectural idea of letting its ceiling vanish into a dark nothingness, done as a dark-blue al fresco painting of a thin cloth," adding that it should have the effect of festivities under a night sky. Hakon Ahlberg has extracted a diary entry by Asplund during his travels in Italy describing an evening carnival at Taormina, with coloured lanterns under a star-filled sky, which can have been his later inspiration.[61] The original, seemingly temporary arrangement in the cinema was round, silk-covered globular lamps hung at different heights. More illusionary than in any other contemporary Swedish formation of space, this induced a feeling of being out of doors.[62]

A year before Asplund began work on the cinema, he published a comprehensive review of the competition for a new *Concert Hall* for Stockholm that was certainly significant in that Ivar Tengbom received the commission. Before this piece was published, in which

Skandia Cinema, Stockholm (1922–23), by Asplund who, partly by using silk-covered lamps, wanted to achieve an open-air festival atmosphere in the auditorium.

Achieved in the completed, but later altered, Stockholm Concert Hall, Tengbom's original sketch (1920) of its main auditorium implies an open-air space and an illusory perspective.

Tengbom's sketch of the Stockholm Concert Hall exterior, rendered in a shining blueish purple, seems weightless, despite its large volume and substantial colonnade.

Asplund deemed Tengbom's resolution of the plan to be unrivalled in its clarity, the prize jury had not designated any clear winner. Asplund emphasised, as so often, the rhythm in the sequence of rooms, which Tengbom had accentuated by a low ceiling over the flight of steps so as to elevate the effect of the "large, light, liberated and airy concert hall."[63] Such as it appears in Tengbom's proposal, this room made Asplund almost lyrical, declaring that it is a something between out and in, but no compromise. "The architecture is light and dissolved, the ceiling hovers unconfined, an effect of a tent à la Gustaviana on light tent poles. The light attractive space that and the perspective towards the orchestra podium draw attention from the architecture into a boundless incorporeal space."

Tengbom had thought of a weightless, floating ceiling and a semblance of a perspective as a backdrop, which is how the concert hall itself was eventually built.[64] As we have seen, this manner of forming space was characteristic of the time, but Tengbom was the first to apply it in premises such as these that were tuned, so to say, for festivities.

Tengbom's drawing from 1920 shows clearly how he wanted the exterior to look: the volume of the building seems to be a large cube with quite smooth, rendered surfaces. It seems very light, almost floating, with its atmospherically shifting rendered surface in a bluish-violet tone. A massive colonnade is applied to its exterior as if it were an independent element. Another monumental arrangement of columns was intended to be part of the immediate vicinity of the building, so its own monumental columns would match the scale of this

urban space, linking the building with the town on a superimposed level. Simultaneously, this colonnade would be a transitional zone between public space and the interior of the building, in a manner that was characteristic for the 1920s.[65] The large lines and smooth surfaces of the exterior are set off by the fine-limbed, elegant detail work. In the early 1920s, and within an encompassing classicism, developments were proceeding in two directions: entire forms proceeding towards a cubic simplicity and abstraction with smooth superficial effects, detailed forms moving towards an increasingly delicate refinement, lightness and slender line drawing.

Swedish arts-and-crafts work, which made an international breakthrough at the 1925 Paris exhibition, was sui generis and came later to be called Swedish Grace. The invited competition that led to the Swedish pavilion in Paris being designed by Carl Bergsten had attracted an entry from Asplund that was much remarked: a cubically simplified building elevated on Doric columns in a way that can now induce thoughts of Le Corbusier. But the forms of its details and its resolution of space are almost theatrical. According to Ahlberg, whose personal opinion of it was high, it was thought altogether too bizarre by the prize jury, which designated Ture Ryberg's proposal as the winner.[66] The committee that was to plan the exhibition, however, fixed finally on Bergsten's proposal on account of the advantages it offered from an exhibition point of view: it was characterised by a severe, beautifully balanced classicistic form with decoratively treated smooth surfaces and a sequence of rooms that was typical of the time.

Swedish Pavilion, 1925 Paris Exhibition, by Carl Bergsten, exemplifying the sort of classicism called 'Swedish Grace' in the 1920s.

Towards a Point of Break

Designing power stations was sensitive job, in which advanced technical facilities directly confronted the most intrinsic elements in a wild undisturbed landscape. The first large modern facility in Sweden had been built at *Trollhättan* in 1906–10 (see also catalogue). Its architect, Erik Josephson, had used a monumental rounded arch in granite over the flow of water to demonstrate its power; he used a similar formal language later (around 1910) in power stations at *Porjus* and *Älvkarleby*.

Ten years later, industrial architecture was developing towards severity and simplification, and particular attention was attracted by Osvald Almqvist's power station at *Forshuvud-forsen* (1917–21): a sharp-cut cubic volume with a slightly sloping roof and high, narrow white-painted fenestration apertures. Making it emphatically factual, he left it looking as if it had derived from a traditional building.

In an article presenting an exhibition of technical and industrial facilities arranged by the Swedish Homestead Society (*Samfundet för hembygdsvård*) in 1924, John Åkerlund asserted that, with both these buildings, specialists in Sweden had got close to the ideal for this type of building. He went on to explain why, following the example of its German equivalent, the hembygdsrörelsen (it might be called the 'local heritage-society movement' nowadays) should concern itself with matters such as these. "If anything is care of one's home tract", he wrote, "it must be to strive to achieve a reverential and beautiful form for these disturbing facilities."[67] But not by forcing what was new into old-fashioned forms: "transformer buildings should not be done as old belfries or water towers nor as fortresses or church towers, no, the new buildings should be given a form suitable to their contemporary purposes."

In principle, this was the point of view Westman had expressed in the early 1890s, but, in the 1920s, the words had a novel implication. The exhibition was reviewed by Gotthard Johansson, who expressed a belief in a form that he appreciated as functionally derived. "Every line of the latest locomotive of the Swedish State Railways is charged with an energy that speaks a language as powerful as that of Michelangelo's figures of prophets on the ceiling of the Sistine chapel.[68]

In 1924, Osvald Almqvist, too, spoke in favour of rational form.[69] In Björn Linn's opinion, his appreciation changed at this time, his architecture became increasingly strongly disciplined, which was a wholly independent development, the roots of which derived from studies of tradition. In two power stations, *Hammarforsen* (see also catalogue) and *Krångforsen* (1925–28), Almqvist did not draw on the store of conventional forms but proceeded from the practical demands of the situation and the dynamism that was developed in the tumbling water (page 85).

As we have discussed, Almqvist did much work of sorts that can now seem trivial: among them housing investigations, kitchen standardisation, power stations. His real importance can thus easily be passed by. He was a most gifted designer. Hakon Ahlberg has pointed out the importance of Asplund, Lewerentz and Almqvist as a trio from the Klara school "of distinct personalities who certainly stimulated one another to a high degree, and worked together on different occasions and in various combinations but, as individuals, they retained their integrity and developed along different lines… But while Almqvist was an out-and-out aesthetic talent, perhaps the most subtle of the three, he always went to fundamentals in his work and never tried to score aesthetic points at the expense of design and economic considerations."[70]

A Point of Break

Lewerentz' *Chapel of the Resurrection* at the Woodland Cemetery was inaugurated just before Christmas 1925. This chapel lies at the further end of an old boundary that has become an important, symbolically charged line through the whole cemetery. It was to stand at the end of the straight road through wooded ground. In an early proposal, this perspective had been dominated by an antecham-

Forshuvudfors Hydro-Electric Generating Station (1917–21), by Osvald Almqvist: traditionalist, despite its geometrically strict, reductionalist form.

ber with its roof borne on columns on the longitudinally sited chapel, which would thus, with a north-south orientation, have departed from ecclesiastical convention and would have been hardly acceptable to the cemetery board.[71] Consequently the peculiar solution was reached of entry through an antechamber on the longitudinal side of the building.

The antechamber stands in front of an extremely high, narrow building, a basic form that Lewerentz himself had introduced in his Helsingborg project, but which by this time had become typical. The tendency to treat the parts of a complete building independently had been pushed to the limit. If Tengbom's columns seemed to have been applied to the wall of his concert hall, Lewerentz' antechamber stand quite free of the chapel, being set at a hardly noticeable angle to it; the two have differing characters. The ornamented capital and relief on the antechamber tympanum ("The Resurrection of Christ", by Ivar Johnsson) contrast with what is behind it, the ascetically smooth rendered surface of the windowless and otherwise featureless wall that extends down to the ground. The flat roof, too, seems to be an independent element lying loosely on the building.

The cemetery board had objected to the proportions and wanted a broader volume and more fenestration apertures, but, fortunately, Lewerentz got the support of the architects of the National Building Board (Byggnadsstyrelsen) that had supervisory powers over churches and cemetery chapels.[72] The proportions were really decisive for the architectural effect. Hans Nordenström has shown how all the chapel's interior and external dimensions and their interrelationships can be analyzed mathematically in detail.[73] This led to a number of interesting observations. Thus the ceiling is higher than the outer ledge of the roof.[74] In Nordenström's view, on entering the chapel, one experiences its ceiling as astonishingly high and floating. Its space has a continuity thanks to the repetition of its mathematically determined basic forms, but, at the same time, undergoes certain transformations.

We have already seen how plasticity vanished and ornamentation grew increasingly superficial during the 1920s. Decoration may not disturb our appreciation of what constitutes the real building: surface and volume. On the other hand, secondary architectural details can seem to come to the fore if they are over-emphasised in body and as to manner. The interior walls of the Chapel of the Resurrection have classicistic divisions between pilasters and cornices in such extremely shal-

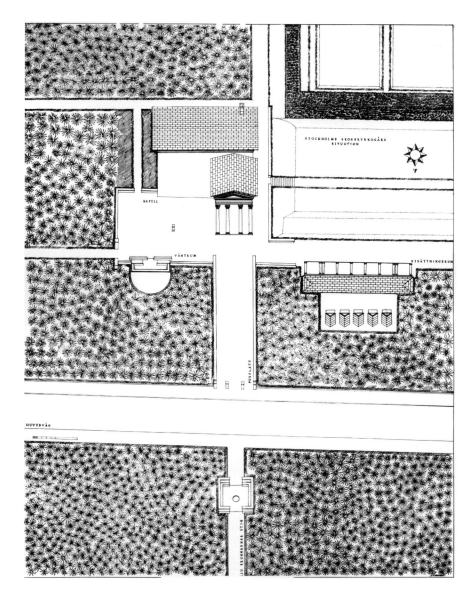

low relief as to approach a straightforwardly drawn graphic line. Only the four seemingly unnecessary window consols impose themselves on the eye. This over-emphasis induces

Lewerentz' naivistic drawing (1923) emphasises how unbridled nature, if in very geometrical forms, differs from the abstract flat surfaces of his Chapel of the Resurrection (1921–25).

The interior's bare simplicity gets its character from the loftiness of the Chapel of the Resurrection, while also concentrating attention on the light from the only window falling over the catafalque.

an awareness of how smooth the surfaces otherwise are, but it does give the window a symbolic role and a status of a dignity equal to that of the altar and the catafalque, the two other most prominent elements in the room. The window is so placed that, at the most usual times for burial services, it admits light falling directly on the catafalque. It is the only window and a mourner can suppose that the soul of the deceased takes final leave of the earth through it.[75] The mourners leave through a door in its short, western side, whence they look over a sunken, open arrangement of graves in a way similar to that of the Woodland Chapel. So, once again, the theme from Lewerentz' chapel in Helsingborg reappears.

The Chapel of the Resurrection was reviewed by Markelius, who saw it as an expression of "the most noteworthy striving" of the time.[76] He was not thinking of the form of its stylistic details that he thought unessential and "the most fleeting of the building's virtues": "in the consistent and monumental purposefully emphasised resolution of the task lies a value of a more enduring nature. On that can the building work survive the day when the classical costume in itself no longer manages to catch our interest."

At the time, Markelius was working on the Helsingborg concert hall, which had become the subject of a second competition; his first proposal had too many then typical classicistic touches, and its reorientation into a functional direction was now begun (page 86).

In an article published in 1927, Uno Åhrén discussed contemporary theatre architecture in light of the challenge posed by the movies for the art of the theatre.[77] In his opinion, theatres now had everything to win by finding their own means of expression, that was to say, not representing reality as films did but by creating a dramatic presence in the space on stage. In his further opinion, this radically changed the view of architecture and its role, which, in principle, also applied to concert-hall premises, and, in this context, the Stockholm Concert Hall had contributed nothing new: in his opinion, "a perspective of columns, garden fences and statues in niches" were merely disturbances.

Asplund formed the main room of his *Stockholm City Library* (see also catalogue) as an immense circular room, which form he justified in an analysis of the building's functions.[78] An open-shelf public library with books freely available was a novelty in Sweden. A large-minded, democratic idea, it still presupposed discreet control in practice: the building is concentrated around the check-out counter,

on either side of which is a narrow exit passage for putative borrowers. A long staircase leads down to the exit from the building onto the street outside.

Writing about the flight of steps in Ahlberg's arrangement at the 1923 Göteborg exhibition, Asplund had called it amazing that it did not frighten off but attract. Now, at the library, he made the staircase one of its principal motifs: sequence by sequence, it penetrates from below one shell of the building after another until it goes straight into the centre of the main room: on entering the main door of the library, ones goes through a vestibule, then, following its main axis, through a further door and up the first flight to the wall of the rotunda, which appears to be a rendered outer wall. In this space, one's experiences alternate between being outside and being inside. Around the exterior of the rotunda rise two opposing narrow flights, each being confined between two high walls as if between two buildings. Similar divisions of a staircase into two flights occur in the Skandia cinema and the Lister courthouse building.

A staircase feels easy to ascend if it leads from darkness towards light. In his comments on the Stockholm Concert Hall competition, Asplund had noted that Tengbom kept the ceiling over his staircase low so as to elevate the experience of the light and liberating height of the hall itself. The Stockholm library stair channels a strong upward pull towards the light room, above which its ceiling seems to float at an immeasurable height.

In 1924–27, when the Stockholm library was being built, architecture was exposed to novel ideas. In his presentation in 1928, Asplund showed a drawing in which the basic geometric forms were given contours as sharp

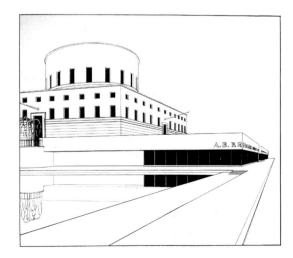

In this sketch, Asplund emphasised the abstract geometry of Stockholm Public Library (1928) and its modernistic row of shops.

as knives, at the expense of the detailing. In the drawing, the ashlar marking has turned into distinct stripes, which induce a sense of horizontality that was typical for the time but hardly expressed as such in the building. The drawing also includes and emphasises a wholly modernistic length of shops.

The library was reviewed by Åhrén, with reservations on principles, in a very critical article. It was aimed at the "formalism" that he considered was still inherent in the building.[79] He announced that neo-classicism was at an end. "The town library stands as a termination and high point of an epoch." Åhrén had begun his argument with the large clock in the borrowing hall: the Roman numerals indicating a "practical division" into 24 hours were placed radially (ie some were upside down or nearly so), which, for Åhrén, was symbolic. He wrote that the decorative appreciation of form had, as long as it could, hindered the liberation of a radically functional outlook.

Åhrén felt a conflict between his own, dynamic time and the classicistic form, and this conflict appeared more clearly to him in Asplund's work than in anyone else's. He wrote that one could walk with indifference past a weaker work, but "the town library forces [the observer] yet once again as one must do time and again to confront him- or herself with the great problem of the day of life and form." In his opinion, this building stood on the boundary between, not two modish directions, but two periods with deep-going differences between their mentality. He wrote further that an era of static appreciation of form that views things decoratively is being succeeded by the awareness of the dynamic essentials of culture.

Åhrén was the most noticed proponent of international modernism among those who debated Swedish architecture in the mid 1920s. Having been greatly impressed by Le Corbusier's Pavillon de l'Esprit Nouveau at the 1925 Paris exhibition, Åhrén presented the Frenchman's work for his Swedish colleagues. In 1926, before the library was completed, Åhrén published a strongly polemical article, expressing a feeling that the times were in transformation: that one had to choose to favour or oppose it.

Spengler's *Der Untergang des Abendlandes* that was then getting a lot of attention in Sweden, including a two-part presentation for the architectural profession, to a certain degree nourished Åhrén's argument.[80] Spengler's thesis that dynamic space was the ur-symbol of western culture aroused interest among architects and came to function as philosophical

From within its entry hall, the Rotunda of the Stockholm Public Library seems another building, circumnavigated by alley-like flights of stairs around its external walls.

Beneath the Rotunda, Stockholm Public Library by Gunnar Asplund: finely appointed open-shelf arrangements in wood and brass beneath a light and airy space under an inconspicuous floating roof.

View towards the street through the colonnade across the semi-circular courtyard of the palatial Swedish Matchstick head-office building (1926–28) by Ivar Tengbom. Fountain by Carl Milles.

As built, the Reception Hall of the Swedish Matchstick head office with its geometric design was a rare example of Swedish Art Deco; it was located in an inner courtyard and was top glazed.

legitimation of the appreciation of space of functionalism, while Spengler's 'decline' was toned down or made dependent on a new aesthetics managing to renew the life-force of culture. Åhrén wrote that "the future or decline of western culture depends on whether it be possible to be modern in a deeply human and fruitful sense."

In 1927, travels to Germany had begun. The Stuttgart exhibition and the new German housing areas were decisive impulses for Swedish architects, of whom some also read the Danish periodical, *Kritisk revy*, that an architect, Poul Henningsen, published from 1926 to 1928. In 1928, the Swedish periodical, *Byggmästaren*, began to print in a functionalistic typography, which was used to present the new building for *Svenska Tändsticksaktiebolaget*. Designed by Ivar Tengbom, it was the culmination of the luxury architecture of the 1920s, a monument to Ivar Kreuger's worldwide safety-match empire that, more than anything else, symbolised economic power and international prestige. Time around the world was indicated by a display of clocks. Behind its exclusive facades, the company was on the way towards one of the greatest economic crashes of the early 1930s, which had far-going consequences for the Swedish economy.

The commission Tengbom got was to design a suitably imposing headquarters building for a worldwide group. Some fifteen years earlier, in 1912, in his Enskilda Banken building, he had demonstrated his ability to express a discreet refinement. Now he conferred a closed and restrained character on the new building. Its very long facade was reduced in scale through a thin striping on its two lateral parts, which is reminiscent of quoins, or can be interpreted as if indicating three different buildings. Tengbom wrote of it that the door leads into a vestibule-like portico and thence to a semicircular courtyard, a cour d'honneur.[81] In the back wall of the courtyard five high, narrow windows are the only indication of the group's most magnificent room: a session hall, which, following the curve of the courtyard, extends upwards in two stories and is exclusively embellished with intarsia and with a large painting by Isaac Grünewald.

Another luxurious interior, designed by Carl Bergsten, was done by the end of the 1920s: the Swedish American Line's liner *Kungsholm*. Here one may speak of the culmination of another epoch, for the custom had been to give such vessels' interiors the pattern of some luxury hotel; as it was to a certain degree here. Bergsten demonstrated an extremely refined interior-decoration art with a slight tendency towards Art Deco, but, at this time, the purely functionally determined forms of maritime vessels had become almost cultist models for the avant garde of modernism inspired by Le Corbusier. Kungsholm was reviewed by Erik Friberger, one of a number of radically inclined architects. "One can hardly enjoy the peculiarity of contemporary life and the creative power of modern technology in a more concentrated form than on board an Atlantic giant", he stated by way of introduction.[82] After having lingered in fascination over the technical and organisational aspects of ship-building, he points out that interior decoration on board remains scene-painting art as long as the job is that of fitting into a vessel the forms of space usually found in buildings on land.

Bergsten had been, at the beginning of the century, the most energetic of the Swedish architects in asserting a rationalistic view of architecture, with a point of departure in design. In his presentation of his work in Kungsholm, he claimed that he had sought to work through the different units of space in accordance with the iron skeleton of the vessel, so that its pillars and beams became logical elements in these various spaces.[83] Friberger recognised Bergsten's attempts in this direction; in his opinion, by commissioning him to do the work, the shipping line had contributed to preparing the way for a sounder shipbuilding culture and had placed itself among the leaders of this transoceanic traffic; Friberger expressed the hope of yet a further step in a direction more in accordance with the time.

Since his relatively isolated, youthful avant-garde position, Bergsten adhered to the new inclinations on rational grounds that manifested themselves during the second decade of the century. He had become one of the most skil-

First-Class Reception Room, M/S Kungsholm, Swedish-America Line (1927–29), designed by Carl Bergsten in typical Art Deco contrasts between ebony and grey lacquering.

ful practitioners of 1920s classicism. But when rationalism was later driven towards a new aesthetics, he did not follow. Unlike his contemporary, Tengbom, he never became a functionalist, thus once again demonstrating his independence. His last major work, Göteborg Town Theatre, which was complete in the 1930s, he was still working to a major degree in the classicism of the 1920s, which is why the building never aroused much interest at the time. Bergsten died in 1935, aged 56.

A Work of Art is Completed

The job of completing the crematorium of the Woodland Cemetery came in question first in the 1930s, although Asplund and Lewerentz had been working more or less continuously on the cemetery throughout the 1920s, when different proposals for chapels in strictly classicistic forms had come into being.[84] In February 1930, when both men were working on the Stockholm exhibition (p. 88), they worked over their previous proposals and finally peeled off classicism so as to get a pure cubic form.[85]

The physical work on the walls, graves and landscape at the Woodland Cemetery had been performed to a large extent by people engaged under relief programmes at times of unemployment, either in 1914–18 or the depression of the early 1930s. During such work in 1930–32, the landscape acquired a novel look, and, probably, the architects perceived new values of beauty in it that caused them to adjust their plans. The ultimate form of the landscape and its large hill was thus not planned but reached step by step. The un-wooded viewing point with soft grassy slopes running down from it appeared in 1932.[86] In drawings, the crematorium and the path leading to it were displaced, so as to focus on the large hill. Lewerentz gave it form with a walled mediation glade and a group of elms (Ulmus glabra); their large downward curving tops make an effective silhouette at a distance.

At this stage, the chairman of the cemetery board, Yngve Larsson, communicated its decision to commission only Asplund to design the crematorium, which evidently agonized him and made him sorrowful and Lewerentz bitter. Behind the decision lay, probably, the board's dissatisfaction with Lewerentz' slow pace of work that was caused by his perfectionism. Thus the points of departure of the large main facility were mainly clear when Asplund began to plan it. The form of the landscape and entry were formed mainly by Lewerentz.

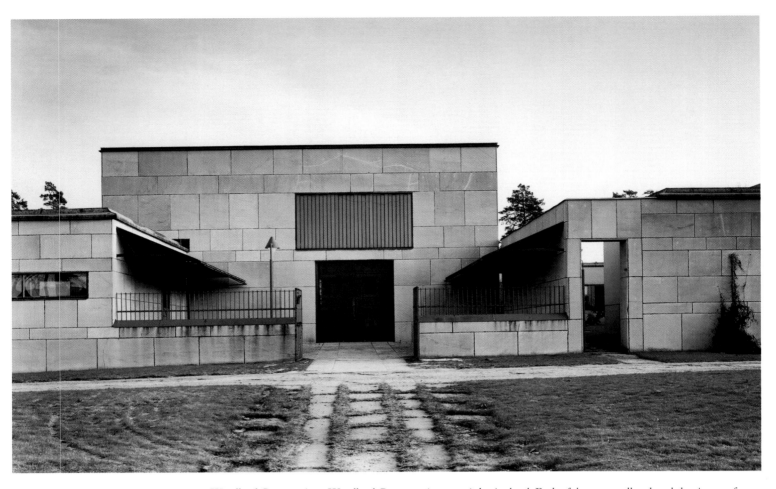

Woodland Crematorium, Woodland Cemetery (1935–40), by Asplund. Each of the two smaller chapels has its own fore-court; the one shown here is to the Chapel of Faith.

There was also a proposal for the crematorium in Lewerentz' hand that is to be understood as their joint point of view, the main characteristics of which accord quite closely with the final form. Asplund concluded his presentation by testifying how he had striven to tone down the buildings in relation to their natural surroundings. He wrote that the strong emphasis on the landscape "was won by letting the buildings sink softly in height from south to north, towards the walls of the columbarium and the main entry."[87]

The facility comprises a larger, main *Holy Cross Chapel* and the two lesser chapels (*Faith*, *Hope*). Each has its antechamber, waiting room and closed courtyard in immediate contact with it. Each is worked out in every detail: floor patterns, seating fittings, artistic embellishment, but the two smaller chapels are, as entities, kept simple. In all three, their space embraces the catafalque, onto which the inward flow of light concentrates.

The main chapel has a softly rounded depth but is cut off cleanly towards its large open pillared hall, which comprises its antechamber. Asplund's intention was that, on certain occasions, it could be transformed into an open-air chapel by causing the iron grill of its doors to sink down into the ground. A sunken, shell-shaped part of the floor adds to the character

Holy Cross Chapel, Woodland Cemetery, with painting by Sven Erixson. Softly curving lines delineaing this space focus attention on the catafalque.

Looking outwards from the forecourt of the Holy Cross Chapel, over a shadow from John Lundqvist's Resurrection Monument, towards the Glade of Meditation, by Lewerentz.

of the room as gently embracing its occupants. Its arched concrete ceiling, the central part of which seems to be carried on pillars that are placed around the catafalque, does this, too. In his review, Ahlberg perceives a certain problem in this: it gives "an impression of a compromise between two systems of design, those of the arch and the columns, from which follows a tension that cannot wholly be obscured by the room's otherwise extraordinary artistic qualities."[88]

He considered it as greatly distinguished by the effects of its coloration and materials, that its details were excellent, original but also discreet. A painting by Sven Erixson, with "bold dynamic lines and intentional·distortions" was as distinguished but did not wholly harmonise with the room.

Ahlberg was thus not unreserved in his view of the crematorium, his comments are independent and reveal his strong integrity, thus making his recognition and praise all the more convincing. He wrote that his final impression was a deep and humble admiration in the face of an exceptionally strong, living and rich building. He considered also that, throughout their work on the Woodland Cemetery,

Asplund and Lewerentz had never lost their leading motif, "the northerly high melody superscribed over their first inspiring vision".

His review appeared in the 19th issue of *Byggmästaren* in 1940. The third number after it appeared contained an obituary over Asplund. After cremation, the burial of his ashes was one of the first such ceremonies to be performed in the cemetery once the crematorium had been inaugurated. In this, his last work, he had left the strongly time-bound forms of international modernism behind him. The crematorium gives an impression of a timelessness that derives from the basic experience he had gained in the second and third decades of the century. The volumes of the crematorium are restrained, and peeled down in their simplicity, and, as they did in his absolutely first, small chapel, they are subordinated to their natural surroundings. In intimate, closed rooms and courtyards, from which open views towards a landscape are almost transcendental in the calm they confer, mourners can find detachment. This landscape became ultimately the centre of power of the whole.

ARKITEKTVR

48 ÅRG ⊛ REDAKTÖR
E G ASPLVND ⊛ REDAK-
TIONSMEDLEMMAR
IVAR TENGBOM
L I WAHLMAN

1918

Cover (1918) of the main professional periodical.

NOTES

1 Gunnar Asplund, "Aktuella arkitektoniska faror för Stockholm, hyreshusen", *Arkitektur* 10/1916, 127 ff.

2 Presented on 26 November 1915 to a meeting of Samfundet S:t Erik and published in its 1916 annual.

3 Carl Bergsten, "Kungsgatans bebyggande", *Arkitektur* 12/1915, 121.

4 Gregor Paulsson, *Den nya arkitekturen* (1916), 116 ff. He refers in this context to W.C. Behrendt, Die einheitliche Blockfront als Raumelement im Stadtbau.

5 The course of the whole series of incidents is described in Hans Nyström, *Hungerupproret 1917* (Ludvika, 1994); see especially 10 ff and 34 ff.

6 Statement by Yngve Larsson, referring to *Arkitektur* 2/1920, 13 ff.

7 Larsson, in *Arkitektur* 2/1920, 14.

8 The drawings for the other quarter, called Ivar, are unsigned. See Sven Drakenberg, *Västerås stads byggnadshistoria från 1800-talets mitt* (Västerås, 1962) 241 ff.

9 The hollow walls were filled with insulating sawdust that attracted bedbugs. See Sven Wallander, "Om kristidens bostadsbyggen", *Arkitektur* 3/1920, 29.

10 Björn Linn, *Osvald Almqvist, en arkitekt och hans arbete* (1967), 56.

11 See *Den svenska egnahemsrörelsen* (1915), 176 ff; *Byggmästaren* 1926, 24; and Hakon Ahlberg, "Sigurd Lewerentz", *Arkitektur* 9/1963, 218 ff.

12 Paulsson (1916), 29.

13 Paulsson (1916), 15.

14 Gregor Paulsson, "Äldre svensk nyttoarkitektur" and "Om konstruktionen som arkitektonisk stilbildare", *Arkitektur* 12/1918, 177 ff, 191 ff.

15 Carl Bergsten, "Arkitekterna och industrins byggnader", in *Arkitektur* 11/1918, 157 ff.

16 *Arkitektur* 11/1918, 160–175.

17 Lisa Brunnström, *Den rationella fabriken* (Umeå, 1990), 167 ff.

18 Erik Hahr, "Verkstadsbyggnad för Asea, Västerås", *Arkitektur* 11/1918, 160.

19 Brunnström, 131 ff, 137.

20 This thesis is advanced by Brunnström.

21 Arkitekten 1920, 168 ff. Reprinted in *Nordisk klassicism/Nordic Classicism* 1910–1930 (Finnish Museum of Architecture, Helsinki, 1982), 40 ff.

22 Nils A. Blanck, "Dansk nutidsarkitektur", *Arkitektur* 3/1918, 33 ff.

23 Called Svenska Likbrännningsföreningen before 1917.

24 The early cremation movement in Sweden is described in Ulf G. Johnson, "De första krematorierna och deras förutsättningar", *Konsthistorisk tidskrift* 3-4/1964.

25 "Here one does not need to ask about the creator, it is so unmistakeably Lewerentz and in addition one of his finest pieces of work," wrote Hakon Ahlberg, in "Sigurd Lewerentz", *Arkitektur* 9/1963, 203.

26 Johnson (1964), 122.

27 Bengt O.H. Johansson, *Tallum* (1996).

28 Johansson (1996), 24; Linn (1967), 54.

29 Gunnar Asplund, "Skogskapellet", *Arkitektur* 7/1921, 87 ff.

30 According to Johansson (1996), 58, this intention was frustrated by the interposition of a cemetery-board member.

31 Both Johansson (1996) and Elias Cornell refer to this review.

32 See, for example, Magnus Olausson, *Den engelska parken i Sverige under gustaviansk tid* (1993), 333 ff.

33 Asplund, *Arkitektur* 7/1921.

34 Caroline Constant, *The Woodland Cemetery: Toward a Spiritual Landscape* (1994).

35 Gunnar Asplund, "Villa i Djursholm", *Arkitektur* 12/1919, 162 ff.

36 Stuart Wrede infers associations to pregnancy in the round-bellied contour. For him, the irregularity of the plan and the incised circle is a metaphor for birth. This type of interpretation, which he makes consistently, seems far-fetched and has hardly aroused a response in the Swedish debate. Stuart Wrede, *The Architecture of Erik Gunnar Asplund* (Cambridge, 1980).

37 See Sven-Ulric Palme, "Tjugotalets samhälle", *Fataburen* 1968, 2–28; the preceding summary derives partly from this source.

38 Palme, 27.

39 Jan Larsson, *Hemmet vi ärvde* (1994), 109. Cited also in notes 6–8, Larsson lived until he was over 90 years old.

40 In an unpublished essay, *Uttrycksmedel i tjugotalets svenska arkitektur*, Richard Brun and Thomas Hellqvist analyzed some 1920s' buildings and described some of the qualities, including the tendency to an anti-hierarchic attitude, that they had in common (University of Lund, 1978).

41 Björn Linn, "En professionell arkitektur", *Arkitektur* 2/1982, 16.

42 Sven Wallander, "Om kristidens bostadsbyggen", *Arkitektur* 3/1920, 29 ff.

43 Markelius had recently changed his name from 'Jonsson'. See also his "Standardiseringsfrågan", *Arkitektur* 2/1920, 6.

44 Sven Jonsson, "Standardiseringskommitténs snickerityper", *Arkitektur* 5/1920. See preceding note.

45 Sven Wallander, "Hyresgästernas Sparkasse- och Byggnadsförening i Stockholm eller H.S.B.", *Byggmästaren* 1/1927, 1; Osvald Almqvist, "Kökets standardisering", *Byggmästaren* 9/1927, 105.

46 Wallander (1927), 7.

47 Axel Dahlberg, "En orienterande redogörelse för den av Stockholms stad bedrivna trädgårdsstads- och småstugeverksamheten", *Nordisk Byggnadsdag* 1927, 166.

48 Hans O. Elliot, "Standardisering av bostadstyper och byggnadsmaterial", *Nordisk Byggnadsdag* 1927, 93 ff.

49 Hans O. Elliot, "Om typer och typserier av mindre bostadshus", *Byggmästaren* 19/1926, 229 ff.

50 Building regulations forbade on grounds of fire prevention more than two kitchens on each on each landing; in addition, the narrowness of the buildings was a factor of

their being built in a relatively simple way in wood; see
Praktiska och hygieniska bostäder, 47.

[51] Åsa Walldén, *Kungsladugård, en arkitekturguide* (Göteborg, 1992).

[52] Hans Arén, *Radhuset som folkbostad*. Doctoral dissertation. (Göteborg, 1980), 65 ff.

[53] Carl Erik Bergold, *Bostadsbyggande i Uppsala, 1900– 1950—en aspekt på folkhemmets framväxt* (Uppsala, 1985), 160–163.

[54] Linn (1982), 16.

[55] Hakon Ahlberg, "Jubileumsutställningen i Göteborg", *Byggmästaren* 1923, 125.

[56] The dissertations by Hans Bjur, *Stadsplanering kring 1900* (Göteborg, 1984), 119 ff., and by Rasmus Waern, *Tävlingarnas tid* (1996), 108 ff., address respectively the competition in general terms, and its proposals and their assessment. See also *Arkitektur* 1/1917, 69, 91 ff; 8/1918, 111 ff.

[57] Gunnar Asplund, "Bilder med randanteckningar från Konstindustribyggnaderna på Göteborgsutställningen", *Byggmästaren* 1923, 277 ff.

[58] Hakon Ahlberg, "Konstindustribyggnaderna på Göteborgsutställningen", *Byggmästaren* 1923, 286.

[59] Who had been assisted by the-then young Finnish architect, Hilding Ekelund, later prominent in architecture in Finland; *Byggmästaren* 1923, 286

[60] Gunnar Asplund, "Skandiateatern i Stockholm", *Byggmästaren* 1924, 185.

[61] Hakon Ahlberg, *Gunnar Asplund arkitekt 1885–1940* (1943), 48.

[62] The cinema has since been rebuilt several times, and its interior has been greatly altered.

[63] Gunnar Asplund, "Konserthuset", *Arkitektur* 1/1921, 1 ff.

[64] This perspective was removed in a later rebuilding.

[65] Björn Linn addresses this in his analysis, *Arkitektur* 1/1982, 16.

[66] Hakon Ahlberg, "Sveriges paviljong på Parisutställningen 1925", *Byggmästaren* 1924, 141.

[67] John Åkerlund, "Vackra verk", *Byggmästaren* 1924, 237 ff.

[68] Gotthard Johansson, "Skönhet och nytta", *Aftonbladet* 1924; also published in *Kritik* (1941), 157 ff.

Modern office building (1929–31), by Cyrillus Johansson, at the intersection of Sveavägen and Kungsgatan; with one of the latter street's two skyscrapers just visible. A mix of classicism and functionalism.

[69] Osvald Almqvist, "Gatubelysningsarmatur. Några reflexioner i samband med lyktstolpstävlingen", *Byggmästaren* 1924, 52; see also Linn (1967), 67,

[70] Hakon Ahlberg, "Sigurd Lewerentz", *Arkitektur* 9/1963, 202.

[71] Johansson (1966), 66.

[72] Johansson (1996), 66.

[73] Hans Nordenström, "Uppståndelsekapellet på Skogskyrkogården", *Hus, 27 arkitekters val ur svensk byggnadskonst* (1965).

[74] Nordenström (1965), 126.

[75] Demetri Porphyrios, "Döden, naturen och antiken". *Lewerentz*. (Museum of Architecture, 1987), 31.

[76] Sven Markelius, "Uppståndelsekapellet", *Byggmästaren* 20/1926, 233 ff.

[77] Uno Åhrén, "Drama, musik och arkitektur", *Byggmästaren* 2/1927, 13 ff.

[78] Gunnar Asplund, "Några uppgifter om biblioteksbygget", *Byggmästaren* 1928, 100.

[79] Uno Åhrén, "Reflexioner i Stadsbiblioteket", *Byggmästaren* 1928, 93.

[80] Gustaf Strengell, "Spenglers historiefilosofi och arkitekturen", *Byggmästaren* 1925, 186 ff, 201 ff.

[81] Ivar Tengbom, "Svenska Tändsticksaktiebolagets nybyggnad", *Byggmästaren* 1928, 166.

[82] Erik Friberger, "Kungsholm", *Byggmästaren* 1929, 1.

[83] Carl Bergsten, "Inredningen av T.M.S. 'Kungsholm'", *Byggmästaren* 1929, 5.

[84] Constant (1994); Johansson (1996).

[85] Johansson (1996), 77.

[86] Johansson (1996), 78–80.

[87] Gunnar Asplund, "Krematoriebygget", *Byggmästaren* 19/1940, 247 ff.

[88] Hakon Ahlberg, "Krematoriet på Skogskyrkogården", *Byggmästaren* 19/1940, 243 ff.

Leading early functionalistic office- and printers' building (1928– 34), Stockholm, by Ivar Tengbom, who used its lighting to emphasise its big-town character.

Under the slogan of "One day the earth shall be ours", the Cooperative Association architects' office proposed this row house to the 1932 Stockholm competition for inexpensive dwellings.

Early Functionalism 1930–40

EVA RUDBERG

The 1930s began with crises in society. The economies of the western world had been shaken by stock-market crashes. In Sweden, underemployment was high and one industrial worker in five was out of work. Cramped living and urban housing shortages were still a scourge; a normal dwelling for a working-class family was a single room, with a kitchen. When the Social Democrats campaigned in the 1932 general election on a programme focusing on unemployment and the housing crisis, this led to victory and they formed a government under Per Albin Hansson.

The People's Home (Folkhemmet) that the new government wanted to create had been launched, as a concept, in a celebrated speech by Per Albin Hansson in 1928. In it, he likened society to the "good home" of a large family in which the better equipped members look after the others who are not so well off. "In the good home obtain similarity, thoughtfulness, helpfulness ... The good home knows nothing of some who have privileges or are disadvantaged, there are no pets and no stepchildren ... One does not look down on another, none tries to acquire advantages at the expense of another, the strong do not oppress and plunder the weak."

A more powerful and more easily appreciated image of a democratic welfare society is hard to think of. At the same time it associated to a tradition of the home as a symbol for security and continuity, and thus spoke in this way even to more conservative values.

Interruption or Continuity

Earlier in Sweden, the central government had taken as little action as possible in public-welfare matters, but, now, to counter the economic crises and get national society moving again, the possibilities of active measures to affect production and consumption were put forward. Welfare payments needed no longer be regarded only as outgoings: they created demand for goods, which increased production. This was a way of thinking that, having been advanced by Keynes, was adopted in Sweden by the man who became the first Social-Democrat minister of finance, Ernst Wigforss. Keynes' ideas became applied more thoroughly in Sweden than in perhaps any other country and have comprised a part of what came to be called 'the Swedish model'.

A further powerful and propagandistic formulation came to acquire importance for the breakthrough of this thought. It appeared in a book, *Kris i befolkningsfrågan*, by Alva and Gunnar Myrdal (published 1934). Numbers of births had shown a disturbing decrease and, in the Myrdals' opinion, this could be explained as unemployment and cramped dwellings scaring people off parenthood. In their opinion, the resolution of unemployment as well as shortages of housing would be to embark on building housing. This would generate jobs not just in the building industry but in all others on which the industry depended: quarrying, timber and so on. Being all domestic industries, this policy would create jobs within the country.

Even if public-sector remedies did not become comprehensive during the 1930s, their aim was at least formulated and the way to reach it indicated in a convincing and powerful manner. And a scenario of a Sweden bereft of its population was something to induce politicians beside Social Democrats to unite. Appointed in 1935, the National Population Commission (*Befolkningskommissionen*) led to remedies that would improve conditions

Per Albin Hansson, Social-Democrat prime minister of Sweden (1932–46) and only symbolically a father figure, outside his Stockholm row house, by Paul Hedqvist in 1932.

for women and children. Gunnar Myrdal was one of the motive forces in it, as he was in the national Housing-Social Commission (*Bostadssociala utredningen*) that had been appointed two years before: it was to lead to an entirely new housing policy.

This new political climate offered space for novel thinking in architecture, planning and building, which could demonstrate something that the representatives for this democracy ought to be keen to make known: signals to the world at large and the Swedish electorate that a new and better society was under construction. At its absolute centre was the need for housing, which became all the more acute on account of rapid urbanisation. Many of the representatives of the new style in architecture centred their interest and ambitions on building housing for the public at large. Actually building real, three-dimensional buildings that were light, airy and hygienic would be a promising image of "the people's home". While the Social Democratic regime did not expressly make the new architecture into a symbol for the new society, it has later, in many ways, and with some justification, been so appreciated. Many leading personalities among Social Democrats showed that it was their clear personal choice, but, even within the Labour Movement, there were some who saw this architecture as an impoverishment, as a challenge to the working class. One who held such views was the influential Arthur Engberg, editor of *Social Demokraten* at the time and later a government minister: "What has the Labour Movement done wrong, that in its ascent it should be made responsible for a direction of taste that implies a descent?".[1]

But the new prime minister showed his sympathy for the new direction by moving into a row house on *Ålstensgatan*, one of the most modern, newly-built sets of terraced houses in Stockholm; its architect was Paul Hedqvist, one of the foremost of those working in the new spirit.

International Contacts

The new architecture had reached Sweden during the 1920s, and one could establish the year as 1925, which was when Le Corbusier's pavilion for the periodical *L'Esprit Nouveau* was shown in conjunction with the big art and industrial exhibition in Paris. Several Scandinavian architects found visits to the pavilion a turbulent experience, one that felt like a liberation and a return to fundamental architectural values. In Denmark, Edvard Heiberg

reported enthusiastically about it; in Norway Lars Backer asserted the need for a new architecture; and, in Sweden, Uno Åhrén wrote that "Here is free space to move in, to speak seriously or banter, just as one pleases, freestanding walls to hang art on, uncluttered floor area to group furniture on, just as you like."[2]

Contacts with the new architecture and its creators were made in various ways. Books and periodicals were important, among them Le Corbusier's *Vers une Architecture* and *Urbanisme*, as well as *Das Neue Frankfurt*. International personal contacts were made by some, including Gregor Paulsson, director of the Swedish Handicraft Association (*Svenska slöjdföreningen*), who became one of the most important protagonists of the architecture that became known in Sweden as *functionalism*. Two others, Uno Åhrén and Sven Markelius, got to know Le Corbusier, Walter Gropius, Fred Forbat and others, besides the people in *CIAM*, Congrès Internationaux d'Architecture Moderne, with whom they also worked.[3]

The large exhibitions named here were places for meetings and inspirations for the Scandinavians. For Swedish architects, exchanges with Germany were most important and inspiring, for those from Norway contacts with Dutch modernists. Many Swedes visited the Stuttgart *Weissenhof* (1927) and *Berlin* (1931) exhibitions, as well as Ernst May's exhibition, *Die Wohnung für das Existensminimum* in Frankfurt (1929).

Swedish architects also entered some of the most noticed international competitions of the

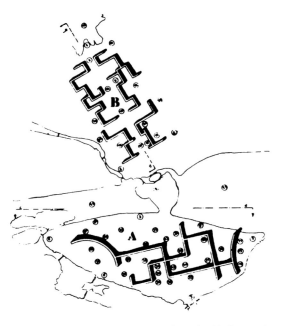

Le Corbusier's competition proposal to rebuild all central Stockholm (1932) except the Old City. Large houses instead of traditional blocks.

time, including that for the League of Nations' building in Geneva (1926); one of the nine prizewinners was Nils Einar Eriksson. Most competition entries, including those from the Swedes, were not of modernism architecture. But those for the theatre (1930) in the town of Charkov, now in the Ukraine, were: many German and Russian ideas about the mutability of space in the theatre characterised entries. A group of Swedish technologists, Jöran Curman, Lars Magnus Giertz, Sune Lindström and Gunnar Pettersson won a prize.

Several of the well-known modernists were invited to Sweden, both Gropius and Le Corbusier visiting Stockholm to lecture. Le Corbusier aroused great attention with his entry for the competition (1932) for *Nedre Norrmalm* in central Stockholm: it proposed that the older buildings should be replaced by modern point blocks.

The Swiss architect, Alfred Roth, an important protagonist of modernism, lived in Göteborg in 1928–30, and, together with Ingrid Wallberg, one of the first Swedish women to become an architect, designed the Simonsson summer place at Kungsbacka (south of the town), and, in Göteborg, the *Helagsfjället* and *Nybygget* developments of 200 apartments in a local type of two- or three-story wooden building on a stone or brick foundation (landshövdingehus); they were commissioned by a local branch of the national Labour Movement housing organisation called HSB. Roth also lectured at Röhsska Museum, Göteborg, in 1928, on Le Corbusier and his work.[4]

Josef Frank, a leading Austrian architect whose wife was Swedish, designed five summer places at Falsterbo, the southernmost tip of Sweden, a fashionable seaside place. Completed by 1927, the *Claesson* and *Carlsten* hous-

The Nybygget apartments for HSB, Göteborg (1930), by Alfred Roth and Ingrid Wallberg.

es were among the first modernist buildings north of the Baltic. The fifth house, and the most exclusive, the *Wehtje* house, was complete by 1936; differing from his earlier, right-angled layouts, its organically irregular, U-shaped ground plan let him realise his ideas (previously only entertained as fantasies) about open links between rooms and movement through the house. With a facade in pink rendered light concrete, this house may be the most interesting of his buildings, of which it was in fact the last to be built. He had moved to Sweden in 1933 and been engaged by Estrid Ericson to join the interior-decoration company, *Svenskt Tenn*, to design furniture and textiles, besides interiors. This, which came to be his principal occupation in Sweden, has made him well known in Sweden and international circles.[5]

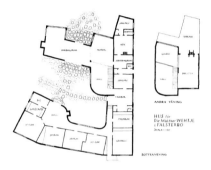

Wehtje House, Falsterbo, by Josef Frank: for 1936, its irregularity and open layout were very interesting.

Swedish Functionalism

Sweden and the other Nordic countries provided the new direction in architecture with fertile ground on which to establish itself, to grow, and to develop continuously.

Functionalism offered many Swedish architects and builders long-awaited answers to a number of problems and of matters that had been called into question. It seemed to be a concerted answer: a seeking after the basic values of architecture; an honest expression; a factual, even almost a scientific, attitude to the work to be done; and rationality, efficiency and standardisation in building were all part of it. Steps had already been taken to be more rational and apply standards.

Light in the northern countries in winter never comes from a point much above the

The Claesson House, Falsterbo (1927), by Josef Frank; one of the first modernistic buildings in Sweden.

Sheltered courtyard of the Wehtje House.

horizon. Access to it, a central architectural question, received an answer in the large individual or serial fenestration or extensive curtain walling favoured by functionalism.

Urban growth, increasing vehicular traffic and all-too-often cramped living quarters sought for resolutions, singly or together. Other countries had undergone this urbanisation process much earlier, and influences originating there may have made Swedish architects receptive to the ideas embodied in functionalism. A culture which combined Swedish poverty and the severity of purified Swedish Lutheranism was also receptive to functionalism.

Of the Swedish architects who first took up functionalism, several clearly preferred the chillier modernism of Gropius to the more sensuous and expressive material, colour and form of the modernism represented by Hugo Häring, Bruno Taut and Hans Scharoun, among others. Early Swedish modernism was characteristically rational, simple and restrained, so it was more than adequate that 'functionalism' should be the name given to this inclination towards studies of function and rational organisation. Everyday problems were emphasised, as they were, from 1931, in the slogans of the Swedish functionalists' manifesto *acceptera*, which intended not to return to "an old culture's outgrown forms" nor to leap from the present "into a future utopia": "Accept the reality before you—only through it do we have any prospect of mastering it, of coping with it so as to alter it, and to create culture that is a handy tool for one's life."

Functionalism in Sweden affected really all types of building, from exclusive to everyday work. The American writer and housing researcher, Catherine Bauer, who visited Scandinavia on several occasions during the 1930s and 1940s, and other foreign observers, have singled out precisely the efforts concerning building of everyday housing as some of the most important Swedish contributions to modern architecture.

But Swedish functionalism was characterised not just by international models. Whenever Swedish architecture and manners of building have been affected by impulses from outside the country, they have in various ways been adapted to domestic conditions. What has often happened has been that these relatively costly models, on becoming subject to modest Swedish resources, have turned into variations that are simpler but with characters and identities of their own. As happened with functionalism: its expressed and desired inter-

nationalism got Swedified, in the sense that the classicism that had prevailed during the 1920s (restrained, simple, pure facades) metamorphosed into a more puritanical functionalism of flat, unbroken and undecorated facades. The differences are as clear as the continuity, while both have origins in late 18th-century and early 19th-century Swedish styles. Timber, the traditional Swedish building material, got used in functionalist buildings, giving the Swedish variant a particular character, for instance vertically panelled facades painted in light colours. Brick was used for larger buildings of which some were rendered in light colours; those that were left untreated could retain a robust character. Timber being relatively scarce, brick was most common and familiar in Skåne (the south), where the Danish brick tradition was not far off.

An older Swedish tradition of form appeared in the long, narrow, freestanding blocks of three or four stories that made their impression on 1930s housing areas; they can be said to follow the similarly simple buildings with pitched or mansard roofs that were common in rural locations and military establishments. The tradition of mid-height fenestration in urban buildings, as was once required by Stockholm regulations, to reflect light down into the street, often reappeared in Swedish functionalist buildings but to achieve flat, light and shining facades.

Debate and propaganda appeared foremost in the *Byggmästaren* periodical, but also in a series of pamphlets (1932–35) called *Arkitektur och samhälle*. Many of the radical architects contributed to *Fönstret* (started 1930), as well as to the publication of the Social-Democratic women's association, *Morgonbris*. The Danish *Kritisk Revy*, started in 1926 by a combative Danish architect Poul Henningsen, accepted contributions to its debates from Swedish architects. It was characteristic that architects, together with doctors, lawyers, economists and writers, tried to cooperate over professional and working boundaries to take part in radical groupings.[6]

Functionalism was taken up primarily in Stockholm, while, in other towns and in the country, the styles of the 1920s persisted into the 1930s. If something there was built in a functionalist style, it was often because a Stockholm-based architect had received a local commission.

The earliest functionalist buildings that were designed by Swedish architects who were inspired by foreign models included the silo (1927) and flour-mill buildings (1928) owned by the Cooperative Movement or KF (as in

The functionalist manifesto (1931) by Asplund, Gahn, Markelius, Paulsson, Sundahl and Uno Åhrén; its title is an imperative: Accept!

Student building, College of Technology, Stockholm (1930), by Sven Markelius and Uno Åhrén, after a competition in 1928: the first significant functionalist public-sector building in Sweden.

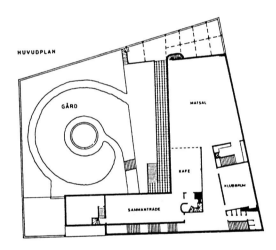

Plan including cafe and dining room of the building above.

Swedish) at *Kvarnholmen*, as it was later called; the *Tiden* office building (1929) on Sveavägen in central Stockholm, designed by the KF Architects' Office; Wolter Gahn's office building (1928) on Drottninggatan, central Stockholm; Markelius' apartment block on Dalagatan-Tegnérgatan (1929), central Stockholm, one of the first in the reinforced concrete that was otherwise used mostly in engineering works and the like, foundations and factories; and Markelius' own reinforced-concrete house in Nockeby, Stockholm (1930) that was strongly influenced by Le Corbusier. One of the earliest public buildings was the *students' building* at Tekniska högskolan,

Stockholm (opened 1930) by Markelius and Åhrén.

The first functionalist buildings but ones hardly influenced by foreign models include Almqvist's power stations at *Hammarforsen* and *Krångforsen* that were built in 1925–28 as straightforward engineering jobs. His responses to them were factual and rational, as well as expressive of the movement of the water and the building's functions. He had been critical of hydro-electric power stations that were pretentious "with a feeling of a castle or church in the middle of the waters and a lot of mechanical equipment… In giving them form, people have often disdained any expression of straightforwardly factual conditions."[7] His success is testified to by Gustaf Näsström, an art critic and one of the protagonists of functionalism; he wrote in Stockholms Dagblad of the expressiveness of the power stations: "Their different buildings are characterised by controlled energy and, through their position, grouping, material, and the dimensions of their windows and surfaces, give a clear and lively impression of the enormous process in their interiors through which the thundering masses of water are transformed into electricity."[8]

Each facility comprises three conjoined shed-roofed buildings with rows of windows: they contain machinery, switch gear and intakes. They differ in that the highest building at Hammarforsen is the central one, and,

Hammarforsen Hydro-Electric Generating Station, by Osvald Almqvist, 1925–28, expressing the movement of the water.

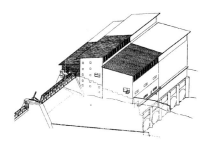

Axonometric view of the same.

at Krångforsen, the one furthest upstream. Relationships between the buildings at each facility, and the angling of their roofs, created dynamism: "in their composition, the buildings seem as it were to follow the mass of water from its hesitancy behind the dams to its release and freedom as it pours downwards."[9]

Almqvist presented the power stations in axonometric parallel perspective, a method of drawing that conferred a pedagogical and mechanical clarity on his subjects, besides making the method a favourite means of presentation among other functionalists. The powerful simplicity of the buildings has given them a self-evident place in Swedish architectural history, and functionalists themselves have often, for example in *acceptera*, asserted that they are exemplary.

Almqvist was to develop his factual attitude further, for example in the work he did for the 1930 *Stockholm exhibition* and in the industrial school at *Domnarvet* (1932).[10]

From Classicism to Functionalism: the Helsingborg Concert Hall

A clear instance of the novelty of functionalism as a marked influence on Swedish architecture is provided by Markelius' proposals for the concert hall at Helsingborg (see also catalogue).[11] A competition had been held in 1925, and the first and second prizes were awarded to two of the best-known architects of the day,

Lars Israel Wahlman and Ragnar Östberg, while the third prize was awarded to the much younger Markelius, whose name had become known thanks to successes in several competitions. Of the three, he was 'the rationalist'.[12]

His competition entry was based on a strict, logical ground plan, decked in a chilly classicist costume. His large main building contained the auditorium, a lecture hall and subsidiary spaces, while the restaurant and kitchens were located in a lesser building linked to the first by a corridor. The municipal company that had commissioned him considered neither his nor either of the other two proposals economically feasible. When the competition was re-held the following year, Markelius won it with a reworked, more economical proposal, which he was commissioned to build. As in his first proposal, its exterior was strictly classical, now with an entry in the form of the gable of a neo-antique temple; the company wanted a less severe exterior, and Markelius and his colleagues worked out a number of alternatives.

The following year, 1927, having received a travelling scholarship to study aerodromes, he and his wife, Viola Wahlstedt, went motoring in Europe through Germany, France, Belgium and Holland. At Dessau, Markelius sought out Gropius, who showed him the recently completed *Bauhaus school* and the terrace house area of *Törten*. This, Gropius' latest experiment, had been built with rational building techniques and a well-thought-out plan and

Two views of Markelius' Concert Hall, Helsingborg (1925–31). A transition from classicistic to functionalist style.

Drawing (1930) in a sprayed-ink technique, reinforcing the sense of sharp-cut surfaces and volumes.

timetable for organisation. This lived up to what Markelius himself had long been interested in, and, in an article in Byggmästaren later that year, he gave an enthusiastic account of this manner of building inexpensive houses of a given type. The following year, Gropius was asked to lecture in Stockholm.

Markelius and his wife continued to the Weissenhof Exhibition in Stuttgart, where he was especially interested in houses by Le Corbusier and Pierre Jeanneret.

The impressions from the trip influenced Markelius strongly in the work of reworking the exterior of the concert hall. His encounters outside Sweden with the new architecture confirmed his own attempts to reach the rationality, simplicity and architectural honesty he had previously implied in his projects and published writings.

In 1929, his ideas for the concert hall were strongly modernist, with a residue of classicist elements: a sort of hybrid he probably disliked. In 1930, the columns of the entry lost their classical capitals, the row of cloakroom windows were more emphasised, and the concrete buttresses in the main building were exposed, so as to become a decisive architectural effect in the completed building. The last of his original ideas to go was the relief on the gable facade. His perspective presentations were changed at the same time: he replaced his earlier gouache technique with one of spraying with ink while masking parts of the drawing. This reinforced the impression of the whole, sharply-delineated surfaces and geometrical volumes that are the ideal in modernist architecture.

Despite these changes, the main lines of his original plan underwent no decisive alteration. It remained a building with a lofty main part containing the concert hall, and a lower part containing the entry and subsidiary spaces, but the reworking gave the whole a clearer, more powerful and purer form: content had found form. With its geometric, white rendered forms, the concert hall was the first genuinely monumental functionalist building in Sweden. More perhaps than any other building of the time, its exterior reveals its design and func-

tions. The buttresses of the main building are clearly visible from outside, and its inner coherence can be deciphered through its various volumes.

The glazed entrance leads via the monumental stairway first to the elegantly rounded, bulging cloakrooms, beautifully furnished in mild, light colours, with looking glass, and top light from fenestration under the roof. The stairs lead thence either down to the restaurant on the lower floor, or up, to the upper foyer.

The north wall of the foyer is entirely glazed. It, and the large undecorated expanses of wall, the huge white lighting globes, the slender handrails, and the whole of the airy volume of the foyer together comprise an excellent example of contemporary formal language. The foyer leads into the concert hall itself, which is a large rectangular room with a slightly sloping seating floor. Its walls are clad in mahogany, which gives the hall a warm look while also contributing to its exceptional acoustics, a result of Markelius' cooperation with Gustave Lyon, whose celebrated Salle Pleyel in Paris was taken as a model for many other contemporary concert halls and auditoria.

Helsingborg Concert Hall (1932), one of the most important works of Swedish functionalism.

National Insurance administration (1932), Stockholm, by Sigurd Lewerentz: this block with windows like holes in a wall contains an oval glazed yard.

The building, completed in 1932, was received enthusiastically, not least by the dominant art critic, Gotthard Johansson, who compared its buttresses with the rhythmic tensions of Gothic cathedrals and took the hall as proof of the strength of the new architecture.

The commissioning company and the municipal building board were upset that approved drawings had been departed from and that decisions had been torn up, and went so far to report the matter to the police, an essential step in Sweden in taking legal proceedings. But the many instances of reworking had demonstrated a result in which the whole and its details are melded into a convincing unity of abiding value.

This transformation of a building from classicist to modernistic has parallels with Alvar Aalto's reworking of his *Finnish Theatre in Turku* and for the *Library in Viipuri*. Close friends, Markelius and Aalto were much in contact and influenced one another; associations between their work were then numerous.

A functionalist building with classicistic elements, begun in 1928 and finished in 1932, was Lewerentz' *Riksförsäkringsanstalten* in Stockholm that originated in a competition. Its cubic volume and clean-cut wall apertures, together with the flat, undecorated facade rendering and its recessed top floor utter the formal language of functionalism, with the weight of its facade on the street and its entrances, its oval inner yard and symmetry of its central axes utter that of classicism. The studies of the functions and lighting of its interior, however, express a purified spirit of functionalism.[13]

The 1930 Stockholm Exhibition

In 1930, the great Swedish manifestation of functionalism took place in Stockholm (see also the catalogue).[14] From its opening in mid May until its close at the end of September, it attracted 4 million visitors (the national population was then a little over 6 million), besides much contemporary popular and media attention at home and abroad. Widespread enthusiasm was mingled with severe criticism by more traditionally-minded architects and designers, but, as a whole, it was a resounding success and has been remembered ever since.

Inspired by the Swedish successes at the 1925 Paris exhibition, the Swedish Handicraft Association took the initiative in bringing to fruition this exhibition of applied art, handcrafts, domestic craft, dwellings and objects for use. Everyday things occupied the centre of attention, as they had done for the Association since its reorganisation in 1915, but much space was devoted to more exclusive objects from handcraft artists.

The Association's director, Gregor Paulsson, general commissioner of the exhibition, believed explicitly in the strength and ability of the new movement, and, through his central position, became one of its most important protagonists in Sweden. As early as 1916, he had, in his book *Den nya arkitekturen*, asserted the need for industrialisation and standard types, technical, hygienic and social rationalism and the beauty of a constructively clear formal language.

Published in 1928, the programme for the exhibition included his declaration of taking exception to 1920s classicism, as well as his view of functionalism: "I should like to state that I have, with pleasure and appreciation," he wrote "become acquainted with [functionalism] because it implies an intellectually and morally straightforward relationship to the artistic problems that feels doubly refreshing after recent years' worship of hazy idols that have borne the beautiful but false museum labels of national tradition or classical beauty. The belief that it would be possible to raise a modern culture of building and living in direct association with a resurrection of older artistic styles and ways of life demonstrates a faulty insight into the values arising out of artistic

Stockholm Exhibition (1930): the colourful breakthrough for functionalism in Sweden; designed by Asplund and many others.

creation… I have taken exception not to the old but to the reconstruction of the old." [15]

The central government and the municipality of Stockholm voted funds for the exhibition, which was built on an idyllic waterside site in central Stockholm. Gunnar Asplund was appointed principal architect. Together with his colleagues, he succeeded in creating an airy, light and shimmering composition, in which water, greenery and buildings worked together in a unity. This impression was reinforced by sophisticated lighting that advertised the exhibition in the evenings. Writing regularly on art in the Stockholm daily paper, Svenska Dagbladet, Gotthard Johansson became one of the most important protagonists of functionalism in Sweden. His response to the exhibition was enthusiastic from the start: "[Asplund] has shown that one can compose poetry as freely in glass, iron and eternit [asbestos-cement roofing material] as in historical styles with columns and minarets. He has shown that pure cubes and clear spaces can be built up into a shining architectural poem of festivities, that functionalism need not, as many still stubbornly insist on believ-

ing it is, be dry, boring and unpoetic, and the question is whether this is not the exhibition's greatest result. What one must admire before anything else in this architecture is its large grasp—large, but also careful. In fact, its interplay between architecture and the natural world is its most captivating side. With genius, Asplund has used the existing idyll of the park by the water to build, under the green vaults of the trees, all the small kiosks and such other buildings as would otherwise threaten to split up the unity of the whole, and, at the same time, to create a wonderfully fresh and lively oasis in the crush of the exhibition. On the other side, in a rhythmic crescendo, the long rows of halls proclaim the main architectural motif of the exhibition that culminates grandiosely in the monumental glazed architecture of the main restaurant that comprises one of our foremost modern buildings, and which, as early as the present moment, one would wish to see preserved after the conclusion of the exhibition." [16]

Asplund's closest colleagues were three architects—Nils Einar Eriksson, Viking Göransson and Hans Quiding—and an engi-

Poster by Sigurd Lewerentz, with a revolutionary red ground; the blue-and-yellow band signifies Sweden.

(Above) View of the Corso and the advertising mast, with Lewerentz' symbolic pair of wings; Stockholm Exhibition, 1930.

(Right) Asplund's Paradise Restaurant was his most impressive single work at the exhibition.

neer, B. Ahlström. Together they designed most of the exhibition buildings: the entry with the Swedish Handicraft Association's executive committee's offices, the exhibition halls, the main restaurant called Paradise, the Park restaurant, the press stand and its lofty advertising mast, as well as most of the pavilions and kiosks. Other architects made individual contributions. Lewerentz (Green Point Cafe), Wolter Gahn (Bridge Cafe), Folke Bensow, (Milk Propaganda Refreshment Premises), Uno Åhrén and Gunnar Sundbärg (Rented Accommodation Hall), Markelius (Hospital Exhibition). Others contributed kiosks, care of graves and exhibited objects of varied use. In addition, there was the Dwellings Department that contained 13 owner-occupier, terraced and detached houses that were products of an architects' competition.

Most of the buildings had timber frames clad with eternit, a seemingly ideal material made since the turn of the century from cement and asbestos that was easy to saw to size and fit together, and afforded adequate protection from Swedish summer weather. Sixty years' hindsight makes it less ideal. The buildings were characteristically extensively glazed and had colourful awnings. Neutral in tone, by contrast, the exhibition halls were, as Asplund put it, "thought of as backgrounds to what is on exhibition."

The Handicraft Association's premises by the entrance had columns equipped with lighting facilities that, when used at night, associated the appearance of the building to a Greek temple in a modernistic style, besides exemplifying the abiding presence in early Swedish modernism of a classical inheritance.

The exhibition halls lay in a long row along the main thoroughfare, the Corso. The Public-Transport Hall stood out among them on account of its convex bowed canopy roof, a form that gave room for a sailing boat placed

under it. Balconies in the hall displayed interior furnishing for boats and railway compartments; an aeroplane was placed on a raised platform. Motor cars were on display and some buses that Lewerentz had designed. Unlike the other halls, this one had a steel frame.

The lofty steel advertising mast included a suspended press stand. It stood at one end of the Corso, in the Festival Square. Its form associated to Russian constructivism. Seventy-four metres above the ground, its top carried the exhibition's symbol of freedom that Lewerentz, whose design was inspired by a winged Egyptian figure of a man, saw as a pair of stylised wings; the public nicknamed it 'the cut-throat razor'.

Nearby lay Paradise, the main restaurant, that, as Johansson mentioned, was architecturally the most prominent building at the exhibition. It was long, and its rounded termination was carried, in part, on pillars, and was glazed with large horizontal rows of windows shaded along its short sides by red awnings, and, on its long sides, by yellow and green ones. From inside, the mezzanine entrance of the restaurant and its thin railings seemed to hover. Its slender construction in steel may have associated to the wings of a dragonfly, but its short summer life was more that of a mayfly: despite Gotthard Johansson's hopes, when summer ended it was torn down and its remains sold as scrap. Its site is now occupied by the *National Maritime Museum* (1934), by Ragnar Östberg. As one may infer from this work, he was one of the most powerful opponents of functionalism, a style he openly stated he would not use here.

The exhibition contained several restaurants and cafes. With three sections, called Puck, Ellida and Böljeblick, around a core of kitchens and subsidiary premises, the Park Restaurant had an elegant solution: an irregular ground plan that left existing trees undisturbed in its midst. Puck, which had a vaulted, glazed roof, also functioned as an art gallery. An artist, Otto G. Carlsund, arranged an exhibition of borrowed works of post-cubist art by important international figures, including Mondrian, Leger and Moholy-Nagy. The public at the exhibition understood little of it, some critics cried down the whole and when, after the exhibition closed, Carlsund could not discharge the debts he had incurred to put it on, the paintings were distrained and auctioned off, but made catastrophically low prices. This darkened Carlsund's life for many years.[17]

Beyond the Paradise Restaurant lay an exhibition of images and texts of Sweden and her people, their social problems and technical progress. Called Svea rike, it was arranged by a writer, Lubbe Nordström, whose name is still a household word. In the late 1930s, his book about rural housing, *Lort-Sverige* (literally 'Shit-Sweden'), recorded what he found. *Svea rike* ('the Kingdom of Svea', a female personification of Sweden) also contained a racial-biological element that was typical of the time; it was arranged by one Doctor Herman Lundborg, head of the National Institute for Race Biology but, unlike the architectural and related features of the exhibition, it led to no comment or article in any newspaper.

Around the exhibition area were located small pavilions and kiosks that advertised various companies. Playfully designed by different architects, they contributed powerfully to the relaxed character of the exhibition. The Pix

Terrace house, Stockholm Exhibition, by Uno Åhrén: this in swedish housing then-unusual form attracted much admiration.

Kiosk, by Viking Göransson, had a rotating advertising text that could be altered, and was one of the most elegant.

The Dwellings Department

No part of the exhibition outdid the Dwellings Department in the debate it aroused.[18] Lying in the east of the exhibition area, it presented the furnished apartments, detached houses, terrace houses and small buildings that were created through a competition that grew out of two investigations into urban planning and into housing possibilities for people in different income categories. Entries were to provide good, well-planned dwellings within given cost frameworks. The thought was that even people in low-income groups should have well-planned dwellings.

The dwellings presented small areas of living space divided by function. The possibility of domestic privacy for separate members of a family was emphasised. The exhibitors' ambition was that a family dwelling should comprise, besides a kitchen and bathroom, two or three other rooms. Merely to include a bathroom raised the usual standards of small 1920s apartments. The smaller apartments at the exhibition saved space by including indirectly lit cooking-and-washing-up spaces that were no novelties, having been a feature of 1920s apartments. They were justified at the exhibition with the argument that kitchen work had become more efficient thanks to simplification of cooking but this was unrealistic; nothing in the Dwellings Department attracted so much criticism.

However, Uno Åhrén, one of those responsible for this Department, stated that building costs and the condition of the country made it impossible to build good housing for families with small incomes. The question was not primarily architectural and technical—to get minimal areas to work in practice—but political.

Even so, the dwellings at the exhibition presented some interesting solutions. Åhrén's terrace house, a type that was then unusual in Sweden, had an open plan: its general and dining rooms were essentially a single space giving directly onto an external terrace. The carefully designed functional kitchen was separated from them; on the upper floor were three bedrooms (two of only 8 m² each) with access to a long balcony, and a bathroom. So the two children in a family of four would have their own rooms.

In his exhibition house, Markelius demon-

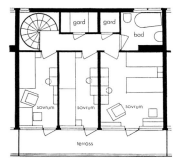

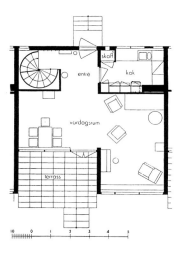

Åhrén put bedrooms upstairs, a living-room, kitchen and terrace downstairs.

strated his attempt to get many rooms into a small area, or, by making use of intermediate walls that could be removed, to get large but fewer rooms. This idea, probably derived from Mies van der Rohe's apartment at the 1927 Stuttgart Exhibition, reappeared as a principle at the 1934 *Standard* Exhibition at Stockholm by Nils Ahrbom and Helge Zimdal.

One of the most functionalist buildings at the exhibition was Kurt von Schmalensee's house in lightweight concrete that was painted yellow and had simple, purely geometric forms, flat facades, and with a simple balcony as an accent; its roof terrace accommodated gymnastic equipment. Inside, its staircase was pure formal language and its protruding mezzanine story showed what building techniques could do.

The Hall for Apartments presented mezzanine solutions, either as an elegant structure of rooms, as in von Schmalensee's contribution, or, in that by Markelius, as an attempt to increase the number of rooms in a given volume.

A Lack of Swedishness?

As the foregoing section makes clear, the exhibition was received with enthusiasm and appreciation among both foreign and domestic critics, but some who represented more traditional values were strongly critical.[19] 'A lack of Swedishness' was one of the repeated accusations. The fear that national and individual characteristics would be spoiled through the new architecture and design was asserted by some besides the most energetic critic, the skilful furniture designer Carl Malmsten, who was a member of the committee of the Swedish Handicraft Association and a well-represented contributor to the exhibition. "In my opinion," he wrote "functionalism contains a tendency towards obliteration of the boundaries and the difference in kind in forming surroundings that ought to be maintained between the sphere of work and production and the domestic circle that is intended for social assembly and recreation."[20]

But protagonists of the new architecture asserted that it had strong roots in what was Swedish. In his book *Svensk funktionalism* (1930), Gustaf Näsström showed that older Swedish building traditions possessed rational technology, standardisation and uniform design. One of Asplund's closest associates at the exhibition, Viking Göransson, asserted that the greater part of older monumental public 'Swedish' architecture was borrowed

'Co-op shop', Nacka (c. 1930); in the country-side, such shops often first signified how the functionalist style was growing.

The Co-op/KF architects also designed shops in the 1930s in traditional styles. They and the modern shops were most often built in timber.

from foreign sources, while what was sought in the new architecture was the honesty and vitality that had existed in the older, anonymous architecture, and that "were it wanted to preserve Swedishness in architecture, once-modern but now out-dated decoration should not be copied but the honesty, alacrity, open-mindedness for new ideas and vitality of the old pioneers and master builders that should survive. Only then can occur a development that is based on tradition and reverence."[21]

These attacks on an alleged lack of Swedishness were in tune with the times. Running counter to the international currents of opinion, of which functionalism was a part, there were national currents that contemporary economic crises strengthened. Similar discussions occurred in Germany.

By claiming that the new architecture was anchored in the various protagonists' own countries, they sought to win its acceptance in several camps. This does not exclude the possibility that this was so—as it was on several counts in Sweden—but the motivation for claiming this was almost a matter of propaganda. In a corresponding way, much of the criticism of the new architecture at the Stockholm Exhibition was propagandistic; its opponents' claim that the organisers did not permit traditional contributions to the exhibition did not square with the facts. In reality, the exhibition was the hitherto most exhaustive account of Swedish 1920s applied art, with important contributions being made by the most critical of the critics.[22] But nothing of the exhibition now remains on the site.

Through the exhibition, Sweden had indicated its leading position in Nordic modernism. In *Architectural Review*, Morton Shand expressed both enthusiasm and criticism, as well as the view that, with "Swedish grace", the exhibition had gone further that the Göteborg (1923) and Paris (1925) exhibitions, while he expected that Sweden would anyway come to be a pathfinder in modernism.[23] It was clear that Swedish functionalism both continued with and departed from the immediately preceding epoch.

Sweden—the Middle Way

The book, *Sweden—the Middle Way*, written by Marquis Childs, an American, in 1937, implied a way between socialism and capitalism. It was a combination that aroused both admiration and suspicion. What came to be called 'the Saltsjöbaden spirit' implied the understanding reached between the national trade-union federation (Landsorganisation or LO) and the Swedish Employers' Federation (SAF) in 1938. But this spirit was not decisive on its own: Childs suggested the importance of contributions by the Cooperative Movement for the development of society in Sweden. Through competition with privately-owned companies, its different parts contributed to lower prices. The most important of them were the national organisations for retailing household goods and food (KF), rented housing (HSB) and a trade-union building organisation (Fackföreningarnas byggnadsproduktion).

The KF Architects' Office

Having been founded in 1899, KF opened its own architects' office in 1924. Its first director, Eskil Sundahl, an architect and convinced functionalist. It attracted other architects interested in socially-directed commissions and work, and cooperative forms of organisation; many of them became well known. After 1927, work was arranged in ten relatively independent departments, each named for the architect who led its work. As a whole, the office had the ambition "clearly and naturally to express the purpose of each building—to give the cooperative spirit a rational expression."[24]

At first, the office designed shops' furniture and fittings, as well as small shops, but it soon did factories, commercial premises, housing, furniture and fittings, household goods and advertising, besides outdoor theatres and local premises for one or more of the component organisations of the Labour Movement that are individually called folkets hus. The KF-designed buildings were characterised as representative of the new architecture and attracted attention within Sweden and in other countries. In central Stockholm, the heights immediately south of the old city were furnished with a lift, *Katarinahissen* (1935), by Olof Thunström; this, the Swedish building that came closest to Russian constructivism, can symbolize the radical attitude of the KF office.

Standardisation was one of the office's aims, and, as applied to the shops, it went so far that even Neufert regarded it as exemplary; he used the standard arrangements of the KF shops in his handbook *Bauentwurfslehre*.[25] With its 70 employees, the office was the largest in Sweden at the time, and contributed greatly to spreading functionalism throughout

View, from within Tage William-Olsson's contemporary road-traffic development, of the Katarina Lift and the KF premises (1935), Stockholm, by Olof Thunström of the KF architecture office.

Kvarnholmen industrial and housing area, Stockholm, by Eskil Sundahl, Olof Thunström and others, KF architects' office.

the country: the KF shops were often the first rural or small-town manifestations of the style. Many rural shops by the Stockholm office were, however, of traditional, with pitched roofs, vertical wooden panelling and, often, with a residential upper floor.

One of the most important of the KF premises was *Kvarnholmen*, just outside Stockholm (see also catalogue). It came to be something of an exemplary society, a democratic modern version of the old privately-owned, hierarchically-arranged works that was typically polarised between the church and the owner's mansion. Dwellings at Kvarnholmen were, instead, terrace houses and two apartment blocks occupying the next most prominent position after the factory premises. There was no church and the private residence of the manager was inconspicuously located. Built between 1927 and 1934, the places of work at Kvarnholmen were the silo, the stores, the mill for porridge oats, a macaroni factory and the rye-crispbread factory.[26]

The *Lumafabriken*, Stockholm, is perhaps the premises that more than any other is associated with work by the KF Architects' Office of the late 1920s. Its products, electric light bulbs, were planned to, and did highly successfully, compete with those from the Philips and Osram in Holland and Germany respectively. Artur von Schmalensee began the Luma-factory project in 1928, and, by 1930, having been built by the cooperative trade-union building company, its compact premises were complete.

Its main building has three wings giving onto the water. Its layout is a lesson in the time-and-motion spirit of Taylor: rationally and logically, the raw materials for manufacturing lamps enter the eastern end of the building, and, working westwards, are treated, made into components, assembled, packed and despatched. The upper part of the western wing contains the glazed bulb-testing room, a shining symbol for the whole facility.[27]

Luma electric light-bulb factory (1930), Stockholm, Artur von Schmalensee, KF architects' office. The illuminated room is where lamps were tested and, in part, how they were advertised.

The building has a steel skeleton encased in concrete, and non-bearing walls in rendered brick. The skeleton system made it easy, as anticipated, to extend the building. Its flat rendered facades, long bands of standard fenestration, flat roof and the easily deciphered functions of its different parts give the whole building an unmistakeable modernistic character. It is related to the van Nelle factory in Rotterdam (1925–31) by Brinkman and Van der Vlugt and with the I.G. Farben office building in Frankfurt-am-Main (completed 1931) by Hans Poelzig.

The Housing Question

Swedish Social-Democratic policy had the housing question at its core, the background being the dreadful housing conditions that had obtained for a long time, with high urban rents and crowding that was still worse than in most other parts of Europe: an urban working family had on average to live in one room, with a kitchen. The Housing Commission (Bostadsutredning) to look into housing conditions was appointed in 1933, with terms of reference that included making suggestions for improvements; several architects took part in its work. A similar but separate investigation into housing and social conditions, the Housing-Social Commission, reported later in the decade, proposing support for less-well-off families with children and for improvements to neglected rural housing.

The first form of support resulted in 'child-rich houses' (*barnrikehus*), sometimes called 'sunny (back)yards', *solgårdar*; their rents were subsidised through national and municipal grants. They were of a high standard and, for those they admitted, were big improvements, but, as only low-income families with three or more children qualified for admission, they led to segregation. Some got bad reputations after 1945, and, as a solution for the housing problem, the concept was abandoned. The proposals that were then made by the investigation were to have decisive importance for future housing policy.

As professionals, many architects addressed the housing question, in which they were both socially and politically engaged. Several saw their main task as bringing into existence good housing for the public at large. Studies of functions in housing were central to this, and furthered the 1920s' striving for rationalisation and standardisation. What got most attention was a kitchen's form and equipment. Osvald Almqvist's investigation into them, a

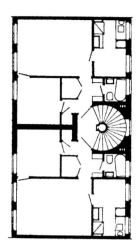

Plan of an apartment in a 'narrow' block shows how it is lit from two, opposing sides.

'Narrow' small-apartment blocks, Hjorthagen (1934–37), Stockholm, by Hakon Ahlberg and Leif Reinius.

result of an initiative in 1920 by the Standardisation Committee (Standardiseringskommittén), was presented as a book called, simply, *Köket* ('The Kitchen') (1934). His conclusions had already been used in several building-and-dwelling exhibitions, among other things, and in preparation for the 1930 Stockholm Exhibition. His studies can be compared with similar contemporary studies of industrial processes, in which machines and work places would be arranged so as to reach the highest level of efficiency. Correspondingly, Almqvist showed how studies of kitchen functions could be studied from the point of view of work processes, and gave examples of good and poor kitchen arrangements. He followed work done in Germany in the 1920s by Bruno Taut, Ernst May, Grete Schütte-Lihotzky and others. He studied measurements and working positions so as to be able to indicate needs of space, and the heights of working surfaces, cupboards, chairs, stools and so on. To make kitchens hygienic and easily cleaned he prescribed flat painted surfaces. All this formed a basis for designing the fixed kitchen joinery that became standard in 1930s Swedish homes.

These studies of function together with technical developments caused small and larger apartments to resemble one another in layout and divisions of functions. Rooms that middle-class families might have reserved for

formal occasions became more everyday, and servants' rooms and passages for serving purposes began to be omitted. Smaller apartments were equipped with 'kitchen corners' separated from eating areas. During the 1930s, bathrooms became standard in large and small apartments even if they were called in question for the least costly apartments. Water closets had become a standard feature of apartments a decade earlier, having replaced shared WCs on staircase landings or in backyards. Replacing wood-burning tiled stoves by central heating liberated ground plans from any need to consider fixed chimneys and heat diffusion from a few sources: radiators could be placed beneath windows, leaving space otherwise unencumbered. The provision of basement laundry (but attic-drying) facilities in apartment buildings, and of bathrooms in all apartments, was given a lead by HSB. Lifts became a standard in apartment buildings of five floors or more.

All this affected only what was built during the 1930s; it would take many years before existing buildings were modernised in anything like the same way.

Criticism of small apartments in older buildings often emphasised their lack of daylight: those that looked only in some northerly direction or at high, nearby buildings were all too often dark and/or shadowed. Studies of the fall of sunlight became an important ele-

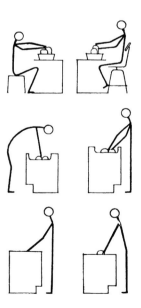

Early ergonomics, from Almqvist's book (1934) on the kitchen.

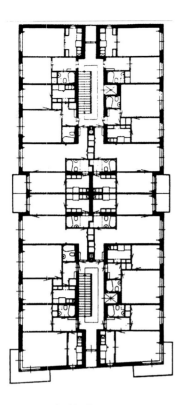

'Thick'-block apartments get light from a single direction: the Marmorn dwellings, Stockholm, by Sven Wallander, head of the HSB architects' office.

ment in urban-planning debates (see further below), but, because the economic possibilities of building apartments of bigger areas and thus better admission of daylight were small, the solution became 'thin' buildings (about 7.5 to 10 m wide) with two apartments on each floor of each staircase (a *tvåspännare*) that could each give onto two directions. When more space between buildings was also increased, sunlight conditions were better indoors and out. For economic reasons, this could be achieved mostly only on urban peripheries. These 'thin' blocks became something of a sign in the 1930s of simpler residential premises that came to characterise many areas that were then suburbs. The layouts of these apartments were often of high quality. One of the best-known areas was *Hjorthagen*, built in 1934–37 to designs by Hakon Ahlberg and Leif Reinius by the socially-concerned building contractor Olle Engkvist.

The less costly 'thick' apartment buildings were erected mainly in more central urban positions, where land prices were higher. To keep costs down, HSB often chose this form. It was the natural solution for blocks containing larger apartments, for example *Ribershus* close to a favoured bathing beach in Malmö, which was initiated and built in 1937–38 by the inventive and legendary builder Eric Sigfrid Persson.[28] The urban plan was drawn up by Eric Bülow-Hübe in cooperation with Hans Westman. The high buildings, between four and nine floors, were by Nils Einar Eriksson, Stig Dranger, David Halldén and others.

'Thick' blocks at Ribershus (1937–38), with large and small apartments, by Nils Einar Eriksson, Stig Dranger and David Helldén, Malmö, and built by Eric Sigfrid Persson. Ribershus was much praised.

Service-apartment block, John Ericssonsgatan (1935), Stockholm, the first in Sweden providing food lifts to all apartments, a child-care centre, etc.

Halldén's mezzanine apartments, and the picture windows that the builder himself invented were parts of the experiment. Ribershus won much attention and praise. Gotthard Johansson called it "the most modern residential area in Sweden";[29] Gustaf Näsström wrote of its "overwhelming impression of what values of beauty and pleasure our modern architecture can give when it is at its best."[30]

The most radical and controversial housing experiment during the 1930s was *kollektivhuset*, 'the collective house'. Alva Myrdal, who had concerned herself with questions about children and families, was a driving force in the matter. Together with the Professional Women's Club (*Yrkeskvinnornas klubb*), she took it up and wrote the first articles about it in 1932. The idea was to resolve the members' needs, and those of other working women, to look after their children and homes. Markelius had presented the idea in *acceptera* the previous year. He already knew Myrdal and the two friends addressed the question jointly, on one occasion at an open meeting arranged by the club, at which Markelius demonstrated a proposal for a large collective housing facility at Alvik.[31] Reactions were mixed, some considering this an assault on society, the family and the individual, others that it was a sensible solution to a real problem.

Eventually there were two collective houses in Stockholm: the first, by Markelius, was (and still is) on *John Ericssonsgatan*, where it opened in 1935 (see also catalogue); the sec-

Tessin Park, Stockholm, plan by Arvid Stille from a competition (1928–29): functionalistic premises laid out in classical symmetry.

Hammarbyhöjden (1930s), Stockholm: the 'houses-in-a-park' style, applied in typically wooded terrain.

ond, *Yrkeskvinnornas hus*, by Albin Stark and Hillevi Svedberg, was opened in 1939 and is still on Furusundsgatan.

Markelius' house has 57 apartments, a restaurant with food lifts serving all apartments, a children's section, a terrace and an outdoor place. Employees looked after all this, as well as the washing and cleaning. Most apartments are small, having one or two rooms, a minimal kitchen corner, and a bathroom. Its exterior is characterised by right-angled bay windows, elegantly curved balconies and ochre-yellow facade rendering. Its initial residents were mostly radical intellectuals.[32]

Novel Thoughts About Urban Planning

Giving the customary lecture on appointment as professor Gunnar Asplund addressed the theme of "our architectural understanding of space" at the Royal College of Technology (KTH in its Swedish initials) in 1931. He spoke of urban space, and made reference to Oswald Spengler's thesis in *Untergang des Abendlandes* that different cultures are characterised by different experiences of such space; that the symbol of western culture was open, endless space. For Asplund and his colleagues, this thesis was philosophical legitimation of the direction taken by modern urban planning: towards this open space, in which space, airiness and light replace closed urban space, with its monumentality for the well off, dark back yards for the poor, and unsolved, growing traffic problems. "On the basis of the old ideas", he said, "we have tried to get more light into [housing] quarters, to make their traffic flow more fluidly, and we must admit some improvement has occurred. But it has also become apparent that no satisfaction of

the demands of large towns and housing is to be expected if we hold fast to our previous architectural understanding of space, to the closed square and the space of the street, to closed space in general."[33]

Some years earlier, a novel way of thinking about urban planning had been launched in Sweden. In 1928, under the headline of 'Elementary urban building techniques', Uno Åhrén discussed the advantages, when a degree of exploitation (the residential:ground-area ratio) was high, of building high at wide intervals rather than low at close ones, because the first would give more open space between buildings; if they were parallel and well oriented, their apartments would receive the most direct sunlight. This would equalise them, unlike apartments in enclosed quarters, where mostly the smallest got the worst lighting. This view of urban planning centred on the quality of individual apartments, not open urban space. Åhrén supported his argument on, among other things, the urban-planning theories of Anton Hoenig, a German.[34]

Markelius applied these principles that year (1928) in proposed high-rise housing on Ladugårdsgärde, Stockholm. He used the German methods of measuring sunlight to gauge it very carefully; the project, which was to include 18-floor apartment blocks, came to look a bit like the high-rise one that Gropius and Hilberseimer were then realising, but it was never built. The competition for *Ladugårdsgärde* (*Tessinparken*) the following year became a break-point, at which the axiality, symmetry and enclosed yards of the 1920s were opposed by the new urban-planning ideal of openness orientated towards the sun and parallel 3–4 story blocks. When the prize board preferred the first of these, and dismissed the second, it attracted the criticism of

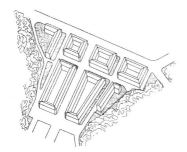

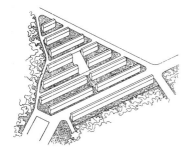

Plans before (above) and after (below) Åhrén became senior urban planner; the latter was what was built on the Söderlingska meadow, Göteborg.

the younger, radical architects. But, later, the second won more and more adherents, particular for use in outer urban areas, where degrees of exploitation were lower, allowing blocks to be only 3–4 stories high. The land between was made use of for planned playgrounds. The unpretentiousness and feeling for the natural world that can be considered to be typical of Swedish architecture characterised many such areas. Two built in Stockholm in the 1930s, *Hammarbyhöjden* and *Traneberg*, exemplify this: their light, flatly-rendered apartment blocks are located in otherwise undisturbed rocky wooded ground. The concept of 'a house in a park' got interpreted in Sweden, where natural preconditions of a site were kept as they were but used, within a constricted framework.

The new urban-planning ideology was applied in Göteborg under the direction of Uno Åhrén, appointed Senior Urban Planner there in 1932; he caused many of the proposals for planning to be altered from the enclosed quarters that formed the town's traditional pattern to parallel apartment blocks. A characteristic of the town was a three-story building on a stone ground floor with wood above: a landshövdingehus. The new urban-planning ideal showed one of its weakness in Övre Johanneberg, where six-story blocks were planned, in marked contrast to some nearby enclosed yards from the 1920s, in an open arrangement with much unused ground intended as a park. The town's housing manager added a floor onto the six, to increase returns on building costs, while no park of any sort was laid out. Novel thoughts about urban planning could clearly be misapplied.

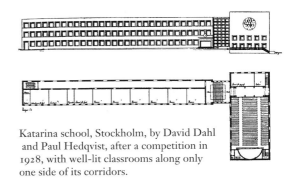

Katarina school, Stockholm, by David Dahl and Paul Hedqvist, after a competition in 1928, with well-lit classrooms along only one side of its corridors.

The open urban-planning system received some support from the urban-planning law that came into force in 1932 after fifteen years' preparation. It emphasised that an urban quarter should be planned as a whole, not by reference to site boundaries. Land use should be given, not just for streets and quarters but also for parks, and areas for traffic and sport. Industrial and residential areas should be screened from one another by protective areas. These hygienic aims had been evolving for a long time and agreed well with the new planning ideas and the division of functions and zoning they emphasised. Criticism arose when these demands were met at the expense of created urban space.

Education, Leisure, Health, Traffic

Between 1918 and 1939, important political steps were taken in Swedish education, working times and health care. School reforms were made, primarily as a result of women's stronger positions in society. An eight-hour working day and a fourteen-day holiday were enforced for most employees and health care was improved. Buildings, including those for increasing traffic, became symbols for a more modern, more democratic society proceeding towards higher welfare.

Schools

Novelties appeared in building schools. Some early examples include the indications of more modern ground plans in schools designed by G.A. Nilsson in the second and third decades of the century. In 1928, in the competition for the *Katarina School* in Stockholm, the new ideas made a conspicuous entry into the public eye: instead of the traditional 'hall school' arranged with classical symmetry, a proposal

Sveaplan girls' school (1936), Stockholm, by Nils Ahrbom and Helge Zimdal. The bodies of the buildings of these purely functionalist premises reveal their functions.

was presented for a division of functions in buildings with parts at right angles with one another, as in Nilsson's schools, but with all classrooms giving onto a south aspect so that they got good natural lighting. Paul Hedqvist, later to be something of a specialist in schools, as well as a very active architect and a consistent modernist, and David Dahl, submitted the winning proposal.

Important school reforms had been given effect in the 1920s. The position of women in society had been strengthened by the introduction of universal adult suffrage in 1921; while women had long been admitted to universities, they were admitted to colleges of technical education only in 1921, and departments of architecture began to attract them. More than anything else, the decision to admit women to higher official posts led in 1927 to a national reorganisation of schools that now permitted female students at national schools to take matriculation examinations, whereas they had previously been referred to fee-paying private schools, which were not within the means of all families. As there was resistance to admitting them to national schools for boys, it was decided to build five schools exclusively for girls in different parts of Sweden; one was to be located at *Sveaplan* in central Stockholm (see also catalogue).

A competition for it conducted in 1931 resulted in one of the most consistently designed modernistic school buildings in the country.[35] It was won a pair of young architects, Nils Ahrbom and Helge Zimdal, who had already had many competition successes but could now put their ideas into practice. Their reworked proposal that resembled the second-prize proposal by Åhrén was built and complete by 1936.

The school demonstrated a consistent application of the functionalist principles of resolving the ground plan. Its division of activities between different parts of the building was clearly decipherable from its exterior. Its entrance had an external pillared and roofed arcade to provide cover during rainy breaks between classes. An extruding, characteristically vaulted form indicated the auditorium. The long narrow section indicated the gymnastics department, with the gymnasium itself as a separate concluding volume. The classrooms, teachers' room, dining room and so on were contained in a more compact section, all extending from the glazed staircase in its centre.

The school's characteristic functionalist formal language includes its horizontal buildings, their clean-cut geometric forms, flat roofs, flat

Built of wooden elements: a summer place, Leisure Exhibition (1936), Ystad, by Erik Friberger.

rendered facades and uniform fenestration, with large south-facing glazed areas indicating classrooms and lesser areas indicating corridors facing north. Chary functional embellishments, or parts of the composition as a whole, includes the external stairs up to the roof terrace, the clocks carefully incorporated in the staircase facades, and the architecturally severe organ pipes in the glazed wall of the auditorium that are easily visible from outside.

But most of all the character and soul of the building comes from the light that floods into its staircase, auditorium, classrooms and corridors. Light has a more than functional importance: it represents commonsense and clarity, which are seldom symbolised in school buildings. The colour blue that, for some, signifies the intellect is the most important chromatic element in the school, appearing on the staircase, on the arcade pillars, on railings, and on the undersides of the auditorium seats that are visible when folded back, and on the auditorium window blinds.

The architects' office designed all the furniture and fittings, including the tables and chairs for all rooms. It introduced a freer furnishing for the classrooms: rather than fixed benches, tables and chairs could be placed as wished, which was a novelty that the press noticed and appreciated when the school was inaugurated.

Schoolchildren of the time used to take food with them from home but this school was the first in Sweden to include a 'school restaurant' arranged as a cafeteria or bar serving take-away food and milk. Propaganda for milk as a drink that would improve public

Flamman, a Göteborg cinema, by Sten Branzell, 1937. Its rounded, closed form and projecting glazed entry and stairs reveal its functions.

Draken, a Stockholm cinema, by Ernst Grönwall, 1938. Panelled in copper beech, its auditorium was one of the most beautiful of the time.

Flamman, a Stockholm cinema, by Uno Åhrén, 1930. Slender pillars and light-blue space in its auditorium exemplify early functionalism's ideals.

health had this result, as well as the establishment of milk bars as alternatives to cafes. The teachers were provided with a dining room that was furnished with the means of preparing food: many women teachers lived as boarders, without access to kitchens. The school, which also included residential premises for two caretakers, in accordance with what was then usual, was re-inaugurated in 1996 after a careful renovation.[36]

Leisure

Two-week paid holidays became established by law in Sweden in 1938. At the time a working day of eight hours was the norm for most industrial workers, but not those in agriculture, nor their wives; even so, leisure had become a factor to reckon with in the national economy. This was illuminated by the Swedish Handicraft Association's exhibition on the subject in Ystad, southern Sweden, in 1936: Hans Westman was the architect for the exhibition and Bengt Gate its director. The most remarkable of the buildings it presented was a putative leisure house by Erik Friberger: built out of wooden elements to allow for individual houses of different sizes, it stood on poles so that the owner's motorcar could be parked beneath it, and was reminiscent of Le Corbusier's Villa Savoye. Examples were erected in some parts of Sweden but the type did not catch on, perhaps because it was too special in relation to Swedish conditions.

Premises for sport built at the time include the Tennis Stadium in Stockholm (1930) by Ture Wennerholm that is a building with a consistency in design, function and form. Its technical designer, Henrik Kreuger, a professor at KTH, Stockholm, often worked with leading architects. In this instance, he designed a frame of iron arches and an interior of painted masonite, a new material derived from compressed wood fibres that had been developed in Sweden and was a favourite object in architects' experimental work. It gave a pleasant warm tone to the interior of the 115-metre long hall. This feature, together with the rhythm of the visible, repeated iron arches, the windows high up in the roof and the longitudinal balcony gave it a strong architectural character.

The popularity of summer bathing increased and even large towns opened outdoor bathing pools. An example in central Stockholm was Vanadisbadet by Paul Hedqvist in 1938: opposite a steep, natural outcrop of rock that caught the sun, he placed low, simple

and rational terrace buildings in concrete painted in light colours for changing rooms and showers; they have large glazed areas in their facades, with details in steel painted blue. Hedqvist had previously worked with bathing premises, winning a competition for one in Eskilstuna in 1930; when it was completed in 1933, it was characteristically rational and severe in his personal style.

When the talkies reached Sweden in 1930, increasing numbers of cinemas were built, but no longer palaces of the exotic. The one in Stockholm called *Flamman*, 'the Flame', by Uno Åhrén that year exhibited a festive atmosphere in its airy vaulted light-blue auditorium, with slender pillars, reflecting metal surfaces in its foyer and a flood of light from its many bare electric-light bulbs. Like many other inner-city cinemas, this one was accommodated in a large building for rented premises.

The large (1,100-seater) Draken, 'the Dragon', by Ernst Grönwall (1938) was one of the freestanding cinemas. Each of the concrete arches of its construction has a slit to let in indirect light and fresh air. Its interior having beech-wood panelling that follows the divisions of the arches, its auditorium feels a bit like a camera bellows. It is enriched by Isaac Grünewald's magnificent curtain motif of a dragon that, with the moving-dragon external neon sign, contributed to making the cinema one of the foremost of its time.

Hospitals

For many years of the 20th century, tuberculosis was a widespread endemic illness in Sweden, and numberless sanatoria had been built by 1930. Some were built later, one being the *Lung Clinic* at Uppsala (1937) by Gustaf Birch-Lindgren; later, as the disease declined, it was used by the Uppsala University Hospital and was finally torn down in 1975.[37] It had been the architecturally most extreme functionalistic building in Sweden and was related to the much bigger sanatorium at Paimio, Finland, by Alvar Aalto.

During the 1930s, hospital building took significant steps in Sweden. A task that could, more than many others, be studied and subjected to a systematic approach, it formed the subject of the first Swedish doctoral thesis in architecture: Birch-Lindgren's *Svenska lasarettsbyggnader. Modern lasarettsbyggnadskonst i teori och praktik* (1934), which surveys the building of domestic and foreign hospitals and gives clear examples of the writing of pro-

Stockholm Tennis Hall (1930) by Ture Wennerholm, 1930. Visible steel design and an interior clad in unpainted masonite, then a modernity.

Swimming baths, Eskilstuna, by Paul Hedqvist (1933): a health-and-hygiene facility of the time.

Seen beneath the railway bridge, Söder Hospital (1938–44), Stockholm, by Hjalmar Ceder-ström, overlooks the waters of Årstaviken.

Karolinska Hospital, Solna, by Carl Westman and others, 1932–40: its many buildings are characterised by their traditional brick.

grammes that grew up as a working method during the period.[38]

So far as completed hospitals are concerned, the *Karolinska* and *Söder hospitals* are the most important in principle, and biggest of the time. Despite being contemporary with one another and of about the same size (over 1,000 beds), they differ in essence, not least architecturally.

Karolinska was designed by Carl Westman, a leading Swedish national-romantic architect. A national committee (appointed in 1919) to look into building hospitals discovered a need for a university hospital and commissioned him to propose a design. He first (1925) proposed an area of Stockholm that later became a park with residential buildings, then

reworked it; applied to a larger site, in Solna, it was eventually built.

Karolinska combines two contemporary hospital principles: a concentrated block or a hospital of more dispersed pavilions. The various specialised clinics and treatment rooms are in the concentrated, central parts, and the wards are in its wings. Building began in 1932, and, when Westman died in 1936, his colleagues Sven Ahlbom and Sven Malm carried on the work, which was finished by 1940.

The architecture in brick and the traditional character of Karolinska forms a link between two important Swedish styles: the early 20th-century national romanticism and its emphasis on the effects of material, and the post-1918 folkhem style, in which similar architectural features were once again taken up and varied.[39]

The Söder Hospital is entirely different, being built between 1938 and 1944 as a product of an expressly functionalistic programme. An engineer, Hjalmar Cederström, was the architect, or organiser, of this immense project. Its designer was Hermann Imhäuser, who had come to Sweden in 1932 after working with Peter Behrens and others. The hospital was strongly concentrated into double, parallel blocks, with functions separated: one block of clinics and treatment rooms, the other of wards that occupied the five wings that each terminate in a light open general room that, facing south, have a marvellous view of the Mälaren lake in Årstaviken. The buildings' characteristically wholly geometrical volumes were originally lightened by placing windows at their corners that, when the hospital was rebuilt in the 1980s, were regrettably blocked up.

Work on Södersjukhuset can be regarded as the apogee of the attempts of Swedish 1930s functionalism to control and make systematic all the functions and measurements in the job of creating a building. Cederström's immense work of investigating and writing a programme for building the hospital outdid anything done previously in Sweden; it formed the basis for the National Commission to Rationalise and Standardise Health Care (Centrala sjukvårdsberedningen).[40] Regarded as a milestone, Södersjukhuset is depicted on the cover of Kidder Smith's *Sweden builds*, a celebrated work from the 1950s.

Traffic

Development of means of communication—primarily aeroplanes and motorcars—became a symbol of modernity and the triumph of

Built 1936, the Stockholm
Bromma aerodrome (Paul
Hedqvist) was long the largest
in Scandinavia.

Ford assembly plant (1931), Frihamnen, Stockholm,
by Uno Åhrén: a rationally planned process housed in
factually formed architecture.

When built (1933), Traneberg Bridge, Stockholm, by
Paul Hedqvist and David Dahl, was the longest single-
span concrete bridge in the world.

technology. It brought new jobs onto
architects' drawing boards.

Stockholm had a regular seaplane passenger
service but the time became ripe for a large
aerodrome: in 1934 invitations to compete for
the design of *Bromma* Aerodrome went to the
elite of Asplund, Lewerentz, Markelius, and
Hedqvist, who received the eventual commission; it was complete by 1936. Bromma was
the largest aerodrome in Scandinavia.[41] Its
main building had an iron skeleton, with
beams and outer walls in clinker concrete,
rendered with mica plaster; it was extensively
glazed, revealed its functions and, thanks to its
awnings and roof terrace, had a relaxed character. Its external factuality and rationality was
somewhat softened internally by the restaurant that extended in a beautiful curve out
over the waiting room. Hedqvist's young col-

laborator, Nils Tesch, later an architect of
importance, did more traditional work in the
following decades.

Motor traffic increased and brought new
tasks, among them the *Ford assembly plant* in
a harbour in Stockholm that Uno Åhrén
designed in 1930–31; in contrast to earlier
Ford premises, this one was clearly modernistic.[42] The bensinmack, the Swedish equivalent
of a petrol (or gas) station, was another task
for the new architectural spirit: many were
designed by architects who used the novel
architectural language to expose and emphasise their functions. What would now be
called parking garages had been built as early
as the 1920s, the largest being the *Automobil-
palatset* in Stockholm (1926) that, commissioned by the Philipsson vehicle-importing
company, which commissioned another in the

town of Jönköping in 1930, accommodated 600 motors.

Site, Time and Building

Functionalists considered that a building ought primarily to meet the demands of the time and its functions rather than those of its site or surroundings. Three examples from Göteborg in the 1930s, and the debate they aroused, illustrate this understanding and expose its nuances.

Extension of the Göteborg Court House

Before Asplund died in 1940, aged 55, he was regarded as the foremost Swedish architect of his generation; his reputation has since only increased in Sweden and other countries. Inspired, like most of his contemporaries, by modernism that acquired a Swedish tone, his work in the 1930s included his and Lewerentz' Woodland Cemetery, the 1930 Stockholm exhibition, the *Bredenberg* Department Store, Stockholm (1935), the *National Bacteriological* Laboratory, Stockholm (1937), and the extension to the *Göteborg Court House*.

His work on this commission can illustrate his entry into functionalism (see also catalogue), while no other work from his hand

generated so much controversy and criticism: an extension (completed in 1936) of a building, originally by the elder Tessin (1670s), that had been heavily restored in the 19th century. An adjoining 19th-century building was pulled down to give space for it.

In 1913, when Asplund won a competition for the commission, he began to address the central question it posed: how should the exterior of the extension relate to the existing building as well as to its central position on a central square in Göteborg, Gustaf Adolfs torg. In 1916, in an article in Arkitektur, he suggested "it is more important to follow the style of the site than [that of] the time."[43] The development of the extension illustrates both Asplund's and contemporary Sweden's changed view of the question.[44]

Asplund's 1913 proposal was to meld the old building with the new into a similarly styled unity that had an expression of weight and stability that accorded with the national-romantic ideal of the time. The building has a uniformly flat pilastered facade.

By 1920, his felt the mass of his first proposal was too much for the site. To reduce its weight and the dominance, and to give it the lighter character and proportions of 1920s classicism, he retained the look of the old building, while its extension became adapted and freestanding, formed in accordance with that of the old one, and with its own main entry being subordinated.

During the rest of the 1920s and into the

Asplund's summer place (1937) on Lisön, a Stockholm skerry. A traditional pitched roof and wooden panelling helped his delicately treated, late-1930s functionalist house fit well into a marine landscape.

Göteborg Court House, with Asplund's extension (1936) that after a long design history expresses contemporary style perhaps more than a sense of place.

1930s, he developed this theme, letting his assistants try variously to adapt it to, but not directly to copy, the old building's symmetry, fenestration, rhythm, embellishments and the roof springing.[45] A variant in 1934 was to lengthen the old building and repeat its facade motif, but the dominating, centrally located entry of the old building unbalanced the proposed lengthened version.

In the ultimate, built proposal, he got a grip on this asymmetric quality: letting the unchanged, old building dominate, he distinguished its extension with a clear identity of its own. Thus he indicated the right of contemporary architecture to express itself in circumstances that include traces of the architecture of former times.

The extension has a steel framework, with horizontal beams of steel and concrete slabs. Built together with the main building, it is entered through the same entrance. Its flat rendered facade has a horizontal relief as its only embellishment. Its floors, vertical divisions and coloration are adapted to the old building, but its windows are square and recessed, and it has no ground floor or roof projection. Its form emphasises the impression of a flat-sided cube, overtly contrasting with the older, articulated building. Despite some adaptation to its site, the extension had mostly met the demands of the time and of its functions.

Asplund's means of building something new in old surroundings was not unique; rather the opposite: similar examples exist in contemporary work, one being Yngve Ahlbom's and Nils Sterner's winning entry to a competition in 1935 for the Halmstad Court House in the town about 160 km south of Göteborg: it proposed a openly modern building in the main square next to a timber-frame building. As with Asplund's extension in Göteborg, this new building has its own identity, while much care has been devoted to causing its volume and proportions to suit its position.[46]

The reactions to the Göteborg extension were powerfully negative, some of the newspaper headlines being "a crime", a disgusting "funkis box", "tragic", a "catastrophe".[47] A professor of art history, Axel Romdahl, considered the facade "irredeemably mistaken", but appreciated the interior of the building even more, an opinion that was shared by many.[48]

The old building had been partly rebuilt internally, and its own entry became that of the two. Internally, they are brought together around a shared courtyard that, in the extension, turns into a large open hall lit by daylight

from the staircase in the south facade and through skylights. This hall, well lit and airy, beautifully lit and with furnishings and fittings in wood, is among the foremost interior spaces created in Sweden in the 1930s. Although the building's business is serious, it feels a relaxed place: through its warm tone of timber, its interior points towards a functionalism of finer nuances. Its court and other rooms also possess these qualities. Carl Axel Acking was Asplund's assistant as interior designer on the project.

Theatre and Concert Hall

Another building in Göteborg illustrates how site, tradition and modernism can meet: the *town theatre* of Göteborg by Carl Bergsten. As a commission, it began in the late 1920s; it was built complete by 1934. Its precondition was to fit into the axial composition of the Götaplatsen square that had a large fountain and statue by Milles in its centre, the art museum on high ground to the south; the projected theatre would face a projected concert hall to the west.[49]

In the two preceding decades, Bergsten had done much creative work, and, in his more modernistic buildings, he had retained a highly personal feeling for unity and details. In its early version, his theatre had a look of a Venetian palace, but he reworked it into the more severe classicism with strong modernistic elements that the completed building exhibits. In its facade, giving onto the square, its pillars alternate in style between modernistic and

Asplund's Göteborg Court House extension, interior: the warm tone of its wood did much to make it one of the 1930s' finest public interiors in Sweden.

Chair by Carl Axel Acking for the Court House: soft but strong forms, with sculpturally formed metal fittings.

Göteborg Concert Hall (1935), by Nils Einar Eriksson. The symmetry and arrangement of pillars of the exterior adapt it to its classicistic surroundings.

Göteborg Concert Hall: Swedish modernism is finely exemplified by the warm tones of the wood-panelled interior that acoustic demands required.

stylised classical with capitals. Beneath them, its entry is glazed and more purely modernistic. Inside, in a fascinatingly complex interplay of opposites, tradition meets modernism, extravagance simplicity, and caryatids patterned velour wallpaper. Although Bergsten is not a man whose work can be assigned to any one particular type, his interior of the Göteborg theatre is one of the very few Swedish buildings to exemplify Art Deco. For Swedish opinion of the 1930s that took modernism as its yardstick, the theatre building appeared to be an uncertain, bewildered creation, and Gotthard Johansson deemed it to be "a modern theatre of an unmodern type."[50]

The site across the square from the theatre was designated for a *concert hall* when, in 1931, a competition was announced to resolve its design. A heated debate then broke out over the task of building on a sensitive site. Critics thought the prize committee included so many traditionally-minded people that it could not put forward younger, radical points of view. Many architects simply refrained from competing on account of the composition of

Carl Bergsten begun his Göteborg town theatre in the late 1920s. Complete by 1934, it mixed modern and classicist elements in a rare Swedish example of Art Deco.

the prize committee, and those who did compete were considered to have accommodated their proposals far too closely to the committee's requirements with respect to the site.[51] The winner, Ville Tommos, worked for the KF Architects' Office, but, after a further competition, the proposal by Nils Einar Eriksson that had come second was commissioned; it was built by 1935 (see also catalogue).

Eriksson, one of Asplund's closest assistants on the 1930 Stockholm exhibition and a overt proponent of functionalism, emphasised in his concert hall its adaptation to the entirety of the Götaplatsen Square. Modernistic internally but with classicistic elements externally, primarily in its marble facade's proportions and capital-less colonnade, the concert hall was clearly linked to the nearby art museum and theatre. Eriksson formulated this dualism by calling his work "a crab in a rectangle": the container being the four-cornered shape of the square and the hall adapted to it, the 'crab' being the hall itself as his architectural answer to the technical task.[52]

A critical comment by Eriksson's younger, radical colleague, Helge Zimdal, was that the concert hall was an unhappy contradiction between its location and the commission to build it, and that the compulsive monumentality of the Square stifled any chance of letting the concert hall become an expressive addition to the image of the town. But Zimdal did think its interior had been wholly derived from Eriksson's resolution of the commission, and expressed his admiration for the way in which audiences move through the foyer and up the stairs, for the great auditorium, and its and the other spaces' beautiful interiors. "This monumental effect has been achieved", he wrote "without falling back on immense or imposing means. On the contrary, every detail has started from human dimensions. The actual form of the building has for that matter been wholly and completely subordinated to the main theme. One finds no interest here for any obviously naked construction."[53]

Unlike Asplund's extension to the Court House, Eriksson's concert hall was well received in Göteborg, being liked for the dualism that Zimdal criticised and because its architect spared the town "the pedagogical nudism that calls for architecture that must, if it is to honest, expose not merely its flesh but its very bones."[54]

A Maturing Functionalism

During the 1930s, Swedish functionalism developed from orthodoxy towards nuances, even while following its guiding stars of rationality and factuality. The expressive multiplicity that exhibited itself on the European continent was hardly represented in Sweden. But straight Swedish lines and cubic Swedish formal language did get softened, forms did become more organic, colours got warmer, and chilly-looking steel fittings and details were done in wood that could be formed and express nuances of feeling.

In the Nordic countries, primarily Alvar Aalto is associated with this freer, more organic functionalism, which he developed to perfection. Asplund, too, expressed a freer formal language in his care for details and treatment of materials, and, in his later work, sought to return to the basic elements of architecture: the architecture of his last work, the Chapel of the Holy Cross, at the Woodland Cemetery, is of a timeless beauty.

Byggnadsförenings House, Stockholm

An early sign of advancing from cold modernism to something less chill and infused with feelings was Markelius' *Lindén House*, Västerås, a town west of Stockholm. Its ground plan is as open and clear as any previous work, but, in contrast to other buildings' the exteriors that were generally rendered in some light colour, its facades oiled fir gave the house a warm, living feeling; the shiny timber emphasised its closed form and rounded, apse-like staircase.

It can be related to Aalto's much later (1938) *Mairea House*.

The interior form of Markelius' building for *Stockholms byggnadsförening* in 1937, is the Swedish example that gets closest to a modernism closely related to Aalto's. Markelius was commissioned to do it after twice winning competitions in 1934.[55] The job was for a building-trade association of individuals and organisations that had been formed in 1848, once the antiquated Swedish guild system of trade control had been ended by legislation. Having been its secretary and then chairman in 1928–32, Markelius knew the association had long wanted premises of its own and also knew what they should be.

His building has an exterior of toned-down restraint characteristic of Swedish modernism; larger fenestration in its light, rendered facade reveals the presence of the association's top-floor club premises. An asymmetrically placed balcony, a flagpole for functionally flying the association's flag, and a representation of its emblem together provide a element of restrained external decoration. Within, Markelius created a warm lively atmosphere on the upper floors that the association occupied (it rented out the others). The top floor but one contains the hall, restaurant, kitchen and offices in an open arrangement. A staircase reaches the top-floor conference room, auditorium and beautifully spacious club room with a vaulted roof making the best use of the building's permitted height; his inspiration for this probably came from Aalto's newspaper building (*Turun Sanomat*, Turku, 1928). Reached by a staircase from the clubroom, a library over the conference room gives onto a small roof terrace. As in so many of his buildings, Markelius created views over the interior and of the surroundings, as well as rooms with character through an open arrangement of rooms, staircases and a mezzanine floor.

Form and material meet most elegantly where the mahogany walls of the auditorium meet the white rendered vaulted ceiling in a soft elegant line. Markelius also used cedarwood, as well as mahogany, in the walls; and, in details and furniture, more cedar, as well as maple, teak, birch, ash and oak. In a feature reminiscent of Aalto's 1935 library at Viborg, he used birch plywood for an undulating, perforated false ceiling in the restaurant that conceals the ventilation. The interiors of the rooms are characterised by warm chromatic tones and a soft interplay of lines.

The building has a steel-and-concrete framework that was designed by Stig Ödeen. Thanks to this, when the building suffered

House (1932) in Västerås, by Sven Markelius: softly organic architecture in wood that Aalto's later work would consummate.

Markelius' Swedish Building
Association premises (1937)
are open, have an elegantly
vaulted roof line and wood-
panelled rooms, giving its
interior an intimate but airy
character.

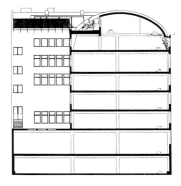

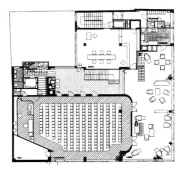

Plan and section of the above,
with club and meeting rooms,
auditorium and a library.

severe damage from a bomb explosion on
New Year's Eve 1982, it could be restored
almost to its original condition.

Karlskoga Town Hall

Functionalists underwent a testing time in the
late 1930s, against a background that included
the criticism of Asplund's Court House extension in Göteborg. In a 1937 editorial piece in
Byggmästaren, readers were advised that the
public at large, being often critical of the new
architecture, preferred work by Ragnar Östberg and Carl Malmsten: "The old architecture had a more intimate contact with the
people as a whole than the modern has, which
has isolated itself in aesthetic respects, where
it has lost itself in spiritual masturbation. We
have reason to look about us and to look for
deeper soil. To do so means neither a step
backwards nor self-effacement, at most a little
self-conquest. It means finding a counterpart
that shall be conquered. Conquered with
work, with houses that are both better and
more beautiful, and—why not?—with some
exhibitions, persuasion, and propaganda."[56]
Although Sune Lindström's editorial formulations were careful, they were clear signs of
the time, for he was a convinced functionalist
with a socialist engagement, who had also
studied briefly at the Bauhaus in Dessau. He
was also at work on the town hall, and a hotel
and its restaurant, at *Karlskoga*, the home of
the Nobel industry group, which was completed in 1940.[57]
In this project, he abandoned the modernist
principle of letting each function have its own
form and expression: on a central site on the

main square, he provided a unified form in
which to locate premises for administration,
formal entertainment, parties and residence.
Through his choice of materials for the facade
giving onto the square—red brick in Flemish
bonding, tarred wooden shingles from Gryt-
hyttan, light sprayed rendering, lead sheeting
and local slate—he made clear the building's
adaptation to its location. Its volumes are
restrained and uniform, with exception for the
restaurant that extended from the main block
and the playfully undulating roof over its
baldachin-like entrance. A pillared aperture
beneath its upper floors linked the beautifully
arranged internal courtyard with the square.
Paving stones used in this courtyard, and its
bricked facade, continued into the lobby of the
hotel. This strong tactile material effect was
reinforced by the robust form of decoratively
formed details.

The impression made by the building is
far from that of early-1930s work in light
rendered abstract volumes with subordinated
details, even if Lindström upheld the planning
principles of functionalism in links between
rooms and studies of functions. The whole
indicates the transition to the architecture of
the 1940s that was characterised by a continued development of the working methods of
functionalism, expressed through a traditionally oriented formal language with regional
associations. Thinking of the Danish equivalent that had strong roots in Danish building traditions, Kaj Fisker coined the expression "the functional tradition".

Before Lindström's work was completed in
Karlskoga, the 1939–45 European war had
broken out and Swedish building work had
stopped. Sweden remained neutral, but German freight trains used the Swedish railway
system. Swedish winters were as cold as ever,
or colder, while Swedish needs of coal were
now dependent on commercial links with
Germany. The chill spread, in more senses
than one.

Town hall and hotel (1940), Karlskoga, by Sune Lindström. It combined traditional and regional elements with
functionalistic working methods.

NOTES

¹ *Socialdemokraten*, 13 July 1931.
² Uno Åhrén, "Brytningar", *Svenska slöjdföreningens årsbok* 1925.
³ In his *CIAM-Dokumente 1928–1939* (Birkhäuser, 1979), Martin Steinmann names as "Delegiert" Markelius (1928–31 & 1933), Sundbärg (1929), Åhrén (1930–31, 1937–39) & Sundahl (1933).
⁴ *Alfred Roth* (Waser Verlag, 1985).
⁵ Berqvist & Michélsen (eds.), *Josef Frank, arkitektur* (1994).
⁶ Eva Rudberg, *Uno Åhrén* (1981), 81 ff.
⁷ Osvald Almqvist, "Nyare kraftverksanläggningar", *Byggmästaren* (1929), 73.
⁸ Gustaf Näsström, *Svensk funktionalism* (1930), 105.
⁹ Elias Cornell, *Ny svensk byggnadskonst* (1950), 22 ff.
¹⁰ Björn Linn, *Osvald Almqvist. En arkitekt och hans arbete* (1960).
¹¹ Eva Rudberg, *Sven Markelius, arkitekt* (1989).
¹² "Konserthustävlan i Hälsingborg", *Byggmästaren* (1926), 117 ff.
¹³ Janne Ahlin, *Sigurd Lewerentz arkitekt* (1985), 147 ff.
¹⁴ Among other sources, see *Byggmästaren* (1930); *Huvudkatalog Stockholmsutställningen* 1930; & P.G. Råberg, *Funktionalistiskt genombrott* (1972).
¹⁵ Gregor Paulsson, "Stockholmsutställningens program", *Svenska slöjdföreningens tidskrift* (1928).
¹⁶ Gotthard Johansson, "Funktionalistisk vernissage", *Svenska Dagbladet*, Stockholm, 16 May 1930.
¹⁷ Oscar Reutersvärd, *Otto G. Carlsund i fjärrperspektiv* (1988).
¹⁸ *Katalog över bostadsavdelningen, Stockholmsutställningen 1930*.
¹⁹ Eva Rudberg, "Rakkniven och lösmanschetten, Stockholmsutställningen 1930 och Slöjdstriden", in Kerstin Wickman (ed.), *Formens rörelse* (1995).
²⁰ Råberg (1972), 174.
²¹ Viking Göransson, "Funk- och nationalism", *Stockholms Dagblad*, 1 October 1930.
²² Råberg (1972), 176.
²³ Morton Shand, "Stockholm 1930", *Architectural Review*, August 1930, 67.
²⁴ Lisa Brunnström, *Den rationella fabriken* (1990), 189.
²⁵ Brunnström (1990), 187–188.
²⁶ *Kooperativa förbundets arkitektkontor 1925–35*, (1935).
²⁷ "Lumafabriken i Stockholm", 1937, 68 ff.
²⁸ Ulla Hårde, *Eric Sigfrid Persson* (1986).
²⁹ *Svenska Dagbladet*, 25 August 1938.
³⁰ *Stockholmstidningen* 7 August 1938.
³¹ See eg Claes Caldenby & Åsa Walldén, *Kollektivhus* (1979), 176 ff.
³² Rudberg (1989) 76, 83.
³³ E.G. Asplund, "Vår arkitektoniska rumsuppfattning", *Byggmästaren* (1931), 206.
³⁴ Uno Åhrén, "Elementär stadsbyggnadsteknik", *Byggmästaren* 1928, 129 ff.
³⁵ Bengt Romare, "Tävling om högre allmänt läroverk för flickor i Stockholm", *Byggmästaren* (1932), 30 ff; & Nils Ahrbom & Helge Zimdal, "Högre allmänt läroverk för flickor i Stockholm", *Byggmästaren* (1936), 341 ff.
³⁶ *Arkitektur*, 2/1996.
³⁷ Anders Åman, *Om den offentliga vården* (1976), 269.
³⁸ Åman (1976), 389.
³⁹ Claes Caldenby, "Byggnadskonst och läkekonst", in Per Bjurström (ed.), *Konsten på Karolinska sjukhuset* (1997).
⁴⁰ Åman (1976), 279.
⁴¹ "Arkitekttävling om Flygstationsanläggning vid Bromma", *Byggmästaren* (1934), 197 ff; & Paul Hedqvist, "Byggnaderna vid Bromma flygfält", *Byggmästaren* (1936), 291 ff.
⁴² Rudberg (1981), 123.
⁴³ E.G. Asplund, "Aktuella arkitektoniska faror för Stockholm, hyreshusen", *Arkitektur* (1916), 130.

Town hotel (1940), Karlskoga, by Sune Lindström. Powerful effects from its materials contrast strongly with the flat surfaces from the early 1930s.

⁴⁴ "Göteborgs rådhus", *Byggmästaren* (1939), 157 ff; & Hakon Ahlberg, *Gunnar Asplund arkitekt* (1943) 72 ff.
⁴⁵ Christina Engfors, *E.G. Asplund, arkitekt, vän och kollega* (1990), 28, 30.
⁴⁶ "Halmstad rådhus", *Byggmästaren* (1939), 177 ff.
⁴⁷ Ahlberg (1943), 75.
⁴⁸ Claes Caldenby, "När kom modernismen till Göteborg?", *Kulturmiljövård*, 1-2/1996, 45.
⁴⁹ "Göteborgs nya stadsteater", *Byggmästaren* (1929), 141 ff; & Carl Bergsten, "Stadsteatern i Göteborg", *Byggmästaren* 1934, 191 ff.
⁵⁰ Caldenby (1996), 44.
⁵¹ Harry Kjellkvist, "Tävlingen om konserthus i Göteborg", *Byggmästaren* (1931), 179.
⁵² Claes Caldenby (ed.), *Göteborgs konserthus, ett album* (1992), 20.
⁵³ Helge Zimdal, "Göteborgs konserthus", *Byggmästaren* (1935), 194.
⁵⁴ Caldenby (1996), 45.
⁵⁵ Sven Markelius, "Stockholms byggnadsförening", *Byggmästaren* (1937), 283 ff.
⁵⁶ Sune Lindström, "Arkitektens anpassning", *Byggmästaren* (1939), 1.
⁵⁷ Sune Lindström, "Stadshus och stadshotell i Karlskoga", *Byggmästaren* (1940), 329 ff.

Baronbackarna, Örebro, 1951, by Per Ekholm and Sidney White, who assumed housewives would, while doing the kitchen work, keep an eye on the kids in the bath.

Building the Welfare of the Folkhemmet 1940–60

EVA RUDBERG

The People's Home (Folkhemmet) that Per Albin Hansson, the Social-Democratic leader, had spoken of in the 1920s, and, as prime minister, had begun to build in the 1930s, was completed after 1945 in the form of the Swedish Welfare State. Once its ideological foundations had been laid, actually building this novel society was the definitive matter in hand. Housing needs were all the more acute on account of an absence of building in 1939–45 and, later, of migration from the land. In 1930, larger and smaller towns had been home to a registered 32 % of the population: by 1950 47 % lived there.

Worked out by Ernst Wigforss, Gunnar and Alva Myrdal and others by 1944, the Labour Movement's postwar programme was the ideological starting point for Social Democratic policy. Its main goals were full employment, fair shares for all and a higher standard of living, as well as greater efficiency and better democracy in industry. These were also the starting points for postwar social planning and the national investigations that were now appointed to look into the housing question, localisation, public-sector power over land and possibilities of steering the planning of its use.[1] This radical and farsighted programme was achieved in part, primarily in respect of housing policy and the increased roles and greater strength of municipalities.

Collective resolutions of individuals' problems had deep roots in Swedish society, a striving towards a loyalty that found partial expression in the cooperative movement. When the neighbourhood idea took root in Swedish urban planning, there was already a stratum receptive to ideas of collective services in housing areas. A national investigation, The Collective-Dwelling Committee (*bostadskollektiva kommittén*), was appointed in the late 1940s to assess the need: a characteristically Swedish manner of proceeding.[2]

Political decisions having led to reforms in schools, and in care of the elderly and general health, extensive building work became necessary. The reforms in 1952 of municipalities created needs for new centralised municipal administrative and related buildings, besides necessitating the building of indoor and outdoor sports facilities, swimming baths, schools, libraries and other premises for meetings. These new centres needed or attracted commercial and industrial enterprises, besides needing to be linked to others by new and improved roads. Capital and labour for building were in high demand, and, although a very great deal of building was undertaken after 1945, the need for buildings remained greater than what could be supplied.

Good Housing

As if an unwelcome inheritance from former decades, but worsened by conditions in 1939–45, the housing question remained central. To counter speculation on account of shortages, rent-control legislation was introduced in 1942, and, as its predecessor had done in 1914–18, the government found justification for action in the need economically to support the building of residential premises. The difference was that this could now, in the 1940s, be developed into a large housing-policy programme.

Once the Housing-Social Commission that had begun work during the 1930 had made its final reports in 1945 and 1946, decisions in 1947 by the riksdag established the social goals of Swedish housing policy: that the whole

A bill posted in Swedish railway stations in 1946 to warn presumptive travellers of the housing shortage in Stockholm.

	1945	1960
Flats in built-up areas (millions)	1,3	2,0

STANDARD	%	%
1 R+kitchen or smaller	44	30
2 R+kitchen	30	31
3 R+kitchen or larger	26	39
Central heating	59	82
Bath	40	71
WC	52	81
Water/Sewage	83	97
Refrigerator	15	70
Gas/Electric cooker	50	82

CRAMPED DWELLING (eg >2 people/room)	%	%
Households	21	8
Residents	29	13
Children	45	21

In the 15 years after 1945, Swedish housing standards were raised substantially: dwellings became more numerous, less cramped and better equipped, especially as to heating and hygiene.

population should be furnished with good, hygienic housing at reasonable prices. The intention was to achieve a high, even housing standard for which rents would not exceed 20% of an industrial worker's income. This implied taking exception to cheap solutions that would entail lower standards for those with low incomes. Special remedies, such as 'child-rich houses', were terminated. Unlike most other countries at the time, which provided what was called social or low-cost housing that often led to segregation and new slums, Sweden embraced the principle of not distinguishing special low-income groups.

Thus, to reach the agreed housing goals, provision was made for nationally-available loans and interest subsidies with respect to building dwellings, as well as rent assistance for pensioners and low-income families with children. But, as had been pointed out in the 1930s, housing policy had another side to it: it became a means of regulating industrial activity, in that central-government stimulation of housing could be regulated by reference to labour-market considerations. Should unemployment threaten, building could be stimulated, while, should labour demand rise, this stimulation could be reduced.

To overcome the huge post-1945 housing shortage, and also create jobs, the riksdag approved a major building programme that was followed but less extensively than had been intended. Things were not as they had seemed: the unemployment that had been feared became a real shortage of labour in the export industries, which also needed capital to compete on the international market that, partly with the help of Marshall Aid, was being built up in Europe. In the domestic competition for capital and labour, the building industry was held back in favour of the export industries, and the housing shortage persisted for decades.

But the new housing policy was already determined. The housing companies that were given priority, in the form of national loans, were the non-profit-making ones owned by municipalities, called allmännyttiga. A few had existed in the 1930s, but most originated after 1945. These companies' jobs were to build and administer without profit. An important motive was that they should furnish even economically weak groups with dwellings. Private-sector companies could choose to refrain from renting their property, for example to families with children, but these municipal companies did not.

As well as these municipal housing companies, those of the cooperative movement, of

which HSB and the Cooperative Housing Union (Svenska Riksbyggen) that had been founded since the 1930s were the largest, were entitled to official loans, if on less favourable terms. Still less favourable terms were offered to private-sector housing companies that had earlier accounted for the greatest part of newly-built dwellings. The political aim was to cause new production to be made by public-sector companies that would thus set prices. On account of this national housing policy, the number of municipal housing companies increased markedly from the early 1950s.

Cramped living quarters was still the largest problem. In 1945, of urban and small-town rented accommodation, 44% comprised one room with a kitchen, or less; while a further 30% comprised two rooms and a kitchen (see table). The definitive goal of the national housing-social policy was an occupancy of no more than two persons to a room, excluding kitchens. A family of four should thus be offered at least two rooms and a kitchen, and it was thought economically possible to achieve family dwellings of, on average, 2 or 3 rooms and a kitchen. This may now seem a modest goal but conditions were then such that it was a major improvement.

Because the size of such accommodation was so limited, it was thought to be impossible to relieve the housing shortage through building small houses: apartment blocks thus became the most usual form, which is a partial explanation for the phenomenon that, in international terms, proportions of apartments are so high in Sweden, despite the country's low population density and its access to large areas of land.

Housing Norms

To guarantee that what was built with subsidized official national loans was of good quality and could retain its creditworthiness, loans were made subject to norms and regulations that, over the years, have been decisive for new housing in Sweden and its high average standards, which are among the highest in the world.

These norms and regulations included demands concerning fire and its resistance but also the functions of furnishing, relationships between rooms that were derived from the knowledge possessed by HSB and other large housing companies, as well as the research begun in Osvald Almqvist's studies of kitchens in the 1920s. This research was further developed during the 1930s and 1940s by the Homes' Committee (Hemkommitté) of the women's organisations, by the Swedish Handicraft Association, the Swedish Architects' National Association (*Svenska Arkitekters Riksförbund*) (founded in 1936), and the Homes' Research Institute (*Hemmens forskningsinstitut*), founded in 1944. Housework and looking after children being regarded as exclusively something for women, it was revolutionary not merely to take it seriously but to base the planning of housing on it.

Founded in 1948, the National Housing Board (*Bostadsstyrelsen*) was responsible for the national norms and approving loans for housing. In 1954, it published a booklet, *God bostad*, that set out the norms, but, in 1942, when the national-loan system had begun, the town architect of Stockholm, Sigurd Westholm, had compiled a collection of norms that was called 'the bible according to Westholm'.

Continuously revised, the 1954 version remained the basis of Swedish housing standards until the 1990s, when the system of national loans was discontinued; by that time it had become less a text for assessing the suitability of a proposed loan than one that addressed the quality of housing. Its assumption was a household was normal that comprised a family with children. It prescribed the minimum dimensions of rooms and required that plans for housing should indicate how dwellings should be furnished. It emphasised the need, in a kitchen, of a place to eat meals; on the premise that any room in an apartment or house should be capable of use as a bedroom, it denied approval for any room that could be treated as a passage.

After 1945, the efforts that were made to improve housing achieved success. It was decisive that economic activity, and levels of employment, and wages and salaries, increased rapidly. In the 15 years ending in 1960, dwellings increased in number by about one third: from 2 million to 2.7 million. In addition, they were roomier, better equipped, much warmer and more hygienic, and fewer people lived under cramped conditions. As a proportion of the total, the smallest apartments were fewer, and those with 3 or more rooms and a kitchen were much more numerous (see table). Even so, the housing shortage continued to be severe, and demands for better housing were strengthened by households' essentially improved economic conditions.

A counterweight or a complement to the subsidised public-sector housing companies that are described above, the Association for Dwellings in Industry (*Industriens bostadsförening*) had appeared in 1945. This organisation was formed by industrial companies joint-

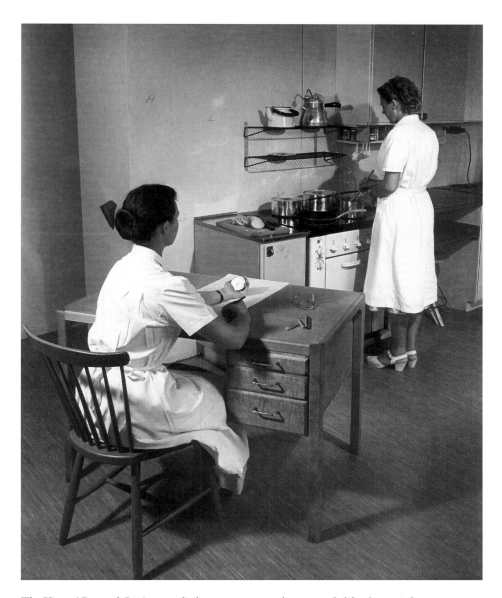

The Homes' Research Institute studied measurements and space needed for domestic functions, as in this test kitchen from 1945.

ly that wished to follow the Swedish tradition of 'the works' providing housing for its employees. With some dating from the 18th century, or even earlier, examples still exist in many, often remote, rural places in Sweden.

The Association was led for many years by its first director, the architect Jöran Curman, who had drawn up and published a report, *Industriens arbetarebostäder*, on national housing stock in 1944. As director, he succeeded in one of his ambitions: to mediate good architectural competence to the companies in question. Thus an otherwise surprisingly number of smaller industrial centres now contain much good or really excellent work by many leading architects, including Ernst Grönwall (Domnarvet, Korsnäs), Backström & Reinius (Bofors), Ralph Erskine (Storviks Hammarby, Gyttorp), Sven Ivar Lind (Väja at Kramfors), Artur von Schmalensee (Bjuv), and Jöran Curman (Uddeholm, Nykroppa).

Row house (1948) for Nykroppa Ironworks, by Jöran Curman, who was an advocate of kitchens with eating places.

Baronbackarna, Örebro: plan. 'All-rooms' were introduced as combined eating and living rooms, while kitchens were made smaller.

Baronbackarna, Örebro, by Per Ekholm and Sidney White, 1951. The meanders of its overall plan enclosed larger and smaller courtyards.

Experimental Apartments

Alongside the establishment of building norms, the layouts of buildings were developed through experimental apartments.[3] The flexible apartment plan, achieved through the use of moveable walls, was a way to let individual tenants decide how they wanted to use the space they rented. The idea had been discussed at the Standard 1934 Exhibition, and was tried out in practice in an apartment block by Tage & Anders William-Olsson at Järnbrott, Göteborg, in 1951: that a family, at different periods of its life, would use its apartment in different ways. In practice, it proved to be so to only a very limited extent.

Another form of flexibility was to provide, conjoined with an apartment, a room that, having its own entrance, could be rented out so as to meet the continuing demand for urban housing consequent on post-1945 urbanisation. Such 'bachelors' rooms' would, it was thought, be transitional.

Another experiment produced allrummet, the 'all-room'. A competition in 1951 for the *Baronbackarna* housing area in Örebro was to create possibilities for more rooms on a limited area by minimising kitchens and making walls moveable. One of the entries, from Per Ekholm and Sidney White, was for an allrum. A housewife doing the kitchen part of her

work could look through a pane of glass in an internal wall to see that a child in the bathroom was bathing, and, through a well-placed kitchen window, that all was well in the playground outside. The 'all-room', placed immediately next to the kitchen, was an attempt to get a family and its members to refrain from treating one of their rooms as 'best', and using it relatively seldom, but to make better use of the space they had.

It was supposed that they would use their 'all-room' for all purposes, including eating meals, doing homework, sewing, reading, and generally being social; but existing living patterns persisted. Later investigations showed that meals were eaten in the kitchen, but in shifts, while the putative 'all-room' was furnished as if it were the 'best room' The conclusion here, as in other cases, was that kitchens should be big enough to provide space for meals round tables, where families could also socialise.[4]

Housing Areas

The plans of the 1930s for parallel apartment blocks (lamellhus) had striven to get a maximum of daylight into the apartments: the key words were open urban plans, light and greenery, but the frequently schematic applications of these well-intentioned ambitions aroused

Caricature of monotonous parallel arrangements of blocks being sown by the Stockholm housing director, Axel Dahlberg. Svenska Dagbladet, a Stockholm daily paper, 20 March 1939.

criticism during the 1940s, not least from the urban planners themselves. The new ideal became roominess and variation. Striving for sheltered places out of doors was natural in the chilly, windy Swedish climate. The natural surroundings in and around the apartment-block areas that seemed undisturbed country-side to some seemed sometimes to sceptics to be neither one thing nor the other.

Housing began to be built instead around enclosed back yards that were now to be airy and green, and many housing areas built in the 1940s and 1950s are distinguished by their generously sized and now-mature back yards that made good use of the terrain and the trees that were growing there, rocky scars and other natural features. The characteristically manual building methods of the time made this sort of thing feasible, but realising it and planting suitable material called for the engaged professional skills of landscape architects and gardeners. This was another theme in which the guideline of functionalism for honesty with material—the terrain and its vegetation—was crucial. Many areas thus acquired a character that came to be regarded as typically Swedish.

Criticism of the parallel rows of apartment blocks led as a result to more varied urban plans, of which perhaps the best-known development was a *stjärnhus* or honeycomb variant, by Sven Backström and Leif Reinius. Having started a joint office in 1936, they were soon among the leaders of Swedish urban planning. They wanted to enrich the formal language of Swedish functionalism and reinforce its impressions of space.[5]

At Gröndal in Stockholm (see also catalogue), where the first honeycomb buildings were erected in 1944–46, their starting point was to achieve a more economical variant of the tvåspännare layout of two apartments on each staircase landing of a 'thin' or lamell apartment building. They angled it to make room for a third apartment on each landing (a *trespännare*), which created a star or honeycomb pattern. Depending on the lengths of such buildings, and how they were located in the terrain, they formed larger or smaller intermediate spaces protected from the wind, and, overall, a varied urban plan. The buildings could also be formed as point blocks. Generally, they retained the good lighting conditions, with light from two or three directions, of the 'thin' apartment building: a valuable quality in a Swedish winter landscape.

Backström and Reinius presented the idea they were realising at Gröndal in Byggmästaren 1945–46. The terrain at Gröndal was a difficult, rocky site facing north and exposed to the wind; a sulphuric-acid factory had lain there and destroyed much of the earth and its vegetation. These difficulties gave birth to the idea of resolving them by placing these honeycomb buildings on this sloping ground, which was easy to do, so that they also gave shelter from the wind as well as good internal lighting.

What was built was a mixture of continuous, long buildings and low point blocks. The work was commissioned and built by Olle Engkvist,

Star house, by Sven Backström and Leif Reinius, 1945: plan. Set in a courtyard, it had three 'narrow' apartments on each floor.

Star-house dwelling area, Gröndal, by Backström and Reinius, 1946: exemplary dwellings with views towards central Stockholm.

Terraced apartments and point blocks, Gröndal, Stockholm, by Backström and Reinius, 1946–52. Besides star houses, this area contained other, equally carefully studied layouts.

Danviksklippan, Stockholm, by Backström and Reinius, 1945: plan. Block with four corner apartments and a small one facing in only one direction.

the presence of the whole Gröndal area which included a combined cinema and theatre.

This innovative set of buildings made Gröndal something of a finger-post on the way taken by Sweden after 1945. Honeycomb layouts were copied in Sweden and abroad. Domestic work was done by Backström and Reinius (at *Rosta* in Örebro, and at *Sickla*), by Torsten Roos and Gunnar Lindman (at *Mellanheden* in Malmö in 1953) and others.

Backström and Reinius made another contribution to urban planning and the building of housing with their housing area at *Danviksklippan* in Stockholm; including the first high point blocks of housing built in Sweden, it was completed in 1945. The terrain at the site was a steep, uneven scar of bedrock, a typical feature of many rural and urban Swedish landscapes that was then difficult to build on. Development in blasting techniques in the early 1940s, however, resolved this difficulty and, in combination with the small site area needed for a point block, made it economical to use such a site. Thus this form of building was a response to a specific terrain.

The nine point blocks each had eight floors, which was the permitted limit for a building containing only one lift; the staircases received no natural lighting, which contribution would have contradicted building regulations had not an exception been made for these blocks. Layouts varied as between the houses. Each floor contained four or five apartments. Each of the four occupied a corner position and could thus get daylight from two cardinal points of the compass; where there was a fifth apartment, it was smaller than the others but faced south.

The exteriors of the blocks were given rough-cast rendering and painted in strong earthy reds, greens and browns. With their

with whom both architects had worked previously. Their skill and inventiveness, and his readiness to make experiments, ensured these novel ideas could be realised.

They augmented their buildings at Gröndal in 1946–52 with a point block, some row-houses and a three-story *terraced house* that was another novel idea in Sweden. Built at the top of a steep slope that would otherwise have been hard to use, its laterally displaced floors provided room for a spacious terrace for each apartment. This form associates to Frank Lloyd Wright's architecture, which seems appropriate: Reinius admired his work and had visited him (see below). Further down the slope, Backström and Reinius placed their 11-floor, trespännare *point block*; its apartments had good natural lighting. Centrally located and with a sculptural appearance, it announced

Danviksklippan, Stockholm, by Backström and Reinius, 1945, contained the first point blocks in Sweden.

Reimersholme, Stockholm, by Fred Forbat, Sven Wallander and others for HSB, 1942–46. High blocks were well suited to markedly uneven terrain.

conical roofs, bevelled corners and marked balconies, the blocks had a sculptural appearance, and, in silhouette, looked remarkable and became a landmark in the town.

Throughout the 1920s and 1930s, the cooperative housing company, HSB, grew in significance, and, after 1945, played a leading part in housing matters. Its influential director, Sven Wallander, had the help of a number of skilful architects. The urban plan and buildings for *Reimersholme* in Stockholm belong to the most important contributions by HSB during the 1940s.[6] It was built between 1942 and 1946. It was an urban plan that skilfully followed and took advantage of the terrain. It had been drawn up by Harry Egler, Fred Forbat and Sune Lindström, some of the leading architects in planning. Sven Wallander, together with Axel Grape, was responsible for the buildings.

An area that illuminatingly demonstrated that the ideals of urban planning had changed from an open to a more closed-off concept of space is *Södra Skallberget* in Västerås. It was made ready during the late 1940s. In three stages between 1945 and 1947, its plan was changed from detached point blocks complemented by some parallel blocks into a open, grouped ring of lamell blocks complemented by a party closely road space, to the actually built resolution of a circular open space surrounded by buildings and a partly closed-off road space. The creators were Nils Tesch and Lars Magnus Gierz.

The Good Neighbourhood

The municipalities were assigned a key role in carrying out the new housing policy. They were to initiate and manage public-sector housing companies, as well as drawing up programmes to build housing, which entailed a requirement that they should assess future needs of housing in their areas and plan to realise them in terms of buildings.

The Powerful Position of the Municipalities

The roles of the municipalities was even more extensive than that: they should steer the direction in which society at large should develop and take responsibility for the social and economic well being of the people who lived in their areas. This entailed municipal policies for housing, the labour market and land use, and municipal organisations grew as municipalities' responsibilities swelled. To create better economic resources and possibilities for investments from larger municipal populations, the number of municipalities was reduced from 2,400 to 800 in 1952. Numbers were reduced still further on a number of later occasions.

The municipalities enjoyed a strong position, too, in physical planning that was established through legislation that came into force in 1948. In accordance with it, a *municipal monopoly* over planning empowered municipalities to decide what, where and when anything might be built in their areas. A means of doing this was the *general municipal plan* that acquired legal status in 1948; in municipalities individually the plans included forecasts of the development of industry and commerce, and households, from which conclusions were drawn as to needs of land and buildings. To facilitate cooperation between adjoining municipalities, *regional plans* were available as a means of help in resolving questions of localisation, of building or extending roads and similar matters.

The local (= municipal) and regional plans demonstrated an ambition to confront the changes that a novel age entailed: increased urbanisation, expanding industry and commerce, and an end to the isolation in 1939–45 forced on Sweden by her neutral position. Previously, only a few instances had occurred in Sweden of general plans being drawn up, but now this work became widespread. The profession had to learn to be competent in a novel area of specialisation.

One of the leading architects in developing this work in Sweden was Fred Forbat, a Hungarian-born Jew who had become internationally known for his work in Berlin and at the Bauhaus. Like many other Jews in the late 1930s, he was indebted to help from profes-

Södra Skallberget, Västerås, by Lars-Magnus Giertz and Nils Tesch, 1945–48. Successive developments changed its plan from an open to an enclosed sense of space.

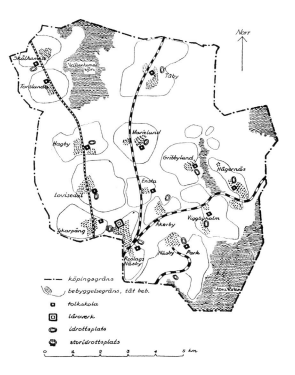

Täby general plan, by Sune Lindström, 1947, exemplifies many post-1945 plans; the part shown here deals with schools and sports grounds.

ern plans that employed forecasting methods for population growth, industrial developments, needs of services, development of standards and changes in traffic. His general plan for *Skövde* 1949 was his most important mainly on account of the novel principles he used in it to present statistics.

The general plan for *Täby* 1947 by Sune Lindström is a clear example of contemporary planning of neighbourhoods with buildings divided into small units of housing, services and a school. Since 1944, Lindström had developed work with general plans in VBB (Vattenbyggnadsbyrån), a engineering company that started an architects' office.

During the war, Swedish architects and planners began to develop an interest in Great Britain, which country replaced Germany as a model. *Neighbourhood thinking*, or division of extensions of large towns into smaller units, *community centres* for communal facilities, shops and services, and independent new or satellite towns: Swedish planners took up these ideas and developed them further.

One of the neighbourhood ideas was that the small units that could be easily surveyed should bear up a sense of community and democracy and counter tendencies imputed to people in the mass—an idea that naturally found a welcome after the war. During the war, Swedish planners managed with some difficulty get access to Patrick Abercrombie's Greater London Plan 1944, as well as other writings on English planning ideas. In 1945, several Swedish planners attended the big urban-planning congress in England, where the first new towns could be seen. Otto Danneskiold-Samsoe presented these new ideas in his *Nutida engelsk samhällsplanering* (1945).

sional colleagues in Sweden for his admission to the country, where he made his home. His first planning work in Sweden, done with Sune Lindström, was a *general plan* for *Lund* (1942), which was one of the first such mod-

Neighbourhood Planning in Årsta

Interest in the social aspects of planning was strong in Sweden in 1939–45 and later, and hopes of being thus able to build a society characterised many planners and architects.[7] They took up not just neighbourhood planning but also superordinate matters of social planning. Interdisciplinary groups were formed with a view of widening the areas of knowledge represented; sociology was an advancing science, represented by Torgny Segerstedt, who, together with Gregor Paulsson, started a group in Uppsala in 1939. They gathered their ideas in a publication *Inför framtidens demokrati* (1944) that included an architectural section on "Gruppsamhällen" by the architects Jöran Curman and Helge Zim-

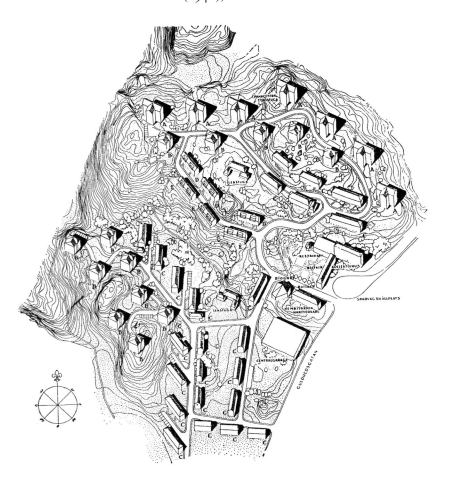

Norra Guldheden, Göteborg, by Gunnar Wejke and Kjell Ödeen, 1945, an area with long and point blocks, common facilities and collective housing; the first neighbourhood unit with a community centre to be built in Sweden.

dal. In 1942, Uno Åhrén had started a group called *Plan* that addressed societal questions; the group was large, and, besides a number of architect and planners, included Alva and Gunnar Myrdal, Alf Johansson and Brita Åkerman. In 1947, the name became that of a periodical published by the Association for Societal Planning (*Föreningen för samhälls-planering*). Employees of the KF architects' office were also strongly in favour of a social content in planning.

The post-1945 extension of the buildings and the centre at Årsta gives a clear image of the application of neighbourhood planning in Sweden (see also catalogue). Årsta, one of the southern suburbs of Stockholm, was where the newly-formed Cooperative Housing Union (Svenska Riksbyggen) had acquired access to land on which to build housing. The Union had been formed in 1940 by building-industry trade unions, primarily to ensure employment while Sweden was isolated by the war, but also to create good housing. Organised as a coop-erative housing company with local branches or associations in various parts of the country, it was a parallel to the HSB housing company.

The building work required by the Union was provided by the Trade Unions' Building Production that had been founded in 1922 with the German building guilds as a model. These two cooperative ventures jointly found-ed the *BPA* Building Company in 1948. Their intrusions into the private market for building and property maintenance exemplify the Swedish median between socialism and capi-talism discussed in *Sweden — the Middle Way*.

The Cooperative Housing Union had its head office in Stockholm. In 1943, Uno Åhrén became its chief executive and head architect.[8] As one of the foremost proponents of func-tionalism and the new ideal of urban planning, he took part during the 1940s in most of the important national investigations of housing matters and social planning. At Årsta, he saw a possibility of realising neighbourhood plan-ning ideas and of causing the Union to be a model for deliberate social planning of its housing areas.

In a self-critical account of housing areas built in the 1930s, he summarised what he and many of his colleagues had come to perceive as deficiencies: "We assumed that all apart-ments should be well lit by the sun", he wrote, "so we arranged housing estates in nothing but rows of apartment blocks. But we over-looked two important things. First, in our haste, we observed too little the factor of pleasure so these areas easily became uniform and dull. Second, we planned housing areas as

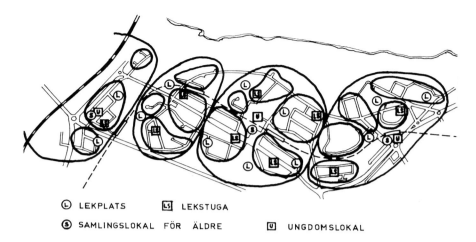

L LEKPLATS   LS LEKSTUGA

S SAMLINGSLOKAL FÖR ÄLDRE   U UNGDOMSLOKAL

if all we had to do was to get a given number of people into a given number of apartments, forgetting that actually living is in reality com-plemented by various forms of communal life involving individuals. We overlooked the need to arrange the residential buildings in groups around local centres where such communal life could be lived: play centres, club premises, rooms for studies, meeting rooms, libraries, cinemas and so on."[9]

In 1943, Åhrén worked out a plan for Årsta in which the projected 28,000 inhabitants were allocated to four main areas. Each such area was divided into smaller units of which most were furnished with play centres, play-grounds, young-people's rooms and premises for grown ups. Small food shops would be dis-tributed about the area. Each of the four main areas would have its centre, but one of them would be larger and, besides shops, a young-people's centre and meeting rooms, would have a 'citizen's house' that would among oth-er facilities include a library, club rooms and a restaurant.

This scheme accorded well with the discus-sions that were then being carried on about small-scale neighbourhoods and centres well-furnished with social and commercial facilities. It proved to be unrealistic, however, for the population was too small to bear all this. By 1944, plans were being made for a single large centre complemented by a certain degree of dispersed services.

The Ahlsén brothers, Erik and Tore, who were both socially-engaged architects and with experience of the KF architects' office, were engaged as consultants to work out plans for Årsta Centrum. Their presentation of their completed work gives an image of the time that is typical in its hopes for what central facilities could achieve in social terms. While emphasising that a housing area of this sort

Årsta housing area, Stockholm, 1943. Uno Åhrén conceived it as four lesser neighbourhoods, each with a playground and adjoining buildings, including a meeting place; it was built with a single large shared cen-tre.

must be regarded as experimental, they wrote that: "We have understood the main purpose with the facilities to be to bring into being a place where personal contacts can be established between individuals and groups, to stimulate discussions and personal contacts. It should at once serve the interests of individual members of the community and the striving of the democratic society." [10]

Commercial facilities, municipal services and leisure premises were located in the central buildings. Their successes were to a high degree the result of the architects' intensive work and persuasive talents. They contacted the shop-owners' association, which resulted in shops and a restaurant being opened in the centre. Municipal authorities were unfamiliar with running services in suburbs, but, through negotiations, the suburb could include a district medical centre, a maternity centre, dentistry services and a health-insurance office. For leisure activities, the architects could engage a number of organisations within the Labour Movement (adult education, housewives, artisans, tenants and other associations), sports' associations and so on in discussions as to what should be provided in the centre. The architects turned the ideas that emerged into sketches as a basis for further discussion. It was clear that they assumed they were engaged in this miniature People's Home

Årsta Centrum, Stockholm: architects and their assistants paint the facades.

on behalf of 'the people'; the efforts they made to realise a social content are impressive. Actually getting things built took time: under post-1945 conditions and in the economic circumstances that obtained, the national authorities wanted first of all to build dwellings and gave low priority to leisure premises.

Årsta Centrum, Stockholm, by Erik and Tore Ahlsén, 1945–54 included a community centre with meeting premises, library, theatre and shops.

But the results of all these discussions were rooms of different sizes for leisure purposes and meetings: the smallest could hold about ten people, the largest, the car-free central square, could accommodate a meeting of five or six thousand people. Two theatres, one large, the other smaller, both mainly for amateur dramatics, a library and a cinema were housed in a building for these purposes. And, to attract more personal cultural activity, a number of studios were built for artists.

Forming the square as a room is emphasised by the human scale of the facilities, by the proportions of the buildings and by the paintings on their facades. Contemporary concretist artists having been inspired to do paintings, the architects and helpers from their office then represented them on the buildings. While the architects had had a straightforwardly functionalist approach to the contents of the buildings, they worked with the surfaces of their facades as an independent part, separate from their designs and functions. They had no intention, either, of expressing the qualities of the materials used, nor of associating or referring to existing buildings, whether traditional or modern.

This work by Erik and Tore Ahlsén, to be understood as a sort of tapestry or collage on the walls of the room comprised by the square, was an interesting personal experiment in post-1945 Swedish architecture, a mixture of traditional elements and boldly imaginative forms. Their intentions may indeed have been to stir up the putative inhabitants, but they certainly stirred up art critics.

The paintings were the subject of a lively debate in cultural circles. Several leading personalities could not understand them at all, and the leading Swedish art critic, Gotthard Johansson, took exception to what he saw as a misunderstanding of the message of the concretist painters. "The architects", he wrote, "have simply attached an abstract image to a facade that has a quite different concept of form. The incongruity of this is raucous, and leaves the absence of style in the wildest 19th-century ornamental excesses far behind it."[11]

Critics attacked the very idea of neighbourhood planning and community centres as such, seeing it as a romantic dream that could create a sense of community and transform people in the mass into active democrats. An art historian, Göran Lindahl, considered that these "collectivistic villages" could just as well create isolation, stagnation and finger-wagging supervision; he recommended instead "the living big town". He saw Årsta Centrum as a warning example. "Perhaps this sort of thing

The facades at Årsta Centrum, given character by means of concretist paintings, set off a violent debate.

would suit little children and pensioners, and maybe even an exceptionally meek victim of asthenia".[12]

Planners, sociologists and politicians resisted this view of neighbourhood planning. Certainly, in planning Årsta Centrum, the architects had strongly emphasised its social content, but the heaviest argument in favour of neighbourhood planning was more practical. The fundamental Swedish motive for it was set out by Göran Sidenbladh, one of the main authors of the general plan for Stockholm 1952: "The functional and architectural reasons for neighbourhood planning are quite sufficient for us and our principals. The practical people who are active are not trying to create some novel sort of human being. We will be wholly satisfied if we can succeed in building so that people are pleased to live and work there."[13]

A visitor today to Årsta Centrum can see at once that the age structure of its population has changed very much. Many shops have closed. Leisure activities now draw on a larger area than previously. Neglected maintenance has caused many deficiencies in premises. Rather than the buildings themselves, technical and organised administration is decisive for continuous use and access. The buildings in Årsta Centrum are clear examples of that.

Örebro as a Model Town

The strong formal and economic positions conferred on municipalities gave them a decisive role in planning post-1945 society. Örebro, a medium-sized town in central Sweden, has been regarded as exemplary, primarily for its building of dwellings. Internationally, too, the town has been remarked for its path-breaking and experimental urban planning and housing. Örebro is a town of workers, and the Social Democrats enjoyed a strong, unbroken tenure of power from the 1930s until well into the 1970s: a replica of the national political condition, so that the town can be seen as a miniature Sweden.[14]

Together with the immediately surrounding rural county of which it was the principal town, Örebro had developed from a farming community into an industrial one quicker than most other towns in Sweden in the first half of the 20th century. By the late 1940s, nearly half the population of the county was engaged in industrial or manual production. The best-known industry was shoe making.

The building of housing flourished in Örebro, as it had elsewhere in Sweden, up to 1939, when it stopped almost completely, but picked up again after 1945. Its extent was limited, as discussed above, with priority going to export industries.

After 1945, people moved in large numbers to Örebro, and, in conjunction with increased nativity, a housing shortage was soon palpable. As economic activity rose in the 1950s, with rationalisation of industrial structures, larger but fewer production units, and official national policy and industrial enterprises calling for greater concentrations of population as the Swedish welfare state was being built, more and more people moved to Örebro. In this way, the town mirrors the development of many Swedish municipalities.

After 1945, its municipal organisation changed and grew in size. The principal responsibility rested on the unit that dealt with economic management (drätselkammare), and re-organisation strengthened its position. A newly-formed property office (fastighetskontoret) had a central role in physical planning, building and management. The body with the political responsibility (byggnadsnämnd) was also responsible for the town architect's office, and, with its help, founded the town's planning office in 1945.

Land acquisition became an important strategy in the municipality's planning and was significant to its possibilities of locating new housing. Formed in 1946, the municipal housing company, Rented Dwellings in Örebro (*Hyresbostäder i Örebro*), was decisive in building municipal housing. Although this increased sharply, dwellings were always too few; they increased by 30% in number, to 25,000, in the ten years to 1955, when the population was 70,000.

A general plan for the municipality's long-term planning of land acquisition and building, as in other municipalities, rested on forecasts of population and industrial development, needs of services and so on. The first preliminary plan for Örebro, drawn up by Herman Hermansson, the town architect, was issued in 1944; a revised version was issued in 1955.

As the municipality succeeded in providing housing, and its building programme created jobs and acted as a motor in the local economy, power concentrated in the hands of a leading personality, Harald Aronsson, a Social Democrat and chairman of the local party district from 1950. His official posts included chairmanships of the economic-management unit (from 1951) and of the municipal housing company (from 1954). In addition, from 1959, he was also employed, part time, together with four others, by the municipality to manage its budget, finances, land and building work. Thus his influence over the municipal property office and its housing agency was direct. As a career, this was something of a record. In 1948, he had left a job in a workshop to be a caretaker for the municipal housing company. Ten years later, he as good as ran the town.

He was something of a patriarch in the old ironworks' manner, but a patriarch with a difference: while holding office thanks to nomination by his party, he was described as 'popularly elected' (folkvald), for, in the Swedish political system, votes are cast for parties, not individuals. The same conditions obtained in other industrial towns in Sweden, including Norrköping, Västerås and Sundsvall, where similar Social Democratic personages played decisive roles in their post-1945 developments. But few of them had the local importance of Harald Aronsson in Örebro, thanks to his capacity, his local roots in the people and his contacts with industry. In addition there was his engagement as a housing caretaker with people looking for housing. His Wednesdays at the municipal housing agency from 1400 to 2200 became a legend that contributed to his characterisation as 'father of the town'. In 1971, resigning all his political and other posts, he accepted the national Social-Democrat government's nomination as governor (landshövding) of the county of Örebro.

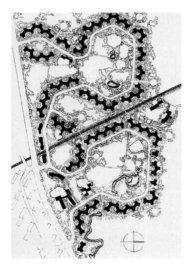

Rosta, Örebro, by Backström and Reinius, 1947–51, following a competition in 1946.

Rosta, Örebro, by Backström and Reinius, 1947–51, with star houses set in small intimate courtyards but separated by large, open stretches of park.

In itself, power was not his goal: his motive for gaining control over the means of governing the public sector was to create a vital society with good housing and jobs for all. He personified post-1945 Social Democratic thinking about the People's Home.[15]

A concentration of power gave great efficiency and tempo in planning and building the town's housing estates, where the municipal housing company became the most important means of achieving this. For ten years from the late 1950s, it accounted for 50%, and in the 1970s, for 60%–70%, of new housing in the town; it also managed much of it, having done so for 10% of all dwellings in Örebro in the mid 1950s. The Örebro branch of HSB had long been established in Örebro, but it was allotted fewer rights to build, and private companies even fewer. The municipality consistently gave priority to its own company, to which it allotted the large areas of land that it acquired. Not all this land was green-field sites. From the mid 1950s, it acquired large parts of the centre (Söder), razed their buildings, and the municipal housing company erected dwellings, offices and shop premises there; in 1963, it moved its administrative offices to premises in the *Krämaren* district.

The size of the housing programmes was a motive for putting them in the hands of the municipal housing company. The first two, and the best known, of the Örebro housing areas, called Rosta and Baronbackarna, contained respectively 1,340 and 1,230 apartments; projects of this size were then unusual in Sweden.

Rosta began with an invited competition in 1946. The first project by the newly-formed municipal housing company, it was important that it succeeded; and it did. An inspiring model for the world around, the competition was an approach that was used several times.

Rosta, Örebro: traditional pitched roofs and pairs of light-coloured painted windows are characteristic of Swedish housing in the 1940s.

Rosta, Örebro: star-house interior, of high quality, well laid out and with good natural lighting.

Four architects were invited to submit entries, and the winning team was Backström and Reinius, perhaps the strongest proponents of Swedish 1940s architecture.

Rosta was built in 1947–51. The architects applied a development of their honeycomb (stjärnhus) idea from Gröndal (see above), to create in Örebro large, coherent park spaces in combination with sheltered playgrounds near the residential buildings that were of three stories with an attic story that was shared by the third-floor apartments.

The open urban plan and the well-lit apartments united the best of contemporary architecture with economical building methods. The municipality's openly and strongly expressed ambition was that the tenants should be from all classes of society in the area; the apartments ranged in size from a single room with a kitchen corner, to those with five rooms and a kitchen, with a possibility of renting out one of the rooms, which was an attempt temporarily to resolve the great housing shortage.

Planned but never built 'collective housing' and domestic-servants' quarters featured in contemporary debate about how to ease things for working wives. An 11-floor point block at Örebro that contained only one-room-and-a-kitchen-corner apartments for people living on their own had something of this function but the building as such formed an architectural accent and a landmark in the area.

Complementary buildings, including schools, shopping centres, laundry facilities and meeting premises were built, and various municipal authorities cooperated to ensure that social services were good. Much effort was devoted to getting a varied population of tenants. Aronsson personally spent much time

in interviewing and contacting those looking for somewhere to live. Families with children were accorded priority and were in the majority, but no segregation that might scare off putative tenants ever occurred. The area was popular from the start.

Rosta was still building when, in 1950, a general competition was announced for the next large housing area, at *Baronbackarna*. Interest was great, 21 entries were received and the winning entry came from the Ekholm and White team.

Their plan was related to that of Rosta but the open spaces around its buildings were larger than those at Rosta, and, together, formed a meandering line around a large, undulating park space. Unlike Rosta, traffic, excluded from the housing area, moved only around its periphery. Buildings comprised apartment blocks of three or four stories. On average, apartments were larger than those at Rosta, and, in this sense, followed the general development in the country towards building larger apartments for families.

Baronbackarna was built in 1953–57; its tendency towards larger living areas became even clearer in the next Örebro housing area, *Tybble*, designed by the Ancker-Gate-Lindegren firm of architects and begun in 1957.

Later housing areas at Örebro were designed with the help of competitions. *Oxhagen I* (built 1962–64) introduced separate and terrace houses as complements to apartments, for which the municipality had hitherto not found economic room. Later housing areas contained many apartments and have acquired a more urban character, with further separation of traffic and more parking space than in the 1950s areas. Thus the extensions to Örebro give a picture of how the preconditions and ambitions for urban building changed in the post-1945 decades.

Apollo and Dionysus — Debates on Form After 1945

Twentieth-century Swedish architecture is generally not monumentally large scale and characteristically individual, being typically rather low key, restrained, everyday and collectively achieved. Clearly traditional elements reappear in post-1945 architecture. During the 1940s and early 1950s, this found expression in a relatively more exuberant formal language in which treatment of material was emphasised. Bay windows, marked eaves, ornamental brickwork, angled roofs, and window surrounds gave buildings a traditional character. The colour, form and rhythm of 1920s' architecture returned. Unrendered brickwork and coarsely rendered surfaces in strong earthy colours and patterns contributed to giving buildings a sensual expression, in contrast to the lightly, flat-rendered easy and almost immaterial buildings of the 1930s.

The traditional elements and emphasis on the intrinsic expression of the material used takes one's thoughts back to the national-romantic period almost a half century earlier, but the architecture of the 1940s had, as little as had turn-of-the-century national-romantic style, a primarily romantic starting point: it was practical, a realism in creating form, while its choice of material was often a consequence of the scarcities of the time. Poor access to reinforcing rods in iron or steel pushed choices away from reinforced concrete towards brick and other more traditional material and building methods. Shortages of asphalt caused flat roofs to be even less able to resist leaks: architects chose the more practical sloping saddle-roofs that shed water and snow much better. Rough-cast rendering was more resistant than the thin flat rendering of the 1930s. Fuel shortages contributed to a reluctance to use large window areas, and, instead of the long rows of fenestration typical of functionalism, lesser, delimited and clearly marked windows were used. Shortages contributed, too, to uncharitably revealing often poorly insulated houses and their often quite inadequate, misnamed insulating material that had result-

Row houses, Torsvik, Lidingö, by Erik and Tore Ahlsén, 1946; variations and material effects were sought in post-1945 housing.

ed from experiments during the 1930s; they further motivated a recurrence to tried methods and materials. The architecture of the 1940s has, as a parallel to the synonym of national realism for the national-romantic movement, been called *neo-realism*.[16]

Even if this pragmatic attitude contributed to post-1945 formal language, it was not decisive for it: form had been undergoing testing since the late 1930s. At the same time, the methodology of resolving plans had been furthered and developed the functionalist way of working with studies of dimensions and associations of functions. Backward glances to the qualities of architecture in past times, for example neighbourhood planning, took up the qualities of small-town and works' communities in terms of scale and content. There was space for a quite variegated flora of regional and local variants within Swedish post-1945 architecture up until the mid 1950s, when formal language became once again impressed by an international modernism.

A number of Swedish variants that experimented with form, colour and material in more or less successful ways appeared in the spectrum between a rather discreet traditionalistic architecture and a more purified functionalist formal language. Despite these differences, there was a common factor in the low-key, playful and undogmatic. The British architect, Michael Ventris, who came to Sweden in 1947 for a six-month period in the KF architects' office, used and illustrated the Swedish adjective "skojigt" when, on returning to England, he described tendencies in Sweden in the British periodical *Plan*.[17] His linguistic talents had enabled him, while working in the office in Stockholm, to snap up this word as used, for example, in att rita något skojigt, 'to draw something playful', and use it

Hägersten, Stockholm, by Ancker, Gate, Lindegren, 1948: a characteristic housing area in wood and brick, well fitted into the terrain.

The Tegelslagaren quarter, Stockholm, apartment block by Backström and Reinius, 1936; an early example of facades with a forceful sense of material, a reaction to light, smooth, dematerialised functionalist facades.

The Tegelslagaren quarter, Stockholm: living room in a well-planned 'thick' building. Note the carpenter's bench.

to signify the unorthodox and sometimes bold use of form and material, for example hexagonal windows, irregular roof lines, imaginative brickwork and powerful effects of colour and pattern. He took exception to the more uncontrolled variants, but was attracted to, among other things, work by Backström and Reinius.

This pair of architects came to formulate some of the ambitions driving contemporary Swedish architecture. They had been early in their criticism of the chilly character of Swedish functionalism. They had expressed this point of view in their first joint project, the *Tegelslagaren* buildings at Nytorgsgatan 36–38, Stockholm (1936): they varied the facade with bay windows and gave it a clear material effect through the use of tiles and oiled teak. In 1943, Backström wrote in *Architectural Review* that "the goal must be to reach the essential, the simple and the objective things in architecture. We want, certainly, to retain all the positive aspects of what the nineteen-thirties gave us. A house should of course function properly and be rational in its design. But at the same time we want to re-introduce the valuable and living elements in architecture that existed before 1930, and we want to add to this our personal contribution. To interpret such a programme as a reaction and return to something that is past and to pastiches is definitely to misunderstand the development of architecture in Sweden."[18]

He signified this architecture as "more human" and took up the concept of beauty that he thought had become overshadowed in the debate on architecture. "I am thinking most about the psychological and irrational factors that confer pleasure on us and, why not go so far, also beauty?"[19]

In Sweden, the discussion on *Apollo and Dionysus*, conducted in Byggmästaren in 1946–47, when Reinius was its editor, expressed the contrast between the rational and the artistic in architecture. A Danish artist, Asger Jorn opened the discussion. Reinius himself considered that the spontaneous and expressive Dionysus had been for too long in the shadow of the analytical and logical Apollo, and, as a Dionysic model, put forward work by Frank Lloyd Wright whom he admired personally. But his hope was still primarily that these two symbolic figures would unite their talents in architectural work.

His reference to Frank Lloyd Wright was not momentary. Interest in his work had grown in Sweden. Reinius had visited his office in the late 1930s, and, in 1944, an American exhibition, in which Wright's work was prominent, was shown in Stockholm.

The New Empiricism

There is further reason to give prominence to Backström's and Reinius' attitude, because

"Skoj": Michael Ventris characterised Swedish architecture in the 1940s as sometimes over-playful with materials and forms; from *Plan*, 1/1948.

their architecture came to belong to that which was most remarked in post-war Europe. Danviksklippan, Gröndal and Rosta were constantly presented during the 1940s in *Architectural Review*, *L'Architecture d'Aujourd'hui*, *Casabella*, *Werk*, *Die Bauzeitung* and other foreign architectural periodicals. Other Swedish work received attention. The most important contribution towards spreading word of Swedish architecture was the book, *Sweden Builds*, by the American, G.E. Kidder-Smith, which was published in 1950, and, in an edition brought up to date, in 1957.

Interest in Sweden was largely a consequence of the country, having remained outside the war, and to some extent kept its building work going, increasing it quickly after 1945. What was built was of interest to a Europe that was trying to raise itself out of the ruins. In addition, there was the hope, or example in Italy, of being able to build a better society, in which the fascism and nazism of the war would be replaced by democracy. Democratic Sweden appeared as a secure model.

The British were those who clearly remarked the Swedish efforts. As mentioned above, Backström made an appearance in Architectural Review, the periodical that gave a name to Swedish, post-1945 architecture, in a heading of an article in 1947 illustrated by Markelius' 1945 house, with some characteristically northern birches in the foreground: of the "New Empiricism, Sweden's latest style". The term signified an architecture that was based on experience and practical knowledge, partly on Swedish studies of housing functions and habits, and partly, which was emphasised in the debate in England, on the domestic artisanal tradition. Adaptation to the terrain and the fine cooperation with natural surroundings were other qualities that the foreign observers noted. A choice of brick and plaster as material appealed to the English and reminded them of the Morris tradition. Eric de Maré was one of those who welcomed the new style's undogmatic attitude, and its humanism.[20] He expressed his interest in Sweden in a book, published in 1955, on Gunnar Asplund. The more definite results of the influence from Sweden were carried through by, among others, architects of the London County Council. "New Town style housing was Swedish inspired" considered Roystone Landau in a review of English post-war architecture.[21] Buildings at Harlow, one of the first new towns outside London has a strong relationship to Swedish suburban building. And the 1950s point blocks on the *Alton Estate, Roehampton*, near London, by Oliver Cox, are directly inspired by the buildings of Danviksklippan and Vällingby. In *Cumbernauld*, Scotland, honeycomb blocks (stjärnhus) derived from Swedish models were built at the end of the 1950s, with Hugh Wilson as architect.[22]

Italy was another of the countries that followed the Swedish models. The theorist of architecture, Bruno Zevi, (who, incidently, also wrote a book about Asplund) belonged to their proponents. When rebuilding was to begin after the war, a distance was to be emphasised from fascist dictatorship architecture, which made Swedish democracy and its building work of interest. Sweden made an impression primarily through its housing policy, and, in Italy, the national organisation INA Casa was formed with similar ambitions. The honeycomb blocks (stjärnhus) built in the *Valco San Paolo* suburb of Rome in the 1950s, for example, were inspired by Swedish buildings. At the same time, the differences are great, for the emphasis placed in Sweden on a low intensity of exploitation and careful interrelations between the buildings and their natural surroundings are absent in Italy.

Austria received Swedish support after 1945 in rebuilding work and Swedish influence is evident in the *Per Albin Hansson Siedlung* on the outskirts of Vienna. The streets in the area are named for well-known Swedes, and its small communal premises are called Volksheim.

The reception by the world around Sweden was not only a chorus of praise. The small-scale, manual and anonymous qualities, with associations to popular feelings, "people's detailing" and the Morris tradition stuck in the craws of a number of younger English architects. James Stirling, a central figure in postwar modernism, sighed resignedly: "Let's face it, William Morris was a Swede!"[23] Sigfried Giedeon, the historian of international functionalism, thought that the direction had led into a cul-de-sac and called it the "New Escapism". But one of the founders of de Stijl, Oud, defended this direction and its need to develop functionalism's formal language by asking whether it were forbidden to give a functionalist building a spiritual form, and by pointing out that his own experiments had taught him that, as a sole principle, function would result in aesthetic exhaustion.[24]

In Sweden, too, critical voices were raised, the speakers being proponents of a more purified functionalism. Gotthard Johansson, who had praised the 1930 Stockholm Exhibition, considered that the architecture of the 1940s expressed a dilemma, in which architects "at one and the same time reacted against the

With his book, "Sweden builds" (1950, new edition 1957), Kidder Smith, an American, aroused foreign interest in Swedish architecture.

The Smith House, Lidingö, by Nils Tesch, 1959. Traditional and modern elements work together; the harmonic proportions of its well-lit rooms induce thoughts of Swedish 18th-century houses.

In his own house at Kevinge, Djursholm, in 1946, in a functionalist tradition, Sven Ivar Lind carefully controlled relationships between its rooms, proportions and materials; it and its garden work as a whole.

ideas of functionalism and declared them to be the only choice for a basis to build on." In his opinion, no new ideas would be born from such a half-hearted attitude.[25]

Another matter that aroused a great disturbance was Erik and Tore Ahlsén's coloration of Årsta Centre, which was also criticised (see above) by Johansson. Backström and Reinius, too, were criticised for their coloration, and Nils Ahrbom expressed the opinion that they had devastated otherwise good qualities at Rosta.

Gunnar Leche, the town architect of Uppsala, was the one who was most sniped at. His housing areas in Uppsala with imaginative forms for roofs, entries and fenestration made easy targets: "If you want to see most of the meaningless features of 1940s architecture concentrated in a single place and to be aston-

ished by their sometimes hysterical playfulness, you ought to take yourself to Tuna backar in Uppsala: it would be an unforgettable outing."[26] Housing areas by Leche have survived well and appear nowadays as carefully worked in both their external surroundings and resolutions of their apartments' layouts.[27]

Nils Ahrbom, the intellectually sharp, rational and factual architect, was one of the sharpest of critics. He was the creator of one of the more important works of functionalism in the 1930s, the girls' school at Sveaplan, and many other significant school buildings. Among them were the extensions to KTH, the Royal College of Technology in Stockholm, in the 1940s and 1950s. He became a professor there in 1948, and, as such, came to have great significance for the generation of architects that took over some years later.

But let us tarry for a moment at one of the foremost Swedish proponents of 'The new Empiricism'. Nils Tesch belonged to those who united Swedish tradition with a functionalism attitude.[28] An example of his striving to create a sense of space is his urban plan for Södra Skallberget in Västerås. His attitude was undogmatic, almost pragmatic, and, together with Artur von Schmalensee, Sven Ivar Lind and others, he forms a link back to the time before the breakthrough of functionalism in Sweden. His production included dwellings, schools, museums, churches and other public buildings. The Swedish tradition of building in brick and wood as characteristic materials was, for him, a living and applicable tradition. His interiors often give a sense of a light atmosphere of 18th-century Swedish Gustavian feeling, which was a source of inspiration he shared with many architects of the time. Classical proportions, firm and harmonic coloration and reflecting fenestration in

Tuna Backar, Uppsala, by Gunnar Leche, 1947–50. Entry from the district square, with a compass rose painted on the ceiling. The identities of the area and each of its houses are emphasised.

facades are other characteristic elements. He was also inspired by foreign models. There is a touch of Tessenow's architecture in Tesch's work, which has associations to Danish work too. One of his sources of inspiration was what Kaj Fisker signified as the *functional tradition* in Danish architecture. Care over details, factuality and intimacy in Danish architecture was admired by many Swedish architects, and, among other work, the University of Århus, designed by Fisker, Povl Stegemann and C.F. Möller, and extended during the 1930s, was a model. But there were also more direct connections with Denmark. During the war years, many Danish architects sought for political reasons to get to Sweden. Among those who made their way to Tesch's office were Egon Möller-Nielsen and Erik Asmussen. Möller-Nielsen was primarily to work as a sculptor and designer. In 1940, he organised an exhibition in Stockholm called "Artists in Exile" that showed the work of many such architects and artists. Erik Asmussen stayed for a long time with Tesch in a partnership that became important for both men, before the former started an office of his own and became the most important architect for the Anthroposophist Movement in Sweden.

The character of intimacy that Tesch sought appears in work by his good friend and colleague, Sven Ivar Lind, in the latter's *Restaurant Byttan* in Kalmar (1939), and in Lind's own house in Kevinge (1946, see also catalogue).

Brutalism

This became the general name for the 1950s architecture of social-realistic modernism that, among other things, emphasised the expressiveness of untreated material, mostly concrete; it allowed elements of design and installations show themselves fully, so as to achieve a realism and an 'honest' result. Social and economic motives were often central. Its sources of inspiration have been widely divergent, from Peter and Alison Smithson in England and Le Corbusier in France to Mies van der Rohe in the US. The architecture can express itself in so many ways that it is doubtful if one should speak of a 'direction', rather an 'attitude' with different centres of gravity. Rayner Banham gives a full account of this in his book *The New Brutalism* (1966). Banham also puts forward a Swedish source, the *Göth House* (1950) by the young Bengt Edman and the young Lennart Holm. While under construction, it was described as brutal by Hans

The Göth House, Uppsala, by Edman and Holm, 1950: the first neo-brutalist building.

Asplund in the course of a visit to English colleagues, who appreciated this characterisation.[29]

Brutalism was a reaction to the easily nostalgic and tradition-bearing architecture of the 1940s. The previously-mentioned criticism had a living background in the strong position of functionalism in Sweden during the 1930s. Edman and Holm, both of them Ahrbom's former students, belonged to the critics; for a long time, Holm especially was prominent in his well-expressed and sharp articles and contributions to debates that carried on the analytical-rational attitude of Apollo. His and Edman's house for the Göth family in Uppsala is a confirmation of this attitude.

The Göth House should perhaps better be designated as "a moralism" than as "a brutalism", and the architects' attitude has been more of an ethic than an æsthetic character.[30] The economic restrictions on the project became a challenge and a source of inspiration. In its sharp-cut form, flat roof, ribboned fenestration and its open ground plan, the building has a characteristically modernist feeling. The choices of its materials are functional and uniform, the brick stands well up to weather. As an ideal, its design is sparse and slender. Its external and bearing interior walls are done in half-brick, a challenge to the possibilities of the material. In the exterior facades, one can decipher the short ends of the interior bearing walls as so many vertical zips. In the facades, too, the steel bearing joists of the fenestration are 'brutally' visible as horizontal lines. And in the minimised dimensions of the beams the architects have striven to place the bearing walls as optimally as possible. At the same time, they sought to make the forms of the rooms functional and harmonic. The result has become the classical golden proportion relationship in the main

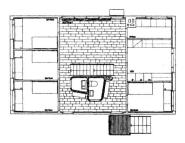

The Göth House; an open layout, in which the 'wet area' has soft forms that differ from the right-angled arrangements of the rest of its plan.

division of the house, united with an open layout. The entry hall leads directly into the combined 'all-room' and dining room that, in its openness, continues in the large living room up a flight of stairs and in roomy play and working spaces in the basement. These common, open rooms are placed around the more separate kitchen and bedrooms. The entry contains and has, as it were, as a watershed, the 'wet facilities' (bathroom, toilets, laundry room), rendered in white and as softly sculptured as a vase by Aalto.

Reactions to it all were strong. Gunnar Leche, the town architect, who represented the traditionalistic direction of the 1940s, commented sourly that "it's fortunate that there are trees", implying that some could hide what others popularly called the 'transformer building.' By now, a preservation order shields its consistency and character of its time.

In an international context, another example of early Swedish brutalism is the roof of the hall of the Social and Economic Council in the UN Building in New York by Markelius, the best-known post-1945, Swedish architect and Bengt Lindroos (born 1918), who created the room; it was inaugurated in 1951.

In planning the UN Building, Markelius was the only Scandinavian architect to be invited to join the group of architects led by Wallace Harrison in 1946–47; it included Le Corbusier and Oscar Niemeyer. As a follow-up to this work, Markelius was commissioned to design the hall. Its dimensions were prescribed. Markelius saw it as a theatrical space with the audience on a floor that, in darkness, sloped down to the illuminated stage on which he placed a large horseshoe-shaped conference table. Further to bring out the arrangement, he made a room that framed the delegates' places with freestanding walls, marked the floor with a particular carpet and set a white internal ceiling over the table that included a pattern of round lighting cupolas; it was hung directly beneath the deliberately exposed technical elements under the roof: beams, ventilation conduits and electrical installations. By placing only the internal ceiling over the delegates' places, he emphasised this, at the same time as it created possibilities of space with a ceiling height in its upper part that was noticeably low. The exposed installations formed a pattern in themselves, which Markelius and his assistants developed further through a flecked coloration in white, black and grey. This 'exhibitionism' in a brutalistic spirit attracted much attention, not least on account of the prestige of the contents of the building. President Eisenhover took part in its inauguration but clearly disliked was he revealed, while Markelius' professional colleagues admired his scenography and the bold exposure of the roof. This roof has since been most variously interpreted; UN guides now assert the ceiling pattern symbolises "the constantly performed, and never-ending work within the United Nations".[31]

Hall of the Social and Economic Council, UN Building, New York, by Sven Markelius and Bengt Lindroos, 1951. The internal ceiling extends over only the delegates' places; elsewhere ceiling installations are left free and wholly visible, which aroused strong reactions.

The Modernist of Regionalism: Ralph Erskine

One of the architects who developed regional architecture in his own very personal way is Ralph Erskine.[32] Born and educated in England, he made his way to Sweden in 1939, where he has lived ever since: Swedish functionalism, not least its social content, had captured his interest. As an architect who came from elsewhere, he posed basic questions about Swedish architecture. The conditions of the Swedish climate inspired him to seek novel solutions. In this way he came to develop an architecture that, while deriving from the methods of modernism in resolving problems, resulted in an original formal language. His architecture became a part of the rich variation of post-1945 Swedish architecture, but was highly independent, and, lacking the contemporary resemblance to traditional forms, was more related to brutalistic expressions. In its way, it can be designated as regional, in that it intended to proceed from local conditions,

Tourist hotel, Borgafjäll, by Ralph Erskine, 1948; the spirit of the place in form and material.

primarily in choices of material. At the same time, it seldom refers to the Swedish tradition of building, and in addition Erskine's personal hand with form is altogether too strong. Sometimes climatic considerations seem almost to be a cover for a wish to bring an expressive architecture into being.

Erskine's *tourist hotel on Borgafjäll* (1948) exemplifies this. Some 100 km from the nearest community, lying in the fells of Lappland, it is built as a part of the terrain; its long sloping roof can be used as a ski run. The angles of its roofs associate to the slopes of the surrounding fells, and, with its terraced immediate surroundings, the buildings form a sort of immense sculpture of the landscape. Much of its building material—stone, timber and sand for concrete—was got on the spot, so as to keep costs low but also to reinforce visually the buildings' links to their surroundings. The whole associates to Frank Lloyd Wright's Taliesin West (1938), where the sculptural effects of the building cooperate similarly with its surroundings. Inside the hotel Erskine worked with mezzanines and rooms on different levels, in public rooms and guests' rooms, which contribute to the building's dynamic expression. On account of its coloration, its timber frame appears clearly and shows Erskine's interest in details of construction. Its open fireplaces are formed as simple, free-standing sculptures. Their expressions as sources of heat and symbolic meaning in the northern climate comprise a theme with which Erskine worked in almost all his buildings.

Erskine was later offered many housing commissions, and the first large facility he designed was *Gyttorp* in Västmanland (see also

catalogue). Here he had an outlet for his ambition to design a "complete small community". In many ways, it was a typically Swedish commission: a job in a rural Swedish works, where Nitroglycerin AB manufactured dynamite and other explosive products based on Alfred Nobel's Swedish invention. At the time, it was an expanding industry in the export sector that had a central position in post-1945 Sweden, where a welfare state was being built up.

As previously mentioned, it had been a tradition in many of these works' communities for the company to put resources into building dwellings for its employees. An industrial association had been formed for the purpose, with the aim of mediating the services of competent architects to interested companies. Erskine's commission at Gyttorp led to designs for a school, a centre and dwellings for employees. Built between 1945 and 1955, they comprised two-story terrace houses and three-story apartment blocks. They were built in

Row houses at Gyttorp, by Ralph Erskine, 1945–55, have concrete shells for climatological reasons.

Row houses at Gyttorp: plans. A small ground-level dwelling, with bedrooms and a bathroom upstairs from the kitchen and living room.

Luleå Shopping Centre, by Ralph Erskine, 1955. Béton brût was characteristic of 1950s' architecture.

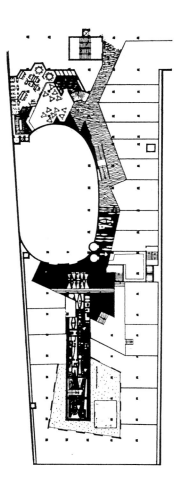

Luleå Shopping Centre, plan: the first indoor shopping centre in Sweden. The oval room houses a cinema.

concrete and had an almost brutalistic expression.

But, in his commissions from these works' companies, Erskine could take good account of older buildings on his sites. At *Gästrike-Hammarby*, built during the late 1940s, he re-enlivened the former works' atmosphere through his choice of on-site material—brick and discarded slag—from 18th- and 19th-century operations.

Completed in 1955, Erskine's shopping centre at *Luleå* was the first modern indoor shopping centre in Sweden. Besides shops, it included dwellings, a restaurant, cafes, a cinema and an art gallery. In winter, the town enjoys a climate appropriate to its close proximity to the Arctic Circle, and the shopping centre was thought of as an extension of central streets through an entry shielded by insulating, hot-air barriers into indoor comfort. Its exterior is dominated by glass, aluminium and concrete. Inside, where Erskine wanted to create surroundings full of varied experiences, he cheerfully mixed different materials and architectural motifs. The plastic form of the egg-shaped auditorium of the cinema was an experiment in design. Indoor streets, galleries, staircases and intermediate-height floor extensions give a labyrinthine impression, full of the raw expressions of concrete cast on site. The premises are a remarkable mixture of traditional architectural elements, experiments in form and brutal material effects: a building that mixes up the social ambitions and formal language of brutalism with playful symbolism. One can view it as an expression of a sort of pleasure in experiment that was typical of the 1950s transition from restrained empiricism to an internationally uniform style, but pri-

marily it is an expression of Erskine's own independent view of architecture.

Public Buildings

The school reforms of the 1940s were important, leading to among other things lengthened of compulsory school attendance: first to seven years, then to nine. Their ambition was both to give children of all classes of society a possibility of education and to meet the national need for a better-educated work force. A uniform school was introduced and the old primary and secondary (folk & real) schools were discontinued. Both rural and urban children would get access to good schooling, and efforts were made to discontinue mixed-age groups in classes, which were common in smaller places. Instead, teaching would be of classes formed by age. This necessitated larger school-catchment areas, and even more numerous and more subject-oriented schools. As a result, schools became larger and more centralised.

In the neighbourhood thinking of the 1940s and 1950s, schools were a decisive starting point: an individual school's catchment area defined neighbourhood size and was one of the preconditions for the general planning of dwellings and services.

The schools built during these decades were still intended for classroom teaching, complemented by rooms for special subjects. The ideal of the 1930s, of classrooms giving off on one side of a corridor was still alive, often leading to resolutions of pavilions, but even the old-fashioned 'hall'-school ideal lived on.

One of the latter was the *Solna School* by Nils Tesch and Lars Magnus Giertz that was completed in 1947. It related more to the big 19th-century schools than anything in the 1930s: a symmetrical building, with its entry and hall on a central axis, and classrooms round it on different floors. Externally, it is

Solna Teachers' College, by Lars-Magnus Giertz and Nils Tesch, 1947; its brush-coated facades, bay windows and leaded glazing look traditional.

restrained, with light, washed facades and a regular fenestration broken only by the lengthy, protruding wooden bay windows of the dining room. Internally, its character is warm, with a strong feeling for materials: patterned red-brick work in the central hall, unpainted wooden inner ceilings, walls and doors. A round and a straight staircase, both freestanding, emphasise the rhythm and movement in the hall. The round, white-rendered staircase with an enclosed lift shaft prompts thoughts of Asplund's staircase in the *National Bacteriological Institute's* building in Solna (1937), while the top lighting of the hall associates to Östberg's Blue Hall of Stockholm Town Hall.

The great changes in central Stockholm (*Nedre Norrmalm* & *Hötorgscity*) during the 1950s included razing in 1958 the building from 1844 of the College of Art that had had various names. Its education continued in the new building for *Konstfack* that began building on Valhallavägen in Stockholm in 1956; it was ready a few years later.[33] Its architect was Gösta Åbergh, who had won the competition for the commission in 1954.

The building well exemplifies the change in architecture from the robust, varying traditionalism of the 1940s to the more uniform, internationally-oriented architecture of the 1950s: eg the low, extended noticeably horizontal buildings around their series of protected yards, in a modernism inspired by van der Rohe. Its walls are experienced as light, sharply-cut screens, in which the powerfully red, moulded bricks contrast in colour and material to the dark and light aluminium-framed glazing that dominates the facades. Where these facades give on to the yard, they form walls to a well-proportioned outdoor room. From outside, they form a shining slender ribboned grid. There is over the building an exactitude, elegance and graphic sharpness. Black wrought iron, mosaic in cement, and white-painted concrete walls form a controlled, neutral background to the colourful people and activities of the building. At the same time, the choices of material and colours of the external bricks and the details in wood in the interior counter any tendency in the building to give a chilly impression. The systematic module system of the building has dimensions of 160 or 16 centimetres. It has been used skilfully to confer a sense of freedom and ease on the design, and on the flexibility of its plan.

One of the few buildings that was directly inspired by Le Corbusier's post-war architecture is *St. Görans Gymnasium* School in Stock-

University College of Arts, Crafts and Design, Stockholm, by Gösta Åbergh, 1959, following a competition 1954: sharp modernistic graphic qualities in volumes and facade materials.

holm that was designed by the husband-and-wife team, Charles-Edouard and Léonie Geisendorf.[34] Built during the late 1950s, it was a school for housework and sewing. Léonie Geisendorf, a Swiss architect, had worked for Le Corbusier before she and her husband came to Sweden. The expressiveness of the raw concrete was well used, and the light shaft in the school, with its high pillars and top lighting, and the floor paving stones, belong to the most characterful and beautiful architectural surroundings of the time. The frame of the building is exposed in other parts of the building. Externally, the alternating dark and light

Solna Teachers' College, by Lars-Magnus Giertz and Nils Tesch, 1947; its central hall has a touch of Asplund's later work.

St. Göran's school, Stockholm, by Charles-Edouard and Léonie Geisendorf, 1956–60: one of very few Swedish buildings strongly influenced by Le Corbusier.

St. Göran's school, Stockholm; interior. Its slender concrete pillars and cobblestoned floor give a powerful sense of material.

parts of the fenestration glazing form a varying pattern that lightens the large, heavy volume of the building.

When the 1958 football World Cup was played in Göteborg, the *Nya Ullevi* Stadium was built as its main venue, its architects being Fritz Jaenecke and Sten Samuelsson.[35] The largest of its sort in Sweden, it accommodated 55,000 spectators. In plan, it forms an ellipse, with most of the seating along the long sides of the pitch, where views are best. An immense, softly curved roof, highest and widest over the long sides, and suspended from pylons over 50-m high, shelters the spectators without obstructing their views of the pitch. The closed form of the whole, its powerful concrete frame, undulating roof and the landmarks of its pylons give a monumental and a dynamic impression. Few other buildings in

Sweden comprise such a strong unity of the engineer's art and architecture. The same architects designed a closely similar but smaller stadium in Malmö the same year.

A consequence of municipal amalgamations was a need for many new municipal premises. Two of them, one built in the early, the other in the late, 1950s can illuminate different ways of adaptation to a site.

Simrishamn is a small coastal town of many old timber-frame houses in south-eastern Sweden. Hans Westman won the competition to design its new *town hall* and chose a drastic means of working. To adapt his building to the town, he employed the timber-frame motif as decoration, not constructional design. Completed in 1953, the town hall was built in brick but given a facade in a black-and-white timber-frame pattern in mosaic: a fundamental challenge to the functionalism principle that a building should reflect its time, its function and its design. So Ahrbom consequently criticised Westman for understanding the tradition metaphorically and to almost eradicate himself in imitating this metaphor. In his view, Westman had "chosen the most questionable alternative, to imitate on the surface a constructional design that existed nowhere else."[36]

But Westman's choice was deliberate: he wanted an illusion and chose to create it with the help of 'make-up' and a 'fool's cap'. Commenting ironically for his colleagues on this, he wrote that "'the people' require play acting and the world one lives in 'is also visual'. We architects build not only for ourselves but to some extent also for the people and their pleasure".[37]

The second example was the new *town hall of Falkenberg*, a west-coast town. Designed by

New Ullevi Stadium, Göteborg, by Fritz Jaenecke and Sten Samuelsson, 1958. A sports' facility that combines the engineering and architectural arts into a stark, sculptural unity.

Town hall, Simrishamn, by Hans Westman, 1953. Its (imitation) timbering is an adaptation to the traditional architecture of the town.

Lennart Tham, it was completed in 1960. It was another approach to the problem of "a new building in an old square".[38] It was to stand next door to the old town hall. Tham had the ambition to fit it to the scale of its surroundings but at the same time to indicate clearly that it was more important than anything else in town. The premises as a whole were large, and Tham sub-divided them into smaller buildings set around a yard. One protrudes and closes off the space of the square. This white cube with its arcade, strict divisions of fenestration and large window areas is unmistakeably modern. In spirit, as it were, it stands aloof from its neighbours, saying it belongs to an age other than theirs, while showing in its scale and rhythm that it is still related to them. The result is a skilful adaptation to its site.

While the Labour Movement, which includes the trade-union and teetotaller movements, called their shared urban premises fol-

kets hus ('the people's house'), their political opponents or some of them built what they called medborgarhus (a 'citizens' house') in a number of towns and other communities after 1945. In 1947, a competition to design one of them in a small town in Skåne called Eslöv attracted 158 entries, of which the declared winner, who also received the commission to build it, was Hans Asplund, Gunnar Asplund's son. His *Eslöv Citizens' House*, one of the most interesting buildings of the 1950s in terms of form, was completed by 1958. It is reminiscent of Erskine's shopping centre in Luleå (see above), although the two buildings are wholly dissimilar: where Erskine is exuberant, Asplund is refined.

Asplund's building contains three main functions, to each of which he gave its own form. Together they balance: the long vaulted cornet with meeting and theatre rooms, the high slab of office premises, and the deck on pillars beneath which lie the foyer, the museum, the cafe, and the study rooms. The three parts surround an oval light well, through the lanterns of which light descends into the foyer. The diagonal of the cornet links the two entries and forms the main orientation of the building.

In the urban plan, too, the three volumes of the building form screens, background and interplay with the surroundings. Their volumes are held together as an entity through the uniform, light marble-chip rendering of their facade.

The building is in concrete cast on site. Internally, it is a building in which form, coloration and material are worked out to the smallest detail. In terms of style, one can find

Town hall, Falkenberg, by Lennart Tham, 1960: modernism adapted to the scale and rhythm of the place.

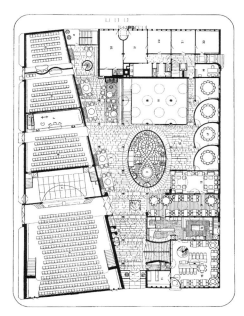

Citizens' House, Eslöv, by Hans Asplund, 1958, after a competition in 1947; exterior and plan. A unity worked out in minute detail.

Vignette from Louis Campanello's publication, "Stadsförnyelse i Gävle" (1953), illustrating contemporary attitudes towards older buildings in town centres.

associations to most of the 20th century without this entailing the loss of the entity of the building. The care devoted to it is impressive but can stifle: everything is ready, nothing can be added or subtracted.

Transformation and Growth of Towns

The cores of many Swedish towns underwent large changes in the post-1945 years.[40] Structural rationalisation in industry and commerce, especially in retailing, together with the rapid increase in car use, were the motive forces for razing older buildings and putting up new ones. In 1947, the national housing-social investigation made a provisional report about the cleaning up of the cores of towns. The ruling attitude was that older buildings, being ripe for cleaning up, should be razed to make way for new ones. Among the motives for this was the need to create work in the face of anticipated post-1945 unemployment. In Gävle, the director of property, Louis Campanello, did an investigation into the town's need for renewal, Urban Renewal in Gävle, (*Stadsförnyelse i Gävle*, 1953). His argument in favour of demolition was heavily motivated by a wish for improved traffic standards and housing, and he put forward the possibilities of getting modern housing into the lightly exploited centre of the town rather than building far outside it.

In his view, renovation would be costly on account of the skilled labour needed, while rationalised new building work would cost less. For the same reason, it would be rational and economical not to renovate individual buildings but tear down whole urban districts and build anew on their sites. Campanello's record of his investigation became something like Holy Writ during the 1950s, when many councils wanted to renew town centres. What happened was that innumerable towns saw their older buildings torn down and their centres undergo great change, with frequent losses of local identity and firm places in history.

The Ordering of the Nedre Norrmalm

This area is now the modern inner-centre of Stockholm (see also catalogue) and its transformation was one of the largest and most comprehensive of all such changes in Sweden.[41] Since the latter part of the 19th century,

shops, companies, administrative and pleasure activities had been attracted to this part of the town, and, for a long time, it had been felt necessary to bring order to its network of streets and buildings. Preparations had been undertaken, and, from about 1910, the urban authorities had systematically acquired property with a view eventually to cleaning up the centre. In a thorough-going plan drawn up in 1928, Albert Lilienberg had proposed a transformation that among other things would have extended the main street through the area, *Sveavägen*, southwards through a considerable hill, *Brunkebergsåsen*, to a square, Gustav Adolfs Torg, opposite the palace and by the water. Geologically a remnant of the last ice age, the hill was both an obstacle to traffic and part of Stockholm's identity.

In 1932, the town authorities, having held an international competition for the whole Nedre Norrmalm area, had 350 entries, of whose authors Le Corbusier and Alvar Aalto were the best known. Their entries both embodied very far-reaching, radical plans for renewal the whole of inner Stockholm, not just of this part of it. The winning proposal, however, was found to be the work of Lilienberg's closest associate, so, as a result, no prize could be awarded to its author.

Work on the plan continued in the town planning office, with alternative proposals being made by others, including Paul Hedqvist and Tage William-Olsson, who were critical of what the office had hitherto proposed. Hedqvist proposed that Sveavägen should swing round, rather than penetrate, the hill, which appealed to a town councillor, Yngve Larsson, who was to play a decisive role not just in the urban plan but in renewing the inner part of Stockholm. This idea became the basis for the decision about a new plan for the area once Sven Markelius had replaced Lilienberg as town planner in 1945.

In 1946, the Proposal for an Urban Plan for Lower Norrmalm (*Förslag till stadsplan för*

Sergelgatan, proposal for realisation, by David Helldén, Stockholm planning office, 1946: pedestrian street with high blocks on one side and low shops on the other.

Sergelgatan, Lower Norrmalm, Stockholm, proposal for a plan, Stockholm planning office, Sven Markelius, 1946: five point blocks, a theatre, shops, a pedestrian precinct.

nedre Norrmalm) was published. Written by Carl Fredrik Ahlberg, it represented a cooperation between the architects, planners and traffic engineers of the town planning office. It included David Helldén's proposal for the form of the area. Over a large area between Hötorget and Brunkebergstorg, new buildings and new traffic routes would replace what was there. A new square, putatively Sveaplatsen but called in fact Sergels torg, was laid out where three traffic arteries, Sveavägen, Hamngatan and Klarabergsgatan, met. A pedestrian precinct, Sergelgatan, linking it with Hötorget, ran between a row (to the east) of five 18-story blocks and a two-story row (to the west) of shops and a theatre. The planners wanted sunlight and airiness in the pedestrian precinct.

Alternative proposals, emanating from inside and outside the planning office envisaged three or four larger, heavier point blocks but what was actually built was the original five that, a clear landmark over the town, were called by Yngve Larsson "the five blasts of the trumpet".

The shopping precinct, a street without wheeled traffic that was reserved for pedestrians, was an important but controversial novelty in post-1945 urban planning. Shopkeepers suspected that, without their cars, customers would not come to the shops. A pedestrian precinct having been successful in 1950, in the southern suburb of Stockholm called *Hökarängen*, it was now included in the plan for the centre. Markelius himself sketched out the form for Sergels torg and took care to give the nearby precinct the character of a long narrow space, slightly widened in its middle. His vision being that of a lively stretch with quiet oases, he added terraces above the shops. These were built but did not really work in the Swedish climate.

In the document on Lower Norrmalm from 1946, one can perceive that the Swedish planners were early adherents of the new ideas. Similarities can be seen between it and projects out in Europe, and the clear relationship between the Sergelgatan precinct and the later commercial stretch, *Lijnbaan*, in devastated Rotterdam. In 1962, Markelius and his closest colleagues were awarded the Patrick Abercrombie prize for the transformation of inner Stockholm and for planning Vällingby (see further below).

Lower Norrmalm continued to be transformed into the 1970s and came to be one of the largest transformations of an old European inner city to be undertaken after 1945. The first stage, Hötorgscity, has been criticised and

admired: criticised because an old familiar part of a town was so totally erased, admired for its success in achieving such a unity, consistency and rhythm in the created surroundings. With its high blocks and the pedestrian precinct, this part of Stockholm belongs without doubt internationally to the most characteristic of the first generation of post-1945 modern city-centre creations. As a confirmation, it embellishes the cover of the fourth volume of Leonardo Benevolo's history of modern architecture, *Il Dopoguerra*.

The General Plan for Stockholm

The need for a long-term plan for the growth of Stockholm was nothing new. In 1928, the-then director of urban planning, Albert Lilienberg, had drawn up what was primarily a plan for the town's traffic. Increased migration to Stockholm had made its housing shortage acute, and the urban authorities even posted warnings at Swedish railway stations to deter

Sergelgatan, Stockholm, 1955–65. One of the first post-1945 modern shopping centres. The high blocks, 'the five blasts of the trumpet', were designed in a curtain-wall technique by different architects; the pedestrian precinct has an abstract design in black and white.

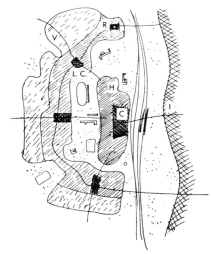

Sketch for an idea of suburban extension of Stockholm, by Sven Markelius, Stockholm planning office, 1945. Buildings are concentrated around a centre, which is surrounded with a belt of parks containing schools, day-care centres, playgrounds and sports' pitches. A rapid tramway system links the suburb to the town itself.

intending travellers from moving to Stockholm. Part of the problem was public transport, and the underground railway that began on a very modest scale to be built during the 1930s, was on the eve of extensive expansion.

The need for a new general plan had long been spoken of, and work on it began in 1944. The town councillor, Yngve Larsson, who was keenly engaged in questions concerning urban building, made great efforts to ensure financing for the work. A working group was appointed that comprised two architects, a statistician and a traffic engineer, respectively Carl Fredrik Ahlberg, Göran Sidenbladh, Erland von Hofsten and Sven Lundberg; their programme for the planning work, *Det framtida Stockholm*, was ready as soon as 1945. As director of building in Stockholm until 1954, Sven Markelius had principal responsibility for the work. He addressed current thinking in an article in Byggmästaren in 1945, where he sketched out a summary of his ideas: "A relatively concentrated extent of rented accommodation could suitably be linked to a centre for shops, social services and premises for common use for leisure occupations and pleasure. A girdle of parks around this central area should provide places for schools, play schools for younger children and day centres for infants, playing fields, playgrounds and sporting facilities. Outside this park belt are terraced housing with smaller local centres for shops for immediate needs, garages, companies running small workshops and the like, children's centres and so on. Houses on their own plots and areas of small houses are to be directed to the more peripheral positions."[42]

Through this pattern it would be possible to achieve variation in the urban picture. To create a varied set of buildings and give a clearly decipherable architectural identity were expressed ambitions in the new ideology of urban planning, and Markelius continued: "Such a differentiation should certainly also contribute to giving the buildings of the town a lively variation and pleasure. Through adaptation to the terrain and its vegetation variations in the manner of building should be able to add liveliness and pleasure to the urban scene."[43]

As mentioned above, contacts with British planners had had great importance for the Stockholm urban-planning office. Under the leadership of Sven Markelius, its planners visited the big town-planning congress in Hastings in 1946, where they could show the plans for the transformation of the Lower Norrmalm area of central Stockholm and an early

sketch of the general plan for Vällingby. The exchange was mutually fruitful, and, later that year, Patrick Abercrombie, Lord Reith, who was chairman of the New Town Committee, and Lewis Silkin, Minister for Housing and Planning, and a number of specialists, visited Sweden and the Stockholm urban-planning office.

The *General Plan* for Stockholm was published in 1952, a comprehensive and simultaneously pedagogical presentation of the preconditions for and thoughts behind the definitive proposals for the extension of Stockholm. It deepened and further developed the ideas of neighbourhood planning with an emphasis on their functional sides. It appears as a straightforward schoolbook in general planning work; few publications give so clear an image of the principles of the post-1945 ruling ideology of urban building in Sweden.

The most important role for the plan was to be the coordinating instrument that made its plans feasible. At an early stage, it deliberately obliged the various urban authorities to cooperate in building the new suburbs and in getting them to function with dwellings, streets, public transport, schools, centres and so on. Its coordinating strength and realism gave the political authorities of Stockholm the possibility of realising a thought-out unity and vision.

The precondition for the town to steer this extension lay also in the deliberate policy for land that had included strategic acquisitions and agreements with neighbouring municipalities. Its main geographical structure was the subway lines, on which, like pearls on a thread, suburbs were interspersed with green areas.

Vällingby

The principles sketched out by Markelius in his 1945 article entailed each built-up area containin the elements of what became called (in Swedish) the 'ABC society', namely Arbetsplatser (work places), Bostäder (dwellings) and Centrum. *Vällingby* became the application of this satellite-town principle, and the clearest and most comprehensive realisation of the ideas presented in the general plan for Stockholm (see also catalogue).[44] Vällingby was part of a planned entirety, comprising a continuous area north-west of Stockholm, the other suburbs in its group being *Blackeberg, Grimsta, Råcksta, Hässelby gård* and *Hässelby strand*, linked to one another, and central Stockholm, by the same subway line. The land comprised fields and meadows, and, for Markelius and his colleagues, it must have been with a unique feeling of freedom that they could embark on planning a novel urban form, with a novel organisation and general form: a whole new 'town' to be built up from the ground.

Over the establishment of work places and commercial activities, however, the planners had least influence. Thanks to two large organisations, the national hydro-electric organisation, *Vattenfallsstyrelsen* and the municipal housing company *Svenska bostäder*, that decided to locate their head offices here, the planners had come far on their way. Prospects for the large central facilities that were to serve all the surrounding areas, were dependent on the association of Stockholm shopkeepers, but, with a population basis of at least 20,000 to 25,000 people, the association could approve the plans.

The building of dwellings in the area also followed to a great extent the ideas Markelius had presented in his 1945 article. High blocks in the centre, 3 or 4-story apartment blocks no further than 500 m from the railway station, and terraced housing and small houses a bit further. This gave a clear visual image to the built-up area, in which each part got an identity of its own and where, thanks to the high blocks, it was clear from a distance where the centre lay. The commission to give form to the plan for the centre facilities went to Sven Backström and Leif Reinius.[45] Certain local centres came into being, one of them being Råcksta, the first area in the Vällingby group to be built. It was also one of the first housing areas in Sweden where traffic was separated from the rest. That vehicular traffic and pedestrians should move in different systems to increase efficiency and to avoid accidents was a thought that Swedish planners and architects had been working on since the 1930s. Their model was the American suburb of Radburn, where these ideas had been put into practice in the late 1920s. At Råcksta they were combined with the ambition to create roominess in its meandering plan. The Stockholm urban-building office was responsible for the plan, while Ernst Grönwall and Adrian Langendal designed the housing.

From Neighbourhoods to a Society of Motorists

As a counterweight to the great efforts made at Vällingby and its group of suburbs and their centres north west of Stockholm, the southern suburbs were built up around the centre of gravity at Farsta. *Farsta centrum* became the

Vällingby Centrum, Stockholm, designed by Backström, Reinius and others, inaugurated 1954. The large-scale patterning of the square is a part of the conceptual whole.

big commercial effort. Following American models during the 1950s, retail trade was much rationalised and concentrated, producing department stores with increasingly large needs of population concentrations. Opened in 1959, Farsta Centrum drew customers from a much larger surrounding area than Vällingby's, infinitely larger than Årsta's, which was now of only local significance. The neighbourhood ideas about a sense of community and keeping an eye on things was replaced by forecasts of the population that could support commercial service. The ABC model was put away: unlike Vällingby, Farsta was no deliberate, satellite town, but primarily a commercial venture built by private-sector companies.

Vällingby Centrum, with surrounding land, Stockholm planning office, Sven Markelius, 1945–54; a realisation of the sketched idea from 1945.

The buildings of its centre, however, were designed by the Backström and Reinius who had designed Vällingby.[46] The square motif was an extended shopping street where department stores used their facades to clearly advertise their characters. To achieve flexibility in layout, the buildings were formed from a prefabricated system of concrete pillars and beams. Their exteriors differed greatly: the light-grey granite exterior of NK said 'quality', the enamelled aluminium sheet of the Konsum building said 'something simpler'. The Tempo facade was the most eye-catching: a pierced white facade in artificial stone hung on the building as an external grid. Having tried it in a large store on an old square in the middle of the university town of Uppsala, where it raised a storm of criticism, the architects now placed it in a less sensitive urban context, thinking of it as a emblem of Tempo shops in rural parts of the country.

The advertising role of the Farsta buildings was greeted with both enthusiasm and criticism. The former critic of the neighbourhood ideas expressed at Årsta, Göran Lindahl, now greeted the Farsta buildings as a signal of a new architecture liberated from the dogmatic demands of functionalism derived from a unity of function, design and form, while, always prepared to argue in favour of factuality, Nils Ahrbom preferred the old morals and regarded the attempt at Farsta as simple prostitution.[47]

Visually, Farsta Centrum was dominated by its parking facilities. Despite having, like Vällingby, its own subway station, the planners anticipated that many visitors would come by car. Since the mid 1950s, motoring

had decisively influenced urban building and characterised it in suburbs and centres. The background was the rapidly increasing car ownership, itself a product of increasing purchasing power. In 1950, the population:car ratio was 20:1; by 1959 it was 6:1, with forecasts pointing steeply upwards. In terms of population, Sweden became the most motor-ridden country in Europe. At the Royal College of Technology, courses were given in 'the motor town', and, in urban-planning work, the separation of vehicular and pedestrian traffic became a dominant theme.[48]

Besides commercial concentration and motoring, the third factor inducing change in planning and building was the industrialisation of the latter. In the mid 1950s, the big building enterprises began to discontinue manual methods in favour of prefabricated elements. Several factories for the purposes were built in Sweden. A housing area at one of the Vällingby group of suburbs, *Grimsta*, was one of the first to be erected with the new technique. Many building contractors and architects had long dreamed of a sort of building box of ready-to-assemble parts that, as a cheaper and quicker means, could assist in solving the housing problem. Hitherto, Swedish building projects had been regarded as too small commercially to justify prefabrication, but, after 1945, housing areas got bigger and this constraint shrank. Shortages of labour were a motivating force: building with prefabricated elements called for far fewer workers, besides reducing the powerful bargaining position of some of them—primarily bricklayers—vis-à-vis building companies.

The new technique entailed problems that were challenging. If they were to fit together, prefabricated elements had to be made accurately. A system of uniform modules with some standard dimensions was elaborated. Elements could be as big as the wall or floor (with suitably placed ventilation channels) of a room; or smaller. Some elements comprised whole rooms, primarily bathrooms and kitchens. Large on-site cranes, stationary or on rails, were needed to lift them into place. The new technique set its mark on layout and urban plans, and the concept of *production-adapted design* was coined by the strong man of the building industry, Sven Dahlberg. The large scale of the results accommodated the novel architectural ideals.

Thus, in the late 1950s, the relatively small-scale, manual practice of building became a large-scale business that made use of untested technical, social and æsthetic means. A novel society began to make itself visible.

Farsta Centrum, Stockholm, Backström and Reinius, inaugurated 1959. The facades of the department stores communicate the identities of the retail chains they belong to.

Östberga, Stockholm, HSB,
1954: the introduction of
industrial building, in which
prefabricated elements are lif-
ted into place by cranes.

NOTES

¹ Eva Rudberg, *Uno Åhrén* (1981), 181 ff.
² See for example Brita Åkerman, *88 år på 1900-talet* (1994), 160 ff.
³ The development of apartments is described in Lennart Holm, "Bostaden som ideologisk spegel", in *Bostadspolitik och samhällsplanering* (1968).
⁴ Lennart Holm & Erik Holm, *Hem, arbete och grannar* (1958).
⁵ Their work is discussed in *Arkitektur* 6/1982.
⁶ See Lennart Holm (ed.), *HSB* (1954).
⁷ Rudberg (1981), 154 ff.
⁸ Rudberg (1981), 158 ff.
⁹ Uno Åhrén, *Arkitektur och demokrati* (1942), 21.
¹⁰ Erik & Tore Ahlsén, "Årsta centrum", *Byggmästaren* 1954, 276.
¹¹ Gotthard Johansson, *Svenska Dagbladet*, 3 October 1951.
¹² Göran Lindahl, "Stadsplanering i det blå" *Dagens Nyheter*, 21 August 1951.
¹³ Göran Sidenbladh, *Dagens Nyheter*, 4 September 1951.
¹⁴ The town' expansion is considered in Bertil Egerö, *En mönsterstad granskas. Bostadsplanering i Örebro 1945–1975* (1979).
¹⁵ Egerö (1979), 68.
¹⁶ Olle Svedberg, "Nyrealismen", *Arkitektur* 2/1988, 28.
¹⁷ Michael Ventris, "Function and arabesque", *Plan* 1/1948.
¹⁸ Sven Backström, "A Swede looks at Sweden", *Architectural Review* 9/1943.
¹⁹ Sven Backström, "Nu och sedan", *Fyrtiotalets svenska bostad*, (1950), 53.
²⁰ Eric de Maré, *Architectural Review* 1/1948.
²¹ Roystone Landau, *New directions in British Architecture* (1968), 23; see also Olle Svedberg, *Planerarnas århundrade* (1989), 135.
²² Eva Rudberg has written on Swedish influence on foreign building in "Sverige provins i Europa", *Arkitektur* 10/1987.
²³ Rayner Banham, *The new Brutalism* (1966), 11.
²⁴ J.J.P. Oud, cited in *Architectural Review* (6/1947), 200.
²⁵ Gotthard Johansson in *Svenska Dagbladet* 21 August

1950; see also the series "Perspektiv på 40-talet", in *Svenska Dagbladet* 1951.
²⁶ Nils Ahrbom in *Svenska Dagbladet* 23 October 1951.
²⁷ Leche's work is described by C.E. Bergold in his *Bostadsbyggande i Uppsala 1900–1950* (1985).
²⁸ For Tesch's work, see *Arkitektur* 5/1991.
²⁹ *Architectural Review*, August 1956; Banham (1966), 10.
³⁰ Lennart Holm, "Villa Göth—en brutalism", *Femtiotalet* (Architecture Museum, Stockholm, 1995 Year Book).
³¹ Eva Rudberg, *Sven Markelius, arkitekt* (1989), 130–131.
³² Mats Egelius, *Ralph Erskine, architect* (1988).
³³ Gösta Åbergh, "Konstfacksskolan", *Arkitektur* 6/1960, 118 ff.
³⁴ L. & Ch-E. Geisendorf, "Yrkesskola i Stockholm", *Arkitektur* 9/1960, 175 ff.
³⁵ Torsten Frendberg, "Två idrottsanläggningar", *Arkitektur* 6/1959, 136 ff.
³⁶ Nils Ahrbom, "Två hus i Skåne", *Byggmästaren* (1954), 25.
³⁷ Hans Westman, "Simrishamns stadshus", *Byggmästaren* 1954, 26; see also Tomas Tägil, *Arkitekten Hans Westman. Funktionalismen och den regionala särarten* (1996) 193.
³⁸ Lennart Tham, "Stadshus i Falkenberg", *Arkitektur* 2/1961, 29 ff.
³⁹ Lennart Holm, "Eslövs medborgarhus", *Byggmästaren* (1958), 141 ff; & Hans Asplund, "Medborgarhus i Eslöv", *Byggmästaren* (1958), 144 ff.
⁴⁰ Bengt O.H. Johansson, *Den stora stadsomvandlingen* (1997).
⁴¹ Of the many accounts of these changes, see Göran Sidenbladh, *Planering för Stockholm 1923–1958* (1981) & Ingemar Johansson, *Stor-Stockholms bebyggelsehistoria* (1987).
⁴² Sven Markelius, "Stadsplanefrågor i Stockholm", *Byggmästaren* (1945), 357.
⁴³ Markelius (1945), 358.
⁴⁴ See, for example, Sidenbladh (1981).
⁴⁵ They presented their plan for Vällingby in *Arkitektur* 4/1956.
⁴⁶ They presented Farsta in *Arkitektur* 3/1961.
⁴⁷ Per-Olof Olsson, "Acceptera Farsta?", *Byggmästaren* (1961), 67.
⁴⁸ Rudberg (1981), 203.

(Top) The Garnisonen block (1972), Stockholm, by the A4 group and (below) Lewerentz' St. Mark's Church (1960), Björkhagen: the dichotomy between large, rationally planned jobs for the state and the 'refuge of beauty' that especially ecclesiastical commissions provided.

The Time of the Large Programmes 1960–75

CLAES CALDENBY

Twenty-five years' uninterrupted economic growth culminated in 1967–68. The export and especially the engineering industries had been its economic motor. Labour was scarce and people were deliberately attracted to industrial centres from rural Sweden and even other countries. Measured in numbers of cars, TVs and charter holidays, welfare had risen quickly. But the 1960s were harvest time for public-sector welfare that was the model of the Swedish People's Home (folkhemmet). The public sector grew to account for over half of GNP. Historically, the Swedish state had been strong since the 17th century: it was now the 'strong society', as Social Democratic politicians were proud to call the means of delivering the benefits of the welfare state; a society of consumers seemed also capable of growing in parallel with it.

Sweden modernised extensively, both economically and socially, with exceptional speed, which was in many ways a triumph for the rationality the Social Democratic Party had stood for since it won power in the 1930s. "The large programmes" were a number of national reforms effected with a planning technique of systems analysis inspired by the "radical rationalism' of the US defense forces.[1] A technique applied in many parts of the world, it suited the national society of Sweden particularly well: besides the Federal Germany Republic, Sweden was the most Americanised country in Europe. The Henry Ford model of modernity suited a small country built on an unusually large-scale industrial base. And its regional re-structuring turned Sweden into a country of green-field building.

The building-industry sector, too, came to be characterised by large-scale programmes. A persistent housing shortage left Sweden, even in the 1940s, with a housing standard that was low in European terms; this and rapid urbanisation combined to cause a great need to build dwellings. The government tried variously to support modernisation of the building industry. Legislation in 1959 created a set of national building regulations. Founded in 1960, the National Swedish Council for Building Research had the mainly technical aim of making building rational. Nationally applicable loan regulations, planning norms and instructions promulgated during the 1960s by various authorities were, in sum, a breakthrough on a broad front for a way of thinking that had been maturing for a long time. During the 1960s, and up to 1975, some fifty national commissions were appointed with terms of reference covering the building of dwellings. What got called the Million Programme was well prepared and entailed no dramatic increase in production. It was needed primarily to fit building on this scale into the national economy. Building one million dwellings within ten years was not to overheat the

"We must replace our old errors with more up-to-date ones." An architect, Mats Erik Molander (MEM), who in satirical drawings made comments on his time and, often and sharply, on bureaucrats.

economy or lead to competition for labour. It presupposed a rational building industry.

This was in the interest of the large building companies; it was no time for small, local builders. The People's Home had led to a development of social building of dwellings; like the National Housing Board, the public-sector housing corporations could order what they chose. During the period, the early-Functionalist architects managed to win a strong position for the profession on national commissions and as independent consultants. During the 1950s and 1960s, building companies moved to retake the initiative and, as novel circumstances obtained, take the lead as builders and property managers. The habit being to take an engineer's perspective, building companies took the engineering industry as a model; as preconditions for rationalisation, they argued for overall contracting (with architects employed as need be), self-contained technical systems and large-scale operations, which was well received by national commissions. Step by step, the architectural profession had to retreat in the building process. During the Million Programme, overall contracting rose to 40% of housing work. With the standard contracting agreement specifying materials and details "or the like", the contractor, not the architect, made the final decisions in the interest of finding a less costly solution.[2]

"... a country and a time with so meagre a general interest in and understanding of architectural quality", a comment by Hakon Ahlberg in an article written in 1963 on Sigurd Lewerentz' work, can seem paradoxical in a country that quite recently had been the object of international architects' interest in architects' social roles. But it must be taken seriously as a perceptive, balanced observer's sorrow over architects and architecture being shoved aside in the building process.[3]

But some architects tried to find a new role while the new national society was being built. A highly conscious view of architecture was developed in work commissioned by the National Building Board for central-government and other national institutions, which was extensive and achieved a high quality. At the time, too, the Swedish architectural profession got a structure of large offices matching the size of commissions and building companies. Most of them were organised collectively, named with sets of initials, and, having been founded in the 1950s, grew large in the 1960s. An investigation in 1996 found that of the one hundred largest firms in the world, four were Swedish and, for example, five German and none French; in proportion to national populations, then, Sweden leads this league.[4]

But one must admit that, during the 1960s, Swedish architects were unhappily attracted to one or the other of the two apparently mutually exclusive poles: "productionadapted design planning" or architecture as an art. The latter was a "haven of beauty" nourished by ecclesiastical work. Although the present account of the 1960–75 period is thus most concerned with the large programmes, it does try to draw attention to good architecture created within them. The old professional culture and its tradition was kept up largely in small firms still working in the master-and-apprentice manner.

The Million Programme

The largest of the large programmes was to erect one million dwelling in 1965–74; it comprised half the volume of all building during these years.

Its background, which has been discussed above, can be summarised here as housing standards in the 1950s that were low in European terms, rapid population growth, internal migration to towns, and general political agreement over a need to build a large volume of housing without attracting labour from export industries. The technical solution was to industrialise building by making it a systematic, mechanical process.

As an image, its results are fixed in Swedish minds as huge housing areas with deplorable architecture and, among their inhabitants, countless social problems. They were deplored even as they were being put up: the one outside Malmö, Rosengård, the 'Rose Garden', was called a "newly-built slum" as early as 1966. In the debate about the modernist view of architecture in the 1970s, the Million Programme came to symbolise all that was wrong with it.

There is ground for this criticism, but, to be fair, it should not be sweeping. The typical Million-Programme housing area is not one of eight-storey blocks in the suburbs of Stockholm, Göteborg and Malmö but one of three-storey blocks in some small town. More than one third of the apartments were in private houses. Some large apartment blocks exemplify a care for small-scale considerations and architectural care for the surrounding terrain and urban space, and the forms of detailing.

LGH 537

Concrete decks with three staircases also carrying all services: individuals built in wood on their "sites". Kallebäck (1960), Göteborg.

Experimental building, Järnbrott (1953), by Tage and Anders William-Olsson. Individual apartments could be individually planned (see right).

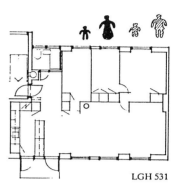

LGH 531

Experimental building, Järnbrott. Apartments have bathroom and kitchen connected to the staircase. The rest is a free plan that can be divided in different ways.

Almost all apartments were well planned, a product of the comprehensive building research that had been done. The architecture of the Million Programme was in many ways consistent with the Functionalist striving not just to form individual buildings but also processes and technical systems. With the obvious risk of averting one's eyes from particular locations and users.

Attempts to Industrialise

In developing industrialised building, work in the west-coast town of Göteborg became in several respects exemplary; a couple of early experimental projects in the town demonstrated a continuity of functionalist ideas. A competition in 1950–51 by a municipal housing company for new types of houses was won by Tage and Anders William-Olsson. On an area of 56 m², they created a third room by making a bar-like arrangement a kitchen opening onto the living room. A system of moveable walls allowed a choice of layouts; it was reminiscent of Mies van der Rohe's apartment building at the 1927 Weissenhof exhibition. One such house, planned by Lars Ågren, was completed by 1953: its bearing concrete frame and its walling elements clad with wood were clearly visible in its facades. The moveable interior wall elements had fully visible joints. The potential for flexibility has been little used, on account of slight interest from the residents and the property owners, together with certain technical difficulties; the house was not repeated.[5]

This principle was taken further in Göteborg with houses to be built on a concrete deck; Erik Friberger, ideologically a functionalist and the county architect, designed them having worked throughout his life to develop an industrial manner of building, using mainly elements in wood and had already retired when his "deck house" was completed in 1960.

On a three-storey concrete deck with stairways between the floors, 'sites' of between 144 m² and 210 m² had individual water and sewage connections. According to needs and resources, families could build simple houses in wood on their sites; most began by building on the entire site. The whole still works well but has not been repeated.[6]

Yet a third site in Göteborg, Mistralen in Södra Biskopsgården, saw the serial application in 1954–57 of a similar principle by Erik and Tore Ahlsén. A non-bearing cladding of corrugated asbestos sheeting protects it from the weather in this windy and rainy part of Sweden. Moveable, prefabricated glazed staircases are located outside the facade, leaving the rest of the concrete decks uncluttered. The bow-shaped houses follow the contours of the terrain that, typically for this part of the west coast, is markedly undulating; they form half-enclosed courtyard spaces.

Industrialised building work was to depart from the open, flexible qualities of this sort of decking towards contractors' own hermetic systems, limited numbers of variants and the ensuing difficulties of fitting buildings into their natural surroundings. In the 1950s, a

The Mistralen block in Biskopsgården, Göteborg. Erik and Tore Ahlsén 1957. Bow-shaped houses follow the terrain. Prefabricated staircases leave the decks free.

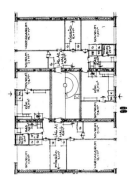

Pennygången in Göteborg. Ekholm and White 1962. Early prefabricated housing. Almost all apartments are four rooms. The "spiral" plan makes all kitchens identical.

Göteborg municipal housing company developed a system of factory-made concrete pillars, beams and floor joists that it used in 1959–62 to build Pennygången, Högsbohöjd, an estate of 761 all but identical apartments. In relation to staircases, apartment layouts on each floor had a spiral, not a mirror-image pattern, so as to minimise variations. Had the town planning office not insisted on providing corners adequately protected against the wind, these four-room-and-a-kitchen apartments that families of the future were deemed to need would have been identical. Their design was by Ekholm and White, via Rune Falk.

Building Low and Densely

According to Ralph Erskine, zoning "is a misunderstanding of functionalism. Production-adapted planning has nothing to do with it either, only with methods of production." He was writing about his housing area, Brittgården, at Tibro, designed and built in 1960–68. His criticism of late modernism has similarities with the ideas of Team X, with which he had contacts. Typically enough, Erskine received no Swedish commission to design a large housing project during the years of the Million Programme, when priority was given to other considerations. Ideas expressed at Brittgården had made fragmentary appearances in his work in the Swedish Arctic mining towns of Kiruna (1961–62) and Svappavaara (1963). The higher gallery houses at Brittgården form a protective wall against northerly winds and the adjacent parking areas. Within the area, buildings are low and densely built: row houses and those around atria. He mixes types of dwellings and forms of occupancy, but includes no workplace in the area. Its architecture is exuberant, with various forms of windows, freestanding balconies and elements of strong colours.[7]

Low, densely-built dwellings of a small-

Erskine's Brittgården: long high buildings shelter the others from north winds and views of parking areas.

town sort characterized Norra Kvarngärdet in Uppsala, built in stages in the early 1960s. Clay foundations made two-storey houses economically interesting. The architects, Ancker, Gate & Lindegren were experienced in designing houses. These had staircases with entries from both sides of the building, which gave easy access to their traffic-free sides.

During the 1960s, Örebro was a precursor. Designed by Bertil Hulten and Lennart Kvarnström, Vivalla was built in 1966–70: a two-storey town of 2,500 apartments in typical undulating conifer and birch woods. Including long access loop roads, relatively large car-parking areas, and, as at Kvarngärdet, a central length of park with shops, day-care centres, schools and sports' fields, its general plan separates traffic more consistently than did Kvarngärdet. Its houses were built in traditional, on-site ways, with bricked facades; a method that proved less costly than assembling prefabricated elements. Costs were kept down by erecting long series of low, simple dwellings. The architects' opinion was that "the individual dwellings are details in a whole and therefore lack expressive values."[8]

The use of prefabricated elements to build a dense, small-scale housing estate that fitted into the terrain was demonstrated in 1966–71 in a seaside municipality to the east of Stockholm. Designed by Jöran Curman and Ulf Gillberg, the Västra Orminge estate at Boo enlarged a community of mainly private houses with 2,600 apartments. Being definite in their demand for limiting the height of the new buildings, the municipal authorities co-operated with the contractors, Ohlsson & Skarne, to develop a system of building elements that included bearing facades and pillars in the middle of apartments that allowed a variable location of inner walls; those of the tenants who were offered the choice showed a preference for open arrangements. The architects worked with staircases as leads in the two-storey buildings, which permitted a close adaptation to the terrain; as a complement, the architects included three-to-five-storey point blocks in the area. All clearly display the character of being built of prefabricated elements: facades are in raked grey concrete, roofs are in vaulted corrugated sheet metal. By keeping to a small scale, and contrasting more urban pathways with undisturbed natural surroundings, the architects achieved a lively architecture in this large area, which, they wrote, "tries to be a consistently applied idea. Some dislike the area, some like it, few lack an opinion of it." Despite showing what can be done, positively, with the use of

Brittgården (1968), Tibro: Erskine worked with various volumes and powerful sculptural balconies; access to duplex apartments in the high building was via external galleries.

prefabricated elements, Västra Orminge inspired little later work in the Million Programme.[9]

Kungshamra in Solna, in Stockholm, a student housing area from 1962–67, combined four-storey buildings containing single rooms with shared kitchens and two-storey buildings of family apartments. The architects were the ELLT firm. Six sub-areas, each containing six buildings, added up almost a labyrinth that, in its dense urban character, contrasted with the old-established park alongside. All the buildings were constructed from the Skarne prefabricated system, and the grey of their raked concrete well set off the strong colours of the woodwork; this and the large square windows contributed to giving the area a playful sense of coming out of some kids' building sets.

The Million Programme included many examples of dense, small-scale, modernistic rented housing that was well adapted to its natural surroundings: several (eg Nyhem, Finspång) were designed by Engstrand and Speek, others (eg Ljuskärrsberget in Nacka) by FFNS.

Adaptation to Production; and Protests

Although the lower apartment blocks comprised the greater part of the Million Programme, especially initially, the image of the whole is usually characterised by the long,

Västra Orminge (1971): concrete elements, small housing units, easy accommodation to the terrain.

high blocks on the outskirts of Stockholm, Göteborg and Malmö. Bredäng to the south of Stockholm, being an early example of a schematic parade of identical eight-storey blocks, was complete by 1965.

A debateable attempt to create "the new monumentality" took the form of seventeen-storey point blocks and eleven-storey bow-shaped slab blocks at, respectively, Näsbydal and Grindtorp, Täby, a Stockholm suburb. Sigfried Giedion had claimed that the tempo of cars demanded this. Beginning in the mid 1950s, Sune Lindström and VBB did the overall plan, the designs for the buildings and that of the large indoor shopping centre at Täby; completion took 10 years, and, when it was done, Täby held 18,000 residents.

Writing in 1966, one of them, Björn Linn, criticised Täby but suggested it unusually clearly reflected its time. "On account of the architects' formal skills, the inability to set up a basic, thought-out programme for building has been so much better illuminated [at Täby] than in many other housing areas that only seem clumsily done and where the reasons are not as apparent. For decades, all these areas will testify as to what could be put up and filled with tenants at a time of housing shortage."[10]

The Million Programme was to build that many dwellings, and it was realised. Its apartments met the demands laid down by the national Housing Board in 1964: for being well capable of being furnished, of containing good kitchen and hygienic facilities, for being light and airy often even in bathrooms and staircases. The functionalist vision of concrete decks kept open for flexible plans through the use of pillars was not realised in more than a small proportion of all buildings.

Overall plans were accommodated to the need of construction cranes to move on straight lengths of rails. In the interest of efficiency and safety, traffic plans rigorously differentiated between a hierarchy of feeder roads, roads to buildings, and approach roads; and separation of different forms of traffic.

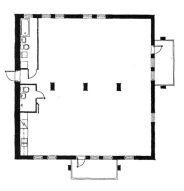

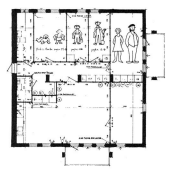

Västra Orminge: bearing walls and central pillars let at least some tenants plan their own rooms.

Kungshamra (1967) student housing, by the ELLT office that used the Orminge system (see above): raked-concrete units, brightly painted joinery.

Kungshamra: six units of four-story 'thick' blocks with single rooms and 'narrow' lower buildings with family apartments; a seventh containing a daycare centre and other facilities has enclosed courtyards.

Together with large generalised parking areas, these made it hard for people to differentiate between one part of an area and another, while buildings were isolated into enclaves.

The terrain for many was the familiar Swedish mixture of farming land interspersed with uneven, often wooded rocky outcrops, of which both had previously not attracted buildings: blasting techniques were applied to flatten them out to take buildings. The spaces in between were planned only schematically and otherwise neglected. As were the details on buildings that had simple geometric forms, with balconies as the sole sculptural element.

Täby (c. 1960), a north-east suburb of Stockholm, by VBB: high point blocks and curved slab-blocks reveal a scale suited to travel by car.

Rosengård, Malmö (late 1960s), with a high proportion of slab-blocks; its central services are located in a building over the central traffic artery, its parking places are on concrete decks between apartment blocks, which contain many unrented apartments. The whole is emblematic of the Million Programme.

As the areas admitted no places of employment, they became dormitories. Most lacked the premises that early post-1945 planners had assumed as essential to anything that called itself a community.

Monuments to this programme that had sunk ideologically by 1968, when its building had just begun, may be seen outside Stockholm at Botkyrka, Hallunda, Rinkeby and Tensta; outside Göteborg at Bergsjön, Gårdsten and Hammarkullen; and outside Malmö at Holma, Kroksbäck and Rosengård.

The ideological shipwreck was a debate on the southern Stockholm suburb, or new regional centre, of Skärholmen in 1968. Its inauguration caused a number of critics to formulate an expression of distaste that won widespread sympathy. "All you can use Skärholmen Center for is to roll one-time glasses between its walls so they sound right shitty. Tear the whole place down!" This was followed up with books of a sort that were then typical: 'The Tensta Report', or 'All you do is to simply get used to it'.[11]

The suburban image was becoming one of social isolation and people made politically and culturally passive. It did not really help when politicians and planners said their intentions had been of the best. The discussion gained in subtlety when an ethnologist, Åke Daun, published a book in 1974 that claimed suburbanites were active but not in their suburbs but, through their work, leisure and friends and relations, throughout the area as a whole: they lived in a big-town culture. It should be said, too, that, internationally, these Swedish suburbs that were products of the national welfare policy were as yet strikingly unsegregated in social or ethnic terms.

Swedish criticism in 1968 was, not unnaturally, flavoured by the politics of 1968. It, as well as demonstrations and occupations, aimed not just at the rationalist planning of the Million-Programme suburbs but also at urban renewal and regional policies. Together with social workers and other working groups, young architects showed that they stood on the side of the tenants. A celebrated combination of these methods occurred in the centre of Stockholm in 1971, when a clump of elms occupying a site deemed to be needed for a subway station were therefore to be cut down. The trees were themselves occupied by mostly young Stockholmers. After a bit, the politicians and planners were forced to take heed of this early example of a 'green' demonstration and did actually change their minds.

The debate inhibited the building of large apartment blocks, and did so all the more on account of an excess of supply over demand on the rented-property market. An annual rate of building 70,000 apartments was reached in 1968–69 but declined to 40,000 in 1974 (the last year of the Million Programme) and below 20,000 by 1980. By then, the unprecedented phenomenon of unrentable apartments had begun to appear, especially in the dormitory suburbs; the market had given a clear indication that left traces in architecture. Throughout the period, about 40,000 private houses were built each year.

From Big Programmes to Small-scale Work

No special official support was given to building private houses but this was favoured by rising inflation and the tax-deductible status of all interest payments. When building costs rose, and fewer people built their own houses, countermeasures were taken in the form of building groups of private houses; during the 1960s these accounted for over half of the private houses built. Ella gård in Täby, designed by FFNS in the mid 1950s, is a set of traditional row houses with cellars on large sites along slightly curved roads but without traffic segregation. In Nordanbygärde, Västerås, the plan and houses were more strict, and the individual plots half the size; this had been designed by Åke Östin and was ready for occupancy in 1961. The Slagstad project, sketched by Hans Fog and Bernt Sahlin was launched by the Stockholm tabloid, Expressen, in 1959, as a 'car town' of one-storey houses that would be the 'town for the 1960s'.

Building of one-off houses was dominated by the companies that sold ready-to-erect houses in wood or light concrete. During the 1960s and 1970s, they developed their production techniques, as well as marketing through catalogues. The slogan of "from owner-built to private house" summed up the change in character about 1960. One-floor houses with bricked facades replaced the traditional houses with cellars with planked facades. Areas increased; four-rooms-and-a-kitchen apartments were now built mostly in small houses.[12]

The building of apartment blocks responded to the reactions to the errors of the Million Programme. For Ralph Erskine the question was one of the continuity of claims for integration and variation, besides the social significance of architecture. He spent much of the time of the Million Programme working in his native England, mostly on his large Byker project (1969–81), which has been celebrated for his striving towards tenants' influ-

Ella gård (1955–70): an area of 500 houses with 4 rooms and a kitchen on their ground floors and an attic that could be furnished.

ence among the former inhabitants of the old, demolished Byker area, and for his Byker Wall that gives protection against the north and an area reserved for traffic. But, above all, Byker was a densely-built, low housing area, with different forms of dwellings.

Erskine developed this theme at Nya Bruket, Sandviken, in 1973–78 (see catalogue), in a town where he had earlier designed a small central quarter with dwellings, shops and offices. Erskine's project has a small wall of houses giving shelter from the north but has otherwise a clear structure of an urban quarter with two-storey houses around yards. Ground-floor apartments have their own outdoor places; those upstairs are reached along galleries. Apertures between houses are closed off by planking and have definitively indicated porticos. A building containing a laundry facility and a general meeting room is sited in the middle of each semi-private yard. The buildings have gabled roofs and characteristically

Byker, Newcastle-on-Tyne (1969–81); Erskine got few Swedish commissions during the years of the Million Programme.

colourful wooden panelling but also clearly belong to an unbridled modernism.

Grimstaby in Upplands Väsby, a suburban community to the north of Stockholm, took these developments further still. Preconditions were special, which led to a far-going integration of activities. The Brunnberg group of architects, which derived from the Curman office, designed it. The housing company, Väsbyhem, was ambitious and made efforts to ensure the centre and its apartments would be united into a structure of small units located along a village street. A school, a kindergarten and a after-school centre are part of it and share open spaces with the dwellings. A public library, post-office and shops are located in a square, and a festival place is provided at one end of the area. The houses have steeply gabled roofs, a highly various and deliberately 'untidy' architecture with light rendering and wooden planking in pastel colours. The character of the whole is traditional.[13]

After the modernism of the Million Programme, the catchwords were integration, variation and tradition. More than anything else, the building of housing became subject to shifts in thinking: from big programmes to small projects, from apartment blocks to private houses, from a producers' to a buyers' market, from assembling prefabricated elements to on-site building, from modernism to post-modernism.

The Transformation of Town Centres

Three forces in town centres caused their buildings to be replaced and the patterns they had formed to be broken: rationalisation of retail-trade structures, increased car traffic, and more office work. Rising wages caused a growing market for consumer goods in general, including ready-to-use food products, as well as self-service shops and department stores, in which employment costs rose. Department stores' catchment areas were large and attracted many customers to come by car to their central locations.

The expanding services' sector generated less car traffic but, especially in the larger towns, led to new office buildings displacing older residential property and small businesses. The situation was well summed up in an article by Göran Lindahl published in 1965.

"During the 1950s, events forced a planning doctrine into existence for practical application. It included virtually no conscious, deliberated defence for the values of the-then existing old town centres, nor any promises for the future about the core of the city. It obtained its character in reality from the cooperation of the two parties that made the decisions: technical-minded municipal tacticians of razing buildings and representatives of commerce and industry, primarily the financially strongest retailers. Retrospectively, a pattern was formed that town after town tried to fit its centre into, a way of if at all possible unifying the claims of trade and commerce with demands for a more-or-less respectable standard of traffic. Normally this meant a highly compressed sales' areas, combined if it could be with a stumpy pedestrian precinct, and surrounded with roads." The writer observed that the same sort of thing emerged in Gävle, Norrköping, Umeå, Uppsala, Västerås and Örebro, without giving rise to any good architecture: "the whole can become a trying combination of demands for commercial expression and half-and-half artistic invention."[14]

Örebro and its 'Citizens' House'

In 1955 an architectural competition won by Erik and Tore Ahlsén inaugurated the razing of the southern part of central Örebro, for its two-storey wooden buildings were regarded as quite impossible to preserve, although a few of them were moved to a museum reservation (Wadköping) outside the town centre; much the same sort of thing occurred elsewhere. The Ahlséns designed two buildings in Örebro that were distinctive not just in the town but in the 1960s.

The Krämaren complex, like many new urban developments, filled a whole urban

Grimstaby (1977), Upplands Väsby, ambitiously integrated schools and other public-sector services into residential property that otherwise contained apartments.

Citizens' House (1965), Örebro, containing offices, theatre, conference centre and hotel; in the background can be seen part of the rest of the new centre of the town.

block and combined various functions: a department store, offices and apartments. To cope with this size, the architects chose as an analogy the four-square late Renaissance castle that lay 300 m north of the site of their building on an island in the centre of Örebro. The department store, built in strongly profiled concrete and with a roof terrace over the edges of which greenery now hangs down, forms as it were a low 'island' from which rise two eleven-storey blocks of apartments below each of which are office premises.

The 'Citizens' House', lying about 100 m south of the Krämaren complex, was built hurriedly to be ready by 1965 for the celebrations of the 700th anniversary of Örebro's founding (see also catalogue). Planned as the local Folkets hus, premises usually owned and occupied by one or more of the constituent parts of the Labour Movement, it was thought of as a civil counterpart to the castle. Thus, besides a theatre, premises for public events, a restaurant, a hotel, offices and shops, it also contains a congress centre.

It is the richest of all the Ahlséns' buildings and exemplifies their 'sensual realism'. It is an out-and-out modern building that fulfils all five of Le Corbusier's points for a new architecture. Its pilotis are exposed around its main entry. Their use in this partly prefabricated building allows an unrestricted plan and facade, so that neither it nor the inner walls are load-bearing. The row of fenestration is marked clearly in the upper floors' rows of repeated rooms. The Fifth Point, the roof terrace, is a pastorally undulating grassed space

above the large rooms. The building's sculptural volume, with its extensions, has similarities with that of Le Corbusier's La Tourette, except that it has none of the raw concrete of the latter. Its material includes red sandstone, plaster, teak, copper, stainless steel and glass; set flush in a collage, its reflections of light are more important that any composition of shadows. Above this tectonic theme of construction and materials, the Ahlséns worked with historical associations, primarily to those of the castle in Örebro: the building has traces of

Citizens' House, Örebro: lower foyer, beneath the theatre's sloping floor, showing a characteristic mixture of "bold" and "polished" material and intentional collisions between modern forms and traditional, banal elements.

PUB department store: half its volume is below ground level.

the castle's corner turrets, extensions, baroque copes as roofs on the turrets, ashlar surrounds of doors and on corners. The simple means of building were, every bit as much as what was formed with artistic freedom, self evident for the Ahlséns, who had come to architecture along a lengthy road; they are among the central figures in a tradition of lyrical modernism or sensual realism that is strong in Swedish 20th-century architecture.[15]

Central Stockholm: Kulturhus and the Bank of Sweden

During the 1960s, the centre of Stockholm was transformed from the former market square of Hötorget southwards to the water. "The reaction came when, in conjunction with the City 62 plan, the administrative authorities of the town wanted a new, extended mandate to continue."[16] This reaction concerned the relationship between preservation and renewal. Comprised mainly of people in the arts, the opponents wanted the continued renewal to have, instead of the "trumpet blasts" of the five point blocks that were the most visible part of the new buildings, the "chamber music" of smaller buildings along typical town streets.

The town plans from 1962, 1967 and 1975 together tell the story of a rising and falling belief in the future, and the sluggish responses of the planning apparatus to this and other changes in the realities of Swedish life. As in other large towns, but in different proportions, the three forces of retail-trade interests, motor traffic and office work were at work in Stockholm. What became called Hötorgscity turned into a 'shopping center' of department stores that, in their building and operations, tried to outdo one other in size, turnover and small numbers of employees. Rationalisation of the structure of commerce was facilitated by this sort of building, which made this centre competitive with those coming into existence on the periphery of the Stockholm region. With about one customer in three coming to Hötorgscity by car, such traffic and numbers of parking places were still being presupposed, in the 1967 plan, to go on increasing rapidly, notwithstanding protests. The 1975 plan eliminated a number of planned but not yet executed street widenings, and reduced the planned eventual total of numbers of parking places to fewer than those envisaged in 1962. Long, wide tracts of the centre were to be razed and excavated to provide tunnels for road traffic and new subway lines.

PUB department store (1960), Stockholm: a wholly glazed store symbolising the open cooperative movement.

Demand for centrally-located offices was a force even greater in Stockholm than elsewhere. Theories of economics posited the importance, which planners accepted, of the location in the centre of a national capital of a country's principal corporations and its main banks' management functions.[17]

The big department stores were a new type of building that departed from previous urban patterns through their size and hermetic character. As early as 1960, the Ahlséns had tried to make the PUB department store, on Hötorget itself, the very opposite of hermetic, namely, a prismatic glazed lantern that should both symbolise the open spirit of cooperative retail trade and make the best use of a restricted site by keeping its external walls thin; this was typical of the brothers' concern for ideological and practical matters. The far larger Åhléns department store, designed by Back-

Department store (1964), providing much wall space and a controlled indoor climate.

ström and Reinius and inaugurated in 1964, was quite a different matter: as hermetic as its American models and occupying what should therefore be called an entire city block, its almost entirely windowless facade was articulated through the use of carefully patterned brickwork and embellished with no more than a single logotype and a decorative clock. Both it and the PUB store have half their volume below ground level.

With the completion of Kulturhuset, the centre acquired a building for a diversity of activities, an *allaktivitetshus*, that looked all the more remarkable for being sited in the middle of a lot of dull complexes of office buildings; the leading Stockholm politician of the day, Hjalmar Mehr, called it "the crowning glory". Between the Kulturhus and the Bank of Sweden there was what was called a "an urban-planning joint", marking a shift from modernism to the "borrowing from the past" exhibited by the Bank of Sweden building.[18]

Both were by the same architect, Peter Celsing. He won the competition for these two buildings, and a town theatre, that was held in 1966. Kulturhuset was built in stages, of which the first was complete by 1971; it was used for 12 years as provisional premises for the Riksdag. By 1974 its second half was completed, and, by 1976, the whole Bank of Sweden building was complete (see catalogue).

The urban-planning conditions on and around these sites were complex. The north-south line of Sveavägen was to terminate here, (rather than to follow an old suggestion and be carried further south to the water, as Erskine, Geisendorf and Tengbom had proposed in a much-discussed competition entry), while

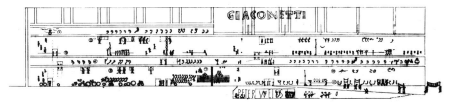

the line between the now open, modernistic Hötorgscity area and the one of close-packed, traditional streets crossed the line of the road. Celsing welcomed the complexity by making it plain, in that he proposed three separate parts: the first two, the screen of Kulturhuset and the cube-like complex of the theatre and hotel give onto the new open space called Sergels torg, while the palatial Bank of Sweden building gives onto the square. Other competition entries, which had been bought in, proposed large-scale, unified structures.

The idea of a 'culture house' grew out of the open, creative activity at the Museum of Modern Art, and its director, Pontus Hultén, helped to formulate a programme for a building with "street atmosphere and a workshop's possibilities". Giving onto the north, the southern, concrete screen wall of the building embraces and terminates the space outside, called Sergels torg. The screen contains all the vertical installations, that emerge in the powerfully sculptural roof landscape. Its facade comprises sheets of glass fitted between the projecting floors, the 'shelves'. The horizontality of the building, and thus all its activities, are emphasised. Its interiors are raw in character, like those of a workshop, pointed up here and there by the use of marble in a corner. Undismayed, Celsing hung, in the foyer to the

Culture House, sketch by Celsing: the building as a musical score, in which a passer-by can read all the activities of the house.

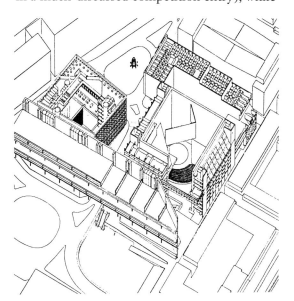

Culture House, Town Theatre and Bank of Sweden, (1966–76): an urban expansion joint.

Culture House: its clear structure includes a closed screen to the south, an open space giving onto the north and a frontal sunken area. Installations appear on the lively roof landscape.

Bank of Sweden. A palatial volume and heavy black-granite facade gives the institution a dignity lightened by small irregularities in the building.

premises occupied temporarily by the riksdag, crystal chandeliers, suspended from the modernist ceiling. The building is an open, modern structure, but without the fright of orthodoxy for contradictions.

The Bank of Sweden building has another character, through its references to the hermetic quality of Renaissance palaces with rusticated stone walls. It embodies memories of the building that previously occupied the site, as well as that of the one in which the bank was originally housed, on Järntorget, in the Old Town. Celsing's earlier proposals showed relatively simple facade grids but, in taking form in black granite, they developed a steadily great weight and complexity. The interior has another tone, being in light birch wood, with walls in stucco lustro. The facade of the interior yard, in folded glass and copper, terminates upwards in the glazed cupola over the top-floor swimming and exercise facilities, which are richly formed. They crowned a building on which an exceptional amount of work had been lavished, including that of artists, Sivert Lindblom, Olle Nyman and Ulrik Samuelson, and a garden designer,

Bank of Sweden. The top-floor recreational facility was formed largely by artists working closely with the architects.

C. Th. Sørensen, a Dane. In all work by architects totalled some 100,000 hours, which makes about 3 hours per square metre, or six times the usual expenditure of time on office buildings. Celsing's ambition level, and the results he and his colleagues achieved, can best be compared with Ragnar Östberg's Stockholm Town Hall, built fifty years earlier.[19]

Wilfried Wang has suggested that, in his work on the Bank of Sweden building and Kulturhuset, Celsing's view of architecture has similarities with both Rossi's typological thinking and Venturi's interest for historical references, while Kulturhuset is a precursor to Centre Beaubourg. Wang interprets Celsing's work as an "inclusive" architecture that is open to the view of its users, besides exhibiting an attempt to cast anchor in its national society and culture.[20] It is remarkable that Swedish commentators, while respecting Celsing, seldom do other than describe the architecture and his work as "exclusive" and, to a high degree, on the margins of his time.[21]

The centres of other swedish towns underwent as drastic a transformation as did central Stockholm in the light of rational planning in the interests of retail trade, traffic and office premises. In the early 1970s, the many small shops and businesses in one fifth of the centre of Göteborg were displaced when this part was razed to build a shopping centre, Östra Nordstan; underground roads gave access for freight traffic; customers used the central, indoor concourse area. Ninety separate sites had become ten. "This latest example of 1960s urban-planning optimism" demonstrated a "catastrophic difference in intensity".[22]

The Philosophy of Structure

The "strong society" that grew during the 1960s called for a rapidly increasing amount of building work to house its administrative apparatus, and new schools and other educational institutions, which led to competition over scarce labour with the industry that was building dwellings. Until 1967, when its work was reorganised, the National Board of Building and Planning was responsible for both public-sector building work and the national administration of planning; later, the board retained responsibility for ensuring central-government needs of premises, including their building and administration, were met, while its responsibility for planning, together with that for building norms, were vested in the new National Planning Board. The acute need for a rational production of premises, and the experienced property administrator's insight into a constant need for rebuilding, led to a novel method or philosophy of planning developed by the board's architects, including Nils Ahrbom and Olof Eriksson, in conjunction with some large consulting companies.

This philosophy of structure, or structuralism, had some simple points of departure that were presented in a report, *Byggprocess och verksplanering*, published in 1966. It departed from the functionalist view of form as a consequence of functions derived from analysis in the work of drawing up a programme. Costly experience showed that activities, and the functions of buildings, could change, often while planning work was still being done; the problems this posed could be worsened by the technical components of a modern building. In addition, the lifetimes of a building's functions and its technical components could differ greatly. Rational administration required that components could be replaced individually.

In its own developmental work, the National Building Board specified parts associated with the context that included the physical divisions of sites, the road network and the public-sector infrastructure; those associated with the building itself, which included its bearing frame, vertical communications, and vertical and horizontal conduits for technical facilities; and those associated to its activities, which included intermediate walls and facilities inherent to the activity. The lifetimes of each of these varied: from centuries for an urban plan to a decade or less for a user.

In presenting this thinking in broad terms, the *Arkitektur-Struktur* exhibition in 1968 had a number of central concepts: generality, coordination of dimensions, separations between parts having different estimated lifetimes, ability to change. The exhibition contained links to the international visionary structuralism of Archigram, Habraken and others, but its other international contacts were few. The special, and in many ways unique, qualities of Swedish structuralism was its pragmatic view and extensive application in national public-sector building work of high quality.

The Office Building Box

The Garnisonen building in eastern central Stockholm (Östermalm) was a pilot project using the National Building Board's office building box that was developed in 1965–66 by ELLT. This firm and the one called A4,

later amalgamated to form Coordinator, became the leaders in applying the philosophy of structure in architecture. As this name suggests, the firm developed a way of working collectively that was typical for the time.

ELLT had spelled out its working principles in an article published in Finland in 1967. This spoke of a society increasingly marked by urbanisation and rationalisation, of more and more general tasks and regulations, of architecture as less concerned with houses, more with urban planning. In architects' offices this demanded systematic planning and participation in developing industrial processes in building. The office was organised collectively in a democratic spirit. It summarises its theme

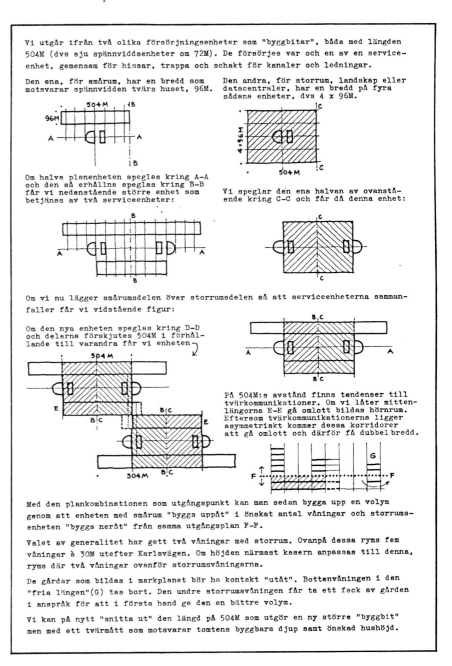

Garnisonen (1972): a carefully worked out accumulation of standard small-office units or office landscapes or computing centres, each with its access lifts, stairs and services.

Training centre, IBM (1970), Lidingö: a clear view of its division into three naves with different types of space, as well as its use of untreated material, including high-fired brick and corten steel, opposed to lacquered parts.

Televerket, Farsta, Stockholm, by Hidemark and Danielson (architects) and Sven Olov Nyberg (landscape architect), 1969. This large facility built of strictly standardised concrete elements became a good working environment on account of its reasonable scale and the careful treatment of its site.

by stating "our belief is that the necessary knowledge does not obstruct but is, by contrast, the basis on which to develop a living architectural art."[23]

The Garnisonen building, which began with a commission to plan in 1964, was completed by 1972. The large late 19th-century properties in the area were to remain in place. The programme declared it was to be office premises for central-government departments with unspecified divisions between conventional offices, landscape offices and computing centres. Planning began with very general studies of the physical structure of the building in relation to its putative users. Its generality showed itself to be large enough to accommodate even the riksdag, which was in fact tested.

Intellectually, the project was a triumph for systematic planning. However, what had been conceived in the 1960s by minds thinking of democratically open central-government administration in a condition of constant change was born, so to say, into the decade of the 1970s when the infant Garnisonen was seen as symbolising a bureaucracy hiding behind anonymous facades. But while Garnisonen had been in the womb, the central government had changed its mind. Giving effect to a riksdag decision in the interests of regional policy, it no longer wanted the immense extension in Stockholm of central-government administration that Garnisonen had been created to house. Instead, this administration was to be despatched, bit by bit, to smaller towns, which was done in the second half of the 1970s.

Until 1965, Swedish police forces were municipal in structure, but they were then brought together into a single national force. A large number of premises for police purposes became necessary. The ELLT architect group designed some of them, the first being the one in Gävle (1967–69). Building-box thinking was applied consistently, and the expressions of the first police buildings were most precise and minimalistic: flat roofs, long rows of fenestration, facades in metal sheet, strong colours. Developments during the 1970s were away from prefabricated building both for economic reasons and because users resisted the application of unconventional resolutions.[24]

At the same time as ELLT was working on the Gävle police building, it was doing the IBM Nordic Education Center at Lidingö (see catalogue), just east of Stockholm, where the architects took a large stride forward both in expressing structuralist thinking and using material in a raw and obvious way. The Center lies on a lovely peninsula jutting out into the Baltic. The building's three naves are separated by high brick-faced installation walls enclosing conduits for technical facilities.[25]

An early, well executed project by the National Building Board that demonstrated the possibilities of building with elements is the Televerket administrative building at Farsta, by Bengt Hidemark and Gösta Danielson; its first stage was completed by 1969. Analyses showed that low buildings around an enclosed yard gave the most efficient and less costly solution. Almost the whole of this large building could be made from three types of facade elements and two wall elements. By staggering the layout of the internal yards, and treating the terrain carefully, an intimate urban environment could be created, despite the severe degree of standardisation.[26]

After the record years at the end of the 1960s, building of office premises for central-government purposes underwent a change as dramatic as that which affected the building of dwellings. Decentralisation of such administrative units from Stockholm to smaller towns has already been mentioned. As a consequence of decisions by the riksdag in 1971 and 1973, a total of 11,000 places of work were moved from Stockholm to dispersed, medium-sized Swedish towns. The new building work undertaken in the mid 1970s followed the building-box thinking already mentioned, but entailed more than anything else a return to building technologies of a more traditional form. When, in 1973, Bengt Hidemark presented the ai-group's project for SMHI, the Swedish Meterological and Hydrological Institute, in Norrköping, he justified his proposal that the buildings should be cast on-site and given a bricked facade by saying "that, within the same cost framework, among other things, this would increase jobs."[27] The shortage of labour that had preceded building with elements had now turned into its opposite.

A number of buildings created for decentralisation purposes and completed in 1976 were all built on-site, and tried in various ways to break down the big-scale effect and adapt themselves to their immediate surroundings, they include SIB, the Building Research Institute, in Gävle, by Erik and Tore Ahlsén; the very extensive facilities at Karolinen in Karlstad, by Gösta Edberg; and the building in Uppsala that houses both the National Foodstuffs Authority and the provincial administration, by Arkitekthuset Götgatan 18.[28]

Building Universities

During the 1960s and 1970s, work by the National Building Board that was as extensive as its work on office premises was building universities and other institutions of higher education. The background was the large increases in nativity in the mid 1940s and a rapidly increasing proportion of young people who, thanks among other things to a system of loans for university studies could afford to undertake further education.

Between 1952 and 1970, the numbers of persons studying at universities increased from 17,000 to 120,000. The task was as if made for the philosophy of structure, with its interest in change. "In reality, the attempts formally to express generality and flexibility in architecture sometimes gave it an unnecessarily schematic character. At the same time, the real flexibility became too limited for it to be able in all parts to capture a novel, different pedagogic consciousness that matured in higher

Southern building, Frescati university (1971), Stockholm. Its first part was criticised for an over-rational view of the pursuit of knowledge that caused students to be strictly separated from their teachers.

education." wrote Olof Eriksson, an architect with the National Building Board, in 1972.[29]

Frescati in Stockholm became a monument to the new ideas, and a target for the sharpest criticism.[30] Plans to move the university in Stockholm away from the town centre had been growing since the 1950s. A competition in 1960 was won by Henning Larsen, a Danish architect, who proposed a big concrete deck with cars below and pedestrians above. David Helldén's more economic and extendable proposal, which won second prize, was in fact the one that was built. Helldén designed the six slab blocks, the abstract and separated functions of which were violently criticised in 1971, when their first users moved in and the area was otherwise incomplete. Since then Frescati has been completed both architecturally and functionally by, among other buildings, Ralph Erskine's Allhus, a general-purpose student building, and adjoining library that comprise freely sculptured meeting places; they were completed by 1981–82. In 1997, Frescati achieved final completion with the opening of Erskine's Aula Magna, its final new building, simultaneously with the planning of a new university to be located to the south of Stockholm (see catalogue).

In 1963, at the Malmö Teachers' Training

Allhuset (1981), Frescati: a restaurant, bookshop and etc in a tent-like building mainly in wood. In contrast to the right-angular character of the other new buildings, this one took account of the terrain and climate of the site.

Teacher Training College (1963), Malmö: long, low and in brick, it had good internal lighting.

College, Carl Nyrén had developed a highly systematic sorting of his programme; he formed a section that, in principle, was repeated at intervals of 300 m. This was architecture of a traditional kind, in brick. One of the most consistent and architecturally successful examples of structuralism is his Arrheniuslaboratorium at Frescati, built in 1973 (see also catalogue): the whole is built from elements restricted to a single pillar, a single beam and a single wall element. External pillars give the building an expressive clarity and relief. The repeated untreated concrete elements of its longitudinal sides contrast with its wooden windows. A similar building box of prefabricated elements was used at the same time by Nyrén in the laboratories he designed for Pharmacia in Uppsala; they continued to be extended throughout the 1980s. Nyrén also chose to make visible the bearing structure on the exterior of an inner-city building in central Stockholm, his Sparbanken on Hamngatan (completed 1975).

The college of higher education in Göteborg became, formally, a university in 1954. Unlike the university in Stockholm, the one in Göteborg remained in the centre of the town,

making do until the 1980s with rented accommodation very variously located in the centre. Building for higher education in Göteborg during the 1950s and 1960s were of premises for Chalmers University of Technology and, on Medicinarberget, those for medical studies; many were designed by Klas Anshelm, who also designed the University of Technology in Lund, where he had his office.

Anshelm is one of the very few architects to have worked both with the large programmes and smaller cultural buildings, always with a straightforward simple architecture in brick with ingenious detailed resolutions. The Technical University in Lund (1960–69) is characteristic for the thinking of the National Building Board. Each section in the school has its own building that can be enlarged by 100%, which is why the buildings are arranged as parallel lengths of different types of premises: lecture rooms, offices, laboratories; each can be extended in either direction along the length. Anshelm refrained from the spectacular expressiveness of element building: "Each attempt failed with the lofty buildings to make them less costly with prefabricated elements." [31]

The University of Technology in Lund included a new School of Architecture that, opened in 1964, was the third in Sweden. Architectural education was expanded greatly to match increased building in general; each of the schools of architecture was furnished with new premises. The one in Lund, by Klas Anshelm, is a robust building in brick, resembling the others in the university. The building in Chalmers University of Technology, by Helge Zimdal (1968), a square building around a courtyard, reflects the four years of an architect's formal education and its four main subjects, and is thus hardly an expression of the thinking of architectural structuralism about generality.

The most particular school of architecture

College of Technology, Lund, laid out with later expansion in mind, on a bit windy open former farming land.

School of Architecture (1969), Stockholm: offices and drawing rooms in an angled, hermetic block that turns its back on the town outside; larger rooms give onto its own courtyard. Its faces are done in concrete, concrete-and-stone, and copper.

is the one at KTH, the Swedish abbreviation of the name of the Royal College of Technology, designed by Gunnar Henriksson and John Olsson and completed by 1969. During his time at the KF architects' office, Henriksson had been responsible for the San Remo bakery in the Stockholm suburb of Västberga (1969): a clearly neo-modernistic industrial building with a thin shell of a facade over activities arranged by reference to function. Another of his buildings at KTH, that for the Institution for Machine Technology and Mining, built in the second half of the 1960s, has a similar character. Simplicity in precise volumes and a restricted choice of materials is more programmed than with Anshelm. The KTH architectural school is located in Östermalm, the east-central area of Stockholm, which comprises mostly compact residential blocks; its uncompact, copper-clad facade, behind which are studios, faces the Engelbrekt church. Its other facades display its concrete framework interspersed with grey concrete and with freely placed small windows.

Among the large high-education buildings of the time were some in newly established universities. Umeå became the fifth Swedish university and was built to a plan by Hans Brunnberg (1962) with yellow brick buildings sited in a landscaped park with an ornamental lake, inspired by Århus University, Denmark. Like all other newly established universities it was located outside the town centre; the A4/Coordinator architects' grouping designed many of its initial buildings. Umeå

was followed, rapidly, by Linköping: the decision was made in 1968, the first users moved in two years later, its premises were complete by 1972. It was a pilot project for the philosophy of structuralism. The architects, the ai-group, were a group of consultants with Hidemark and Danielson as architects. On account of the shortage of time, they chose prefabricated steel designs, with facades in lacquered metal sheeting, which conferred a character of an industrial building on this university.

Other Institutions

The National Building Board was also responsible for commissioning buildings for the national post office, telephone service, air-traffic authority and the Swedish Broadcasting Corporation. Much of what was thus built was characterised by the same thinking and was designed by the same architects. Large new airports were built far outside the main towns. Stockholm Arlanda took over by stages the functions of Bromma during the 1960s; its international passenger terminal, designed by the firm of Bjurström, John and Rosén, was complete by 1976. Coordinator designed both Sturup (1972) outside Malmö and Landvetter (1977) outside Göteborg.

Expansion of public-service radio/TV services called for new buildings. The large premises of these services in eastern central Stockholm, by Gärdet, were further extended during the 1960s and, by 1979, complemented with the nearby Berwald Concert Hall; all was designed by VBB in an internal modernistic style. The radio/TV building in Göteborg (1970), designed by the White office, is more clearly in accordance with structuralist thinking. Its courtyards, openings in a compact grid, are filled with larger studios. Its entry is into a welcoming glazed foyer extending upwards to include two floors.

A focal point in the radio/TV network is the Kaknästornet, by the Borgström and Lindroos firm (see also catalogue), a powerful tower in concrete with a strict geometry of diagonally placed squares containing antennae and a restaurant; the tower is a landmark for the novel technology of the new national society of the 1960s. Lindroos, who had worked with Markelius, represented a clearly modernistic line inspired by Louis Kahn.

New buildings marked by structuralist thinking, besides those built in accordance with central-government policy, included hospitals and other health-care buildings for county administrations and municipal schools.

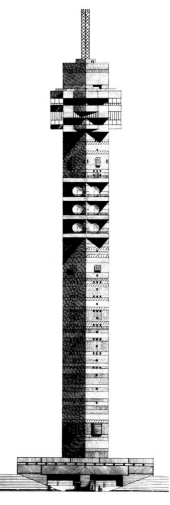

Kaknäs Tower (1967), Stockholm: simple geometric form done in slip-cast concrete, then a novel method.

The compact, chequered structure, with small inner courtyards was a resolution that offered a freedom in re-building, which revealed itself as usual in hospitals that were full of technical equipment. Models existed in international structuralism. In building hospitals, as in building dwellings, thoughts of efficiency often gained the upper hand and led to gigantic establishments: Huddinge hospital, for example, designed by HLLS (1974).

At the end of the 1960s, school building was changed greatly in response to various teaching plans and pedagogical ideas. There was a general interest in large schools built on a single level, with small inner courtyards and classrooms placed around a central study hall. The aim was to get space for teamwork with groups of various sizes. There was also at the time a desire to integrate schools into the local context and to coordinate them with other services to their urban societies. Brickebacken in Örebro, a housing area and combined school and centre (1969–73), designed by White, followed the national service committee's recommendations about integrated service centres.[32]

Compared with the other large programmes of building, the broad activities undertaken for institutions responsible to the central government appear as having a particularly high average level, thanks to an engaged client who commissioned good architects. The structure philosophy was a deliberate architectural expression for a national society in the midst of dramatic change. It was in many ways a characteristic expression for Swedish architecture that emphasises general utility and buildings that are factual and enduring. At the same time, fascinated by the efficiency of the method, and the need for hurry, this philosophy added its own one-sidedness to those of the large programmes.

The rational methods of the thinking in the abstract about planning were inadequate. Many architects sought to cast anchor in history, and what was closest to hand was to search through the "functional tradition" that had been of interest in the 1930s and 1940s. Bernard Rudofsky's *Architecture without architects* (1964) was a timely publication. It is striking how many of the most modern architects in Sweden found inspiration in "the Swedish poverty" of anonymous, simple vernacular buildings. Architects at the White office could find it in the wooden-built Swedish towns or in the 'work's communities'. Bengt Lindroos travelled around the country, documenting old storage buildings; Gunnar Henriksson has had a lifelong interest in the techniques of wooden-frame construction.[33]

This interest in the original and elementary has parallels with the seeking by international structuralists for a sort of anthropological constants, but also has similarities with references to traditions at the turn of the 20th century as an answer in a time of rapid change. It poses the question of the relationship between tasks for society and a proffesional culture, between building and art.

The Double Movement

This chapter has hitherto considered the large building programmes, but, while they were proceeding, building also progressed on a smaller scale and with greater artistic freedom for its architects. Some of them managed to do both sorts of work, but commissions for parts of the large programmes went mainly to the big architectural offices. In Sweden, the 1960s were characterised by an unhappy disparity between the large modern scale and the small and traditional. The choice for architects was between two extremes: to throw away artistic intentions and throw oneself into production-adapted design or to retreat into a haven of beauty that ecclesiastic building came to be seen as.

The "double movement" is an expression signifying modernism's two sides: on one, a society built on commonsense, specialisation, secularisation and social liberation, and, on the other, the aesthetics of the autonomy of art and the artist's self-realisation.[34]

A writer, Stig Claesson, took up such a position, which he formulated in a 1965 number of Arkitektur, imagining an architect caught in this trap. "Thus he prepares a gruel composed of Swedish standard measurements and promulgations from the social authorities and is peculiar enough to be prepared, even if it is popular to claim the opposite, to consume this concoction. Unable even to indulge in pretence, he gives his evenings to designing what will later become a pipe rack or he sketches an anthroposophist chapel that is to be erected in the middle of the green expanses of Gärdet…" Faced, the following year, by yet another such gathering of similarly critical writers, assembled by a journalist, Olle Bengtzon, under a headline of 'Fresh Breezes in Slack Sails', a building-functions researcher, Sven Thiberg, had definitely had enough: "Who is going to settle accounts with the agreeably scented past and put their efforts into a new society with consistent resolutions of functional demands?

Cover by the artist Stig Claesson known as 'Slas', showing his view of a typical Swedish urban scene. The number addressed the question of urban planning deriving from local conditions.

Some have perhaps pinned their hope on writers, on artists, who have allowed themselves time to listen, analyze and formulate. But they, too, looked helplessly about them when asked to give their opinions about the planning of a national society and could manage no more than to display a vision of being awkwardly in two minds: in truth, skulls without skills."[35]

In his book, *Nordisk arkitektur*, Nils Ole Lund points out what for him is typically Swedish, a split between architecture as art and as building. He explains it by reference to the rapid modernisation of Sweden as early as the 1950s, far earlier than in the other, poorer countries of Scandinavia. Swedish architects progressively lost control over the building process, and the "Asplund ideal came into conflict with Swedish reality." Like many other foreign observers, Lund speaks of a "romantic" streak in Swedish architecture, since the days of Östberg and Asplund, a "sensitivity" that, in the hands of less talented architects, becomes in his eyes an altogether over picturesque architecture.[36]

In fact, romanticism and realism can be understood as two sides of modernity. In a description of the 1960s in Sweden, it is easy to over-emphasis the often naive belief in commonsense. At least as important was the process of social liberation and the questioning of authority that brought about the fall of a rationality that had been pushed too far. And just as well as national Swedish society had contained a long tradition of a strong state, a homogenous culture and a moralism of utilitarity derived from a need to survive, it had contained a very strong popular democratic tradition. To a high degree, Swedish farmers owned the land they worked, the aristocracy were the servants of the crown, the middle class relatively weak, and the popular movements of the 19th century an important school in democracy. Sven-Eric Liedman, a historian of ideas, has emphasised, in a text on 'the popular-minded public servant', the unique quality of these conditions, and has traced them back to an 18th-century tradition of popular education. He uses this observation to explain why modernisation of Sweden did not lead to violent clashes, despite taking place much more quickly than it did in the Great Britain or Germany. "The secret of this relatively rapid and still peaceful process lies in the state apparatus—the old brutal Swedish state of superordinate authority with all its concerns for the belief and manners of thought of the people—entered into a union with popular, even, to a certain extent radical, ways of thinking."[37]

The romantic streak in Swedish architecture can be partly understood as an expression of such a popular element, a taking exception to elitism and formalism, an absence of fear for what is banal. But this makes it difficult to distinguish the romantic from the conventional, the everyday, the factual and the practical, and thus also from realism and plain common sense. 'Loyally' and 'inclusively' to proceed from site and programme are other virtues of Swedish architecture that can be understood as both romantic, to the extent that they lead to an informal, 'picturesque' architecture, and realistic, because they derive from the surrounding reality.

"The double movement" is concerned with the relationship between national society and art. "The relative autonomy of architecture" is an expression from international discussions within architecture in the 1960s that claimed an independent significance for the culture of the profession and architectural knowledge, alongside, but not in contradiction of, the tasks of society.[38] Such a relative autonomy was hard to assert in Sweden in the 1960s. On the margin of national Swedish society there were a number of architects, however, who carried a culture professional forward. Some of them can be called romantics, others realists.

An Unconstrained Tradition

Jan Gezelius has spoken of an *unconstrained tradition* in Swedish architecture, in which he places the Ahlsén brothers, Klas Anshelm, Erik Asmussen and Ralph Erskine, and, in a younger generation, Gunnar Mattsson, Göran Månsson and Ove Hidemark. Behind this circle of architects he sees the influence of Sven Ivar Lind, both as an individual and as a teacher. In a text written in the mid 1980s, he proposes this "unconstrained and joy-in-building vein, this 'poetry in things as against

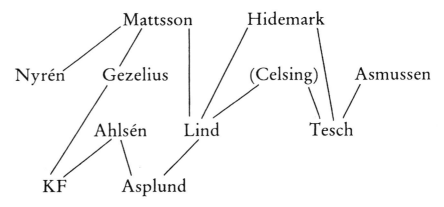

A four-generation structure, growing upwards like a coral reef, of the 'unconstrained tradition', with lines of apprenticeship and influence rising towards its present proponents.

poetry in words'" as an alternative to post-modernistic showers of isms.[39]

It is possible to compose a family tree for large parts of this tradition, in which the architects are related to one another in conditions of masters and apprentices, in the sense that those who are younger have worked under the eye of one or more of their elders. This tree is an image of a culture of a field of work mediated traditionally, to a high degree apart from the tasks of building in accordance with the large programmes. The roots of Asplund and the KF architects' office show something of the interrelationships of this tradition. The tree can be extended in several ways. Erskine had personal relationships with several of these architects. Through his work with Wejke and Ödéen, Anshelm's roots derive from the factuality of the KF architects' office, where these two architects had themselves worked.

Jan Gezelius himself must be included in this tradition to which he has given a name. He had worked in the KF office for Olof Thunström, and admired his ability to resolve plans and his precise and economical way with dimensions derived from German functionalism. But Gezelius is happy to quote Thunström's words to his colleagues that emphasise the popular element and readiness to improvise that Gezelius considered part of a Swedish tradition: "You've got to be banal in conclusion, otherwise people dare not move in."

Gezelius' own work is not extensive, for he taught the art of the garden or of building for long periods. In all he designed just over a dozen buildings: mostly small museums and private houses. They have had great influence. Three lie on the Baltic island of Öland. On its southern point, a gathering place for migrating birds, he built a small migrant-bird museum (1961) that can be seen as a narrowing, side-lit funnel, roofed as if with a kite. On

its northern point he built a house for a fishing family, Fiskarens hus, in 1963, which was one of a number of houses in Sweden commissioned by a magazine from young architects whose work on them it arranged to follow. Living and working with the family, Gezelius interpreted the landscape in a narrow wooden building with a free layout sited alongside a drystone boundary wall, an instance of "disciplined messiness"; its exterior is grey and rustic-looking, its interior strongly coloured and with flowery wallpaper; it is more like something of an Arts-and-Crafts house than anything local. In 1970, he designed the Drake house in Borlänge (see also catalogue): 5-m wide, with two storeys, a shallow roof and lighted windows, it had many imitators among houses built later in the decade. Some of his later work is happily at home in this postmodernist epoch. His museum at Eketorp, Öland, is part of a pedagogical reconstruction of a 5th-to-8th-century fortified settlement, built on its original site and using largely identical material: local limestone for the walls, local reeds for the roof but carried on laminated wooden beams and trusses; and roof lanterns to admit light to the interior.[40]

In 1939, Erik Asmussen, a Danish architect, came to Sweden. He began to work with Nils Tesch in Stockholm, with whom, in the late 1940s, he worked on the school at Solna. He opened his own practice in the early 1960s, having been commissioned to design Kristoffer School, a Waldorf school at Bromma, in western Stockholm, inspired by Rudolf Steiner's pedagogical ideas. Ever since, as the special architect for the Swedish anthroposophical movement, Asmussen has been inter-

Fisherman's House (1963), northern end of Öland: a suitably rugged external appearance.

Migrant-bird Museum (1961), showing its wind-challenging roof. The lighthouse lies on the southern point of Öland; the object to the left of the museum is a bird trap.

Library (1973), Järna. Together with a eurhythmics building, it formed the first large extension of the Anthroposophical Movement's premises at Järna. Like the rest of the Järna institutions, it contains a residential part.

Kristoffer School, Stockholm, by Erik Asmussen, 1965 and later. This Rudolf Steiner school was Asmussen's first commission for the Anthroposophical Movement in Sweden; he has since renewed its architecture.

preting Steiner's ideas about architecture, and, in doing so, he has applied his Danish background, the everyday classicism he absorbed from Tesch, and the Swedish traditions of building in wood. He uses an organic formal language that differs from German architects' interpretations. Compared with theirs, his architecture has a lighter, more restrained sculptural character. Together with Fritz Fuchs, an artist, he has developed the external and internal use of colours.

The Kristoffer school, extended on a number of occasions since 1965, was built in the face of opposition from the National School Board, which demanded greater planning flexibility; but it received the express support of several leading Swedish architects. The school resembles the one in Solna, in that it has a central hall and staircase, which doubles in function as an assembly hall. Asmussen's buildings at Järna (see also catalogue) since the 1960s include teaching premises, dwellings, shops, a cafeteria, larger assembly rooms, a flour mill and a bakery. To achieve a desired mixture of functions, the buildings in which teaching is done contain dwellings. In the Vidar Clinic (1987), Asmussen gave form to the thought that, in such a clinic, the healing process can be helped if patients can enjoy views of the exterior from their sickbeds, and proceed along attractive ways from sickrooms to the sheltered courtyard and thence out into the immediately surrounding farming land. At Vadstena, the municipal housing company commissioned Asmussen's office to design a small housing area (completed 1992; see also catalogue); this work included extensive development of sound materials, which was a part of the ecological thinking that has for a long time been a characteristic of the anthroposophical movement.[41]

For much of the 20th century, Sven Ivar

Lind has had a central place in Swedish architecture, primarily as a writer and teacher, and as an employer of younger architects. He had worked together with Asplund on many occasions, and when Asplund died, he took over his incomplete projects. He did not get the chair of architecture to the Royal College of Technology, Stockholm; the choice of Nils Ahrbom was that of systematic thinking before poetic interpretation.

Lind's volume of work is large, comprising mostly small, unusually well-worked projects but with an extensive range: the Råsunda (Stockholm) football stadium, some power stations, a number of crematoria and their chapels, a few museums. His own house at Kevinge (1946) is a careful study of light, space, relationships to its garden, material. But it avoids any strong form: contemporary opinion called it a self portrait. His buildings have rarely the elegance of Asplund's, but are very sparse and precisely in their form and material. In many respects, his chapels from the 1950s and 1960s are close to contemporary churches by Celsing and Lewerentz but without their strong sense of atmosphere. Lind's chapel in Nässjö (1962) is a simple room in brick from Helsingborg, with a pitched roof; an architecture with an order that is relieved by small, subtle shifts.

In his capacity of Palace Architect for the Royal Palace in Stockholm, Lind did two much remarked museums: the Skattkammaren (1970) and the Royal Armoury (1976). He went further with his earlier studies of light and made the museums murky chambers in which illuminated objects flowed in the dark.[42]

Museums and libraries are buildings of a sort that offer their architects a degree of freedom in giving form to space. Of architects' offices, that of Uhlin & Malm is one with a large production of substantial buildings,

Royal Armoury (1968–75), Royal Palace, Stockholm. Dark premises for light-sensitive objects, with display cases designed after careful studies of light strengths.

often in brick in a spirit like that of Alvar Aalto; their museum at Jokkmokk (1965) is a very simple building with its exhibition space contained in additional cubical volumes. Per-Olof Olsson (in the 1960s a radical editor of Arkitektur), designed the rebuilding of a naval gymnastic building on the island of Skeppsholmen in central Stockholm (1958), which became the Museum of Modern Art; and in 1962 turned a storage building on the same island into the Museum of Far Eastern Antiquities. Immediately across the water, his annex and workshops (1961) for the National Museum reinterpret its neo-Renaissance limestone in cor-ten steel.

Erik Uluot's library in Växjö (1965) is unusual in Sweden for its strongly reduced architecture: an abstract white volume that hovers on white pillars to give a minimalist impression of a classical temple. Jan Wallinder, early in his career employed by Asplund, has a large production of housing in Göteborg but has also designed libraries; that in Jönköping, designed together with Johan Hedborg, has an almost pyramidical design of volumes enclosed within volumes that gives a rich space.

"The Haven of Beauty": Celsing and Lewerentz

Building churches came to be, during the years of the big building programmes, the most important field of work for architects who wished to enjoy greater artistic freedom, which would have amazed people as soon before this happened as the early 1950s. But internal migration and expansion and creation of Swedish suburbs led to the building of an unprecedented number of small churches by the Church of Sweden: over 350 within a few decades.[43]

Celsing's and Lewerentz' archaic dark churches in brick came to set a style for this

ecclesiastic architecture, which was also exhibited by Söderled Church, Farsta (Borgström and Lindroos; 1960), Tannefors Church, Linköping (Axel and John Kandell, who worked with Sven Ivar Lind; 1964); a church in Vikmanshyttan (Jaan Allpere and Claes Mellin; 1966); and others. The most successful church architects, Rolf Bergh and Johannes Olivegren, differed in their architecture, which was more freely sculptural, light and liturgically functional. Bergh developed a type of ready-to-build, portable wooden church, as well as designing, for example, the church at Oxelösund (1957) that had a beacon-like concrete belfry that straddled the entire church. Olivegren's church at Biskopsgården, Göteborg (1961), has a similarly freely formed concrete tower that breaks against its suburban surroundings that are strictly right angular.[44]

The ELLT architects, discussed above in the context of large-scale, building-box work, also designed a couple of churches. As technical students, the four architects won a competition in 1954 for a crematorium in Gävle that was completed by 1960 (see also catalogue). It lies in a fir wood: some simple concrete walls, as high as a man, delimit the space of the chapel, over which its roof, supported on cylindrical steel pillars, seems to sway. The volumes have the simplicity and precision of Mies van der Rohe's work, but the material—beautifully form-cast concrete, cobble stones, oiled steel and wood—has a strength and sensuality in its treatment that few contemporary works could match. Together with Lewerentz' St. Mark's Church and the Ahlsén brothers' PUB department store, it was regarded as Swedish architecture taking a turn for the better after a period of artistic decline.[45] As a firm, the architects designed the Haparanda Church (1967), to replace a wooden church that had burned down. The new building, having the form of a lofty basilica, has a steel frame holding light-concrete planks; its exterior is faced with copper. Its simple, light, constructive

Biskopsgården Church (1961), Göteborg, typical of work by Johannes Olivegren.

Crematorium (1960), Gävle, with a strong material effect: a stone floor, planked concrete walls, steel pillars, a wooden roof and furniture.

Haparanda Church (1967). A classical basilica form expressed in modern materials: light-concrete planking, steel pillars, corrugated sheet metal.

interior space has more in common with 19th-century churches built in wood than with its modern contemporaries.

Härlanda Church in Göteborg was the first church designed by Peter Celsing. The result of a competition in 1952, its completion was delayed by labour-market considerations until 1958. It comprises three distinctive buildings: church, parish offices, belfry; they lie in conjunction with the ruins of a medieval church. In its internal and external walls, dark-fired Helsingborg bricks are laid in Flemish bond. Celsing described his aims, in part, as follows: "Designing the church, a large experience not only practically completed, psychological, in the technique of negotiation, but an artistic research. In secular commissions, the factors by which one steers are the functional, technical and economic, at least such is our belief. In building a church one cannot so easily get away with that. Light in a church cannot be only a light to read hymn books by."[46]

Thus he staked out his position in the debate in 1960 that swirled around his church of St. Thomas (consecrated 1959), of which

Ulf Hård af Segerstad wrote that "a severe fortress of God rears its dark, hermetic square tower beside the throbbing centre of Vällingby." With all respect, he identified practical shortcomings and a hardly inviting architectural language. In an ironical comment, Göran Lindahl mentioned demands for "pleasing churches to sit correctly in", meaning that churches had become "the haven of beauty" and that art was out of step with the welfare society.[47]

At this point in time, Celsing had designed in a short time a succession of other churches, of which most were of the same serious, hermetic and meagrely expressive sort. His chapel in Ludvika (1958) developed his theme from the parish-offices building at Härlanda, with a lean-to roof behind a wall. Almtuna Church, Uppsala (1959) lies on a relatively constricted site in an area of older private houses and forms a rather introverted forecourt on a level reached up a flight of steps. Boliden Church (1960) had been commissioned by the parish as a traditional church; it revives a medieval form usually built in stone, with a nave, choir

St. Thomas', Vällingby (1959), next to the centre. Block-like volumes in highfired Helsingborg brick became exemplary for small suburban churches.

Nacksta Church (1969), Sundsvall: a dark boat-shaped volume, with a steel structure for its bells and rainwater down pipes.

Interior of Nacksta: the church itself can be divided by a folding wall. The entry, sacristy and stairs down to the basement premises form an internal space of their own.

and sacristy beneath a steeply pitched roof. Built much later, the church in Nacksta, Sundsvall (1969), has another character: its exterior is rendered in dark blue, its interior white with light reflected from its fenestration. All activity is accommodated within its boat-shaped ground plan. The interior space of the church is divided by a bow-shaped roof bow and a cross beam. Its architectural references to ships and a cross are rich, and its hymn book light is excellent.

Few other architects of the time could match Peter Celsing in his broad repertoire of references to the history of architecture. In the demands of his programmes and preconditions of sites, he sought for a complexity in a way that foretold much of the discussions about post-modernism during the 1970s. All this is particularly clear in his own residence, Klockberga House, Drottningholm (1969; see also catalogue); it functioned as a sort of three-dimensional sketchbook while he was working on Kulturhuset.[48]

Although Celsing was 35 years younger than Lewerentz, it was he who developed the ecclesiastical architecture that Lewerentz was to take to its ultimate limits. They had come together in the early 1950s, when both worked on the plan—it was never realised—to restore the cathedral at Uppsala. Lewerentz had then been inactive as an architect for almost ten years; he had devoted the time to his factory at Eskilstuna for making his patented windows and parts of walls in stainless steel.

St. Mark's Church, Björkhagen (see also catalogue), a suburb south of Stockholm, was a commission Lewerentz got after a competition in 1956. Completed by 1960, it won an immediate, if greatly delayed acknowledgement of the talent of the now 75-year-old

architect. As in Celsing's churches, he used throughout high-fired Helsingborg brick, but laid in running bond with coarse mortaring that gives its walls a raw, almost ruinous character. In his brief presentation of the church, Lewerentz gives one of his few comments on admitted influences, where he mentions the ancient Persian brickwork. Its main, L-shape building, with wings containing the church itself and parish premises respectively, is inscribed in a square with a smaller square excised from a corner. Lewerentz' fascination with geometry was never dogmatic: its fundamental strictness was constantly getting broken and enriched.

St. Peter's Church, Klippan, in Skåne, was a commission offered to Lewerentz directly in 1963; it was completed by 1967 (see catalogue). It is a variation on the theme introduced in his St. Mark's Church. Its ground plan, too, is square but its parts are differently arranged. The parish offices are L-shaped and, separated only by a narrow passage, surround the church itself. Internally, the church is dark, being lit only through small apertures in its thick walls. Carried on two steel beams supported by a slightly off-centre T-shaped steel pillar, the roof is bricked with flattish vaults. As a whole, the church is in the same dark-fired Helsingborg brick as Lewerentz had used earlier. One of the unconventional technical resolutions is panes of glass fastened directly onto the exterior of the wall. As he had always done, Lewerentz took technical aspects as straightforward points of departure for his architecture, which, as a result, is at once free and compact.

Lewerentz final job was in Malmö, where he had worked since the second decade of the century. His small flower kiosk in Östra kyrkogården (1969) is in concrete, with a

St. Mark's Church (1960), Björkhagen. An archaic, reductionist church by Lewerentz in high-fired brick with broad mortar seams.

St. Peter's Church (1967), Klippan, in dark brick and personal details, such as the insulating glass panes affixed directly onto the outside walls.

coppered lean-to roof. Its architecture extended beyond anything he had done before. In the interior, he used reflecting aluminium-faced board for the ceiling and the electric wires were arranged in flowerlike forms. This reduction to the elemental that his long experience had brought him to was, to be accepted, a demanding message for architects, as well as others; in fact, the interior did not survive its users' desire for a more cosy place of work.

Three in Lund

Lewerentz lived for the last years of his life in Skåne, finally as a tenant of Klas Anshelm, who had built a simple work room for him out of asphalt-impregnate fibreboard: its floor was in scrubbed wood, its ceiling in aluminium-faced board. They shared an interest in inexpensive building and the potential of cheap materials, and the Lund school of architecture of great intensity in brick grew out of their "impassioned realism".

Before Anshelm opened his practice in Lund in 1947, he had worked for Hans Westman, in Lund, and for Wejke and Ödéen, in Stockholm. Besides working on big commission as from the National Building Board, he designed a number of more special buildings that demonstrate his ability to combine a respect for their sites and a tradition of building with a novelty in thinking about function and technical construction. His firmly held thesis, that "architecture cannot be invented",

derived from simple, everyday situations and simple means of building to meet them.

Lund Town Hall (1961–66; see also catalogue) was a winning design from a competition. Anshelm proposed and built a triangle-shaped building with large oval rooms placed freely in relation to the ground plan that appear above the roof as cupolas. This large extension demonstrates its public function clearly but, even so, is retiring, for its volume and material (yellow brick with flush mortar) show respect for the old town hall. The new hall fronts onto a large open square; behind it Anshelm opened a new shopping street.

Malmö Art Hall (1976; see also catalogue) makes a novelty of an art museum as an engineering workshop, with a floor in untreated fine. It gets much top light through 550 small north-facing cupolas fitted with white-painted plywood reflectors; they contain bare electric bulbs that, are easy to replace when they burn out. Anshelm's description reveals his attitudes: "A large, low concrete box, open towards the park and to the light of the sky; 75 m by 30 m, 3.5 m ceiling height, and a 10-m-high lantern. The big problem was to get a good quality of light. The demand we formulated was: obliquely falling light through cupolas… Feasibility of building and low costs were of course absolute conditions."

Something different but showing the same pleasure in building is Anshelm's Oljelund House in Göteborg (1972) that, lying among conventional suburban private houses, looks like something in a kids' adventure playground: facades in plywood painted black; red joinery

Lewerentz' flower kiosk (1969) as a building reduced to bare needs: concrete walls (the squares are from casting frames), glass fixed to walls, a rarely-used back door without entry steps.

Roof of Art Hall (1976), Malmö, showing the array of lanterns that admit an even light to its extensive interior. The line of its facade detours around a tree.

Town Hall (1966), Lund: the old premises are behind the oval emerging from the triangular new building. The tree predates the entry, which deviates to avoid it.

Oljelund House (1972), Göteborg: small-scale exhibition of pleasure in building and an ability unconventionally to reach simple solutions.

for the fenestration; supports for the external stairs at a right angle to their slope, not vertically, so as to save material, something typical for Anshelm. The house is built on plinths that did not entail blasting the bedrock of the undulating site. Its ground plan is structured in rows of small bedrooms, subsidiary spaces and social rooms that have direct contact with the terrace or a view out to sea.[49]

Bernt Nyberg worked first with Anshelm, then from time to time with Lewerentz. From the late 1950s, he ran his own practice in Lund; it had a small production, mainly in brick. Like his masters, he emphasised the qualities of his material, but his geometric clarity is more severe than Lewerentz' and Anshelm's, and his manner of bringing material together has something deliberate about it that makes it almost more art than building. His extension to the County Archive in Lund (1971) is a hermetic brick-built store for compact storage, with bricklaying that recalls the style Lewerentz used at Klippan. Nyberg makes a point of its "honesty" in contrast to the "false pomp" of turn-of-the-century buildings. The only articulation of the extension is at the point where it joins the first building: a round staircase tower and a glazed walkway. Its wrought-iron railing, radiators and electrical switches are all controlled to a degree that is unusual in Swedish architecture. The chapel at the burial ground at Höör (1972; see also catalogue) has the same walling but a freer grouping of volumes than can recall work by both Lewerentz and Sven Ivar Lind.[50]

Bengt Edman can be reckoned as one of the same circle of architects in Lund, where he has been active, both in practice and as a professor of the school of architecture. He came to Skåne in 1956, as an employee of Skånska Cementgjuteriet, to develop a three-dimensional element that would contain all the 'wet' facilities of a dwelling. He has followed his engagement in the early history of brutalism, with Göth House, Uppsala, with a series of buildings. Through ILAUD and Giancarlo De Carlo, he has had international contacts.

He tries to get away from houses and parts of buildings as objects, being in search of an architecture of a pattern of movements, of boundaries set by building materials used "as found", as the Smithsons have put it. In his manner of speaking about architecture, concepts in repeated use include clarity, order, flexibility and context. His Hägerstrand House, Lund (1964; see also catalogue), built for a cultural geographer, can be seen as "a continuation of how landscape is taken into use through the work of farmers." His large student-housing complex, Sparta (1964–71), containing teaching rooms, a restaurant and a sports' hall and built in a brutalist concrete architecture, has a very clear structure built up around its communications; but it was criticised by its users. His architecture does not seek the appealing. "To discuss whether houses are beautiful is as dumb as discussing whether people are beautiful. In both instances, their contents are what signifies something."[51]

Lennart Holm has discussed this dilemma in an article on "three in Lund": Anshelm, Nyberg and Edman. He admits to a conflict between his appreciation of their architecture and his view of houses as tools for a human life; and describes their starting points in the actual grammar of building: "A plan is never an abstraction that is eventually to be clothed in material and techniques. It is from the start material that must be tamed to perform functional tasks." "But," wrote Holm in 1978, "when every user demands influence, can one go on working with this attitude? Probably not. At the same time, one does wonder whether this respect for the inherent logic of building does not put the architect and the individual user more on the same level than anything else: both have to cope with powers that set limits for what is possible."[52]

Student housing (1971), Lund, suitably called 'Sparta'. Erected systematically around lines of communication. A 'brutalistic' character of material.

NOTES

[1] Björn Wittrock, Stefan Lindström, *De stora programmens tid: forskning och energi i svensk politik* (1984).

[2] A well-informed analysis of the development of the building sector during the Million Programme is in Olof Eriksson, *Byggbeställare i brytningstid* 1994.

[3] Hakon Ahlberg in *Arkitektur* 9/1963.

[4] "The Top 250 League Chart", in *World Architecture* No 52 Dec 1996/Jan1997.

[5] Björn Andersson et al., *Experimenthuset i Järnbrott. Erfarenheter från ett hus med flyttbara väggar*. Byggforskningsrådet, 1988.

[6] Lotta Krus, *Funktionalisten Erik Friberger*. Final-year paper in architectural history, Chalmers University of Technology, Göteborg, 1993.

[7] *Arkitektur* 7/1981; Peter Collymore, *The Architecture of Ralph Erskine* 1982; Mats Egelius, *Ralph Erskine, architect* (1990).

[8] Lennart Kvarnström, "Bostadsområdet Vivalla i Örebro", *Arkitektur* 12/1970.

[9] Jöran Curman & Ulf Gillberg, *En elementbyggd låghusstad* 1969.

[10] Björn Linn, "Tankar i Colosseum", *Arkitektur* 8/1966.

[11] The debate over Skärholmen is summarised in Karl-Olov Arnstberg & Lars Ekenborn, *Tio år efteråt. Skärholmen—anteckningar och fotografier*, 1979. The wider debate about suburbs is addressed in Mats Franzén & Eva Sandstedt, *Grannskap och stadsplanering*, 1981.

[12] Leif Jonsson discussed single-family houses in his dissertation *Från egnahem till villa. Enfamiljshuset i Sverige 1950–1980*, 1985.

[13] *Arkitektur* 1/1978.

[14] Göran Lindahl, "Omvandlingen i städernas mitt", *Arkitektur* 5/1965.

[15] Claes Caldenby, *Medborgarhus i Örebro* 1990. The building is presented in *Arkitektur* 5/1965; the Krämaren complex in *Arkitektur* 11/1963. For a monograph on the Ahlsén brothers, see *Arkitektur* 6/1980.

[16] The author had been one of the leading figures in the town planning office at the time; from Göran Sidenbladh, *Norrmalm förnyat 1951–1981*, (1985), 214.

[17] The 1962 plan was thoroughly criticised by some young architects, Mats Edblom, Jan Strömdahl and Allan Westerman, in "Mot en ny miljö", *Arkitektur* 8/1962; with 13 years' experience, they re-addressed this theme in "City 62 och vidare till 75", *Arkitektur* 3/1976.

[18] Lennart Holm, "Stadsbyggets dilatationsfog", *Arkitektur* 3/1976. The Bank of Sweden building is presented and commented on in Bengt O.H. Johansson, "Bank med lån ur det förflutna", *Arkitektur* 9/1976.

[19] Bengt O.H. Johansson, 1976.

[20] Wilfried Wang, *The Architecture of Peter Celsing* (1996), 66, 79.

[21] See eg Olof Hultin's foreword to Wang (1996); Bengt O.H. Johansson, *Arkitektur* 9/1976; Göran Lindahl, "Frågan om vår tid", *Arkitektur* 9/1989; and Henrik O. Andersson, *Peter Celsing. En bok om en arkitekt och hans verk* (1980).

[22] *Arkitektur* 4/1973, a number on the theme of this shopping centre.

[23] Alf Engström, Gunnar Landberg, Bengt Larsson & Alvar Törneman, "Arbetsprinciper", *Arkkitehti* 5/1967.

[24] Gunnar Landberg, "Polishus—några erfarenheter", *Arkitektur* 8/1973.

[25] Bengt Larsson, "IBM Nordic Education Center", in *Arkitektur* 9/1971.

[26] Gösta Danielson & Bengt Hidemark, "Televerkets förvaltningsbyggnader i Farsta", *Arkitektur* 6/1970.

[27] *Arkitektur* 93/1973, a number that addressed the question of decentralisation.

[28] *Arkitektur* 9/1977, another number addressing decentralisation.

[29] *"Din högskola"* exhibition catalogue, Report 97, 1972, from the National Building Board.

[30] Fredric Bedoire, "Högskolans och universitetets bebyggelsemiljö", in *Stockholms universitet 1878–1978* (1978).

[31] *Arkitektur* 7/1979, a monograph issue on Klas Anshelm. A comprehensive catalogue of his work, written by Per Qvarnström, is expected to be published in 1998. See also Olle Svedberg, "Architecture cannot be invented: The Work of Klas Anshelm", in *9 H* 9/1995.

[32] P.C. Gunvall & K.G. Lindqvist, "Perspektiv på 70-talets skolbyggande", in *Skolhus från Ystad till Haparanda* (1982).

[33] Cf. Bengt Lindroos, *Ur den svenska byggnadskonstens magasin* (1989); and Gunnar Henriksson, *Skiftesverk i Sverige. Ett tusenårigt byggnadssätt* (1996).

[34] The Swedish original of this phrase, "Den dubbla rörelsen", appeared as a headline over a series on postmodernism by a literary critic, Mikael van Reis, in the daily newspaper, *Göteborgs-Posten*, in July and August 1985.

[35] Stig Claesson, "För arkitekter att läsa", *Arkitektur* 8/1965; and Sven Thiberg, "Oro utan åror", *Arkitektur* 5/1966. The literal meaning of the second title is 'Dismay without oars'.

[36] Nils Ole Lund, *Nordisk arkitektur* (1991), 107 ff.

[37] Sven-Eric Liedman, "Den folklige ämbetsmannen" in Sven-Eric Liedman & Lennart Olausson (eds.), *Ideologi och institution* (1988).

[38] It is used as a concept in Aldo Rossi *L'architettura della città* (1966).

[39] Claes Caldenby & Åsa Walldén, *Jan Gezelius* (1989), 30 ff.

[40] Caldenby & Walldén (1989). See also "A springboard towards something better ... ", in *arq*, nr. 3, Vol. 1, 1996.

[41] See *Arkitektur* for a monograph number on Asmussen (6/1984); on the Vidar Clinic (8/1988); and on Vadstena (7/1993) See also Gary J. Coates, *Erik Asmussen, architect* (1977).

[42] Tomas Lewan, "Sven Ivar Lind. Arkitekt och pedagog", *Arkitektur* 4/1994. See also the 7/1993 number, on the Royal Armoury.

[43] Lars Ridderstedt (ed.), *Kyrkan bygger vidare ...* (1974).

[44] See Gerd Reimers, "Sex kyrkor av Rolf Bergh"; also Göran Bergquist, "Johannes Olivegren som kyrkoarkitekt" in Ridderstedt (1974).

[45] Björn Linn, "Den svenska arkitekturens ställning", *Arkitektur* 9/1960; the crematorium in Gävle and the PUB department store are presented in *Arkitektur* 12/1960.

[46] See *Arkitektur* 9/1989, 10.

[47] Discussed between Ulf Hård af Segerstad and Göran Lindahl in *Svenska Dagbladet* in March 1960 and reproduced in Lars Ridderstedt (ed.), *Kyrkan bygger* (1961).

[48] The buildings in the foregoing passage are presented in detail in Wang (1996).

[49] For a monograph on Anshelm, see *Arkitektur* 7/1979; see also Svedberg (1995).

[50] Vanja Knocke, "Bernt Nyberg", *Arkitektur* 4/1996.

[51] Gunilla Millisdotter, *Bengt Edmans arkitektur och pedagogik* (1993); see also a conversation with Edman, in Lennart Holm, *Rita hus* (1990); and Claes Caldenby, "Bingospelarna och arkitekten. Samtal med Bengt Edman", *Arkitektur* 4/1978.

[52] Lennart Holm, "Tre i Lund", *Arkitektur* 4/1978.

Stumholmen provides an image of late 20th-century Swedish architecture: working with what is already built, with historical predecessors, in planned forms. Karlskrona, having an impressive 17th-century atmosphere, was the Swedish marine base in the Baltic, but, on land, was long a backwater. Swedish regional policy in 1988 caused the National Housing Authority to relocate there and to start a course of education for planners. The Housing Fair 1993, held on Stumholmen that the Royal Swedish Navy had left, was, with its housing adapted to existing buildings, a great success with the public. The photograph, taken in 1993, predates the new Maritime Museum.

The Middle Way Reaches an Impasse? 1975–98

CLAES CALDENBY

The 1974 oil crisis was a dramatic turning point in 30 years' economic expansion since 1945. For structural reasons, Sweden was severely affected. Competitors in countries that had industrialised later successfully challenged its heavy industries. The shipping building, on which the steel industry depended, was almost eliminated by new eastern Asian yards. The building industry could no longer act as a means of regulating the national economy. Arrested growth and economic support to afflicted industries burdened the national budget, while the public sector continued to expand during the 1970s.

Large political and social changes occurred. Having held national political power for 40 years, the Social Democrats lost office in 1976 to a right-of-centre coalition. At the same time a radicalisation of politics found expression in co-determination legislation (1976), which gave employees great influence in building questions, and, when the Social Democrats had regained office, in employee funds (1983). A tradition of deference to those in authority was eroded from within, especially after the protest movements of the 1960s. 'Green' thinking during the 1970s renewed an interest in popular local history; an author, Sven Lindqvist, coined an apposite slogan: "Dig where you stand."

The unified culture of the country began to splinter. Its frontiers began to be crossed by movements of political solidarity, by waves of political refugees, and by the rapid internationalisation of its economy. Its former isolationist attitudes, which had embodied something of an attitude of self-sufficiency, began to decline into what seems to be an increasingly pluralistic society. Having perhaps been a precondition for this unified culture, the "strong society" began to turn into one of denationalization. Having in general agreement pursued a middle way between capitalism and socialism since the 1930s, Sweden as a whole began to divide up and follow different ways. A divisive factor was the inflation-fuelled years of speculation during the mid and late 1980s, which glittered like gold for the building industry for a few heady years.

By then, Sweden was no longer a society under construction. In 30 years, the average Swedish dwelling area had gone from one of the lowest to one of the highest in Europe. Had the regional plans been as accurate as they were optimistic, the national population would have doubled or tripled within a few decades; it did not but public- and private-sector premises and infrastructures expanded as if it would. The collapse of the programme of a million dwellings in ten years (1965–74) and the oil crisis made it plain that such expansion could not continue and that, for many years, the job would be to adapt actual buildings to actual needs. A new generation of architects would have to acquire a better knowledge of architectural history and building techniques and to learn how to work with the users of existing premises.

As an industrial sector, the building industry had put on weight in response to the big programmes: problematic urban structures and 'sick' buildings were parts of the trouble, but a heavier part was the very large scale of its industrial structures. Building companies were not just physically large, but had got a weighty position in the building process. Not so for architects: their position had weakened, their self confidence was low and those who had put their faith in rational planning techniques had dissipated their professional knowledge. The building sector, having been modernised about as quickly as had the rest of Sweden, found itself faced by problems that had not yet arisen in other countries.

STEFAN ALENIUS
ARKITEKTER MED OMNEJD

Cover by Stefan Alenius to a book published (1986) by the National Association of Swedish Architects depicts architects ironically as equilibristic artists, coping with the weight of history.

For economical and ideological reasons, big-programme building work vanished during the 1970s, although cultural premises continued to be built, even if museums, libraries and music centres took over the role of church building as an aesthetic haven. Architecturally, Sweden became more and more a part of international activity. Although criticised by architects defending functionalism, postmodernism still got remarkably well integrated into a Swedish tradition of architecture open to what was determined by situation, to complexity and popular desires. Increased international exchanges have been positive in bringing a wider awareness of the problem of quality in Swedish building work.

Internationalisation does not mean that what is specifically Swedish is to be eliminated. On the contrary, it can in certain respects be made more evident in an encounter with something different. There are some enduring structures that continue to affect the form of Swedish architecture: among them the long tradition of democracy and popular acceptance, and its significance for an architecture that is loyal to it. Deeply set in Swedish society and its architecture exists a conviction that architects' work must proceed from the needs of eventual users and the practicabilities of using the building. The public sector has, admittedly, been trimmed, and its competence as a strong commissioner of new work has dissolved. Much more has been left to the market. Even so, in the last ten years a good many public building of high quality have been built. Working environments in offices and industries show care and respect for people. Experiments in the building sector proceed with user participation and new forms of living.

Another enduring structure is the Swedish landscape that is the foundation for all building. A thinly populated country, a chilly climate, easy access to the countryside and plentiful supplies of clean water are conditions that will continue to obtain for Swedish architecture. That half the population has access to summer places in the countryside speaks of a closeness to nature and a popular tradition of building, besides signifying widespread practical knowledge of building in wood. The country's sparsely populated condition has been felt as a disadvantage in international competition but has been increasingly described as favouring a society based on environmental sustainability. The project to build such a welfare state accords well with much of what has characterised Swedish architecture during the entire 20th century. It remains to be seen whether the Swedish architectural profession can, as creatively as it did at the start of the century, meet this challenge that it, users and builders all face.

Building in the already built

The return in 1983 of the *Swedish riksdag* to its 1907 premises that had been rebuilt during its 12-year absence was an evidently symbolic event. "As late as the late 1960s, proof of good taste had been", Bengt O.H. Johansson, has written "to demand that [this] showy building in stone should be torn or at least planed down... That was a time when the question of preserving it or building anew turned on whether it took three minutes, or four, to record a vote." In conclusion, he answered those who regretted that 'our time' had not found expression. "But that is what it has

Extension (1983), Riksdag: the new semi-circular plenary hall has been built over the former Bank of Sweden. Beyond the bridge, the earlier Riksdag is now where party groups and committees meet.

done. 'Our time' is to have the benefit of making use of our architectural inheritance. 'Our time' is to go on building but without destroying."

Time and again during the 20th century, the architectural profession had made proposals to improve this neo-baroque building (by Aron Johansson) and put its site into order. In 1971, when the riksdag became unicameral, the need to do something became acute, and when, later that year, it moved to temporary premises a few hundred metres away, an architectural competition was held to decide whether to rebuild or build anew. The winners, two Danish architects, Halldor Gunnløgsson and Jørn Nielsen, had proposed a new building, but the riksdag decided in 1974 to rebuild the old one. Accepting neither Celsing's proposed new assembly hall on the Bank of Sweden site nor an almost invisible rebuilding, as proposed by Hidemark and Månsson, the choice actually made was a compromise. The architectural firm, (Magnus) Ahlgren (Torbjörn) Olsson (Sven) Silow Arkitektkontor AB, or 'AOS', sited the assembly hall above the Bank of Sweden (see also catalogue) as a copper-clad amphitheatre. The old Riksdagens Hus was preserved in its outward appearance, while its interior was restored to almost its original condition. The project included a passage to Clason's and Gahn's chancellery.[1]

The changed attitude manifested by the decision to rebuild the Riksdagens Hus had been preceded by an intensive discussion on preservation and renewal since at least the late 1960s. An important role in this had been played by the School of Architecture of the Royal Academy of Fine Arts (*Konsthögskolan*, also known as *Mejan*), where professors had included Göran Lindahl, a historian of architecture, and John Sjöström, an architect. The school's one-year course of further education concentrated on what was called, literally, 'usage planning' of smaller and medium-sized towns. The concept had been launched in conjunction with an exhibition in 1968 on the industrial landscape of Norrköping, sometimes called Sweden's Manchester. Under Lindahl's leadership, a large project, The Northern Wooden Town (Den nordiska trästaden), began in the early 1970s.

At the same time, a similar ideological discussion in Göteborg concerned the renewal of the town's 19th-century wooden dwellings (landshövdingehus). A municipal company formed for the purpose wanted to raze all areas of such buildings; its head, Louis Campanello, was experienced in doing this (p. 136).

A circle of architects at the *Chalmers University of Technology*, among whom Boris Schönbeck was a leading figure, drew up an alternative plan in 1971 extensively to preserve one such area (Annedal). "The Göteborg model" that was developed led to much work of carefully recording existing building and consulting their occupants.[2] Elias Cornell, a professor in the theory and history of architecture was an important inspiration for a wider point of view on the culture of buildings; it was developed by the first generation of doctoral students in an extension of research into architecture.

In the early 1970s, the only legal possibility of influencing a residential building and achieving its careful renewal was as its owner or a member of a tenants' association. A pilot project of this sort was formed at *Pipersgatan 4*, Kungsholmen, Stockholm, where the residents themselves did parts of the work and also created space for joint use in the building.[3] The concepts of 'careful rebuilding' (*varsam ombyggnad*) and 'careful urban renewal' (*varsam stadsförnyelse*) were increasingly used during the 1970s by researchers and mainly young architects who found this to be a new field for professional work. Studies of such growing practice showed that much unnecessary rebuilding work was done, not on account of official norms and terms for granting loans but, more often, from attitudes towards old buildings and the lack of competence on the part of those managing the work.[4] Conditions for loans and demands for standards to equal those of newly-built premises that, in practice, excluded possibilities of rebuilding, began to be eased; a proposal was made in 1973 by an investigation into the razing of old buildings of the concept of 'lowest acceptable standard' (LGS). It was thus recognised that the preconditions for rebuilding were different, and that such buildings could actually possess other qualities. A general demand for care featured in legislation only in 1987, but the International Building Maintenance Year (inaugurated 1975) can be seen as a shift in ways of looking at things. Since the big programmes had broken down, adapting existing buildings had become the new job.

Re-use of 19th-century Towns

The debate addressed industrial surroundings, both working-class housing of poor standards and industrial buildings made superfluous by structural rationalisation of industry. South of Stockholm, *Norrköping* had many remaining industrial buildings but, unlike Göteborg, very

Pipersgatan (early 1970s), Stockholm: a project of rebuilding and unifying two adjoining stone-built houses. Characteristically for the time, many residents worked on this.

little was left of its former working-class housing. But even though its textile industries had gone out of business in the 1960s, its industrial landscape along the Motala River was compact. Up to 1969, no protests had been made when large premises in Norrköping were torn down. Studies and exhibitions at the Royal Academy of Art, and an article by Göran Lindahl, were important in altering opinion. Two young architects wrote a thesis on how the Drag factory premises could serve as general offices. In the early 1970s, the employees of a national institution that was to be relocated to Norrköping declined with thanks the suggestion that they might move to an old building by the river at Strömmen. Were they anyway obliged to move from Stockholm they wanted to work in new premises!

A renewal began during the 1980s. In 1991, the Museum of Work (Arbetets museum) moved into the building called 'the Smoothing Iron', on the island of Laxholmen; this vertical prism of a building had been designed by Folke Bensow in 1917 (see p. 51). Its rebuilding was designed by Ove Hidemark, the foremost restoration architect in Sweden who was also, however, active in work on new buildings. While respecting wear and tear as evidence of the history of the building, he has nevertheless made additions that are clearly something different.[5] The Holmens bruk factory vacated its premises in the area in the mid 1980s. After a urban-plan competition won by Kai Wartiainen, a Finnish architect, other offices have done some re- and new-building work. A relatively new part of the papermill was used as the shell of a *concert hall* (1994) with a cylindrical auditorium and partly

deconstructionalistic details that are related to the wholly new opera house in Göteborg (1994) which, like the Norrköping concert hall, has been designed by the Lund & Valentin architect firm (see also catalogue).[6] With these additions, the industrial landscape of Norrköping stands out as a very attractive renewed area. By the end of the 1990s, a university college that is integrated into the town is being extended here.

Göteborg, a large Swedish industrial and port town, has also had its characteristic working-class housing areas. One of them lay a few hundred metres from the town centre. In the late 1960s, politicians, urban planners and custodians of national antiquities were agreed in thinking its low wooden buildings were fit only for razing. A stubborn, unconventional urban resistance by residents, among them some young architects, at a time when attitudes in general were felt to be changing, caused at least the streets in *Haga*, as the area was called, to be preserved, along with some 60 of its houses. New buildings in Haga have kept to the scale and general form of the older houses; those designed in the early 1980s by the Haga project group (formed from Arkitektlaget and the Wallinder office) were especially remarked for their care of details and large number of facades in wood. The whole did advance urban renewal, although it was far from the step-by-step rebuilding programme that users would oversee that the original group of activists had argued for.[7]

Across the river from the town centre, the Göteborg shipbuilding industry, and some freight quays, grew up to occupy nearly 5 km of the right, or northern river bank. The freight is now handled in a container harbour outside the river mouth. Still called *Norra Älvstranden*, and during the 1980s in the care of a state-owned company and the Göteborg municipality, this right-bank site became the largest urban-renewal project in Sweden. Its planning has been steered by thinking that a town is 'good' if its functions are mixed, which derives partly from realisations that the Million Programme was only quantitatively a success, and partly from international discussions of reconstructing the Europeian City. Several international architect's competitions about the area have been held; large buildings erected by the shipyards have been rebuilt for various activities; some new dwellings have been put up; the quays have been arranged with careful treatment of their land; and long-term efforts—restaurants, exhibition premises, passenger ferries on the river—have been made to make this, the Eriksberg area, into an at-

Strömmen, Norrköping, Sweden's biggest concentration of early-modern industry, where activity declined fast from the 1960s onwards. Demolition being stopped at the last minute, the buildings have found new uses: one now houses part of a new concert hall by Lund and Valentin 1994.

When Haga, Göteborg, an area of old wooden buildings, was threatened with demolition in the early 1970s, a local group worked unconventionally to save it and its buildings, by (eg) showing a carefully repainted facade.

Having been deemed to be of national interest, Haga's street layout and some 60 buildings were preserved. These (and other) new buildings were fitted into existing scales and surroundings, but individual back yards were amalgamated.

Norra Älvstranden (1997), Göteborg: part of a 5-km stretch of the right bank, now abandoned by superfluous wharfs and shipyards. Since the 1980s, a deliberate policy of marketing it has attracted cultural and other events: a harbour visit during of the 1997 Tall Ships' Race was one of them.

tractive goal for outings (see also catalogue).[8]

The various conditions in this long riverside area have been made use of. Göteborg has been called 'a city of small parts' around its industries. Being near nothing else, and thus not coveted for exploitation, Lindholmen with its wooden houses could be renovated during the 1980s, partly by the residents themselves.[9]

Renewal of the inner parts of *Stockholm* was done in the 1960s through new building in large units, with the same sorts of traffic resolutions as in the suburbs. Done by Göran Bergquist and Sune Malmquist for the Stockholm planning office and published in 1969, *Malmarna* comprised a large inventory of the qualities of 19th-century buildings in central Stockholm.[10] In the early 1970s, *Östra Maria-berget* was the first large urban-renewal project achieved through rebuilding. During the 1980s, Sune Malmquist did a number of infill projects, in which individual properties were

rebuilt; he went far in doing pastiches of houses in the vicinity, using their scales, material and details in an early example of a historicising postmodernism. One of his most recent projects, residential premises at *Oxtorget* in central Stockholm (1995) still uses a classicistic architecture at a time when it is scarcely provocative any more.[11]

Larger urban-renewal projects through new building took urban quarters built in stone as their model. During the 1980s, the southern-central part of Stockholm, *Southern railway-station area*, became an ideological battle-ground. Having been occupied by extensive railway sidings, its rebuilding was made the subject of an architectural competition in 1981: this produced many variants, from Leon Krier's reconstruction of a European town to a lofty proposal, called 'the Manhattan of the South [of Stockholm]'. What was actually built, during the second half of the 1980s,

Oxtorget Residence (1995), Stockholm. Sune Malmquist 1995. Increased density on central sites was one of the few types of building to be feasible in the 1990s; neo-classicism has become typical in Stockholm.

The 'Bågen' Residence by Ricardo Bofill 1991, exhibits a classicistic formal language but with a thin relief suited to light conditions in Stockholm; its apartments are lit from two directions, according to Swedish norms.

with Jan Inghe as planning architect, continued the pattern of existing buildings, except for what was built on the over-decked railway. Among its models were some from the IBA exhibition in Berlin. Attempts to influence the various building contractors and their architects with programmes of quality were not a complete success: the area is now more uneven in character than the parts of the town around it. One theme in the discussions was the large residential building, *Bågen*, by a Spanish architect, Ricardo Bofill, which was completed in 1991. It has been criticised for its monumentality which, it is said, is foreign to Swedish public-sector building. But its apartments have a good Swedish standard and its facades in concrete elements are, in this context, almost restrained and well proportioned.[12]

In a number of other, smaller plans for urban dwelling in Stockholm, the town planning office has tried to recreate an urban space in these plans that follows 19th-century patterns or associates to early functionalism's more open plans. Land exploitation has been consistently high. One of the first was the small housing group at *Sabbatsberg* (1980), with Aleksander Wolodarski as planning architect and the Cooperative Housing Union (Svenska Riksbyggen) designing the houses. Other areas done during the 1980s and 1990s include *Minneberg, Starrbäcksängen, Ruddammen* and the *St. Erik Hospital* area. *Skarpnäck* (former) airfield, on the southern outskirts of Stockholm, was built over with dwellings in the middle of the 1980s; compared with suburban building in the preceding decade, this had closely integrated dwellings and places of work, besides providing a clear street of shops and premises for meetings, but even so the area lies in relative isolation. Architecturally, the most successful part was designed by Arken Arkitekter, Ralph Erskine's heirs: in his style its design interrupted what would otherwise be right-angled corners and straight roof lines, and worked with playful patterns in brick on the facades.

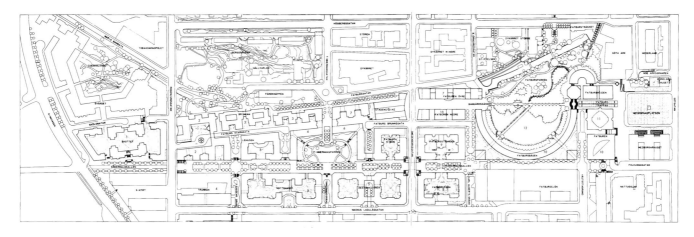

The Southern Station area, once a central marshalling yard, was built over with residential property in the latter 1980s.

Starrbäcksängen (1989–92), Stockholm, an urban neo-functionalist quarter inspired by the open landscape of nearby Gärdet; buildings on the low-lying ground surround a pond. The architects included Nyréns.

Varmfronten (1987), Skarpnäcksstaden, Stockholm, by Arken Architects, 1987, was built as an urban quarter in a suburban location on a disused aerodrome; following Erskine's style, the design impinged on a pattern of right angles.

Suburban Renewal

In the 1980s, renewal through rebuilding reached post-1945 suburbs. After the 1973–74 oil crisis, energy-saving campaigns had led to temporary provisions for loans and subsidies to induce replacements of windows and additional facade insulation. For a time, the building industry's answer was new sheet-metal facades, and, almost without exception, such remedies were applied without reference to the architecture of the buildings. In 1982, when the Social Democrats returned to office after a 6-year absence, unemployment was evident. One of the first building-sector remedies was a *ROT-programme* of repair (Reparation), rebuilding (Ombyggnad) and addition (Tillbyggnad); like earlier, large programmes, it tended more to quantity than to quality. Despite demands for care, its loans often financed work that was over-done. The 1940s and 1950s windows and kitchen fittings that were removed had a higher quality than what replaced them. Rebuilding often caused occupants to be moved, which broke up social networks. But, at the same time, as had happened with 19th-century buildings, knowledge grew and opinions rose of what became known as people's-home dwellings.[13]

The ROT measures were applied also to dwellings of the Million Programme in "turnaround" projects that aimed entirely to reform, socially and architecturally, these increasingly segregated areas. Municipal housing managers were interested in rebuilding premises and raising their rents to effect changes of tenants. During the 1990s, when subsidies were drastically reduced, and turnaround projects became economically infeasible, interest began to rise in understanding the original architectural ideas expressed in the Million Programme, and respecting them.[14]

Some Million-Programme areas have been renewed in socially ambitious processes that have had architecturally interesting results. Early-1970s criticism that many lacked any culture led to the building, in 1979, of a blue-painted cultural centre punningly called *Blå Stället* ("the Blue Place", also "the Blue [working] Overalls") in Angered, a suburb of Göteborg; its dissentingly freely-formed architecture was by Klas Barne and Pietro Raffone (of K-konsult). *Norsborg*, on the southern outskirts of Stockholm, and one of the most monotonous of the Million Programme areas, was renewed in 1988–95 through extensive consultations, which induced residents not to move away; the architects were White and 5ARK. *Upplands*

Upplands Bro, rebuilt centre (1995), by Arken Architects: the novelty here is that a part of the centre that was destroyed in a fire has been rebuilt with dwellings over shops.

Bro, to the north of Stockholm contained low dwellings, of which many remained empty: designed by Arken, a differentiated programme of demolition, simple improvements and total re-forming in different parts has been given effect there; the architects also designed a new, small-town centre of dwellings on a deck over shops. In the mid 1990s, a Göteborg suburb, *Bergsjön*, was rebuilt as an ecological urban district, where out-of-work tenants and immigrants' associations cooperated with its municipal housing companies, schools and other units to apply small but visible remedies that ameliorated this dilapidated area. *Ekoporten*, Norrköping (FFNS, 1996), is a Million-Programme building rebuilt with solar panel's, hot-air heating via facades, and local treatment of waste water. In *Holma*, Malmö, rent reductions have induced tenants to take care of the land around their dwellings, which has greatly improved these surroundings.[15]

Karl-Olov Arnstberg, an ethnologist, has asserted that Swedes who call the Million Programme areas slums do not know what they are talking about. Relying on the opinions of foreign researchers, he has claimed that, "at one time, they were the best dwellings in the world for ordinary people and probably are still." Even so, during the 1990s, a rapid, fully quantifiable social and ethnic segregation is going on in such areas, posing a challenge for architects and antiquarians who have begun to be interested in the architecture of modernism: how can one respect such architecture when, socially, technically and functionally, it needs to be changed?

The Art of Restoration

A diffuse boundary separates rebuilding and conservation, and, on either side of it, the questions to be addressed include the unavoidable aging of material and a need to consider it as an architectural entity. Such, at least, is the understanding that Ove Hidemark has developed as restoration architect and has mediated from the professorial chair in the subject that was established for him at the School of Architecture at the Royal Academy of Art in 1986.

His restoration ideology might perhaps be called unconstrained: it includes that the intellectual history of restoration doctrines must be respected. There is no objective restoration, but, based on careful inventory work, a precondition for restoration of any building is a deep knowledge and understanding of its history and technological way of working.

Drawing (late 1960s) made of damage to plaster at Skokloster, a Baroque mansion between Stockholm and Uppsala, to prepare for restoration (1968–78) by Ove Hidemark.

Hidemark was responsible for the restoration, in 1968–78, of the baroque palace of *Skokloster*, which lies north of Stockholm on an arm of Lake Mälar. Its restoration was "for me", he has written, "together with the technical maintenance of its material, an example of this form of restoration. Here the restoration architect becomes all at once a poet, a historian, an engineer and a conservator. The work of maintenance aims, via the material, to decipher time and aging in the building, and, at the same time, to plan for a continued, genuine aging that will mediate experiences of time and history to the next generation." His work at Skokloster was a part of the shift in perception that occurred during this period. A knowledge of old building techniques emerged, and, for Hidemark himself, simultaneously a scepsis towards contemporary building methods. He has spoken of an ecology and fundamentalism of materials that he has applied in his new-building projects.[16]

Hidemark has worked from the same point of view with other restoration jobs. At *Sätra brunn* he did reconstructions based on detective work into the history of the building, but, at the same time, added new buildings. As Palace Architect at Drottningholm, he has restored *Kina slott* to its original character of a lacquered Chinese box. When, in 1991, *Katarina kyrka*, the church in Stockholm, was destroyed by fire, Hidemark was commissioned to reconstruct the cupola, using the original building techniques, with brickwork and timbered roof trusses (see also catalogue).

Hidemark was succeeded as professor of restoration architecture by Jan Lisinski, a graduate in the late 1960s of the Royal College of Technology. During his education, like others of his generation, he changed from production-adapted design to inventory work on buildings and planning together with users. At a time of unemployment this was one of the few areas of work in which young architects could compete with their established colleagues. A collective style of working being self evident, Lisinski worked with a number of former fellow students: Torbjörn Almqvist, Erik Källström and Margareta Källström, with whom, since 1972, he has run the Arksam office, which has worked primarily with restoration and rebuilding jobs.

This office has done a number of much noticed restoration jobs on functionalistic buildings, including Markelius' collective house at *John Ericssonsgatan* (done 1988–91) and Ahrbom's and Zimdal's *Sveaplan* Girls' School (done 1994–96; see also catalogue). In the first, the main job was to restore origi-

Sveaplan Girls' School, (built 1936) restored 1996 by Arksam as university premises; additions, such as the awnings on its southern facade, have been made in the spirit of the original building.

nal material, while the school had become university premises, a partial change in function. Necessary changes to it followed three principles: additions should be reversible; the building and working routines should "inseminate" one another; anything done should accord with "the spirit of the building". Behind such formulations one can infer Ove Hidemark's presence.[17]

Postmodernism in Swedish

The preconditions for architecture altered in many ways during the 1970s. The period of large-scale building work was over. This entailed not only that what was built had now to take account of its surroundings; demands that future expansion be catered for were no longer so pressing; buildings could be given a final form; and the spaces between them could be deliberately created. Demands to save energy led to thicker walls, so facades were increasingly liberated from bearing members of the buildings. Windows became small holes in walls. Expensively acquired experience of how flat roofs leak brought demands for 'real' ones. Co-determination legislation formalised demands for user influence and, thereby, for a 'popular' architecture.

But architecture is not only a mirror of its preconditions: it is influenced also by developments within the profession of architects. During the 1970s, an intensive discussion of theory that is usually summed up as postmodernism was pursued internationally and reached Sweden with a speed that was in itself

a sign of the country's increasing internationalisation. At the same time, the change was not an import of something international but rather something firmly rooted in a strong Swedish tradition. This is clear in a comparison with the other northern countries: especially Finland came out in defence of modernism, and, on an occasion during the 1980s, the editor of the Finnish periodical Arkkitehti was heard saying "You got the Bofill you deserve!" to some Swedish colleagues.

The competition in 1981 for a new museum in Stockholm for the recovered 17th-century warship Vasa, which was open to architects in the five Northern countries, posed a nice question of the Swedish tradition. The first prize was divided between a Danish and a Swedish proposal. The former, by Fogh and Følner, was characterised by order, simplicity and an almost sacred air. The Swedish proposal, by Hidemark and Månsson, was for its opposite: playfully light, a festive tent in copper, a local ("Djurgård") dialect, to borrow formulations coined by a jury member, Jan Gezelius, who urged that, after a new competition, Göran Månsson and Marianne Dahlbäck should do the job; it was finished by 1990 (see also catalogue).

The building envelops the vessel, which occupies a former dock, in something like a tent. Its plan has a free geometry, as in Hans Scharoun's architecture. The element of imagery in the competition proposal that narrates something of the building's contents is reduced to an abstraction of masts that protrude through its roof. Important points of architectural departure for the museum is its

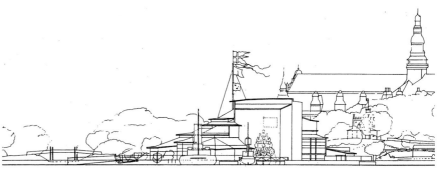

Joint winners of the competition (1981) for a museum in Stockholm for the recovered 17th-century vessel Vasa: (upper) Fogh and Følner's classically simple Danish proposal and (lower) Hidemark and Månsson's Swedish design in a pictorial 'unconstrained' style.

Vasa Museum (1990), Stockholm by Månsson and Dahlbäck: commissioned from the first-prize proposal, it is a tent-like and storage building in wood; the masts are retained from the competition proposal.

relationship to "the spirit of the site" and its "eloquent architecture" that speaks of workshops, quays, storehouses. Collages and complexities in its facade, and, if one will, the building as a "decorated shed", are all concepts at home in the postmodernistic view of architecture.[18]

The ideological testing of modernism was intensive in about 1980, just in time for the 50th anniversary of the Stockholm exhibition. That year, Thomas Hellquist in Lund started a periodical, *Magasin Tessin*, that, lasting until 1987 as a one-man enterprise, published well-filled introductions to the international discussions of the theory of postmodernism, mixed with texts on the history of architecture. Stefan Alenius, Jan Angbjär and Magnus Silfverhielm put on a series of exhibitions, including *Manierismer* and *Åttiorummaren* (1980) and *Villa Lante i huvudet* (1983) that addressed themes in the international discussion. A new, Swedish-language edition of Palladio's four books on architecture was published in 1983. 1985 was the 100th anniversary of the births

of Asplund and Lewerentz, which was celebrated with exhibitions and large monographs. Pragmatical Sweden has never held as an ideal the architect as an intellectual with a work of history propped up on his drawing board, but here seems a change to be on the way.

The 1980s was a market, not just for books about architecture, but for the art itself. The decade's unexpected and unreasonably inflated boom in building came abruptly to a frightening end in the early 1990s. It had been impelled by an accumulation of capital by building contractors, insurance and property companies, pension funds and trade unions: all were looking for something to invest it in. Inflation made property interesting, expectations of rising values drove up prices, and some banks, believing they had money to spare, were over-ready with loans. The private sector favoured office buildings and galleries in large towns. High buildings rose everywhere. Having put up nothing tall in the 1960s, when pressures were great, Göteborg distinguished itself during the early 1990s with three lofty buildings. One, Erskine's *Lilla Bommen* (see also catalogue), provided its builders, Skanska, with a local office on a prime riverside site. The right to stand so obviously tall was got by engaging the services of an indisputable big name.[19]

Building permissions were bought and sold, and 'negotiating planning' became a useful concept. To get permission to build office premises on municipal land, building contractors offered also to put up something of public use. The Stockholm *Globe Arena* (complete 1989) best exemplifies this: the price for building it was 150,000 m² of commercial office, hotel and shop premises. It was projected with contents defined vaguely enough to gull anyone interested into supposing it could

Lilla Bommen (1989), Göteborg by Ralph Erskine, an office building in a maritime style, by the river and near the town centre.

Stockholm Globe (1989) by Berg architects, an arena for ice-hockey, concerts and so on, built in exchange for building rights for commercial premises.

Lilla Aska crematorium chapel (1988), Linköping, by Ove Hidemark. Hidemark's 'material fundamentalism' of heavy brick walls is related to, but is freer in form than Sven Ivar Lind's chapels. Its floor has a life of its own.

Lilla Aska. Its interiors are surprisingly rich in form and colour, which offer mourners, as at Asplund's late chapel at the Woodland Cemetery, many fixed points to look at. The floor lives a life of its own, free from the walls.

fulfil their hopes. But it also was architecture spectacular enough to arouse the media to a degree that could not be denied. The Berg office, through Esbjörn Adamson, Svante Berg and Lasse Vretblad, expressly inspired by Russian constructivism, gave it a clearly modernistic formal language; its detailed work is robust and simple, the very thing for an ice-hockey and rock-music arena.[20]

The decade was also a golden age for architects, who had much to do for clients who wanted architecture. The 'rich' architecture of postmodernism suited this demand, but much of what was done turned out to be bad, on account of rushed work and an absence of knowledge and precision on the parts of clients, architects and builders. The most serious condition during the 1980s was the dissolution of social ambitions in public-sector planning. But it is debateable whether, on average, architecture during the 1980s was worse than that of the 1960s. Modernistic architects may have worried but often only over formalistic matters. In conclusion, one must admit that much good architectural work was done during the 1980s, not least in the many cultural buildings put up then; following German models, this was to see "culture as a factor in localisation."

Simplicity and Pleasure

Ove Hidemark had worked with both Nils Tesch and Sven Ivar Lind; as a student at the Royal College of Technology in the early 1950s, he was one of few interested in the history of architecture, and, as such, became an assistant to Erik Lundberg, a historian of architecture and a restoration architect. Early on, Hidemark was interested in the English Arts and Crafts architecture, and in particular

in Voysey's freely sculpted houses. It is paradoxical that when his *Lilla Aska* crematorium chapel, which was Arts-and-Crafts inspired, was presented in *Architectural Review*, it was seen as regional Swedish work. His suburban church of *St. Birgitta* at Kalmar (1975; see also catalogue) derived from a long gestation that generated material for an essay in fiction: 'the ruins' of a heavy church in an earlier project were built over with a light, glazed construction. Lilla Aska, Linköping, 1988, further develops "material fundamentalism", with massive brick walls, Roman roof trusses, a genuine brick cupola covered with lead.[21]

Having had an office with Hidemark, Göran Månsson and Marianne Dahlbäck set off, starting with the Vasa Museum, on their own road towards a more modernistic architecture. Since the late 1980s, they have been based in Lund, where their *students' association building*, University of Technology (completed 1994) has an architecture in brick that refers to work by Klas Anshelm.

Mattsson, besides being one of a younger generation of architects whom Gezelius signified as belonging to the unconstrained tradition (p. 161), has worked with Sven Ivar Lind, A4, and Carl Nyrén. Together with Gezelius, he won the competition for *Etnografiska museet*, Stockholm, 1972, and later was responsible for planning the building that was inaugurated in 1978. As does Gezelius, he likes to begin with what is many-keyed and full of preconditions that he perceives not only in the site and the programme but in a rich repertoire of older and newer architecture. He then seeks what he describes as a unity of simplicity and pleasure, ease and precision. To him, space is more important than materials and designs. Like Lind's museums in the palace in Stockholm, the Museum of Ethnology is dark, so that its sensitive contents are not

Detail of exterior of Ethnographical Museum (Gezelius and Mattsson, 1978), Stockholm: a large building clad with very Swedish, Falun-red wooden panelling.

Extension (Gunnar Mattsson 1988) to parish building, Leksand: a screen of thin battening in front of a simple rendered building that casts a rich play of shadows.

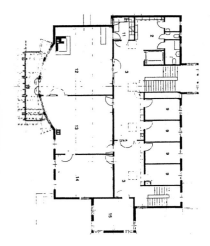

Leksand parish building: an upper floor full of complexities, symmetries and their opposites.

over-exposed to light. Its Falu-red wooden facade, with ochre-yellow windows, lives its own life as an outer surface, referring to Swedish sawmills and brickworks, as well as to Chinese temples.[22]

Mattsson was born in the country town of Leksand, at the heart of the landscape that is national-romantically more Swedish than any other. In designing its Kulturhuset (1985), he gave it Falu-red wooden panelling, lattice windows and broad eaves, causing it to differ from the usual pastiches only in its unusual precision. Its interior, however, is modern, having thin clustered piers that give the library an atmosphere of a light birch glade. His addition (1988) to the national-romantic *församlingshem* across the street is a simple, rendered building but one with an unusually rich use

of battening on its veranda, which faces the street. The relaxed and recognisably everyday quality of the building is united with a most consciously comprehensive plan, with shifts in its axiallity and interruptions of symmetry. Mattsson's *Härnösand Museum* (1994; see also catalogue), lying on the edge of an open-air museum that contains older buildings in wood, is itself a large storage building in brick, with a wooden colonnade like a huge hay-drying hurdle in front of it.[23]

In 1983, Carl Nyrén's office, one of the largest in Sweden, passed into its employees' joint ownership. In this new form, it has maintained its lofty professional culture. In Nyrén's development during the 1970s and 1980s from a modernistic structuralism towards a more complex, classic architecture, one is tempted to see a parallel to an architect such as James Stirling. Nyrén's buildings became types, geometrically simple volumes composed into arrangements well suited to their situations. In his pragmatical manner, he means that a block is as extendible as the structures, quite simply by adding new blocks. The new headquarters in Uppsala for *Pharmacia* (1984) is typical: its extended structure of laboratories has acquired a centripetal hub in the form of two cubes of 23 x 23 x 23 m set corner to corner. Openings in their walls and corners are as it were excised in their brick; their small windows are enlarged by their surrounds.

Two buildings from 1976 illustrate Nyrén's way of building in urban surroundings. *Fersenska terrassen* is a rebuilding and an addition that uses an urban typology. Rows of bay windows came to form a type called 'Stockholm bay windows'. In Nyrén's birthplace, the town of Jönköping, his *Emmanuel Church* is a two-storey, pitched-roof wooden building with traditional windows. A simple plan around a courtyard and a complex section are characteristic elements in his architecture. His small housing area in *Nyköping* (1985) recurs to three-storey 'people's home' dwellings, with double windows, and creates an intimate atmosphere around a courtyard. His *town library in Uppsala* (1986; see also catalogue) is a complex with several parts, a reading room with over-sized lanterns and a large residential building. His *library and concert hall in Nyköping* (1989) opposes a classical rotunda to an extended small-town building in wood. His *museum extension in Jönköping* (1991) is a workshop with a saw-tooth, north-light roof and surprisingly colourful exhibition rooms, inspired by Carl Petersen's neo-classicist museum at Fåborg, on the Danish island of Fyn.

Pharmacia, Uppsala by Carl Nyrén. The oldest laboratory (1973, right) has a structuralistic, incomplete architecture, with external pillars and installations; the newer (1984) office building has a classically completed form.

Fersen Terrace (Carl Nyrén, 1976), Stockholm: an extension, in the form of a modern office building, to a 19th-century building, recreates the rhythm and detailing of the older building.

Of Nyrén it has been said that he is both a mathematician and a Gustavian, but one could also call him a rationalist and a romantic, two sides that coexist happily in him, to make him a most Swedish architect. Gustav III's neo-classical interiors that has become an international mode during the 1990s, was at once simple and elegant, which can also be said of Nyrén's architecture.[24]

Krister Bjurström and Bertil Brodin came from Nyrén's office and have continued to work in its spirit. Their *Källhagen Inn* (1990) is on the site of the 1930 Stockholm exhibition (see also catalogue). Its exterior is calmly rendered in a light colour. Its interiors are calm

and comfortably done in a variety of strong colours. "Above everything, the building is to emphasise and subordinate itself to the natural world of the place and its vegetation, in which flowers, greenery, water surfaces and light are the principal things experienced," as Bjurström himself wrote.[25]

Another former colleague of Nyrén's, Mats Edblom built a new school building for *Nyckelvik School*, Lidingö (1986) that has a factual and intimate character that suits Carl Malmsten's school. His *Överkikaren quarter* (late 1980s) at Slussen, with its hotel and office buildings was a much-discussed decked project in an exposed position; the office building has

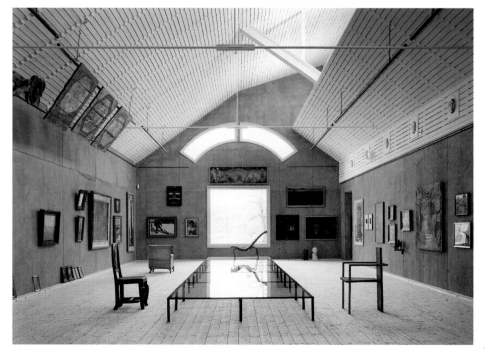

Office building, Överkikaren quarter, Stockholm, by Mats Edblom (1989) is one of the most beautiful glazed atria to have been built during the latter part of the 1980s.

Extension (Nyrén, 1991), Jönköping Museum: the concrete of its interior is stained in powerful colours. From the outside, it looks like a red-rendered workshop with a saw-toothed roof.

a simple, urban facade arrangement that is related to the Fersenska terrace, with a beautiful boat-shaped glazed inner space.[26]

Bengt Lindroos belongs to the same generation as Nyrén. His strongly geometric modernism has demonstrated that it can acquire form from demanding situations. His *Drottningen quarter* (1985; see also catalogue) is surrounded by 18th-century houses in the Söder District of Stockholm; he has assembled narrow, pitched-roof buildings in a free rhythm around small courtyards. His *dwelling in Norrköping* (1987), having thoroughly studied modern, characteristically cubistic forms, has responded to the pinnacles and towers of the turn of the 20th century. Its apartments are clearly arranged with possibilities of moving about in different ways.[27]

At Brunnberg and Forshed (earlier Brunnberg and Gillberg, which had derived from the Curman office), Kjell Forshed has worked for a long time with dwellings in a traditionalistic architecture. A residential building, *Kungshall*, Stumholmen, for the 1993 housing fair at Karlskrona, was much remarked for its plan with only squarish rooms in a narrow building of classical simple Tessenow-ish architecture (see also catalogue). The fair was preceded by ambitious efforts to concentrate building-trade interest on better detailing than what had become routine; Forshed had set this going. In summing up his experiences he wrote in 1994 that "we must get back to simplicity, to a sort of neo-rational architecture, and work with the basic qualities of architecture, in which material, daylight and manual skills must be allowed to play decisive roles."[28]

Neo-modernism

There is a general understanding in Swedish society, and in the larger part of the architectural profession, for the sort of unpretentious and homely architecture exemplified by Forshed's work. An attempt to introduce other perspectives, and to sharpen what is sometimes too sensible a level of discussion, has been made by a circle of younger architects around a periodical called *Mama* (Magasin för Modern Arkitektur) that was started in 1992. Its founders included Lasse Vretblad and Staffan Henriksson, as well as others from the Berg office. As the name of the periodical suggests, they are seeking a contemporary, meaning for them a neo-modernistic, architecture. In an analysis of Terragni's Danteum, Henriksson compares this existentially charged architecture with what he calls Asplund's "day-

Residence, Norrköping (Bengt Lindroos, 1987): a simple geometric plan, combining carefully formed rooms, penetrating lines of vision and possibilities of moving about in the apartments.

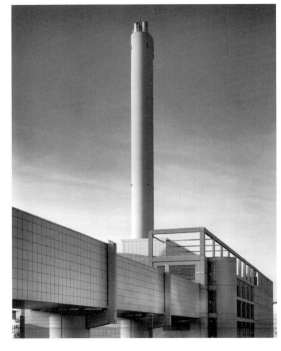

Heating facility (Staffan Henriksson, Berg Architects, 1987), Hammarbyhamn, Stockholm: neo-modernism derived from the strictly formal architecture of the Italian functionalist, Terragni.

care centre rhetoric" that he understands as typically Swedish.[29] Henriksson's *thermal works, Hammarbyhamnen* (Stockholm, 1987), designed while he was with the Berg office, shows clearly, in its white neo-rationalism, influences from Terragni, and makes a worthy attempt to elevate the route taken by hot water through the whole facility to poetry.[30]

Such a purified, 'chilly' neo-modernism is actually not so very usual in Sweden. A striking example of a striving to achieve nuances of modernism is provided by developments within Coordinator, which was formed when A4 and ELLT merged in 1978. Hardly ten years after the Garnisonen quarter was designed, this office did the *Salénhuset* in Stockholm (completed 1978). As a method, structural thinking remained valid, but the building's facades received an impression from their surroundings, and, with their shifting material and broken volumes, became an

Salén Building (Coordinator, 1978), Stockholm. Its facade was influenced by its surroundings.

Postal terminal (Rosenberg and Stål, 1983), Tomteboda, Stockholm: one of the largest and most consistently modernistic of a number of buildings for automatic post-sorting facilities at various points in Sweden.

expression of the contemporary "ideology of variations".[31]

The absence in Sweden of another 1980s tendency, that of high-tech architecture, is striking. It is probably a matter of disinterest in a pragmatical culture of building for symbolic manifestation. In buildings in the 1970s, which were well insulated, it was easier to apply symbolism on their outsides. The *Canon office building* on the outskirts of Stockholm, an early example of high-technology "image of precision", had no successor. It had been designed by the Tengbom office. Its first part was completed in 1979. As an office, the type was novel, with small writing rooms along the facades with places for meetings in the building's interior. Its light character derives from sun shades of metal grids.[32]

The Rosenberg office (until 1987 called Rosenberg and Stål) is one of the few in Sweden that has consistently followed a modernistic line. Its *Postal Terminus, Tomteboda*, Solna (1983), is a huge building designed as a large industrial process, built with high-precision concrete and some wooden elements. Its office for *IBM* (1985) and a clean-room factory for *Ericsson* (1994), both in the Silicon Valley of Sweden, the north-west Stockholm suburb of Kista, have abstract white facades of respectively ceramic tiles and coloured concrete. *SE-Banken, Rissne*, built in white on the large working area of Järvafält, was completed by 1992, just in time for the property and financial crisis (see also catalogue).[33]

The 1950s' Generation

Gert Wingårdh is an architect of the generation that belongs entirely to the postmodernistic period: born during the 1950s, educated during the 1970s. He soon began with his own commissions on a modest scale. In 1978, his *Nordh house* in Göteborg got noticed in the media as the first really postmodernistic house

in Sweden, and, in a loan from Venturi, with a trellis-like screen in front of a large lunette window. For most of the 1980s, Wingårdh designed shop interiors that, despite being noticeably well done and ingeniously detailed, mostly had short lives. His *Yoko Yap* shoe shop in Göteborg (1982), with loans from Japan and Carlo Scarpa, has at least survived the 1980s.

His *Öijared executive country club* (1988), some 20 km east of Göteborg, could hardly have come into existence without the yuppie atmosphere of the late 1980s (see also catalogue): this golf club, Wingårdh's first large building, won him the Kasper Salin Prize for the best building in Sweden, and has its first tee on the clubhouse roof that is partly embedded in the rise. The references may be many and open—Emilio Ambasz' embedded houses, Reima Pietilä's facets and Frank Lloyd Wright's rusticated stone and triangular forms—but they are re-cast into something

PLAN 1 TR 1:500

Office building (Tengbom's, 1979) for Canon, Stockholm: one of the few Swedish examples of hightech architecture in steel and glass. Its plan combines small writing rooms by its facades and meeting places in its interior.

Yoko Yap shoe shop, Göteborg, (Gert Wingårdh 1982); in the 1980s, urban shops became sophisticated design jobs that followed international patterns.

Wingårdh's house at Tofta, Bohuslän (1994) is an extension of an 18th-century 'torp' that has a turfed roof, Falun-red wooden panelling and wood-fibre insulation; it was contemporaneous with the architect's 'high-organic' work for Astra Hässle.

Astra Hässle (Gert Wingårdh, 1989–96), Mölndal, increased the densities of the company's laboratories through a series of new buildings in glass and aluminium .

intrinsic, with a control over both spaces and details.

Astra Hässle (1989–96; see also catalogue) was a large step for Wingårdh, the interior decorator-turned architect, to take: it was a big-league project with technically advanced laboratories. It began as a parallel commission to extend the successful medical-drugs company in Mölndal. Wingårdh won on the basis of his analysis of the pattern of buildings and his structurally considered increased density of the existing facility. Proximity and meetings were important for the company, and its laboratories are compact but even so well lit through strongly glazed facades with sun shading. Astra Hässle is one of the few Swedish examples of actually built high-tech architecture. Wingårdh himself has spoken of his architecture as "high organic", and it is natural to associate its free geometry to work by an architect such as Scharoun.

Parallel with Astra Hässle, Wingårdh designed his own house as an ecological addition to an old torp, or small wooden farm or country building, with a turfed roof, Falu-red

wooden panelling and an interior related to Erik Asmussen's work. Wingårdh's *Ale gymnasium*, Nödinge, outside Göteborg (1995), has yet another character: some 1950s architecture mixed with stained concrete that seems to invite graffiti. Wingårdh himself is evidently very receptive to different, often foreign models, but, at the same time, he can, by adapting them to special situations and listening carefully to his clients' wishes, do work that is very Swedish. It is remarkable that Wingårdh has not designed cultural buildings, although he has anyway designed buildings that challenge Swedish architecture. He has thus thrown a bridge over the divide of the "double movement" in Swedish architecture. Astra Hässle can stand comparison, not least in its interiors, with work by architects including Foster or Nouvel. In an interview, Wingårdh himself has asserted that Swedish architecture is under-estimated because it is neither very photogenic nor delivered in theoretical packaging.[34]

During the 1980s, Anders Wilhelmsson worked with Wingårdh, having earlier worked

Ale School (Gert Wingårdh, 1995): a rebuilt school with premises for 'all-activities' in a pre university-entry school in a municipality north of Göteborg. The dramatically sunken entry give access to a large, light library.

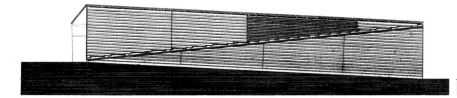
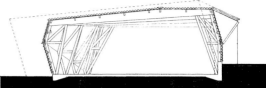

for Jan Wallinder and Bengt Lindroos, two modernists interested in form. His own production is small. His *Gustafson House*, Nacka (1991) has an exterior of Palladian symmetry. Its interior has a more complex, almost Loos-like Raumplan.[35] In his later projects he has readily sought freer forms based on the techtonics. As professor at the Royal College of Art since 1995, he has, in contrast to John Sjöström, his predecessor, devoted much effort to making contact with an international discussion of architecture.

Johan Celsing is son to Peter Celsing. His first larger, completed building was Nobel Forum, Solna (1993; see also catalogue) that unobtrusively takes its place among the 1940s buildings by Ture Ryberg of the Karolinska Institute, its exterior in red brick being as calm and durable as they are. The place and the programme are self-evidently Celsing's points of departure, but, around them, he improvises with the help of a broad register of architectural knowledge. When looked at more closely, Nobel Forum reveals itself as containing a long line of sophisticated details and loans from architectural history. That his ability to give form to space and to be precise in his detailing work in some more everyday commission is demonstrated by his public-sector housing block in central Motala (1993).[36]

Another of the same generation of architects, Anders Landström, was employed by the AOS group that later became the Andersson, Landström AOS firm. His Eke house (1990) is a very large, costly private residence of a sort unknown for generations before the 1980s boom: it exhibits postmodernistic signs, but, in its unrestricted plan and its position in the land around it, it more suggests turn-of-the-20th-century national-romantic houses that owed something to the late 19th-century English Arts and Crafts Movement. Another link to Swedish national romanticism was Landström's 1993 Zorn Textile Chamber at Mora (see also catalogue): it is as self-evidently modern in its use of traditional material as national-romantic treatment was, in its day, of how the farmers in old-fashioned Dalarna then still made their buildings.[37]

Mats Winsa, born in the north of Sweden, but educated in Stockholm and the US, worked for AOS in Stockholm and travelled

for a year in Asia before returning home. In 1990, while with the MAF office, he designed the Stone-Age Museum, Vuollerim, by the Luleälv River, which expresses the passage of time at the near-by archaeological site from 6,000 BP (see also catalogue). The building, with simple detailed work in tarred wood, is formed around a white, top-lit central wall that symbolises the edge of the ice-age coverage of the site. This is a modernism with clearly formulated contents, which has been unusual in Swedish architecture.[38]

A new generation with international experience also includes Christer Malmström. As an assistant to Bengt Edman, he was in touch with the ILAUD summer school at Urbino and with Giancarlo de Carlo. During much of the 1980s, he had an office in Italy. His museum in Växjö (1996) was a rebuilding and extension that "reads the site" in de Carlo's manner. The interior's modernistic pillars and the exterior's climatic-protective wooden panelling contain much of what the ILAUD school calls 'multiplicity'.[39]

Internationalisation

The growing, vitalising international contacts in Sweden were more than a younger generation's travel, study or work outside Sweden. Architects from other countries were invited to consider important commissions in a way that was unprecedented. Nothing of the sort had occurred earlier in the 20th century.

An early example was the new *Volvo Headquarters Building* close to the Torslanda factory. The former main office lay beside the passenger-car factory, and had been designed by Lund and Valentin: remarked at the time as

Garage, Norway, by Anders Wilhelmsson (1997), is an uninsulated shed in which a structure in wood gives its form, and the ribbing of its facade creates a rhythm. The building leans unevenly to match the ground it stands on.

The Eke House, on a skerry outside Stockholm (Anders Landström, 1990): a 500 m² island residence to offer the owners a possibility of living a country life.

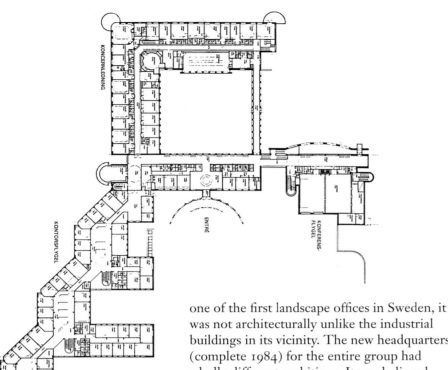

Volvo headquarters (Romaldo Giurgola,1984), Göteborg: arranged as a classical atrium by a semi-circular arcade for group management; a modernistic villa for conferences; and an office wing adapted to the northern terrain.

one of the first landscape offices in Sweden, it was not architecturally unlike the industrial buildings in its vicinity. The new headquarters (complete 1984) for the entire group had wholly different ambitions. It was believed that the combination of quality and restraint that Volvo wanted was beyond the powers of any Swedish architect. Volvo had made contact with Romaldo Giurgola, who had studied with Louis Kahn and was of the same student generation as Robert Venturi. He and Volvo's chief, P. G. Gyllenhammar, formulated the analogy for the new headquarters: "A Roman villa with a northern light." The building lies a little way from the factories. To accommodate itself to this site, it is divided into three parts, of which each has a separate character that tells of its contents. The atrium of the management is the Roman villa, partly a direct borrowing from Domitian's palace on the Palatine Hill. The conference part is white steam-boat, functionalist architecture, with terraces and smokestack motifs. The office part has Aalto's fan-shape and follows the terrain. This eloquent postmodernistic architecture is very restrained and elegantly formed in white concrete, granite, teak, and copper.[40]

The new *SAS Airline Headquarters* building, Solna, followed a Nordic competition won by a Norwegian architect, Niels Torp. Completed in 1987, this large office building avoids the monotony of a systematic building by arranging offices premises in angled wings around a lively central indoor street. The whole building has a precise, high-tech character of a sort that is unusual in Sweden. Mats Edblom has commented on the thin upper crust in Swedish architecture: "If, through a lack of self confidence, an architect dare not or is not strong enough to play his role, or—which is the more probable—is prevented by strong interposing forces, including builders or con-

tractors who unilaterally plead completion and costs … architecture then begins its decline. It is not possible to shake off the suspicion that we in Sweden have gone further down this slope than anyone else in the North." Another building by Torp, his (1996) *bus terminal in Göteborg*, led to similar reflections. While the girders and struts of its elegant hall, and its precise treatment of durable materials contributed to its winning the Kasper Salin prize for the best building of the year in Sweden, Torp himself was dissatisfied in having been overruled in the choice of glass; he expressed his astonishment at the weak position of architects in the Swedish building process.[41] The Kasper-Salin prizewinner of 1997, Henning Larsen, the Danish architect who designed the winning *town library, Malmö*, had much the same sort of thing to say: he had experienced the troubles of a number of cheapening simplifications in the process of completing his building.

The suburb *Hestra*, Borås, an extension planned at the end of the 1980s, announced its ambitions by starting with a well-provided central facility and an area called the 'Northern Quarter', where architects from four of the Northern countries each designed a part. Niels Torp's Norwegian row-houses were particularly remarked, as were the narrow black lengths across the slope of the terrain by Jens Arnfred of the Danish Vandkunsten; both contained very open three-storey dwellings on several floors, a type that was unusual on the

SAS headquarters (Niels Torp, 1987), Stockholm: a large building in beautiful natural surroundings on the route to Arlanda airport; an indoor street would further meetings and creativity, and reduce hierarchies.

(standardised) Swedish housing market, but these found both buyers and tenants.[42] At the time, Arnfred was a professor of architecture at Chalmers University of Technology, Gothenburg, where he was considered provocative; on several occasions, he has criticised Swedish building contractors for their lack of architectural understanding.

The 1990 international invited competition for *Museum of Modern Art*, Skeppsholmen, Stockholm, was won by Rafael Moneo, a Spanish architect. Completed in early 1998, his museum has a simple basic plan; its exhibition room is top lit through marked lanterns (see also catalogue). He tried for an adaptation to the site through an un-rhetorical architecture that he has himself described as related to Swedish culture.[43]

Moneo's design includes new exhibition premises for the *Swedish Museum of Architecture* in the building formerly occupied by the Museum of Modern Art, as well as a new wing for a library and administrative offices. If one will, one can see this as a sign that, after a long decline, architecture is on the way to reoccupying a place in the arts world. Another sign is the official enquiry into culture that was presented in 1995; in it, culture was held for the first time to include architecture. In addition, the riksdag decided to drawn up an architectural policy programme, according to some international models.[44]

In a Swedish perspective it is important to emphasise that architecture is subsumed under 'culture' both as one of the arts and as a part of everyday life. The slogan of the Swedish Museum of Architecture indicates clearly its popular educative job: "architecture concerns all". It does not turn primarily towards the architectural profession but wishes to address questions about architectural matters to users, those who commission work and those who build them, so as to create the preconditions for good architecture. The long Swedish tradition of emphasising general everyday tasks is still asserted strongly.

The Swedish Model

At the end of the 20th century, the specially Swedish form for building a national society, which, as we have seen, has been growing for nearly a century, faces thoroughgoing changes. The public sector is losing ground to various private-sector solutions. General welfare policy is being replaced more and more by specific assistance to those having particular needs.

National planning and steering is being discontinued. The new (1987) Planning and Building Law (*Plan- och bygglagen*) increased municipalities' independence in planning matters and reduced national prescriptions as to buildings' forms. The Planning Board (Planverket) and the Housing Board (Bostadsstyrelsen) merged in 1988 into *Boverket*, which was established in the south-eastern town of Karlskrona; it has since concerned itself more with developing knowledge than directly steering developments. In the early 1990s, the Building Research Institute (*Byggforskningsinstitutet*) that had been moved to Gävle in 1976, was discontinued. The Building Research Council (*Byggforskningsrådet*), which has financed among other things the comprehensive research at the schools of architecture, has been put under investigation and called in question. At the same time, organs financed by the architectural profession—*Arkus* for architectural research, *Arkfort* for further education—were established. The building sector, which has long neglected research and development, is expected to take greater responsibility for it.

Dwellings

The crisis after the Million Programme led to the volume of building being drastically reduced then, and, with a small exception in the late 1980s, ever since: in 1995, fewer than 10,000 apartments were being built, which is less than in any year since 1945. Building is affected by a demand reduced in part by increased supply (dwelling area per capita doubled to 46 m²) and in part by high building costs, reduced subsidies and worsened household economies. Various attempts to lessen building costs—'norm-free building', shrunken areas, technical production changes—must be said largely to have failed.

The 1996 housing-policy investigation summed up the position on the eve of the new century: its title, "From production policy to residence policy" signifies that the question no longer is to build something new but to develop what exists. A central task is seen to be to put right increasing segregation in the suburbs. The investigation was scrutinised critically by researchers in a publication called "Retreat and new values": a retreat from general welfare policies, and seeking "if only in a modest way" for novel values in ecology, equality and architectural quality.[45]

The little being built includes dwellings in categories of different sorts. A market for ex-

Town Library (Henning Larsen, 1997), Malmö, extends an existing library with two simple geometrical buildings: a hermetic entry as a cylinder, and a glazed cube full of books.

Built on sloping ground, the Danish quarter (Vandkunsten, 1992), Hestra, Borås, used bold material (eg corrugated sheets for facades), and had refined proportions. Its gable apartments occupy three levels.

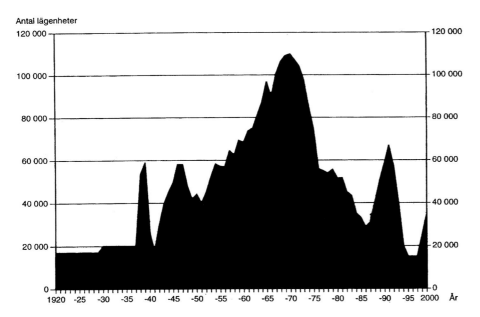

Antal lägenheter

Completed dwellings, 1920–1993 (actual); the later, forecast, figures have proved so over-optimistic that late-1990 levels are below those of the 1920s.

Bo 100: two apartments. Open arrangements were usual, as were large, light bathrooms.

clusive, attractively located dwellings remains in being, not least for inner-city projects, where high-quality plans and materials are feasible. Open layouts and special forms have found a demand on a market over-supplied with good but 'normal' dwellings. Premises for young people, the elderly and handicapped persons have been financed through special measures of support.

A certain form of dwelling that, despite having never won widespread acceptance, has been remarked in Swedish debates has been collective houses. In the 1930s, as on John Ericssonsgatan in Stockholm, the idea was to unburden professional women from housework. The *Hässelby Family Hotel*, designed by

Bo 100 exhibition (Ivo Waldhör 1991), Malmö, achieved a high degree of planning in conjunction with users in this municipal building. Its facade reveals how individual apartments were planned individually.

Carl-Axel Acking and ready for its first tenants in 1955, was a large facility of over 300 apartments, where employees ran dining rooms, day-care centres and hobby rooms. When, after the death of the building contractor, Olle Engkvist, the dining room was closed, a group of residents ran it collectively. During the 1970s, ideological and economical reasons brought about a change from service to community: people spoke of 'small collective houses' of 20 to 50 households that prepared food in common and ran a cooperative day-care centre. *Stacken*, Bergsjön, Göteborg, was the first such project to be put into effect. A professor of architecture at the Chalmers University of Technology, Lars Ågren, who had designed the Million-Programme point block that was now adapted for this purpose, was the motive force behind it. Later, a further 30 or so such houses were so used: some were new, others were rebuilt, some were run in cooperative forms, most were built by public-sector housing companies. One may wonder how it is that collective houses are, except perhaps for Denmark, so usual only in Sweden. The causes probably include rapid modernisation, lack of urban traditions and a sense of urban community, as well a secularised culture that favours social experiments.[46]

A search after new forms existed also in the *Bo 100* housing project in Malmö (ready in 1991), where user planning was carried to unusual lengths; the premises were built by the municipal housing company (MKB). The architect Ivo Waldhör had conceived and driven the project.

A four-year process of planning, including a 'school for dwelling' and a coordination of wishes in several steps, led to highly individual plans for the apartments. Half the 39 households went through the whole process. Open plans, differences in floor levels within apartments and large light bathrooms are some of their features. The building also contains a meeting room, a sauna, over-night guest rooms and hobby rooms. Its architecture has a varied, ad-hoc character that follows the apartments' plans, but also expresses the architect's determination to listen to the tenants and allow form to follow function rather than treat the facade as a part of the public space outside.[47]

Work

User influence and negotiations over working conditions between trade unions and employers has been a part of the Swedish model,

Volvo, Kalmar (AKOS, 1974): a physically compact layout with great care given to working conditions. It had no production line: only teamwork and a certain degree of control by workers over the tempo of their work.

Municipal tram depot and maintenance building, Göteborg, by ABAKO (1985), has good working conditions as well as an architectural dignity in its traditional stonework.

which was further strengthened during the 1980s by the international management trend towards less hierarchical organisations and greater individual responsibility.

The *Volvo Kalmar factory* (ready in 1974) was an early example of "good work" and aroused international interest. Rather than a continuous assembly line the factory used mobile carriers. Work was done by groups of 15–20 employees, which gave each of them longer, more varied tasks; each group had its own rooms for pauses and changing clothes. In the factory as a whole, great care was devoted to natural and artificial lighting, ventilation and acoustic insulation. The whole was formed of hexagonal units in a compact layout which shortened internal transportation distances from the stores. The AKOS firm designed it, the architects concerned being Owe Svärd and Gerhard Goehle. The ideas applied in Kalmar were further developed in the Volvo factory in *Uddevalla* (opened 1989) that was built in a disused shipyard with the help of regional support. In the factory, cycles of work lengthened from a couple of minutes to 2–3 hours, with work teams making most of their own decisions. The Volvo management was overheard supposing it would be possible to make cars in Sweden only if it were done in this way. In Uddevalla, care about working conditions was united with a sophisticated, postmodernistic architecture by Romaldo Giurgola with AKOS and White as the project architects.

Tramway Depot, Göteborg (1985) by the young collective ABAKO firm of architects also exemplifies an industrial building combining care for working conditions with an eloquent architecture. An important part of this project to furnish the municipal tram company with new large central maintenance and repair facilities was to explain its architectural

aims to the municipal officials concerned, the other consultants, the building workers and those who would use the premises. The heavy brickwork architecture as a whole is of a dignity comparable with early 20th-century municipal buildings by Hans Hedlund.[49]

During the 1980s, Swedish architecture absorbed international concepts, 'corporate image', which caused buildings to be more than merely functional shells. Many speculatively erected office buildings featured 'creative streets', while successful Swedish high-tech companies, including Ericsson (telecommunications) and Astra Hässle (pharmaceuticals) began deliberately to commission good architects to compete in parallel. Their buildings outside Sweden symbolise a corporate culture that is less formal and hierarchical than what is common in many other places.

Ralph Erskine's office building *The London Ark* (1992) is very special and erskinian, appearing, as it does, like a vessel stranded on the banks of one of a mass of traffic channels in western London. Introverted towards a funnel-shaped atrium rising through nine floors, it symbolises community, an "old-town" in Hammersmith, with alleys and bridges. Appreciative international comments on this building have often put it forward as representing an un-hierarchical Scandinavian organisation of work.[50]

Institutions

If dwellings and working conditions have been important in the Swedish model, so have the public-sector institutions that have officially provided the cradle-to-grave care of Swedes. Architecturally, however, their post-1975 premises have rarely displayed more than a technical-economic view of building. This lar-

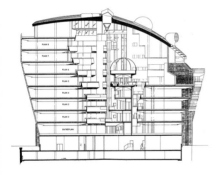

Erskine's London Ark (1992), Swedish-owned offices for rental in a depressed part of western London: an introverted but exemplary working environment. Its facades are in copper, glass and brick; one leans outwards (see section) to accommodate the funnel-shaped atrium.

ge-programme character hangs over very many day-care centres, schools and hospitals, but the late-1980s surge in nativity was matched by a number of interesting schools, many with a clearly ecological profile (page 196). During the 1970s, local long-term health-care centres with places for the infirm elderly were a large building job, with many county councils being actively ambitious.

During the public-sector retrenchment of the 1990s, a large building job has been for universities and other institutions of higher learning where, in contrast to work in the 1970s, architectural quality has been accorded great importance. Knowledge has become important in production, and the mere fact that university towns grow more than others has caused municipalities to compete (often using regional-political means) to give a home to the buildings, staff and students of a university college; the winners include Gävle, Jönköping, Malmö, Norrköping, Sundsvall, Visby and Västerås. Again unlike the 1970s, the new establishments have become what are called 'city universities', being located centrally and, for some, in refurbished industrial or even military premises. Many of the premises, but not all, are owned by a state company (Akademiska hus) established to compete on the market for financing and tenants.

University expansion is typified by developments since the 1980s in *Göteborg*, where new faculty premises of some architectural distinction are dispersed in the town centre; architectural competitions have contributed to their quality. A substantial expansion of the School of Economics and Commercial Law (*Handelshögskolan*) was designed by the Erséus, Frenning & Sjögren firm. It added a ring of new buildings around an inner, half-enclosed courtyard to the existing premises, by Nyrén, from 1952. Completed in 1995 (see also catalogue), the extension has a restrained classic

modernism architecture related to Nyrén's that, in its turn, had borrowed much from Asplund. The interiors of the extension are of a high quality and bear traces of essential donations from private funds. Donations to the medical and mathematics-natural-sciences faculties have resulted in, among other things, the *Congress Center Wallenberg* and the *Lundberg Laboratory*, by Arkitektlaget in 1993 and 1994 respectively. That it is possible to build attractive academic surroundings without donations from private funds was demonstrated by the building, called *Artisten*, for the music and theatre institution, designed by Nyréns in 1992; being open to the public for many performances, others besides students can admire its glazed gallery-like atrium entry. The university's significance for the town, and vice versa, has become progressively clearer. A novel cafe and cultural life is developing; younger generations with habits learned in more urban countries are demonstrating another sort of public life than the one developed by the popular movements of Sweden. Among the more remarkable phenomena of the 1990s is the intense usage of university libraries, the Net notwithstanding.[51]

Communications

Public transport has been an important part of the well-planned Swedish model, at least since the 1950s, when the Stockholm subway sys-

First-floor view of foyer (Nyrén's 1992), Artisten building, the music and drama institution of Göteborg University. Nyrén's work is here becoming almost classical, with strong colours inspired by 1920s Northern classicism.

Subway station (1974–86), Kungsträdgården, Stockholm: designed by the region's traffic company's architects' office, art by Ulrik Samuelsson. One of the stations where art tells more about ground-level surroundings than about the subway system itself.

tem was extended. Perhaps the most architectural public spaces to be added to Sweden during the 1970s were the *subway stations* on the *Järva line*. In their way, they were a sign of a changed way of looking at architecture. The subway-company architects' office developed a model for its underground stations in which the rock was either left untreated or sprayed with a thin layer of concrete; a well-worked-out system of installations, signs and places to sit gave a coherent character to the whole. Artists were invited to work with the entire spaces and thus to give each station a character of its own. Cave-like stations became filled with mythological narratives and more often associated to something on the surface above them than to their being a part in an efficient transportation system.[52]

Not all public-transport surroundings got such careful treatment. During the 1970s, the cold exposed and architecturally bare bus stops were compared often with the costly facilities provided for airline passengers. The 1989 *City Terminus* by the central railway station in Stockholm, an immense arrangement with a large-scale glazed space was designed by Arken, Ahlqvist and Culjat, Ralph Erskine's and Tengbom's offices. But it is reserved for airport buses; the whole was financed by 50,000 m² of office premises in a nice example of negotiation planning. The various new travel centres extended by the state railways were conceived on the same model. The improvement of bus and similar stops were, as for example in Göteborg, financed by companies given the sole right to advertise in them; a typical 1980s resolution.[53]

"Private savings and public luxury", wrote

Johan Mårtelius on the reforming of some urban spaces in central Göteborg: "It sounds like a fundamental maxim, and probably it could be traced back, in some history of ideas, to (may we suggest) Aristotle. In these terms, it is at any rate taken from Swedish turn-of-the-century arguments. In architectural history, such a slogan can be connected to Camillo Sitte's artistic ideal of urban space, and readily (for Sweden) in union with the vision of a dwelling as a little stuga, as with a Carl Larsson or Ragnar Östberg."[54] The formulation can sound much too optimistic at a time more characterised by its exact opposite, but it tries to re-enliven a century-old vision and call attention to the artistic form Swedish architects have managed to give it. And new visions, preferably with roots in history, are needed in late 20th-century Sweden.

"In place of housing, infrastructure is the answer to the search for something to build in the 1990s. One can sense a bit of the political desperation in the face of the emptiness housing policies have left behind them in these efforts towards large road projects and new railways". Writing in 1994, Olof Eriksson, an architect, has retired after a career that gave him a good insight into national planning; he had worked for the National Board of Building during the big programmes, was later head of the Building Research Council and then of the Institute for Future Studies. He now works on environmental and rural questions. His retrospective view of the economical, labour-market and social roles in Sweden played by building dwellings from the 1930s to the 1970s also discusses the efforts towards infrastructures made in the late

City Terminal, Stockholm, by Arken et al. (1989). A bus terminal financed by building even bigger office premises: the 1980s in a nutshell.

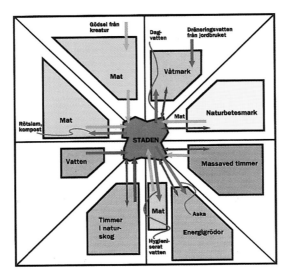

'Sweden in 2009', a vision, sees a symbiotic unity of a town with the countryside around it: giving sewage and compost, receiving food and raw materials. Thus the empty Swedish countryside becomes advantageous.

1980s. As a part of the big-town policies to advance the claims of thinly-populated Sweden to compete on an international market large 'package deals' to extend roads and public transport in the three large towns (Göteborg, Malmö Stockholm) were launched, while the Swedish National Road Administration (Vägverket) also planned "more beautiful roads" and architects came to work with bridges and the forms of traffic routes.

In Eriksson's present opinion, these infrastructures are not credible economically, nor socially or in terms of employment. They need too few employees and, in the worst cases, presuppose dramatic shifts of population. He proposes something else: "Rebuild Sweden into the first ecologically sustainable modern welfare state in the world. It would be a job probably needing 40 years' dogged work, about what the large social-housing programme did that was started in the 1930s and was largely complete by the 1970s."[55]

A Sustainable Welfare Society?

The idea of a durable welfare society fits in well with Swedish political tradition. It has been presented as a large programme with economic and labour-market consequences, but it is also well founded in another durable structure, the Swedish pattern of building with its special character.

A national land-use plan was begun in the 1960s and acquired its political form during the 1970s.[56] Ecological considerations were a part of it, but growth was central as a precondition for welfare. As suggested by the title of the investigation's report, 'Good housekeeping with land and water', the question was not least to resolve conflicts over attractive coastal areas between industry and residential and/or leisure life.

Its visions of the future include alternation between *competitiveness* and *sustainability*, or between 'an efficient society' and 'the good life'.[57] After the 'green wave' of the 1970s, there was the 1980s fascination with big cities and Manhattan. What is sought in the 1990s is a new synthesis between the two, most desirably with the same mythical attractive power as the efficient, good society of the People's Home.

In his study of regional development in Sweden and the Northern countries, Eriksson has launched a scenario he calls *kombi*, as an alternative to the poles of *green* and *turbo*. It relates to the two dimensions of an autonomous or internationalised economy, and dispersed or concentrated patterns of building. Eriksson's thinking is that participation in an international economy can combine with a low density of dwelling, and that such low density has advantages from a sustainable point of view.[58]

Similar ideas can be said to characterise the vision called *Sverige 2009*. Part of the work on a common document for the Baltic countries in 2010, it is in line with studies in other European countries. It works with the vision as a novel instrument for planning, which has been described as planning without power. The vision begins in the Swedish pattern of building, which is a durable structure, with low population densities and small labour markets being two sides of a single problem. Proximity to nature is at once a quality of life and a competitive advantage in a future sustainable society. In relative European terms, and despite its low population density, Sweden has an unusually evenly distributed welfare as between regions. The vision proposes a network of rapid rail transportation that will better link the country into a system of reasonably large places.[59]

Proximity to nature is, in Sweden, both physical and cultural. Urbanisation is, in statistical terms, 84%, assuming an urban area contains at least 200 inhabitants and houses at intervals of not more than 200 m. Other countries put much greater demands on an urban environment. Figures from the past 20 years show that lesser and middle-sized places grow proportionately faster than large towns. Mobility and double house ownership complicate the picture: 600,000 properties in Sweden are second (summer) homes, and, because the several households of a single family often use the same such house, more than half of all Swedes have access to something of the sort.

A typical Swede, speaking of 'my/our summer place', would call it *a torp*, actually a small wooden farmhouse that someone's ancestors

Summer place (Rolf Engströmmer, 1955): a simple unrestricted life in the summer countryside.

'Vistet' (1997), by Anders Landström and Tomas Sandell:
timber building techniques in a new form.

had called home until they could leave it for
something less meagre; unless it were a sort of
perpetual do-it-yourself building site for the
males of the family. Whatever its form, it
would be in the countryside. Architects have
found such houses agreeable exercises in simplicity, small dimensions and traditional architecture in wood. One of the classics is Rolf
Engströmer's *summer place at Söderholmen* that,
in 1955, when dwellings were beginning to be
erected in concrete elements, showed what
can be done with traditional timber jointing.
Stig Ancker's *leisure village, Haverdal* from the
same time (see also catalogue) is one of the
very few examples of summer places built in a
group.

Simple country living, close to nature, was
the ideal for 1970s ecological projects. The
Ararat exhibition (1976, Museum of Modern
Art) was an early manifestation of thinking in
natural cycles, wind power, solar panels and
ecological building. Critically, it saw "a society
becoming more and more demanding, centred
on waste and nuclear power". Ararat's most
interesting architectural features included Klas
Anshelm's small house of blocks of straw held
stably together in an oval form and rendered
inside and out.

At Göteborg University, the *Centre for
Interdisciplinary Studies* addressed ecological
questions. Välsviken in Karlstad was a large
project for an urban district built on user
influence and good housekeeping with
resources. Eventually, in 1985, it became the
small ecological village called *Tuggelite*. It was
designed by EFEM, a collectively owned
architectural office that, having been formed
in 1974, has been much occupied with investigations and research projects on technical
infrastructure and recycling. Their work at
Tuggelite is typical for Swedish ecological
projects: traditional wooden houses, with
large roofs, well-insulated walls and often with
extensions formed as greenhouses.[60]

Håbo Tibble church village is a step-by-step
extension of an old village a hour or two north
west of Stockholm; family houses have been

being added to it since 1978. The whole was
started and has been designed by Sven Olov
Nyberg, who is a landscape architect and lives
in the village. He has emphasised user participation, as well as planning unrestricted, exuberant gardens. The houses have narrow prismatic volumes, well resolved details; they are
related to Jan Gezelius' wooden houses.[61]

Solbyn, Lund, is an ecological village
designed by Krister Wiberg. Its houses are
consistently oriented with greenhouses facing
south west. In 1988 it was still not permitted
to deal locally with sewage. Wiberg's own
house in Lund (1993) develops the heavy
frame of a brick house and the use of sound
materials.[62]

The first ecological village in a more urban
context is *Understenshöjden*, Björkhagen, an
older suburb of Stockholm. The idea for it
came from local residents, and the project has
been characterised by an extensive participation by users. Solar panels, heating arrangements fired by wood-pellets, urine separation
and sound materials are now self-evident features of such areas. Its architecture is traditional, a light classicism (see also catalogue).[63]

Ecological villages are marginal phenomena, pilot projects that presuppose concerned
residents and often resource-demanding long
commuting journeys, but a broader basis for
similar ideals exists in Sweden. During the
1990s, the Housing Authority has argued for
what it calls *Den måttfulla staden*, meaning a
smaller Swedish town that is self contained
and has an identity of its own, where positive
qualities are looked after and developed: a
mixture of functions and nature, within reach
by bike.[64] One could call this view of small
Swedish towns as little *garden cities*, which was
an ideal in the late 1980s: a synthesis of urban
style, sustainability, planning and individual
freedom. Most of the large building projects
that were in the air before the building-industry crash in the early 1990s never got anywhere. Kjell Forshed did some projects (one
was *Eklanda*, Mölndal, 1991) where street
space was carefully prescribed in the detailed

Straw-block house (1976),
Ararat Exhibition, Stockholm
by Klas Anshelm: an early ecological example.

Håbo Tibble (Sven Olov
Nyberg, 1978) varieties of
wooden houses grouped in an
older village, with exuberant
gardens.

planning, as in early 20th-century plans by Hallman and Lilienberg. *Husie gård*, Malmö, by White (1993) was one of the few built projects. Its "low-density housing group ... follows the 1920s' rule book, with beautiful simple houses along roads, where pedestrians and cars get along together in a well-proportioned, tree-planted public space."[65]

Besides dwellings, ecological building has otherwise been exemplified most in schools. The Waldorf schools have been precursors in this work, as well as in their architecture, in some instances copied in a rather schematic way. Christer Nordström is one of the architects who has, on a small scale and with great enthusiasm, run and completed technically creative projects. His *'sun house'*, *Järnbrott* (1986) is a rebuilding of a 1950s building that now has an air-and-solar device on its roof that heats its external walls, as well as a built-on greenhouse that tenants may share. His *Fredkulla* (Waldorf) School, Kungälv, (1992) exemplifies ventilation by induced draughts, a principle also applied in *Riseberga School*, Malmö (1994), for which the White office was the architect.[66]

In the mid 1990s, ecological building and thinking about sustainability seems to be moving from a marginal, alternative culture to something more established. It is possible that this brings a greater freedom to related architectural work, in that ecology and technology become aspects among others to take account of. The White office (1997) *Östra Torn School* pushes ecological principles far: made with re-used bricks and windows, it makes local use of water run-offs, and refrains from glues, fillers and paints to reduce the presence of chemicals. But, in contrast to the careful brick architecture that follows the functional tradition at the Riseberga school, the architecture at Östra Torn is bolder and more brutalist in ways that are unusual, in particular in Sweden in ecological work.

When, in 1996, the Social Democratic Party elected Göran Persson as its new chairman, and thus also prime minister, he made his support for an ecological programme of change surprisingly clear. Olof Eriksson's ideas about rebuilding Sweden as a sustainable welfare state had become official policy.[67] The programme is to be given effect through traditional national measures but also through agreements between all parts of the building industry. An organisation called *Det naturliga Steget* has played an important role in the private sector; its manner of working depends on professional organisations and consensus among researchers. Its goal is to develop Sweden as an attractive, sustainable country. "We have in fact unique possibilities of succeeding, better than any other country in the world," is its confident claim.[68]

This poses the question of whether sustainability is a sufficiently new model that can work under altered conditions and be sufficiently Swedish to maintain continuity and thus be adequately rooted in Swedish society.

Objections have not been lacking to yet another of the large programmes in what is a Swedish tradition; one of the more recent was the (schematically applied) ROT programme for repairs, rebuilding and additions. A vision is good if it is sufficiently vague to admit several different perceptions. We know well enough that sustainability is vital, as well as having a broad popular support in Sweden. And it beckons to those who want or can create a pleasurably sensual architecture.

But it must also coalesce with the aim of building in the already built, with an increasing international exchange between Sweden and other countries, with a loyal architecture that claims that architecture concerns all but that architects possess essential knowledge that must be allowed to contribute to a continued dialogue.

The middle way has no straightforward line of advance. But regardless of which path we take into the future, it begins here, where we are now.

Östra Torn School (White architects, 1997), Lund: extension of a 1970s building using bricks and windows recovered from demolished houses; untreated materials, including brick, concrete and wood, have been used in its interior to minimise the use of chemicals.

NOTES

1 *Arkitektur*, 9/1983.

2 Jonas Göransson et.al., *Vad händer med Kommendantsängen?* (1976). On urban renewal in a longer perspective, see Boris Schönbeck, *Stad i förvandling* (1994).

3 Sture Balgård, Olev Nöu et.al., *Från hyreshus till bostadsrätt på Pipersgatan 4–6* (BFR T 32:1979). Nöu was the architect for the rebuilding work.

4 Ingela Blomberg, Eva Eisenhauser, *Varsam ombyggnad I* (1976), and *Varsam ombyggnad II* (1978). See also *Arkitektur* 2/1983.

5 *Arkitektur* 5/1992.

6 *Arkitektur*, 3/1995; see also *Architectural Review*, 1181, July 1995.

7 *Arkitektur* 9/1985.

8 See *Arkitektur* 9/1990, 1/1992, 2/1994, 4/1994.

9 Birgitta Holmdahl, *Att förnya på Lindholmens villkor* (1988).

10 Göran Bergquist, Sune Malmquist, *Malmarna* (1969). A sign of the interest in the previously neglected architects is Thomas Hall (ed.), *Stenstadens arkitekter* (1981).

11 *Arkitektur* 8/1995, 5/1996.

12 Fredric Bedoire, "Tillbaka till staden", in *Arkitektur* 7/1991.

13 See, for example, Christina Engfors (ed.), *Folkhemmets bostäder* (1986), which was the catalogue for a large exhibition of the Swedish Museum of Architecture.

14 See, for example, the 1996 annual from the Swedish Museum of Architecture, *En miljon bostäder*.

15 *Arkitektur* 9/1986, 8/1993, 6/1996. For Ekoporten, see Sören Thurell (ed.), *SARs Ekoguide: Insikt. 150 ekologiska byggnader i Sverige* (1996).

16 Ove Hidemark, *Dialog med tiden* (1991). For Skokloster, see also *Arkitektur* 4/1972, where Göran Lindahl describes the work there as a "turning point", in contrast to the "taste-restoration" of Uppsala cathedral that was going on at the time.

17 On restoration of Markelius' building, see Eva Rudberg (ed.), *Funktionalismen—värd att vårda* (1992), and for the school at Sveaplan, *Arkitektur* 2/1996.

18 The museum was presented in *Arkitektur* 8/1990. Its relationship to a special Swedish "romantic" tradition is discussed in Nils-Ole Lund, *Nordisk arkitektur* (1991), 107 ff. For Gezelius' formulations, see Claes Caldenby & Åsa Walldén, *Jan Gezelius* (1989), 30.

19 Claes Caldenby, *Höga hus i Göteborg* (1990). Erskine's building was presented in *Arkitektur* 4/1990.

20 *Arkitektur* 4/1989, 1/1990. With the Globe as a case study, the technique of negotiating planning is discussed in Kerstin Sahlin-Andersson, *Oklarhetens strategi* (1989).

21 *Architectural Review* 1125, November 1990. *Arkitektur* 9/1978 (St. Birgitta's), 2/1990 (Lilla Aska). See also Hidemark (1991).

22 *Arkitektur* 8/1981.

23 *Arkitektur* 8/1985 (Kulturhuset, Leksand), 2/1990 (församlingshemmet, Leksand), 8/1994 (museum in Härnösand).

24 See the catalogue for an exhibition at the Swedish Museum of Architecture (1989) on work by Nyrén's office. The museum itself is presented in *Arkitektur* 2/1993.

25 *Arkitektur* 9/1990.

26 *Arkitektur* 9/1988, 8/1989.

27 *Arkitektur* 10/1985, 6/1988.

28 *Arkitektur* 7/1993 (on Stumholmen). See also two articles by Forshed, "Snedsteg och strubbel", *Arkitektur* 8/1988, and "Slut på strubblet, eller?", *Arkitektur* 1/1994. A more comprehensive report on work with windows and roofs is in *Arkitektens utvidgade ansvar* (BFR T16:1993).

29 *Mama* nr. 9, 1994.

30 *Arkitektur* 3/1987.

31 *Arkitektur* 1/1979.

32 *Arkitektur* 4/1979.

33 *Arkitektur* 8/1983 (Tomteboda), 2/1986 (IBM), 7/1992 (SE-banken), 5/1996 (Ericsson).

34 *Arkitektur* 2/1995 (monograph on Wingårdh).

35 *Architecture in Wood* (1992).

36 *Arkitektur* 8/1993 (Nobel Forum), 4/1995 (Motala).

37 *Arkitektur* 3/1991 (Eke House), 1/1994 (Zorn's textile building).

38 *Arkitektur* 1/1992 (Vuollerim), 6/1995 (presentation of Mats Winsa).

39 *Arkitektur* 6/1991 (presentation of Malmström), 7/1996 (Växjö).

40 *Arkitektur* 3/1985.

41 *Arkitektur* 5/1988 (SAS headquarters), 8/1996 (Göteborg bus terminal).

42 *Arkitektur* 7/1993.

43 *Arkitektur* 6/1993, 2/1998.

44 The proposal for action for architecture and design is called *Framtidsformer* (1997) and is at present (early 1998) under formal consideration by interested bodies.

45 The Swedish name of the investigation (SOU 1996:156) is *Bostadspolitik 2000—från produktions- till boendepolitik*; the researchers and their paper are Bengt Turner & Evert Vedung (eds.), *Bostadspolitik för tjugohundratalet. Återtåg och nya värden* (1997).

46 Dick Urban Vestbro, *Kollektivhus från enkökshus till bogemenskap* (BFR T28:1982). See also Claes Caldenby & Åsa Walldén, *Kollektivhuset Stacken* (1984), and Claes Caldenby, *Vad är ett kollektivhus?* (1992).

47 *Arkitektur* 8/1991; see also *Architectural Review* 1141 July 1992.

48 Anders Törnqvist, "Volvo in Kalmar—a First Step Forward" and "Volvo in Uddevalla—Building the Whole Car", in Anders Törnqvist, Peter Ullmark (eds.), *When people matter* (BFR D14:1989).

49 *Arkitektur* 4/1986.

50 *Arkitektur* 1/1993. See also *Architectural Review* 1145 July 1992.

51 Claes Caldenby, *Universitet och staden* (1994).

52 Göran Söderström (ed.), *Art goes underground. Art in the Stockholm Metro* (1988). See also *Arkitektur* 6/1987.

53 For Cityterminalen and Göteborg, see *Arkitektur* 4/1989 and 9/1991 respectively.

54 Johan Mårtelius, "Den offentliga lyxen", in *Arkitektur* 9/1991, 3.

55 Olof Eriksson, "Framtidens svenska modeller.", in *Realism och arkitektur*. Year book 1994, Swedish Museum of Architecture.

56 The basis for the policy was a national investigation called *Hushållning med mark och vatten* (1971).

57 Throughout history, these two concepts appear and reappear in western visions of the future; see Tore Frängsmyr, *Framsteg eller förfall* (1980).

58 Olof Eriksson, *Bortom storstadsidéerna. En regional framtid för Sverige och Norden på 2010-talet* (1989).

59 *Sverige 2009—förslag till vision* (Boverket 1994).

60 *Arkitektur* 5/1986.

61 *Arkitektur* 10/1989. See also Sven Olof Nyberg, *Kan planering tillsammans lösa problem och förverkliga drömmar?* (1990).

62 *Arkitektur* 8/1988, 5/1994.

63 *Arkitektur* 6/1995. See also Sören Thurell (1996).

64 *Den måttfulla staden* (Boverket, 1995:7.)

65 Olof Hultin, *Arkitektur i Sverige 1990–1994* (1994). Johan Rådberg has argued in favour of garden cities in a number of books that include *Doktrin och täthet i svenskt stadsbyggande 1875–1975* (1988) and *Den svenska trädgårdsstaden* (1994). See also Claes Caldenby (ed.), *Trädgårdsstäder i praktiken* (1991).

66 See also Thurell (1996).

67 Olof Eriksson, *Bygg om Sverige till bärkraft!* (1996) describes the relevant programme.

Shown at the 1897 Stockholm Exhibition and published (1899) in his book, 'A Home', Carl Larsson's "Mama's and the little girls' room" dismayed or pleased exhibition visitors and readers for its view of children in a morning rush, of clothes on the floor, of unmade beds and toys everywhere.

Homes

KERSTIN WICKMAN

In Sweden, in contrast to many other countries, a central concern of architects and furniture designers has been dwellings and their fittings and furnishing, but not costly stuff, designed for a small, wealthy class, but of apartments for rent by unexceptional people, even parents of small children.

A mid 19th-century interest in homes grew into cooperation between non-profit-making organisations, big industry and the central government; this favoured the growth of a home-furnishing industry. Culminating in the late 1950s, this long process uniquely combined research, ideology, practical knowledge, aesthetic ambitions, and industrial production.

Overall ambitions declined in the late 1960s. Homes were no longer considered to be the most important means of nurturing the next generation, guaranteeing a democratic development, and giving knowledge of quality and aesthetics. When the demand to make the best use of dwelling areas was no longer necessary, abilities to create closely-examined apartment plans declined. In the late 1990s, we can sense a renaissance for demands for higher quality and a better use of resources.

Rural Culture Becomes Exotic

Historically, misfortune has often decided more success. Whoever falls short in some way has had to make re-evaluations before making new attempts. In summer 1851, the first great world exhibition was held in the Crystal Palace, London, a technical wonder in glass and iron that contained a literally worldwide assortment of objects and technologies. Even if experiences were overwhelming, the exhibition was exposed to "a sharp criticism of quality and civilisation". What was exhibited was considered to be "deficient and without

national characteristics".[1] Interest in many European countries began to turn inwards, to their histories and "exotic" expressions of different regions. The Swedish contribution to the international Paris exhibition in 1867 included tableaux of life-sized dolls wearing traditional dress, together with a "pastiche" of *Ornässtugan*, (an early 16th-century wooden building from Dalarna) that was later displayed in Stockholm, at Ulriksdal.[2] About a decade passed before countryside patterns and objects were to influence middle-class Swedish interior-decoration ideas.

The Swedish Handicrafts Association was formed in 1845; its aims included taking over a Sunday drawing school, newly founded by Nils Månsson Mandelgren, that is the institutional origin of the present University College of Arts, Crafts and Design (*Konstfack*). The Association soon became a hub in contemporary discussions about aesthetics, as well as the centre for a circle of influential personages. In the 1860s, its members elected as their chairman the artistically gifted courtier Fritz von Dardel. His many friends included Jacob von Falke, an Austrian museum official, on whom, in 1867, Swedish vernacular textiles exhibited in Paris made a large impression.

Falke seems to have been the first proponent of the use of traditional rural handwork in wood as models for arts and crafts.[3] In 1870, he was invited to Sweden to catalogue the king's collections of arts and crafts. An interest for textiles was in the air. Published in 1861-63, the great work *Der Stil* by the German theoretician of art, Gottfried Semper, had claimed that textile techniques were the mother of every expression of art.

Formers of contemporary opinion included Lorentz Dietrichson, a Norwegian. In 1868 he gave a series of well-attended lectures in Stockholm on "the application of art in industry". He was a proponent of women's emancipation to the degree that they should develop domestic beauty. "Furniture and household goods should have simple, beautiful forms, so that the eye is both pleased and exercised by them."[4] As did von Falke and Semper, he considered that, in a given object, purpose, material and form should match one another. His opinions spread through his being a teacher and reviewer in the daily press.

The Ladies Receive the Assignment of Giving Form to Their Homes

Jacob von Falke was at home in Stockholm society, where he pleased the ladies by telling them their sense for aesthetics was more developed than that of men. As universities and other institutions of further learning were not in practice open to women of any sort, ladies were restricted to their and their friends' homes, where little more than stitching, sewing and music was correct. Those who wanted to achieve something and be known for it faced many obstacles. A lady who did not allow herself to be obstructed was Sophie Adlersparre, née Leijonhufvud. Writing under the pseudonym of *Esselde*, and together with Rosalie Roos-Olivecrona, she founded *Tidskrift för hemmet* in 1859. That the Academy of Art first admitted women to its teaching in 1866 was largely thanks to Adlersparre, who was powerfully businesslike. In 1871, Jacob von Falke published his *Die Kunst im Hause*. Its text was published in Swedish in *Tidskrift för Hemmet* in 1874–75 and in book form in 1876.

Swedish contributions to the Vienna 1873 world exhibition included domestic industries, a school room and a bathroom, as well as to the section on women's work, upbringing and teaching. The older Swedish countryside textiles aroused great admiration, as did the novel early Nordic element, which included a pattern of interlaced dragons like those on rune stones, designed by Hanna Winge, one of the first women admitted to the Academy of Art. Her husband, Mårten Eskil Winge, an artist, was also interested in early Nordic phenomena.[5] Intended for embroidery onto various furnishing textiles, her design was published in Tidskrift för Hemmet for other women to copy.

In 1873, the magazine published an article about von Falke's ideas of applying work by hand to beautify dwellings. "But what, then, is art—not for artists but for people in general, not for studios but for homes, not for further

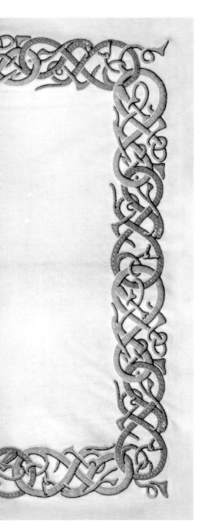

In the 1870s, runes and dragon patterns were a Swedish way to formulate a Northern identity. This pattern, by Hanna Winge, was much noticed at Vienna in 1873.

education but for the nation's life." The article warned readers of the current disdain for what was useful and everyday, and thus anticipated the social-aesthetic debate that would break into flower about, and especially after, the turn of the century.[6] Between 1850 and 1880, developments in the German-speaking world influenced architectural and other cultural manifestations in Sweden. German ideals for furnishing found expression in middle-class Swedish apartments, especially in heavy, often oaken, dining-room furniture and cupboards.

Textiles played an important role. Sheets, towels of all sizes, curtains and similar textiles were produced in industries in Norrköping and the Borås area that became firmly established once the guild system was done away with in 1864. Furniture was upholstered and covered with plush, velvet and silk. Curtains and hangings were arranged fancifully. Large cloths would be topped with smaller, decorative cloths, large carpets with smaller ones, cushions on sofas had cushions piled on them, shelves and cupboards were prinked out with cloths. The source of inspiration was newspaper articles about the Swedish and other royal families.[7] The successes of Swedish textiles at Vienna in 1873 certainly influenced the foundation of the Association of Friends of Textile Art (*Handarbetets Vänner*), a forum where energetic, women could now put their ideas into practice. The treasures of countryside textiles were transformed to suit middle-class urban homes. An ancient Swedish style of weaving, called flamsk, appeared on cushions and the like or became large, newly-created works of art in public places. Viking-age runes inspired designs on damask-woven or embroidered tablecloths and napkins.[8]

In 1884 Mathilda Langlet published her *Husmodern i staden och på landet*. She wanted to reform upper-class homes and shatter lower middle-class dreams of status. Instead of the former's excesses and superfluities, she proposed a tasteful, sober and measured furnishing with clear fields of colour and obvious effects; and she took exception to working-class attempts to imitate on a small scale in their modest dwellings the reception rooms of the middle class. "To pack low, cramped unpretentious rooms with upholstered armchairs, chaise-longues, sofas, cupboards and looking glasses makes such rooms far and away more unpleasant than would a simpler, even an humbler mode of furnishing."[9]

She issued a warning against showy wallpapers, for such things gave a room a "vulgar appearance." Her counsel to middle-class housewives was as follows: "A simple ornamentation, repeated on a ground of mild coloration, is the most beautiful pattern … to 'imitate' oak, birch, walnut and so on ought unconditionally to be rejected. Nothing gains from looking other than what it is … imitations of every sort belong to a falsity of taste."[10] In her view, children should have the largest and most sunny room because "like flowers, children do not thrive without sun."[11] Around the turn of the century points of view such as these were accorded an increasingly hospitable reception.

Young Architects and Painters and Their Families Create a Novel Style

In the 1860s and 1870s, royalty had provided aesthetic and moral models. In the 1890s, this role was assumed by the families of artists and architects. The change occurred a little later in Sweden than in England, where some families belonging to the aesthetic movement created their ideals of living in the country. As early as 1859, William Morris and some friends had created his *Red House*. In 1893, *The Studio* began publication, with the Arts-and-Crafts Movement circles working with it. It won great influence among the aesthetically interested. Its subscribers included the Swedish artists Karin and Carl Larsson, as well Ellen Key, a writer and lecturer, who influenced discussion in Sweden.

German style had become unmodern. Hopes were fixed on England. Ellen Key had expressed her pain over 'the builders' joy' of the 1870s and 1890s that had been "the most awful Teutonic stuff, not just in its looks but in its innards. As a rule, a lot of dark wallpapers with pointless ornamentation, ceilings with glaringly painted plasterwork, gaudy tiled stoves with mirrors and a mass of gewgaws."[12]

The young artists and their families lacked the deep pockets of the 1860s and 1870s industrialists, merchants, doctors and professors, but they were imaginative. Their studios with white-painted walls, country furniture, space enough for creative work, became an ideal way to live. Rather than heavy double curtains behind which symbolically the middle class tried to hide from the rest of the world, the artists' windows were hung with thin white curtains that expressed a longing for sun, air and the natural world. A special aesthetic emerged from this sparse necessity that has ever since influenced Swedish ideals of interior decoration.

The boldest made furniture of packing cases, as Ellen Key has described enthusiastically.

Bunches of wild flowers in workaday glazed stoneware (eg Höganäs) or cheap earthenware pots stood on tables; rather than furniture in costly genuine or imitated wood, things were painted or stained in clear colours, mostly reds, greens or ashy blues. Shaggy pile matting that had been used by country people and fishermen to keep the cold at bay were laid on floors as rugs. Forgotten techniques, materials and patterns were retrieved.

Towards the later 19th century, interest began to flower in domestic slöjd, seen partly as a way for a growing rural population to make a living, partly as a way to promote the care of what was beautiful, as opposed to wretchedly ugly factory-made stuff.[13] In 1899, in conjunction Prince Eugen, Lilli Zickerman, a textile artist, founded the Swedish Domestic Slöjd Association (*Svensk Hemslöjd*). Young urban families could buy at reasonable prices its high-quality domestic furnishings that had their roots in Swedish countryside.

The aesthetic questions addressed around the turn of the century were posed by Ellen Key, Carl G. Laurin and their friends, as well as others in and associated with the Association of Friends of Textile Art, the Swedish Handicraft Society and the Swedish Domestic Slöjd Association. The closeness between the first two of these societies is exemplified by Carin Wästberg, an elected officer of the first who wrote much in the year books and informational publications of the second. In the mid 1890s, its members elected Erik Folcker as its secretary, in reality its managing director. His interest in the English *Arts-and-Crafts Movement* had been aroused in the 1880s. He translated plays and other texts into Swedish, being one of the few contemporary Swedes, who were otherwise much at home in German, who had such a command of English. In 1891 he had a chance of European travel, and, in England, visited Morris at Hammersmith, as well as Walter Crane. The following February, lecturing in Stockholm at his association's meeting, he spoke about English wallpapers and showed designs by Morris and Crane of an aesthetic quality that was then unobtainable in Sweden.[14]

Within his association, Folcker stimulated discussions of design and initiated new products. In 1896, the Rörstrand porcelain factory engaged Alf Wallander as its artistic director, and Folcker arranged a special exhibition in the association's premises of Wallander's work in faience. Thanks to the association, Gunnar G:son Wennerberg, an artist, joined the factory, where he designed a series of wild-flower patterns. A writer, Verner von Heidenstam,

Professor at the Royal Academy of Art, August Malmström, interested in Northern prehistory, designed this oaken chair for the Curman House, Lysekil, in the 1870s.

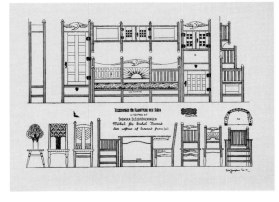

Erik Josephson's furniture for the less well off was part of an 1897 Swedish Handicraft Society series that was presented in full scale at the 1899 Modern Furniture exhibition.

Detail of chair by J.A.G. Acke (1904): organic form typical of Art Nouveau at the time.

and an architect, Carl Westman, had begun a lively debate by proposing that it was wrong to use ornamental elements from antiquity and other cultures rather than flowers that grew wild in Sweden.

The competitions the association arranged to generate new, modern furniture and wallpapers were also important. In 1897, one for 'furniture for a simple dwelling' was won by Erik Josephson, an architect. Asserting it was the first group of furniture in Sweden to be influenced by the novel aesthetics, Folcker thought joiners in all parts of Sweden should be offered free use of the drawings published by the association;[15] some 900 joiners and carpenters ordered them. In 1897, the association began to publish a series of 'drawings for handwork and slöjd', in an ambition to disseminate what it felt were good patterns.

The 1899 Modern Furniture exhibition (*Moderna Möbler*) arranged by Folcker included many newly-designed proposals by sixteen young architects, artists and designers. Among them was a group of Art Nouveau furniture by Johan Axel Gustaf Acke, some chairs by Ferdinand Boberg, a cupboard by Christian Eriksson and furniture in oak by Carl Westman.

Influences from England were strong at the end of the 19th century, which has tended to overshadow the significance of how some Swedish artists settled in Grez, a village south of the Fontainebleau woods, and, among other things, painted landscapes bathed in French light. They got a feeling for what was simple, beautiful, of good quality and rural into the bargain. On returning home, they integrated French eating and living habits with newly-discovered Swedish traditions. As others have done abroad, they discovered what they had at home in the course of a detour through some other culture.

At the 1889 Paris exhibition, Carl Larsson was so impressed by the handicrafts he saw that, under their influence, he wrote enthu-

siastically home to his friend, Viktor Rydberg, a writer, that he should "go out and preach to all the people of the happy, beautiful message of art. Whittle, dip [candles] and cooper [casks], carve doors and cupboards, storm the porcelain factories and drive out the Germans and their boring Lutheran art." He and his wife Karin moved to their house Lilla Hyttnäs, at Sundborn in Dalarna, at the end of the 1880s, where they realised their ideas that excluded all "swarthy Teutonic influence."

At the 1897 Stockholm exhibition, Ellen Key discovered Larsson's watercolours with Sundborn as a motif. The Stockholm critics had received them with no great interest, considering that they exhibited nothing particularly artistic. Larsson's depiction of one of his young daughters in the nursery—stubborn, naked, with stockings drooping down her legs, the floor strewn with toys—aroused moral indignation. But the paintings made Key feel liberated: she saw a home, a real one, where children had room for play and imagination, lively surroundings that welcomed children, rooms in clear colours and a charming mixture of old and new furniture, with textiles woven and embroidered by the children's mother Karin. As an aesthetic, it was remote from the "dusty", 19th-century reception rooms.

This inspired her to write an article, "Skönheten i hemmet" ('Beauty in homes'), in the Christmas 1897 number of the *Idun* magazine. She republished it, and three older texts on the same theme, in book form in 1899: *Skönhet för alla* ('Beauty for all') became almost holy writ for all interested in social and aesthetic matters. One of the most widely-read of the Verdandi series, it acquired decisive significance for generations of Swedish housing ideologues. Her strikingly powerful language and effective metaphors, pointed up its message: "First when nothing ugly is offered for sale; when what is beautiful is as inexpensive as what is now ugly is costly, can beauty for all be a complete reality. As yet work by artists for homes has come to benefit only the rich."[16] This was a claim in her book.

Key heartily loathed white embroidery and crocheting. "It is repulsive to give our rooms similarities with drying attics by filling them with dead white patches in the forms of covers, tablecloths and antimacassars, which, when they are crocheted, anyway get caught in everything and so be doubly repulsive."[17] One senses behind this criticism the almost physical distaste and sense of being smothered that Key and her friends of the same age must have felt in their elders' reception rooms.

Instead, she proposed home-woven textiles as aesthetic models. Disheartening personal experiences perhaps underlay her antipathy to embroidered, crocheted or knitted textiles: the class and surroundings of her childhood prescribed embroidery and lace-making as part of a young lady's accomplishments.

Beauty For All, Even the Workers

How should things meet aesthetic demands? Ellen Key explained: "Each thing shall suit the purpose for which it is provided. One should be able to sit well on a chair, work calmly or eat at a table, rest well in a bed. An uncomfortable chair, a wobbly table, a narrow bed: each is thus already ugly." She also demanded that "things must, as every beautiful object in the natural world does, fulfil its purpose with simplicity and ease, fineness and expression, otherwise it has not achieved beauty, whether or not it meets the demands of utility. Beauty certainly thus implies suitability for the purpose but this does not always lead to beauty"[18]

Two courses of historical events intersected in Sweden during the 1890s. The working class had organised itself and demanded increasing firmly democratisation, rights to culture and better living conditions. The cultural debate in Sweden, as in other countries, was enlivened by national currents of feelings. In turn-of-the-century Sweden, housing standards were lower than in the rest of Europe: working-class families, even those with 5 to 8 children, had most often to live in a single room and a kitchen.

Ellen Key considered home surroundings had a nurturing effect. "The moral and sanitary level of the working class would be raised", she felt, with the help of better homes, "and thus the distress, above all that caused by drunkenness, would be very greatly reduced."[19] In 1899, together with Richard Bergh, an artist, and his wife, and a theoretician of art, Carl Laurin, she staged two exhibitions at the

Workers' Institute in Stockholm. The first, held in the spring, "had the aim of showing how in a quite usual, and usually furnished, room with ugly wallpaper, it would be possible to achieve a beautiful impression."[20] Key hung smooth, thin, quite white curtains with small tufts, laid black-and-white straw mats on the floor, chose china and glass "to show how what is simple and purposeful in form and what is restrained in decoration is stylish."

That autumn she opened the second exhibition, papering the room with an English wallpaper in a pattern of small poppies on a ground with yellow, green and red tones. Carl Westman had designed green-stained furniture that was a mixture of Swedish country and modern English styles. The structure of its pinewood showed through the stain. The sideboard was in red, like that of the one in Carl and Karin Larsson's home. Of the 5,000 visitors to the exhibition, many ordered drawings of the furniture.

It has sometimes been asserted that the Larssons copied the English Arts-and-Crafts Movement, and while they both certainly studied at least the illustrations in *The Studio*, their furniture at Sundborn was either a sort of rural Swedish rococo (including even the new pieces that they had made) or was functionally purified, designed by Karin. She lay cotton rep mats on the floor, flanked the windows with white curtains gathered up by sewn ribbons, and stood red potted geraniums on the window sills. In her textile art, she used either old Swedish techniques or unconventionally interpreted patterns from *Wiener*

'Green Room' (1899) presented at the Workers Institute by Ellen Key, a writer, and friends, of whom one, Carl Westman, an architect, designed the red sideboard and green furniture.

Åhrén's prize-winning kitchen furniture, 1917 Home Exhibition at Liljevalch Art Gallery, in a strict, undecorated factuality.

Asplund's room at the 1917 Home Exhibition was understood as rooted in Swedish vernacular culture, but was really more an aesthetic renewal.

heating in workers' dwellings. In December, the association announced a competition in three classes: for a single room with a tiled-stove cooker; for a one-room dwelling with a kitchen; and one with two rooms and a kitchen. The sizes of the rooms was given, as was the numbers of types of furniture. Two further competitions were arranged: for new ovens, stoves and cookers; and for new furniture and fittings. For the three rooms mentioned above, furniture and fittings should not exceed a cost of, respectively, 260 kronor, 600 kronor and 820 kronor.[28] The result would be put on show at an exhibition.

Elsa Gullberg was employed at the beginning of 1917 and joined the exhibition com-

mittee together with the architect for the exhibition, a furniture designer called David Blomberg, Erik Wettergren and Carl Bergsten, the architect who had designed the Liljevalch gallery the previous year, where the exhibition was to be held. Gregor Paulsson was in charge of relations with the press. In the third year of the war, the treasurer of the Swedish Handicraft Society, August Nachmanson, managed to persuade ten large Swedish companies to contribute 50,000 kronor to the exhibition.[29]

One of the competitions was decided by April 1917, the winners including a number of young architects: Oskar Brandtberg, Carl Malmsten, David Nilsson, Ture Ryberg, Ernst Spolén and Uno Åhrén. Outside the competition, Gunnar Asplund, and, on behalf of *Nordiska Kompaniet*, Harald Bergsten, took part separately in the exhibition. Seventeen furnished apartments and three rooms were represented in the form of drawings and lists of furniture and fittings.

Opening a month later than expected on 15 October 1917, the exhibition was very well received by the press. Some of its ideas that were remarked was that cast-iron stoves were often incorporated in the same unit as a washing-up sink, a cupboard and wall shelves for porcelain, glass and pots; and that several of the items of kitchen furniture had 'kick boards' that would "prevent shoes from being worn against oil paint." Asplund's cosy domestic dwelling was deemed to be charming. Uno Åhrén exhibited the best hand basin of the exhibition, and his painted pine furniture was of a simple, factual, "honest" sort. In anticipation of the exhibition cooperation had been entered into with school teachers of cooking and other informed persons so as to arrive at a more rational planning; superfluous steps that were taken in a kitchen began to be counted.[30]

Besides all the groups of furniture, standard items in cheap pine, birch or oak for putative machine production, lights and light fittings were something of a novelty for the working class. A Stockholm daily paper commented: "We have at last understood that electric lamp fittings are things to bear small glass pears, as light as cotton, not heavy paraffin holders. At this exhibition we are spared heavy-centred copper and iron chandeliers."[31]

This was a democratisation of the concept of beauty: to produce something for modest homes that were 'thought out', not 'worn out'. Thirty years later, Elsa Gullberg looked back on the exhibition, where "there was a lively social interest, a wish to serve the people, but in ways that were variable, and less constricted

Asplund 'stove room' at the 1917 Home Exhibition furnished both heat and a means of cooking.

Paulsson's 1919 pamphlet "More Beautiful Everyday", argued for rational modern industrial production to supply durable beautiful reasonably-priced goods.

craft Society published Gregor Paulsson's *Vackrare vardagsvara*, a book that took the ideas from the exhibition further: industry would realise the idea of beauty for all.

In 1917, the Housewives Association (*Husmodersföreningen*) and the Association for Rational Housekeeping (*Föreningen för Rationell Hushållning*) were formed, both being deeply engaged in developing housing, and how homes should be fitted out so as to be practical and easily run. In 1921, the first official national housing investigation issued its report: Practical and Hygienic Dwellings. Apartment buildings, too, should be low and have access to greenery, sun and air. Traditional Swedish countryside kitchens had hitherto been models for small urban apartments, with a relatively large living room and working kitchen, and, if there was any other room, a small one would be kept for best. This model now began to change: the kitchen shrank and the other room or rooms became larger.

An expert from the housing investigation, Osvald Almqvist, an architect, had studied kitchens' functions and forms. Kerstin Key, a domestic-science expert, accepted a commission from the Housewives Association to create an exhibition kitchen in accordance with the investigation's directives; in coming years, it would "be put on display as an inspiring example."[33]

within a given scheme than they are nowadays. There was a burning wish that, in their everyday lives, people should encounter art."[32] The aim was to form a Swedish style with links to countryside culture, not with middle-class pastiches.

Over 40,000 people visited the exhibition, which had inexpensive entry tickets. Considering the needs of the time, the intentions of those who planned the exhibition have been sometimes called in question by later writers about architecture: yet another almost ridiculously unrealistic attempt from the comfortably-off to put the working class in its place. But contemporary press reports, including those from left-wing papers, were enthusiastic. The exhibition gave hopes of a more beautiful, better life. In Aftonbladet, Nils G. Wollin challenged industry to seize the chance: through standardisation, rationalisation, artistic endeavour and a national identity, Sweden could, once peace had returned, advance to a stronger, more competitive position.

In 1918, some of the leading architects and artists who had been active in the exhibition formed the Workshop Association (Föreningen Verkstaden). Some other leading designers of utilitarian objects also joined. Its chairman was an architect, Hakon Ahlberg. It has its collective eye not on workers' dwellings but on middle-class residences. In 1919 Swedish Handicraft Society published Gregor Paulsson's

Functionalism Takes Form

Carl Bergsten, the architect who had designed the Liljevalch gallery, was one of a circle of architects and artists who characterised the 1920s 'typically Swedish' image. He was the principal architecture for the Swedish pavilion at the *Exposition des Arts Décoratifs Modernes* in Paris in 1925; Asplund showed a gentleman's study, Uno Åhrén a lady's boudoir. Otherwise the furniture was principally by Carl Hörvik and Carl Malmsten.

Bergsten's architecture, which exhibited a classicistic formal language of severe decoration, pillars, symmetry and a clear sense of space that had merged with ingredients from *Wiener Werkstätte*, was appreciated by at least the public as undilutedly Swedish. Thanks to their successes in Paris, Bergsten and the Swedish artists and architects who worked in applied arts were invited to take part in an exhibition to be held in 1927 at the Metropolitan Museum, New York; their work at the exhibition was much remarked and was the first of a number of similarly successful exhibitions outside Sweden.

Asplund's neo-classical, severe 'studio' at the 1925 Paris Exhibition was remarked partly for its de-scaled, minimally decorated chairs.

Responsibility for the pavilion in Paris and the exhibition in New York, having been borne by the Swedish Handicraft Society, led it from success to introspection. In Paris, young Swedish architects could study how, in his *L'Esprit nouveau* pavilion, Le Corbusier had excluded all unnecessary decoration, worked with open spaces for rooms in a cubistic shell of smooth white concrete and glazed surfaces.

Uno Åhrén felt as if his eyes had been cleansed. Once he was home, he wrote in the association's year book a long account of his distaste for overdone decoration that dominated the rest of the exhibition. It is, he wrote, "so heavy to think of having to live in such rooms. The very air seems too thick for a clear thought or a cheerful laugh, forms, forms, forms... Every millimetre of everything prinked out with pretty-pretty forms—in the end such surroundings become unspeakably horrid. With what gratitude did I think of all that which simply did its job without worrying about its looks. The electric-light bulb, the hand basin with hot and cold water." He saw the solution to lie in "artistic form conferred

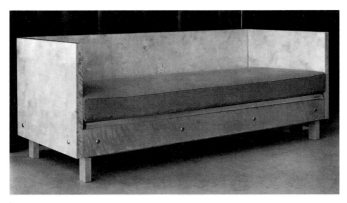

Almqvist's undecorated sofa for the 1930 Stockholm Exhibition, was made by AB Svenska Möbelfabrikerna, Bodafors.

unobtrusively on things of practical use: that is the specific characteristic of modernism."[34]

Otherwise, in Sweden, women's organisations took the lead in discussing housing questions during the 1920s. In each issue of information published for members, Husmodersförbundet reported on local associations' exhibitions all over the country.[35] During the 1920, dwellings built to be rented to middle-class tenants were smaller than they had been and fewer middle-class households employed living-in domestics. Middle-class women had to do more housework.

This information sheet complained about low-quality and impractical dwellings and demanded that apartments should have better access to air and sun, and that windows should open inwards to minimise risks of cleaning their exteriors. In 1927, a miniature dwelling for a household of four was presented with simple, functional furniture from a newly-established furniture shop, *Hyresgästernas Möbelbutik*, at Brunkebergstorg, that was owned by *HSB*. *AB Svenska Möbelfabrikerna i Bodafors* had supplied the furniture. The bare convertible sofa-bed was designed by Osvald Almqvist.[36] Rather than buying a suite, families could now buy furniture to meet their needs.

In 1927, too, the Stockholm Homes and Households Exhibition was opened in the newly built Röda Bergsområdet; it was owned by the Labour Movement tenants' organisation, HSB, and designed by HSB's director, Sven Wallander. The exhibition was arranged by this and other Labour Movement organisations, and the Association for Rational House-keeping. Of the furniture in some exhibition apartments, Carl Malmsten representing the Swedish Handicraft Society had designed some; and some was supplied by HSB.[37] The exhibition also argued in favour of re-use: "It is stupid waste and testifies to poor culture when someone gets rid of old servants in the way of furniture, even if they are no longer a beautiful as they might be."[38]

The problem with small apartments was addressed in a novel way. Criticism was directed at allowing a wish for an imposing appearance to influence furnishing: a dining-room suite squeezed into the one room that was not a kitchen, in which meals were anyway eaten. Instead, furniture was presented that would not obviously reveal the character of a room: sofas with iron rather than wooden frames that were easier to keep clean and free of bedbugs; easily washed curtains hung on wires; detachable chair covers. Propaganda was made for a living room, a combination of dining room, study and bedroom.[39]

These and other Labour Movement organisations were to continue to cooperate over the coming 30 years to lead discussions and developments of the furnishing and fittings of dwelling.

In 1928, Husmodersförbundet declared a war to the death on all old unpractical kitchen details. Some novelties were working surfaces in stainless steel, functional, hygienic crockery cupboards. To be new, a kitchen should also have smooth, easy-to-clean surfaces, oilcloth and linoleum, a high adjustable kitchen stool. An equally fine novelty was the wireless, an object of elevated, literally thoroughgoing status most often placed in the best room, and, left on at top volume, audible everywhere.

When they began planning the 1930 Stockholm exhibition, Gregor Paulsson, director of Swedish Handicraft Society since 1920, and young architects including Asplund, Gahn, Lewerentz, Sundahl and Åhrén found the 1927 Die Wohnung exhibition in Weissenhof, Stuttgart, their greatest inspiration: it presented a novel architecture for dwellings, with smooth rendered facades, flat roofs and interiors purged of details.

The periodical published by the Swedish Handicraft Society reveals how the new ideas became more and more strongly anchored: fewer articles on traditional handwork, domestic slöjd and applied arts, more on standardisation and the new factual architecture.

In anticipation of the 1930 exhibition, and on account of the dearth of furniture in Sweden, a prize competition was announced for items of inexpensive, strong, light, stackable furniture that would go well together and, when worn out, could be destroyed. This furniture was "intended for smaller modern apartments. In the same way that plans of rooms in modern houses ought to offer greater freedom in placing furniture, so the furniture should be neatly adaptable to conditions in the rooms."[40]

Functionalism Gets Criticised and a Hearing

The 1930 Stockholm exhibition offered Swedish architects a chance of realising their slogans about air, light and greenery. The easy designs and light interiors in pure colours agreed well with the new aesthetics. Open spacial resolutions and small 'laboratory' kitchens were launched, the latter as functional as those of Atlantic liners, but thought of as complements to a modern life with tinned preserves, gas stoves and aluminium pots and pans. Large windows would let in as much

light as possible. And everything in the home should be moveable and placed asymmetrically; crockery and saucepans could be stacked.

Eleonor Lilliehöök protested in the periodical of the Swedish National Federation of Housewives (Svenska Husmödrarnas Riksförbund) against the 'laboratory' kitchen: "This exhibition has been planned and put

Apartment, 1930 Stockholm Exhibition, designed by von Schmalensee: birch and jacaranda furniture by Erik Chambert, including the elegant mezzanine-floor chair with a foldback footstool and an adjustable back.

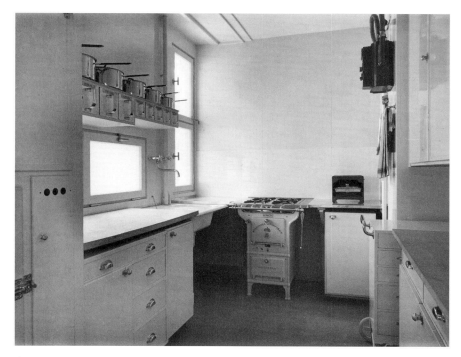

Åhrén's kitchen, one of many things, at the 1930 Stockholm Exhibition; Sara Reutersköld did the combined washing-up and refuse sink.

Tubular-steel furniture is cried down at the 1930 Stockholm Exhibition, but not as copies of work by Marcel Breuer etc. Drawing by Bertil Almquist.

Mathsson's chair (1941) in glued-wood laminates developed since 1933 with arm supports and a better sitting angle.

The shape and supports of G.A. Berg's version (1942) favoured blood circulation and bodyliquids equilibrium.

together by men." She reacted against the art of modern furniture at the exhibition: "No-one is going to force these items of steel furniture onto us."[41] Ingeborg Wærn Bugge, an architect, and Kjerstin Göransson-Ljungman devastatingly criticised the small kitchens in their book, *Bostad och hushållsorganisation. Staden och landet*, published in 1936.

Many items of furniture shown at the 1930 exhibition were not industrial products but prototypes made by craftsmen. But two ideas had been formulated: that furniture should be manufactured rationally and in industrial series; and that apartment plans should be looked at anew. In new furniture, masonite, wood laminates and cellulose-varnished (not shellac) surfaces became increasingly usual.

Only a few furniture factories produced anything new: some neat chairs clad with saddlers' materials, by Axel Larsson (Svenska Möbelfabrikerna i Bodafors), variants of bentwood chairs, by Uno Åhrén and Gunnar Asplund (AB Gemla), furniture in formed steel pipes (A.W. Nilsson, perambulator factory and the Böhlmark lamp factory). Markelius had more or less copied chairs by two Bauhaus architects, Mart Stam and Marcel Breuer. The exhibition interiors were light and airy, with separate, not en suite items of furniture. Erik Chambert's interiors revealed him as a genuine innovator. Carl Hörvik's neat furniture is in the same spirit.

The Stockholm exhibition caused orthodox functionalists and the more traditionally minded architects and furniture designers to disagree publicly; Carl Malmsten belonged to the latter. Known from about 1910 for his inspired, craftsmanlike interpretations of Swedish rural tradition, he had never been reconciled to the functionalist view of things as "mute servants." He thought furniture should have character, express feelings, be masculine or feminine: what was generally

acceptable, standardised and of a given type offended against nature.

His views were opposed to those of Bruno Mathsson, whose first glued-laminate bentwood armchair was produced by 1934: influenced by the German steel-pipe furniture, it was softer and more friendly thanks to its natural materials—birch wood and woven hemp. He had managed to make a stable skeleton for his chair with a minimum of parts and the least possible quantity of wood, with the seat itself being comfortable and having a nice give: a minimalist use of interwoven lengths of what were actually equine harness belly bands. Gustaf Adolf Berg applied more organically extended curves in his Torparen (1942) chair, in which he considered he had reached a physiological and anatomical optimal sitting position, derived from studies of liquid balance and blood circulation in the human body.

Many felt the Bauhaus school's right-angled neo-factual style, with an framework of chromium-plated steel pipes was chilly and technocratic. The Swedish wooden furniture made interiors feel warmer and more friendly. The almost textile-less interiors of the Stockholm exhibition had no provenance in domestic Swedish traditions. During the 1930s and 1940s a number of new textile patterns, often using flowers, came into being.

After the 1934 Anschluss, an Austrian architect, Joseph Frank, emigrated to Sweden where he had had contacts with Estrid Eric-

Axel Larsson's plaited-harness chairs and extendable table (Made by Svenska Möbelfabrikerna, Bodafors), were exhibited at the 1930 Stockholm Exhibition. They met the new demands for flexibility and ease.

Josef Frank, interior and furniture (Svenskt Tenn): a home was not a machine but, with traditional furniture, strong colours and patterns, a source of comfort and domestic pleasure.

son. His move had great consequences for Swedish interior design. Frank's artistically distinguished furniture and textile patterns were (and still are) available from a shop, *Svenskt Tenn*, that Ericson opened. In 1937, the NK textile department got a new chief, a young and talented textile designer, Astrid Sampe. Some years earlier, Elias Svedberg, an interior decorator, had come to the NK furniture department. The pair attracted international attention. Swedish interior decoration was a success at the 1937 international exhibition in Paris, where, as in New York in 1939, Bruno Mathsson made a name for himself.

This style got the name "Swedish Modern" that according to the 1939 catalogue signified a "new version of modernism" characterised by "soundness and sense". The pictures of the interiors show unconventional furnishing solutions. The goal was what had been sought since 1900: to make the everyday state of the homes of unexceptional people and their children more beautiful and pleasant.

Swedes Live Erroneously

Between 1930 and 1950, activities around questions concerning dwellings became more and more intense: investigations into habits,

G. A. Berg's kids' 'boxed', easily stored furniture, New York Exhibition, 1939.

Elias Svedberg and Astrid Sampe-Hultberg exhibited the Swedish Modern.

exhibitions of styles, how-to study-courses, research into the goods of dwellings and kitchen designs, efforts to design everyday things, press and radio discussions. An early example of architects and researchers cooperating with organisations within the Labour Movement extended, in 1944, to include the Industrial Federation.

In 1931, the Social Democratic Women's Association's periodical got a new editor: Kaj Andersson, a working-class woman who had been influenced by the functional and aesthetic programme of the Swedish Handicraft Society. Sven Markelius regularly enlightened readers on how to improve their homes. Osvald Almqvist wrote on planning kitchens, Gregor Paulsson argued that people should become better at setting up house. The editor herself launched the slogan of "the factories' best for domestic needs." The periodical included catalogues of goods to improve readers' knowledge of quality and function. A mid-1930s questionnaire enquiry revealed readers most wanted mattresses: in a school class of thirty, perhaps only four children slept alone in their own beds.[42]

In 1944, Andersson's sister, Margit Hagberg, became the first housing consultant in Sweden; she worked in Stockholm. She had staged her first exhibition in 1933, in some newly-built functionalist residential buildings on Munkebäcksgatan, Göteborg; it was followed by a number of others during the 1930s. When she could not find the furniture she wanted, she had joiners make it. After 1941, she used the set of patterns that Swedish Handicraft Society had published that year with the help of Carl Malmsten, Carl-Axel Acking and Elias Svedberg.[43]

During the 1930s, the Swedish Handicraft Society, too, arranged a series of dwelling exhibitions, of which one was Modern Home (*Det moderna hemmet*), held in conjunction with the inauguration in 1933 of the newly-designed functionalist row houses at Ålstensgatan, Stockholm; another, a Home in a Collective House (*Hem i kollektivhus*) was held when Markelius' 'Collective House' on John Ericsons gata, Stockholm, was completed in 1935. The *Standard* exhibitions (1934, 1936) in the Liljevalch gallery in Stockholm made the repeated point that less costly and better products could be got through standardised industrial production; Åke Hampus Huldt was commissioned to run the first of them as the peripatetic Good Furnishings—Live Better Exhibition (*Bra bohag—bo bättre*), in furniture shops, Labour Movement premises, schools and museums all over Sweden. Furniture deal-

ers were not always so enthusiastic about the Spartan taste of the association. Here you come again, they complained, with your Windsor chairs and 'haywain' furniture.[44]

In 1936, the association arranged a large Leisure Exhibition (*Fritiden*) in Ystad, where one of the novelties was the sportstuga. The 1938 We Live in Ribershus Exhibition was put on in Malmö. The next year, the new 'collective house' on Gärdet, central Stockholm, for the Professional Women's Club was the venue for the Eleven Families Display their Homes exhibition. With irrepressible determination, exhibition after exhibition presented other than en suite furniture, adjustable and revolvable lamps, 'Windsor' chairs and other sturdy items of which most could be used for different purposes, thin, light curtains, steel-frame ottomans on which beds could be made up; all this and room for kids to play.

Before the 1930s, many architects designed both houses and their furniture, but then a specialisation began. Beginning to take over responsibility for interiors and furniture, interior designers formed the National Association of Interior and Furniture Designers (Sveriges inrednings- och möbelarkitekters riksförbund; called SIR).

Alva and Gunnar Myrdal's book, *Kris i befolkningsfrågan*, published in 1934 but never translated, raised an alarm about the low Swedish nativity. A number of social reforms were introduced to induce young persons to marry and to increase and multiply. From 1937, newly-wed couples were entitled to official loans (of 1,000 kronor) on favourable terms; in 1942, having been commissioned to investigate how this money had been spent, Ingeborg Wærn Bugge and Åke Huldt investigated 164 families who had received such loans in 1938–1942.[45]

Many of these young families had not

A Malmsten Windsor-style chair (1942) exemplifies this style's renaissance in this decade: practical, functional and acceptable as general furniture.

When the Ribershus Housing Area, Malmö, was opened (1938), the Swedish Handicraft Society arranged an exhibition furnished with NK's products by Svedberg and Sampe-Hultberg.

Poster (1941) for dwelling exhibitions; in 1937, official loans had been offered to help young couples set up home and form families.

bought the most necessary things, but had spent their loans on heavy dining-room suites in dark-stained birch wood and wine-red plush fabrics. Country kids who had moved, voluntarily or not, to big towns, wanted in this way to show that they were really not yokels, for dining-room suites with sideboards had status. Having moved from the countryside and its culture, these young families had difficulty in seeing the value of what they had left.

Bugge commented laconically on the result of the investigation in *Byggmästaren*, (8/1943). "The unoccupied best room is the symbol of social completion ... the unsuitable furnishings and the absurd living habits are generally hard on children. For them there is not much room in such a sterile paradise for two that parents create for themselves. 'The only place for him is under the kitchen table,' said a mother about her little son."

So that young people should not waste their money, Bugge had written a how-to brochure in 1937: "With slender means we set up house" (*Med begränsade medel ... gå vi att sätta bo*).[46] It was published by the Taxpayers' Association. In 1944, the Swedish Handicraft Society was instructed to cooperate with the National Bank of Sweden to spread information about the most necessary kitchen and cleaning equipment. When the young couples received their loans they would receive this

brochure. New editions were published in 1948 and 1955. This pedagogically undemanding text inspired the similar, 'Worth Knowing' brochures published by KF in the 1960s and 1970s. The starting packets that IKEA now offers young families can be seen as a commercial follow-up to this idea.

Dwellings Must Be Re-planned

Alvar Aalto, the Finnish architect, was engaged in the preparations for a housing exhibition to open in Helsinki in 1939. He contacted his Swedish colleagues and the Swedish Handicraft Society, to ask them to present an apartment for a family with many children. Gotthard Johansson, the association's chairman, has described how uncertain people felt about the form of such a dwelling. While, in retrospect, the Stockholm exhibition apartments were perceived to be less practical and thought out than they seemed at the time, no-one could say for sure what a good apartment and good furnishings should look like.[47]

In 1937, Brita Åkerman had begun her investigation of how 214 young families and their children used their apartments; these families belonged to different social groups, their dwellings were of different types. She concluded that their dwellings were both cramped and wrongly arranged. Although she did not publish until 1941, her work was known to a small circle. Families squeezed themselves into small kitchen corners so as to be able to preserve large rooms as 'best'. Adults' voluntary constrictions were hardest on children: of those living in a single room and a kitchen, 13 per cent shared beds either with siblings or parents; 23 per cent had a bed that had to be hidden away by day.[48]

It was decided in Swedish Handicraft Society and SAR that research should be begun to provide a basis for better dwellings. Gotthard Johansson was a motive force, but, without his young, engaged and inexhaustible colleagues, primarily Sten Lindegren, the job could not have been done. The researchers set to work most thoroughly. They studied the use of dwellings in the slightest details. On behalf of the association, and to get an idea of what it offered, Åke Huldt and Elias Svedberg made an inventory of the furniture market that they published in 1941. In winter 1942–43, Lena Larsson did the fieldwork for an investigation into dwelling by visiting 100 families living in the newly-built Stockholm suburb of Traneberg. Her intentions were to survey how the

ety as a whole would better when homes were. When the Swedish Handicraft Society celebrated its centenary in 1945, Åke Stavenow asserted the slogan: "The best possible for as many as possible."

In 1947, Lena Larsson concluded her work with the association to manage the newly-opened shop at NK, called NK-bo. Elias Svedberg, who was responsible for NK product development of furniture, wanted a direct channel to consumers for the new Triva furniture programme. Larsson continued her pedagogic activity in the shop, with debates and courses for members of the general public.

As time passed, the work of the Dwellings Committee altered. Study leaders were trained who could take over the courses. The association concentrated on studies of domestic furniture and furnishings. The first subject for research was beds: how long, wide and high was the ideal? And how should it be designed to ensure agreeable rest and to resistance to normal strains?

Increased Welfare, Larger Dwellings, Better Net Incomes

Some years after 1945 most Swedish households began to be better off. The ideology and aesthetics of 1940s scarcity became less attractive as an answer to the housing problem. New synthetic materials—paints, regular and plasticised textiles, wallpapers, a greater range of sets of china and other things for the home—tempted people to consume. Modern housing areas catered to individual tastes. There was no longer but one correct way to live. Having urged their readers to *Dwell Better*, furnishing brochures now offered them *A Richer Everyday Life*.

The basis work about dwellings done during the preceding decade now began to bear fruit. God Bostad (1954) defined apartment plans and demands on equipment. In apartments designed during the 1950s, architects succeeded exemplarily in taking advantage of how buildings were oriented, in creating fine relationships between rooms that could be variously furnished without wasting space. More people than ever before knew something about good design and quality. The extensive efforts on domestic science in schools, in courses, on TV programmes and an intensive coverage of domestic things in the daily media stimulated interest.

In 1952, the furniture dealers held their first annual Ideal Home (Önskehem) exhibition, where they presented what was new and desir-

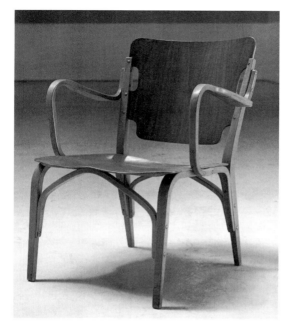

Carl-Axel Acking's technically advanced armchair derived from a 1943 competition arranged by a furniture factory and the Swedish Handicraft Society; 12 chairs fitted into a single carton.

able. Lately popular material had included birch, pine and elm, but in the 1950s much furniture was lacquered in grey-white, blue, red or black.[58] New industrial spray-painting facilities simplified this work. Foam-rubber and plastics became the new frame and padding materials. "Invisible" plastic lacquers eliminated thick yellowish cellulose lacquer.[59] Beds with 'no-sag' frames, writing tables on trestles, kids' furniture from KF called *Växa med läxa*, were novelties that were to survive.

Designers and industries shared ambitions to achieve good quality. Several furniture designers, including Karl Erik Ekselius and Yngve Ekström, owned high-quality furniture factories; skilled craftsmen still played a role in many furniture factories. In 1957, inspired by the Danish Snedkerlauget, some young Swedish furniture designers formed the HI-Group that, they thought, if helped by skilled joiners, could produce unique items of furniture, short series but above all prototypes for industrial manufacture, which would be a way to raise the standard of furniture design. The textile industry, too, wanted to work with novel designs and a high quality of material, weaving techniques and printing.

As in the 1930s, there was a tug-of-war between those who unreservedly accepted the new industrially produced or synthetic materials and those who accepted only what they called natural materials. Carl Malmsten was one of the naturalists and refused to have anything to with the new foam-rubber and synthetic padding and covering material. He went on working with natural materials and tradi-

Malmsten's 'Talavid' series (1955) was considered one of the best of the decade.

tional techniques. His *Talavid* series (1955) was one of the best of the decade.

The Swedish Handicraft Society did resist the consumption euphoria but not so strongly as Malmsten. It devoted itself to research into goods, which resulted in the VDN product declarations for furniture and, in time, for domestic lighting; it still asserted a common-sensical aesthetic and won sympathy for this among designers. The Milan Triennale exhibitions expressed post-war ambitions to create a more beautiful, better world. Many of the Swedish glass, textiles and ceramics designers achieved an "exotic scent" of the natural northern world, a modern organic or bare, severe and pure formal language associated with "Scandinavian Design". Carl-Axel Acking, Yngve Ekström, Elias Svedberg, Nisse Strinning and other furniture designers were among the leaders. Systematic studies by the Swedish Handicraft Society of furniture functions, dimensions, surfaces and designs had led to some practical and functional pieces of furniture.

This elegant minimalist style of tense contours and functional form triumphed at the H55 exhibition in Helsingborg in 1955 that also included new domestic plastics, heat-resistant ceramic materials, stainless steel, combination furniture and cunning storage systems; of these, Nisse and Kajsa Strinning's String Shelves, which originated in a competition arranged by a company in the Bonniers publishing group in 1949, became the best known.[60] These mahogany book shelves had white-lacquered iron supports that could be fastened to any suitable wall, thus saving floor space; once the supports were point welded and plasticised they could be mass produced.

The six 1955-exhibition houses' individual floor area was restricted to 125 m², the maximum that qualified for an official loan; their component parts were factory-made and could be supplied in a ready-to-build package; the houses had neither cellar nor attic. Each had a bar-kitchen, a garage, a protected inner yard and a room for children.

In this context, perhaps the most interesting layout was that of the *Skal och kärna* house by Anders William-Olsson and Mårten Larsson; its furnishing and fittings were designed by Larsson's wife Lena, and Ulla Molin. Its kitchen, bathroom and laundry room formed a kernel around which the other room units could be varied as needed: the children's bedrooms and playroom, and the family living room, lay on one side, the parents' bedroom and a room for the grown-ups on the other. Ulla Molin designed the kitchen, which contained some

Axel Larsson's cupboard, shown at the 'Contact with the Utilitarian Artist' exhibition, 1944, had dimensions and a form derived from the 1933 Housing Commission.

Mid-1950s interior, with Nisse Strinning's 'Stringhylla' shelving. Having been introduced in 1949, it was developed into a complete programme of items constructed in the same technique of plasticised iron.

Kitchen by Ulla Molin for a bungalow-type house at the 'Housing in 1955 Exhibition'; it was more remarked than any other kitchen there.

subtleties, including a kitchen stove with three hotplates in a row and an oven on the wall, so that, as a pleased journalist wrote, "housewives need no longer crawl about on the floor." [61] The most remarked feature was an 'all-room', something first seen at Baronbackarna, Örebro, in 1951: a single room in which grown-ups and kids would eat, play and pursue their various hobbies.

Private consumption rose: sales of household goods rose to an unprecedented height towards 1960. A belief in the future was firm. Technology was mankind's friend, a help in making "good" design less costly and thus accessible for all. No longer was it as important as it had been during the 1940s to look at every detail of a potential purchase and wonder whether it was needed. Children had rooms of their own rather than access to the living room. Domestic furnishing periodicals, such as *Hem i Sverige*, showed boys' and girls' rooms; teenagers were found to comprise a novel group of consumers.

Hitherto setting up home had been a matter of acquiring things to live with happily ever after. Now furnishing became a hobby. First published in 1956, the periodical *Allt i Hemmet* offered readers hints on repainting and changing one's home. Homes were now where personalities were expressed and handy skills demonstrated. Once again, Carl and Karin Larsson's Sundborn became a model: a home that reflected its owners' needs and aesthetics and thus successively changed its appearance.

In their book, *Tingens bruk och prägel* (1956), Gregor and Nils Paulsson assigned consumers

to one of three groups: the keen, the autonomous, the prudent. The first was alert to novelties, the second made choices independently of trends or conventions, the third preferred what was traditionally sure to what might be unsure. Of course the authors wanted more consumers to be conscious and reflective, but all the new goods that in increasing volumes filled the supermarkets and department stores were much too attractive, especially at their points of sale.

Easy, Mobile, Flexible

The 1960s began with animated debate of the get-it-use-it-chuck-it syndrome; köp, slit, släng in Swedish. An article by Lena Larsson set it off; she pointed out the need of changes in fashion and discussed and even prodded the sacred cow-principle of the demands of quality.[62] While some opposed her views, they were more attuned to the time than her opponents. During the 1960s, an easy-going attitude towards things and the words that signified them eclipsed demands for high quality, craftsmanship and sound materials; plywood, masonite and fibreboard were fundamentally to alter production and consumption.

Furnishing changed. 'Best' rooms were changed into living rooms through the addition of large sofa groups, buttoned-leather sofas, mats soft enough to sit on, revolving chairs that could be spun to face the TV and whole walls covered with book shelves (half) filled with audio-visual gear. Increasingly often, washable chair- and sofa covers, and coffee-table surfaces that withstood spilled coffee and fizzy drinks were what were wanted. Furniture got castors so it could be moved easily to one side. Things were no longer to impede the living of sitting or reclining in front of the box: having been started in 1957, the single-channel monochrome state TV service had attracted 2.2 million licence-paying Swedish households by 1967.[63]

Housework was eased by supermarkets, semi-prepared foodstuffs and a less rigidly prescribed code of etiquette. As the medical-drugs industry could cope with increasing numbers of illnesses, demands for hygiene and an aversion to dirt diminished. Many Swedes acquired holiday homes in Sweden or ventured out on charter holidays. Well-kept perfect homes that housewives had prided themselves on in the 1940s lost their attractions, perhaps especially for their daughters. Old objects snapped up at auctions adorned many homes as conversation pieces: spinning

'Joker' (1967) furniture: bits of lacquered plywood that could easily be put together; Börge Lindau and Bo Lindekrantz designed them, Birgitta Hahn did the cushions.

wheels, copper pots, rocking chairs; butter churns served as umbrella stands.

Inspired by Pop Art, some textile designers produced large-scale, colourful playful patterns; Sven Fristedt, Inez Svensson and Birgitta Hahn regarded their late-1960s patterns as cheap alternatives to costly oil paintings: textiles could simply and rapidly transform a home.

Jan Ahlin, Jan Dranger, Johan Huldt and Martin Eiserman fitted a loose padding covered with orange corduroy on their 1967 Multoman sofa; they and other young furniture designers experimented with furniture in folding cardboard, in inflatable plastics, in simple cheap chipboard systems, and lamps that could be built to be altered, raised and lowered. Trestle tables and folding chairs met demands for flexibility. Much of this exemplified köp-slit-släng. Less impermanent but still typical of the 1960s was Bruno Mathsson's revolving Jetson chair (1966), his linen-covered, stainless-steel sofa on castors called Karin (1969), Yngve Ekström's Furubo cupboard (1964) and Stefan Gips Robust child's chair (1962).

In 1965, the Million Programme began of producing that many dwellings in a decade. Despite this gigantic effort to deal with housing queues and cramped living conditions, much of the superimposed interest in homes had already, strangely enough, dwindled away. In some respects, research continued, partly to make dwellings more suitable for handicapped people who, it was considered, should be able to live at home in a wheelchair or with the

help of other means. Designers began to wonder about the demands of other groups, children's needs, how furniture should be able to suit the elderly.

In 1967, the research into and studies of furniture that had been done by the Swedish Handicraft Society's Dwelling Institute was made the responsibility of the new, Furniture Institute (Möbelinstitutet) of which the director was Erik Berglund. It was financed by the central government and industry. Possibilities

The Mathsson 'Jetson' revolving chair (1966) mediated ease, flexibility and contemporary interest in space technology.

of making tests became much better, for it had a well-equipped laboratory.

The association became more interested in the public-sector environment, in collective forms of dwelling, and industrial design. Interior decorators who concentrated on public-sector furnishing and fittings included Gunnar Eklöf, Jack Ränge, Lars Ljunglöf, Sven Kai-Larsen, Björn Hultén, Åke Axelsson, Bo Lindekrantz and Börje Lindau. Increasing numbers of women found employment. Children's nurturing, done formerly at home by families, was taken over by day-care centres, schools, leisure and young-people's centres, sports' organisations and other institutions.

IKEA Absorbed Ideas

This image of the diminished domestic significance must be seen against the unbelievable success of the IKEA store that opened in 1965 in a southern suburb of Stockholm. Its director, Ingvar Kamprad, and his young employees could make use of the tendencies of the time. The department with small things for the home was called Accent. The Swedish loam word from French milieu caused this department store to be a miljövaruhus. Kamprad's comment was that "we think in entire rooms, and, that while others sell furniture, carpets and lamps, we sell home furnishings." The complete interiors of displayed rooms were

As early as the 1960s, IKEA had an eye for families with kids, as it still has; this interior is from the mid-1980s.

models for prospective buyers. The young IKEA staff had got its models from NK-bo, from exhibitions by the Swedish Handicraft Society and from *Allt i hemmet*, then the largest home-furnishing periodical in Sweden.[64]

This IKEA store was established at a time when the many people born in the 1940s were forming families. New suburbs were growing up around the big towns, where small furniture shops were either closing or merging with or being replaced by chain stores and department stores. The few that remained were felt by young people making homes for themselves to be often fuddy-duddy and unmodern. So they preferred untreated wooden storage shelves for their books, inexpensive basketwork chairs, restaurant suppliers' goods in their kitchens, blocks or cushions in plastics out of which they made themselves things to sit on. In protest against their parents' dreams of status, they wished to furnish their own homes simply and without great expense.

In the IKEA stores customers had, as in any other supermarket, to make their selections and take them in large trolleys to the checkouts. Self service was at first a necessity for IKEA, because the initial demands were so great, but the idea agreed well with the spirit of the time.

Kamprad had begun to sell furniture by post order in 1950. The Swedish Handicraft Society circle was highly critical of the quality and the type of his furniture. In the mid 1950s, he began to engage designers, including Erik Wörtz, who had designed the Trivia furniture for NK. In 1964, IKEA employed Karin Mobring, a designer trained at the Carl Malmsten workshop school.

IKEA, a member by 1959 of the Swedish Handicraft Society's producers' section, was also one of the first furniture companies to submit its products to the association's tests conducted under the direction of Erik Berglund. In 1963, IKEA could provide its furniture with the relevant VDN labels. In 1964, Allt i Hemmet, testing the quality of IKEA and other producers' furniture, found the IKEA items were, while costing less than those of other producers, of a quality at least equal to theirs.

IKEA was not the only channel to furniture buyers in the 1960s. KF, too, with its Domus Interior department stores, had a youthful style. Its decorative textiles were colourful, with bold patterns; their designers included Gunila Axén, Carl-Johan De Geer, Ingela Håkansson and Susanne Grundell. Its furniture programme comprised cheap, neo-simple products. Its greatest marketing success was the Spika shelf (1967) made by the company's own factory in Lammhult, which sold 1.3 million units. It was made in the most rational way possible of chipboard. This company and IKEA dominated the furniture market in this decade.

New Demands For a Quality of Life

Ecological awareness began in the late 1960s and grew in the 1970s. Some popular books and article on science addressed the risks entailed by unchecked consumption and the chuck-it-out-when-worn syndrome. Land, sea and air could not cope with so much poisonous chemical and industrial refuse, which was a growing problem. People had to change their patterns of life. Home was where things should be made—bread, for example, well-simmered stews and vegetarian dishes—and re-used. Kitchens were once again their centres; not their living rooms, as in the 1960s. The demand for an improved standard of living and good basic products were mentioned more frequently in the media. Interest grew in old technologies.

Domestic furnishing was increasingly influenced by international trends and TV series. Swedish kitchen standards integrated the German or continental height: cupboards extending up to the ceiling left nowhere for dust and dirt to settle, but now stopped lower down, irrespective of ceiling heights. Formerly bare surfaces became decorative; eg attractive wood replaced utilitarian working surfaces. Kitchen manufacturers declined to follow the standards of the 1950s, but chose to meet emotional needs of variation and status. Frameworks were often made in cheap chipboard and fibreboard, but the visible elements followed a variety of types; what was sold as 'English Colonial style' attracted many. Many Swedish homes were characteristically orange and brown in this decade. In 1977, the periodical Form posed the question of whether the age had any style, and replied that it did not; pastiches, environmental cosmetics, freshly-produced antiques, and heavy clumsy pine furniture dominated the market.[65]

Opposing forces existed but had less effect. Åke Axelsson, whose serious research was to bear fruit, had studied designs and manufacturing methods in classical Egyptian and Greek chairs.[66] He presented his findings in an exhibition in 1974. In the 1976 Stockholm Ararat exhibition, he showed an ur-chair without either screw or nail: only wood and rope. It was stable when sat on. Its straight legs,

woven-string seat and back support of rungs were so simple that, made by craftsmen in Axelsson's workshop, it cost no more than if it had been made industrially.[67]

It would probably not have been awarded the new form of furniture declaration: Möbelfakta, launched in 1973. Berglund had long been dissatisfied with the cumbersome VDN label procedure: would-be buyers did not read the extensive texts, nor were the furniture industry and shops really interested. The new scheme did better. Its brief texts indicated the area and capacity of use of the item, its durability, the quality of its material and the care with which it had been made.[68]

Really novel home furnishings were few. The Swedish Handicraft Society persuaded KF to produce a well-thought-out basic furniture programme "with pleasant, functional and durable products, made without waste of resources in a good working environment, offered for sale at reasonable prices and forms without pretention or borrowings."[69] That, at least, was the intention. Appearing in 1978, the basic furniture met the functional needs

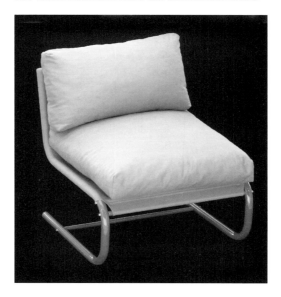

Mid 1970s' new thinking in the Cooperative Association was set off by the Swedish Handicraft Society and led to the 'Bas' sofa or spare bed. Furniture was to be timeless, environmentally friendly and practical.

The 'Stuns' chair (1972) exemplifies bent, lacquered steel tubes and canvas in an unpretentious style. Designers were Johan Huldt and Jan Dranger (of Innovator).

Young 1980s designers wanted to express ideas about furniture as art and concepts: Jonas Bohlin's sculptural 'Concret' chair (1981) was an early (and costly) example.

of homes: to eat, be together, sit, work, sleep, store; etc. Their formal language was northern blond, bare and popular, in some items almost self-righteous. They used normal or curly-grained birch. As a commercial success, the Bas sofa-and-spare-bed piece outdid everything else. Another variety of timeless furniture was designed by Innovator, a company founded by Johan Huldt and Jan Dranger; their furniture in lacquered steel tubes and simple uncomplicated covers, their Stuns chair (1972) and table on castors called Tech Trolley (1974) survived a number of changes in modishness. The same applies to the director's chair by Börge Lindau and Bo Lindekrantz for Lammhults Mekaniska Verkstad (1972).

Symbolic Values Instead of Functional Demands

In 1978, Curt Lagerström and Anders Söderberg were awarded a prize in a Scandinavian furniture competition for a "scarcely usable writing desk with concretist decor in

John Kandell's three-legged stool. First made in 1982, it has appeared in large numbers since, made by Källemo as part of this company's efforts to further a more imaginative, artistic way of regarding furniture.

yellow and red"[70], which signified that other, post-modernistic values were affecting the form of furniture. Of this piece of furniture, its designers thought it more important to satisfy aesthetics and visual feelings than to meet functionalistic demands: it was not merely equipment but a form of image communicating feelings, memories, experiences. Among a new generation of furniture designers, Mikael Löfström, Catharina Nordenstedt, Jonas Bohlin and, later, Mats Theselius, wanted to do their work in a more post-modernistic spirit but the industry was not interested in renewal.

Several young designers chose to go into production themselves, so as to get their ideas for furniture into trade fairs, exhibitions and to potential customers. Thus especially Bohlin and Theselius, having met a growing interest from the public and the media, were taken on by a producer, Källemo. Its director, Sven Lundh, said among other things that "imagination is the enemy of the durable, but it is the spearhead of development and a significant human resource, although often a restricted and under-used one."[71] The climate of the 1980s being generous towards form, the talented designer John Kandell reappeared with furniture with an imaginatively playful richness of form. As a concept, 'furniture as art' brought out the ability of things to have an identity, a personal expression, an ability to stir feelings on a deeper level. Furniture was made in short series and was thus costly and exclusive: nothing for the wider masses.

A wide range of low-price furniture caused IKEA increasingly to dominate Swedish homes. It widened its range to match various tastes. To catch the interest in quality of middle-aged customers, IKEA launched its *Stockholm* series in 1984–85; designed by Karin Mobring and Tomas Jelinek, it was more exclusive and qualitatively distinguished from the rest of the range. Niels Gammelgaard, a Danish architect, and Tord Björklund were among IKEA's leading designers in the 1980s; the first worked in a high-tech spirit, the second in the light Scandinavian style.

Interest in design grew during the 1980s, even if *Sköna Hem* and other interior-decoration periodicals often presented a continental, textile-rich and decorative style of furnishing homes from which children and domestic occupations were conspicuously absent. The furniture industry and the designers' organisations began to feel responsible for the development. A number of new prizes were to be awarded to stimulate new design: Utmärkt Svensk Form and the Forsnäs Prize among them.

Exhibitions about dwelling were few at first, but, repeated exhibitions were held in various parts of Sweden from 1985 onwards, and developments began to change. It is interesting to compare the 1980 Stockholm exhibition of apartments, Ways of Living 1980 (*Boslag 80*) of which Svensk Form was one of the organisers with the 1985 Seven Rooms' Roominess *Sjurumslighet* exhibition held in conjunction with the 1985 Dwelling (*Bo 85*) exhibition in the northern suburb of Stockholm, Upplands Väsby.

The first occupied 104 m² and was furnished with commonsensical and functional ideas, moveable walls and a deep perception of the needs of the three different families whom it was supposed to satisfy. The second was a normal three-rooms-and-a-kitchen apartment rebuilt to contain seven rooms; it was distinguished by a number of scenographic and poetical material effects and unexpected encounters between material. Its plan associated in part to 18th-century pastors' residences, which used to have a large room placed between two smaller chambers; the small sleeping alcoves that were then usual made a reappearance.[72] Media comment and the general public's responses were as polarised as they had been in the face of the 1930 Stockholm exhibition.

In general, this criticism was sharp. "Its incomprehensible mixture of luxury and indigence, its pastel-fresh surface over a reality of many deficiency diseases. Dreamy bits of painted scenery in the 'people's-homely atmosphere." Reviewers complained of poor furnishing materials and poor joinery, and a lack of facilities for the handicapped. One of the few good things mentioned was the Sunda house by the White architect group and Olle Anderson: its "soundness implies that natural materials are used as far as possible, that an ecological balance is sought …"[73]

During the 1980s and 1990s, several young furniture designers have worked consciously in a Scandinavia spirit, with light materials and clear colours, often in a minimalist, compact, multi-functional way, with greater ecological insights than during the 1950s, when Scandinavian design was renowned internationally. But knowledge of the demands of functions is not always now as large as it was then.

With the aims of more easily reaching potential buyers and other interested persons, young designers have formed some more or less temporary groupings; they have often made their furniture for young singles of either sex living in large towns where they must or choose to live in small spaces.

At the large 'Dwelling 1985' exhibition, at Upplands Väsby, the Swedish Society of Crafts and Design transformed an unexceptional three-room apartment into an imaginative 'Seven Rooms' Roominess"; its architects were Stefan Alenius and Magnus Silfverhielm.

An exception to this urban, minimalist and compact domestic culture is the broad, well-thought-out programme of furniture for family life, by Erik Richter, an architect. He first presented it at the 1993 Dwelling (Bo 93) exhibition at Karlskrona, where he furnished an apartment in the west wing of a lovely old building, Kungshall, that Kjell Forshed had renovated. He selected timber for its intrinsic qualities: hardwoods such as oak for table tops, birch in chairs, pine for the lower parts of tables; rubber-backed or natural coconut fibre and horsehair, down for filling and covers. No plastic lacquers, but surfaces treated with oils or painted with egg tempera.

His furniture combines craftsmanship and industrial manufacture. His exhibition programme declared he would "make furniture with simplicity and feeling, at prices that feel reasonable. Furniture that is durable, in material and in function and form… We work mostly in wood, always solid wood, most often Swedish grown. We choose broad planks for table tops, which makes the timber more alive. The oils and colours we use are also pure natural products. All this makes the furniture not look as if it were without blemishes, and that it ages—but in what a lovely way!"[74]

Now, in the late 1990s, it is evident that, in future, homes are going to have perform many more tasks. Many work at home, communicat-

In many language editions, IKEA's furniture catalogue outdoes all rivals, as well as offering an infinity of modest-priced goods. In the 1980s, IKEA began to offer things for older, qualityconscious consumers, eg the 'Stockholm' series (1984–85.)

ing electronically with colleagues. At the same time, because official subsidies have been cut, living costs in Sweden have risen so steeply that many can no longer afford the roomy, recently-built apartments. Growing number of students, even former students, live at home. Demand for smaller, less costly apartments, also for more compact means of furnishing, is growing. Exemplary ecological housing areas are so far few, but now that kitchen refuse must be sorted and preserved, kitchen form is of renewed interest: many ecological and resource-saving demands affect it. Once again, as during the close of the 19th century, the large table round which meals are eaten, hobbies pursued and work done is becoming the central item of furniture in some dwellings.

Interest in Sweden in homes grew during the second half of the 19th century and developed through a unique combination of voluntary organisations, designers, producers, central-government departments and social-political efforts, which culminated in the 1950s. Its results began to be questioned during the economically expansive 1960s. New, easily cared-for materials and easy-going attitudes towards things led to novel patterns of consumption, which were called in question in their turn in the following decade. Demands for thoughtful housekeeping and a greater environmental awareness deepened and expanded during the 1990s.

The Swedish habit of focusing on the home has sometimes been explained by reference to the chilly climate and short gloomy winter days. But winter is as long and dark elsewhere in the world without comparable efforts being directed towards people's homes. As this chap-

By the early 1990s, Erik Richter was designing and producing ecologically conscious goods and child-friendly furnishings: these are from the 'Dwelling in 1993' exhibition. They differ both from the throw-away mentality of the 1960s and from the exclusive pieces of the 1980s

ter has tried to show, the reasons are more complex, and the Swedish concern for homes has been unique when compared with other countries.

'Ängeln' rocking chairs (Thomas Sandell, 1997), associating to both the 1940s 'People's Home' and the novel whiteness of the 1960s; the maker is Källemo.

NOTES

[1] Angela Rundqvist, "Nationella former och ideala normer" in Kerstin Wickman (ed.) *Formens rörelse* (1995), 11.

[2] Rundqvist, 21.

[3] Sofia Danielson, *Den goda smaken och samhällsnyttan* (1995), 36.

[4] Danielson (1991), 42.

[5] Kerstin Wickman, "Bohaget—kvinnans trygghet och verk", in Brita Åkerman et al., *Den okända vardagen* (1983), 239.

[6] Eva von Zweigbergk, *Handarbetets Vänner 100 år* (Anniversary Catalogue 1974).

[7] Wickman (1983), 234.

[8] Kerstin Wickman, "Drømmen om Scandinavian Design lever endnu" in *Louisiana Revy* 2/1996, 19.

[9] Mathilda Langlet, *Husmodern i staden och på landet* (1883–84), 814.

[10] Langlet, 811 ff.

[11] Langlet, 815.

[12] Ellen Key, *Skönhet för alla* (1899; facsimile edition 1997), 5.

[13] Rundqvist, 20.

[14] Elisabet Stavenow-Hidemark, "Förändringens vind" in Wickman (ed.), (1995), 27.

[15] Stavenow-Hidemark (1995), 35.

[16] Key, 6.

[17] Key, 9.

[18] Key, 4–5.

[19] Ellen Key, "Folket och konsten", in *Varia. Illustrerad månadstidskrift* (1900), 38.

[20] Key (1900), 40. See also Ellen Key, *Folkbildningsarbetet särskildt med hänsyn till skönhetssinnets odling* (1906), 139.

[21] Ragnar Östberg, *Ett hem dess byggnad och inredning* (1905), 3.

[22] Elna Tenow, *Solidar. En lifsfråga för hemmen* (1905), 89, 97, 107, 111, 117, 139.

[23] Erik G. Folcker, "Modern möbelkonst på Parisutställningen", in *Svenska Slöjdföreningens Meddelanden* (1900), 62; see also an account of her visit by Clara Hahr, p. 122.

[24] Gunnela Ivanov, "Den besjälade industrivaran", in Wickman (1995), 51.

[25] *Svenska Slöjdföreningens Tidskrift*, Meddelanden (1913), 111–112.

[26] Wickman (1995), 54.

[27] Kerstin Wickman, "Hemutställningen på Liljevalchs" in Wickman (1995), 62.

[28] Hemutställningen catalogue (1917), 17-19.

[29] Wickman (1995), 66.

[30] Press cuttings from the exhibition; see also Wickman (1995), 69–71.

[31] Wickman (1995), 70–71.

[32] "Hemutställningen och dess upptakt", interview with Else Gullberg, *Form* 10/1947, 178.

[33] Kerstin Thörn, "Från kök till rum" in *Hem* (catalogue from Stockholm City Museum, 1996), 65.

[34] Uno Åhrén, "Brytningar" in *Svenska Slöjdföreningens årsbok* (1925), 6.

[35] Wickman (1983), 252.

[36] Wick (1983), 253.

[37] Catalogue for *Utställning för hem och hushåll* exhibition (1927), 6.

[38] Catalogue (1927), 50.

[39] Catalogue (1927), 54.

[40] *Svenska Slöjdföreningens årsbok* (1929), 1–2.

[41] Wickman (1983), 255.

[42] Kerstin Wickman, "Då var bostadsfrågan nästan religion", an article on Kaj Andersson in *Form* 6/1979, 6.

[43] Kerstin Wickman, "Basmöbler och djärva inredningsexperiment redan på 30-talet", an article on Margit Hagberg in *Dagens Nyheter*, 6 September 1979.

[44] Wickman (1983), 259.

[45] Gotthard Johansson, *Bostadsvanor och bostadsnormer*, investigation by Svenska Arkitekters Riksförbund and Svenska Slöjdföreningen (1964), 31.

[46] Wickman (1983), 261.

[47] Unpublished interview with Sten Lindegren; see also Wickman (1983) 261-2.

[48] Brita Åkerman, Familjen som växte ur sitt hem (1941), 39.

[49] Wickman (1983), 263.

[50] Gotthard Johansson (1964), 162.

[51] Lena Larsson, "Lära sig att bo" in Kerstin Wickman (1995), 145.

[52] Lena Larsson (1995), 146; Erik Berglund, *Tala om kvalitet* (1997), 15.

[53] Monica Boman, "Vardagens decennium" in Monica Boman (ed.) *Svenska Möbler 1890–1990*, (1990), 253.

[54] Monica Boman, "1945: Bostadsfrågan i centrum" in Kerstin Wickman (1995), 160.

[55] Boman (1995), 160.

[56] Wickman (1983), 268.

[57] Boman (1995), 161-2.

[58] Lena Larsson, "Ett dynamiskt årtionde" in Boman (1990), 285.

[59] Larsson (1990), 292.

[60] Larsson (1990), 280.

[61] Sven Silow, "Gröningen. Byggnader, bostäder, bosättning på H55" in Wickman (1995), 210.

[62] Lena Larsson, "Köp, Slit, Släng" in *Form* 7-8/1960.

[63] Kerstin Wickman, "Byggbart, utbytbart, flyttbart" in Boman (1990), 336.

[64] Kerstin Wickman, "The traditional heritage: Ikea and the Swedish Home", in Barbro Klein, Mats Widbom (eds.), *Swedish Folk Art. All tradition is change* (1994), 228.

[65] *Form* 4/1977; the subject is discussed in a number of articles.

[66] Kerstin Wickman, "Kunskapens källa", an article on Åke Axelsson in *Form* 3/1974, 136–8.

[67] Monica Boman, "Den kluvna marknaden", in Boman (1990), 393, 397.

[68] Berglund (1997), 75.

[69] Sven Thiberg, "Dags att undvara", "1970-talet. Insikt om de ändliga resurserna", in Wickman (1995), 274.

[70] Boman (1990), 432.

[71] Jill Dufwa, "Nya former, nya uttryck", in Boman (1990), 439.

[72] Bengt O.H. Johansson, "Svensk Forms lägenhet", in *Form* 7/1985, 9–10.

[73] Gunilla Lundahl, "Bo 85", in *Form* 7/1985, 18.

[74] Kerstin Wickman, "Fresh shoots from old roots", in *Form* 6/1993, 95.

Sven Markelius' house (1945), Kevinge, with its new sort of garden, one that took the natural world as its model.

The Functionalism of the Gardening Art

THORBJÖRN ANDERSSON

During the 20th century, the role of the garden designer changed into that of the landscape architect, who, working within wider boundaries, became responsible for urban buildings and large-scale changes to the landscape. In Sweden, this occurred during a time when visionary politicians and their public servants were leading the country affirmatively into the future and remodelling the country in a full-scale experiment in the art of social engineering. Both national society as a whole and individual towns were altered in thoroughgoing ways. But large efforts were also made in the landscape: the natural world was to be tamed for human purposes, power was to be won from the rapids, the country was to be criss-crossed with a network of roads for the rapid transport of goods and people, glacial ridges and craggy scars were to be exploited for large public-sector building works. In this immense transformation of an agricultural country into one that was industrialised, demands arose for the skills of landscape architects, of whom many were women; this profession was one of the earliest in Sweden to include as many women as men.

We shall concentrate here on only a very few of the names and projects of 20th-century Swedish landscape architecture. A handful of projects and their architects show how the form and the content of gardens were changed radically during a period in about the middle of the century. Parks for the bourgeoisie to promenade in were obliged to give way to parks of a novel sort that were laid out as public landscapes that democratically permitted anyone and even their children to enter. During the period, the 1940s and 1950s seem now to have been a harvest-time for the thoughts that had been formulated earlier. For the first time, Sweden made an independent contribution to the international history of the garden-

ing art. When Peter Shepheard published his expose, *Modern Gardens* (1953), he devoted several pages to the Swedish example that aroused interest all over the world.

Two special photographs were essential to the international reputation of Swedish parks. One depicts a private environment: Sven Markelius' *house in Kevinge*, which had been built in 1945.[1] This photograph has become something of an icon for the functionalistic view of the gardening art. It, rather than the garden it depicts, has had a large influence on Swedish landscape architecture. From having been a formal precursor to formal reception rooms in the house, or a separate space for private gardening, the garden is now a space, open to the surrounding landscape and possessed of an intrinsic value, in which one can be or find recreation. The photograph shows the house as a background to the garden, instead of vice versa. Some birch trees, such as may be found in the nearby woods, give us the impression that, behind the camera, the garden has in fact no defined boundary. Instead, the landscape in which Lake Mälaren lies comes rolling up to the very facades of the house. In the centre of the photograph there is a pool of water that seems small, no more than rainwater gathered in a crevice in a scar. A naked girl whose light skin catches the sunlight stands with her back to us. She strikes no pose but feels very much at home in this very special garden that most recalls a forest glade. She stretches out her arms to the shining future and towards the natural world that is her garden and that of Swedish functionalism. The girl represents the first generation that is going to live a completely modern life. Even so, we can track a historical link in this novel appreciation of the garden. The photography testifies to an inherited Swedish view of nature, in which people are at home in the

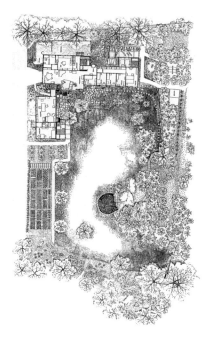

Markelius' house and garden.

Fredhäll Park (1936–38), Stockholm, by Osvald Almqvist: a free, informal urban park spread the reputation of parks in Stockholm all over the world. Photograph by K.W. Gullers.

Affectation in the-turn-of-the century park, as seen by Birger Lundquist, a cartoonist.

wild and live in an intimate relationship with the natural world.

Sven Markelius was hardly a precursor in matters of gardening. The mid-1940s date of the photograph tells us that its message is a confirmation more than a foretelling. Thoughts about the landscape of Lake Mälar as a feasible motif for a garden had been formulated, for example, 20 years earlier by Rutger Sernander, a professor of botany, besides becoming, by 1936, a reality given form by Holger Blom, the town gardener of Stockholm, and his predecessor, Osvald Almqvist.[2] But the strength of the composition of the photograph and Markelius' official town-planning status worked together to give weight to the message. Markelius had many international guests in his home which helped to spread the rumour about this expression of novel Swedish ideas about the new garden; one of them was Le Corbusier.

The second photograph shows a public place in a municipal park. This photograph of the paddling pool at *Fredhäll*, Stockholm, was published in countries including Denmark,

England, and Germany and had a large effect internationally in spreading the message of a novel sort of park. A photographer well known in Sweden, K.W. Gullers, had taken it. The picture shows a peaceful scene in which children play in a sun-drenched pool of water; mature untended ash and oak trees serve to frame it. Meadows extend beneath scattered trees. The place looks as if it were an inlet of the sea or a lake. But for the dwellings in the background, the picture could show a country outing, the landscape and the atmosphere being roughly the same.

The Natural World as a Garden

The 1930 Stockholm exhibition powerfully marked the break-through for functionalism. The new values that emerged concerned gardens as well as housing and other matters. Among the gardening concepts on which people definitely turned their backs were the late 19th-century British-influenced Arts-and-Crafts' garden. This sort of garden with its showy flower beds, detailed rock gardens and introverted nature belonged to what a new age saw as a musty, dusty middle-class ballast of an outmoded culture erected on individual ownership. The demand of the time for ideological renewal, with new, modern material, and a wish for rational care, showed itself to lead to difficulties in the world of horticulture. If it were large, a garden represented individualistic manifestation, or a conservative view of the development of culture, because garden culture came from cultivation and an agricultural society, which was precisely what Sweden was leaving. If one chose to see gardens as an aspect of utility, they were small separated units of cultivation, or, if seen as aspects of pleasure, decorative forms composed of plants; neither was a fitting image of a rational society on its way into the age of industry.

The vision of the new garden implied among other things that it should be natural, open, airy and locally anchored. Such a vision was to be found immediately outside the garden fence, in the Swedish landscape. The new garden was to be formulated more by the natural world than by horticulture. The natural world became a garden. And the garden went, not just stylistically but also ideologically, outside its traditional domains: a garden that so clearly made itself fast in the landscape comprised in fact an image of the country. A well-known Swedish writer, Carl Jonas Love Almqvist, had stated aphoristically a century earlier that "only Sweden has Swedish gooseberries."

A cultural characteristic of Sweden can be expressed in a limited register of descriptive words, including restraint, calm, sparseness, order. What they signify occurs characteristically in Swedish poetry, prose, film, painting, architecture and the gardening art. Few have described this peculiarity as well as Almqvist. His principal work, *Törnrosens bok* (1833–51), includes a text, *Svenska fattigdomens betydelse*, in which he uses the country's flora as an image of what is Swedish; more closely, the wild brier or dog rose: "formed of poverty, wild pleasure and chastity." As an eloquent comparison, Almqvist describes the "hotly red, lust-recalling sleepy southerly rose" with its narcotic vapours, in contrast to the "light-red dog rose with its fine, soft scent."

Almqvist, who was active within a broad field including literature, music, journalism, theology and social science, chose to let the Swedish flora illustrate the national identity in a broad sense. This is easy to understand. Swedish culture follows the rhythms of nature, and even its evolutionary principles, where changes are slow and comprise constant adap-

tations. In this harmonic cultural climate, the landscape has always been there as sounding board. To be sure, landscape architecture all over the world is subject to sites and the conditions of production that obtain there. But in few other countries can one see a country's culture so deeply impressed by the natural world it contains, and in few other countries can one see so clear a similarity between created garden art and the natural landscape.

Perhaps it is a Swedish peculiarity that the Swedish garden was born so clearly on the borderline between culture and nature. Sven Hermelin, the nestor of Swedish landscape architecture puts it like this: "The transition between bound and free has often occupied my imagination."[3] This is an attitude that goes straight into the history of the gardening art. Within important periods such as the renaissance and the enlightenment, nature was taken as the starting point for interpreting both human beings and their societies. It was a consequence of the break-through in the 14th century of the natural sciences. Nature was considered to possess the answers to all the questions that both scientists and humanists could pose. In its turn, on account of its ability to decipher nature, the gardening art became the great scene on which the great puzzles of life could be illuminated. Interpreted by poets, painters and architects, the Swedish view of nature often demonstrates a similar belief in landscape. It, and its worked form, the gardening art, are thus a bearer of significance for Swedish culture.

As all landscapes are, the Swedish landscape is specific. It possesses some special basic characteristics that are derived from the circum-

The Stockholm skerries. Their geology causes a characteristically regular landscape.

An ancient farming landscape kept open by grazing animals.

stances out of which it has grown. These characteristics are both simple and evident, and saturate most of the variations displayed by the landscape. They comprise a sort of a set of playing rules for what is possible and impossible to carry out and change in the landscape. Whoever is in different ways active in this landscape is subordinated to these rules: farmers and foresters, but also those who use the land for other purposes, urban planners and landscape architects.

One such quality is its clear light, noticeable especially in the vicinity of large expanses of water, where the horizon can seem as sharp as a knife. In relation to misty Mediterranean horizons and that flat sky, the northern bowl of heaven really is a bowl, and on land its light is apparent even in its long, mild shadows. The shifting light of the seasons comes to expression in long-drawn-out dawns and dusks. Their coloration comprises dull nuances of greys, greens and blues. The reason for this light and the sharp horizons over marine horizons is chilly water that lowers humidity and sharpens the distinction between sky and sea, and makes the air transparent.

Another quality is a restricted typology of plant species. Hugo Sjörs, a botanist, has been able to classify the whole of the Swedish landscape into only a dozen main botanical communities. This creates a sparseness in expression that in its turn has brought out a united tradition of giving form. In its character, this tradition is on the boundary to the severe. An explanation of this narrow natural typology can be found in the relatively cold climate, with long winters and lessened possibilities for rich biological life, but also in the generally meagre soil, which reduces vegetation in the numbers of its species and development. Not only the gardening art, but also architecture, painting, textiles and studio glass love to use this special landscape as the foremost source of their inspiration.

The third and perhaps most important peculiarity of the landscape is a geomorphological regularity. Its cause is the ice masses of the last ice age that sculptured the country as recently as 10,000 years ago. The movement of the ice has given a structure to the landscape that, in its surface features, is concave here, convex there: lines along and across the lines of ice movements, with extended ridges of glacial gravel and excavated watercourses. Of the bedrock, its structure is revealed as far down as the level that is the crystalline order. The landscape obtains its logic through this. These three qualities—clear light, limited natural typology, glacially modelled country—

form the natural-geographical base from which the Swedish arts of gardening art and landscape architecture have emerged.

This need not have been so. History demonstrates several examples of how peculiar geographical conditions have produced an art of the garden that instead describes a counter-movement. In desert-like climates gardens have often comprised a separate enclosed, walled world with rich vegetation and a generous use of water as motifs, which is shown in the earliest Persian gardens. This is one of the basic types of the gardening art, a paradise contrasting with an inhospitable outer world of natural conditions beyond control.[4] Here the garden expresses the dream of a better life, basically an escapist phenomenon, a flight from the real world.

Swedish gardening art takes up an almost contrasting position. To form a garden has always and with few exceptions been a question of carefully choosing a place, and rather strengthening and refining its inherent qualities than changing them. This is one of the reasons why, in Sweden, the concept of landscape architecture is used instead of the gardening art. This attitude, to get closer to the landscape than to oppose it, expresses itself also in a number of phenomena in Swedish culture. The collective right to make use of the landscape, stipulated in the ancient principles of allemansrätten, is one of them: it comprises eleven separate rights and eleven duties and constitutes a freedom subject to personal responsibility to proceed across and even to remain on land owned by another. One of the rights is to overnight on such land in a tent placed so that it is not in sight or within hearing of the nearest house. Another right is to pick flowers and berries, but not nuts and growing twigs that are the landowner's winter provisions and fuel.[5]

Allemansrätten has been formed in a sparsely-populated country with unrestricted access to uncultivated land. It is a customary right that presupposes care. It is a part of a tradition, of a popular culture. It derives from a view of nature that embodies not only a physical but also a spiritual attitude towards the landscape. Swedes have an understanding that the natural world plays a decisive role in people's striving after both physical and also spiritual well-being.[6] A central-European Jesuit active in Sweden expressed it as: "A continental person meets God in another person. One who lives in the North meets God in the natural world."[7] Dag Hammarskjöld, the UN general secretary from 1953 to 1961, formulated this view of nature in his post-

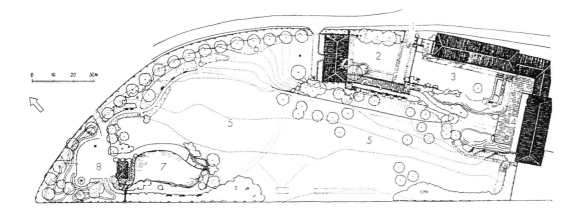

Marabou Park (Sven Herme-
lin, 1945), Sundbyberg:
brought into existence
to fulfil an ambition to compensate industrial workers for
their monotonous working
surroundings.

humously-published diary, Markings. "A sunny day in March. Within the birch-tree's slender shadow on the crust of snow, the freezing
stillness of the air is crystallised. Then—all of
a sudden—the first blackbird's piercing note
of call, a reality outside yourself, the real
world. All of a sudden—the Earthly Paradise
from which we have been excluded by our
knowledge."[8]

A deeply religious man, Hammarskjöld
explains here why the Christian creation myth
is, in part, not valid for Swedes, or, perhaps
more correctly, illuminates how the most
archetypical of all accounts of a garden, that of
Eden, and the expulsion thence of the first
people, requires revision if it is to apply to the
Swedish view of nature. Hammarskjöld finds
his paradise out in untamed nature rather than
in the garden of Eden. He suddenly discovers
that, having been excluded from one paradise,
he has found another.

comprising counterweights to the thickening
urban mass.[9] Parks should be capable of use
by all citizens and the activities in them should
be adapted to everyday needs. "Go easy with
flowers, it is easy to have too many good
things … I think a lawn full of happy children
is more beautiful than one full of colourful
flower beds."[10] His conviction that parks could
have a positive effects on people's health and
well-being found expression in his work at the
Marabou chocolate factory in Sundbyberg, in
the north-western suburbs of Stockholm. In
1937, he designed a park of an area of 5 hec-
tares adjoining the factory buildings, for the
recreation and enlivenment of the workers
after their monotonous work.

He had good international contacts. He
received most of his education in Germany,
where had come into contact with the *Schön-
heit der Arbeit* organisation, which proposed
beautification around factory buildings and
even arranged architectural competitions with

Sven Hermelin and the Socialising of the Art of the Garden

Hermelin is the most important figure in
Swedish landscape architecture in the 20th
century by virtue of his many working roles:
as well as being a teacher, a writer and agita-
tor, he was the first architect in Sweden to run
a straightforward consultancy practice.
Draughtsmanship had always previously been
combined with the physical work of laying out
gardens. His career was a lifelong striving to
give his work a new definition. He enlarged
the role of a gardener with drawing skills into
that of a landscape architect.

Hermelin had a strong social engagement,
which accorded with the-then spirit of the
times in Sweden. An aristocrat (a baron), he
spoke of the "socialisation of the art of the
garden" in an attempt to describe the new role
of parks as open and generally accessible,

Marabou Park.

this aim. The park at the Marabou chocolate factory is as much Hermelin's work as that of its owner, the far-seeing and interested industrialist, Henning Throne-Holst, a Norwegian.[11]

The site at the time had a strong character, with great differences in level, mature park trees and open areas of grass, sheer rocky cliffs but also areas with good gardening soil. This persuaded Hermelin to take on the job with great confidence. The buildings located on the upper, northern level had been arranged to form a half-open space. This suggested laying out in their sheltered vicinity a formal, ordered garden, but, towards the south, there was undisturbed nature in the form of an extended lengthy scar, darkly dramatic, and shaded by mature deciduous trees, and with a difference in height of almost 10 metres. Here was an excellent opportunity to create the contrast between undisturbed nature and a garden that had so fascinated Hermelin that he chose the career of garden architect. He saw possibilities of achieving effects that would be impossible on level ground. The resolution he perceived was self evident to him.

The entrance garden by the building was given a relatively formal arrangement, with the two buildings being complemented by a pergola in a yellow brick like that of their facades. A circular pool was placed in the courtyard thus formed. The pergola deliberately obscures the view and the dramatic edge of the scar towards the large expanse of grass below. To reach it one must proceed beneath the pergola and then descend steps down the dark edge of the scar towards the sun-drenched expanse of grass that was thought of as being an inviting area for "play and other physical movements."[12] At its farther end, a pavilion could be seen reflected in a pool that seems to have been impressed into the earth by a gigantic thumb: no abrupt edge separates the water from the grass that surrounds it. The single trees standing here and there on the grass give a sculptural play of shadows that moves as the sun moves. Park seats are located along the northern edge of the grass below the steep scar and make it possible to rest in the shade of the tree tops. The dark steeps of the scar contrast with the sun-drenched grass but also form a backing and support for whoever chooses to take a rest at their foot.

Hermelin saw the Swedish landscape as an artistic possibility to develop the gardens in a new direction. Ever since the continental art of gardening had been introduced during the 16th century by the German and Dutch gardeners engaged by Gustav Vasa, Sweden had followed the international trends. The bosquet, cascade and parterre had been elements of the art of the garden, sometimes not without certain difficulties in Sweden. The box that was so vital for formal dividers, for example, did not really thrive in the northern climate and, in Sweden, short-clipped dividers of pine or whortleberry were planted instead.[13] In his turn, Hermelin replaced the entire baggage of classical gardening art and, instead, took images from the landscape. Forest edges and glades, lake inlets and meadows were stylised in his landscape architecture and were used to give form. Horticulture and cultivation as conditions for a garden were erased and replaced by a novel idea of style. In seeking for the content of the modern garden and its aesthetic identity, Hermelin's attitude offered an excellent possibility.[14]

In the art of the garden, 'nature' is normally seen as the antithesis of 'garden', the terrain that shall be colonised, shall be forced, shall be changed and given new, better qualities that, in their turn testify to human presence and control. When Hermelin returned from a study trip to Denmark he reacted to Danish keenness to build up gardens as directed interplays of horticulture and artifacts. "Within these intimate areas, refined, detailed work is presented than lacks any equivalent in the average garden in the part of Sweden where Stockholm lies. In Denmark an idyll is to be created, and the idyll is often valued more highly than any architectural composition. At least for me the riches of plants and love for all that flowers were obvious in the private gardens in Copenhagen. … Danish gardens exhibit examples of how even the cracks between paving stones are filled with so many high and low perennials that in some cases one has difficulty in proceeding through the area without trampling on the plants."[15]

Hermelin made use instead of the natural assets of the landscape of central Sweden. He notes the important differences he thinks he sees between the two neighbouring countries. "Gardens in central Sweden are extroverted, and the natural world around them holds so much that, into the bargain, the landscape architect's job is carefully to compose buildings in their natural surroundings and to give order to the mediating area in between. In Denmark such a natural world is unfortunately not at hand, and gardens become a compensation for it. Gardens are instead introverted, with their boundaries beyond which lies agricultural land marked by thick vegetation."[16]

Hermelin sees and interprets. In one way he maintains and carries on a tradition based on a

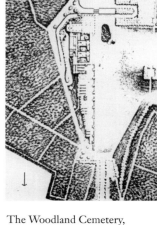

The Woodland Cemetery, Enskede: Asplund's and Lewerentz' landscape was made into an inspired place where not only sorrow but also hope and happiness could find a home.

The Woodland Cemetery, Enskede; 1940 plan by Asplund.

Swedish way of seeing the natural world. But his way entails a radical introduction: he brings the landscape inside the garden fence. Where the natural or wild landscape has always been seen as an antithesis to paradise or the garden, he sees the forests as Swedes' secure home.

The etymologies differ curiously of Swedish skog and its equivalent in English, 'forest', which word derives from a Latin word signifying 'outside, exterior'.[17] Skog, however, derives from Early Icelandic and relates etymologically to Sw. skydd, meaning 'shelter'. Skog as the home of those who live in the North runs as a concept through the Swedish view of nature. It got a metaphysical content in one of the country's most important landscape monuments, the Woodland Cemetery in Enskede.

The Woodland Cemetery

In 1915, Gunnar Asplund and Sigurd Lewerentz won the international architectural competition for the extension of the old burial ground of Sandsborg, south of Stockholm. The motto for the winning proposal was Tallum, a sort of dog Latin coined on the Swedish word for a pine tree, a "tall". Their competition proposal was much more orthodox than the design that was eventually built.[18] It shows the whole covered with trees, mostly pines, and the road system is an adaptation to the landscape rather than an idea about four-square quarters.

During the ensuing twenty years, and in parallel to the drawing work, an intensive debate was conducted about the form to be given to the burial ground; Asplund and Lewerentz worked continuously on producing new, revised proposals. The debate engaged people on high levels, often with the inclusion of politicians appointed to the cemetery board. The architects, each aged 29 at the time of the competition, seemed to be slightly alarmed at the uproar caused by their proposal and, in the first period after the competition, they drew alternative versions that clearly swung back towards a classicism.[19]

The Woodland Cemetery, as it gradually took form, lacked the overall framework of regulation for how the visitor should feel and behave that is so clear in the classicising cemeteries exemplified by Père Lachaise in Paris. Instead, there are in it feelings of landscapes of many different sorts, such as hope and happiness, sorrow and despair, death and resurrection. It is an environment full of feelings that facilitate contact between the inner and outer landscapes.

It is a comforting place. This former pine-covered disused gravel pit has acquired a new meaning. Nature dramatises the burial ground, the graves give nature a soul. The shadows of the dark pine wood alternate with light, sun-lit glades.

Seen formally, it is a mixture of most things, which well reflects its long and changing process of coming into existence. Its place of entry and way upwards are strongly classicis-

(Top) *Swift* (1885), Bruno Liljefors. Oil on canvas, privately owned. Functionalist gardens recurred to a Swedish feeling for the natural world.

(Lower) *Fox and crows* (1884), Bruno Liljefors. Oil on canvas, privately owned. Liljefors depicts natural scenes without romanticism but with the factual tone of reports.

ing. On taking a single step beyond the entry way and the walls that surround it, one feels that the whole space explodes, causing a widespread landscape apparently without any limit to open. Few examples of landscape architecture so clearly demonstrate a central aspect of modernism: dissolved space, a fluid transition between contexts, a wish to accentuate movement. Placed asymmetrically but despite that free in space, the meditation glade on its hill, crowned by hanging elms, the tree of sorrow, standing against the sky. The monument, the three chapel facilities, are arranged to one side, towards the periphery, so as to subordinate themselves to the landscape.[20]

On leaving this open space the visitor encounters a planted birch wood that, with its regularly spaced white-flecked trunks, plays

with the irregularity of patches of light that penetrating shafts of sunlight create: a Swedish national romance. This sentiment, dominant at the turn of the 20th century, is exhibited in painting, in part through the work of Carl Larsson. Having passed through the birch wood, the visitor enters a cathedral-like space of columns formed by lofty fir trunks that throw long straight shadows across the grass-covered ground. Here lie the graves, freely, in their forest home, without any seeming arrangement into marked places.

The conceptual forest is also a point of departure for Bruno Liljefors, a painter whose motifs are exclusively Swedish. For him, the natural world was the space for life. In it he found a context of an existential sort. In his painting of swifts, or *Tornseglare*, from 1885, he depicts the close-packed myriad forms of life in a Swedish meadow in summer. The black swifts swoop over the meadow's carpet of flowers and dancing insects. In his *Räv med kråkor* (1884) he reports from the natural world of central Sweden: the vegetation of its hilly terrain, the intricate patterns formed by walls of boulders separating fields, the fox and the cawing crows. Liljefors was an interpreter of the symbolic charge that the natural world has for his fellow Swedes. His accounts are factual, his details sharp. They lack elements of dreaminess or romance. His paintings often depict the natural dramas that are nowadays classified under the concept of ecology. The forest as the secure place, with protection and fodder is shown in *Rapphöns i snö* (1903), where the juniper bush is the painterly centre, as well as the shelter and source of food for the flock of partridges in their winter landscape. "Organic life, especially that of animals, is the high point of creation, and movement is the highest expression of life in the natural world," said Liljefors.[21] This was in close accordance with an aspect of Swedish functionalism. Movement through semi-dissolved spacial contexts, as we have seen in the Woodland Cemetery, became a recognisable characteristic of the new landscape architecture.

The Garden and Painting

In his paintings, Liljefors a form to, and interpreted, the Swedish feeling for nature. Carl Larsson, for his part, was an important early proponent of the new view of the garden that emerged from precisely this feeling for the natural world; his home, Sundborn, functioned as a laboratory for thoughts about how a domestic environment could be formed.

He and his wife Karin received their stuga, called *Lilla Hyttnäs*, in *Sundborn*, as a gift from her father, in 1888. Few places in Sweden have had such significance for a view of the domestic environment. A counterweight to the bourgeois ideal of a heavily pretentious formal language, Sundborn, as created by the Larssons, was an easy, light and straightforward everyday environment, evident throughout their house, from the wall hangings that Karin wove to the informal garden environment on the banks of a stream. Carl's paintings and drawings disseminated this image of Sundborn widely and thus came to spur on an altered attitude towards both style and an ideal life. The garden is here a cultivated landscape liberated from late 19th-century imperative formalities. People eat breakfast under a birch tree on the unmown meadow outside the house. A harmonic family lives its fortunate life here.[22]

Out in Europe, too, painting had helped to generate a new direction in landscape architecture, but from a quite different starting point than that of the Swedish lyricists of nature. In the 1920s, experiments were made with gardens in France but in a way that was evidently impressed by modern painting quite different from work by Liljefors and Larsson. Simplified, elementary geometric patterns and the use of a few uniform areas of clear colour distinguished these cubistic gardens.[23] Perhaps Villa Noailles, in Hyères, designed in 1926 by Gabriel Guevrekian, is the best known, because among other things it has been preserved best. And, at the international art and industry fair in Paris in 1925, there were many of these two-dimensional, flat-surfaced gardens that recalled more than anything the unrepresentational painted investigations of form by Mondrian.

And Swedish garden architects took an interest in the novel attitudes in other countries that so radically rejected all that had once been learned to be essential: an embracing effect of space, clear relief, use of perspective, the ability of plants to change with the season. Gunnar Martinsson was one of the Swedish garden architects who was most tuned to international currents of thought. In 1955, he entered a competition at Wilharditurm in Bremen on the form of the modern garden with a proposal of large unfilled surfaces, concentration on the centre instead of delimitation around the periphery, a reduced, jerky geometry and a focus created by a collection of triangular flower beds, not unlike those at Villa Noailles. It won the second prize. It differed sharply from the other entries that were

Villa Noailles (Gabriel Guevrekian, c. 1926), Hyères, France: a garden clearly inspired by modern continental painting.

Composition No. 5, Piet Mondrian (1919); oil on canvas. Reduction of coloration and form was typical not just for modernism's painting but also for its gardening art.

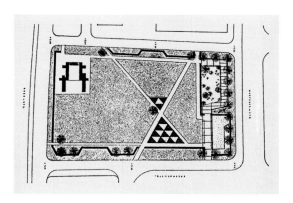

Wilharditurm, Bremen, competition entry 1955; Gunnar Martinsson was almost alone in Sweden in being inspired more by geometry than by the natural world.

Martinsson: garden for a private house. This hard-floored, architecturally-formed and easy-to-keep garden was typical of the man and of modern, continental garden designers.

Råcksta Cemetery (Gunnar Martinsson, 1962). Following a gravel ridge, the visitor suddenly sees a valley opening. To induce movement in this way was typical of modern garden design.

awarded prizes, which were still derived from the English landscape garden, with sweeping lines and harmonic, half embraced spaces.[24]

Martinsson belonged to those who broke with the old tradition and sought new ways. This change of style occurred late in northern Europe, or, more correctly, the French cubistic gardens by the Mediterranean were very early, emerging as they did not far from where the leading artists in modern painting were working. Throughout his career, Martinsson was to remain interested in the problem of form in gardens. In certain instances in his work he reduced colour, form and material down to close to an absolute zero of aesthetic appreciation. An often-heard citation is that "with flowers I can make [anything] very ugly".[25] Martinsson's broad register that, with his reductive way of working, he did not always choose to use, is shown by among other things the fact that his public breakthrough occurred when, together with Lena Larsson, he wrote a book full of flowers and details, *Mitt hem och min trädgård* (1963). It is a book full of Martinsson's special plans and drawings with an almost etched line and flattened perspective pictures, but also full of the pleasure of cherry trees in flower and lush rhododendrons. With flowers Martinsson has also done a great deal that is beautiful. Larsson is represented in this book with his painting of the captivating flower window at Sundborn.

Gunnar Martinsson's graphical simplicity is perhaps most effective when he translates it into a larger scale. This stylised way of working from surface / decoration goes over into

being spatiality / landscape art. And it is here that the peculiarity of the Swedish landscape as described above—clear light, sparse means of expression, topographical regularity—really enters as a reinforcing factor in Martinsson's work. The *burial-ground at Råcksta* west of Stockholm (1962), a commission won in a competition, is such a place: along a gravel ridge running east-west, relatively small burial fields have been laid out on a rolling grassy slope. Hedges, individual trees of different species and protruding scars of bedrock create a varied and free form. Walking along the northern side of the ridge, an artificial opening in it suddenly reveals an unlimited perspective: a huge expanse of grass, a valley floor planted with only a single species of willow (Salix alba). The effect is strong: the small and separated against the widely extended; the varied against the distilled and simplified; and all conducted in movement, a revelation in a single step.

Gunnar Martinsson's international orientation was one of the reasons that he was offered a professorial chair at the university in Karlsruhe in 1965; he lived there until the end of his active working life. In Sweden, he seems to have been alone in a search for a clarified form and in his way of translating modern painting into the art of the garden. In his thoughts, he is at home with kindred spirits on the continent.

The art of the garden in both Sweden and out in Europe was influenced by modern painting but from two different points of departure and with two different results.

European artists, including Klee, Kandinsky, Picasso and Mondrian, get a resonance in the art of the garden where Gunnar Martinsson is one of the few Swedish proponents. Exclusively Swedish in at least their best-known motifs, Larsson and Liljefors depicted a wholly different style of garden, which Hermelin represented.

Policy for Parks

The 20th century was also the time when parks were made democratic. The history of the public park is not longer than that of the democratic society. The first public park in Europe, the *Englischer Garten*, in Munich was laid out as late as during the 1790s.[26] As an urban necessity and in fact also as a medicament for the body, parks had become relevant in conjunction with the thickening towns of industrialism, where it was difficult to keep health and hygiene in order, difficult to survive.

The City Beautiful movement in the USA, and the gigantic *Central Park* on Manhattan in 1858, after a competition that Frederick Law Olmstedt and Calvert Vaux won, left traces in thinking about urban matters throughout the western world.[27] In Sweden the park in Malmö called Pildammsparken was one of the more remarked examples of an old form with a novel social role. Even earlier examples were *Slottsskogen* in Göteborg and *Folkpark in Norrköping*, the result of a donation in 1893.[28]

Its donator, the chairman of the town council, John Philipson, a consul, wrote in a motion on the question that "few towns in our country exceed Norrköping in the multiplicity and size of general plantings and promenade facilities... However many and far-extended these facilities may be, they do not afford chances for families to spend all their days of rest there, while they do not either offer playgrounds for children and young people. The need of some larger park or wood outside the town but in its immediate vicinity, where, in summer, the general public can spend the whole of their days of rest, is thus felt by many, and it is to meet this need that I now with respect dare to solicit the kind engagement of the town council."[29]

The park was opened in June 1895 to the tones of patriotic songs sung by a choir. Almost 20 years later, there was another feast, when the *Baltic Exhibition* opened in the same park. After the dramatic end to the exhibition, when the outbreak of hostilities in August 1914 found some exhibitors on opposing sides,

planning began for a park in the area. Its core was the partly artificial lakes called Pildammarna that served as a reservoir. A well-qualified Danish garden architect, Erik Erstad Jørgensen, got the commission, which was transferred in 1921 to the newly appointed town engineer, Erik Bülow-Hübe, who was interested in parks. He and the town's head gardener, Birger Myllenberg, were the brains behind this extensive park with green grassy boulevards that, converging on a central star in a classicistic way, hold the whole together. If the Folkpark in Norrköping was one of the last larger parks to be laid out in the English landscape style, then Pildammsparken was one of the last to find inspiration in the classical periods. But both had democratic and social elements that distinguished them from their predecessors, but the huge central star of the latter was intended as a festival place for the people of Malmö and also came to symbolise the Social-Democrat rise to power that had just occurred in Malmö.[30] Some time was yet to pass, however, before the novel park ideology found a physical form that departed from the old understandings.

A book called *Stockholms Natur* (1926) by Rutger Sernander, a professor at Uppsala, had great influence. The author argued in favour of a new form for planning the capital's parks, in which the regional landscape should be taken as their point of departure. An extensive polemic followed. One of its targets was the *park of Ålsten*, west of Stockholm, that the principal gardener of the town, Mauritz Hammarberg, had planned as a classical promenade park, with winding gravel walks set in mown lawns, furnished with flower beds. Sernander's line was the one that was carried through and, in the late 1920s, this park became the prototype for those that were built during the next

Pildamm Park (Erik Bülow-Hübe, 1926). This plan does not reveal it as an early Swedish urban park that, being modelled on classicising German sports' parks, was deliberately made democratic.

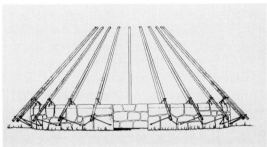

Humlehyddan (Holger Blom, 1941), Norr Mälarstrand.
Hops once grown as a crop become a motif in a modern
urban park.

Norr Mälarstrand (Blom and Glemme, 1941–43). Despite being narrow, the park contains many functional
and aesthetic elements.

The Director of Gardens,
Holger Blom, directs his
workers. Illustration by
Birger Lundquist.

30 years. With their special ideas and form,
they later came to give a name to a style: the
Stockholm school.[31]

Ålstensparken has stands of mature forest
trees, fringed with sloes (Prunus spinosa) and
wild roses (Rosa canis). Its roads, which are
more like paths through the woods, join sunny
glades with south-facing shores of Lake Mälar
and dark patches of woods. Expanses of bed
rock have been raked clean of earth, boulders
mark particular places or changes of direction.
This pattern was followed in building up this
type of stylised natural world in many places
in Stockholm, even in the built-up centre
where nothing of the sort existed.

Fredhällsparken, mentioned above as a subject of a photograph by K.W. Gullers, became
a well-known representative for the Stockholm school. In these parks, the natural world
and the regional landscape were taken as
aesthetic points of departure. Examples of
elements of the landscape that occurs around
Lake Mälar are the expressive glacially pol-

ished crags and scars, dark forest tarns and
aromatic pine woods; Stockholm lies where
the lake debouches into the Baltic. The aesthetic programme of the Stockholm school
was built up on these bases. But the new parks
differed from the old not just in form but in
content. The parks were now seen as active
urban elements, not mere oases of greenery.
During this period of Social-Democrat political strength the parks were formulated as a
social right for Stockholmers, a public one,
along the private rights to standards including
water closets, balconies and running hot and
cold water. Provided for active use, the parks
permitted walking on the grass, ball games,
picking flowers, sun-bathing and picnicking.

The man who was to develop and carry
through these ideas was Holger Blom, the
principal gardener of Stockholm from 1937 to
1971, and, as such, unusual in various ways.[32]
When he took up this post he was 31 and did
not know much about gardens. After qualify-
ing as an architect, he had worked for Lars

Tegnérlunden (Erik Glemme, 1941–42) was laid out first as a 'crag park' in the 1890s but was re-done later to meet the demands of a new society.

Israel Wahlman in Stockholm, with Krüger & Toll in Amsterdam and Le Corbusier in Paris. His contributions had two centres of gravity. One was his park programme, which in its ideas had been laid down by his predecessor Osvald Almqvist. Blom was the first to formulate and carry through a park-political programme, which helped to give his thoughts ideological strength. The other was that, as a town official, he successfully carried through an idea about a park system: that parks should exist at strategic places and extend as a net over larger parts of the town. The concept is relevant at present in ecological contexts: a green structure, which thus received an early application.

Perhaps the best example of how a park can enter into this role is *Norr Mälarstrand*, a fin-ger of green about a kilometre long but hardly fifteen metres wide along the northern lake shore on Kungsholmen. It contains the world of ideas of the Stockholm school almost in miniature. A walkway winds in soft curves through it, past places to sit, sunny spots, jetties, a look-out terrace, small pools, play-grounds, small patches of garden, sculptures, a small cafe over the water. At one point, the natural line of the beach has been scooped out to give a small inlet, only for the pleasure of bridging it to increase the sense of being close to the water.

When the park was laid out, in 1941–43, Sweden was isolated by war. In consequence, the park became very regional and locally associated. As nothing could be imported, only plants that could be got in Sweden were planted in it. Some of the many types of Lake-Mälar landscapes were re-created here: enclosed grazing land with birches, a grove of hazel bushes, wetland with alders. Human influence on the landscape is represented by a courtyard surrounded with a drystone wall, a small fisherman's stuga in wood and painted white, and Humlehyddan, an example of a union between tradition and renewal; its intimate garden is framed by a low stable stone wall, with the airy complement of hop bines growing on a hut-shaped superstructure.[33]

Blom was an ideologist of parks. The architect who gave form to many of the parks of the Stockholm school was Erik Glemme. There are hundreds of environments in Stockholm and in many of the 1950s suburbs that bear Glemme's artistic signature. In 1952, the International Federation of Landscape Architects held its annual congress in Stockholm.

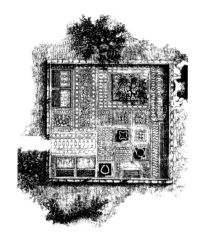

One of three cliff gardens (1947), Vasa Park, Erik Glemme. Detailed garden spaces placed in an unrestricted context became characteristic of the Stockholm school.

Vällingby Center (Erik Glemme, 1953–55): an ideal town built on a concrete deck over a subway line. The circular pattern on the ground was applied consistently.

Grindtorp, Täby. The garden is transformed into elementary functions inscribed in geometrical figures.

With his country as host, Blom could, not without pride, show off the town and the most progressive parks' policy in the world.

Thus, in practice, the Swedish garden tradition at the close of the previous century became uprooted and replaced by two opposites. The main stream was the reality given by the natural world that the Swedish landscape offered, but, equal with it, there was the design of the geometrically formed garden. Glemme was first and foremost a lyricist of the natural world.[34] But in certain work, as in the square at *Vällingby*, a "New Town" located about 10 km west of Stockholm, he laid out a pattern of large circles in red, black and white paving stones that dominated the whole surface of the square. All other elements, including benches and other seating, fountains and street lights were subordinated to the circular pattern that seemed to continue out and beneath the buildings erected there. Vegetation is almost entirely absent; being hard to master, biological life accorded ill with the ambitions of modernism to understand, influence and steer. The political ideologists of the time strove for perfection in their constructed visions of national society. The good life comes as a result of careful planning.

To formulate methods for this planning architects, among others, were turned to. Architects took part and defined the necessary properties for a family to be able to live a happy normal life. But on not all occasions were

the results of the same high class as at Vällingby. During the 1960s and 1970s outdoor surroundings were designed that, nowadays, belong to the worst one can find in the country.Ideal apartments were designed and joined together in immense multiples blocks in the undisturbed natural world. But novel values followed a novel use of language: something called "a green surface" (grönyta) was born, and a number of square metres of it was deemed to be sufficient for each citizen. On it, such a citizen should pursue his or her "leisure" (fritid), another of these novel words that would have lacked any meaning for earlier generations. The dimensions of infants' sandboxes, and other playground facilities were determined. Scientifically calculated, the new environment was thus in all respects correct.

Blom was an employee of the town administration, Hermelin active in an office of his own. Their knowledge had different backgrounds. Hermelin was a landscape designer with training in horticulture, Blom an architect with experience of urban planning. Despite the difference, these two became frontal figures most active in working in ways that established a new garden and park style in Sweden that actually excluded gardens. The art of the garden thereby returned with this to its popular tradition and liberated itself from the styles that had been developed as aristocratic surroundings in the courts of various continental monarchies.

We shall conclude, as we started, in a domestic environment: Per Friberg's summer place at Ljunghusen, Skåne. It was built in 1960. Two glazed boxes are borne into the landscape as if by a helicopter. They rest on pilings, hovering over the sandy terrain. These small light houses crouch below pine trees, on the boundary between an enclosed wood and the large expanse of heath. Friberg's summer place captures and concentrates what is and will always be an important theme in Swedish landscape architecture: the ability to draw the inherent qualities out of the natural world and to let them stand out unobscured. Sometimes —as here at Ljunghusen—this means of working entails choosing a location.

Friberg said: "The sky, the sea, the heath, the house: we built as simply as possible, primitively, ascetically, we felt the heath demanded this purism. An unpretentious frame around the delightful life in summer that we, as people who live in the North, want to live in intimate contact with nature during some intensive summer weeks."[35]

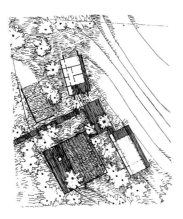

Summer place (1960), Ljunghusen, by Per Friberg.

Summer place (Per Friberg, 1960), Ljunghusen. Easy summer living as Northerners want to live it.

NOTES

[1] Eva Rudberg, *Sven Markelius, arkitekt* (1989).

[2] Bertil Asker, *Stockholms parker* (1986).

[3] Letter (23 April 1983) to Sven-Ingvar Andersson, who had worked for Hermelin and later became a professor at the Royal Academy of Art, Copenhagen.

[4] *Utblick Landskap* 2/97. "Paridaeza—islams trädgårdar".

[5] Torvald Wermelin, Ute (1962).

[6] Patrik Grahn, Om parkens betydelse (1991), 37 ff.

[7] Utblick Landskap 2/95, 4.

[8] Dag Hammarskjöld, *Markings*, translated by Leif Sjöberg & W.H. Auden (London 1964), 74.

[9] Sven Hermelin, "Hemmet, trädgården och vi själva", in *Allmän Svensk Trädgårdstidning*, 6/81.

[10] Lotte Möller, "Det långsamma skådespelets regissör" in *Vi* (40/1982), 12, 18.

[11] Inger Wedborn, "Rekreationsanläggning vid Marabou-fabriken", in Gregor Paulsson, Sven Hermelin, Walter Bauer & Holger Blom *Trädgårdskonst* (II, 1948), 484 ff.

[12] Sven Hermelin, "Trädgårdsanläggningen vid Marabou chokladfabrik" in *Lustgården* (1939), 119–123.

[13] Gösta Adelswärd, "Vad menade André Mollet? Ljung eller lingon?", in *Lustgården* (1994), 47 ff.

[14] *Utblick Landskap* (1/1985); a monograph number on Sven Hermelin.

[15] Sven Hermelin, "Dansk trädgårdskonst och svensk. Några intryck från Föreningen Svenska Trädgårdsarkitekters exkursion till Danmark", in *Havekunst* (1934) 25 ff.

[16] Hermelin, 1934. In this argument Hermelin finds support in an earlier article in *Havekunst* written by Emma Lundberg. Together with her son, Erik Lundberg, a professor, she had created a number of gardens, mainly in the Stockholm area.

[17] Ronny Ambjörnsson, "Skogen står i vägen", *Dagens Nyheter* 27 December 1997, 4.

[18] The main extension of the Woodland Cemetery at Enskede continued until 1940.

[19] 'Classicism' is a problematic term in garden art. The landscape of antiquity was in fact hardly formal but taken from assumptions about the undulating landscape of Arcadia. The fact that the art of the garden has been categorized by art historians rather than historians of the art of the garden has led to the basically erroneous by nevertheless frequently advanced belief that a classicising landscape has a formal geometry.

[20] Caroline Constant, *The Woodland Cemetery: Towards a Spiritual Landscape* (1994).

[21] Allan Ellenius, *Bruno Liljefors. Naturen som livsrum* (1996).

[22] Carl Larsson, *Ett hem* (1899).

[23] Dorothée Imbert, *The Modernist Garden in France* (1993).

[24] Gunnar Martinsson's role in modern landscape architecture has been analyzed in Bengt Isling and Torbjörn Sunesson, *Gunnar Martinsson, landskapsarkitekt* (1996).

[25] Oral communication from Gunnar Martinsson, in 1995.

[26] Geoffrey Jellicoe, Susan Jellicoe, Patrick Goode & Michael Lancaster, *The Oxford Companion to Gardens* (1986).

[27] Norman Newton, *Design on the Land* (1971) 271 ff.

[28] Stig Hellerström, *Folkparken. En beskrivning av dess tillkomst och utveckling* (1996).

[29] Signed by John Philipson, this motion was dated 17 September 1893.

[30] Per-Jan Pehrsson, *Malmö parkernas stad* (1986).

[31] In the 1980s, the-then principal gardener of Stockholm, Anders Sandberg, and Clas Florgård, a professor, began to designate this tradition from central Sweden as 'the Stockholm school' or the 'Stockholm style'. This was an attempt to formulate it and give it emphasis, because the parks exhibiting its work were becoming dilapidated.

[32] Asker (1986).

[33] Thorbjörn Andersson, "Erik Glemme and the Stockholm Park System", in Marc Treib (ed.), *Modern Landscape Architecture: A Critical Review* (1992).

[34] *Utblick Landskap*, (2/1988), monograph number on Erik Glemme.

[35] *Arkitektur* (4/1992); monograph number on Per Friberg.

Buildings

Dickson Public Library

Gothenburg 1892–97

HANS HEDLUND

The Dickson Public Library was Sweden's first public library. Like the other public institutions built in Gothenburg during the 19th century, it was funded by private endowment. Architect Hans Hedlund, like his benefactor, was absorbed with issues of popular education. Impressed by the animated stone architecture of Henry Hobson Richardson, Hedlund traveled to the United States in 1893 to see Richardson's work in person. Richardson's influence is apparent in the library's asymmetrical composition, semi-circular arches, and rustic treatment of materials. The Dickson Library came to symbolize the end of the academic 19th-century preoccupation with styles. Shifting the entrance to one side gave the building a diagonal organization, revitalizing a plan which early sketches show to have been locked in symmetry. The building functioned as a library until 1967, when it was replaced by the Gothenburg Public Library at Götaplatsen.
R.W.

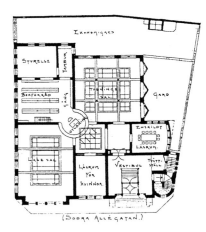

Train stations

on the Stockholm-Västerås-
Bergslagen Line and
the Ängelsberg-Vansbro Line
Dalarna, Västmanland, and
Stockholm, 1900–07.

ERIK LALLERSTEDT

In the 1890s, the architecture of the Swedish railroad
was liberated from the stylistic standardization that dictated appropriate forms for public buildings. Train stations began to take on the characteristics of pre-Func-
tionalist residential architecture, with free plans and
facades that expressed the often asymmetrical disposition of rooms. Among the foremost examples are a number of buildings by Erik Lallerstedt for the great private
SWB Line between Stockholm, Västerås, and Bergslagen, including stations in the rural counties of Dalarna
and Västmanland as well as the Stockholm area. A few
of them, like Smedjebacken Station, were rendered and
adorned with ornamental tiles in patterns inspired by
Viennese prototypes; many were wooden structures influenced by the decorative art of Carl Larsson, with a red,
white, and green color scheme accented by details such
as hand-painted flowers.
B.L.

Literature: Björn Linn: Svensk järnvägsarkitektur in:
Bebyggelsehistorisk tidskrift 12, 1986. Karin Winter
ed.: *Erik Lallerstedt — arkitekt under fem årtionden*
(Arkitekturmuseet 1982).

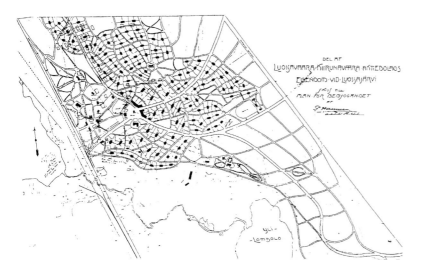

Kiruna

1890s to the present

GUSTAF WICKMAN / RALPH ERSKINE / HAKON
AHLBERG / ARTUR VON SCHMALENSEE AND
OTHERS

In the far north of Sweden, Kiruna is a unique example of
early 20th-century urban planning. Here lay an untouched
wilderness until a wealth of iron ore deposits brought the
first settlers in the 1890s. With the arrival of the railroad
at the turn of the century, Kiruna began to grow rapidly.
A geologist named Hjalmar Lundbohm led the city's development, employing many of the foremost artists and
architects of the day. Between 1899 and 1900, Per Olof
Hallman and Gustav Wickman produced a city plan which
was unusually well-adapted to the local terrain. Over the
short span of the next few years, Wickman designed a
home for Lundbohm, a hotel for his company (LKAB),
and homes for its engineers, as well as worker housing,
offices, schools, a fire station, hospital, bath house, post
office, and a bank building, among other projects. Kiruna
Church (1903–12) is considered Wickman's most significant work—a synthesis of American wooden architecture, the Norwegian stave church, and the Laplander's
conical hut. The church's artistic decoration included
paintings by Prince Eugen and Christian Eriksson. Important recent buildings include housing by Ralph Erskine
from the 1950s and '60s, buildings for LKAB by Hakon
Ahlberg and Artur von Schmalensee's 1963 City Hall.
R.W.

Literature: Lasse Brunnström: *Kiruna — ett samhällsbyg-
ge i sekelskiftets Sverige*, Part I, 1981, Part II, 1980.

Villa Tallom

Långängen, Djursholm 1904–06

LARS ISRAEL WAHLMAN

In his own home, the Villa Tallom, architect Lars Israel Wahlman utilized his studies of traditional stacked-timber construction, particularly in his native county of Dalarna, and his first-hand experiences of working with knowledgeable craftsmen. The natural drying and settling of the timbers that results in a tight building required that all vertical elements such as doors, windows, stairs, and piping be flexibly installed to allow for movement. The floor plan was in part determined by the maximum available length of timbers—about ten meters. To allow for effective splining of the timbers, Wahlman believed, a smaller central room should be inserted between two larger, preferably protruding from the building as in the Villa Tallom. The timbers were left unfinished inside and out. "Having dwelt at Tallom for roughly two years, I now know what wealthy recompense a true, robust genuinity makes for the loss of the circuitous, veiled, stale potpourri we have inherited from preceding centuries," wrote Wahlman in 1908. "Timbers are trees whose lives have become sagas." He shared his knowledge and conviction with several generations of architects as lecturer and professor at the Royal College of Technology until 1935.
C.C.

Literature: *Arkitektur* No. 10, 1908.

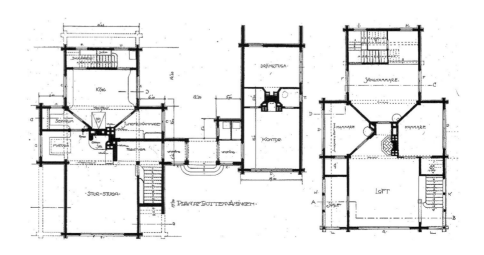

Central Post Office

Malmö 1899–1906

FERDINAND BOBERG

Ferdinand Boberg called his Malmö Central Post Office "probably the building that I would consider my best work." It stands in the harbor, a dignified symbol of modern society's expansion of the urban infrastructure. It is one of a group of similar commissions from the turn of the century that also includes a fire station, gas works, and electrical power plant in which Boberg's penchant for monumentality could be indulged to good effect. The Central Post Office is characteristic of Boberg's architecture—a powerful volume with two towers crowned by cupolas. The architects of the National Romantic Movement admired the brick building's massing and the treatment of its materials, but never accepted the rather oriental than Swedish character of the towers and ornamental reliefs. His colleagues' criticism prompted Boberg to retire early from professional practice.
C.C.

Literature: Ulf Sörenson: *Ferdinand Boberg, Arkitekten som konstnär*, 1992; Ann Walton: *Ferdinand Boberg — Architect. The complete work*, 1994.

Adolf Fredrik's Northern Elementary School

Stockholm 1898–1902

GEORG A. NILSSON

Several new elementary schools were built in Stockholm around the turn of the century in response to the city's rapid expansion. Georg A. Nilsson planned Adolf Fredrik's Northern Elementary School for 2,200 children. The young architect was awarded the commission soon after graduating from architecture school, and the project's success led to a long string of other school buildings. Nilsson's adjective treatment of materials and the building's simple, rational plan—a U-shape that encloses a south-facing courtyard—broke new ground in school design and made a profound impression on contemporary architects. The classrooms face outward, the single-loaded corridors filled with light from the courtyard side. The school includes several unusual spaces: two gymnasiums, a swimming pool, and craft shops. The building's machine-made brick walls rise from a granite plinth; its floor plates are of reinforced concrete—a technique that was new at the time. The architecture is free of Classical forms, its ornamentation restricted to figures and proverbs painted on rendered surfaces.
C.C.

Literature: Martin Rörby and others: *Georg A. Nilsson arkitekt*, 1989.

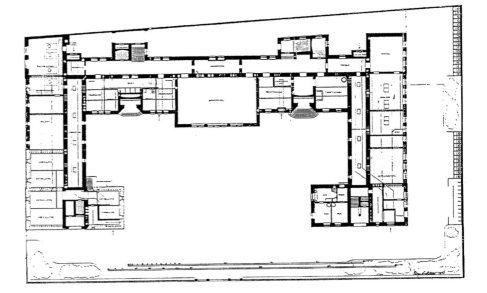

St. Olof Elementary School

Norrköping 1903–08

CARL BERGSTEN

In 1903, a young architect named Carl Bergsten was asked to draw up facades for a new elementary school in Norrköping. After his 1904 tour of European architecture, Bergsten was commissioned to design the school in its entirety. He was then twenty-five years old and had been powerfully influenced by the new architecture he had seen in Vienna. The impressions of his travels are recorded in the St. Olof Elementary School and other buildings he designed in Norrköping at the time. The school combines simple, stereometric forms in a single precisely-cut volume. Its brick facades are raised on a monumental concrete base. The entrance is crowned by a decorated window pediment that fills the entrance hall with daylight. The plan is organized around double-loaded corridors which are unusually well lit due to their generous width, the high bay windows at their ends, and the windows of the indrawn central portion of the principal facade. Bergsten designed all of the interior, including the furniture. The school was later altered and most of the furnishings lost.
E.E.

Literature: Bengt O.H. Johansson: *Carl Bergsten och svensk arkitekturpolitik under 1900-talets första decennium*, 1965.

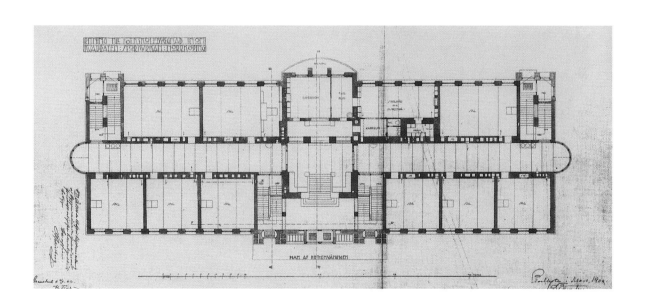

251

Lagercrantz Residence

Djursholm 1909-10

ELIS BENCKERT

The Lagercrantz residence established Elis Benckert's architectural career and became an admired prototype for his generation. It illustrates the ideal of an era with uncommon clarity. The house is a clean and simple volume devoid of decoration, but the materials in each part are treated with the greatest care. The thick, lime-washed brick walls and small window openings give it a reserved and archaic demeanor. Benckert's plan was based on a traditional central cross. The kitchen area and maid's quarters were to the northwest. The entry, stair hall, and a secluded library occupied the southwest, where the evening sun provided an atmosphere of tranquillity. Bedrooms and spaces for entertaining faced the garden to the east. The play of daylight throughout the house was calculated with utmost precision so that the sun would fill the rooms at the particular time of day appropriate to the function and desired ambiance of each. On the exterior, the windows appear haphazardly arranged, but were in fact carefully aligned for each room inside. The thick walls' deep window niches were splayed to the inside, providing more surface area for the play of daylight and making the windows seem larger inside than out.
E.E.

Literature: Elisabeth Stavenow-Hidemark: *Villabebyggelse i Sverige 1900–1925*, 1971.

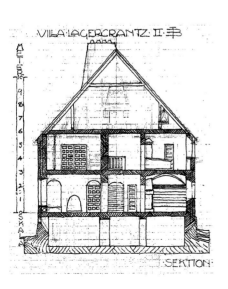

SEKTION

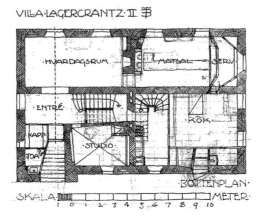

BOTTENPLAN

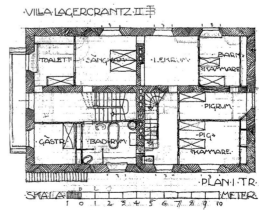

PLAN·I·TR·

252

Olidan Power Station

Trollhättan 1906–10

ERIK JOSEPHSON

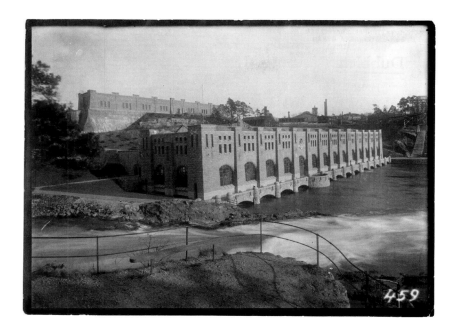

The government assumed ownership of the mighty falls in Trollhättan in 1905 and began to develop Olidan Power Station, the nation's first hydroelectric plant. It was the first project undertaken by Vattenfall, the State Power Board, and remained for many years the largest. The architectural commission went to Eric Josephson. Though hardly a radical pioneer, Josephson was always among those considered "modern". The plant consists of three blocks, the foremost of them a granite-clad machine room. It was finished in 1910 with nine monumental window bays; a decade later five more bays were added to the south. Its turbines are fed through tunnels from the intake block, also clad in granite. The third block, the bridge signal cabin, was faced with brick. The Trollhättan plant remains a uniquely complete work of industrial architecture. Even Svante Dyhlén's housing for the workers was designed with great feeling and care. R.W.

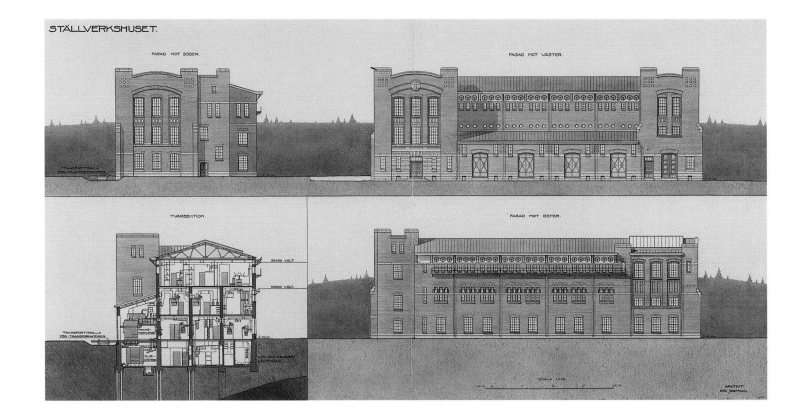

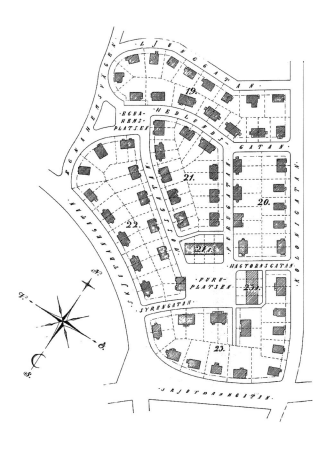

Landala Egnahem Residential District

Gothenburg 1908–22

ALBERT LILIENBERG / CARL WESTMAN

The turn-of-the-century Home-Owner's Movement was a government attempt to curb emigration from Sweden by offering responsible workers loans toward the construction of their own homes. It was a reform program related to the Garden City Movement. The Landala egnahem residential district is one of the movement's earliest and most thoroughly-designed neighborhoods, comprising grouped standardized single-family homes and duplexes and creating the kind of urban uniformity coveted by contemporary planners. The development includes 105 homes in a total of 63 buildings. Albert Lilienberg's master plan follows the rocky terrain with clearly-defined streets and small urban spaces in the spirit of Camillo Sitte. Carl Westman and Sigfrid Ericson were commissioned to develop standard home plans for the area, and Westman's were chosen. He designed several different prototypes: single-family homes or duplexes with gable or gambrel roofs and one to three bedrooms. There are also two row houses facing one of the public spaces. Westman's buildings are simple and robust plank houses. He intended them to be rendered, but in the end they were clad in wooden siding and painted a uniform brown. C.C.

Literature: Olle Lind: *Landala egnahem*, 1992.

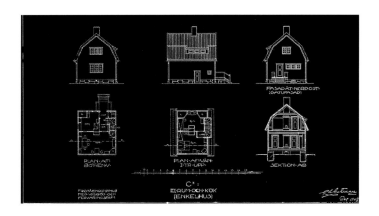

Stockholm Stadium

Stockholm 1909–12

TORBEN GRUT

Torben Grut's Stockholm Stadium was built for the 1912 Olympic Games, and is today the oldest Olympic stadium still in use. Its classic horseshoe form seats 22,000. A temporary wooden grandstand was built across the open north end for the Olympics; these bleachers remain today, though the architect intended for them to be torn down later to give spectators a view through the monumental arcade to a rocky ridge surmounted by a planned college of athletics. The exterior is reminiscent of the city wall that surrounds Visby: two octagonal towers flank the great main entrance to the south, and two taller, square-sectional towers mark the ends of the horseshoe to the north, the easternmost providing a focal point for Sturegatan. The walls are of dark Helsingborg brick with repeating arches that span between pilasters; the permanent stadium seating was constructed of reinforced concrete. The architecture of the stadium is a modern structural application of the medieval art of brick masonry as found in Sweden's ancient city walls, fortifications, monasteries, and churches. Each part develops organically from practical requirements and the structural system— nowhere does one find superficially-applied architectural motifs. The building is a cut-and-dry composition, something like a boat or a bridge, whose "aesthetics" reside in its materials and proportions.
C.C.

Literature: *Arkitektur* No. 7, 1912.

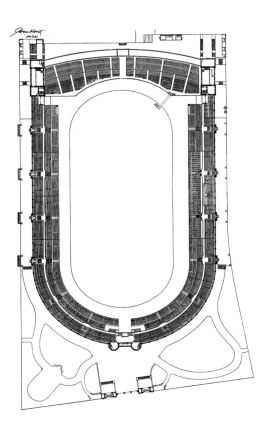

Geber Residence

Embassy District, Stockholm,
1911–13

RAGNAR ÖSTBERG

Brick facades unify the exclusive Embassy District, whose irregular property lines typify early 20th-century urban planning in Sweden. In the Geber residence, architect Ragnar Östberg used flat, machine-made bricks with thick bed joints to give the walls a beautifully varied texture. The house is a large, narrow block cut slightly askew in response to the irregularities of the site. The architect exploited and even exaggerated these distortions in the interior plan. A door in the nearly windowless entrance facade leads to an interior courtyard. One side is completely blank, concealing the kitchen wing, while on the facing side the house proper opens onto the courtyard through Venetian windows and a second-floor terrace. Östberg used the Geber residence as a proving ground for new ideas in anticipation of his masterpiece, the Stockholm City Hall. The house also reveals the era's new fascination with the architecture of the Italian Renaissance, particularly in the courtyard flanked by arcades — a theme that would reappear in the City Hall. Opposite the courtyard, the house opens to a rear garden and the water through great windows, its ground-floor rooms for entertaining aligned along a formal axis. The graceful curves of the roof line alleviate the weight of the huge volume and lend the house an exotic ambiance.
E.E.

Literature: Elias Cornell: *Ragnar Östberg svensk arkitekt*, 1965.

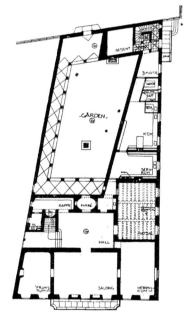

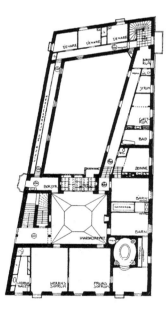

Masthugget Church

Gothenburg 1907–14

SIGFRID ERICSON

Masthugget's precipitous cliffs culminate in the mighty walls of Sigfrid Ericson's Masthugget Church. Its sixty-meter-high tower is a powerful icon throughout the city and is visible far out to sea. Despite its dramatic silhouette, the church seems smaller and more intimate up close. Except for the gables, the walls are at most just over seven meters high. The building has a tangible materiality, its exterior forged almost exclusively of rough granite and brick. Raw blocks of uncut stone join the church to the rocky bluff; the walls above are of oversized hand-made bricks. The interior is dominated by an enormous timber-framed roof structure that rises from white-washed walls.

R.W.

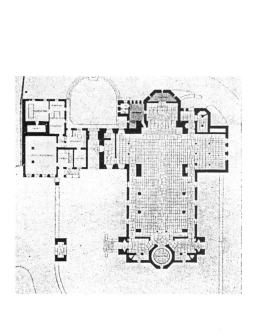

Engelbrekt Church

Stockholm 1905–14

LARS ISRAEL WAHLMAN

In 1905–06, a competition was held for a new church and parish house atop a rock promontory on the northern edge of Stockholm. Lars Israel Wahlman's submission, though it won first prize, astonished the public and alarmed the jury: while all of the churches in Stockholm's recent past were in Gothic or Baroque style, Wahlman's lofty church was a free composition. The huge cruciform plan held about 1,500. The shortened arms of the transept form enormous niches that lack the raked seating of the nave, and whose vast windows fill the sanctuary with a solemn, glare-free light. The red-brown brick exterior frames periodic blind windows and decorative surfaces rendered with stucco. The interior is more unified: the nave is spanned by a granite-ribbed parabolic vault, and the light in the space is colored by plaster in a grayish yellow tone that approximates that of the granite. Architect Carl Bergsten's appraisal of the building was appreciative but critical: he called Wahlman "an old-fashioned master builder of churches with a sense for the essential in the ancient traditions, though he is not content with merely reproducing those traditions—he develops them and adapts them to the needs today." Bergsten also emphasized the importance of the fact that Wahlman had been in control of the entire project, including construction management and the project's economy—a situation, even then, which he said was "still quite unusual, of course."
C.C.

Literature: Arkitektur No. 2, 1914, Bengt Romare: *Verk av Lars Israel Wahlman*, 1950.

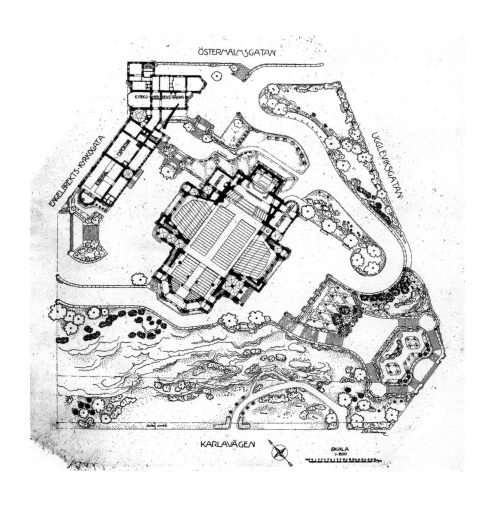

Liljevalch Art Gallery

Stockholm 1913–16

CARL BERGSTEN

With an endowment from saw-mill magnate C.F. Lilje-valch, Carl Bergsten built a large art gallery next to Skansen, the open-air park on the island of Djurgården. The young architect was awarded the commission after sharing first place in an architectural competition. Poor soil conditions compelled him to use a reinforced concrete frame with load-bearing columns and light-weight partitions. The jury liked the simple structure, which they said made the building unmistakably at home on Djurgården, though they thought it had a somewhat temporary character more suited to wood-framed construction. The Liljevalch Art Gallery's graceful rationalism came to typify much of the Classical architecture of the 1920s in Sweden. The lofty sculpture hall, with its coffered ceiling and clerestory windows, reflects the work of Tessenow, who was highly esteemed by the Swedish architects of the day. The plan is compact and easily comprehensible, with exhibition spaces aligned along an axis and top-lit through roof lanterns. Behind these rooms lies an enclosed courtyard with restaurant seating.
C.C.

Literature: *Arkitektur* No. 9–10, 1919, Rasmus Waern: *Tävlingarnas tid*, 1996.

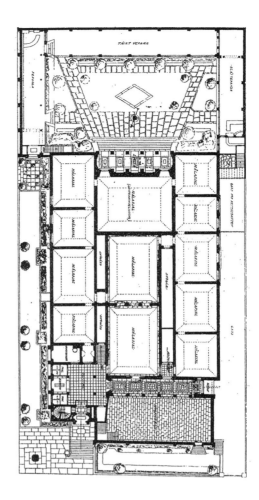

Röhsska Museum of Applied Arts

Gothenburg 1910–16

CARL WESTMAN

The Röhsska Museum of Applied Arts in Gothenburg was
built between 1912 and 1914 following an invited competition that Carl Westman won in 1910. The apparently
simple volume reveals upon closer scrutiny great complexity. Westman's uncompromisingly compact facade
gives the impression of a sealed case. The second-floor
windows are not vertically aligned with those on the
ground floor—a structural eccentricity commonly used
to downplay the bearing capacity of the facade wall, making the building seem a solid, sculpted mass pierced by
window holes. Corbie-stepped gables give it a slender,
lofty appearance from the street below. The hand-made
brick is incised with naivistic imagery (as well as the
architect's initials, CW) to underscore the sense of handicraft and give the building an amiable playfulness. The
facade makes no allusion to the functional requirements
of the plan, such as the varying elevation of the ground
floor. The building disregards demands for continuity of
form with content to invoke instead the observer's immediate experience of form—it appeals to his feelings
rather than his knowledge of classical traditions.
R.W.

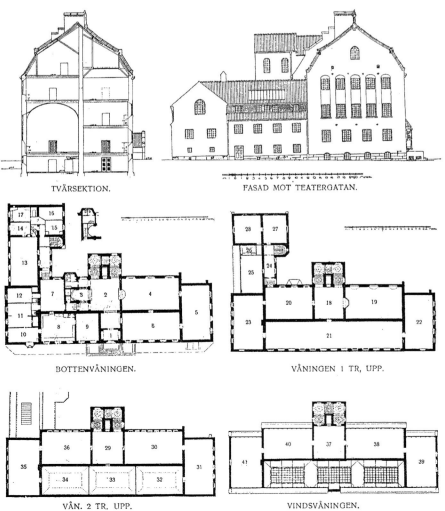

TVÄRSEKTION.

FASAD MOT TEATERGATAN.

BOTTENVÅNINGEN.

VÅNINGEN 1 TR. UPP.

VÅN. 2 TR. UPP.

VINDSVÅNINGEN.

Enskilda Banken

Stockholm 1912–15

IVAR TENGBOM

Enskilda Banken marked the start of Twenties Classicism and of the brilliant carrier of its young architect, Ivar Tengbom. The site for the bank was part of Stockholm's ubiquitous pattern of orthogonal courtyard blocks, but opened onto Kungsträdgården. Tengbom chose to make the private bank's facade first and foremost a wall for the park by rendering it in smooth, gray terras stucco. While stucco is the typical wall surface in Stockholm, the building is distinguished by a powerfully rusticated base and other details in black granite. Since city ordinances forbade the projection of free-standing columns into the street space, Tengbom designed ovular engaged columns, and crowned them with sculptures by Carl Milles.

Inside, the main hall is a modern, glass-roofed space with columns that extend through its two-story height. The liberally-interpreted Classicism of the interior and the simple, stereometric exterior form reveal the influence of Austrian architect Josef Hoffmann. With the commission for Enskilda Banken, Tengbom's office grew from four to twenty, making it the country's largest at the time. His systematization of the design process brought him admiration in architectural circles and appreciation from builders and the many influential clients who commissioned him.
C.C.

Literature: *Arkitektur*, 1915, Björn Linn: Ivar Tengbom och arkitektyrket in: *Stenstadens arkitekter*, 1981.

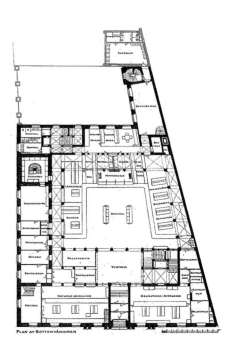

Bergslagen Village

Borlänge 1915–20

OSVALD ALMQVIST

Osvald Almqvist was commissioned by Stora Kopparbergs Bergslags AB, a mining corporation, to design a village to house workers and administrators on five hundred parcels of land. The scheme, which replaced an earlier plan by Per Olof Hallman, prescribed deep, narrow lots connected by a system of differentiated streets. Apartment houses lined the streets of Bergslagen, periodically enclosing informal urban spaces and giving small dead-end streets an interior character. Smaller detached homes for one or two families stood perpendicular to the rear of the apartment blocks, creating a traditional courtyard atmosphere closest to the apartments and leaving the back of each lot for communal green space. Almqvist incorporated standardized elements in a pair of simple and robust house types. All the windows were extremely simple, with either four or six lights and molded trim above and below only. The architect thus united an economic construction system with the charm of a traditional village atmosphere, making the most of both established local traditions and modern English planning in the spirit of Unwin. The area includes a custom-designed home for the company president, with a progressive and cleverly refined plan behind a deceptively simple, traditional facade.
E.E.

Literature: Björn Linn: *Osvald Almqvist, en arkitekt och hans arbete*, 1967.

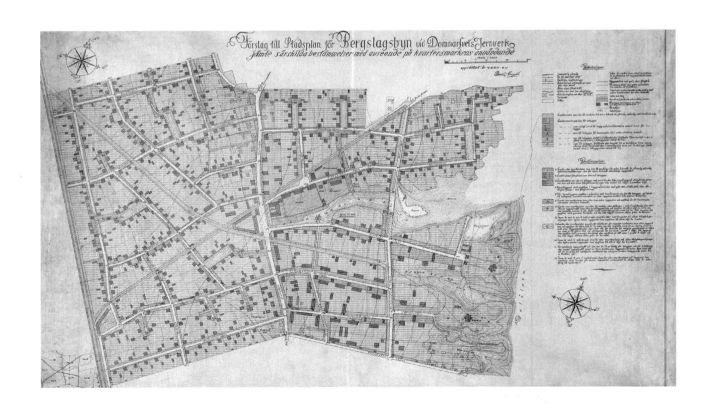

Lister District Courthouse

Sölvesborg 1919–21

GUNNAR ASPLUND

This courthouse plainly demonstrates the popular fascination of the Teens for early 19th-century Classicism in
its pale, smoothly-rendered surfaces and precise detailing. Asplund worked here with elementary geometric
forms. The round courtroom is the building's core, a
cylindrical void inscribed within the rectangular building
volume. The broad gable of the main facade provides
a dramatic focal point for the end of the long, straight
street that ascends the hill to the courthouse. The monumental semi-circular arch of the entrance was a popular
motif about 1800 that returned to vogue with the Classical revival of the 1920s. Details such as the courtroom's
corpulent balusters and windows that protrude from the
walls of the rear facade give the building a curious
demeanor. Several of its themes later appeared in the
Stockholm Public Library, including the central cylinder
wrapped on either side with staircases. One of the meeting rooms inside the courthouse is adorned in pure
Empire style.
E.E.

Literature: Claes Caldenby and Olof Hultin eds.:
Asplund, 1985.

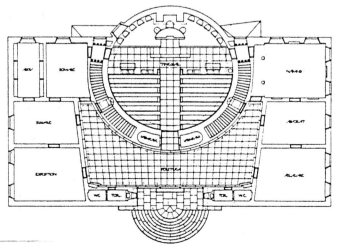

Götaplatsen

Gothenburg 1916–23

ARVID BJERKE / R.O. SWENSSON / ERNST
TORULF / SIGFRID ERICSON AND OTHERS

Götaplatsen was created in 1923 in conjunction with an exposition commemorating the three hundred year anniversary of the founding of Gothenburg. At the end of the city's main boulevard, Kungsportsavenyn, the site was to be a place for celebration and an entrance to the fairgrounds behind. It was the nation's most monumental urban planning initiative since Tessin's plan for the area surrounding the Royal Palace in Stockholm.

City Engineer Albert Lilienberg's preliminary studies formed the basis of an open competition held 1916–17. Lilienberg saw in the project an opportunity to firmly define the city's southern edge just where the terrain begins to rise sharply. Together the buildings around the new square would form an important focal point for Kungsportsavenyn. Ragnar Hjorth and Ture Ryberg won the original competition, but the runners-up, Arvid Bjerke, R.O. Swensson, Ernst Torulf, and Sigfrid Ericson, were also invited to continue developing their proposal, and in the end it was the latter scheme that was chosen.

Only the Museum of Art, the Art Gallery, the monumental terraces, and the square with its yet stateless fountain pool were finished in time for the 1923 exposition. The other buildings came later, following architectural competitions: the City Theater (Carl Bergsten, 1934), Concert Hall (Nils Einar Eriksson, 1935), Park Aveny Hotel (Eriksson, 1950), and the Public Library (Lund & Valentin, 1967). The original concept of a unified architectural space was gradually replaced by an approach that treated each building as an individual urban element. R.W.

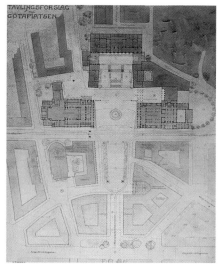

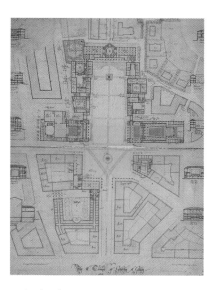
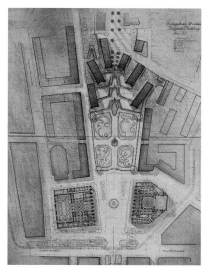

Ares 1917   Asplund 1917   Lewerentz 1917

Stockholm City Hall

Stockholm 1902–23

RAGNAR ÖSTBERG

Few of Stockholm's public buildings can boast such a monumental site as its City Hall. The building Ragnar Östberg built here has ambitions that extend far beyond the borders of the capitol city. Its tower culminates in three crowns—a symbol inherited from the old Royal Palace, known as the Three Crowns, as if to proclaim the building's national significance. The original commission for a municipal courthouse had engaged Östberg since the early 1890s. The planning had commenced with the country's first two-stage competition, in which six proposals were chosen from the first round to continue to a second. Östberg's scheme was clearly influenced by Carl Westman's idea of pressing the building to the water's edge and by Tengbom & Torulf's disposition of the plan; its procession of rooms is designed for ceremony.

The architecture of the City Hall juxtaposes the rustic with the elegant. The detailing was for the most part finalized during construction: the blue-tinged plaster of the "Blue Hall," for example, was left off at the last minute in favor of pick-hammering the bare brick walls. Georg Pauli, Einar Forseth, Axel Törneman, Axel Wallert, and Prince Eugen were among the contributors to the building's interior; Sidney Gibson, Ernst Spolén, Melchior Wernstedt, and Carl Malmsten designed its furniture; and Maja Sjöström designed the textiles.
R.W.

Literature: Elias Cornell: *Ragnar Östberg svensk arkitekt*, 1965.

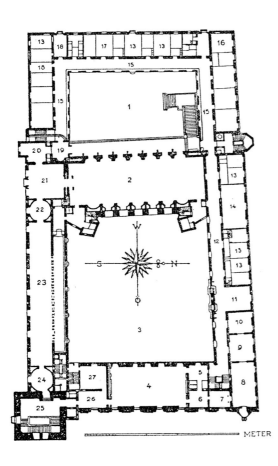

Swedish Match
Corporate Headquarters

Stockholm 1926–28

IVAR TENGBOM

"The Match Palace" was the popular name for the head-quarters of Ivar Kreuger's internationally expansive company, the Swedish Match Corporation. Ivar Tengbom was the natural choice for an assignment that warranted great dignity as well as discretion. The complex replaced a 17th-century palace on stately Västra Trädgårdsgatan, just next to the great park Kungsträdgården. Tengbom said his intention was to "preserve the unity that has always distinguished this street, and the quiet reserve that has given its buildings a unique character." He divided the site into three courtyards to provide the offices with daylight: a semi-circular formal entrance court at the center flanked on one side by a glass-roofed cashier's department and on the other by a garage court. The architect later made a point of noting that the client did not want the beam-and-column structure and glass walls typical of modern office buildings—the rooms were to be spacious, clearly defined, and warm and comfortable. The building's structure incorporates load-bearing walls of brick with composite floor systems that combine steel beams with reinforced concrete. The facades are rendered; facing the courtyards, the ground floor is clad in green Kolmård marble, with paving and columns of granite. The fountain is by Carl Milles.
C.C.

Literature: *Byggmästaren* 1928, p. 166.

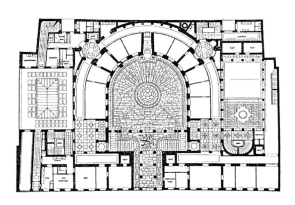

Stockholm Public Library

Stockholm 1918–28

GUNNAR ASPLUND

The Stockholm Public Library was one element in a master plan for the area surrounding Observatory Hill, and thus was naturally integrated with the university institutions which were expanding there. When Gunnar Asplund was hired to develop a program for the library, he traveled through Europe and the United States, where he came upon the scheme of surrounding a central hall of books with reading rooms. The completed library is close to Asplund's original Classicist proposal of 1922—its round, cupola-crowned central space was easy for librarians to oversee, and courtyards provided the flanking reading rooms with plenty of daylight. But as design work progressed, the building became increasingly abstract and simplified. A row of shops built into the library's base and a fourth wing of book stacks to the west, added in 1932, demonstrate the transition from Classicism to Functionalism. Two decorative elements stand out against the smoothly rendered walls: the Egyptian entrance portal, inspired by Thorvaldsen's museum in Copenhagen, and a frieze of home-made hieroglyphics.
C.C.

Literature: *Byggmästaren* 1928, p. 100, Kirstin Nielson: Stockholm Public Library, in: A. J. *Masters of Building, Erik Gunnar Asplund*, 1988.

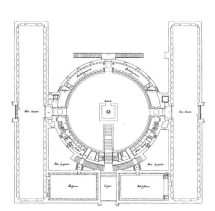

Stockholm Exhibition

Djurgården, Stockholm 1930

GUNNAR ASPLUND AND OTHERS

In 1930, the Swedish Handicraft Society arranged a grand exhibition of Swedish handicrafts, furniture, and industrial design, including a housing exposition, on the waterfront of Djurgården in Stockholm. It was a break-through for Functionalism, introducing the movement to a broad public for the first time in Sweden. The exhibition met with great acclaim mixed with harsh criticism. Chief architect Gunnar Asplund and his collaborators united beauty with inspired fantasy—exhibit halls, restaurants, pavilions, and news stands mingled gracefully with trees and vegetation. The festivities extended out over the water in boats, diving platforms, fountains, and fireworks. A 74-meter-high advertising mast proclaimed the new spirit of the exhibition far and wide. Asplund worked closely on the project with Nils Einar Eriksson, Viking Göransson, and Hans Quiding. Modern masters Sigurd Lewerentz, Sven Markelius, and Uno Åhrén also made substantial contributions, and many of the leading archi-tects of the day took part in the housing expo. The most elegant building was Asplund's restaurant Paradiset. Like many of the others, it was unmistakably Functionalist; much of the handicraft work on display, however, still embraced the aesthetic ideals of the 1920s. At the end of the summer, all of the buildings were either moved or demolished, so that traces of a garden and some ter-races are all that remains today of the celebrated event. E.R.

Literature: P. G. Råberg: *Funktionalistiskt genombrott*, 1972, Eva Rudberg: *Uno Åhrén*, 1981, Kerstin Wickman ed.: *Formens rörelse*, 1995.

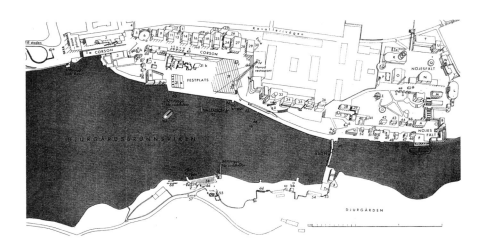

Concert Hall

Helsingborg 1925–32

SVEN MARKELIUS

Sven Markelius's Helsingborg Concert Hall, with its geometric forms in white stucco, was the first truly monumental Modernist building in Sweden. Markelius's original competition-winning proposal, however, was robed in classical garb; his first confrontation with the new European architecture induced a dramatic reworking of the project. The structural buttressing of the main volume is revealed on the exterior, and the relationships between the various interior spaces are clearly expressed in the building's differentiated volumes. From the fully-glazed entrance, visitors are led up a grand stair to be met by the convex form of an elegantly curved cloakroom. The stair continues to an upper lobby that opens to the north through a wall of glass. With its expanses of unadorned white wall surface, large white hanging light globes, delicate handrails, and airy volume of space, this sequence is an excellent example of the formal language of the era. In the auditorium, mahogany wall paneling and a warm color scheme create an intimate atmosphere. E.R.

Literature: Eva Rudberg: *Sven Markelius, arkitekt*, 1989.

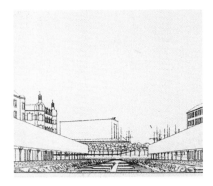

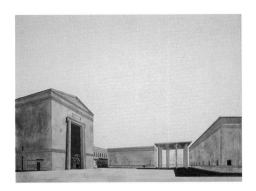

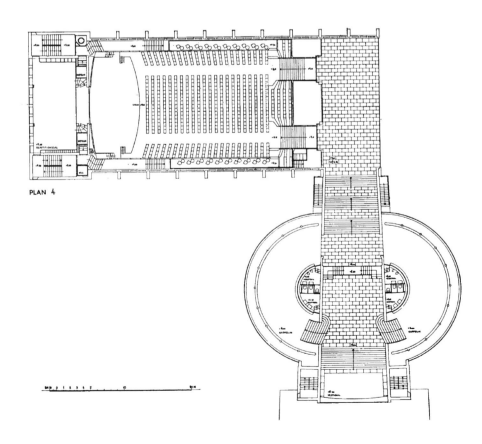

PLAN 4

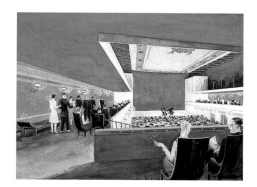

Kvarnholmen Complex

Nacka 1927–34

THE SWEDISH COOPERATIVE UNION AND
WHOLESALE SOCIETY'S OFFICE OF ARCHITEC-
TURE, PROJECT ARCHITECTS ESKIL SUNDAHL,
OLOF THUNSTRÖM, AND OTHERS.

The enormous Kvarnholmen complex was a modern version of the old manufacturing estate in Functionalist
style. Its workplaces included silos, warehouses, an oat
mill, and factories for making macaroni and crispbread.
Workers were housed in four row-house chains and two
apartment buildings. The scheme included the obligatory
company store. The 1927 grain silos were modeled on
American prototypes. The floors of the drying tower are
stacked like boxes one atop the other. Together the
tower and the repeating silo cylinders create a powerful
sculptural effect. The row houses from 1930 are oriented uniformly for optimal daylighting. The 7.3-meter narrow apartment blocks also have excellent interior lighting
conditions. They have characteristic facades cleanly rendered in pale stucco, with strip windows, windows that
wrap around corners, and shallow-pitched roofs.
E.R.

Literature: *Kooperativa förbundets arkitektkontor
1925–1935*, 1935.

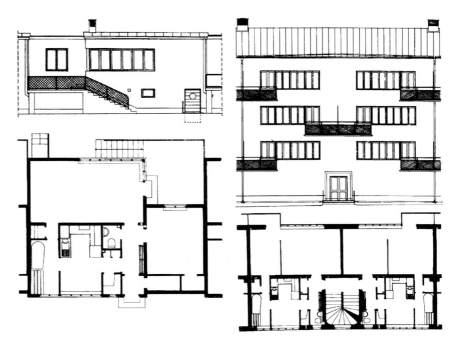

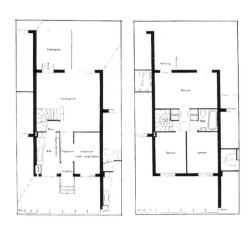

Row Houses

Bromma, Stockholm 1932

PAUL HEDQVIST

In 1932, Paul Hedqvist built about a hundred row houses outside of Stockholm in a zigzag pattern that afforded partially-protected outdoor spaces along the street. The precisely-cut and smoothly-rendered pale forms and shallow-pitched roofs give the buildings a decidedly Functionalist character. Each has two floors, with living room, kitchen, and a third room below, three more rooms above, and a private garden at the rear. The developer was a social activist and eager experimentalist named Olle Engkvist. Per Albin Hansson, prime minister in the social democratic government of 1932, lived in one of the houses.
E.R.

Concert Hall

Gothenburg 1931–35

NILS EINAR ERIKSSON

Nils Einar Eriksson's Concert Hall completed Götaplatsen, Gothenburg's stately fine arts center. The building's monumental base and colonnade show respect for the Classicist grammar of the square. The audience's experience follows a carefully-orchestrated path up the broad entrance stair, through a coat-check area, up to an upper promenade lobby that curves around the auditorium and overlooks the square. The auditorium itself is a Modernist shell sculpted into an acoustically optimal stepped funnel. Eriksson employed the foremost science of the day to produce a space of exceptional acoustic clarity. The complicated multi-layered wall system supports a surface veneer of sycamore maple, which gives the hall a warm, golden tone. The opulent interior is clad in fine wood and polished plaster in green and yellow hues. The building is complemented with an abundance of artistic embellishments. Interior architect Axel Larsson's substantial furniture was praised by a contemporary as "not excessively Functionalistic."
C.C.

Literature: Claes Caldenby, ed.: *Göteborgs konserthus, ett album*, 1992.

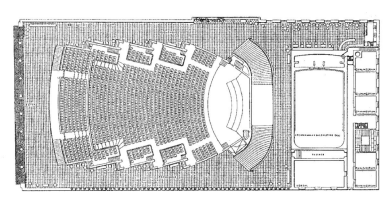

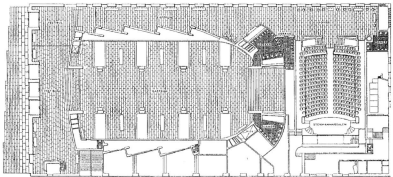

Collective House

John Ericssonsgatan 6, Stockholm
1935.

SVEN MARKELIUS

Sweden's first full-fledged "collective house" or apartment hotel was built in Stockholm in 1935. The project was conceived by architect Sven Markelius together with the Working Women's Club and women's activist Alva Myrdal. Most of the fifty-seven apartments are tiny, equipped only with minimal kitchenettes. The building had a ground-floor restaurant with dumbwaiters connecting it to each apartment, a day-care center, and a staff that cleaned and did laundry for the residents. The exterior is distinguished by the protruding planes of cant-bay windows that angle to give views down the street to the nearby water, by its elegantly-rounded balconies, and by the striking ocher color of its stucco walls. Among the building's first residents were many of the intellectual radicals of the day, including Markelius and his family; a Nazi resistance group, the Cultural Front, conducted its meetings here. After a period of neglect, the building has been restored essentially to its original condition. In 1995 it became a registered historical monument.
E.R.

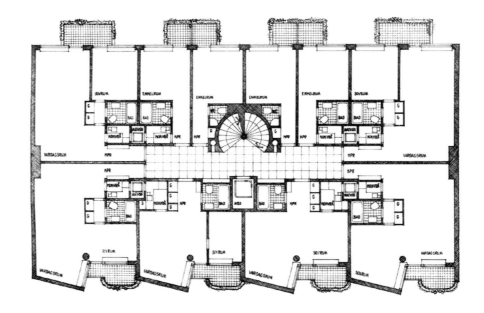

Sveaplan Girls' High School

Stockholm 1936

NILS AHRBOM, HELGE ZIMDAL
STRUCTURAL ENGINEER: STIG ÖDEEN

The girls' school at Sveaplan was one of the first public schools to be built following the educational reform of 1927, which made higher education more accessible to girls. Architects Ahrbom and Zimdal employed the formal language and organizational principles of Functionalism uncompromisingly, assigning to each school activity a single clearly-articulated building volume. They used modern building materials such as reinforced concrete columns and walls, with exterior insulation of foamed cellular concrete—an American invention developed in Sweden during the 1920s. The roof of the boldly projecting auditorium is carried by two arching welded-steel beams. Uniform window sizing helped minimize costs in a limited budget. The modern interior included new features such as movable benches and tables and provisions for a school meal service. The building was commendably renovated in the mid-1990s by Arksam.
E.R.

Literature: *Byggmästaren* 1936, p. 340.

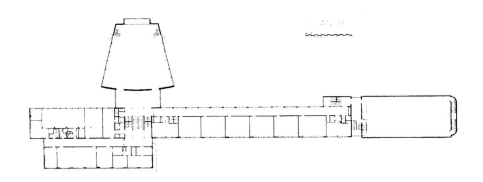

Gothenburg City Hall Extension

Gothenburg 1913–37

GUNNAR ASPLUND

Gothenburg's original wood-framed City Hall was replaced in 1672 with a stone building designed by Nicodemus Tessin the Elder. The building was remodeled and expanded several times during the 18th and 19th centuries, but the arcades that surrounded the courtyard in 1672 still stand today. The growing administration established a committee to investigate the possibilities for a major expansion. The investigation lasted twenty-seven years, until finally an architectural competition was announced in 1912. Gunnar Asplund won, and despite the committee's dissatisfaction with his scheme—which turned an undistinguished facade toward Gustav Adolfs Torg (the city's formal political square) and its entrance toward the Harbor Canal—he was commissioned to develop the proposal. In 1915 Asplund submitted a scheme that would connect City Hall on the west side of the square with the Stock Exchange on the north side in a monumental whole. The building's National Romantic garb had by this time been replaced with Classicism in pale yellow, white, and green. In a 1918 invited competition for the design of the square, Asplund divided the building into two volumes for the first time, one for a municipal courthouse and the other for the city's administrative offices. He submitted several more variations during the Twenties, and in 1934 the project for an addition to City Hall to house the municipal courts at last entered the final stages of design development. The changes continued, however, through construction, including the distinctive lateral shift of the windows and the minimizing of the roof's overhang in order to emphasize the building's cubic volume. The interior is generously bathed in natural light through the fully-glazed south-facing courtyard facade and a strip of clerestory windows above the main hall. The direct light is intercepted by a floor system along the south facade, diffused by the white-painted scoop of the clerestory roof monitor, and modulated by the soft curves of columns and wood-veneered walls. The Art Nouveau-inspired forms of the luminaires mix with Constructivist allusions in the elevator tower and telephone booths.
R.W.

Literature: Björn Fredlund: E.G. Asplunds om- och tillbyggnad av Göteborgs rådhus in: *Göteborg förr och nu* (VI 1970), Peter Blundell Jones: Gothenburg Law Courts in: *A.J. Masters of Building. Erik Gunnar Asplund*, 1988.

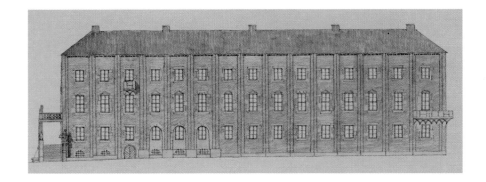

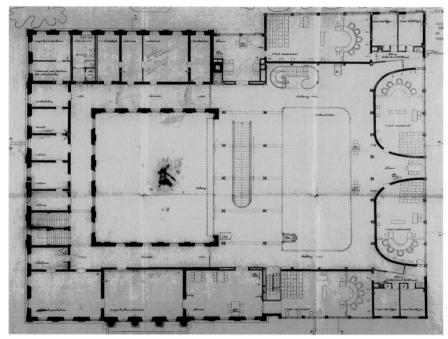

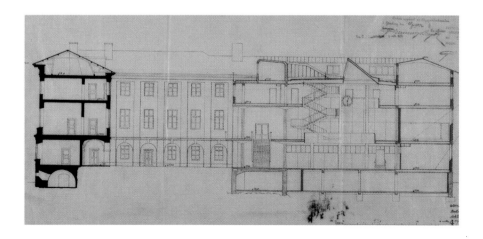

Woodland Cemetery

Stockholm 1915–40

GUNNAR ASPLUND / SIGURD LEWERENTZ

Gunnar Asplund and Sigurd Lewerentz's Woodland Cemetery is perhaps the most widely publicized work of Swedish architecture. Its long approach path leads through a classical landscape replete with biblical references—an open field with a hilltop grove of trees for meditation, a mighty free-standing crucifix, and at one edge the monumental, abstract portico of the crematorium. Asplund and Lewerentz's original 1915 competition-winning proposal, however, was rather a Nordic landscape with small clearings in a pine forest and a romantically leaning cross as a focal point. The two architects worked together on the cemetery's master plan and took turns designing its small chapels. Lewerentz also assumed the primary responsibility for the landscape design. Asplund's little Woodland Chapel (1920) is like a cottage in the woods with a simple shake-clad roof borne by Doric columns. Lewerentz's extremely subtle Chapel of the Resurrection (1925) is a slender and strictly-formed building with an entrance portico just barely detached from and slightly canted in relation to the main volume. It was a terrible disappointment for him that the building committee in the end commissioned Asplund alone to crown the composition with the crematorium and its great Chapel of the Holy Cross, on which the two had done preliminary design work together. The travertine building unites the Functionalistically abstract volumes of the smaller chapels with a Classical colonnade that supports an elegantly-shaped concrete barrel shell roof.
C.C.

Literature: Bengt O. H. Johansson: *Tallum*. 1996.

Chapels of St. Knut and St. Gertrud

Malmö Eastern Cemetery 1943–44

SIGURD LEWERENTZ

Sigurd Lewerentz's Chapels of St. Knut and St. Gertrud are additions to a crematorium at Malmö's Eastern Cemetery, with which the architect had been involved since winning a 1916 competition. The two small chapels rise from the flat landscape with open entrance porticoes whose columns spring directly from the ground without a podium, following the curve of the earth like the trees that surround them. The facades are cloaked in thin bands of marble shards; on the interior, the walls take on an almost textile texture—a weave of marble strips, yellow brick, and pine ribs. The informal grouping of the building volumes and their intense materiality are typical of Swedish building in the 1940s.
C.C.

Literature: Janne Ahlin: *Sigurd Lewerentz, arkitekt*, 1985.

Lind Residence

Danderyd 1945–46

SVEN IVAR LIND

In an article in Byggmästaren, Leif Reinius asserted that Sven Ivar Lind's own home was a self-portrait—an environment created with the greatest care and deliberation for a couple with no children and a love of cooking and gardening. The simple gabled oblong is closed on the north side toward the street, the primary spaces opening on the garden to the south. The freely-placed chimneys and varied fenestration indicate subtle changes in floor level and show the rooms within to be uncompromisingly tailored for domestic comfort. The dining room at the heart of the building opens to an outdoor room, which leads to a terrace and then the garden. At one end lies a living room with more generous ceiling height. The dimensions throughout the house are spare but thoroughly studied and well proportioned. Lind's choice of materials is straightforward, with gray plaster and gray-painted woodwork dominating. The atmosphere is as timeless as in a French country home.
C.C.

Literatur: Tomas Lewan: Sven Ivar Lind. Arkitekt och pedagog, in: *Arkitektur* No. 4, 1994.

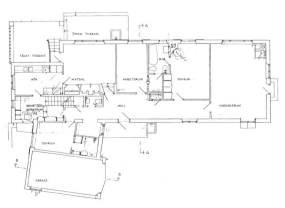

Norra Guldheden Residential Development

Gothenburg 1945

GUNNAR WEJKE, KJELL ÖDÉEN

Norra Guldheden had Sweden's first "community center," presented to the public in the "Better Living" housing exposition in August, 1945. The exposition was organized by the City of Gothenburg, The National Housing Loan Office, and the Swedish Handicraft Society. Architects Gunnar Wejke and Kjell Ödéen planned the area and designed most of its buildings. The rocky Landala promontory is crowned with the striking silhouette of Raketgatan's seven-story apartment towers. Behind the towers, lower oblong apartment buildings face Guldhedstorget, the area's little commercial square. An apartment hotel was built on the square with single rooms, a restaurant, and shops on the ground floor, and apartments for "household employees" on the floors above. Wejke and Ödéen incorporated an existing garden into the square to provide the modern space with well-established vegetation and a manifest connection to the history of the place. The development also included a nursery school. The apartments have between one and three bedrooms. The T-shaped towers in particular are known for the quality of their apartments.
R.W.

Literature: Malin Larsson: *Norra Guldheden. Kulturmiljö av riksintresse*, 1993.

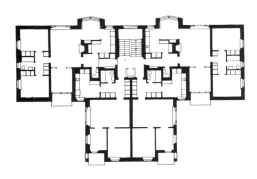

Södra Guldheden Residential Development

Gothenburg 1950

SVEN BROLID, JAN WALLINDER

The southern part of Guldheden is exemplary of the "city beautiful" ideal of 1940s urban planning—placing free-standing buildings in a park environment. High-rise apartment buildings were rare at the time: the vast majority of multi-family housing consisted of three- or four-story blocks. Vertical slabs and towers became common first in the 1950s. Among the earliest were Sven Brolid and Jan Wallinder's elegant high-rises up on Södra Guldheden, deftly sited among green lawns, leafy trees, and outcroppings of rock in a park-like landscape. The clever floor plan links two slender apartment towers with a common vertical circulation core. The kitchens are small, with separate dining areas, according to the custom of the day. The balconies can be reached from both living room and bedroom, and still let daylight into the bathroom between them.
E.R.

Literature: *Arkitektur* No. 10, 1953.

Friluftstaden Residential Development

Malmö 1944–1950s

ERIC SIGFRID PERSSON AND ERIK BÜLOW-HÜBE (MASTERPLAN).

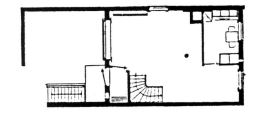
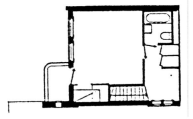

It took some time before Swedes considered the row house an acceptable dwelling form, but in the 1940s and '50s several high-quality row-house neighborhoods were built. One of the most interesting is Eric Sigfrid Persson and Erik Bülow-Hübe's Friluftsstaden ("Open-Air City"), developed in stages to include a total of two hundred homes. The rows of houses cross a softly undulating park landscape in parallel lines, the terrain deftly sculpted with careful excavation and free of fences. The houses are staggered one to the next, creating small private outdoor rooms facing either east or west; the remaining land is shared by the residents. The uniformity of the scheme is tempered by steep tile roofs and by alternating rendered and bare brick facade surfaces. The area includes a small commercial district with shops and services. The same builder developed similar row-house neighborhoods in Nässjö and Huskvarna in the 1950s. E.R.

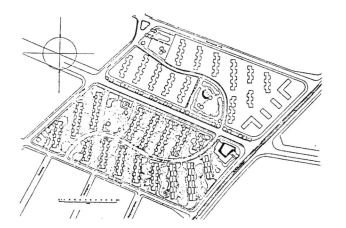

Literature: Ulla Hårde: *Eric Sigfrid Persson*, 1986.

"Honeycomb" Apartment Buildings

Gröndal, Stockholm 1944–46

SVEN BACKSTRÖM, LEIF REINIUS

Sven Backström and Leif Reinius's innovative "honeycomb" plan was a development of the narrow apartment block, whose units span from facade to facade and thus receive daylight from two or three directions. The honeycomb's stairwells gave access to three apartments on each floor instead of two—an important economic improvement. It also afforded new variations in urban planning patterns, with protected courtyards of different sizes. The idea was born of the difficulties of a wind-swept, north-facing site in Gröndal. Its realization was due to the architects' ingenuity and developer Olle Engkvist's enthusiasm for experimentation. The buildings were given gabled roofs and rendered in rich earth tones of burnt sienna, green umbra, ocher, and brown; the windows were trimmed in white. These aspects gave the buildings a traditional character in spite of their innovative form. The honeycomb had successors in Sweden and abroad, one of the most well-known among them Rosta in Örebro. E.R.

Literature: *Arkitektur* No. 6, 1982.

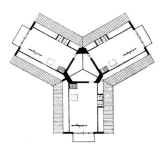

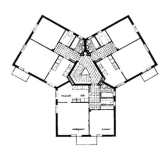

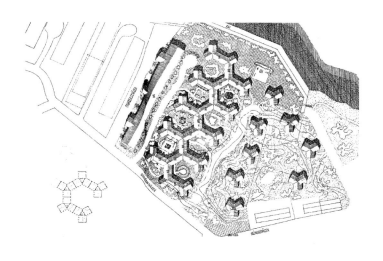

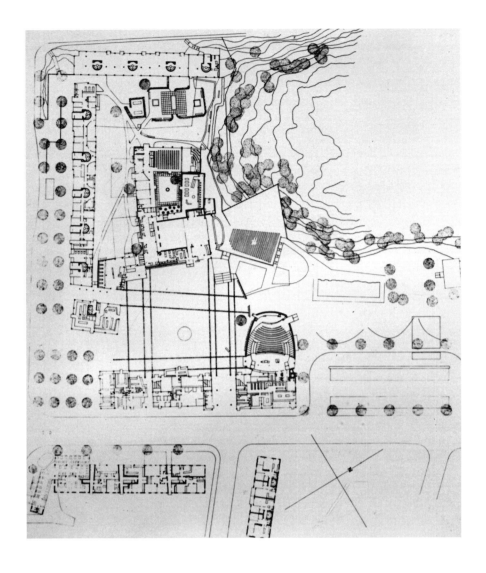

Årsta Community Center

Stockholm 1943–53

ERIK AND TORE AHLSÉN

Årsta, a suburban satellite of Stockholm, had one of the country's first examples of neighborhood planning. Society's investment in the arts is the heart of this project: Erik and Tore Ahlsén planned the community around a core that includes a theater, a library, artists' studios, a cinema, and meeting rooms of varying size. They designed the main square as a public assembly space that holds thousands. The architects provided for social services, including a maternity clinic and a dental care center. There are shops and restaurants, but these do not dominate the center of town in the manner of later suburban communities. Årsta center is set off from the surrounding town by its distinctive architecture. Its facades are wrapped in a colorful graphic pattern that belies the function and structure of the buildings behind, but strives instead to arouse the curiosity and create a festive atmosphere. The proportions of the buildings establish a comfortable, human scale. After many years of population decline and gradual deterioration, the area has once again begun to flourish.
E.R.

Literature: *Byggmästaren* No. 12, 1954.

Sala Backar Residential Development

Uppsala 1950–53

GUNNAR LECHE

When he designed Sala Backar residential area, Gunnar Leche had been City Architect in Uppsala for three decades, and had left his mark both as planner and building architect on much of the city. Sala Backar was his last major project, and is among the finest examples of "Folkhem" architecture in Sweden. It is a satellite community on the hills overlooking the city. The central incinerator's chimney provides a landmark next to which an assembly hall, retail stores, and workshops are grouped around a public square. The three- and four-story apartment blocks conform to the terrain, forming three courtyards. There are imaginatively designed pavilions for children's play, and each of the entrance doors to the apartment buildings is unique. The apartments are planned to be "elastic"—three small units can be rearranged to form two larger.
C.C.

Literature: Carl Erik Bergold: *Bostadsbyggande i Uppsala 1900–1950*, 1985.

Housing, School and Commercial Center

Gyttorp 1945–55

RALPH ERSKINE

The town of Gyttorp, in Västmanland, exemplifies the many important contributions made by architects in small towns across Sweden following the Second World War. Ralph Erskine designed for the town several two-story row houses and three-story apartment buildings of reinforced concrete with an unusual barrel-roofed form. Their concrete construction was a security precaution against the risk of explosion and fire from a nearby explosives factory. To minimize thermodynamic stress in the material, Erskine separated the heated interior structure from the exterior shell that was exposed to the cold— a characteristic expression of what he called "climatic architecture." He left the air bubbles that develop when concrete is poured into forms unaltered, allowing the unique nature of the material to contribute to the charac-

ter of the facades—an early example of beton brt architecture in the spirit of Le Corbusier. The powerful balcony facades pierced with circular holes became something of a signature for Erskine, a pattern to which he would return in other projects. One critic accused the architect of violating the idyllic little village and proclaimed that putting a stop to Erskine was "the most urgent task now facing cultural preservation in Sweden." In 1996 the Central Board of National Antiquities announced its plan to landmark the buildings and invest in their renovation.
E.R.

Literature: Mats Egelius: *Ralph Erskine, arkitekt*, 1988.

Baronbackarna Residential Development

Örebro 1951

PER-AXEL EKHOLM / SIDNEY WHITE

In the late Forties, Örebro was a model city that benefited greatly from a successful series of architectural competitions for new residential developments. The competition for a neighborhood called Baronbackarna was won by the team of Per-Axel Ekholm and Sidney White. Their scheme used a continuous, meandering three- to four-story chain of apartments to separate protected outdoor space from a street side with automobile traffic and parking. This allowed them to preserve and enhance the trees and rocks and rolling hills that make up the natural landscape behind the buildings—a strategy typical of Swedish landscape planners. There are also smaller courtyards equipped for children's play. Baronbackarna became known for using the qualities of well-planned shared outdoor space to compensate for the space limitations of minimized apartments. In Ekholm and White's competition submission, a quarter of the units were to be experimental mini-apartments. A full-scale model of these was built on the site to help potential tenants understand the ideas behind the new scheme. Their floor plan was carefully designed to facilitate the housewife's work in the home. Like many of the residential developments of the day, the area includes a high-rise with small apartments for single residents.
E.R.

Literature: *Byggmästaren*, 1959.

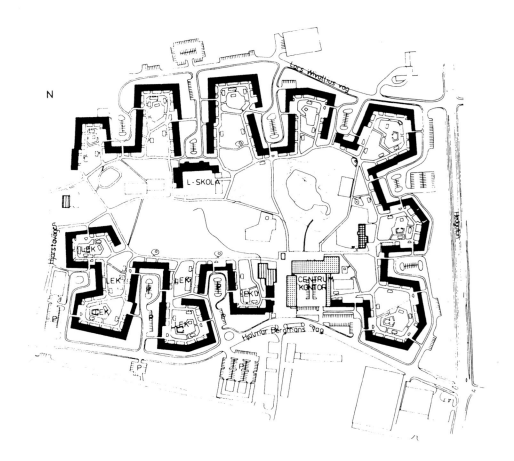

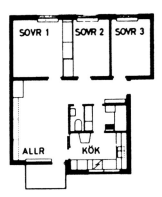

Water Tower

Örebro 1954–58

SUNE LINDSTRÖM / POUL KYHL (VBB)

The economic expansion that followed World War II required local governments in Sweden to invest heavily in developing the urban infrastructure. Migration to the cities, the growth of industry, and improvements in hygienic standards in the home rapidly multiplied the cities' need for fresh drinking water. VBB architects Sune Lindström and Poul Kyhl's water tower in Örebro remains a sculptural manifestation of the new era of urban technology. Water towers had long been designed with high aesthetic ambitions, but the advancement of pre-stressed concrete technology provided new expressive possibilities. The large-scale form was a favorite motif for Lindström and Kyhl. The Örebro tower's continuous shell could be constructed without scaffolding. The slight relief and oscillating gray tones of the surface intensify its powerful gesture. The shallow-pitched lid covers a viewing platform and restaurant. VBB built several similar towers in the years to come, including a number in Kuwait between 1969 and '73 which are strikingly arranged in groups of various colors.
R.W.

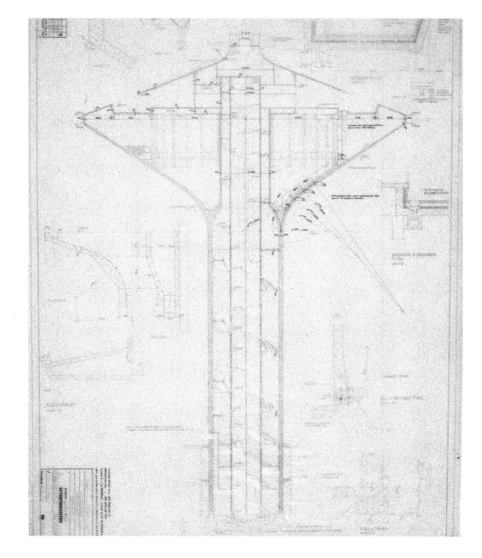

Vällingby Town Center

Stockholm, dedicated 1954

SVEN BACKSTRÖM / LEIF REINIUS, AND OTHERS

Vällingby is the hub of a group of suburban communities northwest of Stockholm which incorporated residential, commercial, and industrial development. Backström and Reinius were commissioned to plan the center of Vällingby, and to design its civic center and cinema. They gave the town square a strong architectural identity by paving it with large white rings on a black background; one ring holds a fountain. The sprawling expanse of the square provides a deliberate contrast to the town's narrow pedestrian shopping streets. Unlike at Årsta, commercial buildings form the heart of Vällingby, while its cultural buildings (which include Peter Celsing's Church of St. Thomas) are more peripherally sited. The area is among the most internationally recognized works of postwar Swedish planning, and visitors still travel to Vällingby to experience modern planning history in person.
E.R.

Literature: *Byggmästaren* No. 4, 1956.

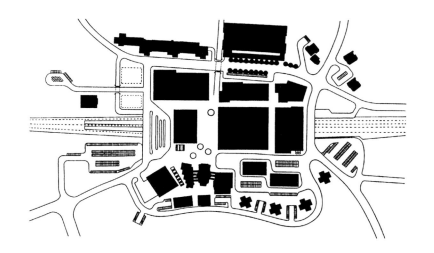

H 55 Exhibition

Helsingborg 1955

CARL-AXEL ACKING AND OTHERS

In 1955, the Swedish Society of Industrial Design held an exhibition in Helsingborg harbor called simply H55. It was a concise demonstration of Sweden's elegant post-war Modernism, but also marked the end of an era as society began to depend upon the automobile, undertake physical planning and development at a vast scale, and prioritize the means of production over the interests of the consumer. Carl-Axel Acking was the chief architect of the H55 exhibition. He designed a pavilion for the shipping industry that looked like a command bridge and, together with Per Friberg, a garden pergola that cast striking graphical shadow effects. Bengt Gate designed the Parapet restaurant and several of the exhibition spaces. Much attention was given to an apartment building with the motto "Shell and Kernel" that was planned around the needs of children by Ulla Molin, Lena Larsson, Mårten Larsson, and Anders William-Olsson.
C.C.

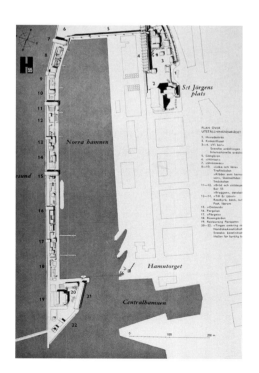

Vacation Houses

Haverdal, 1953

STIG ANCKER

In 1953, Stig Ancker built a group of vacation houses
arranged in rows along a ridge overlooking a sandy
beach on Sweden's southwest coast. Based on year-
round residential prototypes, this "summer village" was
built as a tenant-owners' society with a shared technical
infrastructure and a unifying appearance. The homes are
atrium houses, a form that was being utilized for single-
family homes at the time but never achieved lasting popularity. A 100-m^2 walled-in square holds a kitchen and living space, four small galley bedrooms, and a little bath
house in an L around a private, wind-sheltered courtyard.
The walls of the perimeter square were of white-painted
concrete block, while the interiors and the walls separating the rooms from the courtyard were assembled from
prefabricated wood-framed elements. Tenants were free
to paint their own homes, but the architect was to
approve their choice of color.
C.C.

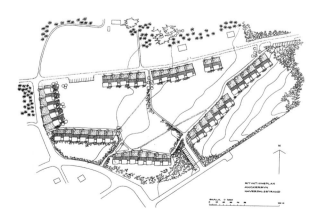

Sjögången Residential Development

Gothenburg 1959–61

BENGT FORSER / JARLE OSNES / NILS SUNNER-
HOLM / LENNART BERGQVIST

Sjögången is one of many relatively low occupancy row-
house communities built in Sweden during the 1950s.
The area was planned to include homes for the
architects' own families. The outdoor spaces vary widely
in their degree of privacy, from the central communal
green to private gardens. To the north and east lie narrow chains of two-story row houses with small back
yards. Because all the windows on the second floor face
the opposite direction, these yards are completely private. The atrium houses to the south and west also have
sheltered outdoor spaces. With most of their rooms
opening directly onto the courtyards, these homes max-
imize indoor-outdoor contact.
R.W.

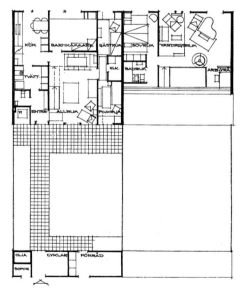

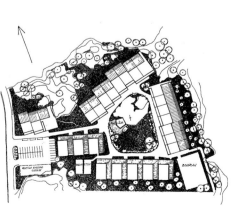

High-rise Office Buildings

Hötorgscity, Stockholm 1955–66

D. HELLDÉN / A. TENGBOM / S. MARKELIUS /
L-E. LALLERSTEDT AND S. BACKSTRÖM /
L. REINIUS

"The five trumpet calls" was what City Commissioner Yngve Larsson called the five vertical slabs that marked Hötorgscity, Stockholm's new commercial center. Their sleek and slender geometric forms, washed by light and air, manifest the principles of Modernism. The lean appearance was achieved by breaking each into two planes that seem to shift vertically and laterally. The broad sides are individual interpretations by five architects of the Modernist curtain wall unified by windowless white narrow sides. The first four slabs are simply glazed to reflect the sky, while the fifth, which faces Sergels torg, has a more articulated surface. Hötorgscity was one of the earliest and most thorough urban renewal projects in the world. The first sketches, by David Helldén under supervision of Sven Markelius, were reviewed by the city planning department as early as 1946. Sergel gatan became one of the first pedestrian streets in Sweden—a long, narrow plaza lined on one side with the tower slabs and on the other with a low row of shops. The paving's large-scale black-and-white rectangular pattern emphasizes the axiality of the scheme. The original project included a market hall and movie theater. The row of shops has since been substantially expanded.
E.R.

Härlanda Church

Gothenburg 1952–58

PETER CELSING

Härlanda Church was the product of an architectural
competition. It was the first in a series of churches by
Peter Celsing, constructed of the dark, hard-fired Helsingborg brick, that inspired a substantial following
in Sweden. The administrative office wing presents a
simple brick wall to the church yard, its flat surface
drawn up above the roof line in a parapet. A free-standing
cubist bell tower defines the other side of the yard. The
entire project is infused with an archaic sense—the
church of Torcello, outside Venice, was one of the prototypes that inspired Celsing. Härlanda Church bears the
scars of an imagined long history: its door and daylight
openings are asymmetrically placed, and although the
transept has no north apse to match the south, there are
corner quoins to suggest that one has been removed
and walled over. With uncompromising sobriety, the dark
exterior brick recurs in the austere interior of the sanctuary. Behind a mighty pier, light floods the transept from
the south. The parish hall lies below in a basement that
opens to the west.
C.C.

Literature: Wilfried Wang: *The Architecture of
Peter Celsing*, 1996.

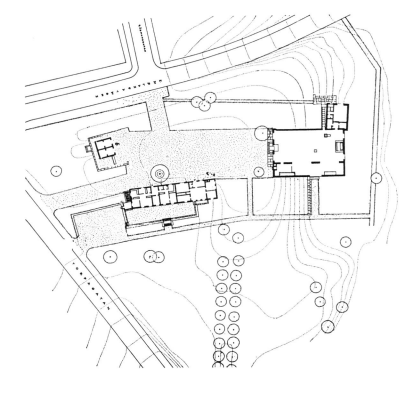

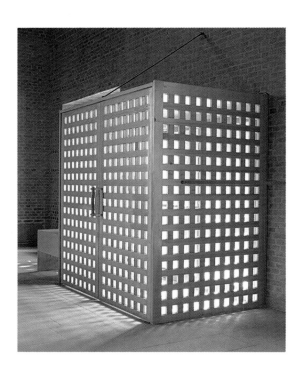

Crematorium

Gävle 1954–60

ELLT

In 1954, four young architecture students named Alf Engström, Gunnar Landberg, Bengt Larsson, and Alvar Törneman won the competition to design a chapel for Gävle's new forest cemetery. They called their submission "Forest Light." Their idea was to "let the natural stillness and devotional spirit of the pine forest build a framework of light and freedom for the burial ceremony." They inserted a system of walls among the pine trunks to create two chapels. An open forecourt and waiting room provide a transition from the forest to the chapels. Their roof planes seem to float above cast-concrete walls that are striated with vertical ridges and channels left by the random-thickness boards of the formwork. The floors, inside and out, are paved with broad slate slabs and smaller stones. The steel structure of the chapel roofs is clad in pine paneling, and held aloft by steel columns. Cremation takes place below in an underground room. The free-standing bell tower next to the approach road was constructed of common steel beams. The grounds around the chapel were landscaped by Per Friberg. Bernt Nyberg designed the cemetery's service buildings.
C.C.

Literature: *Arkitektur* No. 12, 1960.

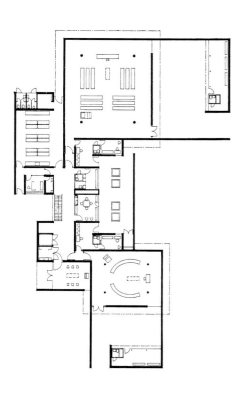

St. Mark's Church

Björkhagen, Stockholm 1956–60

SIGURD LEWERENTZ

The 1950s Stockholm suburb of Björkhagen provides an
everyday background for the first of two churches of
dark-fired Helsingborg brick designed by Sigurd Lewerentz
long past the age of retirement. The pale trunks of the
low-lying site's birch grove stand out against the dark wall
of a reserved main facade whose windows are abstract-
ed to holes overlaid with glass. The speckled pattern of
bricks in mortar resonates with the dappled bark of the
trees. The somber brick and archaic character of the outside continues in an interior marked by the contrast
between daylight and darkness. The roof is spanned by
three-segmented shallow brick vaults. The parish hall,
with its bowed laminated-wood canopy, and a wing for
administrative offices and bell tower enclose a small
courtyard.
C.C.

Literature: Janne Ahlin: *Sigurd Lewerentz, arkitekt*,
1985.

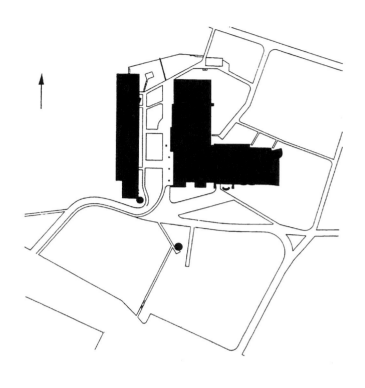

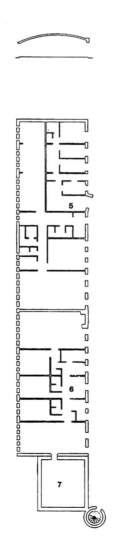

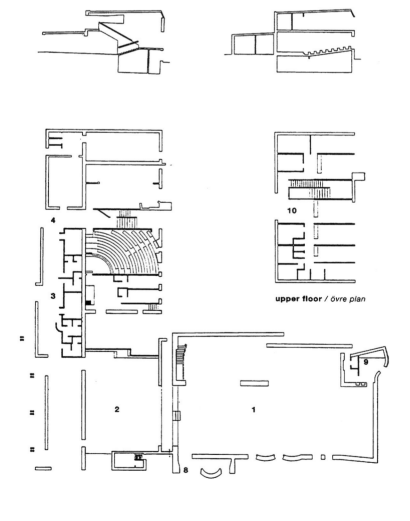

upper floor / övre plan

Smith Residence

Lidingö 1959

NILS TESCH

There is an atmosphere of 18th-century Sweden about
the simple, harmonious, and well-proportioned interiors
of Nils Tesch's Smith residence. Tesch kept the traditional art of building alive. The house's island site slopes
down to meet the waters of Stockholm's archipelago.
The warmth of the brick walls glows through a gray lime-
washed surface, blushing against a slate roof that nearly
replicates the cold gray of the bay below. Tesch designed an L-shaped building, and added a third wall along
the street to enclose a sheltered courtyard, which he
paved partially with stone. One of the Smith residence's
many qualities is the contrast between the intimacy of
this little courtyard and the grandeur of the garden
beyond, with its panoramic view over the bay. The architect chose to limit views to the water rather than captur-
ing them through huge windows, thereby preserving their
dramatic impact. His closest associate on the project
was Erik Asmussen.
E.R.

Literature: *Arkitektur* No. 5, 1991.

Crematorium Chapel

Nässjö 1957–62

SVEN IVAR LIND

Sven Ivar Lind's scheme for Nässjö's Name Crematorium surrounded a simple, gable-roofed chapel with a number of lower buildings, all of it in Helsingborg brick. The interior walls were white-washed and then scrubbed with red bricks to give them a rosy glow. Lind placed the windows freely, setting them in deep, splayed niches. The roof structure is revealed on the inside—it seems to float above the walls, and the two sides part along the peak as though the roof might open to the sky at any moment. The encircling subsidiary spaces step down from the higher chapel to grasp the earth with a series of walls. C.C.

Literature: Tomas Lewan: Sven Ivar Lind. Arkitekt och pedagog, in: *Arkitektur* No. 4, 1994.

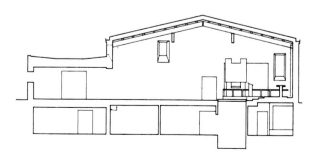

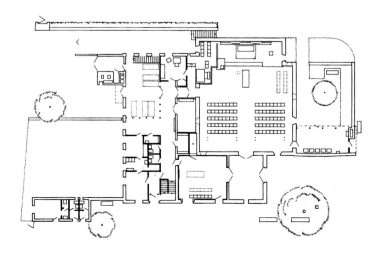

Hägerstrand Residence

Lund 1964

BENGT EDMAN

When Torsten Hägerstrand, a professor of cultural geo-
graphy, hired Bengt Edman to design his home, he gave
the architect a clearly defined program, but appreciated
Edman's desire to let the form of the house be determined by the inherent configuration of the site and the
building materials. The result is a central kitchen flanked
on either side by a series of small rooms for children and
parents. The property lines dictated the perimeter, forcing the rooms to wrap around a small courtyard, as in
the local vernacular architecture of Scania. Part of the
courtyard was roofed over to become a high-ceilinged
living room. All the walls were laid up with free flawed
bricks rejected by the factory in Helsingborg. The raw
brick was left unaltered inside. The masonry walls were
given an intrinsic value independent of the rooms: one
continues unabated through a window wall into the garden.
C.C.

Literature: Gunilla Millisdotter: *Bengt Edmans arkitektur
och pedagogik*, 1993.

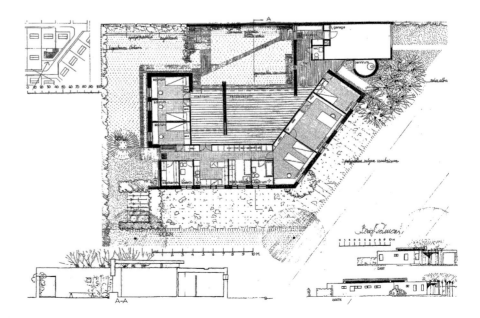

Kaknäs Tower

Stockholm 1964–67

BORGSTRÖM & LINDROOS

The television transmission tower was a new building
form in the 1960s. Both its function and its bold new
methods of construction captured the spirit of the day.
Borgström & Lindroos's 161-meter-high Kaknäs Tower
is unusual in that its technical prowess is overshadowed
by its sculptural power. The square-sectional concrete
shaft was poured in slip forms. It is rotated 45 degrees
in relation to its square base, and to the tower are
attached angled platforms for service spaces and a
restaurant. The dramatic entrance sequence leads
visitors down a ramp into a cave that glitters with reliefs
by Walter Bengtsson. The rough texture of raw concrete
is offset by the tower's gold-toned heat-reflective glass
windows.
C.C.

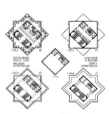

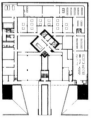

Civic Center

Örebro 1957–65

ERIK AND TORE AHLSÉN

The construction of a new civic center was part of the urban renewal of the south side of Örebro. Erik and Tore Ahlsén fit the center's complex program within a single city block. They lined the exterior facades with small assembly and meeting rooms, surrounding a courtyard filled by three large auditoria. The building is divided vertically, with public functions on the two lower floors that take in the street and square through window walls, and two more enclosed office levels that cantilever out above. The shops along Drottninggatan are reminiscent of the appentice sheds that ringed medieval cathedrals. The building's facades are composed with a rich palette of materials—red sandstone, stucco, teak, copper, stainless steel, and glass—that juxtaposes the rustic and the refined. The mix of coarse and polished continues inside. Above the theater lobby, the smooth rake of the underside of the theater's seating was rendered and burnished by artist Olle Nyman. The room's ribbed concrete walls are adorned with elegant luminaires plated with gold leaf.
C.C.

Literature: Claes Caldenby: *Medborgarhus i Örebro*, 1990.

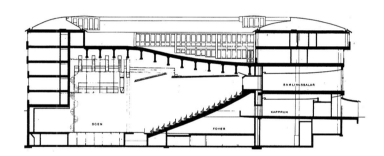

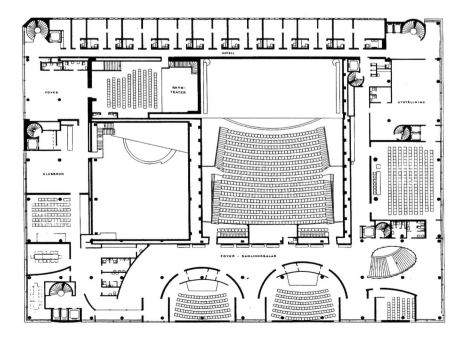

City Hall

Lund 1961–66

KLAS ANSHELM

Klas Anshelm won the competition to expand the Neo-classical city hall in the medieval heart of Lund with an innovative proposal that was at once Modernist and sensitive to its surroundings. The reserved front of Anshelm's triangular addition remains subordinate to the adjacent original building, while contributing at the back a new shopping street to downtown Lund. The new building's materials match those of the old, but its detailing has a distinctive character. The entrance protrudes with a decidedly Modern steel-framed awning that seems to both support and give way for an old tree. Two oval-shaped auditoria rise through the roof to proclaim their public significance like huge glass roof monitors resplendent with rows of naked light bulbs that line the edge between the wall and ceiling inside. These clerestory windows also admit light from above into the auditoria, which are clad in pale wood veneer with acoustic reflectors suspended from the ceiling.
C.C.

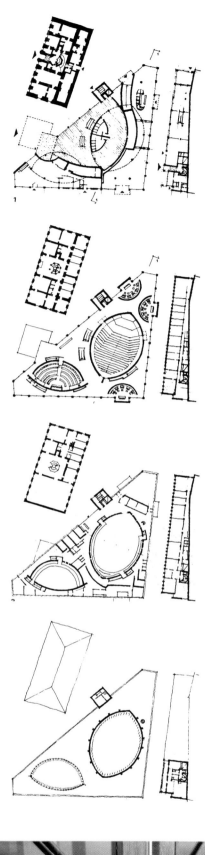

St. Peter's Church

Klippan, Scania 1963–67

SIGURD LEWERENTZ

In St. Peter's Church, Sigurd Lewerentz revived the themes on which he based St. Mark's, reinterpreting them and reducing them to a more pure essence. The sanctuary is dark, its thick walls pierced with small holes sealed by thermopanes clamped to the outside. The roof is spanned by shallow brick vaults carried on two steel beams; these in turn are borne by a steel column and beam, somewhat eccentrically placed, whose T-shape suggests the cross. The baptismal font is a gigantic sea shell. The floor, spread with a carpet of various ceramic pavers and tiles, swells and pitches under foot. The freely-laid running-bond cavity walls are of the same dark Helsingborg brick as Lewerentz used at St. Mark's. C.C.

Literature: Janne Ahlin: *Sigurd Lewerentz, arkitekt*, 1985, Sigurd Lewerentz: *Two churches/Två kyrkor*, 1997.

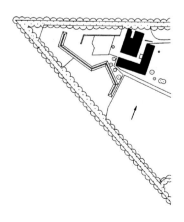

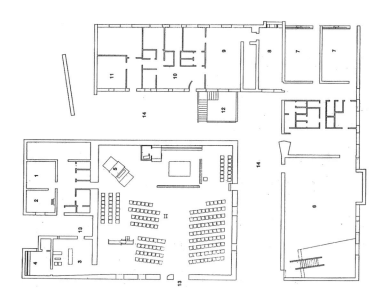

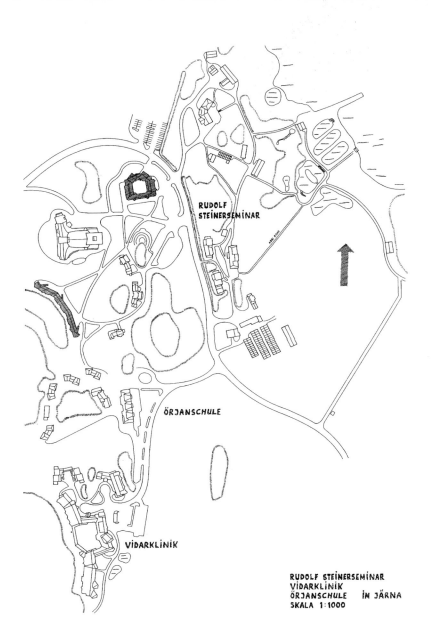

RUDOLF STEINERSEMINAR
VIDARKLINIK
ÖRJANSCHULE IN JÄRNA
SKALA 1:1000

The Rudolf Steiner Seminary

Järna 1968–92

ERIKS ASMUSSEN

The Anthroposophical Society's first Nordic seminary, a counterpart to that in Dornach, Switzerland, was established in the artist Bruno Liljefors's former studio, distance kilometers south of Stockholm in Järna. Starting in the 1960s, Architect Erik Asmussen added a long series of buildings to the seminary over a twenty-five year period. First there were a few student dormitories, a eurythmics building, a library, and a music building; then came the Ormen Långe dormitory, a dining hall, and a shop in nearby Robygge; and finally the institution's main building, the Fine Arts Center, with its great hall. The buildings' organic forms might be described as metamorphic transformations of one another, each of them clearly inspired by Steiner's own expressionist architecture of the 1910s. Other important sources were the local vernacular architecture of Järna Bay and traditional Swedish wooden construction. The buildings are distinguished, however, by the sculptural forms of roofs cut flush with facades clad in dramatically-colored wood or stucco. Each of the institution's buildings contains at least one dwelling. Asmussen designed several other buildings in the vicinity with ties to the Anthroposophical Society— a mill, a bakery, a school, and the health care center Vidarkliniken.
C.C.

Literature: *Arkitektur* No. 6, 1984, Gary J. Coates: *Erik Asmussen, architect*, 1997.

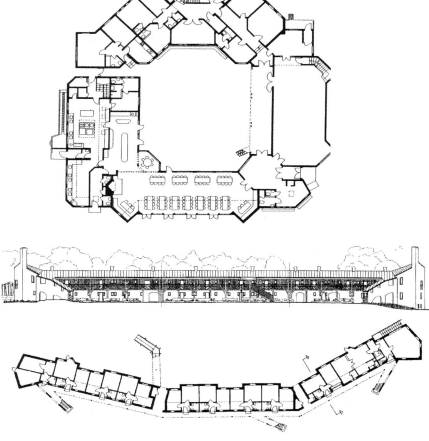

Flower Stand

Malmö 1969

SIGURD LEWERENTZ

Sigurd Lewerentz's final commission was for a small flower stand at Malmö's Eastern Cemetery, where he had worked since his youth. It is an extremely simple little box with a steep copper shed roof that extends far out over the street facade on the low south side to provide shade from the sun. The concrete walls were poured into forms with chamfered edges, leaving a raised grid pattern across the surface. The windows are simple thermopanes set flush to the facade with steel fasteners. There is no stair for the elevated door to the seldom-used refrigeration room. While he strove unceasingly for reduction to the most essential, Lewerentz also took pleasure in "the flow of poetry through Romex", letting serpentine electric cables meander freely across the bare concrete of the interior walls.
C.C.

Literature: Janne Ahlin, *Sigurd Lewerentz, arkitekt*, 1985.

Chapel

Höör 1972

BERNT NYBERG

Bernt Nyberg's Chapel at Höör is built on the simple idea of two square roofs, each borne aloft by four crosses built up of rusty structural steel members. One roof shelters a place to gather outdoors at the cemetery's highest point; the other seems to float within the walls of a room for ceremonies. These are freely composed spatial volumes, though they are disciplined by the waffle slab roof's strict modular grid of concrete coffers and bare light bulbs. Daylight grazes the coarse brick walls of the ceremonial room from above through automotive glass panes fitted with electrical conductors to prevent snow accumulation. The light is reflected further into the space by a strip of aluminum foil that wraps the top of each wall, accentuating the distinction between roof and wall structures. The windows are simply thermopanes adhered to steel frames—an obvious reference to Nyberg's mentor, Sigurd Lewerentz.
C.C.

Literature: *Arkitektur* No. 4, 1996.

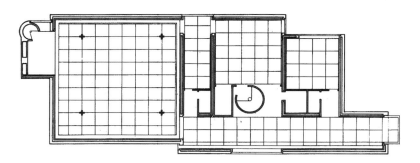

Villa Klockberga

Drottningholm, Stockholm 1969

PETER CELSING

Peter Celsing designed his own home, the Villa Klockberga, while he worked on the plans for Stockholm's new
Fine Arts Center. It is an exercise in complexity and contradiction full of historical references. The entrance
facade of the remodeled existing house, clad in sheet
metal, is a baroque composition of subtly disaligned axes
and half-round windows that cut into its broad cornice.
The architecture at the rear of the house is more intimate, with wood siding and a windowed veranda. Inside,
the architect experimented with axis shifting, mirror
images, and reflections. The ceiling of the enlarged living
room is hung with a carpet that hides a beam. Another
exquisite oriental rug climbs from the floor up onto a
couch.
C.C.

Literature: Wilfried Wang: *The architecture of
Peter Celsing*, 1996.

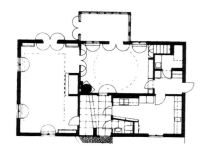

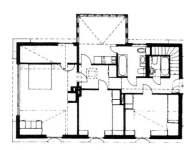

Drake Residence

Borlänge 1970

JAN GEZELIUS

Drake, a local public official, played an active role in the planning of his new home, but never allowed "the overly personal to distort the universality that is the foundation of every simple house." The lending regulations for new home construction at the time favored 1 1/2 stories, but architect Jan Gezelius proposed instead a slender two-story structure only five meters wide. The Drake residence established a new standard of quality for wooden architecture and was imitated regularly during the 1970s, but its graceful proportions never supplanted the stout 1 1/2-story house. The Japanese strain that runs through the home is evidence of the influence of Greene and Greene and other architects of the Arts and Crafts movement who were among Gezelius's favorites. The facades are clad in board-and-batten siding painted with red distemper with square, ocher-colored divided-light windows; the roof is covered with corrugated asbestos-cement sheeting. The interior is simply detailed and well lit throughout, with windows facing more than one direction in nearly every room to follow the course of the sun. C.C.

Literature: Claes Caldenby, Åsa Walldén: *Jan Gezelius*, 1989.

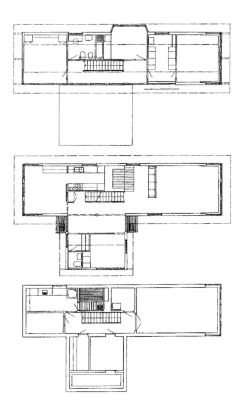

Garnisonen Office Complex

Stockholm 1964–72

A4

In the 1960s, the National Board of Public Building developed a Structuralist philosophy in collaboration with several large consulting firms. The Garnisonen ("Garrison") block, on the site of an old barracks area on Östermalm in Stockholm, became a proving ground for emerging concepts such as the standardized office building box, systematic planning, and generalization to expedite construction and facilitate later changes. This Garrison was to provide enough space to house all the offices of the National Board of Public Building under one roof. The scheme developed by the firm of A4 divided the complex into two enormous building blocks, one for individual office cells and one for open-plan offices. Each had its own service core with elevators, stairwell, and shafts, and each was 50 meters long—in terms of its modular system, 7 x 72 M = 504 M. This structure provided enough space for 2600 office workers. The sleek, unrelieved facade toward Karlavägen stretches over 300 meters, clad with bronze-toned anodized aluminum panels and flush strip windows to form a single, unbroken plane hovering above a ground-floor arcade that is punctured to afford views to a series of entrance courts. The interior of the complex is livelier, animated by adjective service towers, courtyards adorned with artwork, corridors with exposed mechanical systems, and abundant glossy primary colors.
C.C.

Literature: *Arkitektur* No. 1, 1972.

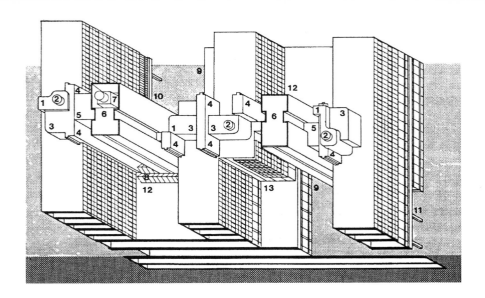

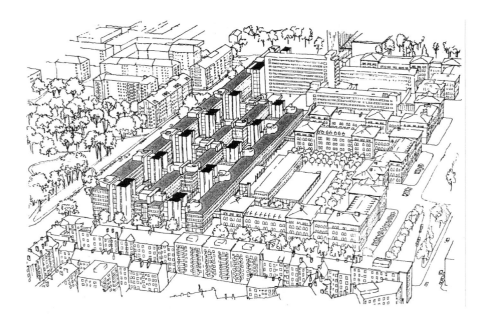

IBM Education Center

Lidingö 1968–70

ELLT

ELLT's Nordic Education Center for IBM in the Stockholm suburb of Lidingö is thoroughly and pedagogically planned, and a typical example of the 1960s philosophy of Structuralism. All of the center's functions were consolidated into a single building volume to preserve the natural beauty of the site and to create for conference participants the intense community atmosphere of a cruise ship. The structure is organized into three zones separated by high, brick-faced cavity walls. The central bay holds large lecture halls, while the flanking aisles contain offices, hotel rooms, a restaurant, and spaces for socializing. The building's prefabricated concrete frame is clad with auburn rusted steel. The rusty sheet metal and dark manganese brick was intended to age gracefully and allow the huge structure to conform over time to its natural surroundings. Red-lacquered detailing stands out sharply against this background of subdued earth tones.
C.C.

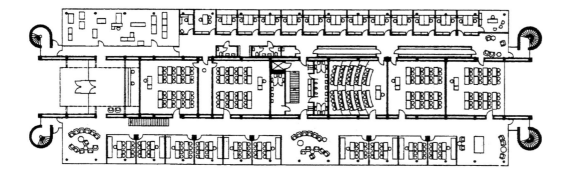

Arrhenius Laboratory

Stockholm 1968–70

CARL NYRÉN

The Arrhenius Laboratory, on the Frescati campus of Stockholm University, was Carl Nyrén's first prefabricated building. "The National Board of Public Building wanted prefab concrete elements that could be repeated infinitely and sandwich panel walls. It was the cheapest alternative. That generated the building. The goal was one column, one beam and one floor unit, one flight of stairs and a single railing unit. Of these components we could build the entire north campus, I thought." Outside, exposed shouldered columns illustrate the prospects for future expansion and give the building formal clarity and articulated vigor. The entrance facade offers a complete cross-section of the structural system, and can thus afford a look of its own without confounding the logic of the whole: aluminum panels, a continuous sun screen, and an arcade with a sloping glass ceiling that gives views to the interior. Mechanical systems are carried in the corridors and distributed to each room above dropped ceilings, allowing ample freedom to reorganize the office spaces.
C.C.

Literature: *Nyréns arkitektkontor AB*, Arkitekturmuseet 1989.

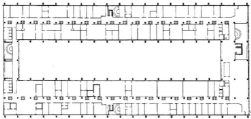

Malmö Gallery of Art

Malmö 1971–75

KLAS ANSHELM

Klas Anshelm won the commission for the Malmö Gallery of Art in an invited competition. He conceived the gallery as a simple concrete box—a large, open workshop. Visitors enter the space directly, with no intervening air lock, through a canted entrance with Anshelm's trademark doors, whose diagonal struts bulge to become handles. The rear facade folds in to accommodate an existing tree, a gesture Anshelm called "an irrational enhancement." The floor is made of raw two-inch-thick spruce decking. Exhibit partitions can be fastened directly to the floor and to a system of steel piping suspended from the ceiling. The space is lit by a large north-facing clerestory roof monitor that also raises the ceiling, and by a network of 550 small dome lights, each fit with a reflector and easily-changed lamp. In 1994, White arkitekter annexed the neighboring building, thus adding a new restaurant to the gallery.
C.C.

Literature: Per Helander, Per Qvarnström eds.:
Klas Anshelm/Malmö konsthall, 1994.

Student Union, Library, and Auditorium

Stockholm University
1974–82, 1997

RALPH ERSKINE

Ralph Erskine's distinctly public buildings for Stockholm University in Frescati provide a playful contrast to the campus's severe, Structuralist office and laboratory buildings. His library was the product of an architectural competition. From a barrel-roofed hall the library connects through an array of parallel corridors to the various departments in the South Building. On one side, the library's broad floor plates project through the facade to clutch aerial reading nests; on the other they enfold several stately old oaks. The student union provides students with a central meeting place. It is distinguished by the soaring extension of its roof to form a lofty canopy that covers the primary pedestrian axis. The opposite side presses into a hillside, where a great amphitheater-shaped auditorium, Aula Magna, designed by Erskine and dedicated in the fall of 1997, completes the campus. The auditorium is a variation and development of familiar Erskine themes—its freely-composed geometry, richly-patterned exterior brickwork, and the deep relief of its interior ceiling paneling. The lobby opens toward the hill and connects to the student union. Erskine also designed the neighboring law school building and the university's athletic complex.
C.C.

Literature: Mats Egelius: *Ralph Erskine, arkitekt*, 1988, *Arkitektur* No. 1, 1998.

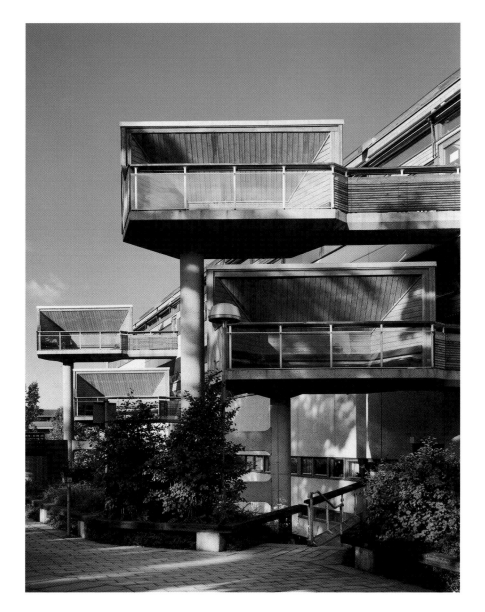

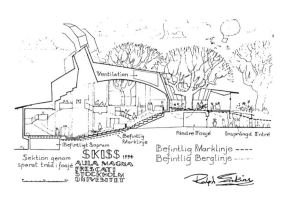

Sektion genom
sparat träd i foajé

SKISS 1994
AULA MAGNA
FRESCATI
STOCKHOLM
UNIVESITET

Ventilation

Befintlig Soprum   Befintlig
                    Marklinje

Nedre Foajé   Insprängd Entré

Befintlig Marklinje -----
Befintlig Berglinje ------

Ralph Erskine

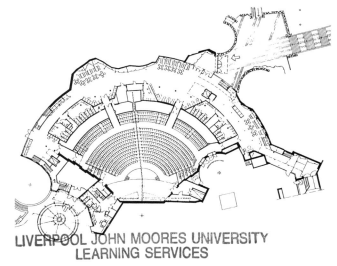

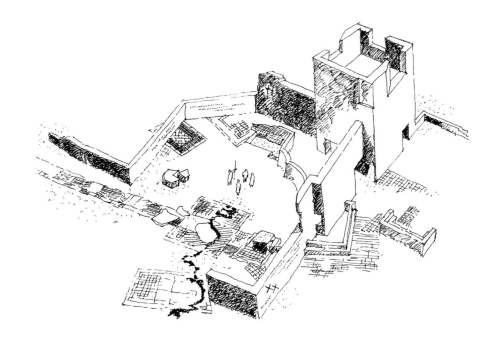

St. Birgitta's Church

Kalmar 1965–75

OVE HIDEMARK

St. Birgitta is a suburban church on the northern edge of Kalmar. Despite a late change of site, the building committee declined to abandon its plans for a massive brick building. Architect Ove Hidemark preserved the history of the project in the church's many layers, lending a fabricated antiquity to its modern suburban surroundings. A light superstructure of glass and steel rises from the fragments of the original brick building. The floor pattern suggests an archeological excavation that extends beyond the facades. There are traces of Celsing and Lewerentz, but also of older painted "country Baroque" churches and the Art Nouveau interiors of Erik Lundberg. The brick bell tower is a cubist sculpture crowned by an old-fashioned gold-leafed weathervane. These are the freely-woven fables of a sage historian recorded in the fabric of the building—and recounted in the church caretaker's guided tours.

Literature: Ove Hidemark: *Dialog med tiden*, 1991.

Eketorp Ancient Fortification Museum

Öland 1977–82

JAN GEZELIUS

When in the 1960s and '70s archaeologists excavated the ancient ruins at Eketorp, on the south end of the island of Öland, they discovered the remains of fortifications dating to three different centuries. It was decided that parts of the seventh-century fort would be reconstructed, including a ring wall lined on the inside with various small buildings. In the middle a chain of new buildings would be built to display the finds from the dig. Jan Gezelius' museum rises from an ancient foundation in the same materials used for the reconstructed buildings—a lofty thatch roof sheltering thick limestone walls. The roof is carried by arching laminated wood beams. The walls that would separate the row of spaces one from another were replaced by display cases top-lit through roof lanterns—there is no electric light in the museum. In 1996 Gezelius added an entrance building with larch facades and stone slab roof.
C.C.

Literature: Claes Caldenby, Åsa Walldén: *Jan Gezelius*, 1989.

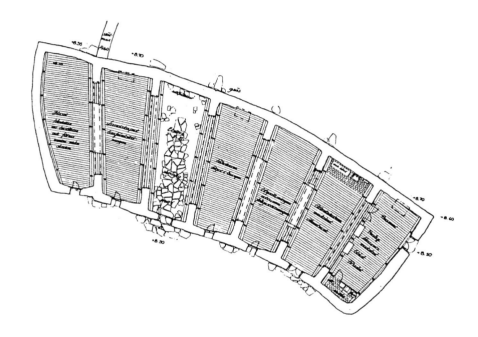

Cultural Center and Bank of Sweden

Stockholm 1966–76

PETER CELSING

When Stockholm's new commercial center was completed in the early 1960s, it was criticized both for its Modernist plan's preferential treatment of the automobile and for its lack of cultural components. The competition for a new cultural center and headquarters for the Bank of Sweden, won by Peter Celsing in 1966, put an end to the controversy. Celsing's scheme resolved the conflict between the Modern Hötorgscity district and the traditional urban structure of the adjacent lower Norrmalm: a composition of three distinctly different buildings with the Fine Arts Center's open Modernist screen facing one way and the more reserved masses of the bank and a new performing arts theater facing the other. The Fine Arts Center's Modernist concrete-and-glass curtain wall is interrupted only by the red-lacquered restaurant that projects from the rear toward the pedestrians on Drottninggatan.

Celsing's Bank of Sweden, finished in 1976, carries the weight of past traditions. The multi-layered facade is dominated by a rugged outer mantle of cleft black granite. Behind this framework, recessed windows are set in a sheath of the same stone smoothly sawn; the repeating pattern of windows seems to glide behind the rougher exterior. A few details break this well-articulated but otherwise unvarying order: the asymmetrically-placed entrance, which is sealed at night by stainless steel cylinders, and the contrasting heights of the facets cut from either corner. The interiors were richly worked in collaboration with various artists.
C.C.

Literature: *Arkitektur* No. 9, 1989, Wilfried Wang: *The architecture of Peter Celsing*, 1996.

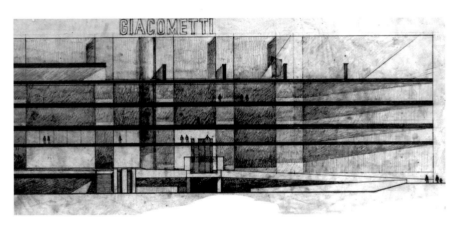

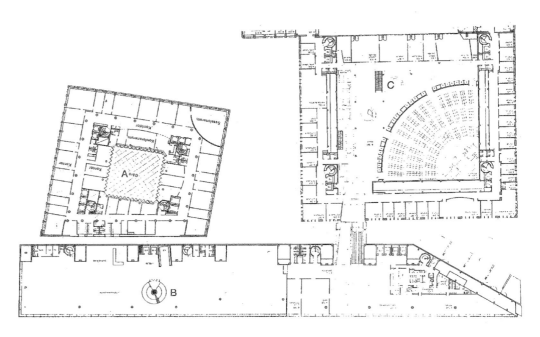

Nya Bruket Residential Development

Sandviken 1973–78

RALPH ERSKINE

Ralph Erskine's Nya Bruket apartments replaced a semi-urban neighborhood of antiquated worker housing. The new development preserved the original building scale and pattern of streets with partially enclosed blocks, but the number of units increased from 500 to 750. A few buildings rise above the two-story norm, including a six-story assisted-living home for retirees. Balconies cling loosely to stucco facades that are complemented with wood siding variously oriented and painted in different colors. Erskine combined thoughtfully designed outbuildings, playgrounds, benches, and fencing to create an intimate and eventful neighborhood environment. The area was built by a single developer at the close of the "Million Program," when the quality standards of large-scale development hit bottom; Nya Bruket was touted as an alternative prototype and a reminder of what might have been.
C.C.

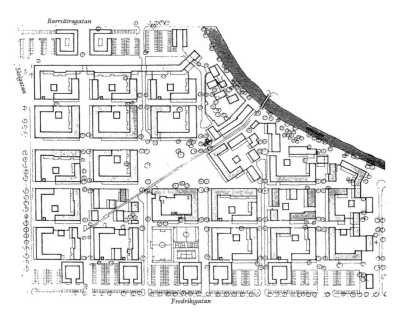

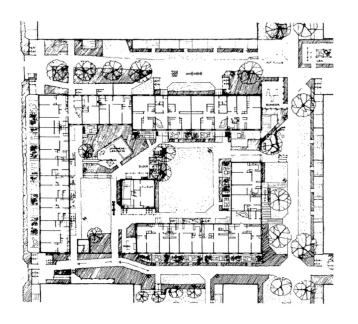

Parliament Building Renovation

Stockholm 1974–83

AHLGREN / OLSSON / SILOW

Sweden's transition from a bicameral to a single-chamber parliament in 1971 required a new space. Following an architectural competition, it was decided that Aron Johansson's 1907 Parliament Building and Bank of Sweden on Helgeandsholmen would be renovated. It was a historic decision that acknowledged the importance of adding to rather than replacing the past. Much of the Baroque Revival interior was restored to its original appearance. Ahlgren Olsson Silow's new parliamentary assembly hall was built on top of the amphitheater form of the bank building. On such a spectacular site, against the backdrop of the magnificent old interiors, the assembly hall is remarkably subdued, infused with a requisite informal tranquillity.
C.C.

Literature: *Arkitektur* No. 9, 1983.

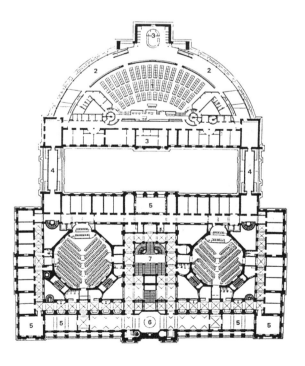

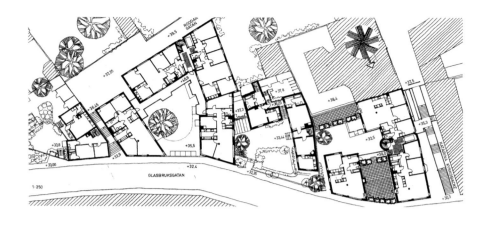

Drottningen Block

Stockholm 1985

BENGT LINDROOS

On the heights of Södermalm, overlooking the glittering bays and waterways of downtown Stockholm, amidst simple 18th-century buildings, lies a small block called Drottningen—"the Queen." Architect Bengt Lindroos fit the site with narrow, shed-roofed, intimately-scaled apartment buildings that enclose small courtyards. The apartments have square bedrooms and their kitchens are integrated into living rooms that open toward a breathtaking view. In the base of one of the buildings, the architect took the liberty of mounting his name plate to a concrete door cast from the mold of an old wooden panel door. Aside from that, there is nothing pastiche or Post-Modern about this place.
C.C.

Uppsala Public Library

Uppsala 1980–86

CARL NYRÉN

The site of an old brewery in downtown Uppsala was chosen as the location for the city's new public library. After an invited competition, Carl Nyrén was commissioned to design both the library and an apartment building. The former Structuralist emerged here as a Post-Modernist. He preserved two older apartment buildings along the pedestrian street side, incorporating them into the library but leaving little space for a prominent entrance. Nyrén exploited these constraints in the manner of Venturi—with a playful juxtaposition of architectural elements and contradictory scales. The library is announced by an exterior stair and a large rose window that presses through the roof. A narrow passage leads from the street to a small courtyard, where visitors confront the huge reading hall. The great height of this space, lit from above by an array of over-sized dormers, exemplifies the 1980s trend toward treating the library as a vital public space rather than a department store. Nyrén's carefully-detailed exterior brickwork, with periodic courses of black brick, pays homage to Uppsala Cathedral, whose walls are similarly patterned.
C.C.

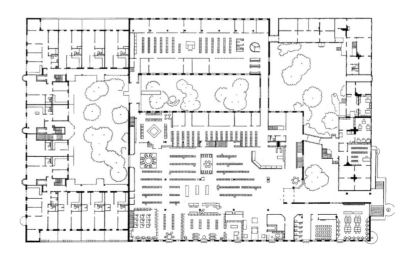

Olby Residence

Lerdala, Västergötland 1986–87

TORSTEN ASKERGREN

Torsten Askergren's Olby residence sits on a north slope with a view across the level landscape below. Its symmetrical massing is strongly reminiscent of Palladio: wings spread from a central gabled living room to detached outbuildings at either end. The building's form, like its oval and half-round windows, belongs to the decade of Post-Modernism. The owner is a furniture maker, and wood is the primary material of the house—wood carefully chosen and carefully treated. The windows have the kind of old-fashioned moldings that reflect varying nuances of light. The Olby residence is painted with traditional linseed-oil paint, calcimine distemper, egg-and-oil tempera, or lime-wash. It was awarded the 1988 Wood Building Award.
C.C.

Literature: *Arkitektur i trä*, 1988.

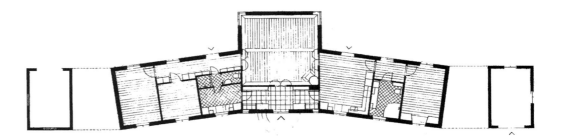

Källhagen Inn

Stockholm 1990

KRISTER BJURSTRÖM / BERTIL BRODIN

Almost no traces remain of the 1930 Stockholm Exhibition, but on its site, in a rural environment on the edge of the big city, and with a view over the waters of Djurgårds-brunnsviken, lies Bjurström and Brodin's Källhagen Inn. The inn conveys its exclusivity by striving to enrich the lives of its guests with timeless values: landscape, water, light, fire, and sequences of elegantly-finished rooms. The building combines Functionalism's crisply-rendered pale forms, fabric awnings, and delicate roof overhangs with Arts and Crafts elements such as broad chimneys and divided-light windows and the skewed plan and irregularities of Asplund's Snellman residence. Love Arbén designed the interiors. The grounds were landscaped by Sven-Olov Nyberg.
C.C.

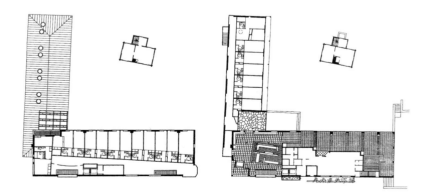

Clubhouse, Öijared
Country Club

Öijared, Lerum 1988

GERT WINGÅRDH

At Öijared Country Club, golfers tee off for the first green
from the roof of Gert Wingårdh's clubhouse, which is partially buried in a hill. The roof emerges from under its
grassy carpet as a wood-framed trellis that doubles as a
safety net along the edge of the hill and a sun screen for
the faceted south-facing glass facade. The interior rises
with the terrain in terraces of limestone slabs finished variously over the entire spectrum from cleft to polished. Far-
thest in, and highest up, the stone terraces dissipate in the
reflective surface of an indoor pool lined with deep blue
tile. Wingårdh used CAD software and a system of triangular modules in designing the building, and built it with prefabricated concrete elements. He named several sources
of inspiration, including Frank Lloyd Wright as interpreted
by Hans Erland Heineman in Wingårdh's home town of
Skövde.
C.C.

Literature: *Arkitektur* No. 2, 1989.

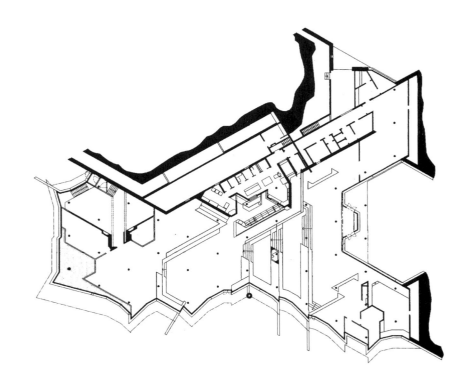

Lilla Bommen Office Complex

Gothenburg 1989

RALPH ERSKINE

Lilla Bommen, historically a gateway from the Göta River into Gothenburg's Harbor Canal, is today the endpoint of the city's main public axis, which begins at Götaplatsen. During the building boom of the late 1980s, this riverfront district was developed for office buildings. The most controversial among them was a tower for the giant construction corporation Skanska—the project was approved in large part because the company chose a famous architect. Ralph Erskine had long been interested in tall buildings as landmarks. He designed an extraordinary red-and-white-striped building that calls forth images of ships and navigational buoys. The tower culminates in a viewing deck with forms that jut out like smoke funnels and periscopes. The reclining lower wing of the building has the most successful of the many glass-roofed spaces built in Sweden in the '80s—it is at once lively and intimate, a far cry from the ubiquitous mirrored galleries and flamboyantly technical roof systems. Skanska's offices occupy the lower wing, while the tower was intended to be rented to smaller businesses that would be less hindered by its limited accessibility.
C.C.

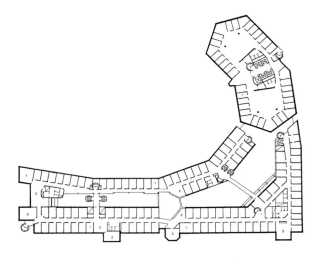

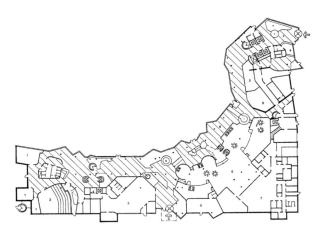

Astra Hässle Pharmaceutical Laboratory Complex

Mölndal 1989–96

GERT WINGÅRDH

When the successful pharmaceutical company Astra Hässle needed to expand its laboratories, it held an invited architectural competition. The winner, Gert Wingårdh, proposed a consolidation of the company property, which was scattered with diverse buildings. To improve proximity and social contact within the organization, he added tall, compact laboratory buildings with fully-glazed facades and exterior sun screens. Barrel roofs provide ample space for mechanical equipment, but also create an easily-recognizable image for the flourishing company. At one end of the complex, a crescent-shaped dining hall enfolds a small hill. The interior of the hall is a landscape of terraces with sunny corners that overlook the natural landscape outside. Wingårdh prioritized the dining hall's interior atmosphere—its facades form an expressionless shell for the more important meeting place inside. The office building is a funnel-shaped main entrance to the axis that now unifies the entire complex. Its north-facing facade, unaffected by solar heat gains, is a sleek sheet of glass; the wood paneling inside adds warmth to the building's metallic sheen.
C.C.

Literature: *Arkitektur* No. 2, 1995.

346

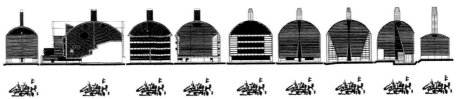

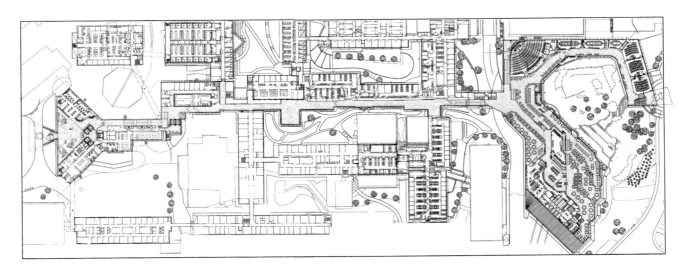

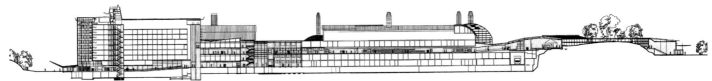

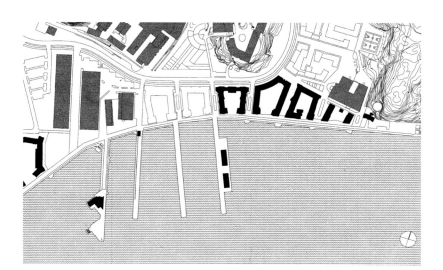

Eriksberg Mixed-use Development

Gothenburg 1989 to the present

ARKITEKTLAGET / WHITE ARKITEKTER
AND OTHERS

Until the 1970s, Gothenburg was among the most important harbors and shipyards in Europe. When the ship-building industries closed, the city was left with a five-kilometer stretch of riverfront property just across the river from downtown Gothenburg. Since the late 1980s, the area has undergone a gradual renewal. Eriksberg, its largest shipyard, has evolved into an urban neighborhood with an attractive location—a mixed-use development along the lines envisioned by the city planning department. In 1993, White arkitekter converted the enormous old machine hall into a hotel, preserving its steel frame and leaving a vast central space encircled by hotel floors. At the end of the western-most pier, Arkitektlaget's Pietro Raffone completely rebuilt a little workshop into a first-class restaurant in 1990. In 1991 the same firm designed a new headquarters for the harbor's tugboats on another pier. It neighbors a group of newly-constructed apartment buildings arranged in partially-enclosed courtyard blocks that present tall gables to the river. The apartments by Arkitektlaget for the property management company Eriksbergs Förvaltnings AB, under the engaged direction of Vice President Bengt Tengroth, are notable for their wealth of details, durable materials, and vivid interior color scheme.
C.C.

Literature: *Arkitektur* No. 2, 1995.

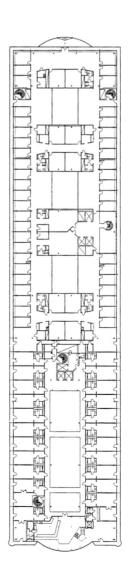

Vasa Museum

Stockholm 1981–90

GÖRAN MÅNSSON / MARIANNE DAHLBÄCK

The king's flagship Vasa sunk in Stockholm harbor on its catastrophic maiden voyage. The regal vessel was raised from the depths more than three hundred years later to be preserved in a temporary museum on the nearby island of Djurgården. After a huge open competition and subsequent repeat competition, the jury selected Hidemark and Månsson's proposal for a permanent ship's museum. Its informal massing and festive tent character seemed both typically Swedish and true to the site. The exterior is a collage of varied wood siding stained red and black with traditional red distemper and creosote. The building's dark coloring and diffuse contours are intended to meld with the natural surroundings and defer to the palatial Nordic Museum next door. The interior is dim, allowing the ship to shine. The architects are reluctant to speak of prototypes for the building, but were inspired during the design process by images from Le Corbusier, Scarpa, Lewerentz, Anshelm, Picasso, Matisse, and Brancusi.
C.C.

Literature: *Arkitektur* No. 8, 1990.

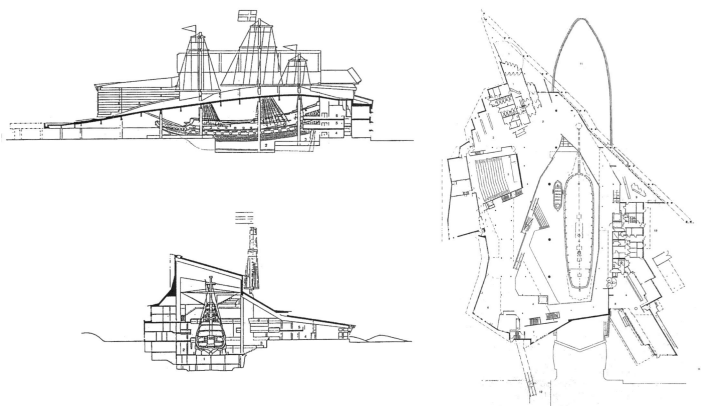

Stone Age Museum

Vuollerim 1990

MAF ARKITEKTKONTOR

When the inland ice receded from northern Sweden
nine thousand years ago, people settled at the conflu-
ence of two rivers called the Lilla Luleälv and Stora Luleälv. In the 1980s, a Stone Age settlement was excavated
here, and in 1990 MAF arkitektkontor built a small museum for the dig's finds. The site is shaped like an hour-
glass with a timeline of poles to represent its age in 500-
year increments. Visitors proceed from a reception area
to the exhibition space, then through a white wall into a
film viewing room. After the video presentation, the walls
open to reveal the dig site amidst a landscape of waterways. The materials are rustic—creosoted wood, local
stone, and moosehides to sit on; the form is Modern
and abstract.
C.C.

Literature: *Arkitektur* No. 1, 1992.

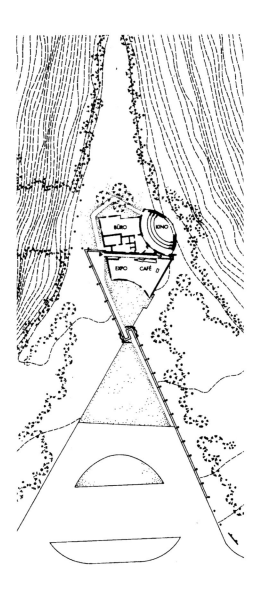

Sjökvarteren
Residential Development

Vadstena 1989–92

ERIK ASMUSSEN

In one of his few commissions outside the Anthroposophical Society, Erik Asmussen designed a number of apartments for the public housing corporation on the seaside in the small town of Vadstena after winning an invited competition. The building commission distinctly specified healthy buildings. The colorful exterior walls are of lightweight concrete rendered with lime stucco and lime-washed. The floors are of linoleum or oiled wood. The attic floors are insulated with cellulose fiber. The ventilation systems are simple and can be shut off. Each apartment has its own fireplace. The building form is characteristic for Asmussen: roofs with no overhang, glazed doors flanked by slant-topped windows, and deeply-colored stucco walls. Not satisfied by the narrow, two-story buildings' conformity to the scale of the old neighborhood, the local planning commission required a more conventional architecture than the architect intended.
C.C.

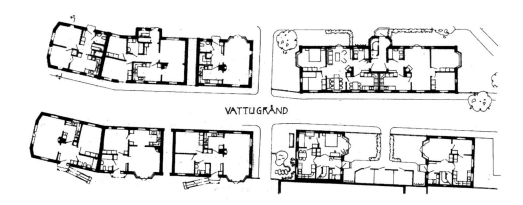

VATTUGRÅND

SEKTION "A-A"

SE-Banken Data Headquarters

Sundbyberg 1987–92

ROSENBERGS ARKITEKTKONTOR

In the late Eighties, Skandinaviska Enskilda Banken wanted to move its data unit, which required little outside communication, from downtown Stockholm to a cheaper and more effective location on the urban periphery. The site chosen was a commercial district at one of the city's northwestern entrance points. The company defined its objectives thus: "expressiveness, effectiveness, simplicity, and timeless elegance." Rosenbergs arkitektkontor designed a two-part complex. One building strikes an arc that follows the curve of the passing highway with a blank facade of white-glazed ceramic tile. Its generalized layout has double corridors lined with rows of office cells. Inside the arc, the second building is more loosely structured to accommodate spaces with special height and free-span requirements. It also includes a shopping gallery that offers the 1,600 relocated employees such restaurants and other amenities as an "edge city" can.
C.C.

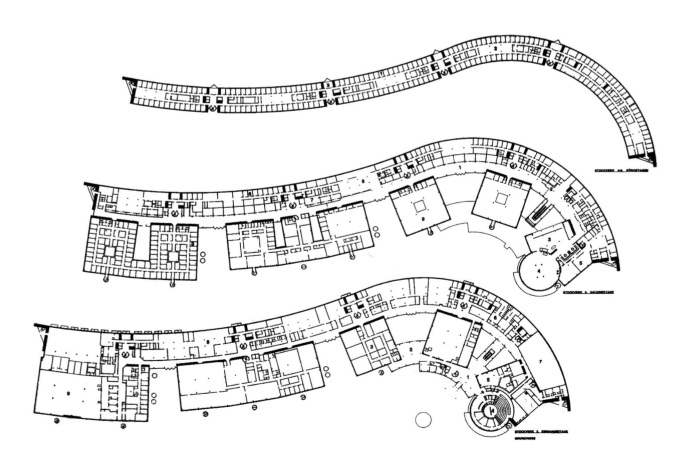

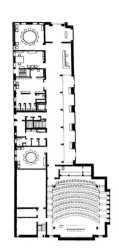

Nobel Forum

Solna 1983–93

JOHAN CELSING

Johan Celsing's Nobel Forum in Solna provides offices
and an assembly chamber for the deliberations of the
selection committee for the Nobel Prize in medicine. It
is aptly located on the grounds of the Karolinska Institute
of Medicine. The Forum is a narrow, red brick block with
appended auditorium, its material and plan form borrowed from neighboring institutional buildings. The interi-
or offers a sequence of spaces of varying intimacy and
increasing color. Most of the building's furnishings were
custom designed by Celsing's office. Its thorough detailing reveals an extensive familiarity with and understanding of architectural history. The details are never intrusive, but convey an aloofness that only heightens the
presence of the building.
C.C.

Literature: *Arkitektur* No. 8, 1993.

Zorn Textile Collection

Mora 1993

ANDERS LANDSTRÖM

After achieving great acclaim as a painter, Anders Zorn
returned to his rural home town of Mora in year to build a
home and raise a number of old timber structures gathered from various parts of the country. After the artist's
death, Ragnar Östberg designed a Zorn Museum for the
site, which was completed in 1939, when the entire property was bequeathed to the public. Zorn shared a National Romanticist's interest for folk culture with his wife,
Emma, who collected textiles. In 1992, a grant from the
County Labor Board made it possible to create a museum to display her many weavings and regional folk
costumes. Anders Landström's barn-like building is clad
in black creosoted wood with windows painted English
red. To protect the light-sensitive textiles, the windows
were fitted with wooden shutters that sift a soft light
between their boards, and contribute to the museum's
image as a simple repository. The reserved interiors
accent the objects on show.
C.C.

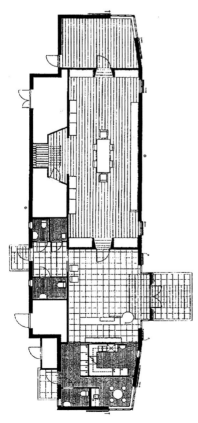

Concert Hall

Norrköping 1992–94

LUND & VALENTIN

Norrköping was the center of the Swedish textile industry until the 1960s. Then its riverside industrial landscape was abandoned and gradually began to be demolished. In the '70s, interest in conservation and adaptive re-use started to develop. In 1987, an urban planning competition was held for the area, and won by the Finnish architect Kai Wartiainen. After a conflict-filled process, a number of old buildings were remodeled by other architects. The most spectacular of these projects was the transformation of Ivar Tengbom's huge 1950s paper mill into a concert hall and convention center. Architects Lund & Valentin projected one bay toward the river for the restaurant. They inserted the round auditorium, which seats 1,300, into the old building as a free-standing steel cylinder. The interior's dramatic steelwork detailing has a Deconstructivist flair typical of the time.
C.C.

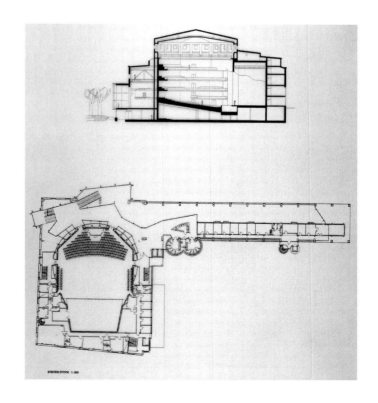

Stumholmen Island Redevelopment

Karlskrona 1989–97

HEDERUS MALMSTRÖM / BRUNNBERG &
FORSHED AND OTHERS.

The town of Karlskrona was long the chief port of call for
the Swedish navy. A large part of the naval base on the
island of Stumholmen has with time become available for
civilian use. In 1989, Stumholmen became the subject of
an architectural competition. The winning master plan
was by the firm of Hederus Malmström. Several new and
renovated apartment buildings were finished in time for
the 1993 housing exposition in Karlskrona. Brunnberg &
Forshed's building, called Kungshall, received particular
public acclaim for the familiar Classicism of its exterior
and for its square-roomed apartments furnished by Norr-
gavels möbler. Several of the buildings were part of a
Swedish Council for Building Research project to develop
architectural details, particularly windows and roof accou-
terments such as chimneys and access ladders. Hederus
Malmström's new Naval Museum, opened in 1997,
extends like a pier out over the water.
C.C.

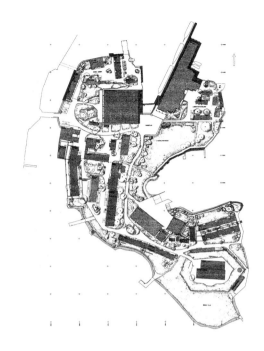

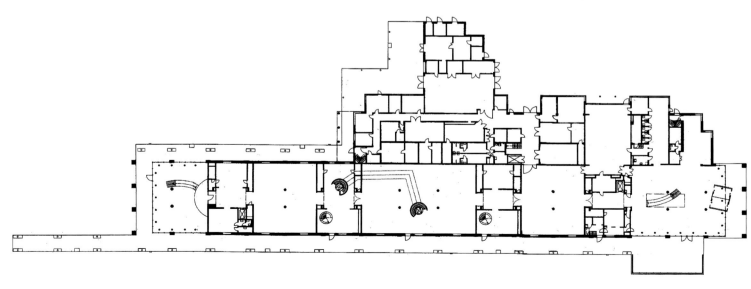

Western Norrland Regional Museum

Härnösand 1991–94

GUNNAR MATTSSON

Until the early 1990s, the county museum in Härnösand was merely a collection of old timber buildings in an open-air park exhibit. Then Gunnar Mattsson built a proper museum on the hill above the park—a large warehouse structure that includes exhibition space, workshops, and a café. The museum required a heavy, enclosed building, and three of its facades are of raw brick with simple, wood details painted with traditional red distemper. However, the carefully-worked wooden front, painted light gray, puts a more refined and festive face on the otherwise artless warehouse and ties it to the older buildings below. Its monumental portico alludes to the many formal Neoclassical buildings that adorn this seat of provincial government. The museum's repetitive structure is animated by a number of distinctly asymmetric features, such as the angling of the stair to the café and the lateral shift of the entrance. The windowless basement provides a reliquary for valuable objects, while the exhibition spaces above are light-filled and pleasant. The roof of the two-story central exhibition hall is carried by slim, paired columns and studded with great loosely-placed free-form dormers that funnel light into the space. Locals refer affectionately to it as "the hay fence."
C.C.

Göteborg University College of Business

Gothenburg 1989–95

ERSÉUS, FRENNING, SJÖGREN

Since 1952, the College of Business at Göteborg University had occupied a building designed by Carl Nyrén. Over the years, the growing college had spread into various neighborhood buildings. An invited competition in 1989 awarded Erséus, Frenning, Sjögren the commission to expand Nyrén's building to fill the entire city block. Their scheme positions a series of distinct volumes along the perimeter, one for each department in the college; the lecture halls' lobbies face a more unified courtyard on the interior of the block. On the most public corner, an imposing cylinder houses the library and principal auditorium. The library's reading room is reminiscent of Asplund's Stockholm Public Library, and turns an enormous window on the park opposite. The addition's exemplary limestone-faced Modernism radiates the self-assurance of its institution. Substantial private donations provided for a high quality of materials and detailing. C.C.

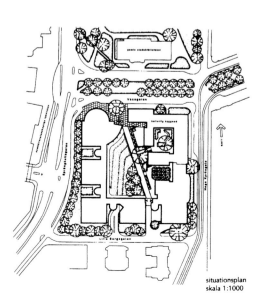

situationsplan
skala 1:1000

Understenshöjden Residential Development

Stockholm 1990–95

HSB:S ARCHITECTS OFFICE

The initiative for Understenshöjden, a residential development in the south Stockholm suburb of Björkhagen,
came from a group of people with an enthusiasm for ecological building. They were turned to HSB, the National
Federation of Tenants' Savings and Building Societies,
for the project's realization. HSB's own architectural staff
planned forty-four tenant-owned row houses with extensive resident input and personalized design. They are
perched on column foundations to minimize the need for
blasting of the bedrock. The homes are heated with solar
collectors fortified by a pellet-fired furnace located in a
common utility shed. Separation toilets extract urine for
use as agricultural fertilizer. Greywater is cleaned in an
on-site biological treatment system. Tenants sort their
household garbage and compost food scraps from the
kitchen. Construction materials were limited to products
that have been thoroughly tested for their impact on
human health: the wood frame is insulated with cellulose
fiber, the interior painted with egg-and-oil tempera and
linseed-oil paint, the exterior stained gray with iron vitriol,
and the roof covered with clay tiles. The architecture is
traditional with hints of 1920s Classicism.
C.C.

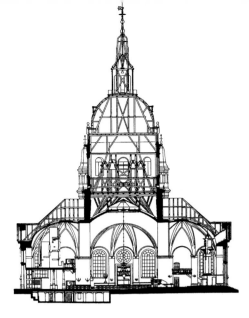

St. Catherine's Church Restoration

Stockholm 1990–98

OVE HIDEMARK

The central-plan Church of St. Catherine was built on Södermalm in Stockholm in 1656–95 by Jean de la Vallée. Its original massing formed a pyramid with a relatively low cupola. The great city fire of 1723 destroyed the church, and it was rebuilt by Göran Josuae Adelcrantz with a cupola raised on an octagonal drum. In 1990 the church was again struck by a fire that destroyed the woodwork and ravaged the interior, though the portable furnishings could be saved. Ove Hidemark's restoration returned St. Catherine's to its prominent position in the urban fabric. Hidemark emphasized the importance of relying on original materials and construction methods: the cupola is an authentic masonry structure and the roof framing has the same dimensions as the original. For the interior, however, he chose a more liberal interpretation as a contribution from our own time.
C.C.

364

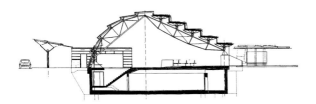

Nils Ericson Bus Terminal

Gothenburg 1996

NIELS TORP

The Nils Ericson Bus Terminal is the only part realized of
a planned extensive new transportation complex adjacent
to the old Central Train Station in Gothenburg. The competition for the project held in the late 1980s was won by
Norwegian architect Niels Torp. His bus terminal is a long
pier that separates the train yard from the turnaround for
buses. The long and narrow interior space is divided into
a zone for movement punctuated by small free-standing
shops and a zone with seating areas for waiting at the
gates of the various buses. The roof is a high-tech asymmetric steel-and-glass structure, while wood and stone
dominate the lower region of the space, making it at
once comfortable, robust, and precise.
C.C.

Literature: *Arkitektur* No. 8, 1996.

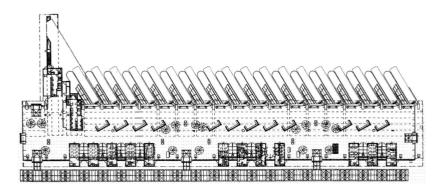

Swedish Museums of Modern Art and Architecture

Stockholm 1990–98

RAFAEL MONEO

The international invited competition for the new national Museums of Modern Art and Architecture on the island of Skeppsholmen in central Stockholm was won by Spanish architect Rafael Moneo. His scheme is a compact, top-lit volume partially excavated from the bedrock to suit the natural terrain and the old navy buildings that surround the site. The bearing idea is a square space with a pyramid roof and a chimney-like lantern that animates the roof landscape. Moneo brings together rooms of various size in a labyrinth, dividing them into three groups with openings that give views over the Sound. The restaurant occupies the best spot, hanging like a shelf along the side toward the water. The old navy's exercise hall that in the past served as the Museum of Modern Art now provides exhibit space for the Museum of Architecture. The administration building for the Museum of Architecture is a white-rendered Functionalist coda at the end of the composition and Moneo's tribute to Swedish Functionalism.
C.C.

Literature: *Arkitektur* No. 2, 1998, *Moderna Museet och Arkitekturmuseet/The Museum of Modern Art and the Museum of Architecture*, 1998.

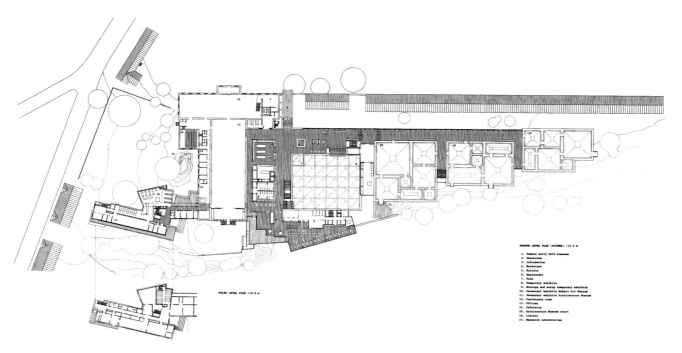

THIRD LEVEL PLAN +18.4 m

FOURTH LEVEL PLAN (ACCESS) +14.3 m

1. Common entry both museum
2. Checkroom
3. Information
4. Bookstore
5. Toilets
6. Restaurant
7. Void
8. Temporary exhibits
9. Storage and setup temporary exhibits
10. Permanent exhibits Modern Art Museum
11. Permanent exhibits Architecture Museum
12. Conference room
13. Offices
14. Cafeteria
15. Architecture Museum court
16. Library
17. Research laboratories

A4 ARKITEKTKONTOR

The A4 group of architects was started in 1957 by Tage Hertzell (b. 1928), Lennart Lundström (b. 1930), John Sjöström (b. 1931), and Ragnar Uppman (b. 1929). Sjöström was a professor at KKH, 1965–95. Uppman became a professor at KTH in 1963. The four combined to produce an office that led the development of Structuralism in Sweden together with the National Board of Public Building. In 1978 they merged with ELLT to become Coordinator arkitekter.

Important works. Row houses in the Omega block, Vällingby, 1958. Karlshamn oil factories, starting in 1958. Visby District Courthouse, 1962. Forum student apartments, Stockholm, 1962–68. Garnisonen office complex, Stockholm, 1963–71. Umeå University, starting in 1964. Sturup Airport, 1968–72. Landvetter International Airport, outside Gothenburg, 1972–77.

RUDOLF ABELIN (1864–1961)

Abelin was a landscape architect and pomologist. He studied landscape architecture in Denmark. Designed and built the Norrviken Gardens outside Båstad, 1906–28, in addition to a number of landscaping projects for large estates, primarily in Södermanland and Östergötland Counties. The Classical style of his work made frequent reference to the Italian Baroque. Abelin also started a landscaping school for women at Norrviken.

CARL-AXEL ACKING (born 1910)

Degree in Interior Architecture from the Higher College of Applied Art, Stockholm, 1934. Then made the transition to designing buildings. Internship at KF:s arkitektkontor. Worked for Gunnar Asplund, where he designed the furniture for the Gothenburg City Hall extension.

Important works. He has designed several furniture series for Svenska Möbelfabrikerna, Nordiska Kompaniet department stores, and the Swedish Cooperative Union and Wholesale Society (KF). Some of his more important interiors are the Malmen Hotel in Stockholm (1951), the Swedish Embassy in Tokyo (1959), Suite of rooms for the prime minister in the Government Office Building in Stockholm (1962), Continental Hotel in Stockholm (1962). In 1955 he was one of the principal architects of the H55 exhibition in Helsingborg. Head teacher in the Furniture and Interior Design Department of the University College of Arts, Crafts, and Design in Stockholm, 1947–57.

HAKON AHLBERG (1891–1984)

KTH, 1914; KKH, 1917. Worked in the office of Ivar Tengbom 1914–17. Taught Ornamentation at KTH, 1918–28. Own architectural practice, 1917–73. Palace Architect at Gripsholm Palace, 1933–70. Founder and Chairman of SAR, 1936–45. Dean at KKH, 1954–62. Editor of *Arkitektur*, 1921–22 and *Byggmästaren*, 1922–24. Ahlberg was a central figure among Swedish architects who united humanism and rationalism in his architecture.

Important works. Brännkyrka Rectory och Parish Hall, Stockholm, 1917–20. Church in Stora Sköndal, Stockholm, 1927. Mälarhöjden Chapel, Stockholm, 1928. Masonic Boarding School in Blackeberg, Stockholm, 1928–31. Hjorthagen housing development, Stockholm, 1934–40 (with Leif Reinius). Art Industry Pavilion at the Gothenburg Exhibition of 1923. Brunnsvik College, 1928–1950. Art gal-

Ahlberg

lery in Falun, 1936. Sidsjön Mental Hospital, Sundsvall, 1939. Malmberget Church, 1945. University Hospital in Maracaibo, Venezuela, 1946–54. LKAB Mining Company main facility, including an iron dressing plant and production office, Kiruna, 1953–60. LKAB office building, Stockholm, 1960.

Writings. *Modern Swedish Architecture* (1924). *Gunnar Asplund Arkitekt* (1943).

Further reading. Eva Rudberg, Eva Paulsson (ed.), *Hakon Ahlberg arkitekt och humanist* (1994).

AHLGREN OLSSON SILOW ARKITEKTER

AOS was founded in 1950 by Magnus Ahlgren (born 1918), Torbjörn Olsson (born 1916), and Sven Silow (born 1918). The office produced an extensive number and a wide variety of buildings. Silow was a professor at KTH, 1964–81. In the 1980s a few of the younger associates opened their own office under the name of Andersson Landström AOS ARC.

Important works. Sparbankernas Bank building, Stockholm, 1963. Swedish Embassy in Madrid, 1963. County Administration Building, Örebro, 1967. Sheraton Hotel, Stockholm, 1971. County Administration Building, Linköping, 1973. City Government Administration Building, Gävle, 1973. Haga 'Copper Tents,' Solna, 1977. Renovation of the Parliament Building, Stockholm, 1983. Postal Museum, Stockholm, 1986.

ERIK AHLSÉN (1901–88) AND TORE AHLSÉN (1906–91)

The Ahlsén brothers stuck together throughout their long and productive lives. Both studied civil engineering at KTH and, after building site apprenticeships, went to work for KF:s arkitektkontor—Erik in 1926, Tore in 1929. Each took time off from work periodically to study architecture at KTH—Erik graduating in 1933 and Tore in 1934. Tore also worked for Gunnar Asplund, 1933–36. In 1936 they opened their own office together, though Erik continued to work at KF until 1946. The Ahlsén brothers worked primarily with apartments, town centers, and assembly halls. They often collaborated with artists, and their sensuous and straightforward Functionalism, which they called 'sensual realism,' had a profound effect on post-war Swedish architecture.

Important works. Kristianstad City Hall, 1936–40. Årsta town center, outside Stock-

Erik & Tore Ahlsén

holm, 1944–54. Torsvik row houses, Lidingö, 1945–46. PUB department store, Stockholm, 1948–60. Uppsala City Hall, 1949–64. Apartments in Kortedala, Gothenburg, 1951–57, and in Biskopsgården, Gothenburg, 1954–57. Krämaren department store and mixed-use development, Örebro, 1955–63. Örebro Civic Center, 1957–65. Student Union, Uppsala, 1956–66. Apartments in Henriksdalsberget, Nacka, 1946–72. National Institute for Building Research, Gävle, 1972–76.

Further reading. *Arkitektur 6/1980.*

NILS AHRBOM (1905–1997)

KTH, 1927. Professor of Architecture at KTH, 1942–63. Director of the National Board of Public Building's Development Department, 1963–67. Palace Architect at Vadstena Palace, 1968–85. Architectural practice with Helge Zimdal, 1932–50; own practice 1950–80. Editor of *Byggmästaren*, 1934–36. Ahrbom was a rationalist and Functionalist, an intellectually keen critic and a skilled pedagogue.

Important works. Sveaplan Girls' High School, Stockholm, 1935. Eriksdal School, Stockholm, 1937. Skanstull High School, Stockholm, 1943. Linköping Museum, 1939. KTH expansion, 1944–61. Swedish Embassy buildings in Tokyo (1959), Ankara (1961), Beijing (1971), and Cairo (1976).

Writings. *Radhusets planläggning och ekonomi* (1953), *Svensk strukturalism* (1980), *Arkitektur och samhälle* (1983).

OSVALD ALMQVIST (1884–1950)

KTH, 1908; KKH, 1910; together with Asplund and Lewerentz was one in a group of students who started the Klara School, 1910–11. Worked for Ivar Tengbom, 1910–11. Almqvist was a versatile designer who undertook a variety of commissions including furniture, street furniture, and buildings, as well as master plans and urban development studies. He played a central role in an important housing study, the results of which were published in 1921 as *Praktiska och hygieniska bostäder*. He contributed to the standardization of kitchen furnishings in Sweden, 1922–34. Stockholm Parks Superintendant, 1936–38, and City Planning Architect in Södertälje, 1940–48.

Important works. Together with Gustaf Linden, Almqvist designed several homes in Stockholm between 1911 and 1913 and the Standard Hotel in Nyköping in 1913. His independent works include a highly-acclaimed competition proposal for the Woodland Cemetery in Stockholm in 1915. Master plan and worker housing in Bergslagsbyn, Borlänge (1915) for Stora Kopparbergs Bergslags AB in Domnarvet, 1915–20. Hydroelectric power plants at Forshuvudforsen (1917–21) and Hammarforsen and Krångforsen (1925–28). Row houses, furniture, and lighting for the Stockholm Exhibition of 1930. Master plans for many communities.

Further reading. Björn Linn, *Osvald Almqvist. En arkitekt och hans arbete* (1967).

ANCKER GATE LINDEGREN ARKITEKTER

Stig Ancker (1908–92), Bengt Gate (1909–88), and Sten Lindegren (1906–89) started an architectural practice together in 1936. The office maintained a careful Modernist precision that often incorporated brick facades. They designed a number of significant housing developments.

Important works. Apartments in Torsvikshöjden, Lidingö, 1943. Anckerbyn summer cottages, Haverdal, 1954. Gröna gatan housing, Uppsala, 1955. Norra Kvarngärdet housing, Uppsala, 1963.

SVEN-INGVAR ANDERSSON (born 1927)

Landscape Architect. Professor at the Royal Academy of Fine Arts School of Architecture in Copenhagen, 1963–94. As a pedagogue, author, and practicing landscape architect, Andersson has renewed and developed the art of landscaping in Scandinavia, emphasizing its poetic and artist aspects.

Important works. Several competition entries, such as Karlsplatz in Vienna, 1971. Realized projects include the Tête Defense in Paris, 1984; Brunnspark in Ronneby, 1985–87; and Hamntorget in Helsingborg, 1995. Andersson has also restored several historically significant gardens, such as Damsgård Grove in Bergen, 1983, and Uranienborg on Ven, 1992. His artistry has been rewarded with both Scandinavian and international citations, including the Bavarian Academy of Fine Arts' Sckell Ring (1988).

Writings. Andersson is a frequent writer, author of, among other books, *C Th Sørensen — en havekunstner* (1993), written together with S Høyer.

Further reading. S Høyer, A-M Lund, S Møldrup: *Tilegnet Sven-Ingvar Andersson* (1994).

KLAS ANSHELM (1914–1980)

CTH, 1940. Interned with Hans Westman in Lund, 1942–45, then with Wejke and Ödeen in Stockholm. Started own architectural practice in Lund in 1947. Anshelm is known for his simple, easily-constructed objects, but also for his innovative spirit. He designed about a hundred buildings, many of them major institutions. Among them a few materials and details recur frequently: load-bearing walls of brick, square window openings, and flat roofs. His approach to architecture was related to that of Sigurd Lewerentz, whose final home Anshelm designed.

Important works. Lund University, 1948–78. Rausing residence, Lund, 1953. Lund Art Gallery, 1954–57. Faculty of Medicine, Gothenburg, 1954–59. Chalmers University of Technology, Gothenburg, 1960–63. Lund University of Technology, 1960–69. Lund City Hall, 1960–68. Sjömansgården, Malmö, 1969. Oljelund residence, Gothenburg, 1972. Ararat straw house, Stockholm, 1976.

Further reading. *Arkitektur* 7/1979, Per Qvarnström, *Klas Anshelm arkitekt* (1998).

ARKEN ARKITEKTER

When Ralph Erskine began to scale back the scope of his work in 1981, twelve of his former employees founded Arken arkitekter. In 1998 the office has six partners and continues to a great extent Erskine's approach to architecture and a belief in small scale development that blends a variety of functions in an urban atmosphere.

Important works. Varmfronten block in Skarpnäcksstaden, Stockholm, 1987. Cityterminalen, Stockholm, 1989. Bro Town Center, Upplands Bro, 1994. Åkroken College campus, Sundsvall, 1997.

ARKITEKTLAGET

Three former employees of K-konsult in Gothenburg founded Arkitektlaget in 1979 as an member-owned architectural office. The firm has had a number of large commissions in the development of the North Shore of the Göta River in Gothenburg. Their work is characterized by rich detailing and the expressive use of color. In the early 1990s the firm divided its business into several smaller offices.

Important works. Bohuslän Regional Museum, Uddevalla, 1983. Apartments in Haga, Gothenburg, 1984–90. Westra Piren restaurant, Gothenburg, 1990. Apartments in Eriksberg, Gothenburg, 1992. Wallenberg Hall, Gothenburg, 1993.

ARKSAM

Started in 1973 by a group of former classmates at KTH, Arksam was one of the first collectively-owned architectural offices. They began with inventory and conservation programming assignments. The firm has worked primarily with restorations, but has had a few small new construction projects. One of its partners, Jan Lisinski (born 1947), succeeded Hidemark as professor in the art of restoration at KKH.

Important works. Restoration of Sven Markelius' 1935 apartment hotel at John Ericssonsgatan, Stockholm, 1988–91, and of Nils Ahrbom and Helge Zimdal's 1936 Sveaplan Girls' High School, 1994–96. Apartment building on Stumholmen, Karlskrona, 1993.

Further reading. *Arkitektur* 5/1986, Lennart Holm, *Rita hus* (1990).

ERIK ASMUSSEN (born 1913)

Born in Copenhagen, where he studied at the Technical College, finishing in 1936 and going on to a year at the Royal Academy of Fine Arts. Interned in Denmark with Flemming Lassen and Kaj Fisker. Emigrated to Sweden in 1939. Worked for David Helldén, Ahrbom and Zimdahl, for Nils Tesch from 1942 until 1960. That year he began his own architectural practice with the St. Christopher School, a Waldorf school his own children attended in Stockholm. Asmussen became the architect of the Swedish Anthroposophical Movement, living and working since 1976 in Järna, where its seminary lies, all of its buildings designed by Asmussen. He has built a number of Waldorf schools in Sweden and abroad. He has succeed in giving Anthroposophical architecture a distinctive character influenced by Tesch's intimate Classicism and traditional Nordic wooden construction.

Important works. St. Christopher School in Bromma, Stockholm, 1965–67 and later. Rudolf Steiner Seminary buildings, Järna, starting in 1973. Vidarkliniken health care center, Järna, 1985–92. Cultural Center, Järna, 1992. Waldorf schools (starting in 1972) in Järna, Norrköping, Nyköping; Odense, Vejle, Danmark; Düsseldorf and Hannover, Germany; and Fredrikstad, Norway. Apartments in Vadstena, 1992.

Further reading. *Arkitektur* 6/1984, Gary J. Coates, *Erik Asmussen, architect* (1997).

GUNNAR ASPLUND (1885–1940)

KTH, 1909. Was one in a group of students who started the Klara School in protest against the conservatism of the faculty at KKH, 1910–11. Study trips to Italy, 1913–14, and Denmark, 1918. Editor of *Arkitektur*, 1917–20. Professor of Architecture at KTH, 1931. Asplund quickly emerged as a leader of his generation and achieved a unique position in Scandinavian architecture during the 1920s. He was a main source of inspiration for the Classicism of the Twenties and the breakthrough of Functionalism; in the Thirties he was a leader in the moderation of the Modernist vocabulary toward a greater continuity with architectural traditions.

Important works. Intermediate school in Karlshamn, 1912–18. Won the competition for the Woodland Cemetery in Stockholm together with Lewerentz, 1915; his early works at the cemetery were the Chapel of the Forest (1918–20) and a utilitarian building (1922–24). Competition proposal for Götaplatsen in Gothenburg, 1917. Residential kitchen design for the 1917 Home Exhibition in Stockholm. Snellman residence, Djursholm, 1917–18. Lister District Courthouse, Sölvesborg, 1917–21. Skandia Cinema, Stockholm, 1922–23. Karl Johan School, Gothenburg, 1915–24. Competition proposal for a pavilion for the Paris Expo of 1925. Stockholm Public Library, 1920–27. Chief architect for the Stockholm Exhibition of 1930. Bredenberg department store, Stockholm, 1933–35. State Bacteriological Laboratory, Stockholm, 1933–37. Gothenburg City Hall, 1913–37. The architect's own summer house at Stennäs, Sorunda, 1937. Crematorium, Woodland Cemetery, Stockholm. 1935–40.

Further reading. Holmdahl et al (ed.), *Gunnar Asplund arkitekt 1885–1940* (1943). Stuart Wrede, *The Architecture of Erik Gunnar Asplund* (1980). Claes Caldenby & Olof Hultin (ed.), *Asplund* (1985). "Asplund 1885–1940", *Arkitekturmuseets Årsbok 1985*. Christina Engfors, *EG Asplund. Arkitekt, vän och kollega* (1990).

SVEN BACKSTRÖM (1903–1992)

KTH, 1929. Worked at KF:s arkitektkontor, 1929–32; for a short time with Le Corbusier, 1932–33; and for Hakon Ahlberg, 1934–35.

Asplund

Assistant at KTH under Gunnar Asplund during the 1930s. Editor of *Fyrtiotalets svenska bostad* (*The Swedish Home of the Forties*), 1950. Palace Architect at Strömsholm Palace, 1951–78. Architectural practice together with Leif Reinius, 1936–92. See also Leif Reinius.

WALTER BAUER (1912–1994)

Studied landscape architecture in Sweden, Denmark, and Austria. Worked for City of Stockholm Parks Department in the early Forties. Started own practice in 1946. Bauer was responsible for a long series of highly-acclaimed restorations of historically-significant palace and manor house grounds, including the Tessin Palace (1965), Drottningholm Palace Gardens (1969), and Forsmark Estate (1978). The Rosendal Terrace gardens on Djurgården, Stockholm, 1969. Riksplan, the square before the Parliament Building, Stockholm, 1985. A number of projects in other countries.

ELIS BENCKERT (1881–1913)

KTH, 1904. Internship in Ragnar Östberg's office. Benckert was considered the most promising architect of his generation. During his short professional career he established one of the most uncompromising expressions of the early-20th-century strive for simplification and craftsmanship.

Important works. Lagercrantz residence, Djursholm, 1910. Exhibition buildings in Arvika, 1911. Renovation of Skuru Castle, 1911. Thiel residence, Saltsjö-Duvnäs, 1912. Norrgården, Ägnö, 1912–13. De Jounge residence, Gävle, 1913.

ERIK BERGLUND (born 1921)

University College of Arts, Crafts and Design; Carl Malmsten's Workshop School. Started designing furniture for Malmsten in 1943. Became an academic advisor for the Swedish Society of Industrial Design's Bo-skola (School of Home Design) in 1945. Berglund conducted the first functional survey of furniture in 1948, studying beds and later tables, chairs, and cabinets. In the Fifties he developed the first standardized methods of testing furniture, and worked on a system for objectively describing color. Secretary of the Institute for Informative Labelling's Furniture Committee (VDN), 1953–67, which led to the VDN furniture labelling system. Founded *Möbelinstitutet* in 1967. The VDN label was replaced in 1972 by the 'Möbelfakta' approval label, which Berglund also developed. He became an honorary doctor of technology at CTH in 1985.

CARL BERGSTEN (1879–1935)

KTH, 1901; KKH, 1903. Taught at the Klara School, 1910–11. Editor of *Arkitektur*, 1912–15; later contributed numerous articles to that journal. Director of NK department store's furniture department, 1917–21. Became professor at KKH in 1931. Strong inspiration from turn-of-the-century Vienna combined with an indefatigable sense of artistic integrity to give Bergsten's early work an *avant-garde* character. With the influx of Classicism into Swedish architecture about 1910, he found a way to give expression to his buildings' reinforced-concrete structure and thus to the rationalism that was a fundamental element in his approach to architecture.

Important works. Exhibition buildings, Norrköping, 1906. St. Olof's School, Norrköping, 1903–08. Bank building for Skandinaviska kreditbanken, Norrköping, 1906–08. Hjorthagen Church, Stockholm, 1904–09. Liljevalch Art Gallery, Stockholm, 1913–16. Swedish pavilion for the World's Fair in Paris, 1925. Interior of the royal ship M/S Kungsholm, 1927–29. Gothenburg City Theater, 1927–35.

Further Reading. Bengt OH Johansson, *Carl Bergsten och svensk arkitekturpolitik under 1900-talets första decennium* (1965).

BJURSTRÖM & BRODIN ARKITEKTER

Krister Bjurström (born 1948) and Bertil Brodin (born 1939), both one-time employees of Carl Nyrén, started their own office in 1987. They share space and service facilities with three other architecture firms in the Architect Building at Götgatan 18 in Stockholm. They have had a variety of commissions, much of their work in the spirit of graceful simplicity that characterizes Nyrén's architecture.

Important works. Långholmen Junior College (renovation of an old prison), Stockholm, 1990. Källhagen Inn, Stockholm, 1990. Duplex homes, Saltsjöbaden, 1990. Scheele Laboratory at the Karolinska Medical Institute, Solna, 1997. Djäkneberget restaurant, Västerås, 1997.

Backström & Reinius

HOLGER BLOM (1906–96)

Blom was both a landscape architect and an architect. Educated in Stockholm, he interned in Stockholm, Amsterdam, and Paris. Worked for the City of Stockholm Planning Department before being named the city's Parks Superintendant in 1938—a position he held until retiring in 1971. Blom was a gifted strategist, and during his long career as a public official he thoroughly expanded Stockholm's system of parks. His work was informed by Functionalist theory and gave rise to a new style, known as the 'Stockholm School' of park design. Blom was also known as an enthusiastic debator of urban planning issues.

FERDINAND BOBERG (1860–1946)

KTH, 1882; KKH, 1884. Internship with Isak Gustav Clason. Boberg was a key figure in the renewal of Swedish architecture in the 1890s. He was particularly influenced by the work of Henry Hobson Richardson. Boberg was one of the country's most highly-acclaimed architects at the turn of the century, having developed a personal style based on the interplay between large unadorned surfaces and imaginitive ornamentation in shallow relief. He was a gifted designer who produced a vast number of buildings as well as furniture and utilitarian objects. In 1915 he retired from architecture to concentrate on making documentary drawings of historical monuments and landmark environments.

Boberg

Important works. Several buildings at the Stockholm Exhibition of 1897. Fire station in Gävle, 1889–91. Rosenbad commercial complex, Stockholm, 1899–1902. Central Post Office, Stockholm, 1899–1906. Thiel Gallery, Stockholm, 1904–05. Various commissions for Stockholm's electical, water, and gas authorities in the 1890s and 1900s. Central Post Office, Malmö, 1905. Church of the Revelation, Saltsjöbaden, 1910–13. Nordiska Kompaniet (NK) department store, Stockholm, 1912–15. Pavilion at the 1909 Exhibition in Stockholm. Pavilion at the 1914 Baltic Exhibition in Malmö.

Further reading. *Bobergiana* (1958). Ulf Sörenson, *Ferdinand Boberg. Arkitekten som konstnär* (1992). Ann Walton, *Ferdinand Boberg—Architect. The complete work* (1994).

ULLA BODORFF (1913–82)

Studied landscape architecture in Sweden and in England. Worked during the 1930s for the City of Stockholm Parks Department. One of the nation's first female landscape architects, Bodorff opened her own office in 1937. Her work is charcterised by Functionalist thinking and an informal style based on the given qualities of the natural landscape. Her lyrical naturalist side came out in projects such as Reimersholme in Stockholm, 1942–46. She also designed nearly a hundred city parks throughout Sweden, as well as cemetearies, industrial parks, and private gardens.

Further reading. C Nowotny, B Persson, *Ulla Bodorff Landskapsarkitekt 1913–82* (1988).

BRUNNBERG & FORSHED ARKITEKTKONTOR

Descends from the office that until 1973 was known as Curmans arkitektkontor; 1973–77 it was called Brunnberg & Gillberg; and from 1977 until 1988 Brunnberggruppen. Håkan Brunnberg (born 1940) and Kjell Forshed (born 1943) started working under their current title in 1988. Their primary contributions have been the design of apartments with an intimate scale and formal variety and master plans that are a development of the Garden City. Forshed has headed research projects on the importance of detailing and building components and urban typology.

Important works. Grimsta, Upplands Väsby, 1976–79. Carlslund, Upplands Väsby, 1985. Apartments at Terra Nova, Visby, 1986. Minneberg, Stockholm, 1987. Trädskolan Enskede, 1990. Redevelopment of Boda village, including a library and apartments, 1991. Apartments on Stumholmen, Karlskrona, 1993. Apartments at St. Erik, Stockholm, 1997.

ERIK BÜLOW-HÜBE (1879–1963)

CTH, 1895–98; Polyteknikum, Zürich, 1900. Chief engineer at the Office of Municipal Engineering in Stockholm, 1904–10. Director of the Real Estate Department for the Stockholm-Saltsjön Railroad, 1913–20. Chief City Engineer in Malmö, 1921–46. Bülow-Hübe's greatest contributions are in Malmö, where he developed modern, widely-admired master plans for such areas as Ribersborg and Friluftstaden. He also worked as a landscape architect, designing parks such as Pildammsparken in Malmö, surroundings of Malmö Castle, and the Citadel in Landskrona.

PETER CELSING (1920–74)

KTH, 1943; KKH, 1945. Internships with Ivar Tengbom, Paul Hedqvist, and Sven Ivar Lind. Worked in Beirut, 1946–48. Worked as subway station architect for the Stockholm Transit Company, 1948–52. Collaborated with Sigurd Lewerentz on the renovation of Uppsala Cathedral, 1951–55. Professor at KTH, 1960–69. Celsing's professional practice was concentrated to two areas—sacred architecture, where he established a distinctive church type, and the transformation of downtown Stockholm, where his Fine Arts Center and Bank of Sweden defined the limits of Modernist urban planning. Among his generation of architects he was one of the most interested in architectural history. The elementary classicism of his work was mitigated by a Post-Modern contingency on the characteristics of the site—an approach that has been described as 'inclusive purity.'

Important works. Friis residence, Drottningholm, 1955. Härlanda Church, Gothenburg, 1952–59. St. Thomas Church, Vällingby, 1953–59. Ludvika Crematorium, 1954–58. Olaus Petri Church, Stockholm, 1955–59. Almtuna Church, Uppsala, 1956–59. Operakällaren restaurant, Stockholm, 1961. Stockholm Student Society at Uppsala University, 1963–68. Nacksta Church, Sundsvall, 1963–69. Film Center, Stockholm, 1964–70. Fine Arts Center and Bank of Sweden, Stockholm, 1965–76. Villa Klockberga (Celsing residence), Drottningholm, 1966.

Further reading. Lars Olof Larsson m. fl. (ed.), *Peter Celsing. En bok om en arkitekt och hans verk* (1980), Wilfried Wang, *The Architecture of Peter Celsing* (1996).

ISAK GUSTAF CLASON (1856–1930)

KTH, 1879; KKH, 1881. Study trips to France, Italy, and Spain. Professor at KTH, 1890–1904. He was the leading authority during Swedish architecture's last phase of historicism, and led the way toward the turn-of-the-century emphasis on materials and the National Romantic Movement in the early years of the 20th century. Clason used his comprehensive understanding of architectural history in striving to incorporate the lessons of history in new buildings.

Important works. Bünsow Mansion, Stockholm, 1886–88. Östermalm Market Hall (with Kasper Sahlin), Stockholm, 1888. Hallwyl Palace, Stockholm, 1893–98. The Nordic Museum, Stockholm, 1889–1907. Brandstods-

bolaget office building, Stockholm, 1899–1901. Swedish Private Central Bank, Stockholm, 1912–15. Renovation of palaces and manor houses in Lejondal (1889–91), Castenhof (1890–91), and Adelsnäs (1912–22).

Further reading. Hans Edestrand & Erik Lundberg, *I. G. Clason* (1968).

COORDINATOR

Coordinator was formed in 1978 in a merger of A4 and ELLT. The two offices had shared administrative personnel, an internal development program, and office space since 1966. They have approached their work together in a systematic manner and in the spirit of Modernism. In 1991 Coordinator merged with White arkitekter.

Important works. Salén Building, Stockholm, 1973–78. Göteborg University Library and School of Humanities, Gothenburg, 1977–85. Apartments in Traneberg, Stockholm, 1980–84. Ministry for Foreign Affairs, Stockholm, 1979–88. South Station, Stockholm, 1985–89. The Cupola arena, Borlänge, 1988–91. Electrum offices, Kista, 1984–92.

JÖRAN CURMAN (1907–1972)

KTH, 1931. Worked in the Gothenburg City Planning Department, 1933–36. Assistant County Architect in Gävleborg and Uppsala County, 1936–39. County Architect in Uppsala, 1939–44. Worked for Uddeholms AB, 1944–49. Own architectural consulting practice, 1949–72 (see also Brunnberg and Forshed). Founded the Industrial Housing Association, 1945.

Important works. Housing and housing areas Uddeholms AB (1940s), Strandliden, Hässelbystrand, Stockholm (with N Gunnarz 1956–57), Orminge, Stockholm, 1960s.

Writings. "Gruppsamhällen" (with H Zimdal) in *Inför framtidens demokrati* (1944), *Industriens arbetarebostäder* (Uppsala 1944).

Further reading. *Industribostäder* (IBF, Stockholm 1950), Ann Mari Westerlind, *Industribostäder i bruksorter, industriens bostadsförening 1945–1982* (1950).

MATS EDBLOM (born 1936)

KTH, 1962; MPhil, KTH, 1967. One of the young critics of the Modernist plan for downtown Stockholm in 1962. Worked for Carl Nyrén, 1967–82. Editor of *Arkitektur*,

Celsing

1971–74. Started own architectural practice in 1982. Dean of the Tessin School, KKH's department of road and bridge building.

Important works. Nyckelvik School, Lidingö, 1985. Association of Swedish County Councils Building, Stockholm, 1990. Höga Kusten Bridge over the Ångerman River, 1997.

BENGT EDMAN (born 1921)

KTH, 1948. Collaborated with Lennart Holm, 1949–52. Then worked at HSB in Stockholm until 1956, when he moved to Skånska Cementgjuteriet, where he did developmental work. Started his own practice in Lund in 1958. Professor at LTH, 1972–81. Professor at KTH, 1981–86. Since the late Seventies, Edman has been involved in ILAUD's summer study programs in Italy, which helped him establish a network of international contacts that centers on Team X. Edman's work is clearly structured and has a tangible materiality in which brick plays a prominent role.

Important works. Göth residence, Uppsala, 1950. Apartments and shops in the Hästen block, Uppsala, 1957. Group of single-family homes, Partille, 1960. Hägerstrand residence, Lund, 1964. Student housing in the Vildanden block, Lund, 1966. Sparta Student Center, Lund, 1964–71. Lund City Park, 1964–77.

Further reading. Gunilla Millisdotter, *Bengt Edmans arkitektur och pedagogik* (1993).

ELLT

ELLT architects' office was started by four students of KTH— Alf Engström (1932–83), Gunnar Landberg (b.1933), Bengt Larsson (b.1932) and Alvar Törneman (1930–67) —after winning the 1954 competition of Gävle crematorium. Their architecture has been modernistic with a brutalist character of materials. For the National Board of Public Building they developed the so called office building box, used eg for police stations. Merged with A4 to become Coordinator.

Important works. Gävle crematorium (1954–60), Saltsjö Duvnäs row-houses (1961–64), Kungshamra students' housing, Solna (1961–67), Ålidhem housing, Umeå (1962–65), Nyköping psychiatric clinics (1962–69), Haparanda church (1963–67), IBM education centre, Lidingö (1966–68), Police stations in Gävle, Östersund, Falkenberg, Visby, Ystad, Kristianstad, Norrtälje (1967–79), Luleå university students' centre (1974–80), PTK education centre, Djurönäset (1976–81), Housing Oxievång, Malmö (1976–81).

OLLE ENGKVIST (1889–1969)

Engkvist started his own construction business, Bygg Oleba, in 1922. The company grew to become Sweden's leading building corporation for many years. Engkvist collaborated with the nation's most prominent architects on residential, commercial, and industrial projects. His concern for social housing issues and passion for experimentation led to the construction of numerous collective houses. Engkvist was also a member of the National Social Housing Study of 1933–47.

Important construction projects. Rowhouses in Ålsten, Stockholm, 1932. Narrow apartment buildings in Hjorthagen, Stockholm, 1934–37. Star-shaped buildings, terraced apartments, and residential towers in Gröndal, Stockholm, 1945–52. Hässelby Family Hotel, Stockholm, 1955. Gothenburg City Hall extension, 1935–37. Gothenburg Concert Hall, 1935.

Further Reading. *Olle Engkvist Byggmästare* (1949)

SIGFRID ERICSON (1879–1958)

CTH and KKH, 1895–1902. Taught at CTH and the Gothenburg School of Arts and Crafts; became Dean of the School of Arts and Crafts in 1913. Practiced architecure in Gothenburg. His Masthugget Church was a clear illustration of the ideals of the National Romantic Movement.

Important works. Masthugget Church, Gothenburg, 1910–12. One of four architects on the team of ARES, which took second place in the 1917 competition for Götaplatsen in Gothenburg; after the competition's second phase, ARES was commissioned to design the Gothenburg Museum of Art, 1919–23. Buildings for the Gothenburg Jubilee Exhibition of 1923 (with Arvid Bjerke).

NILS EINAR ERIKSSON (1899–1978)

KTH, 1922; KKH, 1923–25. Worked for Carl Åkerblad, 1918–19; Cyrillus Johansson, 1919–21; Hakon Ahlberg, 1924; and Gunnar Asplund, 1928–30. Own practice in Stockholm, 1930–32; thereafter in Gothenburg.

Important works. One of nine proposals that shared first prize in the 1927 competition for the League of Nations Palace in Geneva (not built). Collaborated with Asplund on the Stockholm Exhibition of 1930. Gothenburg Concert Hall, 1935. Thule office building, Gothenburg, 1936. Centrum office building, Gothenburg, 1938. Torpa housing development, Gothenburg, 1948. Gothenburg Community Center, 1949. Park Aveny Hotel, Gothenburg, 1950. Tidens förlag publishing house, Stockholm, 1929 (with Sigurd Westholm). Folksam Insurance Building, Stockholm, 1959 (with Yngve Tegner).

Further reading. Claes Caldenby (ed.), *Göteborgs konserthus, ett album* (1992).

OLOF ERIKSSON (born 1926)

KTH, 1949. Worked for Lennart Tham in 1950. Head architect at the Building Construction Society of the Federation of Swedish Farmers' Association, 1952. Started his own architectural practice in 1957. Building advisor and later technical director at the National Board of Public Building, 1962–73. Head of the Swedish Council for Building Research, 1973–80. Chairman of the Secretariat for Futurological Studies, 1980–87. Chairman of the Dalarna County Research Council, 1988.

Writings. *Bortom storstadsidéerna. En regional framtid för Sverige och Norden på 2010-talet* (1989), *Byggbeställare i brytningstid* (BFR T 20: 1994), *Bygg om Sverige till bärkraft* (1996).

ERSÉUS, FRENNING & SJÖGREN ARKITEKTER

Peter Erséus (born 1952), Pelle Frenning (born 1943), and Magnus Sjögren (born 1952) started their own office in 1987 after working together for White arkitekter. They work within the tradition of Modernism, with classical features and genuine materials.

Important works. Akribi Print, Mölndal, 1991. School of Economics, Gothenburg, 1995. Restoration of the Course and Newspaper Library, Gothenburg, 1995. Gunnared Church, Gothenburg, 1997.

RALPH ERSKINE (born 1914)

Architectural education London, 1931–37; KKH, 1946. Started own architectural practice in Sweden in 1942. Erskine is a Modernist whose buildings are rooted in the regional and climatological conditions of the site. He has had an extensive professional career with many international commissions.

Important works. Apartment buildings and other ancillary facilities in Gyttorp, 1945–55; Hammarby, Gästrikland, 1947–57; Tibro, 1956 and on; Kiruna, 1961; Byker, Newcastle, England, 1968–82; Nya Bruket, Sandviken, 1973–78; Myrstugeberget, Stockholm, 1977–85; and Tappström, Ekerö, 1983–89. Engström residence, Lisön, 1955. Architect's own home on Drottningholm, Stockholm, 1963. Detached homes and row houses at Esperanza, Landskrona, 1969. Borgafjäll Ski Lodge and Hotel, 1948. Cardboard factory at Fors, Avesta, 1953. Shopping center, Luleå, 1954. Library, student center, Aula Magna and law student union, Stockholm University, Frescati, 1974–90.

Further reading. Mats Egelius, *Ralph Erskine, arkitekt* (1988).

FFNS

FFNS was established in 1958 by Bertil Falk (born 1925), Carl Erik Fogelvik (born 1920), Gunnar Nordström (born 1929), and Erik Smas (born 1915). It has grown into the largest architectural office in Sweden with 555 employees in some twenty locations (1996). In 1987 it became the first architecture firm on the stock exchange. FFNS initially focused on residential work, but has for many years now designed all types of building.

Important works. Apartments and single-family homes at Ella Gård, Täby, 1955–70. Akalla Garden City, Stockholm, 1974. Trosa Public Library, 1985. Office building and shopping gallery, Stockholm, 1986. Norrbotten County Theater, Luleå, 1986. The Forum (Nacka town center), 1989. Apartments, Umeå, 1989. Swedish contribution to the Hestra inter-Nordic housing development, Borås, 1992.

FRED FORBAT (1897–1972)

Born in Hungary. Received a degree in engineering at Munich, Germany, 1920; studied at the Bauhaus, 1920–22. Practiced architecture in Berlin, where he designed apartments in Siemensstadt and Haselhorst, 1925–32. Taught at the Ittenschule, Berlin, 1929–31. Community planning commissions in Karaganda and Magnitogorsk (the latter with Ernst May), Soviet Union, 1932–33. Practiced architecture in Hungary, 1934–38. Fled to Sweden in 1938 to escape the persecution of the Jews with the help of Swedish collegues. Worked in the City Planning Department in Lund, 1938–42; for HSB in Stockholm, 1942–45; and the Egler

Office of Urban Planning, Stockholm, 1945–69. Professor *pro tempore* at KTH, Stockholm, 1959–60. Forbat was an internationally-recognized architect whose work in Sweden developed the process of long-range comprehensive community planning.

Important works in Sweden. Borgmästaregården housing development, Lund. Master plan for HSB's housing development on Reimersholme, Stockholm, 1942–46. Several city plans, including Lund, 1942 and Skövde, 1949. Planned a model city for the Interbau Exhibition, Berlin, 1957 (with Stefan Romare).

Further reading. *Fred Forbat* (Arkitekturmuseet, 1970), Kristina Mezei, *Fred Forbat och principerna för hans byggande* (1975).

JOSEF FRANK (1885–1967)

Technical University in Vienna, 1908. Internship with Bruno Möhring, Berlin, 1908–09. Professor at Wiener Kunstgewerbeschule, 1919–25. Own interior design firm with Oskar Wlach called Haus und Garten, 1925–38. Wrote *Architektur als Symbol* (1931) and articles for several journals. Participated in CIAM's first meeting in 1928. Immigrated to Stockholm in 1933, where he worked primarily with furniture, textiles, and interiors for the firm Svensk Tenn. Contributed to the Paris World's Fair of 1937 and the New York World's Fair of 1939. Frank was a prominent figure in the Modern Movement in central Europe until forced into exile in 1933. His undogmatic, reflective approach and carefully modulated architecture provided a counterpoint to the more rigid tendencies of the contemporary *avant garde*.

Important works. Worker housing development in Ortmann, Pernitz, Germany, 1919–21. Contributed to a number of residential projects in Vienna between 1919 and 1931. Took part in 1927 Weissenhof exhibition in Stuttgart; head architect of the 1932 housing expo *Werkbundsiedlung* in Vienna. Two single-family homes in Falsterbo, Sweden, 1924–27. Beer residence, Wenzgasse, Vienna, 1929–31 (with Wlach). Bunzl residence, Chimanistrasse, Vienna, 1936. Three more single-family homes in Falsterbo, 1934–36.

Further reading. Hermann Czech & Johannes Spalt, *Josef Frank 1885–1967* (1981), Christoffer Long, *Josef Frank and the Crises of Modern Architecture* (1995), Mikael Bergquist & Olof Michélsen (ed.), *Josef Frank arkitektur* (1994), Kristina Wängberg-Eriksson, *Orkidé i vinterlandet* (1994).

Frank

PER-ÅKE FRIBERG (born 1920)

Studied both landscape architecture and architecture in Sweden, Denmark, and the United States. First ever Professor of Garden Design and Nature Conservation at the Swedish University of Agricultural Sciences, 1964–85. Friberg designs gardens, parks, and landscapes as well as buildings and master plans through his own office.

Important works. Cemeteries at Görväln in Jakobsberg, 1969–75, and at Augerum in Karlskrona, 1970–74.

Further reading. *Arkitektur* 4/1994.

ERIK FRIBERGER (1889–1968)

KTH, 1912; KKH, 1914. Worked for Stockholm City Hall building office, 1914–17, and the Gothenburg City Planning Department, 1921–26. County Architect in Gothenburg and Bohus County, 1927–54. Started own architectural practice in Gothenburg in 1917. Chairman of the Association of County Architects, 1933–38. Friberger was a Functionalist and social activist who developed prefabricated houses, vacation homes, and apartment buildings.

Important works. Betel apartment building for HSB, Gothenburg. Row houses on Munkebäcksgatan, Gothenburg, 1934. Lange residence, Gothenburg, 1938. Apartment building with expandable units on concrete decks, Gothenburg, 1960. Prefabricated vacation homes for the Leisure Time exhibition in Ystad, 1936.

Writings. *Regionplanering i England* (1924), *Mekaniserad bostadsproduktion* (1945), *Elementbyggda enfamiljhus i Göteborg* (1958)

Further reading. Lotta Krus, *Funktionalisten Erik Friberger* (CTH 1989), Marianne Dahlbäck, "Erik Fribergers elementhus", in *Arkitektur* 7-8/1971.

LÉONIE GEISENDORF (born 1914)

Born in Switzerland and educated at ETH in Zurich. Worked for Le Corbusier. Immigrated to Sweden in 1938, where she worked for Sven Ivar Lind, KF:s arkitektkontor, and Paul Hedqvist. Started own practice with her husband Charles Edouard Geisendorf (1913–1985) in 1950. Geisendorf's work follows in the spirit of Le Corbusier.

Important works. Villa in Ranängen, Djursholm, 1951. Bagarmossen row houses, Stock holm, 1956. St. George's High School, Stockholm, 1961.

Further reading. Charlie Gullström (ed.), *Léonie Geisendorf. Arkitektur* (1990).

NILS GELLERSTEDT (1875–1961)

Degree in civil engineering, KTH, 1898. Started the engineering firm Kommunaltekniska byrån in Stockholm in 1902. Undertook several assignments as a member of the Stockholm City Planning Commission. Gellerstedt was one of the leading proponents for the new concepts in urban planning at the turn of the century.

Important works. Prize-winning submissions to major urban planning competitions for communities such as Gothenburg, 1901 (second place). Gellerstedt developed a great many plans for various cities throughout Sweden.

JAN GEZELIUS (born 1923)

MA, 1949; KTH, 1953; KKH, 1960. Worked for William Holford in London, Bengt Hidemark, the City of Stockholm Planning Department, and KF:s arkitektkontor. Head architect in the City of Stockholm Parks Department, 1964–67. Guest professor in Graz, Austria, 1976–77. Professor at CTH, 1981–88. In his own small practice, Gezelius' commissions have been limited in scope to private residences and a few museums, but his work has had a profound influence on Swedish architecture. Most of his buildings are wood-framed.

Important works. Migratory Bird Museum, Öland, 1961. Fisherman's House, Öland, 1963. Drake residence, Borlänge, 1970. Ethnographic Museum, Stockholm, 1972–78 (with Gunnar Mattsson). Eketorp Ancient Fortification Museum, Öland, 1977–82. Post office prototype, 1982–86 (with Arksam).

Further reading. Claes Caldenby, Åsa Walldén (ed.), *Jan Gezelius* (1989), Jan Gezelius, 'A springboard towards something better', in *arq*, spring 1996, number 3, volume 1.

ERIK GLEMME (1905–59)

Practiced both landscape and building architecture. Worked for the City of Stockholm Parks Department, 1936–56. Glemme was one of the most prominent figures of the 'Stockholm School' of park design. He produced some of the country's finest examples of Functionalist landscape architecture, such as Norr Mälarstrand (1941–43) and the renovation of Tegnérlunden (1941) and Vasaparken (1947), all in Stockholm. His comprehensive talent for design was expressed in parks and public squares as well as street furniture, news stands, luminaires, and other refining elements in the urban environment.

Further reading. 'Landskapet i staden', special issue *Utblick Landskap* 1988.

TORBEN GRUT (1871–1945)

KTH, 1894; the Royal Academy of Fine Arts in Copenhagen, Denmark; KKH, 1898. Worked for Isak Gustaf Clason in 1893 and '96 and for Ferdinand Boberg as Project Architect for the Central Post Office in Stockholm. Editor of *Arkitektur*, 1904–07. Inspired by the the Danish architecture with which he was so familiar, Grut played an important roll in the emergence of the National Romantic Movement.

Important works. Second place in city planning competition for Gothenburg, 1901 (with Gellerstedt). Designed mostly single-family homes at the start of the century, including Solliden, a summer house for the Royal Family, 1906; Villa Sunnanlid, the architect's own home, Stockholm, 1906; and a standard house for small farms, 1905. Grut designed Stockholm Stadium for the 1912 Olympic Games, a rationally-planned sports arena within a powerful brick structure. He thereafter specialized in athletic complexes, designing several in Sweden and abroad.

ERIK HAHR (1869–1944)

Higher College of Applied Art, Stockholm, 1891. Internship with Lilljekvist. Started own architectural practice in Stockholm in 1897. Hahr made his greatest contribution as City Architect in Västerås, 1909–35. As planning professionals took an increasingly global approach to the urban environment, Hahr's work in Västerås was recognized as exemplary. He also became known as an industrial architect by virtue of his buildings for Asea, the Swedish General Electric Company.

Important works. City Hall and City Hotel, Västerås, 1902–07. Mimer workshop, Västerås, 1911–15. Several buildings for Asea in Västerås, including a headquarters building, 1916–19. Steam power plant and accompanying housing, Västerås, 1915. Theater, Västerås, 1915. Savings bank, Västerås, 1916. Worker

Glemme

housing (Kåre, Julius, and Oscaria blocks), Västerås, 1917. Various other commissions in Västerås, including apartment buildings, single-family homes, and schools. Gothenburg College, 1907 (with Ernst Torulf). Villa Ekbacken (Dahlén residence), Lidingö, 1912–13. Worker housing for Dahlén's company, AGA, Lidingö, 1913.

Further reading. Sven Drakenberg, *Västerås stads byggnadshistoria från 1800-talets mitt* (1962).

PER OLOF HALLMAN (1869–1941)

KTH, 1890; KKH, 1893. Comprehensive study trip to some forty cities in Germany, Austria, and France in 1895. Worked on the Stockholm Building Commission starting in 1894. Expert member of the Stockholm City Planning Commission starting in 1909. Assistant City Architect, Stockholm, 1913. Director of the Stockholm City Planning Department, 1922–27. Taught Urban Planning at KTH, 1897–1932. Jury member for several urban planning competitions in Sweden and other Nordic countries. Authored countless lectures and papers. Hallman was a leading proponent for the new urban planning ideals at the turn of the century.

Important works. First place in the 1901 city planning competition for Gothenburg (with Fredrik Sundbärg), the event that marks the breakthrough of the new urban planning in Sweden. Developed a long series of master plans for various districts in Stockholm, including Lärkstaden, Enskede, Blecktornsparken, Rödabergsområdet, and Helgalunden. Submitted some sixty different plan proposals for communities throughout the country.

Further reading. Thomas Paulsson, *Den glömda staden* (1959, 1994).

HANS HEDLUND (1855–1931)

CTH and KKH, 1871–79. Started his own architectural practice in Gothenburg in 1881. Study trip to the United States in 1893. Taught at Gothenburg School of Arts and Crafts, 1881–87, and at CTH starting in 1887. Became Professor of Building Construction at CTH in 1911 (the first outside of Stockholm). Under the influence of Henry Hobson Richardson, Hedlund developed a picturesque architecture based on asymmetrical composition and the expressive use of materials.

Important works (all in Gothenburg). Dickson Public Library, 1897. Gothenburg Public Library, 1900. Carnegie Sugar Refinery, 1901.

Electrical plant, 1907. Union of Clerical Employees Building, 1908. Telephone company building, 1909–12 (with son Björner).

PAUL HEDQVIST (1895–1977)

KTH, 1914; KKH, 1918–20. Worked for Ragnar Östberg and Cyrillus Johansson. Started own architectural practice in 1921. Worked for the National Board of Public Building from 1925. Professor at KKH, 1938–48. Chairman at the Academy of Arts, 1963–71. A prominent school architect, Hedqvist was a professed Modernist whose extensive professional career had a marked influence on the movement.

Important works. St. Catherine's Intermediate School, Stockholm, 1928–31 (with David Dahl). Västerbron bridge, Stockholm, 1931–35 (with Dahl). Traneberg Bridge, Stockholm, 1933–35 (with Dahl). Row houses Ålstensgatan, Stockholm, 1932. Vanadis Swimming Pool, Stockholm, 1936. Bromma Airport, Stockholm, 1936. Income Tax Department Building, Stockholm, 1955. Johanneshov Ice Arena, Stockholm, 1955 and 1963. Dagens Nyheter newspaper office building, 1960–64. Eskilstuna Public Swimming Hall, 1933. Uppsala Biomedical Center, 1961–77.

Further reading. Sune Malmkvist, "Paul Hedqvist 1895–1977", in *Arkitektur* 10/1977.

BJÖRN HEDVALL (1889–1982)

KTH, 1916; KKH, 1918–20. Worked for Osvald Almqvist, Aron Johansson, and Gustaf Linden. Started own architectural practice in 1921. Head architect at the Royal Naval Material Administration, 1939–43. Hedvall was an accomplished Classicist in the Twenties and an early Functionalist in the Thirties.

Important works (all in Stockholm). Metropol Restaurant and Lyran Cinema, 1926. Eden Hotel, 1928–30. Apartment building at Norr Mälarstrand 20, 1931. Paraden Cinema, 1932. Ekhagen housing development, 1935. Royal Cinema, 1937. School of Naval Warfare in Näsbypark, 1942. Ängby Church, Blackeberg, 1959.

Further reading. Ingeborg Ouvrier, *Björn Hedvall* (Stockholm univ. 1982).

DAVID HELLDÉN (1905–1990)

KTH, 1927; KKH, 1929–30. Worked for Erik Lallerstedt, 1927–35. Thereafter started own architectural practice. Helldén was an uncompromising Functionalist in the spirit of international Modernism.

Important works. Apartment buildings in Ribershus, Malmö, 1937–42. Apartment buildings in Hökarängen, Stockholm, 1944–51. Malmö City Theater, 1933–44 (with Erik Lallerstedt and Sigurd Lewerentz). Contributed to the city planning of Stockholm with master plans for lower Norrmalm in 1945, Hötorgscity in 1951–60 (including the first of the district's five towers and its market hall), and Sergelstorg in 1958–60. Stockholm University, Frescati, 1961–73.

Further reading. Martin Rörby, *Samtal med David Helldén, arkitekt SAR* (1991).

GUNNAR HENRIKSSON (born 1919)

KTH, 1949. Worked for KF:s arkitektkontor, 1949–57. Professor at KTH, 1957–70. President of KF:s arkitekt- och ingenjörskontor, 1970–73. Stockholm City Architect, 1973–84. Henriksson's buildings follow the Functionalist standard of clear delineation of functions. He studied traditional post-and-plank construction in his spare time, leading to the book *Skiftesverk i Sverige. Ett tusenårigt byggnadssätt* (1996).

Important works. San Remo Bakery, Stockholm, 1960. Schools of Mechanical Engineering and Metallurgy and Materials Technology, KTH, Stockholm, 1966–67. School of Architecture, KTH, Stockholm, 1969.

SVEN HERMELIN (1900–1984)

Studied landscape architecture in Sweden, Denmark, and Germany. Started his own practice in 1926; collaborated 1941–68 with Ingrid Wedborn. First ever teacher of Garden Design in the Horticulture Program at the Alnarp Institute, 1934–54. Hermelin was one of the first to unite garden design and landscape architecture with a modern ecological awareness. He was an enthusiastic polemicist and frequent contributer to professional journals. Also made significant contributions to professional organizations and environmental protection groups. Established the Järna Foundation in 1954, a full-scale laboratory for studying environmental and landscape issues. Hermelin's professional office developed into a nursery for future generations of landscape architects.

Important works. Marabou Park, Sundbyberg, 1945. Lötsjön Recreation Area, Sundbyberg, 1952. Sandviken Church Park, 1947.

Restoration of Hässelby Palace Park, 1961, and Strömsholm Palace Park, 1947.

Further reading. *Utblick Landskap* 1/1985.

BENGT HIDEMARK (born 1924)

KTH, 1949. Architectural practice with Gösta Danielson and with ai-gruppen, a large architectural and engineering consulting group. Professor at KTH, 1972–89. Hidemark spent much of his career designing office and laboratory buildings in the spirit of the National Board of Public Building's Structuralist philosophy; in recent years he has addressed issues of energy conservation.

Important works. Televerket office building in Farsta, Stockholm, 1969. Linköping University, 1972. SMHI offices, Norrköping, 1973. Apartments, Smålands Taberg, 1981. Terraced apartments, Tyresö, 1986. Apartment buildings in Ladugårdsängen, Örebro, 1992.

OVE HIDEMARK (born 1931)

KTH, 1956; KKH, 1962. Worked for Nils Tesch, 1950–56, and Sven Ivar Lind, 1957–62. Architectural practice with Göran Månsson from 1962 until the early 1980s. Became professor of the art of restoration at KKH in 1986. Palace Architect of the Royal Palace in Stockholm and Drottningholm Palace since 1989. Hidemark showed an early interest for the history of architecture and for construction technology under the inspiration of one of his teachers, Erik Lundberg. Hidemark also designs for new construction.

Important works. Restoration of Skokloster Palace, 1968–80. Restorations and new construction at Sätra Spring, 1969. Hallstavik Community Center, 1970. St. Birgitta's Church, Kalmar, 1975. Lilla Aska Crematorium, Linköping, 1988. Restoration of the China Palace, Drottningholm, 1990–96. Restoration of St. Catherine's Church, Stockholm, 1991–97.

Further reading. Ove Hidemark, *I dialog med tiden* (1991).

LENNART HOLM (born 1926)

MArch, KTH, 1949; PhD Arch, KTH, 1955. Holm is an astute and well-spoken researcher, teacher, organiser, and polemicist in the field of community planning and housing issues. Taught at KTH, 1957– 67. Head of the National Institute for Building Research, 1960–69. Director of the National Board of Physical

Planning and Building, 1969–89. Chairman of the Swedish Council for Building Research, 1975–91. Contributed to several government studies, including the Housing Cooperative Committee of 1949–56, the Housing Construction Study of 1961–65, and the 1965 Museum Assessment MUS 65. Editor of HSB's journal *Att bo* (*Living*), 1951–69.

Important works. The Göth residence, designed in 1950 with Bengt Edman.

Writings. *Familj och bostad*, 1955; *Hem, arbete och grannar*, 1958; *Stadsbygd*, 1959; *Strategi för kultur*, 1964; *Land i sikte*, 1971; *Rita hus*, 1990; *Han, hon och huset*, 1995.

Further reading. *Vision och perspektiv. En bok om planverket och Lennart Holm* (1988), Ulf Sandström, *Arkitektur och social ingenjörskonst* (Linköping univ. 1989).

JAENECKE–SAMUELSON ARKITEKTFIRMA

Fritz Jaenecke (1903–78) graduated from architecture school in Berlin in 1928. He worked there for Hans Poelzig, 1926–30, and had his own practice in Berlin, 1930–36. Started a firm with Sten Samuelson in 1951. Became a professor at the university in Aachen in 1961. Sten Samuelson (born 1926) graduated from KTH in 1950. He was a professor at LTH, 1964–83. Their work together is characterized by an elegant and expressive Modernism.

Important works. Ullevi Stadium, Gothenburg, and Malmö Stadium, both 1958. Ronnebybrunn Hotel, 1961. IBM offices, Lidingö, 1966.

CYRILLUS JOHANSSON (1884–1959)

CTH, 1905; KKH, 1908. Started his own architectural practice in Stockholm in 1906. Johansson developed a highly personal architecture with a genuine and timeless character. He worked primarily with simple brick buildings. The windows are typically framed in thin relief for emphasis. Johansson was a versatile designer with a wide variety of commissions from master plans to industrial plants, water towers, office and apartment buildings, and single-family homes.

Important works. Stockholm's Cotton Spinning and Weaving Mill, 1916–17. Central Wine and Spirits Company warehouse, Stockholm, 1920–23. Several water towers, include one in Vaxholm, 1923. Årsta Bridge, Stockholm, 1923–24. Värmland Regional Museum, Karlstad, 1926–29. Swedish Tobacco Monop-

oly warehouse, Gothenburg, 1928. Centrumhuset commercial building, Stockholm, 1929–31. Royal Military Record Office, Stockholm, 1942–48. Church and parish hall at Stora Essingen, Stockholm, 1959.

Further reading. Cyrillus Johansson, *Byggnaden och staden*, (1936). *Cyrillus Johansson 1884–1959* (Arkitekturmuseet 1979).

KOOPERATIVA FÖRBUNDETS (KF:S) ARKITEKTKONTOR

(The Swedish Cooperative Union's Architecture Office). Known after 1958 as Kooperativa förbundets arkitekt- och ingenjörskontor (KFAI). KF:s arkitektkontor was the largest in Sweden in the 1930s, with over seventy employees, and an important force in the history of Swedish architecture. The firm brought together young, radical architects and prominant professionals such as Olof Thunström, Artur von Schmalensee, Dag Ribbing, Olof Hult, Eric Rockström, Erik Ahlsén, and principal Eskil Sundahl.

Important works. The office designed factories, shops, department stores, apartments, and assembly halls throughout the country, as well as furniture and packaging. Functionalistic straightforwardness and social activism combined with a powerful sense of form to produce a great many distinguished works; among the most important are the industrial communities on the island of Kvarnholmen, Nacka (1927–34), and in Gustavsberg (1937–1950s).

Further reading. *Kooperativa förbundets arkitektkontor 1925–35* (1935), *Kooperativa förbundets arkitektkontor 1935–49* parts 1–2, (1949), Lisa Brunnström, *Den rationella fabriken, om funktionalismens rötter* (1990), P G Råberg, *Funktionalistiskt genombrott* (1972).

ERIK LALLERSTEDT (1864–1955)

KTH, 1886; KKH, 1889. Architectural practice in Stockholm, 1890–1944. Professor at KTH, 1905–29. As a practicing professional Lallerstedt demonstrated a profound sensitivity to the changing trends of the day. His openness to innovation allowed for close relationships with younger architects, and his office was highly coveted by interns.

Important works. Among many other churches, the Jäth Church in Småland County, 1897–98. Many buildings for the Bank of Sweden, the postal service, and the telephone company in various communities including

Västerås (1908–11), Växjö (1909–11), and Kristianstad (1911–16). Train stations for diverse private railway companies (1899–1909). Trygg Insurance Building, Stockholm, 1906–09. KTH master plan and buildings, Stockholm, 1911–40. Thule Building, Stockholm, 1915–17 (with Ture Ryberg). Stockholm College, 1918–27. Row house development for telephone company employees, Norrköping, 1922. Bank of Sweden building, Norrköping, 1932. Malmö City Theater, 1933–44 (with Lewerentz and Helldén).

Further reading. *Erik Lallerstedt Arch. Arkitekt under fem årtionden.* (Arkitekturmuseet, 1982).

AXEL LARSSON (1898–1975)

Studied furniture design at KTH in Stockholm. Worked as a drafting assistant for Carl Malmsten. Designer for the Association of Swedish Furniture Manufacturers in Bodafors, 1925–56. He was quick to embrace the Functionalist approach, and showed a number of Functionalist pieces at the Stockholm Exhibition of 1930.

Important works. Furnishings for the Gothenburg Concert Hall (1936), the Terminus Hotel in Stockholm (1938), and the Swedish American Line's ships Stockholm (1938) and Kungsholm (1953). Interiors for the Park Aveny Hotel in Gothenburg (1950) and the Folksam Insurance headquarters in Stockholm (1960).

LENA LARSSON (born 1919)

Studied furniture making at Carl Malmsten's Workshop School and interior architecture at the Higher College of Applied Art and KTH in Stockholm. Worked for Elias Svedberg, where she collaborated on a series of furnishings for the government and one for the Triva-Bygg company. Commissioned by the Swedish Society of Industrial Design and the National Association of Swedish Architects in 1942 to study home customs. Course director at the Swedish Society of Industrial Design Bo-skolan, 1943. Head of Nordiska Kompaniet department store's furniture department, 1947. Highly-acclaimed interior for the H55 Exhibition in 1955.

Writings. *Heminredning,* 1947 (with Elias Svedberg), *Barnens Vrå, Bo idag, Mitt hem och min trädgård, Mitt liv är ett skåp.* She has been a regular contributor to the journal *Form* since the 1940s. Has written many articles for the newspaper *Expressen*. Became an editor of the magazine *Allt i Hemmet* in 1956, and an editor at *Vi* magazine in 1968.

GUNNAR LECHE (1891–1954)

KTH, 1915; KKH, 1916–18. Worked in the Gothenburg City Planning Department under Albert Lilienberg. Uppsala City Architect, 1920–54. Leche built a large number of apartments and buildings for various public institutions in Uppsala, all in a traditional style. Member of the board of directors of the Swedish Association of Municipal Technology. Important works (all in Uppsala). Vaksala School, 1925. Tuna backar housing development, 1946–51. Sala backe housing development, 1950–53.

Further reading. CE Bergold, *Uppsala. Stadsbyggande 1900–1960* (1989).

SIGURD LEWERENTZ (1885–1975)

CTH, 1908; internship in Germany, 1907–10; among the group of students who founded the Klara School, 1910–11; internship with Carl Westman, 1911. Architectural practice together with Torsten Stubelius, 1911–17; thereafter independent practice, with long-standing collaboration with Gunnar Asplund on the Woodland cemetery. Started a company in 1933 that made steel-framed windows and doors according to his own 'Idesta' system. Lewerentz's architecture is characterized by a 'passionate realism' combined with a deep fascination for materials and a strive for simplicity.

Important works by Lewerentz & Stubelius. Worker housing colonies for Nyvångs Coal Mines, Scania County, 1912, and for the City of Helsingborg, 1912. Proposal for a crematorium chapel, Helsingborg, 1914. Ahxner residence, 1914. Diverse designs for furniture, luminaires, and other utilitarian objects.

Important works by Sigurd Lewerentz. First place in the competition for the Woodland cemetery in Stockholm, 1915 (with Asplund). Lewerentz worked primarily with the cemetery's landscaping as well as designing the Chapel of the Resurrection, 1921–25. Several burial monuments and chapels at Malmö Eastern Cemetery, 1916–76. Contributed a single-family home and an apartment to the Stockholm Exhibition of 1930, as well as the event's emblem. National Social Insurance Board Building, Stockholm, 1931. Edstrand residence, Falsterbo, 1936. Won the competition for Malmö City Theater, 1932 and '35, but

Lewerentz

was forced to share the commission with Lallerstedt and Helldén (not built until 1944). Competition proposal for the restoration of Uppsala Cathedral; later commissioned study with Peter Celsing. St. Mark's Church, Björkhagen, Stockholm, 1956–60. St. Peter's Church, Klippan, Scania County, 1962–66.

Further reading. Janne Ahlin, *Sigurd Lewerentz, arkitekt* (1985), Claes Dymling (ed.), *Sigurd Lewerentz Architect*, Band I–II (Stockholm 1997), *Arkitekturmuseets Årsbok 1986*. Hakon Ahlberg, "Sigurd Lewerentz", in *Arkitektur* 9/1963.

ALBERT LILIENBERG (1879–1967)

Civil Engineering degree, KTH, 1903. Worked for Per Olof Hallman, 1903–04. Chief City Engineer in Gothenburg, 1907–27. Guest instructor in Urban Planning, CTH, 1916–27. A frequent lecturer and prolific writer of professional papers. Honorable Member of the Town Planning Institute and Chairman of the international urban planning congresses in New York, 1925, and London, 1935. Director of the Stockholm City Planning Department, 1927–44. Along with Hallman, Lilienberg assumed a leading role in the field of urban planning in Sweden during the first decade of the 20th century. He was better able than Hallman to incorporate new developments in planning, particularly the changing demands of traffic.

Important works. Produced a multitude of master plans for new neighborhoods in Gothenburg during a period of great success early in the century, including Bagaregården (1908), Landala egnahem (1908), and Kungsladugård (1916). Parallel to his work in Gothenburg, he developed some sixty plans for other communities. His principal work in Stockholm was a proposal for the 1928 general city plan.

Further reading. Hans Bjur, *Stadsplanering kring 1900* (CTH, 1984).

Lindroos

SVEN IVAR LIND (1902–80)

KTH, 1925. Worked for Ernst Torulf and for Gunnar Asplund, 1925–28. Independent architectural practice in Paris designing for the Swedish company AB Kreuger & Toll, 1928–30. Editor of *Byggmästaren*, 1932–33. Took responsibility for Asplund's work during his illness and after his death in 1940. Completed several of Asplund's ongoing projects— the Kviberg Chapel, Skövde Chapel, and the

Stockholm City Archives. Professor at KKH, 1948–58. Palace Architect at the Royal Palace in Stockholm and Drottningholm Palace. Lind was a leading figure in Swedish architecture for many years as a teacher and as one of the field's most prominent authors. His office was highly coveted by interns. Lind's architecture was simple, strict, and thoroughly designed down to the smallest detail; he never strove for spectacular effects.

Important works. Råsunda Stadium, 1937. Swedish pavilion for the World's Fair of 1937 in Paris. Byttan restaurant, Kalmar, 1939. Marieberg apartment hotel, Stockholm, 1943. Kevinge, the architect's own home in Danderyd, 1946. Six hydroelectric power plants and surrounding landscaping and housing, Norrland, 1950–62. Chapels in various communities, including Flen, Nässjö, Iggesund, and Stockholm, 1953–69. Skattkammaren and the Royal Armoury of the Royal Palace, Stockholm, 1967–76.

Further reading. *Arkitektur* 4/1994.

GÖRAN LINDAHL (born 1924)

MPhil in Art History from Uppsala University, 1953; PhD, 1970. Professor in History of Architecture at KKH, 1961–91. Lindahl is an art historian, author of several books and widely published in professional journals as well as newspapers. He has had a strong influence on architectural thought in Sweden. During his professorship at KKH he focused primarily on conservation issues and the history of settlements. He made important contributions to the debate over urban renewal in Sweden during the 1970s. He led a research project called 'the Nordic Wooden City.'

Writings. *Högkyrkligt, lågkyrkligt, frikyrkligt i svensk arkitektur* (1955), *Universitetsmiljö* (1957), *Grav och rum* (1969), *Konstakademiens byggnadsskola* (1987).

GUSTAV LINDEN (1879–1964)

KTH 1906; Royal Academy of Fine Arts, Copenhagen, 1907; KKH, 1909. Started his own architectural practice in 1909. Linköping City Architect, 1912–25. Taught Urban Planning at KKH, 1919–21. Director of the National Board of Public Building's City Planning Department, 1930–44. His architecture is characterized by a restrained traditionalism.

Important works. Early work with Osvald Almqvist (see Almqvist). Linden's most important work as a practicing architect is in

Linköping. He began his career designing buildings and master plans for smaller developments, such as the worker housing on Konsistoriegatan (1918) and a series of row houses on Lindengatan (1924). This work was summarized in a comprehensive 1923 general city plan for Linköping, which had a profound influence on Swedish city planning during an era in which new methods in the field were being developed.

BENGT LINDROOS (born 1918)

KTH, 1945. Worked for Sven Markelius in 1941. Started own architectural practice in 1954; collaborated with Hans Borgström, 1954–68. Lindroos carries well the mantle of Modernism he inherited from Markelius with a penchant for powerful sculptural geometric forms in the spirit of Louis Kahn.

Important works. Unesco Library, Paris, 1958. Farsta Church, Stockholm, 1960. Kaknäs Tower, 1967. Lappkärrsberget student housing, Stockholm, 1968. Apartments in the Drottningen block, Stockholm, 1985. Apartment building, Norrköping, 1987. Urban Mortgage Bank Building, Örebro, 1987.

Further reading. Litteratur: Och så vidare... (1989).

SUNE LINDSTRÖM (1906–1989)

KTH, 1931; studied at the Bauhaus in 1928. Lindström was an internationally-oriented Modernist, an urban designer and city planner, and an enthusiastic polemicist. Worked for the National Board of Public Building's City Planning Department, 1937–39. Taught Urban Planning at KTH, 1938–47. Regional Director in the Gothenburg City Planning Department, 1940–44. Head architect at VBB (the Office of Hydraulic Enginnering) starting in 1944. Professor of Urban Planning at CTH, 1956–69. Conducted research on traffic safety and urban planning economics during the 1960s. Editor of *Byggmästaren*, 1936–40.

Important works. Karlskoga City Hall and Hotel, 1939. Buildings for the Swedish Broadcasting Corporation, Stockholm, 1956. Master plans and apartment buildings in Täby 1959. Wennergren center offices, 1959. Water towers in Örebro (1954–58) and Kuwait (1969–73). Many city and regional plans in Sweden and abroad through the consulting firm VBB. Some of his writings have been collected in a book called *Sagt av Sune Lindström* (*Said by Sune Lindström*), 1966.

ERIK LUNDBERG 1895–1969

MA, 1917; MPhil, 1921; and PhD in Art History, Stockholm College. KTH, 1923. Lundberg made a strong impact as a teacher, an art historian, and through his restoration work. Headed the Cultural History and Design Departments at Skansen open-air museum in Stockholm, 1919–32. Antiquarian at the Central Board of National Antiquities, 1932–46; Director of that institution's Historic Landmarks Department, 1938–46. Professor of the History of Architecture at KKH, 1946–61; taught History of Architecture and Landscaping at KTH during the same period.

Important works. Several church restorations, including Västerås Cathedral, Götene Church, and Spånga Church.

Writings. Lundberg was a prolific writer whose important books include *Svensk bostad* (1942), *Arkitekturens formspråk* parts 1–10 (1945–61), and *Trä gav form* (1971).

CARL MALMSTEN (1888–1972)

Malmsten was a furniture designer, polemicist, author, and the founder of schools. His professional career began in 1916 with first place in the competition for designing the furniture for the Stockholm City Hall. Interiors for the Stockholm Concert Hall (1928), the Waldorf Astoria Hotel in New York City (1930), Marabou Chocolate factory, Sundbyberg (1936–43), the Supreme Court Building, Stockholm (1947–49), and the Folksam Insurance headquarters, Stockholm (1956–60). Established the craftsman schools Carl Malmsten's Workshop School in 1933 and Capellagården on the island of Öland in 1958. In 1936 he was awarded the title of Professor. Consolidated a number of small factories under the name of Nyckelverkstäderna in 1955 to produce the furniture he had designed. Among his most successful furniture series are Vardag, 1944, and Talavid, 1955.

SVEN MARKELIUS (1889–1972)

KTH, 1913; KKH, 1913–15. Head of carpentry for the National Committee for Building Industry Standardization design department, 1920. National Board of Public Building's Research Department, 1938–44. Director of the Stockholm City Planning Department, 1944–54. Own architectural practice from 1910. Markelius was one of the most significant architects of the Modern Movement in Sweden.

Important works. Master plan and single-family homes on Lidingö for the Bygge och Bo housing exhibition of 1925. KTH Student Union, Stockholm, 1930 (with Uno Åhrén). Helsingborg Concert Hall, 1932. Collective house, Stockholm, 1935. Building for the Stockholm Building Association, Stockholm, 1937. United Nations Economic Council Chamber, New York City, 1952. Linköping Community Center, 1953. Stockholm Community Center and City Theater, 1960. Third tower in Hötorgscity development, Stockholm, 1963. Sweden House, Stockholm, 1969.

Writings. Contributing author of *acceptera*, 1931. Editor of the Spektrum series *Arkitektur och samhälle*, 1933–35.

Further reading. Eva Rudberg, *Sven Markelius, arkitekt* (1989).

GUNNAR MARTINSSON (born 1924)

Martinsson is a landscape architect who opened his own office in 1956. He was a professor at the University in Karlsruhe 1965–92. He works in an expressive, consistent style that gives the landscape architecture a powerful intrinsic value.

Important works. Råcksta Cemetery, outside Stockholm, 1962. Garden at the Swedish Embassy in Moscow, 1964. Palace Garden in Rastatt, Germany, 1987, as well as urban spaces in a number of German cities. Wrote several books, including *En bok om trädgårdar*, 1957.

BRUNO MATHSSON (1907–88)

Mathsson was a furniture designer known for his pieces of laminated form-pressed wood, a technique he developed himself. His debut exhibition came in 1936 at the Röhsska Museum of Applied Arts, and his breakthrough came the following year at the international exhibition in Paris.

Important works. Grasshopper easy chair for Värnamo General Hospital, 1931. Eva chair, 1934. Pernilla easy chair, 1944. Freestanding bookcase, 1943. Super-ellipse table (with Piet Hein). Jetson easy chair, with steel piping and a free-hanging basket seat, 1966. Karin wheeled easy chair, 1969. In the 1950s, Mathsson built a few single-family homes with large surfaces of triple-paned glazing for passive solar heating according to his own patent.

GUNNAR MATTSSON (born 1937)

KTH, 1962. Worked for Sven Ivar Lind, A4, and Carl Nyrén, 1961–73. Started own architectural practice in 1973, collaborating with Jan Gezelius until 1978. Mattsson strives after an architecture of simplicity and grace, precision and ease. He has primarily worked in wood, giving a modern interpretation of traditional building practices based on a comprehensive knowledge of architectural history.

Important works. Ethnographic Museum, Stockholm, 1978 (with Jan Gezelius). Leksand Library and Museum, 1985. Övre Martinagården, Tällberg, 1986. Addition to Parish Hall, Leksand, 1988. Härnösand Regional Museum, 1994. Swedish and Finnish Embassies, Dar es Salaam, Tanzania, 1990–96. Museum, Björkö, 1996. Apartments, Växjö, 1996.

GÖRAN MÅNSSON (born 1933)

KTH, 1957; KKH, 1962. Started architectural practice with Ove Hidemark in 1962. Has collaborated with Marianne Dahlbäck (born 1943) since 1988. Månsson has made many clearly-defined additions to existing environments.

Important works. Addition to Gävle Theater, 1985. Vasa Museum, Stockholm, 1990. LTH Student Union, Lund, 1994. Renovation of the Hippodrome Theater, Malmö, 1994.

GEORG A. NILSSON (1871–1949)

KTH, 1895; KKH, 1898. Principal (with civil engineer Ivar Nyqvist) of the architectural and engineering firm Arkitekt- & byggnadsbyrån, 1904–12. Head of the administrative offices at the National Board of Public Building, 1922–37. Like Carl Bergsten, Nilsson was inspired by the followers of Otto Wagner in Vienna and took a rational approach to design. He was primarily active as a school architect.

Important works. Matteus Elementary School, Stockholm, 1899–1901. Luth & Roséns elektriska AB, Stockholm, 1904–09. Architect's own home at Regeringsgatan 88, Stockholm, 1906–07. Elementary School, Eksjö, 1910. Felix Sachs office building, Stockholm, 1911–12. A long series of schools, mostly in Stockholm, including Djursholm Coeducational School (1910), Adolf Fredrik Elementary School (1910), Enskede Elementary School (1915), and the School at Fridhemsplan (1925).

Further reading. Martin Rörby and others, *Georg A Nilsson arkitekt* (1989).

BERNT NYBERG (1927–78)

KTH, 1952. Worked for Klas Anshelm in Lund, 1952–57. Started architectural practice in Lund in 1957, working with Karl Koistinen until 1964. Nyberg was a close friend to Sigurd Lewerentz during last years of the latter's life. He contributed to Lewerentz's work on the flower stand at Malmö's Eastern Cemetery and they collaborated on several competitions. Each strove to reduce architectural detailing to the powerful essential, and both worked primarily in brick, but Nyberg went farther in simplifying building geometry to circles and squares.

Important works. Row houses, Lund, 1961. Leander residence, Lund, 1963–74. County Administration Building, Malmö, 1965–74. County Archives, Lund, 1969–71. Chapel, Höör, 1972.

Further reading. *Arkitektur* 4/1996.

CARL NYRÉN (born 1917)

KTH, 1942. Worked for the Royal Naval Material Administration, 1942–44, and Paul Hedqvist, 1944–48. Started own architectural practice in 1948; reformed the office as an employee-owned business, Nyréns arkitektkontor, in 1983. It is one of Sweden's larger firms, with an extensive production of high-quality buildings of all types. Nyrén's early work followed in the footsteps of Gunnar Asplund. In the Sixties he was strongly influenced by Structuralist theory, developing typologies for everything from building sections to interior details. Since the 1980s Nyrén has pursued a more classical architecture of simple geometric blocks that are nonetheless always modulated by site conditions.

Important works. School of Economics, Gothenburg, 1948–52. Balder School, Danderyd, 1954. Västerort Church, Vällingby, 1957. Södra Vätterbygden Junior College, Jönköping, built in several stages. Malmö Institute of Education, 1963 and 1973. Trygg-Fylgia office building, Stockholm, 1965. Värnamo City Hall, 1961–70. Arrhenius Laboratories, Stockholm, 1973. Pharmacia offices and laboratories, Uppsala, starting in 1970. Stockholms Sparbank building, Stockholm, 1975. Fersen Terrace, Stockholm, 1976. St. Immanuel's Church, Jönköping, 1976. Gottsunda Church, Uppsala, 1980. Jönköping Train Station, 1984. Apartments, Nyköping, 1985. Public Library, Uppsala, 1986. Bank of Sweden, Linköping, 1988. Nyköping Concert Hall and Public Library, 1989. Klara office building, Stockholm, 1989. Jönköping Regional Museum, 1991. Apartments at Starrbäcksängen, Stockholm, 1992. Artisten (Göteborg University School of Performing Arts Building), Gothenburg, 1992. Mälardalen College, Västerås, 1994.

Further reading. *Arkitektur* 6/1983, *Nyréns arkitektkontor* (Arkitekturmuseet 1989).

GREGOR PAULSSON (1889–1977)

MA, 1909; MPhil (1911) and PhD (1915) in Art History. Worked for the National Museum of Fine Arts in 1913; curator of the museum, 1916–20. Parallel to his museum work, Paulsson was an art critic. He also authored several significant manifesto-like books. President of the Swedish Society of Industrial Design and editor of its journal, 1920–34. Professor of Art History at Uppsala University, 1934–56. Swedish General Commissioner at international industrial arts exhibitions in Paris in 1925 and New York in 1927, and for the Stockholm Exhibition of 1930. He did his MPhil and PhD studies in Berlin, where the socio-political ideas of German Modernism and the Deutscher Werkbund's agenda left a powerful impression. He was a central figure in industrial arts and architecture issues in Sweden, particularly between 1915 and 1930. Paulsson then concentrated his efforts on art history, writing the book *Svensk stad* (*The Swedish City*), in which he together with a group of doctoral students tried to create a picture of the physical and social environment of the Swedish city.

Writings. *Den nya Arkitekturen* (1916), *Vackrare vardagsvara* (1919), *accepters* (1931, with Asplund, Gahn, Markelius, Sundahl, Åhrén), *Konstens världshistoria 1–4* (1942–52), *Svensk stad 1–2* (1950–53), *Die soziale Dimension der Kunst* (1955), *Tingens bruk och prägel* (1956, with N. Paulsson).

ERIC SIGFRID PERSSON (1898–1983)

Persson was an innovative and productive builder who introduced the picture window to Swedish homes in the 1930s. Working primarily in Scania County, he built many prominent housing developments, including Ribershus (1938), and Friluftsstaden (1944–48), both in Malmö. The row-house development at Friluftsstaden was closely immitated in Huskvarna and Nässjö in the 1950s.

Further reading. Ulla Hårde, *Eric Sigfrid Persson* (1986).

Nyrén

LEIF REINIUS (1907–1995)

KTH, 1929. Worked for Hakon Ahlberg, 1929–35. Architectural practice with Sven Backström, 1936–92. Editor of *Byggmästaren*, 1944–50. Backström and Reinius combined functionality and sensuality in their architecture; they are also among the nation's most prominent residential planners.

Important works. Narrow apartment buildings at Hjorthagen, Stockholm, 1934–40 (with Hakon Ahlberg). Tegelslagaren residential block, Stockholm, 1936. Danviksklippan housing development, Stockholm, 1945. Star-shaped apartment buildings, towers, and terraced apartments in Gröndal, Stockholm, 1944–62. Women's apartment building, Stockholm, 1938. Elfvingegården housing, Stockholm, 1940. Nockeby Family Hotel, Stockholm, 1952. Rosta housing development, Örebro, 1947–52. Court of Appeals, Sundsvall, 1948. Vällingby town center, 1948–54. Farsta town center, 1956–60. Fifth tower in the Hötorgscity development, Stockholm, 1962. Åhléns department store, Stockholm, 1964.

Further reading. *Arkitektur* 6/1982.

GÖSTA REUTERSWÄRD (1892–1980)

Studied garden design in Denmark. Through his own firm Reuterswärd designed a series of parks in his Neoclassical style and restored many others, most notably Ulriksdal Palace Gardens north of Stockholm. He became head garden designer of the Swedish State Railways in 1938. During his twenty-year stint there he oversaw the renovation or new construction of about two thousand parks and plantings at train stations around the country. Reuterswärd remained faithful to his Neoclassical ideals throughout his career. He wrote several books, including *Blomstergårdens rika möjligheter* (1925).

GUSTAF ROSENBERG (born 1925)

KTH, 1925; KTH, 1952. Architectural practice with Olle Stål 1987, then worked independently as Rosenbergs arkitekter. Throughout his career, Rosenberg has remained an uncompromising Modernist.

Important works. Swim Hall, Sollentuna, 1972. Postal terminal, Solna, 1983. IBM office building in Kista, Stockholm, 1985. Skandinaviska Enskilda Banken data headquarters, Rissne, Sundbyberg, 1992. Office of Technical Works, Linköping, 1993.

TURE RYBERG (1888–1961)

KTH, 1912; KKH, 1912–14. Worked for the Stockholm City Planning Department, 1922–47. Taught Architecture to painting and sculpture students at KKH, 1918–53. Ryberg was successful in architectural competitions, most importantly that for the Karolinska Institute.

Important works. Thule Building on Kungsträdgårdsgatan, Stockholm, 1917 (with Erik Lallerstedt). Elementary School Teachers' Training College, Linköping, 1927. Single-family home for the Stockholm Exhibition of 1930. Town Hall, Saltsjöbaden, 1931. Swedish Church in Helsinki, Finland, 1932. Single-family homes in the Ysäter block, Djursholm, 1934. Two apartment buildings in the Mullbärsträdet block, Stockholm, 1935–38. Karolinska Medical Institute, Solna, 1936–61. Employee housing for the Southern Hospital, Stockholm, 1953.

Further reading. Johan Celsing, "Ture Ryberg 1888–1961", in *Arkitektur* 8/1993.

ARTUR VON SCHMALENSEE (1900–1972)

KTH, 1923; KKH, 1927–29. Worked for a short time for Sigurd Lewerentz, Gunnar Asplund, Sven Markelius, Gunnar Wetterling, and Schulze & Weaver in New York City. Worked for KF:s arkitektkontor, 1926–37. Started his own architectural practice in 1937. Began teaching freehand drawing and sculpture at KTH in 1939. Von Schmalensee was one of the leading architects at KF:s arkitektkontor, a Modernist with a penchant for Swedish 18th-century architecture.

Important works for KF:s arkitektkontor. Oat mill on Kvarnholmen, 1928. Apartment buildings on Kvarnholmen, 1934. Luma light-bulb factory, Stockholm, 1930. PUB department store on Drottninggatan, Stockholm, 1933–40.

Important independent works. Government office building annex in Gamla stan, Stockholm, 1945–50. Housing and offices for the Findus company in Bjuv, 1945. Student housing in Uppsala, 1945–53. Laboratory, pavilion, and offices for the Marabou chocolate factory, Sundbyberg, 1942–63. Kiruna City Hall, 1958–62. Union of Local Authorities Building, Stockholm, 1961. Restoration of Klara Church, Stockholm, 1965 (with John Sjöström).

Further reading. John Sjöström, "Arkitekten Artur von Schmalensee", in *Sankt Eriks årsbok 1974*.

KURT VON SCHMALENSEE (1896–1972)

KTH, 1922; KKH, 1924. Worked for KF:s arkitektkontor, 1925–29. City Architect in Norrköping, 1929–61.

Important works. Shops and other commissions for KF. Single-family home for the Stockholm Exhibition of 1930. Crematorium, Norrköping, 1938. Fire station, Norrköping, 1940. Water works, Norrköping, 1945. Norrköping Museum of Art, 1947. Motala Church, 1954. Crematorium, Motala, 1958. Kila Church, Södermanland County, 1963. Crematorium in Berthåga, Uppsala, 1965. Restoration of Växjö Cathedral, 1956–60.

HENNING SEGERROS (1916–95)

Studied landscape architecture in Sweden and Germany. Worked as a road maintenance advisory officer for the Swedish Homestead Society, 1944–59. Own professional practice, Henning Segerros Office of Nature Conservation, 1959–85. During the massive expansion of the road system in the Forties and Fifties and the exploitation of the rivers for hydroelectric power generation in the Sixties and Seventies, Segerros worked to incorporate these vast man-made structures into the natural landscape.

Important works. Ljunga Power Plant in Västernorrland County, 1969–80. Expansion of the Ljunga and Ljusna plants, 1972 and 1975. Restoration plan for the Slite Lime Quarry on the island of Gotland, 1977–82. Further reading. *Utblick Landskap* 4/1996.

ERNST STENHAMMAR (1859–1927)

KTH, 1882; KKH, 1884. Internship with Isak Gustaf Clason, 1884–87. Started own architectural practice in 1887. Taught at KTH, 1887–1905. Most of Stenhammar's commissions at the turn of the century were for commercial projects such as retail and office buildings and banks. After 1909 the focus of his work shifted to hospital design. He was among the first architects who looked to construction as the basis for a modern expression free from stylistic features.

Important works. The Central Palace office complex, Stockholm, 1895–98. Myrstedt & Stern department store, Stockholm, 1909. Tjänstemanna Bank, Stockholm, 1906–08. Grand Hôtel Royal, Stockholm, 1905–09. A long series of hospital buildings.

ESKIL SUNDAHL (1890–1974)

KTH, 1914; KKH, 1916–18. Worked for Isak Gustaf Clason and Erik Lallerstedt. Started his own architectural practice in 1920. Worked on the Committee for Standardization in the Building Industry, 1923–26. Principal of KF:s arkitektkontor, 1924–58. Professor of Building Construction at KTH, 1936–57. Contributed to the manifesto *acceptera*, 1931.

Important works. Sandström School, Stockholm, 1923. Swedish Tobacco Monopoly factory buildings (facades), Stockholm, 1924–27. Bus garages at Hornsberg, Stockholm, 1933 and 1939. For KF:s arkitektkontor. Konsum complex in Stockholm, 1930–33; Konsum department store, Borlänge, 1931 (with Eric Rockström).

Further reading. Lisa Brunnström, *Den rationella fabriken, om funktionalismens rötter* (1990).

IVAR TENGBOM (1878–1968)

CTH, 1898; KKH, 1901. Internship with Erik Lallerstedt, 1901–03. Editor of *Arkitektur*, 1908–11. Taught at the Klara School, 1910–11. Architectural practice with Ernst Torulf, 1906–12; Tengbom was responsible for the firm's commissions in Stockholm, Torulf those in Gothenburg. Opened his own office in 1912. Professor of Architecture at KKH, 1916–20. Head of the National Board of Public Building, 1924–36. Member of several professional societies. As early as 1914 Tengbom's office had grown to the largest in Stockholm. The firm's high standards of quality and ability to organize assignments rationally have contributed to its strong reputation. His office has survived several generational shifts in personnel and remains one of the country's oldest.

Important works. With Ernst Torulf: Prizewinning submission to the competition for Stockholm's Courthouse (later the City Hall), 1902–04. Arvika Eastern Church, 1908–11. Borås Town Hall, 1909–10. By Tengboms arkitektkontor: Enskilda Banken, Stockholm, 1912–15. Enskilda Banken, Borås, 1912–15. Högalid Church, 1917–23. Stockholm Concert Hall, 1923–26. School of Economics, Stockholm, 1925–26. Tändstickspalatset (Swedish Match Company headquarters), Stockholm, 1928. Esselte printing press and publishing house, Stockholm, 1928–34. Citypalatset commercial building, Norrmalmstorg, Stockholm, 1930–32. Örebro Savings Bank,

Tengbom

Tesch

Örebro, 1932–34. The Swedish Institute in Rome, Italy, 1940. Bonnier Publishing House, Stockholm, 1946–49 (with son Anders Tengbom). By Tengboms arkitektkontor under the leadership of Anders Tengbom (born 1911): Skogshem Conference Center, 1959. Svenska Dagbladet Building, Stockholm, 1962. Löwenström Hospital, Upplands Väsby, 1968. Swedish Embassy in Moscow, 1972. Trygg Hansa Insurance Company, Stockholm, 1975. Canon office building, Stockholm, 1978–84. After reorganization in 1989 as Tengbomgruppen: Sagerska huset restoration, 1990. Tyréns office building, Stockholm, 1997.

Further reading. *Tengboms. Ett arkitektkontors utveckling sedan 1905* (1991).

NILS TESCH (1907–1975)

KTH, 1930; KKH, 1932–34. Worked for Birger Jonson, 1930–34, and Paul Hedqvist, 1934–36. Started architectural practice with LM Giertz in 1936. Tesch's architecture synthesized tradition and functionalism in a unique manner.

Important works. Wehtje residence, Djursholm, 1940. Solna Grammar School, 1947. Row houses and apartment buildings, Västerås, 1944–50. (All with Giertz) Smith residence, 1959, and Mölna row house development, 1954–60, both on Lidingö. Örebro Regional Museum, 1940–64. Umeå Home Economics Teachers' Training College, 1951–60. Loen block offices in Stockholm, 1970. Collaborated with Peter Celsing on a few commissions and competitions.

Further reading. *Arkitektur* 5/1991.

OLOF THUNSTRÖM (1896–1962)

KTH, 1922. Worked as Project Architect for KF:s arkitektkontor, 1925–62, where he was one of the office's most talented residential architects.

Important works. Row house development on Kvarnholmen, Nacka, 1929. Prize-winning submission entitled to the City of Stockholm affordable housing competition of 1932. Katarina Elevator and Kooperativa förbundet's offices at Slussen in Stockholm, 1935. Housing development and office building, Gustavsberg, 1937–1950s.

Writings. *Ombyggnad* (*Renovation*), 1955 (with Ingrid Johansson).

Further reading. Connie Norenstedt, *Olof Thunström* (Stockholm univ. 1980).

Wahlman

ERNST TORULF (1872–1936)

CTH, 1893; KKH, 1896. Worked in collaboration with Ivar Tengbom in Gothenburg, 1906–12. Then started own architectural practice, which grew to become the largest in Gothenburg around 1920. Member of the ARES group of architects (see Ericson).

Important works. Gothenburg College, 1902–07 (with Erik Hahr). By Tengbom & Torulf: Arvika Eastern Church, 1908–11. Borås Town Hall, 1909–10. With other architects in the ARES group: Gothenburg Museum of Art, 1923. Independent works: Hvitfeldt Grammar School, Gothenburg, 1915. Museum of Natural History, Gothenburg, 1916–23. Central Post Office, Gothenburg, 1923.

LARS ISRAEL WAHLMAN (1870–1952)

KTH, 1893. Started own architectural practice in 1893. Began teaching at KTH in 1894; Professor at KTH, 1912–35. Also taught Garden Design at KKH. Numerous lectures and papers for professional journals. Wahlman was one of a group of leading architects who developed the new material-conscious architecture in the early 20th century. Among them Wahlman had been the most influenced by the British Arts and Crafts Movement.

Important works. Hjularöd Palace, Scania County, 1894–97 (with Clason). Tjolöholm Palace, including worker housing, gardens, and other ancillary elements, 1897–1904. Trevnan residence and Trotzgården residence in Hedemora, 1900–01. Architect's own home, the Villa Tallom, Stocksund, 1904–05. Wahlman's most important work was the Engelbrekt Church, Stockholm, 1909–14. Thereafter many other churches, chapels, and church restorations in communities such as Oslo (1917–26), Tranås (1930), and Östersund (1940).

Further reading. Bengt Romare and others, *Verk av LI Wahlman* (1950).

SVEN WALLANDER (1890–1968)

KTH, 1913; KKH, 1913–15. Worked for a short time (1916–17) for Ivar Tengbom, Lars Israel Wahlman, and for the Stockholm City Planning Commission, where under the direction of Per Olof Hallman he worked on the development of Kungsgatan and designed the northern of its paired towers. Then started his own architecural practice. Wallander was an important organizer. He founded the nation-wide cooperative housing development company HSB (the National Federation of Tenants' Savings and Building Societies) in 1923, and was both president of the company and head of its architectural office from 1923 to 1958. Member of the social housing comission of 1933–47. Became Chairman of the Committee for Standardization in the Building Industry in 1950 and a member of the National Committee for Building Research in 1953. Some of the most important HSB projects in Stockholm are the Hedemoratäppan block (1926), the Metern block (1926), the Färjan block (1929), the Marmorn block (1932 and '39), the Kungklippan block (1936), and the Reimersholme housing development (1942–46).

Further reading. Sven Wallander, *Mitt liv med HSB* (1968), Kerstin Thörn, *En bostad för hemmet. Idehistoriska studier i bostadsfrågan 1889–1929* (Umeå 1997).

INGRID WALLBERG (1890–1965)

Did not have a formal degree in architecture. Wallberg was one of the first female architects in Sweden. Her sister Lotti married Albert Jeanneret, brother of Le Corbusier, which helped Wallberg land an internship with the master in the spring of 1928. There she met Alfred Roth, who followed her to Gothenburg, where they started an architectural practice together in 1928. Roth left the firm in 1930.

Important works. Apartment buildings in the Helagsfjället and Nybygget blocks for HSB, Gothenburg, 1929–30. Simonsson summer house on Särö, Kungsbacka, 1930. Single family home in Örgryte, 1932 and row houses on Brödragatan, both in Gothenburg, 1935.

Further reading. Eva Rudberg, "Kvinnor blir arkitekter (1)", in *Arkitektur 2/1983*, Karin Winter, "Ingrid Wallberg", in Gunilla Lundahl (ed.), *Kvinnor som banade väg* (BFR T 6:1992).

JAN WALLINDER (born 1915)

KTH, 1939; KKH, 1950. Worked for Gunnar Asplund, 1938–40. Architectural practice with Sven Brolid in Gothenburg, 1948–54. Professor of Theoretical and Applied Aesthetics at CTH, 1959–80. Wallinder designed apartments with unusual and well-thought-out layouts, as well as town centers, schools, and libraries. He represents a cultivated development of the Functionalist tradition.

Important works. Apartments at Södra Guldheden, Gothenburg, 1950. Apartments and town center at Järnbrott, Gothenburg, 1951. Doktor Fries torg, Gothenburg, 1955. Axel Dahlströms torg, Gothenburg, 1956. Apartments in Kortedala, Gothenburg, 1956. Karlskrona Public Library, 1959. Jönköping Public Library, 1969. Ljungby Public Library, 1978.

VBB

VBB is a large technological consulting firm that is descendant from Vattenbyggnadsbyrån (the Office of Hydraulic Engineering), which was founded in 1897. The architectural design department represents only a small part of the business of the office. See also Sune Lindström.

GUNNAR WEJKE (1905–57)

KTH. Worked for KF:s arkitektkontor. Architectural practice with Kjell Ödeen, 1935–53. Contributing expert in research projects for the National Housing Loan Office. Became general director of the National Board of Public Building in 1951.

Important works. Central Gymnastics Institute, Stockholm, 1944. Norra Guldheden housing development, Gothenburg, 1943–47.

SIGURD WESTHOLM (1871–1960)

KTH, 1898. Internship with Isak Gustaf Clason. Architectural practice with John Alban Bagger until 1915. Acted as interim City Architect in Stockholm, 1909–16. Stockholm City Architect, 1916–40. Westholm contributed a great deal to architecture and urban planning in Stockholm. Westholm served as an expert witness in various investigations of housing politics and construction legislation. He formulated the conditions for state-subsidized home loans in a 1942 booklet known popularly as 'Westholm's Bible;' he had a profound influence on housing construction in Sweden.

Further reading. Lennart Holm (ed.), *Stockholmsbyggen 1916–1940, skildrade av Sigurd Westholm* (1993).

CARL WESTMAN (1866–1936)

KTH, 1889; KKH, 1892. Internship in an office in the United States, 1893–94. Started

Westman

own architectural practice in 1897. Westman played a leading role in the development of a new architecture in which the building's expression was conveyed by its materials and construction. More than any of his generation of architects, Westman strove relentlessly to make robust buildings with a characteristic straightforward simplicity. He made critical contributions to the development of the architectural theory of the day. One of his lectures launched what became an important literary work, *Gamla svenska städer* (*Old Swedish Cities*). Westman also made significant contributions as a furniture designer and graphic artist. In 1916 he went to work for the National Board of Health, and concentrated on hospital design for the remainder of his career.

Important works. Worker housing in Åtvidaberg and Bjärka-Säby, 1900–1905. Several single-family homes in Saltsjöbaden, 1903–04, including the Pressen residence, 1901–02. Swedish Society of Medicine Building, Stockholm, 1904–06. Romanäs Sanatorium, Tranås, 1905–07. Nyköping District Courthouse, 1907–10. Stockholm City Law Courts, 1909–15. Villa Högberga, Lidingö, 1909–13. Röhsska Museum of Applied Arts, Gothenburg, 1910–14. Houses for the Landala residential development, Gothenburg, 1913–14. Bünsow residence, Diplomat City, Stockholm, 1917–20. St. Mary's Hospital, Helsingborg, 1917–27. Norrköping General Hospital, 1922–26. Red Cross Nursing Home, Stockholm, 1922–07. Karolinska Medical Center, Solna, 1928–40. Umedalen Hospital, Umeå, 1929–34.

Further reading. Bertil Palm, *Arkitekten Carl Westman 1866–1936* (Lund 1954).

HANS WESTMAN (1905–91)

KTH, 1929. Worked for Wahlman and Ahlberg, 1929–31, and Hedqvist, 1931–33. Worked in the Malmö City Planning Department under Erik Bülow-Hübe, 1932–36. Own practice in Malmö and Lund, 1936–83. Westman was a Functionalist who strove to anchor his work in the regional architectural traditions.

Important works. 'Leisure Time' Exhibition in Ystad, 1936. Swimming Hall in Lund, 1938. Architect's own home in Lund, 1939. Linnéstaden development, Lund, 1945–48. Simrishamn City Hall, 1944–53. Sketch Museum (an archive for the decorative arts), Lund, 1947–59. Several student apartment buildings in Lund during the 1950s. Sports building, Linköping, 1956. Catholic church, Malmö, 1960.

Further reading. Tomas Tägil, *Arkitekten*

Hans Westman, funktionalismen och den regionala särarten (1996).

WHITE ARKITEKTER

White arkitekter takes its name from its founder, Sidney White (1917–82), born in Gothenburg to a family of English descent. After winning the competition for the Baronbackarna housing development in Örebro, he collaborated with Per-Axel Ekholm (born 1920) in the firm of Ekholm and White, 1951–59. White's independent practice was called WAAB for a time before becoming White arkitekter. Since its dramatic growth in the 1960s, the employee-owned office has been the next-largest in Sweden, with 274 employees in 1996. Most of White arkitekter's commissions have been for governmental clients such as public housing corporations and county councils. White arkitekter's work carries on Sweden's Functionalist tradition, informed by a committment to research and development.

Important works. Baronbackarna housing development, Örebro, 1957. Tynnered housing development, Gothenburg, 1967. Addition to the Gothenburg Museum of Art, 1968. Östra Nordstan shopping mall, Gothenburg, 1969. Swedish Broadcasting and Television Corporation complex, Gothenburg, 1970. Varberg Hospital, 1972. Vara Nursing Home and Health Care Center, 1977. Lingatan Conference Center, Lysekil, 1982. Apartments in the Mjölnaren block, Gothenburg, 1984. Gothia Hotel, Gothenburg, 1984. Postal terminal, Gothenburg, 1978–87. 'The Healthy Home', Upplands Väsby, 1985. Halmstad Hospital, several phases. Asken office building, Gothenburg, 1986. Volvo automotive manufacturing plant, Uddevalla, 1988. IBM office building, Gothenburg, 1988. Hotel 11, Gothenburg, 1993. Riseberga School, Malmö, 1995. Östra Torn School, Lund, 1997.

Further reading. *Arkitektur* 5/1987.

GUSTAF WICKMAN (1858–1916)

CTH, 1880; KKH, 1884. Worked for Isaeus & Sandahls arkitektkontor, 1883–7. Wickman was at the turn of the century the leading bank architect in Sweden. He also received a long series of commissions for the development of the mining town of Kiruna. His ecclectic architecture combined Baroque and Art-Nouveau forms with the style of modern American retail buildings and innovative technology, particularly in commercial construction. Wickman's talent for creating space is particularly apparent in his bank buildings. He spent his final years, 1913–16, designing hospitals for the National Board of Health.

Important works. Nacka Church, 1888–91. Swedish pavilion at the Chicago World's Fair of 1893. City of Stockholm pavilion and other assignments for the Stockholm Exhibition of 1897. Skånes Enskilda Bank, Stockholm, 1897–1900. Fåhreus residence, Saltsjöbaden, 1898–1900. Norrköpings Enskilda Bank, 1899–1902. Several commissions for the City of Kiruna, including worker housing, starting in 1899. Sundsvalls Enskilda Bank, Stockholm, 1900–02. Skånska Banken, Malmö, 1903–06. Kiruna Church, 1903–12. Stockholm Public Maternity Hospital, 1904–13. Långbro Hospital, Stockholm, 1905–10. Örebro Enskilda Bank, 1909–12. Skandia Insurance Company, Gothenburg, 1909–11.

Further reading. Fredric Bedoire, *En arkitekt och hans verksamhetsfält kring sekelskiftet* (1974).

TAGE WILLIAM OLSSON (1888–1960)

Studied and practiced professionally in the field of mining engineering. After designing mine head frames together with architect Melchior Wernstedt, Olsson determined to return to school to study architecture, and graduated from KTH in 1925. Worked primarily as an urban planner. Head of the City of Gothenburg Planning Department, 1943–53.

Important works. Second place in the 1927 international competition for the League of Nations Palace in Geneva. Slussen traffic hub, Stockholm, 1931–35. Experimental apartment building in Järnbrott, Gothenburg, 1950–53.

GERT WINGÅRDH (born 1951)

CTH, 1975. Started own architectural practice in 1977. Collaborated with Anders Wilhelmsson during the 1980s. Wingårdh started small with a few residences and a series of shop and restaurant interiors. In the late Eighties he began to receive increasingly larger commissions, and today the office is one of Sweden's most successful. Wingårdh was one of the country's first explicitly Post-Modern architects and has continued to demonstrate great aptitude for adopting and adapting current prototypes to his work. He strives for the unexpected and surprising, but details his buildings with high precision.

Important works. Nordh residence, Gothenburg, 1978. Yoko Yap shoe store, Gothenburg, 1982. Öijared Executive Country Club, Lerum, 1988. Nilson residence, Varberg, 1992. Astra Hässle pharmaceutical laboratories, Mölndal, 1989–96. Ale High School, Nödinge, 1995. Ericsson office building, Lund, 1997. Swedish Embassy in Berlin, 1998.

Further reading. *Arkitektur* 2/1995.

HELGE ZIMDAL (born 1903)

KTH, 1927; KKH, 1930. Professor of Architecture at CTH, 1951–70. Architectural practice with Nils Ahrbom, 1932–50. Thereafter independent practice.

Important works. With Ahrbom: Sveaplan Girls' High School, Stockholm, 1935. Eriksdal School, Stockholm, 1937. Skanstull High School, Stockholm, 1943. Linköping Museum of Art, 1939. Independent works: ABF Building, Stockholm, 1958. CTH School of Architecture, 1968. Swedish Embassy in Brasilia, Brazil, 1974.

Writings. *En arkitekt minns* (1981).

UNO ÅHRÉN (1897–1977)

KTH, 1919. Åhrén was one of Sweden's most prominent architectural polemicists and theoreticians, a leading proponent of Modernism, and one of the driving forces behind the 1931 Modernist manifesto *acceptera* and the movement's popular breakthrough at the Stockholm Exhibition of 1930. He was editor of *Byggmästaren*, 1929–32. Chief City Engineer of Gothenburg, 1932–43. President of Riksbyggen, the Cooperative Building Organization of the Swedish Trade Unions, 1943–45. Professor of Urban Planning at KTH, 1947–63.

Important works. Interiors in the style of 'Swedish Grace' for the Exhibition of 1925 in Paris. Flamman Cinema, 1930. KTH Student Union, Stockholm, 1930 (with Markelius). Row houses for the Stockholm Exhibition of 1930 and in Norra Ängby for HSB, 1931. As president of Riksbyggen, Åhrén was behind Årsta town center (1943–53), the first comprehensive community center development in Sweden.

Writings. Åhrén was a prolific writer whose primary subject was community planning issues. His books include *Arkitektur och demokrati* (1942), *Bygg bättre samhällen* (1943), and *Ett planmässigt samhällsbyggande* (1945).

Further reading. Eva Rudberg, *Uno Åhrén* (1981)

Åhrén

JOHN ÅKERLUND (1884–1961)

Educated to be an electrical engineer. Architectural internship with Torben Grut. Contributed background field research for the book series *Svenska Allmogehem*. Built housing for various industries, most notably in Norrland. Designed a long series of mountaineering stations and standardized huts for the Swedish Touring Club. Secretary of the Swedish Homestead Society, 1916–23. Åkerlund stood for a simple and functional architecture based on traditional prototypes.

Important works. Sörängen Junior College, Nässjö, 1912–15. Worker housing including the Josef block, Västerås, 1913–15. Standard house proposal for single-family home developments in several communities, including Borås, 1914–17. Buidings for the Sigtuna Foundation, 1915–24, and Sigtuna Grammar School, 1925–29. Housing for workers for various industrial companies, such as Boliden, 1926–34. Churches in a number of communities, including Brevik on Lidingö.

Writings. Contributed to *Svenska allmogehem* (1909) and *Gamla svenska allmogehem* (1912). Lone author of *Arbetarbostäder vid industriella bruk* (1917).

BRITA ÅKERMAN (born 1906)

MPhil in Literary History, Stockholm University, 1933. Conducted important research on the home, housework, and housewares that led to improvements in housing and community planning as well as helping to inform consumers. Contributed to the public interest organization Active Housekeeping, 1940–46. Became Secretary of the Women's Delegation to the National Census in 1941. Chairperson of the Home Research Institute, 1944–51. Worked for the Swedish Society of Industrial Design, 1946–56 and 1962–67. Member of the National Committee for Women's Issues in Stockholm, 1967–75. Served as either expert witness or secretary in several public investigations of family life, housework, general women's issues, consumer advocacy, and social planning from the 1940s through the 1970s, including the Housing Collective Committee of 1948–56.

Writings. *Familjen som växte ur sitt hem* (1941), *Makt åt konsumenterna* (1968), *Den okända vardagen. Vi kan, vi behövs, Kunskap för vår vardag* (with others, 1983, 1984), *88 år på 1900-talet* (1994).

Further reading. Gunilla Lundahl, "Brita

Östberg

Åkerman", i Gunilla Lundahl (ed.), *Kvinnor som banade väg* (BFR T 6:1992).

RAGNAR ÖSTBERG (1866–1945)

KTH, 1989; KKH, 1891. Study trip to the United States in 1893. Interned in several offices, most importantly with Isak Gustaf Clason, 1891–96. Östberg began his independent architectural practice with a series of residences in the first decade of the century. Participated in the 1903–04 competition for a new district courthouse for the city of Stockholm. The assignment, later changed to a city hall, would occupy the architect until 1923. Professor at KKH, 1922–32. Östberg soon became a central figure in architectural circles during the early 20th century. He fought for a new ideal based on the expressive use of materials and a strict interpretation of the functional program and building structure. Within this framework he contributed more than any other Swede to the enrichment of architecture's expressive potential through innovative floor plans, eventful sequences of rooms, and evocative detailing.

Important works. Brudnäs residence, Östanå, 1900–01. Ebbagården residence, Stockholm, 1901–03. Summer house for Eva Bonnier on Dalarö, 1904. Pauli residence, Djursholm, 1904–05. Villa Ekarne (Laurin residence), Stockholm, 1905. Östermalm Grammar School, 1906–10. Yngve Larsson residence, Storängen, 1907. K. O. Bonnier residence, Manilla, 1909. Stockholm City Hall, 1909–23. Villa Elfsviksudde, Lidingö, 1910–11. Geber residence, Stockholm, 1911–13. Odd Fellow Building, Nyköping, 1911–13. Patent Office Building, Stockholm, 1911–21. Carl Eldh Studio, Stockholm, 1918. Crematorium, Helsingborg, 1924–25. Värmland County Student Society House, Uppsala, 1926–30. National Maritime Museum, Stockholm, 1931–34.

Further reading. Elias Cornell, *Ragnar Östberg — svensk arkitekt* (1965).

ABBREVIATIONS

CTH (*Chalmers tekniska högskola*). Chalmers University of Technology, Gothenburg.
KTH (*Kungliga tekniska högskolan*). The Royal Institute of Technology, Stockholm.
KKH (*Kungliga konsthögskolans arkitektskola*). The Royal University College of Fine Arts School of Architecture, Stockholm.
LTH (*Lunds tekniska högskola*). Lund University of Technology, Lund.

Photo Credits

AM = Svedish Museum of Architecture

A.B. Aeronautic: 279 c
Aero Materiel AB: 53 a
Ahlsén, Tore: 152 b
Andersson, Henrik O.: 31 c, 249 a
Andersson, Thorbjörn: 229, 230, 231 b, 233 a,
    235 a, 236, 238 c, 241
Andersson, Yngve: 92 b
Arbetarrörelsens Arkiv: 81
Arken Ark. k.: 177 c
Arvidsson, in AM: 108 a
Asplund, Gunnar: 41 a
Barthelsson, Arne: 329 b
Benno: 69 c
Berg Ark. kontor, C.H.Tillberg: 180 c
Berglund, Torsten: 352 a
Bergström, Beata: 163 a
Bergström, Per: 172, 355 b
Bladh, Oscar, Aerofoto: 123 a, 139 b, 148 a,
    240 a, 293 b
Bonde, Per, in AM: 20, 24 a, 77
Borg Mesch/Kiruna Komm.: 246 a
Breitholtz, Björn: 186 c, 346 c
Caldenby, Claes: 10 c, 28 c, 37 b, 121, 128 c,
    145 b, 149 b, 164 b, 166 c, 173, 174, 175 a,
    180 a, 180 b, 182 b, 189 a, 189 b, 190 c, 192 a,
    195 d, 196, 244 a, 244 b, 244 d, 251 a, 256 a,
    256 b, 257 a, 257 c, 290 a, 290 b, 295 a, 308 a,
    310 b, 314 b, 318 a, 318 b, 318 c, 319 b, 319 c,
    319 d, 323 a, 323 b, 340 c
Carlén, Lennart J:sen: 145 a
Celander, Ulf: 175 c
Peter Celsingarkivet: 153 c, 154 a, 154 b, 306 a
    (Fabio Galli), 307 a, 307 b (F.G.), 307 c
    (F.G.), 326 a, 326 b, 326 c (F.G.), 326 d
    (F.G.), 336 a, 337 a, 337 b, 337 c, 337 d (F.G.)
Dahlström, Rolf: 177 b, 335 a, 335 b, 335 d
Ekestang, Hans, from SL: 193 a
Ellqvist, Oscar, in AM: 41 b
Ericksson, Bengt: 186 b, 346 b, 347 a
Erskine, Ralph: 131 c
Esselte: 96 b
Feininger, Andreas: 100 b
Fotomonopolet: 67 a, 67 c
Föreningen Svensk Form: 202 a, 202 c (Ateljé
    Sundahl), 205 (Håkan Alexandersson), 206 a,
    206 b, 208 a, 208 b, 209 a, 209 b, 210 b, 210 c
    (Bengt Carlén), 210 d (Schultz), 211 b, 211 c
    (Holmén), 212 a, 212 b (A. Feininger), 215 a,
    215 b (Ateljé Wahlberg), 216 a (Lars Eklund),
    216 b, 217 a (Ateljé Wahlberg), 217 b, 218
    (Lindberg-Foto), 219 a (actionbild), 219 b
    (Karl-Erik Granath), 220 (IKEA), 221 a,
    221 b (Innovator Design), 223 a (Fabio Galli),
    223 b (IKEA), 224
Galli, Fabio: 313 a, 313 b
Goodwin, Henry B: 259 b
Gullers, K.W.: 115 c, 228 a (in Nordiska Museet)
Göteborgs Konstmuseum: 19 (Ebbe Carlsson)
Göteborgs Stadsarkiv: 14
Hallberg, Stefan: 344 b
Halldin, Oscar: 278 c
Hallén, Lars: 187 b, 289 a, 289 b, 289 c, 350 a,
    350 b, 350 c, 350 d, 351 a
Hedö, Kurt: 165 b
Hennos, in AM: 56 b
Hernried, in AM: 304 a
Hidemark, Ove: 364 c

Hintze, Rolf: 300 b
Hjertén, Thomas, in AM: 176 b
HSB: 363 a
Hultin, Olof: 277 e, 325 a, 325 b
Hultzén, G: 135 a
Håkansson, Mats: 179 a, 283 a, 283 b
Håsonbild: 139 a, 300 c
Jalkman, Per: 352 b, 352 c
KF:s bildservice: 93 b, 94 (Elvegård), 278 b
Kidder Smith, G.E.: 92 a, 99, 117 a, 128 b, 288 a,
Källemo: 222 a, 222 b, 225
Larsson, Kjell-Arne: 354 a
Larsson, Lennart, Reklambyrå: 191 a
Leandersson, Bert: 362 a
Liljedahl, Jappe: 358 d
Lindén, Mats: 305 c
Lindhe, Jens: 359 a, 359 b
Lindman, Åke E:son: 50 c, 83 d, 164 a, 177 a,
    195 b, 266 c, 279 b, 286 a, 286 b, 287 a, 287 b,
    287 c, 287 d, 333 a, 333 b, 333 c, 349 a, 349 b,
    349 c, 355 c, 355 d, 356 a, 356 b, 357 b, 360 a,
    360 b, 360 c, 361 a, 362 b, 362 d, 366 a, 366 b,
    366 c, 367 a, 367 b, 367 c
Mattsson, Gunnar: 182 a
Metria: 2, 170
Nationalmuseum: 198, 200
Nilsson, Pål-Nils: 128 a, 147 c, 312 a, 312 c
Nitro (Dyno) Nobel: 297
Nordiska Museet: 18, 201 (Mats Landin), 203
Stig Nyberg's collection: 245 c
Unknown photographer: 10 a, 44 b, 52, 66 b, 79
    a, 93 a, 104 a, 131 b, 147 a, 148 b, 149 a, 153 c,
    154 a, 154 b, 158 b, 166 a, 192 c, 195 c, 255 c,
    262 a, 270 a (FFNS), 307 a, 307 b, 307 c, 314 a,
    324 a, 324 b, 328 d (Coordinator AB), 329 a
    (Coordinator AB), 330 a, 332 a, 343 a, 358 a,
    358 b, 358 c, 363 a (HSB), 370, 375, 385,
    389, 390 a, 394 a
Unknown photographer, in AM: 22 a, 22 c, 25 b,
    26 a, 31 a, 31 b, 37 d, 39, 46, 48 a, 51 a, 56 a,
    58 a, 62 a, 62 b, 66 a, 68, 71 b, 74 b, 83 a, 83 c,
    86 a, 87 c, 88, 89 a, 90 a, 97 b, 98 c, 101 a, 101
    b, 102 a, 102 b, 103 a, 103 b, 103 c, 104 b, 105
    a, 105 b, 106 a, 106 b, 106 c, 107, 109, 110, 116
    c, 120 a, 126 b, 132 a, 132 c, 145 d, 150, 156 b,
    157 a, 166 d, 167 b, 185 a, 195 c, 207 a, 246 c,
    247 a, 251 b, 252 b, 255 a, 255 c, 261 b, 263 a,
    263 b, 263 c, 264 a, 266 b, 270 b, 271 a, 274 a,
    274 c, 275 a, 275 b, 275 c, 275 d, 275 e, 277 d,
    278 a, 282 b, 285 b, 288 b, 293 a, 299 a, 302 a,
    304 b, 306 a, 320 b, 321 c, 321 d, 331 b, 331 d,
    339 b, 339 c, 339 d, 372, 378, 379, 391
Olson, Lennart/TIO: 114 a, 133 a, 135 c, 162 a,
    246 d, 298 a, 301 a, 301 b, 301 d, 305 b
Olsson, Jan: 135 b, 175 b, 303 a, 303 b, 345 a, 345 b
Olsson, Karl Erik: 167 a, 167 c, 168 b
Olsson Snogeröd: 383 a, 383 b
Pehrson, Lars/FLT-PICA: 364 d
af Peterséns, Lennart: 137, 252 a
Plunger, Max: 10 b, 13, 15, 32 a, 54 b, 63 a, 64 a,
    64 b, 65 b, 73 a, 73 b, 76 a, 76 b, 96 c, 123 b,
    125 a, 133 b, 151 a, 151 b, 157 b, 163 b, 166 b,
    168 a, 176 a, 181 a, 181 b, 183 c, 183 d, 184 a,
    185 b, 191 b, 243, 247 b, 248 a, 248 b, 254 b,
    258 a, 258 b, 258 c, 259 c, 260 a, 261 a, 265 a,
    265 b, 266 a, 268 a, 268 c, 269 a, 269 b, 269 c,
    272 a, 272 c, 273 a, 273 c, 273 d, 280 a, 280 b,
    280 c, 281 a, 281 b, 284 d, 285 a, 292 a, 296 a,
    296 b, 305 a, 308 b, 308 c, 309 a, 309 b, 310 a,
    310 c, 311 a, 315 b, 316 a, 316 b, 316 c, 317 a,
    317 b, 317 d, 320 a, 320 c, 321 a, 321 b, 322 b,
    327 a, 327 b, 328 c, 330 b, 330 c, 331 a, 331 c,
    332 c, 334 a, 334 c, 334 d, 338 a, 338 b, 340 a,
    342 a, 342 c, 343 c, 364 b, 384 a, 387 a

Pressens Bild: 393 a
Price: 124
Priivits, Hugo: 152 c, 373 a
Robinson, Victor, in AM: 142 b, 188 b, 332 a
Rombo, Gunilla: 353 b
Rosenberg, Anders: 364 e
Rosenberg, C.G., in AM: 30 b, 40, 74 a, 79 b,
    90 b, 95, 100 c, 239 a, 270 c
Sandqvist, Christer: 193 b
Schultz, Karl: 85 a, 91 b
Sjödén, Nils-Olof: 346 a
Sjöstedt foto: 134 c
Stickelmann, Rudolf: 75
Stockholms Stadsmuseum: 21, 22 b, 23 a, 23 c,
    24 b, 25 a, 26 b, 27, 28 a, 28 b, 29, 30 a, 37 a,
    37 c, 44 a, 48 b, 97 a, 250 b, 256 d, 374 a,
    390 b
Stora Kopparbergs Bergslags AB: 70
Sundahl, Sune, in AM: 17, 113 a, 116 a, 120 b,
    125 b, 126 a, 132 a, 134 a, 134 b, 140, 141,
    142 a, 146 c, 156 a, 158 a, 162 b, 165 a, 165 c,
    183 a, 183 b, 239 c, 291 c, 294 b, 295 b, 295 c,
    302 c, 341 a, 341 b, 341 c
Svenska Bostäder AB: 300 a
Svenskt Tenn: 211 a
Sörvik: 100 a
Törngren, Bo: 226
Unations: 130
Wahlberg: 108 c, 301 c
Vattenfall: 253 a
Westergren, Staffan: 49 b
Westerman, Allan: 184 c
Wichmann, Per: 357 a
Widén, Mats in AM: 56 c
Wiking (Foto-): 276 c
Wilken, Ingrid: 282 a
Vilson, Sten: 159 a
Wingårdh, Gert: 186 a
Winter, Karin: 58 b
Volny, Ingrid: 369
Wretling, Hans: 348 a, 348 c, 365 a, 365 c, 365 e
Wærn, Rasmus: 262 b
Yeh, Thomas: 185 d, 344 a, 344 d
Zätterlund, Håkan: 353 a

Selected Bibliography

Ahlberg, Hakon *Gunnar Asplund arkitekt* (1943)

Ahlin, Janne *Sigurd Lewerentz arkitekt* (1985)

Améen, Lennart *Stadsbebyggelse och domänstruktur. Svensk stadsutveckling i relation till ägoförhållanden och administrativa gränser* (1964)

Andersson, Henrik O & Bedoire, Fredric *Stockholms byggnader* (1973, 1988)

Andersson, Henrik O & Bedoire, Fredric *Bankbyggande i Sverige* (1980)

Andersson, Henrik O & Bedoire, Fredric *Svensk arkitektur. Ritningar 1640–1970 / Swedish Architecture. Drawings 1640–1970* (1986)

Arkitektur 6/1982 (Backström & Reinius)

Arkitektur 6/1983 (Carl Nyrén)

Arkitektur 6/1984 (Asmussen)

Arkitektur 5/1987 (White arkitekter)

Arkitektur 5/1991 (Nils Tesch)

Arkitektur 4/1994 (Sven Ivar Lind)

Arkitektur 2/1995 (Gert Wingårdh)

Arkitektur 4/1996 (Bernt Nyberg)

Arkitektur 6/1998 (Jan Wallinder)

Asplund, Gunnar a.o. *acceptera* (1931)

Backström, Sven & Ålund, Stig (eds.) *Fyrtiotalets svenska bostad* (1950)

Bedoire, Fredric *En arkitekt och hans verksamhetsfält kring sekelskiftet. Gustaf Wickmans arbeten 1884–1916* (1974)

Bergold, Carl Erik *Bostadsbyggande i Uppsala 1900–1950 — en aspekt på folkhemmets framväxt* (1985)

Bergold, Carl Erik *Uppsala. Stadsbyggande 1900–1960* (1989)

Bergkvist, Michael & Michelsen, Olof (eds.) *Josef Frank, arkitektur* (1994)

Bjur, Hans *Stadsplanering kring 1900* (1984)

Brun, Richard & Hellqvist, Thomas *Uttrycksmedel i tjugotalets svenska arkitektur* (1978)

Brunius, August »Kolorism och kubism i svensk arkitektur«, in *Färg och form* (1913)

Brunnberg, Hans m.fl. (eds.) *Trettiotalets byggnadskonst i Sverige* (1943)

Brunnström, Lisa *Den rationella fabriken, om funktionalismens rötter* (1990)

Caldenby, Claes & Walldén, Åsa: *Kollektivhus* (1979)

Caldenby, Claes & Hultin, Olof (eds.) *Asplund* (1985)

Caldenby, Claes & Walldén, Åsa *Jan Gezelius* (1989)

Caldenby, Claes *Medborgarhus i Örebro* (1990)

Caldenby, Claes (ed.) *Göteborgs konserthus, ett album* (1992)

Cornell, Elias *Ny svensk byggnadskonst* (Stockholm 1950)

Cornell, Elias *Ragnar Östberg. Svensk arkitekt.* (1965)

Cornell, Elias *Stockholms stadshus* (1992)

Curman, Jöran & Zimdal, Helge »Gruppsamhällen«, in *Inför framtidens demokrati* (1944)

Curman, Jöran *Industriens arbetarebostäder* (1944)

Drakenberg, Sven *Västerås stads byggnadshistoria från 1800-talets mitt* (1962)

Edestrand, Hans & Lundberg, Erik *Isak Gustaf Clason* (1968)

Edling, Nils *Det fosterländska hemmet* (1996)

Egelius, Mats *Ralph Erskine, arkitekt* (1988)

Ekström, Anders *Den utställda världen* (1994)

Engfors, Christina (ed.) *Folkhemmets bostäder 1940–1960* (1987)

Engfors, Christina (ed.) *E.G. Asplund. Arkitekt, vän och kollega* (1990)

Eriksson, Eva *Den moderna stadens födelse* (1990)

Eriksson, Olof *Bortom storstadsidéerna. En regional framtid för Sverige och Norden på 2010-talet* (1989)

Eriksson, Olof *Byggbeställare i brytningstid* (1994)

Femtiotalet. Arkitekturmuseets årsbok 1995 (1995)

Findal, Wenche (ed.) *Nordisk funktionalism* (1995)

Fred Forbat (Arkitekturmuseet 1970)

Funktionalismens genombrott och kris. Svenskt bostadsbyggande 1930–80. (Arkitekturmuseet 1976)

Gullström, Charlie *Léonie Geisendorf Arkitektur* (1990)

Hidemark, Ove *Dialog med tiden* (1991)

Holm, Lennart (ed.) *HSB* (1954)

Holm, Lennart »Bostadens form som ideologisk spegel«, in *Bostadspolitik och samhällsplanering* (1968)

Holm, Lennart *Rita hus* (1990)

Holm, Lennart (ed.) *Från bostadsnöd till önskehem. Stockholms kooperativa bostadsförening 1916–1991* (1991)

Holm, Lennart (ed.) *Stockholmsbyggen 1916–40, skildrade av Sigurd Westholm* (1993)

Holmdahl, Gustav a.o. (eds.) *Gunnar Asplund arkitekt 1885–1940* (1943)

Hultin, Olof a.o. *Guide till Stockholms arkitektur* (1998)

Hus. 27 arkitekters val ur svensk byggnadskonst (1965)

Hårde, Ulla *Eric Sigfrid Persson* (1986)

Høyer, S a.o. (eds.) *Tilegnet Sven-Ingvar Andersson* (1994)

Johansson, Bengt OH *Carl Bergsten och svensk arkitekturpolitik under 1900-talets första hälft* (1965)

Johansson, Bengt OH & Ullén, Marianne *Hjorthagens kyrka.* (Sveriges kyrkor 182, 1980)

Johansson, Bengt OH *Tallum* (1996)

Johansson, Cyrillus *Byggnaden och staden* (1936)

Johansson, Gotthard *Bostadsvanor och bostadsnormer* (1964)

Jonsson, Leif *Från egnahem till villa. Enfamiljshuset i Sverige 1950–1980* (1985)

Kooperativa förbundets arkitektkontor 1925–35 (1935)

Kooperativa förbundets arkitektkontor 1935–49 del 1–2 (1949)

Larsson, Jan *Hemmet vi ärvde* (1994)

Larsson, Lars Olof a.o. (eds.) *Peter Celsing. En bok om en arkitekt och hans verk* (1980)

Larsson, Mårten (ed.) *Ny arkitektur i Sverige / New Architecture in Sweden* (1961)

Larsson, Yngve *På marsch mot demokratin* (1967)

Lewerentz (Arkitekturmuseet 1987)

Lind, Sven Ivar a.o. (eds.) *Verk av L I Wahlman* (1950)

Lindahl, Göran *Högkyrkligt, lågkyrkligt, frikyrkligt i svensk arkitektur 1800–1950* (1955)

Lindroos, Bengt *Och så vidare …* (1989)

Lindvall, Jöran (ed.) *Den svenska byggnadskonsten* (1992)

Linn, Björn *Osvald Almqvist. En arkitekt och hans arbete* (1960)

Linn, Björn *Storgårdskvarteret* (1974)

Linn, Björn »Ivar Tengbom och arkitektyrket«, i Thomas Hall (ed.), *Stenstadens arkitekter* (1981)

Lund, Nils-Ole *Nordisk arkitektur* (1991)

Lundberg, Erik *Svensk bostad* (1942, 1978)

Lundberg, Erik *Arkitekturens formspråk*, Volume X (1961)

Lundahl, Gunilla (ed.) *Nordisk funktionalism* (1980)

Lundahl, Gunilla (ed.) *Kvinnor som banade väg* (Byggforskningsrådet T6:1992)

Millisdotter, Gunilla *Bengt Edmans arkitektur och pedagogik* (1993)

»Modernismens byggnader« *Kulturmiljövård 1-2/1996*

Museet och 30-talet (1985)

Mårtelius, Johan *Göra arkitekturen historisk* (1987)

Nordisk klassicism / Nordic Classicism 1910–1930 (1982)

Nowotny, C & Persson, B *Ulla Bodorff Landskapsarkitekt 1913–82* (1988)

Nyréns arkitektkontor AB (1989)

Olle Engkvist Byggmästare (1949)

Palm, Bertil *Arkitekten Carl Westman 1866–1936* (1954)

Paulsson, Gregor *Den nya arkitekturen* (1916)

Paulsson, Gregor *Svensk stad 1–2* (1950–53)

Paulsson, Thomas *Den glömda staden* (1959, 1994)

Praktiska och hygieniska bostäder (1921)

Qvarnström, Per *Klas Anshelm arkitekt* (1998)

Ridderstedt, Lars (ed.) *Kyrkan bygger vidare…* (1974)

Rudberg, Eva *Uno Åhrén* (1981)

Rudberg, Eva »Kvinnor blir arkitekter«, in *Arkitektur* 2-3/1983

Rudberg, Eva *Från mönsterplan till kommunöversikt. Den fysiska översiktsplaneringens framväxt i Sverige* (Byggforskningsrådet 1985)

Rudberg, Eva »Sverige provins i Europa« in *Arkitektur* 10/1987

Rudberg, Eva *Sven Markelius, arkitekt* (1989)

Rudberg, Eva *Folkhemmets byggande* (1992)

Rudberg, Eva & Paulsson, Eva (eds.) *Hakon Ahlberg arkitekt och humanist.* (1994)

Råberg, PG *Funktionalistiskt genombrott* (1972)

Rådberg, Johan *Den svenska trädgårdsstaden* (1994)

Rörby, Martin a.o. *Georg A Nilsson arkitekt* (1989)

Sandström, Ulf *Arkitektur och social ingenjörskonst* (1989)

Sax, Ulrika *Den vita staden. Hammarbyhöjden under femtio år* (1989)

Sidenbladh, Göran *Planering för Stockholm 1923–1958* (1981)

Sidenbladh, Göran *Norrmalm förnyat 1951–1981* (1985)

Sjöberg, Lars, Sjöberg, Ursula & Snitt, Ingalill *Det svenska rummet* (1994)

Stavenow-Hidemark, Elisabet *Villabebyggelse i Sverige 1900–1925* (1971)

Sverige 2009 — förslag till vision (1994)

Sörenson, Ulf *Ferdinand Boberg. Arkitekten som konstnär* (1992)

Tengboms. Ett arkitektkontors utveckling sedan 1905 (1991)

Thurell, Sören (ed.) *SARs Ekoguide: Insikt. 150 ekologiska byggnader i Sverige* (1996)

Thörn, Kerstin *En bostad för hemmet. Idehistoriska studier i bostadsfrågan 1889–1929* (1997)

Tägil, Tomas *Arkitekten Hans Westman, funktionalismen och den regionala särarten* (1996)

Törnqvist, Anders & Ullmark, Peter (eds.) *When people matter* (BFR D 14:1989)

Walldén, Åsa *Kungsladugård, en arkitekturguide* (1992)

Vestbro, Dick Urban *Kollektivhus från enkökshus till bogemenskap* (BFR T 28:1982)

Westerlind, Ann Mari *Industribostäder i bruksorter, industriens bostadsförening 1945–1982* (1950)

Wickman, Kerstin (ed.) *Formens rörelse* (1995)

Vision och perspektiv. En bok om planverket och Lennart Holm (1988)

Wærn, Rasmus *Tävlingarnas tid* (1996)

Zimdal, Helge *En arkitekt minns* (1981)

Åhrén, Uno *Arkitektur och demokrati* (1942)

Åhrén, Uno *Ett planmässigt samhällsbyggande* (1945)

Åkerman, Brita a.o. *Den okända vardagen* (1983)

Åman, Anders *Om den offentliga vården* (1976)

Östberg, Ragnar *En arkitekts anteckningar* (1928)

Literature in English and German

Andersson, Henrik O & Bedoire Fredric *Svensk arkitektur. Ritningar 1640–1970/Swedish Architecture. Drawings 1640–1970* (1986)

Andersson, Henrik O & Bedoire, Fredric *Stockholm — Architecture and Townscape* (1988)

Aufbruch und Krise des Funktionalismus 1930–80, Bauen und Wohnen in Schweden 1930–80 (Arkitekturmuseet 1976)

Caldenby, Claes & Hultin, Olof (eds.) *Asplund* (1985)

Childs, Marquis *Sweden — the Middle Way* (1937)

Coates, Gary J. *Erik Asmussen, architect* (1997)

Collymore, Peter *The Architecture of Ralph Erskine* (1982)

Constant, Caroline *The Woodland Cemetery: Toward a Spiritual Landscape* (1994)

Dymling, Claes (ed.) *Architect Sigurd Lewerentz*. Vol. 1. Photographs of the work. Vol. 2. Drawings. (1997)

Engfors, Christina *E.G. Asplund. Architect, friend and colleague* (1990)

Fyrtiotalets svenska bostad/Swedish Housing of the 'Forties (1950)

Holmdahl, Gustav a.o. (eds.) *Gunnar Asplund, Architect* (1950)

Hultin, Olof (ed.) *Sigurd Lewerentz Two Churches/Två kyrkor* (1987)

Johansson, Bengt OH *Tallum* (1996)

Kidder Smith, GE *Sweden builds* (1950, 1954)

Larsson, Mårten (ed.) *Ny arkitektur i Sverige/New Architecture in Sweden* (1961)

Lectures and Briefings from the International Symposium on the Architecture of Erik Gunnar Asplund (1986)

Lindvall, Jöran *The Swedish Art of building* (1992)

Lundahl, Gunilla *Recent Developments in Swedish Architecture* (1983)

Nordisk klassicism/Nordic Classicism 1910–1930 (1982)

Ny svensk arkitektur/New Swedish Architecture (1947)

Ny arkitektur i Sverige/New architecture in Sweden (1961)

Rudberg, Eva *Sven Markelius, architect* (1989)

Rudberg, Eva »Schweden — eine europäische Provinz/Sweden — a province of Europe«, in Raumdenken/Thinking space, *Bauart* 4/1996

Walton, Ann Thorson *Ferdinand Boberg — Architect. The Complete Work* (1994)

Wang, Wilfried *The architecture of Peter Celsing* (1996)

Wrede, Stuart *The Architecture of Erik Gunnar Asplund* (1980)

Yerbury, FR (ed.) *Swedish Architecture of the Twentieth Century* (1925)

Index of Names